Western Technology and Soviet Economic Development 1945 to 1965

Third volume of a three-volume series

By

ANTONY C. SUTTON

HOOVER INSTITUTION PRESS

STANFORD UNIVERSITY, STANFORD, CALIFORNIA

1973

Hoover Institution Publications 113
International Standard Book Number: 0-8179-1131-6
© 1973 by the Board of Trustees of the Leland Stanford Junior University
All rights reserved
Library of Congress Catalog Card Number: 68-24442
Reprint Edition ISBN 978-1-939438-76-8

FOR

Jane and Elizabeth

Preface

The considerable financial burden for this three-volume study has been borne by the Hoover Institution on War, Revolution and Peace established by former President Herbert Hoover at Stanford University. The Institution's extensive archival holdings, a library in excess of one million volumes, first-rate research facilities, and the unique freedom given to individual researchers make it an unparalleled center for original research. The Institution is, of course, in no way responsible for my errors and omissions, nor does it necessarily accept my argument.

Of the many at the Hoover Institution who have contributed to this study special mention should be made of Dr. W. Glenn Campbell, Director of the Hoover Institution since 1960; Mr. Alan H. Belmont, Associate Director for Administration; and Dr. Roger A. Freeman, Senior Fellow. The assistance given by the expert curators and an efficient Library staff is also gratefully acknowledged.

The Hoover Institution Press, headed by Mr. Brien Benson, handled the publication chores for the series and particular acknowledgment is due the editorial staff: Miss Michelle Hogan, former production editor; Miss Liselotte Hofmann, assistant editor; Mr. London G. Green, the editor directly responsible for the first two volumes; and Mrs. Carole Norton, who supervised the editorial work on volumes One and Two and undertook the detailed editing of this final volume. Miss Marcia Taylor compiled the bibliography and Mrs. Joan Johanson compiled the index for this volume.

To these and others who have given their assistance—thank you.

Stanford, California   A. C. S.
June, 1970.

Contents

Tables

Figures

Introduction

This is the third volume of an analysis of the impact of Western technology and skills on the industrial development of the Soviet Union. With this volume, which covers the years 1945-1965, the original hypothesis that by far the most significant factor in the development of the Soviet economy has been its absorption of Western technology and skills[1] is substantially supported over a period of 50 years.

The reader should bear in mind the distinctions made in this analysis between science and technology and between invention and innovation. Science is here defined as theory and laboratory development of theory, while technology is the selective application of scientific findings to industrial production. Similarly, invention is the process of discovery and the prototype development of discovery, while innovation is the selective application of invention to industrial production. Usually there are many inventions available for selection in any industrial system; but in practice only a few are applied to become innovations.

No fundamental industrial innovation of Soviet origin has been identified in the Soviet Union between 1917 and 1965, and preliminary investigation suggests that this situation continued throughout the decade of the sixties.[2] Soviet innovations have consisted, in substance, in adopting those made first outside the U.S.S.R. or using those made by Western firms specifically for the Soviet Union and for Soviet industrial conditions and factor resource patterns. A comparative statement of Soviet innovation—to the limited extent that it exists—is made in chapter 25.

The question now is: Why does the Soviet Union lack major indigenous innovation? Up to about 1957 the explanation could well have been posed in terms of "catching up," i.e., it was cheaper and less time-consuming for the U.S.S.R. to adopt Western technology than to institute the innovative process herself. After about 1957 the catching-up hypothesis cannot be supported; the

[1] See A. C. Sutton, *Western Technology and Soviet Economic Development, 1917 to 1930* (Stanford: Hoover Institution, 1968). Hereafter cited as Sutton I.

[2] The cut-off date varies according to the amount of information available for each industrial sector; for chapter 21 (shipbuilding), information was available to July 1967, while for chapter 9 (non-ferrous metals) information is scarce after the early 1960s.

Soviet Union had caught up technically in the thirties and once again in the forties by "borrowing" in one form or another from the West.

In 1957 came the era of "peaceful competition between systems," when Khrushchev challenged and threatened to "bury" the United States economically. This challenge may well have been a bombastic cover for Soviet intent to increase—not reduce—the acquisition of Western technology. On the other hand, Soviet economists may have concluded that the years 1957-58 represented the zenith of technical assimilation from abroad and that Sputnik would usher in an era of Soviet innovation. Some Soviet innovation did indeed evolve in the late 1950s—in fact examples appear to be concentrated in these years—but it did not survive in the face of dynamic Western technical advances.[3]

Today it is no longer a question of "catching up." It is a question of the innate ability of the Soviet system to innovate at all. On the basis of the research findings elaborated in this three-volume series, we conclude that a society with the kind of central planning that guides the Soviet Union has virtually no capability for self-generated indigenous innovation.

Yet Soviet propaganda concerning Soviet technology has by and large been successful. In the face of the empirical evidence in these volumes, the Soviets have convinced a large proportion of the Free World, and perhaps the Communist Party of the Soviet Union itself, of their technological prowess.

Although the record of foreign technological dependence is largely expunged from Soviet writing, it is possible from time to time to find frank and open statements bearing on the issue. For example, at the Twenty-third Congress of the CPSU in 1966, the report on the directives delivered by Kosygin included the straightforward statement:

> The Soviet Union is going to buy ... over a thousand sets of equipment for enterprises and shops in the chemical, light, food and other industries. Deliveries from the fraternal countries will cover 48 percent of our needs in sea-going freighters, 40 percent of our needs in main line and industrial electric locomotives, about 36 percent of our needs in railway cars.[4]

As the Soviet definition of "sets" of equipment equals complete plant installations and the period covered by the statement was five years, the magnitude of the planned assistance may be readily seen.[5]

This Soviet dependence on foreign countries has largely escaped the attention of the Western world. For example, a survey conducted by the U.S. Information

---

[3] Among many examples, see chapter 15 and synthetic fibers.

[4] Novosti, *23rd Congress of the Communist Party of the Soviet Union* (Moscow, 1966), p. 256. See also A.C. Sutton, *Western Technology and Soviet Economic Development, 1930 to 1945* (Stanford: Hoover Institution, 1971; hereafter cited as Sutton II), p. 3; and A.C. Sutton, "Soviet Merchant Marine", U.S. Naval Institute *Proceedings*, January 1970.

[5] These figures coincide with the material presented in chapter 21 (for ships) and chapter 20 (for locomotives).

Agency on European opinion concerning the relative success of U.S. and Soviet scientific and technical achievements[6] had extraordinary results. Accepting that the layman does not make a distinction between science and technology, then in 1961 more people in Western Europe believed the Soviet Union was technically ahead of the United States than vice versa. This opinion varied by country: in Great Britain 59 percent thought the Soviet Union was ahead and only 21 percent thought the United States was, while in West Germany one-half of the interviewees thought the United States was ahead compared with 19 percent for the Soviet Union. Where further questions were asked of those who thought the Soviet Union ahead, the answers were not in terms of Soviet use of Western technology but rather in terms of factors not supported by this study. Only about 15 percent of the German responses mentioned "captured German scientists" as a key factor in Soviet weapons and atomic energy programs. But most "Soviets-ahead" answers tended to be negative about the United States rather than positive about Soviet "success"; i.e., there were such observations as "Americans like a good time," "no coordination in America," "insufficiency of good scientists in the U.S."[7]

The paradox, or perhaps dilemma, that remains with us is that this study presents detailed and profuse evidence not only at variance with the Soviets' own interpretations of their achievements—despite their exceptional statements that hint otherwise—but also at complete variance with the beliefs of a majority of the Free World, including its academic communities. The confusion may even extend into U.S. Government departments. To illustrate this point, it may be profitable to explore the views of the U.S. State Department concerning Soviet technology and Soviet economic achievements because the State Department, as the senior U.S. executive department, has excellent sources of information and plays the paramount role in the establishment of U.S. economic policy toward the U.S.S.R.

Published State Department papers and statements made by State Department officials to Congress suggest conclusions directly opposed to those of this study. In brief, the State Department has consistently argued from 1918 to the present time—but more importantly in the years since about 1960—that Soviet industrial development has little connection with Western technology, and specifically that it has no vital connection with trade or with the other mechanisms discussed in this study as technology transfer vehicles.

In *The Battle Act Report: 1963*, submitted by the State Department to Congress, it is stated that trade with the West had made "[an] obviously limited contribution to Soviet economic and industrial growth" and that denial of trade could not affect basic Soviet military capability. The report continued to the

---

[6] Leo P. Crespi, "The Image of U.S. Versus Soviet Science in Western European Public Opinion," in R. L. Merritt and D. J. Puchala, eds., *Western European Perspectives on International Affairs: Public Opinion Studies and Evaluations* (New York: Praeger, 1967).

[7] *Ibid.*

effect that the Battle Act embargo program was not as extensive as in the early 1950s on the grounds that "the inevitable process of industrial and economic growth during those 12 years has meant that the Soviets have developed their own productive capability in many of the areas where a restraining impact was necessary and possible 10 years ago."[8] This State Department report was made precisely at a time when the Soviets were midway in a program to purchase complete industrial sectors in the West—concentrated fertilizers, synthetic rubbers and fibers, engines, computers, electric locomotives, and automobiles—all for industrial sectors either nonexistent or very backward in the U.S.S.R. in 1963.

A great deal of information for this study was derived from reports made by various U.S. industry delegations to the Soviet Union under the auspices of the State Department, although not all such delegation reports have been declassified. Some delegations commented adversely on the value of their visits insofar as the United States is concerned, and indeed from the technical viewpoint there has been little U.S. advantage. For example, the American Gas Industry Delegation was greeted in Leningrad by a number of prominent officials, and

> ...a major part of their presentation included a discussion of a butane regeneration plant in the city and of its use in the local gas distribution supply operations. It was with extreme difficulty that a visit to the butane regeneration plant was finally arranged. The plant had not been in operation for two years.[9]

An American petroleum industry delegation was shown four refineries in August 1960[10]— three of them (Nuovo Ufa, Novo Kuibyshev, and Syzran) Lend Lease refineries,[11] and the fourth (Novo Baku) either a Lend Lease refinery or a Soviet copy of a U.S. installation.[12] The reports made by this delegation have been of particular value to the study. A skilled observer—and members of the delegation were skilled observers—cannot be easily fooled. Although

---

[8] U.S. Dept. of State, *The Battle Act Report: 1963*, Mutual Defense Assistance Control Act of 1951 (Washington; 1963), p. 8. See Sutton II, pp. 3-6, for other State Department and academic statements on this topic; also see p. 211 for Assistant Secretary of Commerce Jack N. Behrman's denial of Soviet "copying" of agricultural machinery.
This writer is of course by no means the first to have raised serious doubts about the analytical performance of the State Department. A well-qualified critique which touches on some aspects of this study has been made by a former assistant chief of the Division of Research of the State Department: Bryton Barron, *Inside the State Department*, (New York: Comet Press, 1956). See p. 417 below.

[9] "U.S.S.R. Natural Gas Industry," Report of the U.S. Natural Gas Delegation, July 1961, p. 38.

[10] Robert E. Ebel, *The Petroleum Industry of the Soviet Union* (New York: American Petroleum Institute, June 1961), p. 107.

[11] U.S. Dept. of the Interior, *A History of the Petroleum Administration for War, 1941-1945* (Washington, 1946), p. 270.

[12] See p. 135.

[13] All delegations, without exception, commented favorably on the hospitality.

the delegation was given a cordial reception,[13] written information was not forthcoming in abundance[14] and plant visits were difficult to arrange. Despite such problems, however, the reports display the observers' great perspicacity and technical skill.

The restrictions imposed by U.S. Government classification of data were only partly countered by the excellence of private reports, however; sometimes an alternative and more circuitous approach had to be applied to determine process origin. The most direct alternative was to isolate exports of technology to the Soviet Union by U.S. and foreign manufacturers and trace such exports to specific locations in the Soviet Union—this was the *modus operandi* in volumes One and Two. (State Department files provided detailed information for the period 1917-1945.) It was not possible to rely entirely on the same procedures for the period 1945-1965, since for this period the U.S. Government has restricted information pertaining to such transfers.

Hence another alternative was used in preparing volume Three. In addition to starting with Western firms and tracing technology to the Soviet Union, the author examined and traced back to a possible Western origin (within reasonable limits of time and space) major processes or equipment items known to be in use in the Soviet Union. When a technical link was thus established, a search was begun for a specific Western export or contract; by this means it was found that the Soviet synthetic rubber "Narit," for example, is a chloroprene rubber that traces back to the export of Dupont technology under Lend Lease. Much work originated in U.S. military departments and required only search and collection. For example, the "Moskvich" and "Leningrad" television sets had already been traced by the U.S. Air Force to East German origins, and turbojet engines had been traced to German BMW 003 and Junkers 004 and British Rolls-Royce engines. The Stalinets S-80 was found to be the Caterpillar D-7 in an extensive study by the Caterpillar Tractor Company.

Not all technical links could be fully confirmed. For this reason, two degrees of identification accuracy have been established and are referred to throughout the text. Where positive identification has been made, i.e., where a specific process or piece of equipment is identified in acceptable sources as of Western origin, it is classified as a "positive identification." On the other hand, if identification had to be "inferred" it is so noted; inferred identification includes the category for which information has been provided on a confidential or background basis. The YaAZ truck engine of 1947, for example, is inferred to be a General Motors engine on the basis of comparisons of technical data and the knowledge that such engines were exported to the U.S.S.R. under

[14] U.S. Congress, *Hearings*, Special Committee on Atomic Energy, 79th Congress, 1st session, November 27, 28, 29, and 30, 1945, December 3, 1945; Part I (Washington: U.S. Government Printing Office, 1945).

Lend Lease. Soviet adoption of some nonferrous metals processes has been indicated to the writer on a confidential basis.[15]

Khrushchev's challenge to the West in the late 1950s for peaceful competition coincided with the beginning of a massive Soviet program to purchase complete plants from the West. The year 1957 is central to our study. Up to that time the Soviets had been duplicating technology imported in the 1930s and under Lend Lease; no indigenous progress of any magnitude had been achieved, while certain industries, such as chemicals and synthetic fibers, were perhaps 40 years out of date. Consequently, rates of growth were slipping.

In 1957 several books were published in the Soviet Union proclaiming the benefits of socialist production and the role of Lenin and the Communist Party in bringing about the wonders of socialist Russia. An examination of some of these books[16] suggests several factors germinal to our study. First, little specific information is given; Moskatov, for example, uses multiple or percentage statements rather than absolute figures. Secondly, and of more interest for our purposes, data concerning qualitative factors—somewhat more difficult to disguise—suggest there was an extremely limited product range in Soviet industry in the late 1950s; a situation confirmed by the present study. Sominskii[17] lists a number of machines by model number, and the origins of these machines are presented in the text below. Moskatov covers similar ground and in one or two cases gives a quantitative framework for the number of models actually in use; e.g., in 1957 there were six basic models of tractors. There is, of course, no mention of the origins of this tractor technology.

In brief, Soviet publications on the question of technical progress make statements that, while greatly abbreviated, are not inconsistent with the findings of this study in the sense that no statement is made concerning types of equipment not covered in this text. The technology for types not mentioned did not even exist; such is consistent with subsequent purchase abroad as outlined in this study.

Finally, in a study full of paradoxes let a supreme paradox be suggested. The Soviet Union is the dedicated enemy of the Free World—this by the admission of its own leadership. There is no question that since 1917 there has been a continuing advocacy of the overthrow of capitalist systems. Yet the technical transfers described in these volumes have been the lifeblood of the Soviet industrial process and of the Soviets' ability to back up their avowed campaign of world revolution.

---

[15] Many aspects of the transfer have been more adequately discussed elsewhere. For example, the transfer of a duplicate set of plates for printing currency (from the U.S. Treasury to the Soviet Union, thus giving the Soviets the ability to print unlimited quantities of currency redeemable in U.S. dollars) has been well described and documented in Vladimir Petrov, *Money and Conquest* (Baltimore: Johns Hopkins Press, 1967).

[16] V. S. Sominskii, *O tekhnicheskom progresse promyshlennosti SSSR* (Moscow, 1957), and P. G. Moskatov, *Po puti tekhnicheskogo progressa* (Moscow, 1957).

What is more, the technical transfers have not only been allowed by Western governments but have in fact been encouraged and sometimes even singled out for acclaim. For example, the builder of the first modern Soviet trawlers—Brooke-Marine, Ltd., of Lowestoft, England—was honored by Queen Elizabeth with an M.B.E. (Member of the Order of the British Empire) for Charles Ernest White, the assistant general manager in charge of production.[18] In 1946 Swedish firms were reportedly threatened by their government's ministry of industry and commerce if they refused to take Soviet orders.[19] In Germany in the 1950s and 1960s the Howaldtwerke shipyards in Kiel, owned by the German Government, was a prominent builder of ships on Soviet account. Then in the mid-sixties came President Johnson's "bridges for peace," which opened wider the floodgates of American technology for the Soviets, although, to be sure, a similar argument had been used by Edwin Gay of the War Trade Board in 1919 to initiate trade with the Bolsheviks ("trade would bring the Bolsheviks into the civilized world").

Such, then, is the confused political arena for the transactions discussed in this study.

---

[17] Sominskii, *op. cit.* n. 16, p. 95.
[18] *The Shipbuilder and Marine Engine Builder* (London), February 1956, p. 119.
[19] *Electrical Review* (London), vol. 139, p. 890.

PART I

The Transfer Mechanisms: 1945 to 1965

CHAPTER ONE

Lend Lease and the "Pipeline Agreement," 1941 to 1946

There are two aspects to Lend Lease transfers: (1) shipments made under the five Supply Protocols of 1941-45 and related programs and (2) shipments made under the October 1945 "pipeline agreement"—after the end of the war with Japan and covering goods in inventory or procurement on September 2, 1945.[1]

U.S.S.R. LEND LEASE PROGRAM: THE SUPPLY PROTOCOLS

Negotiations on the First Supply Protocol began on December 7, 1941, but they were postponed until December 28 due to the entry of the United States into war with Japan. A few Soviet military requests in the First Protocol could not be fulfilled or had to be scaled down, and while the War Department was able to meet most commitments it could not at first supply all requests for trucks, guns, and light bombers, antiaircraft guns, antitank guns, and mortars. The War Department did supply tanks, trucks and planes, 100,000 field telephones, 500,000 miles of field telephone wire, 20,000 tons of toluol, 12,600 tons of leather, and 1,500,000 pairs of army boots. Approximately 1,752,000 tons of supplies were made available under this protocol.

[1] Data used in this chapter are from the unpublished U.S. Dept. of State, "Report on War Aid Furnished by the United States to the U.S.S.R." (Washington: Office of Foreign Liquidation, 1945). The published Supply Protocols are not a guide to actual shipments, only to anticipated ones. The reader should also consult George R. Jordan, *From Major Jordan's Diaries* (New York: Harcourt, Brace and Company, 1952), based on Soviet copies of the delivery notes; in most categories Major Jordan's report is consistent with the State Department publication, but sometimes he includes details to be found only in the Lend Lease invoices stored at the Federal Records Center, Suitland, Maryland.
The "pipeline agreement" of October 1945 is published in *Documents on American Foreign Relations*, VIII, July 1945-December 1946 (Princeton: Princeton University Press), pp. 127-32. It should be noted that Schedules A and B to the "pipeline agreement" have not been published but are available from the Department of State; a copy of these schedules has been deposited in the Hoover Institution Library.
The reader should also consult a manuscript of unknown but clearly authoritative authorship in the Hoover Special Collections: *"U.S.S.R. Lend-Lease Program"* (1945). This has data on the virtually unknown "special programs."

The Second Supply Protocol, known as the "Washington Protocol," was signed December 6, 1942, and approximately 770,000 short tons of material were made available by the War Department and 3,274,000 tons by all U.S. agencies. The War Department delivered planes, jeeps, antiaircraft guns, explosives, toluol, tractors, radio sets, clothing, field telephones and wire signal equipment, battery charging sets, tubes, and radio components. Items requested by the Soviets but not offered by the U.S. in this protocol included tarpaulin material, field glasses, radio locators, radio beacons, stereoscopic observation instruments for artillery, radio repair trucks, and light field repair shops for tanks and trucks.

The Third Supply Protocol, known as the "London Protocol," was signed in London on October 19, 1943. The War Department made substantial offerings against all Soviet requests except in teletype apparatus and in locomotives where it offered 500 to 700 locomotives against requests of 2000 to 3000. The total supplied by the War Department was 1,466,000 tons, including substantial quantities of locomotives, railroad cars, industrial lift trucks, tractors, cranes (mobile construction and port use types), power shovels, and teletype apparatus. The United States also began production on Soviet account of 600 steam locomotives and procurement for 10,000 flatcars and 1,000 dump trucks.

The Fourth Supply Protocol, signed in February 1944, covered the last half of 1944 and 1945. It included substantial deliveries of radio locators, tractors, large radio stations, cranes, shovels, shoes, and medical supplies; the main new item under this protocol was mobile construction equipment. U.S. offerings totaled 1,700,000 tons as well as port equipment (valued at $10 million) that included floating, portal, and mobile cranes for the Black Sea ports and heavy cranes for Murmansk and Archangel. The following U.S. offers were turned down by the Soviets: nonstandard combination power supply units, mainline electric locomotives, and nitroglycerin powder.

The Fifth Supply Protocol, signed in March 1945, included motor vehicles, cranes and shovels, tractors, road construction equipment, locomotives, some signal equipment but mainly industrial equipment.

There were in addition programs subordinate to the main Lend Lease Supply Protocols. These included an Arctic program for the supply of Soviet arctic ports, the "Outpost" program for construction of ports in the Soviet Far East, and the highly important Northern Siberian Air Route Program, as well as "Project Milepost" in support of Soviet Far Eastern operations.

The Northern Siberian Air Route program to establish a trans-Siberian airways system was initially suggested to Ray Ellis, director of the Radio and Radar Division of the War Production Board, while he was on a visit to the U.S.S.R., and was handled separately from the main Supply Protocol arrangements. Equipment comprising transmitters, receivers, and range equipment for eight major and 50 minor stations, and valued at $12 million, was requested and substantially assigned by March 30, 1945, for 7000 miles of airways with five 200-mile feeder lines.[2] The relationship of this program to Allied wartime operations is obscure.

COMPOSITION OF LEND LEASE SUPPLIES TO THE SOVIET UNION

About 98 percent of U.S. exports to the Soviet Union between June 1941 and September 1945 consisted of Lend Lease supplies. Table 1-1 shows the major categories of supplies and the approximate amounts shipped; this section describes the content of each of these supply categories in more detail.[3]

Table 1-1   MAJOR CATEGORIES OF LEND LEASE SUPPLY
TO THE SOVIET UNION

Category	Description of Category	Amounts (Arrived in Soviet Union)
I	Aircraft and equipment	14,018 units
II	Vehicles (including tanks and trucks)	466,968 units
	Explosives	325,784 short tons
III	Naval and marine equipment	5,367,000 gross registered tons of shipping
		7,617 marine engines
IV	Foodstuffs	4,291,012 short tons
V	Industrial machinery and equipment	$1,095,140,000
VI	Materials and metal products	2,589,776 short tons of steel
		781,663 short tons of nonferrous metals
		1,018,855 miles of wire
		2,159,336 short tons of petroleum
		820,422 short tons of chemicals

Source: U.S. Dept. of State, *Report on War Aid Furnished by the United States to the U.S.S.R.* (Washington: Office of Foreign Liquidation, 1945), pp. 20-28.

Category I included aircraft and aircraft equipment. A total of 14,018 aircraft was shipped under Lend Lease; these aircraft included pursuit planes, light bombers, medium bombers, one heavy bomber, transport planes, flying boats, observation planes, and advanced trainers. In addition, link trainers and a considerable quantity of aircraft landing mats and communications equipment were shipped.

Category II comprised military supplies of all types. Some 466,968 individual vehicle units were supplied to the Soviet Union. Combat vehicles included

---

[2] See anonymous manuscript, *op. cit.* n.l, in the Hoover Institution.
[3] Date from U.S. Dept. of State, *op. cit.* n.l. Figures are for "arrived," i.e., exports minus losses.

1239 light tanks, 4957 medium tanks, about 2000 self-propelled guns, 1104 half-tracks, and 2054 armored scout cars. The 2293 ordnance service vehicles included 1534 field repair trucks and 629 tank transporters. Trucks included 47,728 jeeps, 24,564 three-quarter-ton trucks, 148,664 one-and-one-half-ton trucks, 182,938 two-and-one-half-ton trucks, and smaller quantities of two-and-one-half-ton amphibian trucks, five-ton trucks, and special purpose trucks. Also shipped were 32,200 motorcycles and 7570 track-laying tractors with 3216 spare tractor engines. All equipment was provided with spare parts and ammunition in accordance with U.S.Army standards.

A total of 325,784 tons of explosives included 129,667 tons of smokeless powder and 129,138 tons of TNT.

Wireless communication equipment comprised a sizable portion of total shipments and included no less than 35,779 radio stations (one kilowatt and less). Related equipment included radio stations of higher power, radio locators, 705 radio direction finders, 528 radio altimeters, 800 radio compasses, 63 radio beacons, and large quantities of radio tubes, component parts, accessories, and measuring and testing equipment.

Construction machinery valued at over $10 million included $5,599,000 of road and aircraft construction equipment and $2,459,000 in tractor-mounted equipment, together with $2,099,000 worth of mixers and pavers and $635,000 worth of railroad construction equipment.

Railroad equipment included 1900 steam locomotives, 66 diesel-electric locomotives, 9920 flat cars, 1000 dump cars, 120 tank cars, and 35 heavy machinery cars, for a total of 13,041 railroad units.

Other military items shipped included 15 cableway bridges, five portable pipelines, 62 portable storage tanks, 100,000 flashlights with dry cells, and 13 pontoon bridges.

Category III comprised naval and marine equipment. Noncombat ships included 90 dry-cargo vessels, ten oceangoing tankers, nine Wye tankers, three icebreakers, 20 tugboats, one steam schooner, 2398 pneumatic floats, one motor launch, and two floating repair shops.

Combat ships sent to the Soviet Union included 46 submarine chasers (110 ft.), 57 submarine chasers (65 ft.), 175 torpedo boats in addition to another 24 torpedo boats supplied from the United Kingdom, 77 minesweepers, 28 frigates, 52 small landing craft, and eight tank-landing craft (and another two tank-landing craft from the United Kingdom) together with six cargo barges.

The marine propulsion machinery group included 3320 marine diesel engines, 4297 marine gasoline engines, 108 wooden gas engines, 2150 outboard motors, $254,000 worth of shafting and ship propellers, $50,000 worth of steering gear, 40 storage batteries for submarines, and parts and equipment (valued at $2,774,000) for marine propulsion machinery.

Special ship equipment included $1,047,000 worth of salvage stations and diving gear, $109,000 worth of jetting apparatus, one submarine rescue chamber, distilling apparatus valued at $36,000 and miscellaneous special shipping equipment valued at $44,000. Also sent were trawling equipment for minesweepers valued at $3,778,000, mechanical and electrical equipment for tugboats valued at $545,000, and mechanical and electrical equipment for ferry boats valued at $1,717,000. A large quantity of naval artillery and ammunition included 1849 Oerlikon guns and $2,692,000 worth of equipment for naval guns.

Over 4.2 million tons of foodstuffs was consigned in Category IV. These supplies included 1,154,180 tons of wheat, wheat flour, grain mill products, and seed; over 672,000 tons of sugar; 782,973 tons of canned meat, including 265,569 tons of "tushonka"; 730,902 tons of sausage, fat, butter, and lard; 517,522 tons of vegetable oil; and 362,421 tons of dried milk, eggs, cheese, and dehydrated products. Also sent were 9000 tons of soap and 61,483 tons of miscellaneous food products.

The shipments most significant to this study were in Category V—machinery and equipment valued at over $1 billion.

Groups V-1/3B included general-purpose engines and turbines, compressors, and pumps to a total value of $39,287,000.

Groups V-4/7 comprised equipment valued at $50,644,000, including crushing, screening, and mixing machinery ($8,048,000); conveyers and conveying systems ($1,651,000); marine winches ($460,000); cranes, derricks, hoists, and similar equipment ($33,272,000); and industrial trucks and tractors ($7,213,000).

Groups V-8 A/11 totaled $38,791,000, including fan and blower equipment ($3,702,000), mechanical power transmission equipment ($111,000), bearings ($25,813,000), and valves and steam specialties ($8,521,000).

Groups V-12/13B3 included general-purpose industrial machinery valued at $197,820,000. These groups comprised miscellaneous machinery ($4,508,000), electric rotating equipment for marine use ($1,867,000), electric rotating equipment for other uses ($17,700,000), military generator sets ($26,803,000), marine generator sets ($12,852,000), and other types of generator sets ($134,090,000).

Groups V-14/17 included $16,685,000 worth of electrical equipment. These groups comprised primary electrical power transmission equipment ($7,107,000), power conversion equipment ($6,923,000), marine secondary distribution equipment ($1,325,000), and motor starters and controllers ($1,260,000).

Groups V-18/22, totaling $5,902,000, included electric lamps ($101,000), miscellaneous equipment ($3,722,000), food products machinery ($735,000), textile industries machinery ($977,000), and pulp and paper industry machinery ($367,000).

Groups V-23/26, valued at $33,283,000, included printing trade machinery and equipment ($52,000), a tire plant from the Ford Motor Company ($8,675,000), rubber-working machinery ($115,000), wood-working machinery

($1,233,000), and metal-melting and heating furnaces ($23,208,000).

Groups V-27/30B, totaling $53,724,000, included blast and reverberating furnaces ($5,186,000), foundry equipment ($2,132,000), special industrial furnaces, kilns, and ovens ($3,268,000), several petroleum refinery plants ($42,610,000), and petroleum refinery machinery and equipment ($528,000).

Groups V-31/34B included special machinery for the glass industry ($671,000), special machinery for chemical manufacturing ($1,460,000), gas-generating apparatus ($13,677,000), miscellaneous specialized industrial equipment ($6,550,000), and cartridge manufacturing lines ($29,855,000). The value for this group totaled $52,213,000.

Groups V-35/39 included machine tools and metal-forming machinery valued at $404,697,000. These groups comprised machine tools ($310,058,000), rolling mills and auxiliary equipment ($25,356,000), drawing machines ($2,412,000), other types of primary metal-forming machinery ($304,000), and secondary metal-forming machinery ($66,567,000).

Groups V-40A/43B included welding and metal-working machinery valued at $15,199,000, comprising various welding machinery ($9,049,000), testing and measuring machinery ($2,830,000), miscellaneous metal-working equipment ($107,000), and various types of portable metal-working machines ($3,213,000).

Groups V-44A/47 comprised a total of $50,420,000 worth of various types of cutting tools and machine tool accessories. These groups included cemented carbide-cutting tools ($5,904,000), metal cutting tools ($34,878,000), other cutting tools and forming tools ($758,000), attachments and accessories for machine tools ($3,945,000), and tool room specialties and equipment ($240,000).

Groups V-48/52 included various types of agricultural machinery and drilling equipment. The total value of these groups was $51,570,000 and included agricultural machinery ($751,000), mining and quarrying machinery ($1,763,000), earth and rock boring and drilling equipment ($8,983,000), well and blast-hole drilling equipment ($9,023,000), and excavating and dredging machinery ($31,050,000).

Groups V-53/58CI included miscellaneous equipment and machinery for a total value of $23,488,000, and comprised miscellaneous construction equipment ($797,000), office machines ($58,000), miscellaneous machinery ($1,195,000), teletype apparatus ($4,470,000), and 380,135 field telephone units ($16,968,000).

Groups V-58C2/59B, telephone and communications equipment valued at $28,630,000, included telephone and telegraph apparatus ($14,419,000), sound equipment ($543,000), automatic block and signaling system equipment ($10,880,000), industrial-type locomotives, cars, and spare parts for cars ($1,655,000), and mine-type locomotives and rail cars with appropriate spare parts ($1,133,000).

Groups V-60/63, valued at $3,885,000, included vehicle parts ($582,000), air conditioning and refrigeration equipment ($593,000), marine lighting fixtures

($1,045,000), other types of lighting fixtures ($421,000), and photographic equipment ($1,244,000). The photographic equipment group is interesting in that $393,000 of a total of only $1,244,000 for the group was en route to the Soviet Union as late as September 20, 1945; in other words, one-third of the allocated photographic equipment was en route to the Soviet Union after the end of the war with Japan.

Groups V-64A/67 included various types of scientific equipment to a total value of $12,431,000, comprising optical, indicating, recording, and control instruments ($6,902,000), navigation instruments ($727,000), professional and scientific instruments ($1,596,000), miscellaneous equipment ($396,000), and nonpowered hand tools ($2,810,000).

Groups V-68/71 consisted of miscellaneous tools and equipment valued at $22,493,000, and included mechanics' measuring tools ($3,672,000), marine power boilers ($90,000), industrial power boilers ($15,880,000), agricultural tractors ($2,773,000), and other miscellaneous equipment ($78,000).

These data show that Lend Lease supplies of industrial machinery and equipment to the Soviet Union between 1941 and 1945 were not only large in amount —i.e., in excess of one billion dollars—but also of a remarkably varied and extensive character and included equipment for all sectors of the civilian and military-industrial economy.

Category VI included materials and metal products. A total of 2,589,776 short tons of steel was shipped, and included 4857 tons of stainless steel wire, 3827 tons of special alloy wire, 56,845 tons of steel alloy tubes, 12,822 tons of stainless steel, 160,248 tons of cold-finished bars, 233,170 tons of hot-rolled aircraft steel, and large quantities of polished drill rod, armor plate, wire rope, pipe and tubing, wire nails, hot-rolled sheet and plate, railroad rails and accessories, car axles, locomotive car wheels, rolled steel car wheels, and other steel products. In addition, a total of 16,058 short tons of ferroalloys was shipped, including ferrosilicon, ferrochromium, ferrotungsten, and ferromolybdenum.

Shipments of nonferrous metals totaled 781,663 short tons, including a remarkable 339,599 short tons of base-alloy copper and large quantities of electrolytic copper and copper tubes. This group also included quantities of aluminum ingot and wire bar, and fabricated aluminum, zinc, lead, cadmium, cerium, cobalt, mercury, and nickel including 261 tons of pure nickel shapes.

Group VI-4A included a large quantity of miscellaneous metals and metal products including molybdenum concentrates, pig iron, and an incredible *one million miles* of telephone wire and submarine cable. The 2,159,336 short tons of petroleum products largely comprised aviation gas and gas-blending agents to raise the octane level of Soviet domestic gasoline. Large quantities of inorganic chemicals were shipped, including ammonium nitrate, caustic soda, potassium nitrate, soda ash, sodium cyanide, sodium dichromate, and similar basic chemicals. In the organic chemical field, shipments included quantities of acetone, butyl acetate, a large quantity of ethyl alcohol (359,555 short tons), ethylene glycol, glycerin, hexamine, methanol, phenol, and 113,884 tons of toluol (a base for manufacture of TNT).

Group VI-10C included $67,000 worth of compressed and liquefied gas. In addition about 12,200 tons of paints, varnishes, carbon, lampblack, and other pigments were shipped. Plastic shipments included 1139 tons of resins and 593 tons of cellulose film base; miscellaneous chemicals included ammonia rubber paste, boiler compounds, reagents, and chemicals used in the photographic industry.

Textiles included 102,673,000 yards of cotton cloth, 60,138,000 yards of woolen cloth, and 53,803,000 yards of webbing. In addition, quantities of tarpaulin, cordage, twine, and fish nets were supplied. Leather shipments included 46,161 tons of leather and $362,000 worth of specialized small lots of leather products.

Rubber shipments included large quantities of rubber products, among them shock absorber cord (166,000,000 yards), about seven million tires and tubes, and $7,784,000 worth of rubber hose.

In large-lot leather goods, 14,572,000 pairs of army boots, 221,000 pairs of ski boots, and other miscellaneous boots and shoes were shipped, in addition to leather apparel including leather jackets, belts, and miscellaneous leather goods.

Abrasives totaled 17,711 short tons, and abrasive products were valued at over $15 million.

One interesting item included in Groups VI-22A/22C comprised carbon and graphite—of interest because of possible utilization in atomic energy. Shipments of graphite powder totaled 3,017 tons; graphite and carbon electrodes totaled $20,933,000; and other graphite material totaled $1,532,000.

Finally, about 14,000 tons of paper and paper products comprised Groups VI-23A/24 with $1.8 million worth of photographic material, asbestos material, button, and miscellaneous other products.

U.S. Army equipment was shipped from the Persian corridor. This equipment included two truck assembly plants, 792 ten-ton Mack cargo trucks, 21 cranes, and 1751 short tons of 75-pound railroad rails plus accessories. The U.S. Army Air Force shuttle bases in the Soviet Union were turned over to the Soviet Union, and 51 storage tanks used by the British Army in the Caspian Sea area were transferred to the Soviet Union.

THE PIPELINE AGREEMENT OF OCTOBER 15, 1945

Undelivered Lend Lease material in inventory or procurement at the end of World War II was made available to the Soviet Union under the so-called "pipeline agreement" of October 1945. Under this agreement the Soviet Union undertook to pay the United States in dollars, with only a small amount of interest, for additional material.

The goods shipped under this agreement were valued at $222 million and comprised only industrial machinery and equipment with some spare parts. A large proportion of the equipment consisted of electrical generating stations, boilers, engines, motors, and transformers for the electric power industry. Other large shipments included machine tools—such as hydraulic presses, hammers, mechanical presses, shears, flanging machines, and bending machines. Large amounts of mining equipment included mine hoists, ball mills, jaw crushers, and hammer mills. The machine tool shipments comprised lathes of all types, including engine lathes, precision lathes, semiautomatic machines with special tools, universal machines, turret lathes, chucking machines, and large quantities of spare parts and specialized equipment ancillary to such machine tools. Spare parts for vehicles previously shipped under Lend Lease were also included in the agreement.[4]

The Soviet Union has not maintained its payments schedule under this agreement.

Table 1-2   TOTAL AMOUNT OWED AGGREGATE PAYMENTS, AND
              TOTAL OUTSTANDING ON SOVIET LEND LEASE
              "PIPELINE" ACCOUNT AS OF DECEMBER 31, 1967*

Obligation under agreement of October 15, 1945	$222,494,574.01
Interest accrued	$107,171,641.28
Total amount owed	$329,666,215.29
Principal paid through December 31, 1967	$47,023,534.57
Interest paid through December 31, 1967	$107,171,641.28
Balance to be repaid	$175,471,039.44
Past due (as of September 1968)	$77,024,968.00

Source: Letter from U.S. Department of State.

* This table does not include amounts due on the $11 billion Soviet Lend Lease account.

UNITED KINGDOM LEND LEASE TO THE U.S.S.R.

War material furnished by the United Kingdom to Russia—free of cost after Russia entered the war against Germany—was regularized in an agreement signed on June 27, 1942.

---

[4] The equipment lists were not published by the State Department, but see Schedules A and B deposited at the Hoover Institution.

By the end of May 1943, a total of 4690 complete aircraft had been sent to Russia, with appropriate supplies of spares, including engines, airframes, and other articles of equipment.[5] Other supplies shipped to Russia included material for all sections of the Soviet fighting forces: 1042 tanks, 6135 miles of cable, over two million meters of camouflage netting, and 195 guns of various calibers with 4,644,930 rounds of ammunition.

The United Kingdom also shipped the following between October 1, 1941, and March 31, 1946: 28,050 long tons of tin, 40,000 long tons of copper, 32,000 long tons of aluminum, 3300 long tons of graphite, and £1,424,000 worth of industrial diamonds.[6]

UNRRA SUPPLIES TO THE UKRAINE AND BELORUSSIA[7]

In August 1945 the United Nations agreed on a $250 million United Nations Relief and Rehabilitation Administration (UNRRA) program for Ukraine and Belorussia, and in a statement of rather twisted logic[8] promptly suspended payments for such supplies. After numerous delays, two small U.N. missions arrived

Table 1-3   UNRRA DELIVERIES TO BELORUSSIA AND THE UKRAINE

Categories	Belorussian SSR		Ukrainian SSR	
	U.S. Dollar Equivalents	Gross Long Tons	U.S. Dollar Equivalents	Gross Long Tons
Food	$29,591,800	101,396	$99,437,700	315,748
Clothing, textiles, and footwear	7,044,200	5,784	17,207,700	16,225
Medical and sanitation	991,100	646	2,445,500	1,037
Agricultural equipment and seeds	5,412,100	8,050	16,988,900	38,069
Industrial equipment	17,780,800	25,977	52,119,500	95,970
Total	$60,820,000	141,853	$188,199,300	467,049

Source: G. Woodbridge, *UNRRA*, II (New York: Columbia University Press, 1960), p. 250.

---

[5] Source: Great Britain, *Accounts and Papers*, 1942-43, XI, Command 6483 (November 1943).
[6] U.S. Bureau of Mines, *Mineral Trade Notes*, (Washington) vol. 22, no. 6 (June 1946), p. 49.
[7] This section is based on George Woodbridge, *UNRRA* (New York: Columbia Univeristy Press, 1950), vol. II, pp. 231-56.
[8] The U. N. subcommittee granting the suspension gave the following reason for suspension of payment: "Information supplied to the Subcommittee by the representatives of the Byelorussian Soviet Socialist Republic indicated that in accordance with the constitutional provisions of the Union of Soviet Socialist Republics, this constituent republic has no foreign exchange

in Russia to administer the program; the missions reported that supplies were equitably distributed, although with no indication that they originated with the United Nations, and mission reports were submitted concerning their distribution. By March 1947 the supply program was about 99.61 percent fulfilled, only $982,700 remaining of the one-quarter billion dollar allotment.

Top priority was given to fats, oils, and meats. These were followed by industrial equipment, with emphasis on equipment for restoration of public utilities and communications together with equipment for basic industries such as peat extraction equipment, a brick-making plant, an asphalt plant, and a mineral wool plant. Almost half of the industrial procurement program was devoted to "protocol goods," mainly electric power stations ordered by the U.S.S.R. in the United Kingdom under the Third Protocol of 1942 but not delivered by 1945. Industrial goods not requiring manufacture (e.g., small locomotives, raw materials, electrical systems, and military vehicles) were by and large delivered before the end of 1946.

SOVIET REQUESTS AND SOVIET RECEIPTS

The Soviet view of Lend Lease in historical perspective is highly deprecatory. A. N. Lagovskii, for example, suggests that the first deliveries arrived only in February 1942, in very insignificant quantities, and "even this delivery was far from being first class."[9] After pointing out that the United States subsequently increased its deliveries to a total of "several billions," Lagovskii suggests that very little was in the form of needed tanks and aircraft and that the U.S.S.R. was "one of the best economically developed countries in the world" on the eve of World War II.[10] Lagovskii concludes that deliveries were "very modest" and that the "Soviet Armed Forces defeated the Fascist German Armies with domestic weapons, developed by our designers, engineers, and workers at our plants."[11]

Other Soviet accounts also maintain that Lend Lease was a minor factor in defeating the German invaders, and no mention has been found in any of them of the deliveries of over $1 billion of industrial equipment.

A comparison of Soviet requests with actual U.S. deliveries does not support

assets of its own, such assets being entirely in the hands of the government of the Union of Soviet Socialist Republics. Nevertheless, in view of the great destruction in the Byelorussian Soviet Socialist Republic, the Subcommittee recommends that the government of the Byelorussian Soviet Socialist Republic be considered at this time not to be in a position to pay with suitable means of foreign exchange for relief and rehabilitation supplies which the Director General will make available." Woodbridge, *op. cit.* n.7, p. 234.

9 A. N. Lagovskii, *Strategiia i Ekonomika*, 2d edition (Moscow, 1961), pp. 113-14.

10 *Ibid.*, pp. 116-17.

11 *Ibid.*, pp. 115-16.

the Soviet position in any manner whatsoever. For example, the initial Soviet request for 3000 pursuit planes was sizable; however, the combined U.S. and British offers under the First Protocol were 2700 pursuit planes, obtained by stripping every other front of its requests. Initial Soviet requests for tanks were for 9900 light and medium tanks, and combined U.S. and British supply on the First Protocol was 4700 tanks. Other items were filled, and indeed overfilled. For example, the Soviets initially requested 20,000 submachine guns—they were offered 98,220 under the First Protocol alone.[12]

We may therefore conclude that Lend Lease with its associated and supplementary postwar programs injected about $1.25 billion worth of the latest American industrial equipment into the Soviet economy. This figure does not include the value of semifabricated materials, foodstuffs, industrial supplies, and vehicles of indirect benefit. This industrial equipment comprised machines and technologies generally in advance of Soviet wartime capabilities (as will be described in later chapters), and the greater proportion was of significant value to the postwar economy.

[12] Based on data in anonymous, *op. cit.* n.1, p. 30. A comparison of the other protocols and Soviet requests could be constructed from the data given in Robert H. Jones, *The Roads to Russia* (Norman: University of Oklahoma Press, 1969), pp. 119, 167.

CHAPTER TWO

World War II Reparations
for the Soviet Union

OBJECTIVES OF THE SOVIET REPARATIONS POLICIES

A prime objective of the Soviet Union during World War II was to exact from its enemies the maximum of reparations in kind to rebuild the war-torn and occupied areas of Russia. U.S. Secretary of State Edward J. Stettinius recalled the great importance attached to such reparations: "Stalin, on the question of German reparations, spoke with great emotion, which was in sharp contrast to his usual calm, even manner."[1]

Only those reparations acquired in the form of plants and equipment transferred to the U.S.S.R. from enemy countries come within the scope of this study.

Table 2-1   SUMMARY OF ORGANIZATIONAL FORMS USED BY THE
SOVIET UNION TO TRANSFER REPARATIONS AFTER 1944

	Capital transfers (reparations in kind)	Trophy brigades (war booty)	Joint stock companies (financial penetration)
Italy	Yes	No	No
Austria	Yes	Yes	Yes
Manchuria	Yes	Yes	A few only
Finland	Yes	No	No
Korea	Probably No	No	Yes
Japan	No	No	No
Rumania	Yes	Yes	Yes
Hungary	Yes	Yes	Yes
Bulgaria	Yes	—	Yes (a few)
Germany (East)	Yes	Yes	Yes
Germany (Western zones)	Yes	No	No
Yugoslavia	—	No	Limited

Source: J. P. Nettl, *The Eastern Zone and Soviet Policy in Germany, 1945-50* (London: Oxford University Press, 1951); and N. Spulber, *The Economics of Communist Eastern Europe* (New York: The Technology Press of M.I.T., and John Wiley & Sons, 1957).

---

[1] E. R. Stettinius, Jr., *Roosevelt and the Russians: The Yalta Conference* (New York: Doubleday, 1949), p. 263.

Some other forms of reparations—the "trophy brigades", for example, and the operation of plants in occupied areas on Soviet account like the SAGs (Soviet companies in East Germany) and the SOVROMs (Soviet companies in Rumania)—are not fully discussed, as they do not fall directly within the scope of our examination.[2]

Capital goods and technology that were transferred to the U.S.S.R. under the reparations agreements and that contributed both industrial capacity and technology will be described on a geographic basis in this chapter. Various chapters in Part II include descriptions of the impact of reparations on individual sectors of the Russian economy.

In monetary terms, reparations claims were substantial; in fact, a figure of $20 billion in 1938 dollars is commonly cited as the Soviet objective. The claims can be approximately and more cogently summarized on a country-by-country basis as follows:[3]

Germany	$10,000 million (plus one-third of the German fleet)
Austria	400 million
Finland	300 million
Italy	100 million (plus one-third of the Italian fleet)
Rumania	300 million
Bulgaria	70 million
Hungary	300 million
Manchuria	800 million (allocated to the Chinese reparations account but arbitrarily removed by the U.S.S.R.)

The figure of $20 billion for total Allied reparations, of which about one-half was to go to the U.S.S.R., was apparently arrived at with only passing objection from the United Kingdom and none from the United States. The original Molotov submission at the Yalta conference was that the amount be fixed at $20 billion with $10 billion to go to the U.S.S.R.[4] Stettinius reported that he himself suggested 50 percent should go to the U.S.S.R.[5], but that there was no final agreement on total absolute amounts:

[2] These are discussed in two excellent books. See J. P. Nettl, *The Eastern Zone and Soviet Policy in Germany, 1945-50* (London: Oxford University Press, 1951) for Germany, and Nicolas Spulber, *The Economics of Communist Eastern Europe* (New York: The Technology Press of M.I.T. and John Wiley & Sons 1957), for excellent, very detailed material on the other East European countries.

[3] Estimates of actual, in contrast to planned, transfers suggest a total of about $10 billion. For example, the U.S. Central Intelligence Agency stated: 'The economic gains accruing to the U.S.S.R. as a result of the European bloc arrangements was greatest during the 1945-55 period when direct and indirect reparations netted the U.S.S.R. an amount estimated at roughly 10 billion dollars.' It should be noted that this excludes Manchuria and possibly Finland. U.S. Congress, *Comparisons of the United States and Soviet Economies*, Joint Economic Committee, Sub-Committee on Economic Statistics, Prepared by the Central Intelligence Agency in Cooperation with the Department of State and the Department of Defense, Supplemental Statement on Costs and Benefits to the Soviet Union of Its Bloc and Pact System: Comparisons with the Western Alliance System, 82nd Congress, 2d session (Washington, 1960).

[4] Stettinius, *op. cit.* n.1, p. 165.

[5] *Ibid.*, p. 231.

It should be understood that there was absolutely no commitment at Yalta that the total sum of reparations should be twenty billion and that fifty percent should go to the Soviet Union. We made it clear that these figures were merely a basis for discussion.[6]

Stettinius added that Russia claimed "incorrectly" that Roosevelt agreed to the $20 billion figure.[7] It is noticeable that no one suggested a measure of relative war damages as a basis for reparations, nor were any engineering or economic studies made to support relative damage claims.[8]

According to one authority, J. P. Nettl:

It is clear that the Soviet authorities were working on a separate plan, prepared before the long drawn-out discussions in the Allied Control Council had even begun. The plan was in operation at a time when the Western Reparations Agency had only begun to register the individual claims of participating powers and was tentatively having particular works earmarked for dismantling.[9]

The method used by the Soviets to arrive at specific country reparations demands differed according to Soviet military and political relationships with the respective countries. Reparations from Germany, Austria, and Italy were settled at discussions by the Big Three; the Soviet share was first taken out on a priority basis by the Moscow Reparations Commission and the balance transferred to an Allied Reparations Commission in Brussels for further distribution, including a second cut for the U.S.S.R. This arrangement worked well—for the Soviet Union.

Finland, Rumania, Hungary, and Bulgaria made bilateral peace agreements with the U.S.S.R. and their reparations were also determined by bilateral agreements. Manchurian industry was actually a charge against the Chinese reparations account; however, the Soviets unilaterally moved into Manchuria just before the end of war in the Far East and removed some $800 million worth of equipment before the U.S. Inspection Commission arrived.[10]

The Soviet reparations program, as pointed out by Nettl, contained definite indications of detailed long-range planning with clearcut objectives, and although each country (Finland, Hungary, Rumania, Germany, Italy, Korea, and Manchuria) was treated differently, some basic parallels can be drawn.

First, the reparations programs were designed to supply capital goods to the Soviet economy, but only modern units of technology were to be supplied.

[6] *Ibid.*, p. 266.
[7] *Ibid.*, p. 231.
[8] *Ibid.*, p. 231. The UNRRA studies of damage in the Soviet Union were not based on first-hand information, and are extremely vague.
[9] Nettl, *op. cit.* n.2.
[10] Edwin Pauley, *Report on Japanese Assets in Manchuria to the President of the United States, July 1946* (Washington, 1946).

Obsolescent plants were ignored. The intent was to gear acquisitions to the future needs of the Soviet economy.

Second, there are some unusual parallels. For example, the Finland reparations program was similar to that of Korea, while the German program was similar to that of Manchuria. There is no question that the Soviets had a plan, but scattered evidence also suggests they tried to cover their steps and obscure the plan. In Manchuria, for example, they encouraged Chinese mobs to wreck the plants after Soviet dismantling had removed desirable equipment.[11]

Third, equipment choices are interesting as they parallel deductions about weaknesses in the Soviet economy; however, such choices puzzled the Pauley Mission engineers in Manchuria, who could not understand, for example, why the Soviets left electric furnaces and cement kilns and removed ball bearings.

SALVAGE VALUE OF DISMANTLED PLANTS

It has been widely suggested that dismantling of plants and removal to the U.S.S.R. was wasteful, inefficient, and of minor economic and technical value.

Statements of a general nature can be found by American officials concerned with Soviet policy in the late 1940s. For example, Walter Bedell Smith, U.S. Ambassador in Moscow, made the following comment:

> The destructive and unskilled methods used by the Soviet Army in dismantling German industrial plants had been enormously wasteful, and it had proved difficult for the Russians to reestablish these plants in the Soviet Union.
> Foreigners who traveled by rail from Berlin to Moscow reported that every railroad yard and siding was jammed with German machinery, much of it deteriorating in the rain and snow.[12]

A similar statement was made by Lucius Clay, U.S. military governor in Germany:

> The Soviet Government soon found that it could not reconstruct these factories quickly, if at all. Reports verified by photographs reaching U.S. intelligence agencies in Germany showed that almost every siding in East Germany, and many in Russia, contained railway cars filled with valuable machine tools rusting into ruins.[13]

Closer observation may be gleaned from Fritz Löwenthal,[14] a former Com-

---

[11]   *Ibid.*
[12]   W. B. Smith, *My Three Years in Moscow* (Philadelphia: J. B. Lippincott, 1950), p. 224.
[13]   Lucius D. Clay, *Decision in Germany* (New York: Doubleday, 1950).
[14]   Fritz Löwenthal, *News from Soviet Germany* (London: Victor Gollancz, 1950), p. 207.

munist official in charge of the Control Department of the Central Legal Administration in the Soviet Zone:

> In Odessa, Kiev, Oranienbaum, Kimry, and other places, where the dismantled factories were to be reassembled, it often turned out that vital machinery was missing or had been damaged beyond repair, as the dismantling is invariably carried out by the Russians at top speed and without proper care.[15]

Vladimir Alexandrov, a Russian refugee, makes even stronger statements. For example: "The dismantling of German industry ... was characterized mainly by the almost complete absence of any overall direction, particularly with regard to the technical questions involved in dismantling complicated industrial equipment."[16] Alexandrov adds that shortage of railroad equipment, disorganized loading, weather, and general inefficiency greatly reduced the value of the dismantled equipment.

Other writers have viewed this inefficiency as the reason for a change in Soviet policy and the establishment of the SAGs to provide current reparations for the Soviet economy in lieu of the transfer of capital equipment. For example, Almond reports the following:

> At first they believed this purpose [i.e., the transfer of capital equipment] to be served best by the removal to Russia of large quantities of industrial equipment. It soon became apparent, however, that the Russians generally lacked the skilled labor and technical know-how required to dismantle, reassemble, and operate this equipment efficiently; consequently, this method of exacting reparations proved to be even more wasteful than would normally be expected. Soviet policy then switched to reparations out of current production. Roughly one-third of the industrial capacity remaining in the zone was transferred to Soviet ownership, but left in place to be operated for Soviet account using German labor, fuel, and raw materials.[17]

Two conclusions can be drawn from the foregoing statements: (1) the Soviets were hasty and unskilled and consequently may have damaged machinery and equipment, and (2) weather, particularly rain, may have corroded machinery.[18]
On the other hand, Nettl observes: "Against this is the fact that the Soviet

---

[15] *Ibid.*
[16] Robert Slusser, ed., *Soviet Economic Policy in Postwar Germany* (New York: Research Program on the U.S.S.R., 1953), p. 14.
[17] Gabriel A. Almond, *The Struggle for Democracy in Germany* (Richmond: The William Byrd Press, 1949), p. 158.
[18] Rainfall in Eastern Europe tends to be less than in Western Europe and precipitation for the years 1945-48 was normal. Average rainfall at Berlin from 1938 to 1950 was 594.7 mm per year; in 1946 it was slightly below this (570.6 mm) and in 1945 and 1947 slightly above (629.8 and 626.9 mm, respectively), *World Weather Records, 1941-50.* (Washington, U.S. Weather Bureau), p. 677.

Government had great experience of removing and reassembling complete factories. Much was done during the war, but the principle goes back to Tsarist days!"[19] Examination of the evidence of installation of equipment in the Soviet Union suggests that the Soviets did indeed reerect these plants in the U.S.S.R. and that the plants in fact made a significant contribution to Soviet industrial development in the late 1940s and early 1950s.

The amount of waste, however, cannot be determined on the basis of the evidence at hand. As the physical removals were numerous, it is essential to determine accurately the possibilities of successful dismantling in order to arrive at a more accurate assessment of its potential contribution to the Soviet economy. If dismantled plants could not be reerected in the U.S.S.R., or if they were lost or heavily damaged in transit, then regardless of how many plants were dismantled and transferred, the economic impact would be insignificant.[20] Some consideration is therefore given to this question, and the arguments are summarized in the next sections.

The first factor that has to be taken into account is the condition of the plant as inherited by Soviet occupation forces, particularly whether Allied bombing—extremely heavy in the later phases of the war—had damaged factories beyond usefulness. Reports of the U.S. Strategic Bombing Survey, a series of highly detailed postwar ground examinations of 25 target plants, concluded that large tonnages of bombs had not, for several reasons, reduced these plants to a completely unusable condition. The effect of heavy bombing was to halt production temporarily, not to destroy productive capacity. For example:

> Physical damage studies point to the fact that machine tools and heavy manufacturing equipment of all kinds are very difficult to destroy or to damage beyond repair by bombing attacks. Buildings housing such equipment may be burned down and destroyed but, after clearing away the wreckage, it has been found more often than not, that heavy equipment when buried under tons of debris may be salvaged and put back into operation in a relatively short time and with comparatively little difficulty.[21]

Since the Soviets transported only less damageable items (e.g., machine tools and equipment rather than utility lines, steel-fabricated structures, and

[19] Nettl, *op. cit.* n.2, p. 205.

[20] This is a technical question. The economics of dismantling, as many commentators have suggested, are obscure. For example, John Hynd, M.P.: "I have never been able to understand the economics of putting 2000 men at work for twelve months—2000 man years— dismantling a rusty old steel factory, breaking it up, marking up the parts, packing them up into crates, and sending them to some other country, where it will probably take two or three years to rebuild the factory, and when, in four or five years' time, someone will have an out-of-date and rusty factory, whereas, if we had left it in Germany producing steel, we should probably have been able to build in the same time, and without any loss, a new modern, well equipped up-to-date factory" (Great Britain, *Parliamentary Debates*, October 27, 1949, p. 534).

[21] U.S. Strategic Bombing Survey, *Aircraft Division: Industry Report*, no. 84, January 1947.

gas holders) it may be asserted that strategic bombing had very little effect, and probably reduced the number of even the most desirable machine tools available for reparations by only about ten percent.

The next question concerns the extent of damage incurred in dismantling and removal procedures. Most Western commentators on dismantling have stated that Soviet dismantling policy was inept and wasteful, and that ultimately the Soviets were induced to switch to a policy of leaving industry in place to be operated by captive companies on Soviet account. This may be a rather superficial view.

At the end of hostilities in Europe the Russians had a great deal of experience in dismantling and the West had very little—this assertion may be highlighted by examining those categories which were subject to little dismantling. The Soviets concentrated on plants containing equipment and machines that could be safely transported. Close comparison of removals in Manchuria and East Germany indicates that almost 100 percent of removals had a high salvage value and were easily removed and transported, i.e., machine tools, precision instruments, and small items of equipment *not* made of fabricated sheet metal. On the other hand, the Western Allies in Europe appear to have concentrated their removals on plants with a relatively low salvage value. One cannot, for example, satisfactorily remove an iron and steel plant to another location, which is exactly what the Allies tried to do. In fact, the Western Allies reduced German steel capacity by 25 percent and concentrated removals in this sector.[22] Although the Soviets did try cutting up and removing cement kilns in Manchuria, the mistake was not repeated in East Germany.

Soviet proficiency in dismantling and shipping plants to Russia is exemplified by events in 1944 in Persia. There the United States used two truck assembly plants (TAP I and TAP II) to assemble U.S. trucks that had been "knocked down" before on-shipment to the U.S.S.R. under Lend Lease. Almost 200,000 trucks were finally assembled in these two plants. Apart from the vehicles assembled, the plants themselves were allocated to the Soviet Union under the Lend Lease agreement, and on December 7, 1944, orders arrived to dismantle and transfer to Russia. A Soviet Acceptance Committee arrived three days later. One plant was divided into small segments, each in charge of one U.S. officer, one Soviet officer, and one interpreter. By January 17, 1945, the entire plant had been dismantled, labeled, loaded onto 115 flatcars, and shipped by rail to the U.S.S.R. Thus in a little over four weeks what U.S. Army spokesmen described as a "considerable consignment" was handled with no trouble. The second plant followed in April on 260 flatcars and was handled with equal dispatch.[23]

[22] See n. 20, comments of Mr. Hynd, M. P.
[23] T. H. V. Motter, *The Persian Corridor and Aid To Russia* (Washington: Department of the Army, Office of the Chief of Military History, 1952).

It should be noted also that 20 years later, on the testimony of Juanita Castro Ruz (sister of Fidel Castro of Cuba), Cuban sugar mills were "dismantled and shipped to the U.S.S.R. as collateral for Cuba's imports of Soviet arms and ammunition."[24]

Therefore, we may have imputed to the Soviets the same mistakes we made ourselves due to lack of experience in dismantling and removing plants. Further, although dismantling is a very inefficient method of developing capacity, the Soviets may have partly avoided or at least offset this factor by long-range planning and greater dismantling experience gained in the 1940-42 movement of more than 1300 large industrial plants behind the Urals, including all aircraft, tank, and motor plants; 93 steel plants; 150 machine tool plants; and 40 electrical plants.[25]

Thus the change in policy in May 1946, when the Soviets announced that dismantling in the Soviet Zone was almost completed, was probably not the result of "inefficiency" but of a knowledge born of experience that remaining plants could not be removed successfully and would better serve the Soviet purpose by operation in place.

We can learn something of Soviet dismantling policy by examining those plants left in place and *not* removed to the U.S.S.R. Five dismantling patterns emerge:

1. Plants with a low salvage value were not removed *in toto*, although individual pieces of equipment and instruments from such plants were selectively removed. Thus the Soviets avoided removing iron and steel furnaces and cement kilns, for example.
2. Machines and equipment with a high salvage value and a high value-to-weight ratio were prime targets for removal. Thus machine tools of all types, textile, papermaking, and food processing machinery, instruments from all industries, and electrical equipment received first priority. Such equipment can be easily removed, easily prepared for shipment, and easily crated and loaded, and it withstands transportation relatively well.
3. The first two observations are modified in one important way: choice of removals was selective in terms of obsolescence. This came out clearly in Manchuria, where the older machines were almost always left and the more modern machines always removed.
4. Selective removals were supplemented by items in short supply in the U.S.S.R., particularly rubber conveyer belts (used for shoe repair), electric motors of all types and sizes, hand tools, laboratory equipment, and hospital equipment.

[24]   U.S. House of Representatives, *Annual Report for the Year 1965*, House Committee on Un-American Activities, 89th Congress, 1st session (Washington, 1966).
[25]   R. H. Jones, *The Roads to Russia* (Norman: University of Oklahoma Press, 1969), p. 222.

5. The planned nature of the removals is emphasized in several ways. It is particularly notable that sufficient equipment to produce the power needed for the dismantling operation was left in place; a casual program would have removed such equipment.

It has been suggested that much reparations equipment was damaged in removal or that bad packing resulted in damage in transit. Contrary evidence can be drawn from two areas, Manchuria and Germany. The Pauley Mission obtained photographs and information concerning the dismantling of Manchurian equipment. The work was undertaken by Soviet troops under the direction of officers who were presumably civilian specialists temporarily in army uniform. Photographs of these troops at work indicate that they were young, but their work appears, from the photographs, to have been methodical. The equipment was removed from its bases, placed on wood skids, and then crated. Heavy damage was done to factory walls only to remove equipment. American engineers on later inspection trips noted several points which lead to the conclusion that the dismantling was not done in great haste. Certain plants were subjected to dismantling several times at intervals of several months. (See Table 2-2.)

Table 2-2   THE SOVIET DISMANTLING SCHEDULE IN MANCHURIA
(MAJOR PLANTS ONLY)

Manchurian Plant	Reported start of dismantling	Reported finish of dismantling
Mukden Main Arsenal	August 15, 1945	March 7, 1946
Manchuria Machine Tool Co.	August 20, 1945	November 14, 1945
Manchurian Gas Co.	August 20, 1945	December 1945
Mukden Refinery	August 21, 1945	February 1946
Fouhsin Power Plant	August 26, 1945	November 1945
Japanese Army 1st Fuel Depot	September 15, 1945	November 10, 1945
Fushun Power Plant	September 20, 1945	October 30, 1945
Molybdenite Mine	Two weeks in September 1945	
Manchuria Machine Tool Co.	September 1945	November 1945
Manchu Wire Rope Co.	Mid-September 1945	Mid-November 1945
Manchu Iron Co.	September 1945	February 1946
Southern Manchurian Railway Co. Repair Shops	October 12, 1945	October 25, 1945
Nippon Air Brake Co.	October 12, 1945	October 25, 1945
Manchu Rubber Co.	October 12, 1945	November 19, 1945
Manchurian Light Metal Co.	October 1945	Early November 1945
Tafengmen Power HEP	Three weeks in October 1945	
Anshan Teto Transmission Tower Co.	October 1945	November 1945
Taiping Hospital	End October 1945	End November 1945
Manchu Otani Heavy Ind. Co.	November 1945	November 1945

Source: Reconstructed from Edwin Pauley, *Report on Japanese Assets in Manchuria to the President of the United States, July 1946* (Washington, D.C., 1946), Appendix 3.

Sometimes the Soviets made it more difficult for later repair work, e.g., by bending over hold-down bolts; such effort is unlikely to be expended in a hasty operation.

Photographs of the crates and the crating process in Germany suggest careful work under Soviet supervision.[26] Crates were marked for Stankoimport, an organization with extensive experience in importing foreign equipment. There is no reason to suppose these shipments would not be handled like any other Soviet imports of machinery. It also must be borne in mind that Soviet practice is to place complete responsibility on the individual in charge, with harsh penalties for failure, and there is no reason to believe that any other procedure was followed in the reparations removals. There was certainly pressure on the 70,000 or so individual German and Chinese laborers recruited to assist in removals.

Another factor to be considered is whether damaged equipment could have been restored to its former usefulness; and there is evidence that Soviet engineers have exerted great ingenuity in such efforts.[27] A practical view of the possibility of this type of recovery was seen in a 1946 German exhibition in the British sector of Berlin with the theme ''Value from under the Ruins.'' Exhibits included lathes, stamping dies, presses, gears, and even more delicate apparatus such as electrical equipment, typewriters, sewing machines, and printing machines retrieved from under debris (where they had lain for two years or more) and returned to original working order. Acid baths and abrasives were used to remove rust, high-penetration oils freed interior working parts, and badly damaged parts were replaced. Precision bearings were brought back by electrodeposition of chromium, and sandblasting was used on larger metal parts.[28] This, then, is a practical example of recovery of *delicate* equipment subjected to far greater abuse and more adverse conditions than any equipment removed from Germany to the Soviet Union. There is no reason why Soviet technicians could not have performed as well on weatherbeaten equipment or on equipment damaged in transit.

Support for this argument may be derived from reports on German equipment moved during World War II across national frontiers and sometimes underground to avoid bombing damage. For example, in a claims letter from Bussing NAG Flugmotorenwerke to Reichsluftfahrtministerium in July 1944 the company—obviously for claims purposes putting on the worst front—stressed that moving caused a lot of wear and tear, but ''this damage was done chiefly when the machines were being moved into the salt mines.'' Further explanations suggest that chemical action in the salt mines and operation by unskilled labor did

[27]   See p. 30 below.

[26]   *A Year of Potsdam* (n.p.: Office of Military Government for Germany (U.S. Zone), Economics Division, 1946).
[28]   ''Recovery of Machinery from Ruins,'' *British Zone Review* (Hamburg), April 26, 1946 p. 15.

more damage to the equipment than lowering it into the mines, although many pieces had to be up-ended for this purpose.[29]

In general, it is suggested that pessimistic interpretations of Soviet ability to make good use of reparations equipment are not founded on all the available evidence. In fact, reparations equipment was a valuable addition to the Soviet economy.

ORGANIZATIONAL STRUCTURE OF THE GERMAN REPARATIONS PROGRAM

The organization of German reparations was from start to finish favorable to the Soviet Union. The initial Soviet share was determined by the Moscow Reparations Commission, whose work was undertaken in "strict secrecy," with Dr. Isadore Lubin as the U.S. representative on the Moscow Reparations Committee.

The Allied Control Council for Germany at Potsdam, through its Coordination Committee, made allocations of reparations in the Western zones of Germany; plants and equipment in the Soviet Zone were not handled through the Allied Control Council, only by the Soviet authorities. The Coordination Committee allocated reparations from the "Western portion" between the Soviets and an Inter-Allied Reparation Agency (IARA). The Soviets then dismantled their allocations immediately, while the remaining 18 allies had to wait until further distribution had been determined by the IARA.

In this manner the Soviets, by virtue of having only to bid against IARA and not 18 individual allies, had the cream of Western zone plants as well as all plants in the Soviet Zone; even at the IARA level, bargaining was bilateral rather than multilateral (Figure 2-1).

Finally, under the program known as "Operation RAP" the Soviets were given priority in removing Western zone plants allocated under this preferential procedure, so that at the end of 1946, 94 percent of shipments from the U.S. Zone had been sent to the Soviet Union.

The formal Soviet claim in the Western zones was determined as follows (Section 4 of the allocation agreement):

(a) 15 percent of such usable and complete industrial capital equipment, in the first place from the metallurgical, chemical and machine manufacturing industries, as is unnecessary for the German peace economy and should be removed from the Western Zones of Germany in exchange for an equiva-

---

[29] U.S. Strategic Bombing Survey, *Bussing-NAG Flugmotorenwerke*, Number 89, GmBH (Brunswick, Germany, January 1947), pp. 9-10.

lent value of food, coal, potash, zinc, timber, clay products, petroleum products, and such other commodities as may be agreed upon.

(b) 10 percent of such industrial equipment as is unnecessary for the German peace economy and should be removed from the Western Zones, to be transferred to the Soviet Government on reparation account without payment or exchange of any kind in return.

Removals of equipment as provided in (a) and (b) above shall be made simultaneously.[30]

Figure 2-1   ALLIED ORGANIZATIONAL STRUCTURE FOR
GERMAN REPARATIONS

Moscow Reparations Committee	— Selected 50 percent for U.S.S.R. in Eastern Europe
Allied Control Council for Germany (Coordination Committee)	— Selected 25 percent for U.S.S.R. in West Germany
"Operation RAP"	— Priority for Soviets

Source: Inter-Allied Reparation Agency, Report of Secretary-General for the Year 1946 (Brussels, 1946), annex X, pp. 61-62; Germany, Office of Military Government (U.S. Zone), Economics Division, A Year of Potsdam: The German Economy Since the Surrender (n.p.: OMGUS, 1946).

In return for equipment dismantled under Section 4(a) the Soviets agreed to make reciprocal deliveries of raw materials valued at 60 percent of the equipment received from the Western zones. In October 1947 the U.S.S.R. presented a first list of reciprocal commodities, which was accepted, and deliveries were duly made.[31] In May 1948 the U.S.S.R. presented a second list of commodities, also accepted by the Western Allies. A dispute then arose over delivery points and the Soviets made no further deliveries.

Therefore, the Soviets delivered a total of 5,967,885 RM (1938: about $1.5 million) against a commitment of the 50 million RM which would represent 60 percent of the value of industrial equipment received by the Soviet Union under Section 4(a). In other words, the Soviets paid only 12 percent of their commitment for reparations received under Section 4(a).

REPARATIONS PLANTS SHIPPED FROM WESTERN ALLIED ZONES TO THE SOVIET UNION

A total of 25 percent of industrial plants in the Western Allied zones was allocated to the U.S.S.R. under Sections 4(a) and 4(b) of the allocation agreement,

[30] Inter-Allied Reparation Agency, Report of Secretary-General for the Year 1949 (Brussels, 1950), p. 3.

[31] For a list of Soviet reciprocal deliveries see ibid., p. 17.

and dismantling of these plants was expedited on a priority basis. The Soviet allocation status as of November 30, 1948, is given in Table 2-3.

Table 2-3   PLANTS FROM WESTERN ZONES ALLOCATED
                 TO THE U.S.S.R. AS OF NOVEMBER 30, 1948

Zone of occupation	War plants	Reparations plants
U.S. (the RAP program)	20	4½
British	6	4½
French	3	1
	29	10

Source: Germany, Office of the Military Government (U.S. Zone), *Report of the Military Governor*, November 1948, p. 25.

Probably the most important single plant dismantled for the Soviet Union was the Bandeisenwalzwerk Dinslaken A.G. in the British Zone.[32] This plant was the largest and most efficient hot- and cold-rolled strip mill on the European continent. The effect of the removal on German productive capacity was a reduction of 15 to 30 percent in strip steel, 20 percent in sheet steel, and 50 percent in tinplate strip steel.[33] Another important steel plant removed to the Soviet Union was Hüttenwerk Essen-Borbeck; dismantling required the services of 3000 workers over a period of two years to prepare for shipment.[34]

By August 1, 1946, a total of 156 plants in the U.S.Zone had been confirmed for reparations by the economic directorate of the Allied Control Council; of these, 24 had been designated in October 1945 as "advance reparations" under the swift appraisal plan known as Operation RAP. As described officially, "this [designation] represented an attempt to make available in the shortest time possible a number of reparations plants to the Soviet Union and the Western Nations."[35] The dismantling status of these "advance reparations" plants as of September 1, 1946, suggests that the Soviet Union indeed benefited. Inasmuch

[32] Wilhelm Hasenack, *Dismantling in the Ruhr Valley* (Cologne: Westdeutscher Verlag, 1949).
[33] *Ibid.*
[34] *Ibid.*, p. 51. The Hüttenwerk Essen-Borbeck plant was still being dismantled in May 1949; see *British Zone Review*, May 20, 1949, and *Neue Zuercher Zeitung*, December 10, 1947. Note these are rolling mills, not blast furnaces with low salvage value.
[35] *A Year of Potsdam, op. cit.* n.26, p. 35. The *New York Times* reports on this question are not accurate. For example, see *New York Times Magazine*, December 7, 1947, p. 14: "Also there was a short period when, for technical reasons, the American zonal authorities gave priority to the shipment of a small amount of equipment to the Soviet zone, a situation that resulted in such misleading headlines as "Russia Obtains 95 percent of Reparations from U.S. Zone." This statement is, of course, inconsistent with the evidence presented here. The same issue also reports (p. 56) that U.K. and U.S. reparations shipments to the U.S.S.R. stopped in May 1946. However, shipments were continuing as late as February 1948 according to Dept. of State *Bulletin*, February 22, 1948, p. 240. In May 1949 the Borbeck plant was still being dismantled for the U.S.S.R.; *British Zone Review*, May 20, 1949.

as 95 percent of all dismantling shipments up to the end of 1946 went to the Soviet Union and the U.S.S.R. was allocated twenty-four and one-half plants, it could be argued that the RAP program existed virtually for Soviet benefit. (see Table 2-4.)

The RAP operation moved swiftly. Dismantling of the huge Kugelfischer ball bearing plant in Bavaria for the U.S.S.R. started only on March 1, 1946, but the first shipment of equipment—which was the first shipment of reparations equipment from the U.S. Zone to any destination—was made on March 31, 1946. By August 1946 a total of 11,100 tons of reparations had been made from the RAP plants allocated to the U.S.S.R.[36] Of 40,374 tons of reparations equipment shipped from the U.S.Zone in 1946, the Soviet Union received 38,977 tons, or 94.3 percent.[37] In all, nearly one-third of reparations removals from the U.S. Zone of Germany went to the Soviet Union. Between March 30, 1946, and March 31, 1947, a total of 209,655 tons of equipment (valued at RM 190,279,000, 1938 prices) was removed. Of this total, 66,981 tons (valued at RM 45,246,000) went to the U.S.S.R.[38]

Other removals from Germany during 1944-51 can be understood only in the context of the way in which occupations took place within the inter-allied zonal borders. The U.S. Army had stopped at the Elbe River while the Soviets occupied the whole of Berlin,[39] and this worked in favor of the Soviet dismantling policy.

The historic and geographic factors have been treated in great detail elsewhere and may be but briefly summarized here. In the closing days of the war the Soviet armies moved up to the Elbe River, facing the U.S. and British armies, and occupied the whole of Berlin including what were to become the U.S., British, and French sectors of the city. They then proceeded to strip Berlin of its industry, including the highly important electrical equipment factories, *and including plants in all sectors.* This removal was probably completed by June 1945 because when the Western Allies suggested moving into their Berlin zones—the Soviets in turn to occupy the whole of their zone west of the Elbe—the Soviets asked only for a few days delay, until July 1.

In the meantime, i.e., from late April to July 1, 1945, the Americans and British maintained industry in their territory, so that when the Soviets moved into the rest of their occupation zone they received yet more factories including a highly important sector of the aircraft industry and, of course, the Nordhausen

---

[36] *A Year of Potsdam, op. cit.* n. 26, p. 37.

[37] *New York Times,* January 23, 1947, p. 13.

[38] *Report of the Military Governor,* Office of the U.S. Military Governor (Germany), no. 45, March 1949.

[39] See Cornelius Ryan, *The Last Battle* (New York: Simon and Schuster, 1966), on the "drive to Berlin" controversy. The official U.S. Government account of this controversy is soon to be published under the title *The Last Offensive.*

Table 2-4   STATUS ON ADVANCE REPARATIONS PLANTS FOR THE U.S.S.R. AT THE END OF 1946

Plant No.	Name of plant	Location	Product	Dismantling started	Percent dismantled at end 1946
1	Kugelfischer Georg Schaefer	Schweinfurt, Bav.	Ball-bearings	1 Mar. 46	97*
2	Bayerische Motorenwerke No. 1	Munich, Bav.	Aircraft engines	1 Mar. 46	82
3	Deutsche Schiffs- & Maschinenbau AG (Deschimag shipyards)	Bremen (Werk Weser)	Ship-building	1 Mar. 46	27
4	Grosskraftwerk AG	Mannheim, W/B	Power plant	—	—
5	Kloeckner-Humboldt-Deutz	Oberursel, Gr. Hesse	Diesel engines	15 Nov. 45	61
6	Fritz Mueller	Oberesslingen, W/B	Machine tools	3 Oct. 45	5
7	Bohner & Koehle	Esslingen, W/B	Machine tools	8 Oct. 45	4
9	Hensoldt & Soehne	Herborn, Gr. Hesse	Fire control	10 Oct. 45	100
10	Gendorf	Gendorf, Bav.	Power plant	16 Jan. 46	40
11	Hastedt	Bremen	Power plant	17 Oct. 45	88
12	Toeging AG Innwerk	Toeging, Bav.	Power plant	11 Feb. 46	8
13	Daimler-Benz (Goldfisch) (underground)	Mosbach, W/B	Aircraft engines	1 Mar. 46	80
14	Bayerische Motorenwerke No. 2	Munich, Bav.	Aircraft engines	2 Oct. 45	100
15	Fabrik Hess. Lichtenau	Hess. Lichtenau, Gr. Hesse	Explosives	6 Feb. 46	24
16	Deutsche Schiffs- & Maschinenbau AG	Bremen-Valentin	Ship-building	1 Jan. 46	100
17	C.F. Borgeward	Bremen	Torpedoes	22 Jan. 46	62
18	Norddeutsche Huette AG	Bremen-Oslebshausen	Steel manufacturing	—	0
19	Hahn & Tessky Indexwerke	Esslingen, W/B	Automatic screw machines	25 Oct. 45	60
20	Fabrik Kaufbeuren	Kaufbeuren, Bav.	Explosives	19 Oct. 45	100
21	Fabrik Aschau	Muehldorf, Bav.	Explosives	27 Oct. 45	30
22	Fabrik Ebenhausen	Ebenhausen, Bav.	Explosives	15 Oct. 45	100
23	Wehrmacht ordnance plant	Strass, Bav.	Shell loading	1 Mar. 46	100
24	Wehrmacht ordnance plant	Geretsried-Wolfratshausen, Bav.	Shell loading	1 May 46	2
25	Wehrmacht ordnance plant	Deschnig, Bav.	Shells	1 Mar. 46	100

Source: *A Year of Potsdam*, (n.p.: Office of Military Government for Germany [U.S. Zone], Economics Division, 1947), p. 36.
* U.S.S.R. portion only.

V-1 and V-2 rocket plants. Thus the Allied drive to the Elbe gave the Soviets the opportunity, willingly taken, to acquire the extensive German electrical equipment industry in Berlin[40] and find the German aircraft industry waiting intact when the zonal frontiers were rearranged a few weeks later.[41]

PLANT REMOVALS FROM THE SOVIET ZONE OF GERMANY

At the end of 1944 a special committee was organized under the Soviet Council of Ministers and under the leadership of Malenkov. Its twin tasks were the dismantling of German industry and the expansion of Soviet industry by the use of the equipment removed.[42] The committee's central headquarters in Moscow was staffed by members of the Central Committee of the Communist Party of the Soviet Union and divided into departments with staff drawn from Soviet industry, given military ranks. As individual targets were located, instructions passed to military units for actual dismantling then were carried out by German prisoners of war and local labor under Soviet officers.[43]

Dismantling of East German industry began with the arrival of the second wave of Soviet forces, first in Berlin (all zones) and then throughout the provinces of Silesia, Brandenburg, Thuringia, and Saxony.

Although the facts of dismantling have been strictly censored by the Soviets and no Allied observers were allowed into the Soviet Zone at the time, information of reasonable accuracy has filtered through the Iron Curtain. In particular the SPD (Sozialdemokratische Partei Deutschlands) in West Germany collected dismantling information on a plant-by-plant basis and published this information in 1951.[44] Further, reports by former Soviet officials add to our knowledge, although some of these leave the impression of being more enthusiastic than accurate.

Dismantling involved several thousand plants and included the best of industry

---

[40] For a description see U.S. Strategic Bombing Survey, reports by A. G. P. Sanders, Capt. Nichols, and Col. Ames on electrical equipment targets in Berlin, July 1945.

[41] In the interval of two months numerous U.S. and British intelligence, army, navy, air force, and civilian teams explored the technical side of Germany industry in the Soviet Zone. This exploration was conducted in the following directions: (a) interviewing German technicians, (b) acquiring papers and materials for reports on technological and economic structure, (c) obtaining drawings, instruments, and samples, and (d) acquiring V-1 and V-2 samples and engine samples. There were no equipment removals. The plants were left intact, and some were even repaired for the Soviets. So the Soviets obtained the productive capacity *intact*, but did not obtain engineers or papers. The papers were acquired under the FIAT programs.

[42] Slusser, *op. cit.*, n. 16, p. 18.

[43] Some 10,000 local Germans were assigned to dismantle the brown coal plants at Regis-Breitingen, and another 5000 dismantled the Lauta works at Hoyersworda; 12,000 Germans were used at the Giessches Erben works; and 20,000 were used at the large plant at Brona. Löwenthal, *op. cit.* n. 14, pp. 182-85.

[44] G. E. Harmssen, *Am Abend der Demontage; Sechs Jahre Reparationspolitik*, (Bremen: F. Trüjen, 1951).

moved to East Germany during the war to avoid Allied bombing. All together, a total of about 12,000 trainloads of equipment was removed to the U.S.S.R.

Table 2-5   REDUCTION OF INDUSTRIAL CAPACITY BY DISMANTLING
IN THE SOVIET ZONE OF GERMANY

Industry	1936 Production	Nettl's percentage estimate of capacity reduction	Equivalent in tonnage terms
Vehicles	532,706 units	65	346,259
Cement	1,687,000 tons	40	674,800
Rubber goods:			
Tires	176,000 units	70-80	123,000-140,800
Tubes	148,000 units	70-80	103,600-118,400
Paper and cardboard	1,195,000 tons	40	478,000
Cellulose	205,400 tons	40	82,160

Sources: J. P. Nettl, *The Eastern Zone and Soviet Policy in Germany, 1945-50* (London: Oxford University Press, 1951), p. 202.   Wolfgang F. Stolper, *The Structure of the East German Economy* (Cambridge, Mass.: Harvard University Press, 1960), pp. 146, 180, 196, 207.

Details of this dismantling in the Soviet Zone have been included in the chapters on industrial activities (chapters 8 through 24).

DEPORTATION OF GERMAN SCIENTISTS AND TECHNICIANS

One significant aspect of the reparations transfer process was the deportation of German scientists and technicians to the Soviet Union, on a mass scale concentrated in the fall of 1946. The major program was completed during the night of October 28, 1946, when trainloads of Germans from aircraft and armaments plants were moved with their families and furniture to the Soviet Union.[45]

Deportations were concentrated among the staffs of key German plants. According to Fritz Löwenthal, more than 300 scientists, technicians, and skilled workers were deported from Zeiss; 26 chemists, seven engineers, and several skilled mechanics were co-opted from the Leuna works; and technicians and workers were drawn from the Junkers works at Dessau, the Oberspree cable works in Niederschoenweida, the Schott glass works in Jena, the optical works in Saalfeld and Poessneck, and the Gera workshops.[46] Löwenthal also cites

[45] For descriptions of deportation, see Löwenthal, *op. cit.* n. 14, and V. L. Sokolov, *Soviet Use of German Science and Technology, 1945-1946* (New York: Research Program on the U.S.S.R., 1955).

[46] Löwenthal, *op. cit.* n. 14, pp. 203-4.

a U.S. Navy report to Congress stating that 10,000 German scientists and technical specialists had been absorbed into Soviet industry by May 1947.[47]

These German workers began to filter back home in the early 1950s together with German, Austrian, and Italian prisoners of war and deportees. In January 1952 *The Times* (London) reported that there was a continuing flow of Germans from the optical and precision instruments industries: "It seems to show that Russia can now do without these craftsmen."[48] The report particularly noted the return of 310 highly skilled workers from the Zeiss works in Jena, after five years in Russia. It is probable that all German deported workers were returned by 1957-58.

REPARATIONS FROM FINLAND, 1944 TO 1955

The Finnish-Soviet Peace Treaty of December 17, 1944, required Finland to transfer goods to the Soviet Union valued at $300 million in 1938 prices over a period of eight years. The amount was similar to that for Hungarian and Rumanian reparations, but in the Finnish case there was little Soviet interference in the manufacturing and delivery—this being entirely a Finnish responsibility whereas in Hungary and Rumania the Soviets formed "joint companies" to carry out the task. Some 60 percent of the indemnity comprised metallurgical and engineering products, the balance being ships, cable, and wood products—amounting in all to a considerable proportion of the Finnish national product.[49]

The technical nature of this huge indemnity required Finland to establish major new industries and to expand engineering industries that were of only negligible importance before the war. This was done with credits and equipment from the United States and Sweden, and thus provides some excellent examples of "indirect transfers."

A. G. Mazour sums up Finnish achievements in reparations deliveries to the U.S.S.R. as follows: "Mere survival was a miracle. To meet the obligations and still manage to survive was an achievement which commands profound respect and admiration."[50] Jensen has calculated the reparation payments as a percentage of net national product as follows:[51]

[47]   *Ibid.,* pp. 205-6.
[48]   *The Times* (London), January 29, 1952, p. 4g.
[49]   Bartell C. Jensen, *The Impact of Reparations on the Post-war Finnish Economy* (Homewood, Ill: Richard D. Irwin, 1966). See also A. G. Mazour, *Finland Between East and West* (Princeton: Van Nostrand, 1956), p. 173.
[50]   Mazour, *op. cit.* n. 49.
[51]   Jensen, *op. cit.* n. 49, p. 18.

Year	Reparations as percentage of NNP	Reparations as percentage of state expenditures
1944	0.3	0.7
1945	7.6	20.9
1946	4.8	13.7
1947	4.1	13.7
1948	3.2	10.7
1949	3.2	10.8
1950	1.6	6.1
1951	1.8	6.8
1952	1.1	4.1

The major deliveries under the program comprised about two-thirds of Finland's prewar ship tonnage plus considerable new construction. Ships transferred included 70 cargo vessels, one tanker, seven passenger ships, two icebreakers, and 15 barges from the merchant marine. In addition, substantial new deliveries of wooden and metal ships were required. During the first four years of the reparations period Finland delivered 143 new ships and two floating docks valued at $25.8 million, while the program for the second four years called for 371 ships and two docks valued at $40.2 million.[52] In all, about 359,000 gross registered tons of shipping with a total valuation of $66 million in new ships and $14 million in existing ships was delivered, requiring a significant expansion and modernization of the Finnish shipbuilding industry.[53]

The next largest category, comprising $70.7 million, was made up of industrial equipment and a number of complete plants. Among other things, this segment included 17 complete industrial plants to establish mills for the production of prefabricated wooden houses. This is of particular interest because instead of themselves supplying a plant specification, the Soviets requested that the Finns supply it (the delays involved in this procedure subjected Finland to a monthly fine of $45,000 payable in supplementary deliveries). The plants delivered (Table 2-6) were complete with sawmills, lumber kilns, conveyers, power plants, and repair shops.[54]

The remaining major categories included 2600 km of power cable, 34,375 tons of bright copper wire, and 1700 km of control cable ($12.9 million), pulp and paper products ($34.9 million), and wood products ($28 million).[55]

[52] J. Auer, *Suomen sotakorvaustoimitukset neuvostoliitolle* (Helsinki: Werner Söderström Osakeyhtiö, 1956), p. 318.
[53] *Ibid.*, p. 327; for a listing of ships by type see Urho Toivola, *The Finland Year Book 1947* (Helsinki, 1947). p. 84.
[54] Toivola, *op. cit.* n. 53, p. 335.
[55] *Ibid.*, pp. 84-85.

of Japan caused disruption of production centers and trade channels and upset the entire economic structure of the Far East; Soviet occupation further disrupted the industrial structure.

The findings of the Pauley Commission were that the wrecked condition of Manchurian industry evident between the time of the Japanese surrender and the visit of the Pauley Mission was due directly to Soviet removals and pillage, and to a lesser extent to indirect consequences of the Soviet occupation. The Soviets had concentrated their efforts on certain categories of supplies, machinery, and equipment: functioning power-generating and transforming equipment, electric motors, experimental plants, laboratories and hospitals, and the newest and best machine tools. The wrecked condition was due mainly to Soviet removals and partly to Soviet failure to preserve order.[60] (See Table 2-7.)

At the Fushun power plant, four 50,000-kw steam-electric generators plus the condensers, auxiliary equipment, stokers, and drums were removed. Thirty-four low-voltage transformers for electric furnaces were taken from the aluminum plant at Fushun (there were 36 transformers at the plant, but two outside on skids were left behind), and the Sodeberg electrodes were removed.

All machine tools from the Fushun coal hydrogenation plant were removed.

From the Manchu iron works (Anshan) power house, one 25,000-kw Siemens Halske turbogenerator and one 18,000-kw turbogenerator were removed, leaving 30,500 kw of capacity in place. From the plant's boiler house, four complete boilers with equipment were removed plus equipment for two more boilers. All rolling equipment was removed from the blooming mill. Ball mills and motors were removed from the sponge iron plant. Magnetic separators were removed from the iron ore treating plant; bearings on the roasting kiln were removed; chargers, pushers, and valve mechanisms were taken from the coke ovens; motors and trolleys from the blast furnace stockyard crane and skip hoists, and blowers and auxiliaries for six of the nine blast furnaces were also removed.

Practically all the machine tools and electrical equipment, seven cranes, and all electric motors were removed from the Mitsubishi machine plant in Mukden. In addition, all equipment (except one large press) and three overhead cranes were removed from the forging shop; cranes, machinery, and a large electric furnace were taken from the foundry. All equipment from the welding shop and all equipment for manufacturing steel tubes were taken from the seamless tube mill at the Mitsubishi plant.

Equipment removed from the coal hydrogenation research institute included high-pressure compressors, machine tools, and the distillation apparatus. All

---

[60] For example, one report states: "Mukden, the largest city in Manchuria, has been left without power for light, water, and other utilities, endangering the health and lives of its two million inhabitants." "Selected Photographs from Pauley Mission to Manchuria: June 1946," Special Collection in the Hoover Institution, Stanford University.

machinery (except lens polishers and some grinders) was removed from the optical instrument plant at Mukden.

Boilers and heavy rubber processing equipment were taken from the belt-making building of the Manchu Rubber Company (Liaoyang), as were tire manufacturing equipment, hydraulic presses, rubber mills and collandars as well as bicycle tires, power and transmission belt manufacturing equipment, and machines for the manufacture of shoes and raincoats.

All tire-making machinery was removed from the Toyo Rubber Tire Company operation at Mukden, all cotton spinning equipment from the tire cord plant, and four nitrators for picric acid removal together with four centrifuges from Arsenal 383.[61]

REPARATIONS FROM ITALY

Under the Soviet Treaty of Peace[62] with Italy it was agreed that reparations amounting to $100 million were to be paid during a period of seven years. The reparations were to include part of Italy's "factory and tool equipment designed for the manufacture of war material"; part of Italian assets in Rumania, Bulgaria, and Hungary with certain exceptions; and part of Italian current production together with one-third of the Italian naval fleet.[63]

REPARATIONS AND REMOVALS FROM AUSTRIA

An estimated $400 million worth of capital equipment was removed by the Soviets from the Soviet zone of Austria in 1945-46.

The Austrian oil industry was exclusively in the Soviet zone, as were many finishing industries and most of the electrical industry. At Zistersdorf in Lower Austria, Soviet occupation forces removed and shipped to Russia about $25 million worth of oil well supplies and equipment. The Alpine Monton company in Styra, with steel plants at Donawitz and finishing plants at Kreiglach and Kindberg, had much of its equipment removed by the Red Army—all together 75 trainloads, including a new blooming mill, two 25-ton electric furnaces, one turbogenerator, and hundreds of machine tools.

There was extensive removal of equipment from the electrical equipment industry, including the wire and cable industry where almost all production facilities fell into Soviet hands. The two Vienna electrical plants, Simmering

---

[61] *Ibid.* Photos for this report were taken by U.S. Signal Corps during the inspection of Japanese industries by American industrial engineers.

[62] United Nations *Treaty Series*, vol. 49, no. 747 (1950), pp. 154 *et seq.*

[63] For details see Giuseppe Vedovato, *Il Trattato di Pace con l'Italia* (Rome: Edizioni Leonardo, 1947), pp. 127-30, 317-31, 363, 561.

and Engerthstrasse, were partially dismantled by the Soviets. The Goertz Optical Works, the leading manufacturer of optical lenses, was seized and removed in 1946.

In transportation industries the plant of Weiner Lokomotiv Fabrik, a manufacturer of locomotives, was dismantled and one thousand of the twelve hundred machine tools in the plant were shipped to Russia. The largest of Austria's motor vehicle producers, Steyr-Daimler-Pusch A.G., suffered extensive equipment removals (however, the largest agricultural machinery producer, Hofherr-Schrandz, was left intact and operated under Soviet control). Numerous plants in the clothing, fertilizer, and chemical industries also had extensive equipment removals to the Soviet Union.

In addition to the dismantling and removal, major deliveries of goods to the Soviet Union were required by the treaty under which Austria regained her independence. The value of such deliveries, largely industrial and transportation equipment, totaled $150 million in six years (plus ten million metric tons of crude oil valued at about $200 million in ten years).[64]

REPARATIONS AND REMOVALS FROM RUMANIA

Under the armistice signed September 12, 1944, Rumania agreed to provide Russia with reparations valued at $300 million, in addition to acceding to Soviet annexation of Bessarabia and Northern Bucovina. The Soviets then proceeded to remove the entire Rumanian Navy plus 700 ships, barges, and tugs comprising the major part of the Rumanian merchant marine, about one-half the country's rolling stock, all automobiles, and large quantities of equipment from the Rumanian oil fields.

Particular emphasis was placed on removal of oil refineries and equipment owned by American and British companies. In November 1944, the following was reported to the U.S. Secretary of State:

> The Russians have been working with all possible speed, even at night, to remove oil equipment of Astra Romana, Stela Romana, and another oil company in which both British and American companies are interested. This equipment is being taken to Russia.[65]

In addition, 23,000 tons of tubes and casing was removed from oil company warehouses. The Soviets claimed that this material was actually the property of German companies sent to Rumania during the war and therefore was not

---

[64] *The Rehabilitation of Austria, 1945 to 1947* (Vienna: U.S. Allied Commission for Austria, [1948?]; F. Nemschak, *Ten Years of Austrian Economic Development, 1945-1955*, (Vienna: Association of Austrian Industrialists, 1955), p. 8.

[65] U.S. Dept. of State, *Foreign Relations of the United States*, vol. IV (1944), p. 253.

owned by the American and British companies. In any event, Andrei Vyshinsky, then the Soviet assistant people's commissar for foreign affairs, suggested it comprised only a small amount of the equipment required for rehabilitation, and "the amount of equipment was so small it might be written off as a minor Lend Lease shipment."[66]

It was later reported that the Russians had occupied more than 700 factories in Rumania, and that considerable amounts of industrial equipment and supplies including oil drilling equipment, actually the property of British and American oil companies, were being removed to Russia.[67]

Diplomatic protests by the United States led to the establishment in 1945 of a Joint U.S.–Soviet Oil Commission to consider the problem. This commission was dissolved in August 1947 without apparently arriving at any agreement. It was then stated that the Soviets had removed 7000 tons of equipment at the end of 1944 from Romana-Americana, a U.S. subsidiary of Standard Oil of New Jersey. This equipment was valued at $1,000,000.[68]

There is no question that there were sizable Soviet equipment removals from occupied areas after World War II; a minimum value figure in excess of $10 billion in 1938 prices can be set for equipment thus removed. The unresolved question concerns the usefulness of such removals in the U.S.S.R.

The argument against usefulness, which also assumes irrationality on the part of the Soviets, is built on no hard evidence except observations of rusting equipment along rail lines from Germany to the U.S.S.R.

On the other hand, the fact that dismantling was spread over a number of years suggests that there was a continuing demand for the equipment. We can also trace delivery of important processes and equipment to the U.S.S.R., and the Berlin Ambi-Budd plant negotiated back to the West was found to have been carefully numbered and guarded for a period of some years although not used by the Soviets.

Furthermore, by the time the war ended the Soviets had extensive experience in dismantling, and after the war they took pains to disguise their intentions and actions. In Manchuria there is evidence that Chinese mobs were encouraged to loot buildings after Soviet removals, and it is not unlikely that such decoy actions were undertaken in Germany.

It is concluded, therefore, that the Soviets removed extensive industrial capacity from a number of countries under a carefully planned program executed with reasonable care. This capacity had the potential to make a significant contribution to Soviet postwar industrial production, and this contribution will be examined in more detail in Part II.

[66] *Ibid.*, p. 263.
[67] *Ibid.*, vol. V (1945), pp. 542, 629.
[68] U.S. Dept. of State, *Bulletin*, August 3, 1947, p. 225.

CHAPTER THREE

Trade as a Transfer Mechanism

The prime means for transfer of Western technology to the Soviet Union has been through normal channels of commerce. Since 1918 Russian foreign trade has been a state monopoly, and this monopoly power has been utilized in a superbly efficient manner to direct the most advanced of Western technological achievement to the Soviet economy. Its monopolistic position, of course, allows the Soviet state to play one foreign country against others and individual Western firms against firms in all other countries in the acquisition process.

Table 3-1, based on United Nations data, presents the percentage of machinery and equipment (U.N. category SITC 7) contained in total Soviet trade with major Western countries between 1953 and 1961. The most significant observable feature is the consistently large percentage that SITC 7 forms of total Soviet imports. Although the high point (97.56 percent of 1959 Danish exports to the U.S.S.R.) is today unusual, the percentage is usually in excess of 60 percent of Soviet imports from almost all major Western industrialized nations, and percentages in excess of 70 percent are not unusual.

Figure 3-1 presents data for the single year 1959 in schematic form and indicates at a glance the high proportion of machinery and equipment from all Western countries. Figure 4-2 illustrates the significant lack of Soviet capital goods exported to the West; only Greece imported Soviet machinery and equipment in 1959. The Soviet Union normally exports machinery and equipment only to underdeveloped areas as part of barter deals; even foreign assistance projects financed by the Soviets have a major foreign machinery component.[1]

In the 1920s and 1930s over 90 percent of U.K. and German shipments to the Soviet Union came within the SITC 7 category; since that period such high percentages are less frequent, but they have remained sizable enough over a period of almost 50 years to suggest the key relationship between trade and Soviet industry.[2]

---

[1] See chapter 7.

[2] Even well informed commentators have taken positions directly opposed to this factual presentation. For example, Senator Jacob Javits of New York comments: "Trade with the West as a general matter, must necessarily be a marginal factor in the performance and potentialities of the Soviet economy." *Congressional Record, Senate*, vol. 112, pt. 9 (89th Congress, 2d session), May 24, 1966, p. 11233.

Table 3-1

PERCENTAGE OF TOTAL EXPORTS TO THE SOVIET UNION
COMPRISING MACHINERY AND EQUIPMENT (SITC 7), FROM 1953 TO 1961

Country	1953	1954	1955	1956	1957	1958	1959	1960	1961	Average 1953-1961
Switzerland	—	—	—	—	—	—	73.51	83.41	91.50	84.73*
Sweden	46.90	62.62	61.02	70.40	55.04	54.47	58.28	39.93	49.21	54.17
Finland	—	48.14	58.25	53.43	50.23	47.89	60.38	61.74	46.25	53.29
Denmark	25.48	2.47	68.64	95.78	42.72	39.10	97.56	78.93	40.64	50.04
Germany	58.13	75.80	64.03	54.24	37.40	69.29	35.86	44.32	56.52	49.87
United Kingdom	53.97	39.52	46.37	37.09	28.53	25.12	43.91	53.54	62.87	43.95
Austria	93.86	50.92	83.94	5.55	54.16	47.15	32.20	42.30	45.68	42.56
United States	17.65	0.93	2.89	59.49	12.71	19.95	60.81	48.82	36.78	41.86
Netherlands	12.32	44.27	63.76	60.08	69.36	2.72	9.87	44.39	36.58	39.50
France	2.56	9.95	23.27	52.98	21.45	25.80	41.97	48.69	52.24	38.16
Japan	—	—	15.96	84.43	14.20	15.81	43.33	29.01	39.12	32.53
Italy	16.09	31.05	15.36	2.10	13.58	10.94	11.08	21.90	32.46	20.42
Norway	—	9.49	—	0.16	0.07	0.62	0.33	0.06	5.42	2.12

Source: *U.N. Yearbook of International Trade Statistics* (New York, 1958).
* Three years only.

Figure 3-1   EXPORTS OF MACHINERY AND EQUIPMENT, AS PERCENTAGE OF TOTAL TRADE, FROM CAPITALIST COUNTRIES TO THE SOVIET UNION (1959)

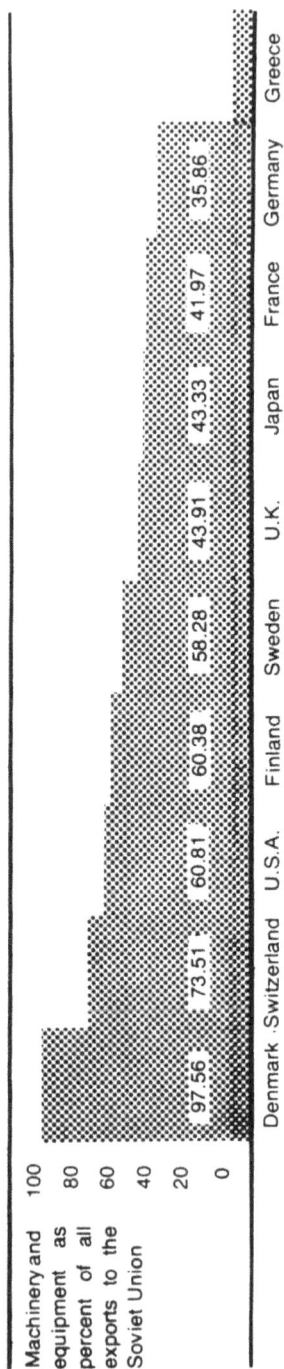

Machinery and equipment as percent of all exports to the Soviet Union										
100										
80										
60										
40										
20										
0	97.56	73.51	60.81	60.38	58.28	43.91	43.33	41.97	35.86	
	Denmark	Switzerland	U.S.A.	Finland	Sweden	U.K.	Japan	France	Germany	Greece

Source: United Nations, *Commodity Trade Statistics,* Statistical Papers, series D, vol. IX, no. 4 (January-December 1959).

Figure 3-2   EXPORTS OF MACHINERY AND EQUIPMENT, AS PERCENTAGE OF TOTAL TRADE TO CAPITALIST COUNTRIES FROM THE SOVIET UNION (1959)

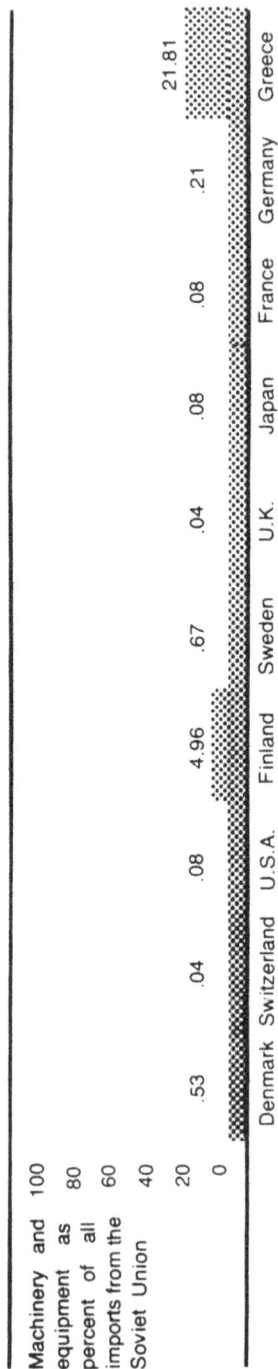

Machinery and equipment as percent of all imports from the Soviet Union										
100										
80										
60										
40										
20										21.81
0	.53	.04	.08	4.96	.67	.04	.08	.08	.21	
	Denmark	Switzerland	U.S.A.	Finland	Sweden	U.K.	Japan	France	Germany	Greece

Source: United Nations, *Commodity Trade Statistics,* Statistical Papers, series D. vol. IX, no. 4 (January-December 1959).

The following selection of trade agreements made by the Soviets with Western nations illustrates that Soviet exports consist almost entirely of raw materials:

Date and trade agreement	Soviet exports under the trade agreement
1953 Denmark trade agreement	"Wheat, oil cake, soya beans, cotton, timber, pig iron, asbestos, apatite concentrate." (U.N. *Treaty Series*, vol. 125, no. 2292, p. 10)
1956 Japan trade agreement	"Lumber, coal, mineral ores, oil, metals, fertilizer, asbestos and fibers." (*Japan Times* [Tokyo], October 20, 1956)
1957 Denmark trade agreement	"Grain, apatite concentrate, potash, pig iron, coal, coke, petroleum products, timber, cotton, chemicals, agricultural equipment, 150 autos, 150 motorcycles." (U.N. *Treaty Series*, vol. 271, no. 3912, p. 132)
1959 United Kingdom trade agreement	"Grain, timber and timber products, wood pulp, manganese ore, asbestos, ferroalloys, non-ferrous metals, minerals, fertilizers, flax and other goods." (U.N. *Treaty Series*, vol. 374, no. 5344, p. 305)

This pattern of Soviet foreign trade, a consistent pattern since about 1922,[3] may then be seen as essentially an exchange of raw materials for Western technology.

More detailed examination of the impact pattern on a country-by-country basis for the period after 1945 illustrates the manner in which the Soviet foreign trade monopoly has been superbly used to induce a flow of modern technology into the Soviet economy to fill numerous gaps and offset persistent shortfalls in the planning process. Complementary to this process has been a propaganda campaign, obviously very effective, to obscure the exchange pattern. This campaign has succeeded to the extent of informing U.S. State Department statements to Congress and the public.[4]

UNITED KINGDOM AS A SUPPLIER OF CAPITAL GOODS TO THE SOVIET UNION

The first postwar trade and payments agreement between the U.S.S.R. and

---

[3] See chapter 21, Sutton I: *Western Technology . . . 1917 to 1930;* cf. Sutton, "Soviet Export Strategy," in *Ordance,* November-December 1969. A complete list of Soviet trade agreements at June 1, 1958, may be found in *Spravochnik po vneshnei torgovle SSR* (Moscow: Vneshtorgizdat, 1958), pp. 91-92.

[4] See, for example, testimony of former Secretary of State Dean Rusk, U.S. House of Representatives, *Investigation and Study of the Administration, Operation, and Enforcement of the Export*

the United Kingdom was signed at Moscow on December 27, 1947.[5] The agreement included both short- and long-term arrangements. Under the short-term arrangement the Soviet Union agreed to supply from its 1947 harvest 450,000

Table 3-2   UNITED KINGDOM DELIVERIES TO THE SOVIET UNION
UNDER THE 1947 TRADE AGREEMENT

Deliveries under Schedule I			Deliveries under Schedule II		
Item Number	Quantity	Description	Item Number	Quantity	Description
1	1100	Narrow gauge 750-mm locomotives	1	£150,000 value	Scientific and laboratory apparatus
2	2400	Flat trucks, 750-mm	2	4	Pile drivers mounted on pontoons
3	2400	Winches (2 and 3 drums)	3	4 sets	Winding gear
4	210	Excavators	4	1	Electro dredger
5	54	Caterpillar loading cranes	5	18	Ball mills for copper ore grinding
6	250	Auto timber carriers	6	8	Ball mills for grinding apatite
7	14	Tugs	7	3	Rod mills for grinding ores
8	4	Dredgers	8	8	Spiral type classifiers
9	200	Locomobiles	9	2	Gyratory crushers
10	150	Mobile diesel electric generators, 50 kw	10	3	Railway steam cranes
11	24	Steam power turbine stations, 500 kw	11	48	154-kv Voltage transformers
12	£1,050,000 value	Plywood equipment	12	6	Complete distributing sets
13	£400,000 value	Timber mill equipment	13	45	Isolating switches (154 kv)
			14	10	Oil purifying apparatus
			15	300	100-kw electric motors

Source: Great Britain, *Soviet Union No 1 (1948)* Command 7297, (London: HMSO, 1948).

Control Act of 1949, and Related Acts, 87th Congress, 1st session, October and December 1961, (Washington, 1962), and *ibid.,* 2d session, Hearings, part. III, 1962.
[5] Published as Great Britain, *Soviet Union No. 1 (1948),* Command 7297 (London: HMSO, 1948).

tons of barley, 200,000 tons of maize, and 100,000 metric tons of oats. In return the United Kingdom agreed to ensure the supply of 25,000 long tons of light rails with fishplates, nuts, and bolts, with an additional 10,000 tons to be supplied from U.K. military surpluses.

The long-term arrangement was more extensive. It included U.K. delivery of materials listed in Schedules I and II (Table 3-2) and supplies of wheat, pulses, pit props, cellulose, and canned goods from the Soviet Union in exchange for oil well tubes and tinplate from the United Kingdom.

Schedules I and II consist entirely of equipment and machinery. Two separate categories may be isolated: (1) sizable quantities of such equipment as narrow-gauge locomotives, flat trucks, winches, auto timber carriers, locomobiles, and generators—clearly intended for production purposes; and (2) four pile drivers, sets of winding gear, two gyratory crushers, and three railway steam cranes—materials in much smaller quantities for which it is unlikely the Soviets had production uses in mind. The spare parts and maintenance problem for a few equipment items is too great to make such purchases worthwhile; these items were probably intended for examination and technical information on British manufacturing methods.

Two major agreements were made with British companies a few years later, in 1954. In January of that year, 20 trawlers valued at $16.8 million were ordered from Brooke-Marine, Ltd. The specifications for these trawlers included the most advanced features available in the West (see chapter 21). In May 1954 a $19.6 million agreement was made with Platt Brothers for supplying textile equipment (see chapter 15).

Another five-year trade agreement between the United Kingdom and the Soviet Union came into force on May 24, 1959.[6] Again, in exchange for raw materials[7] the Soviet Union agreed to place orders with British firms:

> ... for equipment for the manufacture of synthetic fibres, synthetic materials and manufactures from them, and also other types of equipment for the chemical industry; equipment for the pulp and paper industry; forging, stamping and casting equipment; metalworking machine tools; equipment for the electro-technical and cable industry; equipment and instruments for the automation of production processes; pumping, compression and refrigeration equipment; equipment for sugar beet factories and other types of equipment for the food industry; equipment for the building industry, light industry and other branches of industry as well as industrial products and raw materials customarily bought from United Kingdom firms.[8]

There was also a comparatively small exchange of consumer goods in the agreement, to the value of $2 million.

[6] United Nations, *Treaty Series*, vol. 374, nos. 5323-5350 (1960), p. 306.
[7] See page 43.
[8] *Op. cit.* n. 6, p. 308.

The 1959 agreement was extended for another five years in 1964, and the quotas for the ten years between 1959 and 1969 provided for a continuing supply of United Kingdom technology to the U.S.S.R. This included machine tools, earthmoving equipment, mechanical handling equipment, equipment for the Soviet peat industry (there is no peat industry in the United Kingdom), mining equipment, gas and arc welding equipment, chemical, refrigeration and compressor equipment, and a wide range of scientific and optical instruments.[9]

The use to which some of this equipment has been put may be gleaned from a Soviet booklet published by NIIOMTP (Scientific Research Institute for Organization, Mechanization, and Technical Assistance to the Construction Industry) detailing the technical characteristics of British construction equipment.[10]

GERMANY AS A SUPPLIER OF CAPITAL GOODS TO THE SOVIET UNION

The German-Soviet trade agreements of the 1950s comprised the exchange of German equipment and machinery for Soviet raw materials, continuing the prewar pattern. For example, the 1958 trade agreement called for West Germany to export to the Soviet Union "mainly ... capital goods, including equipment for mining and the metallurgical industry, heavy and automatic machine tools for metalworking industries, equipment for the chemical industry, whaling factory ships."[11]

The German-Soviet trade agreement of December 31, 1960, affords a good example of the general composition and implementation of German-Soviet trade; this agreement provided for mutual trade from January 1, 1961, through December 31, 1963, and the form in which it was to be carried out. Two lists, A and B, were attached to the agreement providing commodity quotas for imports into both Germany and the Soviet Union, and both governments agreed to take "every measure" to enable fulfillment of these quotas. List A, comprising German imports from the Soviet Union, consists entirely of foodstuffs (grain, caviar, fish, oilcake, and vegetable oils), lumber products (sawed timber, plywood, and cellulose), and mineral materials (coal, iron ore, manganese, chrome, and particularly platinum and platinum group metals.). No products of a technological nature are included among German imports from the Soviet Union.

---

[9] For a complete statement of the quotas and the agreement see Peter Zentner, *East-West Trade: A Practical Guide to Selling in Eastern Europe* (London: Max Parrish, 1967), pp. 152-57.

[10] V. M. Kazarinov and S. N. Lamunin, *Zarubezhnye mashiny dlia mekhanizatsii stroitel'nykh rabot,* (Moscow: Niiomtp, 1959).

[11] *East-West Commerce* (London), May 7, 1958, p. 11.

List B, comprising commodity quotas for imports from West Germany into the U.S.S.R. for the years 1961 to 1963, consists almost entirely of goods of a technical nature. Table 3-3 lists the machinery and equipment items included

Table 3-3   COMMODITY QUOTAS FOR IMPORTS FROM WEST
GERMANY TO THE U.S.S.R. UNDER THE TRADE
AGREEMENT OF DECEMBER 31, 1960

Commodity	Value (In DM)
Machine tools for metal cutting (turning lathes, grinding machines, gear cutting machines, jig-boring machines, vertical lapping machines, machines for the processing of piston rings, component parts for passenger cars and tractors)	31,000,000
Machines for noncutting shaping (mechanical and automatic presses for the metal powder industry, embossing machines, hydraulic stamping presses, vacuum presses, forging manipulators, casting machines)	10,000,000
Power equipment and apparatus for the electrical engineering industry (water eddy brakes, furnaces, diesel power stations, silicon rectifiers for electric locomotives, electric dynamometers)	10,000,000
Coal mining equipment, equipment for metallurgical and petroleum industries (coal preparation plants, equipment for open-pit mining, agglomeration plants, rolling mills for cold rolling of tubes, rapid-working cable percussion drilling plants, loading machines)	110,000,000
Equipment for the food industry, including three complete sugar factories	126,000,000
Refrigeration plants	52,000,000
Equipment for light industries	5,000,000
Equipment for the chemical industry, Complete plant for production of polypropylene Crystallization of sodium sulfate (four plants) Hydraulic refining of benzene (one plant) Production of di-isozyanatene (one plant) Production of phosphorus (one plant) Production of simazine and atrazine (one plant) Manufacture of foils from viniplast (two plants)	11 complete plants
Equipment for the cellulose and paper industry (vacuum evaporating plants, supercalenders)	26,000,000
Equipment for the building materials industry (veneer plants [Ueber-furnieranlagen] for pressed boards made of wood fiber, assembling machines, equipment for the production of mineral wood)	21,000,000
Pumping and compressor plants (pumps and compressors of various kinds, glassblowing machines, ventilators)	63,000,000
Equipment for the polygraphic industry	10,000,000
Equipment for the cable industry	15,000,000
Fittings and component parts for high-pressure pipelines	44,000,000
Main track electric locomotives	20
Ships	157,000,000
Miscellaneous apparatus, including precision instruments and optical apparatus	16,000,000
Miscellaneous equipment, including special-type automobiles	21,000,000

Source: U.S. Senate, *East-West Trade*, Hearings Before the Committee on Foreign Relations, 88th Congress, 2d Session, March 13, 16, 23 and April 8, 9, 1964, p. 110.

in List B; these items, totaling 717 million DM, comprise machine tools and advanced equipment for the mechanical, mining, chemical, paper, building material, and electrical industries. The list also includes eleven complete plants for the chemical industry not included in the total of DM 717 million. The remaining DM 600 million of the agreement comprises specialized iron and steel products—rolled stock and tubes, for precisely those areas in which the Soviet Union is backward.

Thus the 1960 German-Soviet agreement is an excellent example of the nature of Soviet trade with industrialized countries. The Soviet Union imports from Germany goods with a technological component or of unusually difficult technical specification, and in return provides raw materials produced with equipment formerly imported from Germany and other Western countries.

ITALY AS A SUPPLIER OF CAPITAL GOODS TO THE SOVIET UNION

Italy has been a major supplier of industrial equipment to the Soviet Union since the 1920s. The 1953 Italian-Soviet agreement, for example, required the export of Italian machinery for manufacture of steel plate, textiles, foodstuffs, electrical cables, and fibers. Also under this agreement Italy contracted to supply cargo ships, refrigerated motor ships, tugs, cranes, and equipment for thermal electric stations.[12]

The Italian-Soviet trade agreement for 1958 required a far greater quantity of Italian industrial equipment, including equipment for complete production lines and plants. A partial list of the equipment supplied by Italian firms is as follows:[13]

> 530 interior and centerless grinders
> 25 horizontal boring machines with mandrels of 75-310 mm
> 44 repetition turret lathes
> 20 automatic thread-cutting machines of the "Cridan" type
> 43 vertical milling machines with table measuring 500 by 2500 mm
> 75 die-casting machines
> 26 crawler-mounted diesel electric cranes with grab buckets having a capacity of 25 to 50 tons
> Cranes and excavators (470 million lire)
> Two water turbines of 10,000 kw
> Pressure pipe for hydroelectric power stations (610 million lire)
> Three throttle valves for hydroelectric power stations
> Three hydraulic brakes
> Spares for thermoelectric power stations (625 million lire)

[12] *The Times* (London), October 28, 1953.
[13] *East-West Commerce*, V, 4 (April 8, 1958), 9.

One plant equipment for manufacture of sugar from molasses
10 production lines, complete, for tomato puree
Two production lines for tin boxes with tongue and key
Machinery for light industry (5500 million lire)
One cement manufacturing plant, complete with ovens
One plant for manufacture of reinforced concrete poles for electric transmission lines and lighting purposes.
One machinery plant for manufacture of asbestos cement tubes
Spare parts for ships (235 million lire)
High-frequency tools (780 million lire)
Miscellaneous machines (4700 million lire)

SCANDINAVIA AS A SUPPLIER OF CAPITAL GOODS TO THE SOVIET UNION

Finland has been a major supplier of equipment to the Soviet Union since 1945. For example, no less than 95 percent of all ships manufactured in Finland since World War II have been on Soviet account.

Major deliveries under the Finnish reparations agreements[14] were continued throughout the 1950s and 1960s by annual trade agreements. In exchange for Soviet raw materials, Finland was committed to supply not only ships but power plant equipment (including 25 boilers annually from 1956 to 1960), woodworking and paper-making equipment including complete plants for manufacture of paper and cardboard, plants for manufacture of cellulose, sawmills, veneer-making plants, frame saws, and wood planers. Hoisting equipment, including large bridge cranes, railway cranes, and freight elevators, comprise a significant portion of Finnish supplies.[15]

Sweden has been an important supplier of equipment for the Soviet chemical, food, and building industries under annual trade agreements since 1946. For example, the 1950 trade agreement between Sweden and the Soviet Union called for Swedish delivery of the following equipment[16]:

Equipment for building industry and manufacture of building materials (Sw. Kr. 23,500,000)
Equipment for food industries (Sw. Kr. 9,000,000)
Equipment for chemical industry (Sw. Kr. 12,000,000)
Power and electrotechnical equipment (Sw. Kr. 6,500,000)
One unit of mine elevator gear

---

[14] See chapter 2.
[15] United Nations, *Treaty Series*, vol. 240, no. 3403 (1956), pp. 198-204.
[16] *East-West Commerce*, V, 4 (April 8, 1958), 6.

Four units of excavating machinery and spare parts for deep drilling machinery (Sw. Kr. 1,300,000)
Spare parts for ships (Sw. Kr. 1,300,000)
Miscellaneous machinery and equipment (Sw. Kr. 3,250,000)

Denmark has also been a major supplier of equipment, particularly of diesel engines and cargo ships. The 1959 Danish-Soviet Trade Agreement included the following items of equipment:[17]

Cargo ships of 11,500 tons d.w. carrying capacity and with a minimum speed of 17.5 knots
Refrigerator ships of 1500 tons d.w.t.
Ship's equipment and spare parts (3,500,000 D. Kr.)
Components and parts for ships' diesel motors (6,000,000 D. Kr.)
Machinery for chemical industry and equipment (26,000,000 D. Kr.)
Machinery and equipment for food industry (17,000,000 D. Kr.)
Machinery and equipment for manufacture of cement and other building materials (3,500,000 D. Kr.)
Various machinery and equipment (3,500,000 D. Kr.)
Instruments and electronic apparatus (7,000,000 D. Kr.)

JAPAN AS A SUPPLIER OF CAPITAL GOODS TO THE SOVIET UNION

During the decade of the fifties, Japan, unlike the Soviet Union, developed a first-rate capability to build and export complete plants using in a few cases an indigenous Japanese technology (as in the case of Kanekalon) or more often an adapted or licensed foreign technology. Although Japan at first lacked experience in certain areas (e.g., the ability to guarantee complete performance for a plant in contrast to performance of individual items of equipment), this ability was gained during the 1960s.

Thus the late 1950s saw the beginning of a considerable export of advanced Japanese equipment to the Soviet Union. The first postwar trade and payments agreement between the Soviet Union and Japan was signed concurrently with the joint declaration ending the state of war between the two countries on October 19, 1956.[18]

The trade agreement provided for most-favored national treatment and included a list of products to be exported by each country. Soviet exports were, typically, raw materials, with a small quantity ($1 million) of metal cutting

[17]   *Ibid.*, VI, 9 (September 28, 1959), 6.
[18]   *Japan Times (Tokyo), October 20, 1956.*

equipment. On the other hand, Japanese exports to the Soviet Union were almost completely in the form of machinery or equipment, with significant proportions of specialized metal products. Marine equipment included two herring packing ships, two tuna fishing boats, and two floating cranes, in addition to marine diesels presumably for installation in Soviet vessels; also provided were ten sets of canning facilities for crab-packing ships and ten for salmon and trout. Moreover, provision was made for Soviet ship repairs in Japanese yards. Other transportation equipment included 25 locomotives (diesel, electric, and steam) with 25 passenger and freight cars in addition to 100,000 kw of mercury rectifiers for Soviet electric locomotives.

Other general machinery included mobile cranes and textile machinery, communications equipment, and various machine tools. Specialized metals included rolled steel products, tin plates, steel wire, and uncoated copper wire and cable. Various medical supplies and fiber yarns made up the balance.

A subsequent Japanese-Soviet trade agreement (1959) further demonstrated the continuing Soviet interest in Japanese capital goods—for example, in paper mills, cold storage plants, chemical plants, and related areas. About 60 percent of the later agreement comprised export of Japanese plants and equipment in exchange for Soviet raw materials.

Japanese exports may be described, then, as falling into two categories: advanced machinery, particularly transportation equipment; and specialized materials related to sectors where the Soviet Union has a very limited and antiquated capacity. Some exports, such as mercury rectifiers for electric locomotives and marine diesels, reflect sectors in which the Soviets have known weaknesses.[19]

EAST EUROPEAN COUNTRIES AS SUPPLIERS OF CAPITAL GOODS TO THE SOVIET UNION

The communist countries of Eastern Europe have been consistent and major suppliers of machinery and equipment to the Soviet Union since 1945. After extensive dismantling in 1945-46, the SAGs and similar joint stock companies were used to ensure a continuity of equipment to the Soviet Union. In the 1950s supply was placed under annual trade agreements.

In 1953 East Germany signed a trade agreement that had as its chief component the provision to the Soviet Union of electrical equipment, chemicals, machinery for the manufacture of building materials, and mining equipment.[20] The 1957 East German trade agreement with the Soviet Union called for the supply of

---

[19] See below, p. 221. A good description of the 1960 exports is in *The Oriental Economist*, (Tokyo), October 1960, pp. 552-57.

[20] *The Times* (London), April 29, 1953.

rolling mill equipment, hoisting equipment, forges, presses, raw stock, and a large quantity of seagoing vessels and river craft.[21]

Under the agreements for 1960-65 supply, signed on November 21, 1959, East Germany was required to supply the Soviet Union with engineering products, refrigerated vans and trains, main line passenger coaches, passenger ships, fishing vessels, a number of complete cement plants, equipment for the chemical industry, machine tools, and forge and pressing equipment.[22]

Poland under its trade agreements with the Soviet Union has been a major supplier of machine tools and equipment, rolling stock, and oceangoing ships.[23] Czechoslovakia has probably been the most important East European communist supplier of equipment. The Skoda Works in Pilsen has been a prominent supplier of machine tools and diesel engines for marine and locomotive use. Other Czechoslovak plants have sent electric locomotives, power plants, and general industrial equipment.[24]

During negotiations between the U.S.S.R. and Yugoslavia in the summer of 1947 the Soviets agreed to grant Yugoslavia $135 million in capital goods, including iron and steel plants, coking ovens, refineries, a zinc electrolysis plant, a sulfuric acid plant, copper and aluminum rolling mills, and molybdenum processing installation.[25] The resulting agreement (July 1947), which specified in great detail the equipment to be provided by the U.S.S.R. to Yugoslavia, included equipment of obvious Western origin, such as Dwight-Lloyd belts, Blake and Symons crushers, Dorr concentrators, Dorko pumps, Abraham filter presses, Sirocco ventilators, Sweetland filter presses, Dix hammer crushers, MacCully crushers, Junkers saws and Geller saws.[26] This was in addition to unnamed equipment for which, from material presented elsewhere, we know that the Soviets utilized a Western design—i.e., drill rigs, sulfuric acid and plant equipment, furnaces, rolling mills, and so on. However, concerning this 1947 agreement Vladimir Dedijer, a former member of the Yugoslav party central committee, comments: "The agreement was a mere ruse, for the Soviet Union had no intention of honoring it.... Of the 135 million dollars promised, the Soviet Union sent us installations valued at only $800,000."[27]

Since the 1950s Yugoslavia has been a supplier of advance equipment to the U.S.S.R., including numerous large and fast cargo ships and scarce copper sections.

---

[21]   *East-West Commerce*, IV, 3 (March 12, 1957), 12.
[22]   *Ibid.*, VI, 12 (December 8, 1959), 11-12.
[23]   *Ibid.*, V, 5 (May 7, 1958), 7.
[24]   *Ibid.*, V, 1 (January 3, 1958), 9.
[25]   V. Dedijer, *Tito* (New York: Simon & Schuster, 1953), p. 288.
[26]   United Nations, *Treaty Series*, vol. 130, no. 1732 (1952), pp. 374 *et seq.*
[27]   Dedijer, *op. cit.* n. 25, pp. 288-89.

WESTERN RESTRICTIONS ON TRADE WITH THE SOVIET UNION

Attempts by Western countries to restrict export of goods with a strategic value to the Soviet Union have taken two main legislative forms. One is exemplified in the U.S. Export Control Act of 1949 and similar national acts in allied countries, and the other in the Mutual Defense Assistance Control Act of 1951 (known as the Battle Act) in the United States.

The Battle Act represents an attempt to prevent export of strategic items with capability of strengthening the military power of the Soviet Union from Western countries to the Soviet Union. At the time the act was introduced, at the end of the 1940s, the Free World had legislative control over export of strategic materials. The Battle Act provides for United States participation in the coordination of these national controls through an informal international committee, meeting in Paris and known as CoCom (Coordinating Committee). Essentially, the act reinforces the system of international controls in effect prior to its enactment and provides a link with U.S. strategic trade controls under the Export Control Act of 1949.

The Battle Act forbids U.S. aid to any country that knowingly permits shipment of strategic items to the Soviet bloc when such items are listed for embargo by the administrator of the act, i.e., by the State Department. The CoCom embargo lists are not made public, but the United Kingdom has published from time to time an embargo list as it relates to British exports to the Soviet bloc. This list gives an idea of the erosion that has taken place in restrictions since 1950. For example, on August 15, 1958, it was announced in the United Kingdom that certain goods had been freed from CoCom embargo control:

> All electrical generating machinery (other than mobile generators of more than 5 mw); all electrical motors (except those specially designed for submarines); all turbines; spectrographs, spectrometers (other than mass spectrographs and mass spectrometers); X-ray diffraction and electron diffraction equipment; electron microscopes; radio valve making machinery (except certain advanced types and those designed specially for making embargoed types of valves); civilian vehicles and aircraft; compressors and blowers; many types of machine tools; and ships (with certain restrictions on speed).[28]

The U.S. State Department for its part has never requested the President to apply sanctions under Section 103(B) of the Battle Act, and scores of violations have been made by Western countries without imposition of the sanctions required by law. In fact, inasmuch as the Battle Act has been violated from its inception, it has never provided an effective restraint to the export of strategic goods

---

[28] *Electrical Review* (London), August 22, 1958, p. 342.

from the West to the Soviet Union.[29] It is arguable that the measure is simply a badly conceived instrument, that it is for various reasons unenforceable. But certainly lax administrative action and gross administrative ignorance concerning Soviet technical capabilities and the use of Western processes and technologies have been major contributory causes to its failure and to the decline of coordinated export control.

The Export Control Act of 1949 as extended and amended to 1969 (when it was replaced by the Export Administration Act of 1969), provides for restrictions on materials whose export may have an adverse effect on the national security of the United States. Section 3(a) provides that rules and regulations shall be established for denial of exports, including technical data, to any nation "threatening the national security of the United States" if the President determines that such export "makes a significant contribution to the military or economic potential of such nation."[30]

This power is administered by the Department of Commerce for most exports, by the Department of State for munitions, and by the Atomic Energy Commission for nuclear materials.

EFFECT OF WESTERN EXPORT CONTROL RESTRICTIONS

The general assessment appears to be that Western export controls have not been effective.[31]

An excellent example of their ineffectiveness may be found in the supply of transportation equipment to the Soviet Union and its subsequent use against the United States and its Asian allies in the Vietnamese war. Whereas the Battle Act of 1951 and the more restrictive Export Control Act of 1949 include an embargo on "transportation materials of strategic value," an analysis of merchant vessels utilized by the Soviet Union to carry armaments to South Vietnam[32] and leased by Poland to Red China for similar purposes indicates that such ships and technology were acquired after the passage of the two export control acts.

Of 96 ships known to have been used by the Soviets on the Haiphong run, 12 have not been identified since construction is too recent for listing in ship registers. Of 84 ships positively identified, only 15 were even partly built in Soviet yards, and one of these was a small tug on a one-way trip

---

[29] For further material, see Battle Act reports to Congress and Gunnar Adler-Karlsson, *Western Economic Warfare, 1947-67* (Stockholm: Almquist & Wiksell, 1968).

[30] U.S. House of Representatives, *op. cit.* n. 4, 1st session, October and December 1961, Section 3(a).

[31] Adler-Karlsson, *op. cit.* n. 29, pp. 83-139.

[32] The State Department has pointed out that the Soviet vessels carry the armaments while leased Western vessels carry the economic supplies.

to Haiphong. The other 69, all tankers and cargo ships, were built outside the U.S.S.R.

Of these 69 ships, only 13 were built before the Battle Act embargo of 1951—*in other words 56 were built after the embargo and outside of the U.S.S.R.* Six of the 13 built before 1951 are Lend Lease ships.

The most important component of a ship is its propulsion unit, i.e., its main engine. None of the 84 identified ships on the Haiphong run has a main engine designed and manufactured in the Soviet Union. (There is one possible exception, where complete positive identification of a Sulzer steam turbine has not been made.)

Small marine diesel engines (2000 hp and less) are made at the prerevolutionary Russky Diesel works in Leningrad, under a 1956 technical-assistance agreement with the Skoda firm of Prague, Czechoslovakia. Larger and of course more important marine diesel engines, up to 9000 bhp (the largest made in the U.S.S.R.), are of Burmeister and Wain (Copenhagen) design. Although Denmark is a member of NATO and presumably supports the NATO objective of an embargo on war materials to the Soviet Union, the Burmeister and Wain firm was allowed (in 1959) to make a technical-assistance agreement for manufacture of the B & W series of marine diesel engines at the Bryansk plant in the U.S.S.R. These diesels are massive units, each 60 feet long by 35 feet high and almost 1000 tons in weight, with obvious strategic value.

Under such circumstances it may be asserted that attempts to control export of strategic goods have not been successful. Indeed there has been a massive and identifiable flow of military equipment to the Soviet Union from Western countries through the CoCom control net. As each member of CoCom has a veto over any shipment, it appears that the information utilized by the State Department and comparable Allied government offices is grossly inadequate and inaccurate.[33]

---

[33] This argument is expanded in chapter 27.

CHAPTER FOUR

Technical Assistance
and Foreign Prototypes

Formal technical-assistance agreements with the Soviet Union are far less publicized today than they were in the early 1930s and therefore little public information is forthcoming. This information scarcity is compounded by the refusal of the U.S. Departments of State and Commerce to release precise information concerning U.S. assistance to the U.S.S.R. It is estimated, however, that since the 1930s the Soviets have had about 100 technical-assistance agreements in force with Western companies at any given time. This assertion applied as recently as late 1968, and it is unlikely the situation has changed since then or will change in the foreseeable future.[1]

Quite apart from formally contracted technical assistance there is a transfer of assistance through the medium of equipment sales and installations. Sometimes provision for such assistance is included in a formal agreement to supply an installation. For example, the 1968 agreement whereby Olivetti of Italy (a subsidiary of General Electric) undertook to build a $90 million plant at Oryol, south of Moscow, for manufacture of automation equipment and office machines was an outgrowth of a technical-assistance agreement in 1965.[2] Another such agreement—one of many that could be cited—was that between the Soviets and Fisher-Bendix of the United Kingdom in 1967, under which the British firm agreed to provide technical documentation and know-how to produce the Bendix automatic commercial washer in the Soviet Union.[3]

However, in the final analysis, any sizable sale of plant or equipment entails technical assistance. Such a sale usually includes not only equipment but also assistance for preparation of the specification, installation, training, and start-up. This was the case in the misnamed "Fiat deal" in which the supply of U.S. equipment was supplemented by Italian technical assistance including the printing of training manuals (in Russian) for Russian operatives in Italian printing plants. Quite clearly, then, technical assistance need not be formalized into an agreement;

---

[1] *Business Week*, October 5, 1968, p. 124. According to this source, in 1968, "100-odd ... Western companies ... have technical accords with the Soviets."
[2] *Ibid.*
[3] *East-West Trade News* (London), III, 7 (April 15, 1967).

it is more realistically viewed as part of any sale of technology, regardless of whether or not it is the stated subject of a written agreement.

Apart from formal technical assistance, there is the allied consideration of Soviet imports of single items of equipment for use as prototypes. There is no question that the Soviet Union draws an almost unbelievably large quantity of such prototypes from the West, primarily from the United States and Germany. It might not be rash to assert that the Soviet Union attempts to purchase one of every major industrial product manufactured in the West for analysis and possible reproduction. Examples extracted more or less at random from Soviet imports from the United States in 1960 and 1970 illustrate the magnitude of this flow of single items. In the third quarter of 1960[4] the Soviet Union imported the following items from the United States (almost all single items):

	Value
Industrial power sweeper	$ 2,001
Gas turbine engine	17,830
Centrifugal separator	19,850
Ultracentrifuge	15,645
Analytical balance	1,993
Air compressor	83
Centrifugal pump	1,700
Fluid stream analyzers	28,500
Hard gelatin capsule machine	309,631
Hydraulic presses	27,273
Industrial sewing machine	1,508
Mixing and blending machines	4,538
Percussion type drill	95,000
Plastics molding press	12,490
Vertical turret lathe	95,970
Tracklaying tractor (and blade)	15,000
Beet harvester and topper	8,055
Haying machine	4,970
Police motorcycle (with accessories)	1,944
Potato planters	6,093
Airplane tug and engine starter	86,450
Klischograph	8,950
Wattmeters	596

These small-lot imports are almost certainly for design purposes. Indeed, there never has been export of more than one or two items to the U.S.S.R. of agricultural equipment of the types listed (beet harvesters, haying machines, potato planters, and tractors) since the early 1930s (with the exception of Lend Lease items charged to the U.S. Treasury). Single imports of such equipment, when continued

---

[4] U.S. Dept. of Commerce, *Export Control*, Fifty-third Quarterly Report (Third Quarter 1960), p. 10.

over a lengthy period and not followed by substantial orders, are clearly for prototype use.

Ten years later we find a similar pattern of Soviet imports. In the second quarter of 1969 the U.S.S.R. imported from the United States the following items:[5]

	Value
Airborne navigation equipment	$ 18,116
Electronic computer	169,334
Spectrophotometer	169,334
Diesel engines	13,495
Atmospheric furnace system	92,944
Water filtration system	54,128
Sweep generator	18,358
Industrial weighing scales	15,752
Radiation detection and measuring instruments	208,410
Automatic typewriter	6,800
Power sweeper	6,283

That this process of single-item import has extended over a considerable period of time is determined by examination of the statistics of Soviet foreign trade. Soviet Trade Group 145 is "Excavators and road construction equipment"; imports in this group from the United States have been as follows:[6]

	Value in rubles	Estimated number of units
1949-56	None	None
1957	80,000	2
1958	122,000	3
1959	46,000	1
1960	57,000	2
1961-65	None	None
1966	55,000	2

The tabulation shows that import of small batches or single units is followed by a gap with no imports and then small-batch imports are resumed.

The manner in which such single items are analyzed in the Soviet Union may be inferred from Soviet technical manuals. Such books fall into two basic categories: (1) those that describe in a detailed, comparative manner individual items of foreign equipment, and (2) those that describe the single item that

[5] U.S. Dept. of Commerce, *Export Control*, Eighty-eighth Quarterly Report (Second Quarter 1969), p. 12.
[6] Values taken from *Vneshniaia torgovliaia SSSR: Statisticheskii sbornik, 1918-1966* (Moscow, 1967), pp. 146-47; units calculated at approximately 25,000 to 45,000 rubles per unit.

has been chosen as the Soviet standard, i.e., for duplication on a large scale. Selected data from several such Soviet publications will make the argument clear.

Soviet technical literature has always contained a sizable number of books —usually paperbacks issued in editions of between 2000 and 10,000 copies—making comparative studies of foreign machines. The Soviet Academy of Construction and Architecture, for example, issued in 1959 a 62-page paperback entitled *Zarubezhnye mashiny dlia mekhanizatsii stroitel'nykh rabot*, consisting of a detailed examination of foreign mechanical equipment used in the construction industry. On pages 19-20 a detailed table provides comparative figures on capacity, load, type, and model of engine, speed (converted to kilometers per hour), number of speeds, and total weight in kilograms for 38 foreign models of mechanical dump cars. These models include Aveling-Barford (U.K.); Road Machines (U.K.); Benoto (France); Bates (U.K.); Dart (U.S.A.); Koering (U.S.A.); Orenstein Koppel (West Germany). In other words the Soviets acquired one of virtually every foreign dump car and made a detailed comparative study of characteristics. The booklet is complete with photographs and diagrammatic blowups of the mechanical features. Several of the more interesting Western models are examined in more detail by comparing such features as chassis construction, brakes, and engine characteristics. Finally technicoeconomic efficiency factors are calculated. It might be argued that such comparative studies may be a prelude to Soviet purchase, except that this type of equipment has not been imported in quantities larger than small batches of one to six since the 1930s and (as will be indicated later) Soviet equipment is based with only minor exceptions on such Western models.

A similar hard-cover publication (3400 copies) was a book issued in 1968, authored by N. N. Kalmykov and entitled *Burovaia tekhnika i tekhnologiia za rubezhom*. Pages 20 to 27 contain numerous photographs of United States tri-cone drilling bits—supposedly denied export from the United States to the U.S.S.R. under export control laws. Figure 7 illustrates the Globe Type S-3; Figure 8 the Globe Type SS-2; Figure 9 the Hughes Type OWV; Figure 10 the Smith Type SV-2; Figure 11 the Globe Type MHY-3; Figure 12 two views of the Type EM and two views of the Type EM-1C manufactured by Chicago-Pneumatic; Figure 13 the Reed Type YS and Type YM; Figure 14 the Security Type M4N; Figure 15 the Globe Type M-3; Figure 16 the Chicago Pneumatic Type ER-1; Figure 17 the Chicago Pneumatic Type ER-2; Figure 18 Security Types S4 and S-4T; Figure 19 the Reed Type YR; and so on.[7]

The rest of the volume is a detailed discussion of American oil well drilling equipment. Some of the diagrams suggest that copying of the equipment is the objective: for example, the diagram on page 199 compares tooth profiles

---

[7] The model letters were not transliterated from the original English to the Russian; therefore, they have not been transliterated into English but are given as in the Russian text.

on various tubes. In brief, the book is a clear comparative exposition of the technical features of U.S. oil well drilling equipment.

In the field of U.S. coal mining practice and equipment, a recent Soviet book is R. Yu. Poderni, *Ugol'niia promyshlennost' SShA* (Moscow, 1968; 2600 copies). This book contains comparative performance and technical data on U.S. equipment that would be difficult to find even in the United States. For example, pages 132-33 detail operating characteristics of all Bucyrus-Erie and Marion excavators currently in production; page 146 has comparative data on the seven walking draglines produced by the Marion Company, and is followed by details on the method used by the firm to calculate excavator productivity. If the book were to be translated into English it would provide a useful little manual for excavator and dragline operators in the United States. A similar book on mining practice also was published in 1968, entitled *Rekonstruktsiia, mekhanizatsiia i avtomatizatsiia shakht za rubezhom*, by K. K. Kuznetsov and others (Moscow, 1968; 2700 copies). This book provides information on development and mechanization of foreign mine shafts. The bibliography suggests the scope of Soviet acquisitions; it includes company catalogs and literature (that of the Hibernia and Westphalia firms) and company journals. Soviet interest is reflected in the issue of foreign developments in the field as "Express Information."

The refinement of technical details given in this type of book is suggested by the following translation of Table 1 in a publication entitled *Analiz rabot po avtomatizatsii pitaniia utkom tkatskikh stankov za rubezhom* by Yu. P. Sidorov (Moscow, 1968; p. 10). The table compares operating characteristics of foreign-made stitching machines:

Operating Angles of Automatics

Model of machine and firm	Start stitching operations	Light (no load) stitching	Transfer to new bobbin	Shift spools	Full operating angle
Northrop, England	311	2	14	33	49
Ruti, Switzerland	325	2	8	25	35
Draper, U.S.A.	312	9	13	26	48
Sohengo, West Germany	306	4	17	33	54
Saurer, Switzerland	320	4	10	26	40

In the electronic sector, one type of publication includes operating characteristics of foreign equipment, no doubt as a guide to purchases by Soviet organizations. For example, a booklet issued in 1968 includes details on over 2000 American, Japanese, East German, and West German transistors—*Zarubezhnye transistory shirokogo primeneniia*, by V. F. Leont'ev. Another type of publication includes data on utilization of equipment in the West and obviously provides more than mere information on available equipment. For example, G. G. Sitnikov's *Transzistornye televisory SShA i Iaponii* (Moscow, 1968) is a selection of articles either translated from American and Japanese sources, or detailing circuits reproduced from such sources; pages 68-70 are entitled "TV 120771 firmy EMERSON (SShA)."

These precise examinations of foreign abilities are by no means limited to technology in the narrow sense. They also include analyses of Western management systems. For example, one booklet of 143 pages (9000 copies printed) describes the operations of Olivetti–General Electric plants in Italy—N. A. Salomatin's *Organizatsiia i mekhanizatsiia upravleniia proizvodstvom na predpriiatiiakh italii* (Moscow, 1969). It provides information on the Italian plants of Olivetti–General Electric that would be difficult to find in a well-stocked Western business library. After a brief introduction (without the usual Marxist-Leninist prefixes), it discusses organization of production in each of the G.E. plants (with photographs), including reproduction of documents used, types and numbers of business machines, organization charts, work programs, and a small section on the use of the PERT management system.

An examination of plastics used in buildings, but compiled without benefit of the courtesy extended by Olivetti–General Electric at the plant level, is entitled *Polimernye stroitel'nye materialy* (Moscow, 1968). This 102-page booklet (7000 copies issued) details Western uses of plastics in building, and includes three rather bad color photographs and a discussion of products by trade name and physical properties.

With the help of such fairly common publications it is possible to trace import of foreign equipment in small batches, and its subsequent use first as prototype then as duplication of the prototype for series production of a "Soviet" machine or piece of equipment.

The Soviet production of electric locomotives provides an excellent example of this evolution. Small batches of electric locomotives were imported from the West in early 1930s—first General Electric and Brown-Boveri, followed in the 1950s by Skoda, Japanese mercury rectifiers, and Schneider-Alsthom locomotives from France. More recently these imports have been supplemented by batches of Krupp silicon rectifier electric locomotives and another group of Czech locomotives. Figure 4-1 illustrates the process by which these batches of imported prototype locomotives have been converted into Soviet classes of electric locomotives.

It is unlikely that export of technical data, a normal accompaniment to sales, by itself provides information for "copying." The Export Control Act of 1949 provides specific authority for controlling export of data for national security reasons, and in 1951 stringent controls were put on data for Soviet bloc destinations; since then validated export licenses have been required for shipment of data not generally available in published form. General license

Figure 4-1   FOREIGN ORIGINS OF SOVIET ELECTRIC LOCOMOTIVES

Date	Foreign locomotive type imported	Number imported	Soviet utilization: Russian class	As proto- type for	Date
1930					1930
1932			"S" Class		1932
	General-Electric (U.S.A.)	29	Ss		
	Brown-Boveri (Italy)	7	Si		
1934				VL-19	1934
1936					1936
1938				VL-22	1938
1940				VL-22 (340 kw)	1940
1942					1942
1944	Electric locomotive axles (VI-1-108) U.S. Lend Lease				1944
1946				VL-22m (400 kw)	1946
1948					1948
1950					1950
1952				VL-8 (N-8)	1952
1954			"NO" Class		1954
	Skoda (Czechoslovakia) mercury rectifiers		N-60		
	silicon rectifiers		N-62		
	Japanese (mercury rectifiers only)		N-60 electric mechanical equipment	VL-23	
1956	Skoda (Czechoslovakia) mercury	50	chSl		1956
1958	Schneider-Alsthom (France)	40	F (T)		1958
1960	Schneider-Alsthom (France)		FP (TP)		1960
	Krupp (Germany) silicon rectifier	20	K		
1962	Skoda (Czechoslovakia)		chS2		1962
1964					1964
1966					1966
1968					1968
1970					1970

Legend: — — — — ▶ Prototype development
———————▶ Production

Sources: Association of American Railroads, A Report on Diesel Locomotive Design and Maintenance on Soviet Railways (Chicago: AAR Research Center, 1966); and Association of American Railroads, Railroads of the U.S.S.R. (Washington, D.C., n.d.).

GTDP permits export of data generally available in stores or by subscriptions, or of unpublished data "not directly and significantly related to design, production, and utilization in industrial processes" and available in academic institutions and laboratories.

It is also unlikely that firms would freely ship data to the U.S.S.R. given the Soviets' long history of retaining such material or making unauthorized use of it. Moreover since June 1959 all U.S. exporters of certain specified types of unpublished chemical data and services relating to petroleum and petrochemical plants and processes must obtain written assurances from the importers in friendly countries that neither the technical data nor the resultant machine, equipment, plant, process, or service is intended to be sent to a Sino-Soviet bloc destination or to Poland.

Thus in the third quarter of 1960 the Department of Commerce approved only 18 licenses for export of technical data to the Soviet bloc, including those for rolling mill accessory equipment, a phosphoric acid plant, compressors for urea plants, drawbenches for tubes and bars, superchargers for vehicles, and instructions manuals for communications equipment.[8] Given the restrictions and the limited exports of such data, then, it is probable that the import of prototypes provides the more valuable source for copying.

Import of prototypes and subsequent copying is advantageous to the Soviet Union in several ways: it minimizes internal research and development investment, provides a quick answer to the Party's demands for instant technology, and above all eliminates the cost of investing in processes that will fall by the wayside.

In a market economy numerous processes and products, perhaps several hundred alternatives for any one product, may move from invention to innovation and enter the marketplace for sale to consumers. Consumer demand and technical efficiency (or inefficiency) eliminate the least desirable, and normally there is only a relative handful of survivors. The elimination of those that fall by the wayside, those products and processes sometimes called the "wastes of competition," is, however, a necessary step along the road to achieving efficient economic and technical choices. Socialists may criticize the waste involved, but the alternative is either to choose a single process arbitrarily without going through the market or to depend on technology tested in a foreign market-place.

The time lag between selection of a specific foreign process and its subsequent production in the U.S.S.R. (via import of prototypes and copying) is significant. Figure 4-2 illustrates the approximate time lags for some of the more important types of marine diesels adopted from foreign designs; between six and eight years appears to be the average time between import of the first foreign model

---

[8] U.S. Dept. of Commerce, *op. cit.* n. 5, p. 7.

Figure 4-2   MARINE DIESELS: TIME LAGS IN
                     CONVERTING FOREIGN TO SOVIET MODELS

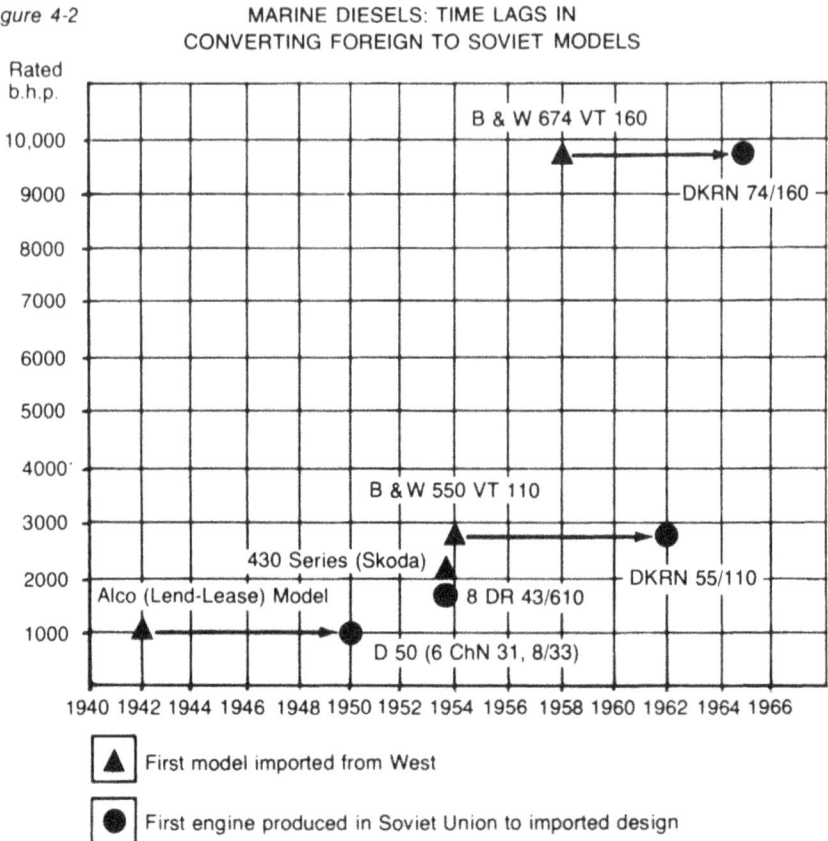

Rated b.h.p.

B & W 674 VT 160
DKRN 74/160
B & W 550 VT 110
430 Series (Skoda)
Alco (Lend-Lease) Model
8 DR 43/610
DKRN 55/110
D 50 (6 ChN 31, 8/33)

10,000 9000 8000 7000 6000 5000 4000 3000 2000 1000

1940 1942 1944 1946 1948 1950 1952 1954 1956 1958 1960 1962 1964 1966

▲ First model imported from West

● First engine produced in Soviet Union to imported design

Source: Registr Soyuza SSR, Registrovaya kniga morskikh sudov soyuza SSR 1964-1965 (Moscow, 1966).

and its initial production in the U.S.S.R. (The exception is produced under joint technical-assistance agreements set up in COMECON.) This lag is favorable when compared to the alternative of developing a suitable technology inside the U.S.S.R. without a background of research and development experience and without the guidance of the marketplace. There is little question that without such imports the Soviet Union (unless it were to effectively decentralize the innovative function and adopt a market economy) would have great difficulty in advancing from its present technological levels. It may be noted in this regard that even Yugoslavia, a socialist country with a quasi-market influence which supplies important technology to the U.S.S.R. (see the Skoda example cited in Figure 4-2), is itself still dependent on Western technology in the marine diesel sector.[9]

[9] More detailed information concerning marine diesels is given in chapters 6, 17, and 21.

We may infer from this brief discussion a point that will be further illustrated later: the degree of indigenous technical innovation in an economy appears to be directly related to the structure of the economy. The greater the influence of market forces, including a demand-supply price system, the profit incentive, and free entry and exit, the greater the degree of indigenous innovation. Conversely, the greater the degree of centralized technical decision-making and lack of personal profit incentive and disciplinary marketplace forces, the less the degree of indigenous innovation.

CHAPTER FIVE

Financial Aspects of Technical Transfers

Previous volumes of this study have only cursorily mentioned the financial means by which technical transfers have been effected. These financial factors are generally beyond the scope of this study, but a summary outline is perhaps in order at this point.[1]

The financing of technical assistance has not normally taken the form of government-to-government transfers; until recently, it was usually accomplished through private loans and credits guaranteed by a Western government, but several large French and German long-term loans in the late sixties may herald a change. Although the role of Western governments has been obscure it has also been fundamental: it is unlikely that individual Western firms, financial institutions, and banks would have continued to provide long-term credits or loans without government guarantees. For example, in discussing British Government support, Paul Einzig points out how the Soviets have reneged on payments. Soviet arrears on United Nations payments, he writes, are a breach of the "most solemn pledge imaginable," and "were it not for the guarantees given by the official Export Credit Guarantees Department most industrial firms would not dare to risk granting such credits and would find it difficult to finance them."[2]

---

[1]   The relations between Western financial houses and the Soviet Union have been explored in the literature of only one country—France. Henry Coston, a well-known French writer of reference books, has also published detailed studies on French financiers and their financial support of the U.S.S.R. The following in Coston's "Lectures Françaises" series are of interest: *Entre Rothschild et Moscou; Les Financiers appuint l'Axe Paris-Moscou; L'Alliance avec Moscou; Les Allies capitalistes du communisme internationale; La Haute finance et les revolutions.* See also two longer studies by Coston: *Les Financiers qui menent le monde* (Paris: Librairie Française, 1958), and *La Haute Banque et les trusts* (Paris: Librairie Française, 1958).

A vast unexplored research field awaits some ambitious economist in the financial relations between American, British, and German financial houses and the Soviet Union. There is a great deal of raw archival material available for such a study or studies. The writer has been unable to locate any full-length published studies on these topics, and the article literature is limited to the subject of Western government financing of the Bolshevik Revolution; see for example George Katkov, "German Foreign Office Documents on Financial Support to the Bolsheviks in 1917," *International Affairs*, April 1956, pp. 181-89.

[2]   *Commercial and Financial Chronicle* (London), February 20, 1964, p. 14. In a later article Einzig takes the British Government to task for favoring the Soviets over the Western countries;

66

The financing of U.S. equipment for the Volgograd automobile plant, to cite a recent example in the United States, was not of interest to private sources, and the original intent was to finance Volgograd through the Export-Import Bank. When this approach was rejected by Congress, other means were found by the administration to provide U.S. Government backing for construction of the largest automobile plant in the U.S.S.R. It is useful, then, to trace the main threads of such financing from the time of the Bolshevik Revolution to the present day, for without Western government and private assistance the technical transfers described in this analysis could not have taken place.

The Bolshevik Revolution itself was financed by "a steady flow of funds" from the German Foreign Ministry.[3] A memorandum to the German kaiser from Baron R. von Kuhlmann, minister of foreign affairs, dated December 3, 1917, reported that German objectives were to support the Bolsheviks financially in order first to remove Russia from the European war as an ally of Britain and France, and then "to provide help for Russia in various ways ... rehabilitation of the railways [and] provision of a substantial loan."[4] The first volume of this series describes how such German assistance was a key factor in bringing about Soviet recovery from the economic depths of 1922.

All banking institutions in the Soviet Union were nationalized under a decree of December 14, 1917. All banking business was declared to be a state monopoly, and all existing private joint stock banks and branches of foreign banks were merged into the State Bank. A subsequent decree, of December 2, 1918, liquidated foreign banks in the U.S.S.R.

Sometime before September 1919 the American-Russian Industrial Syndicate Incorporated was formed in New York by the financial interests of Guggenheim and Sinclair in order to trade with Russia.[5] The long-time interest in Soviet

he suggests that it is one thing to finance routine Soviet transactions but "it is a totally different thing for the British Government to go out of its way to provide additional special facilities for credits up to fifteen years to a maximum of £ 100 million for the exclusive benefit of the U.S.S.R. and other Communist countries." *Ibid.*, March 12, 1964, p. 11. Unfortunately, Einzig does not detail Soviet defaults; these are both numerous and substantial, although there is a prevailing myth to the contrary.

[3] Kuhlmann memorandum; see G. Katkov, "German Foreign Office Documents on Financial Support to the Bolsheviks in 1917," *International Affairs*, 32 (April 1956), 181-89. These "political funds" went through several routes to the Bolsheviks; one route was to the Nye Banken in Sweden and then to the Siberian Bank in Petrograd. The Nya Banken was headed by Olaf Aschberg, who was rewarded after the Revolution with the Russian Bank of Commerce concession in Russia. See also the roles of Alexander Israel Helphand (Parvus) and Kuba Furstenberg as reconstructed from German documents and other sources in Z. A. B. Zeman and W. B. Scharlau, *The Merchant of Revolution* (Oxford and New York, 1965). It should be noted on Parvus that his considerable wealth was acquired suddenly, and that no record exists as to its origins and no trace of it was found after his death.

Another flow of funds for revolution in Russia reportedly was from U.S. and European bankers (Schiff, Warburg, Guggenheim); see A. Goulevitch, *Czarism and Revolution* (Hawthorne, Calif.: Omni, 1962), pp. 230-34.

[4] Katkov, *op. cit.* n. 3.

[5] U.S. State Dept. Decimal File 316-126-50.

finance of the Guaranty Trust Company of New York also began in 1919, with a letter to the State Department inquiring about the legal status of Soviet banking institutions.[6]

In October 1921 the Soviet State Bank (Gosbank) was formed in Moscow with branches in Petrograd, Kassan, and elsewhere. Later in the same year the Guaranty Trust Company of New York was approached by Olaf Aschberg, a former director of the Nya Banken in Stockholm,[7] and the New York bank in turn went to the federal administration with a proposal to open exchange relations with Gosbank.[8] The views of Secretary of Commerce Herbert Hoover on this question were concisely stated: "This seems to me to be entirely in line with our general policy not to interfere with commercial relations that our citizens may desire to set up at their own risk."[9]

However, Charles E. Hughes, then U.S. secretary of state, pointed out that the Bolsheviks could acquire foreign credits by such an arrangement with the Guaranty Trust Company; and (although the secretary did not place much weight on this point) he suggested that the United States might not be able to protect representatives of Guaranty Trust in the Soviet state. Hughes concluded his memorandum: "Particularly I should like to know how it is proposed to secure an effective control of the use by the Bolsheviks of the foreign credits which would be made available in the new State Bank."[10] It was Hoover's subsequent recommendation that any such credits accruing to the State Bank be used for the purchase (question mark "purpose" in original memorandum) of civilian commodities in the United States, and thereby consistent with the humanitarian objectives previously established by the United States with respect to Bolshevik Russia.

In February 1922 overtures were also made to the Irving National Bank of New York to enter into business relations with the State Bank of the U.S.S.R.[11] This does not appear to have been pursued; the State Department files contain only a draft copy of an agreement between Guaranty Trust Company and Gosbank.[12] Under this agreement the Guaranty Trust Company assisted Gosbank in "establishing and maintaining an adequate system covering remittances from the United States of America to the Republic of Russia and [agreed to act] as its agent." The State Department took a noncommittal attitude and apparently disappointed Guaranty Trust Company because "it did not help them very much."[13]

[6]   *Ibid.*, 58. Directors of Guaranty Trust at this time included W. Averell Harriman and Thomas W. Lamont; see Sutton I: *Western Technology ... 1917 to 1930.*
[7]   U.S. State Dept. Decimal File 316-126-663.
[8]   *Ibid.*, 136.
[9]   *Ibid.*
[10]   *Ibid.*, 141.
[11]   *Ibid.*, 158.
[12]   *Ibid.*, 160-169.
[13]   *Ibid.*, 174.

This link with Guaranty Trust in the United States was followed in 1922 by the establishment of an international bank—the Russian Bank of Commerce in Moscow—by a foreign syndicate including the Krupp and Stinnes interests in Germany, and Danish, Dutch, Swedish, and American banks and banking institutions including Guaranty Trust. The head of the Russian Bank of Commerce was Olaf Aschberg.[14] The board of the concession included A. D. Schlesinger (formerly chief of Moscow Merchant Bank), Kalaschkin (chief of the Junker Bank), V. V. Ternovsky (former chief of the Siberian Bank), and Max May of the Guaranty Trust Company of New York. May was designated director of the foreign division of the new bank.[15] A report on an interview with him contains the following statement: "In his opinion, besides its purely banking operations, it [the concession] will of course largely finance all lines of Russian industries."[16]

At that time Aschberg had severed his connection with Nya Banken and was president of the Economic Bolaget bank in Stockholm, which acted as the Swedish representative of the Russian Commercial Bank. In Germany the Russian bank was represented by Garantie- und Credit Bank für den Osten of Berlin. At the end of December 1922 the U.S. legation at Riga referred to this Aschberg concession as the "only real effort made by a foreign group of capitalists" to finance the Soviet Union.[17] It was also pointed out that a group with German capital was working on a project—the Central Asiatic Financial Project—to finance German export trade in Turkestan.

There is in the State Department files an excellent contemporary report by A. Michelson entitled "Private Banks in the Republic of Soviets."[18] Michelson points out that the Russian Bank of Commerce, i.e., the bank operated by Aschberg and linked to Guaranty Trust in New York, was the largest such private bank in the U.S.S.R. and the first bank that had succeeded in establishing itself "partly through the assistance of foreign capital." Michelson adds the interesting comment that "there are, however, serious reasons to suppose that the capital of the Russian Bank of Commerce constitutes the sums belonging to the Bolsheviks themselves which are deposited with Swedish banks." This report also refers to Aschberg as an "agent of Soviet power for all sorts of its financial combinations." The Russian Bank of Commerce was clearly the largest such bank in terms of balances—232.6 million rubles in 1923 as compared to 128.8 million rubles for the Industrial Bank (Prombank) and 80.9 million for the Municipal Bank of Moscow. In March 1923, however, the Russian Bank of Commerce failed.[19] The U.S. Legation in Stockholm reported in 1924

14 *Ibid.*, 209-211.
15 *Ibid.*, 237; see Report 2437 from U.S. Legation in Stockholm, Sweden, October 23, 1922.
16 *Ibid.*, 249.
17 *Ibid.*, 264.
18 *Ibid.*, 432. Michelson was general secretary of the committee of representatives of Russian banks in Paris.
19 *Financial Times* (London), March 3, 1924.

that Aschberg had been dismissed from his connection with the Russian Bank of Commerce in Moscow and that "a large portion" of Soviet funds had been employed by Aschberg for investments on his personal account.[20]

The Gosbank, established in 1922, also depended heavily on foreign consultants for its establishment. Sweden's Professor Gustav Cassel, a leading European authority on banking who was appointed advisor to Gosbank in 1922, provided a public statement to the effect, "I do not believe in a negative policy.... To leave Russia to her own resources and to her own fate is simply folly."[21]

The creation of both Gosbank and the Russian Bank of Commerce was made in close consultation with European and American bankers. For example, in May 1922 Wittenberg, head of the National Bank of Germany, acted as consultant in the Soviet Union,[22] and in October 1922 a group of bankers including Aschberg, Wittenberg, and Scheinmann (chief of Gosbank) arrived in Stockholm to conduct further negotiations with foreign banks.

Finally, an agreement between the Guaranty Trust Company of New York and Gosbank was signed on August 1, 1923. It was agreed that all transactions would be in dollars, with the Guaranty Trust Company acting as a clearing house.[23] The Guaranty Trust Company so advised the Department of State in a letter dated September 14, 1923.[24] Thus the Guaranty Trust was uniquely connected with the establishment of banking in the U.S.S.R. and the financing of trade with the West.

BANQUE COMMERCIALE POUR L'EUROPE DU NORD

In January 1923 it was reported that the Soviet Union had acquired all the shares of the Chinese Eastern Railway formerly held by the Russo-Asiatic Bank; two French financial institutions, the Société Générale and the Banque de Paris et Pays Bas, were the main owners of the Russo-Asiatic Bank.[25] By June 1923 the Soviets had acquired 60 percent of the shares of the Russo-Asiatic Bank while French holders retained the balance.

Negotiations between representatives of the Soviet Union and French banking interests for the formation of a joint Franco-Soviet bank in France broke down in May 1925. Thereupon the Soviets purchased a small bank in Paris, Banque Commerciale pour les Pays du Nord, with a main office in Paris. This bank, founded in 1920 by Russian banker A. Khaiss with a capital of one million francs, was purchased in 1921 by the Wissotski interests, important prerevolution-

---

[20]   U.S. State Dept. Decimal File 316-126-534.
[21]   *Ibid.*, 235-236.
[22]   *Ibid.*, 182.
[23]   *Ibid.*, 424.
[24]   *Ibid.*, 459.
[25]   *Ibid.*, 285.

ary Russian merchants. The reported purchase price paid by the Soviets to the Wissotskis was £130,000 sterling.[26]

After purchase of the bank the brothers D. V. Wissotski and F. Wissotski continued to serve on the board temporarily, while two new directors, Volidsky and Sharov, were appointed to represent Soviet interests; also appointed as directors were Reisen and Iablokov, two former officers of the Azov Bank; Coön, formerly chairman of the Trade and Industry Bank; and Kempner, formerly of the Central Mutual Credit Bank. The American Consulate in Paris reported on August 20, 1925, that the Soviet intention was to issue new stock on the French market and so indirectly secure foreign participation in the enterprise.

During the 1930s the Banque Commerciale was accused of financing Communist Party activities in France. By 1964 there had been a slight name change and assets had grown to $562 million. There were 268 employees, of whom only three were Russian. A similar bank in London, also founded in the early 1920s, was the Moscow Narodny Bank, which had a remarkable growth from only $24 million in assets in 1958 to $573 million in 1964; by the late 1960s this bank was the fourth largest dealer among the London banks in the Eurodollar market. Only the five directors were Russian, the balance of 200 employees being British.

In 1966 the Soviets opened the Woxchod Handelsbank in Zurich, Switzerland. The Soviets also own an insurance company in Vienna (Garant Versicherung) and have attempted to convert it into a full-fledged banking operation. The Austrian Government has so far objected to such operations on the grounds that Garant Versicherung has illegally bought into Western companies to influence their commercial policies.[27]

Thus although Western skills are still heavily utilized in banking, the scene of operations has been transferred from the Soviet Union, where foreign banks are forbidden to operate, to Europe and the United States, utilizing foreign employees under Russian control. One of the key advantages to the Soviets is that such penetration assists the task of influencing and directing the trade policies of Western firms on sales of Western technology to the Soviet Union.

CHASE NATIONAL BANK[28]

In the 1930s the Chase National was one of four American banks and financial houses to institute relations with the Soviets (in addition to Equitable Trust, Guaranty Trust, and Kuhn, Loeb). Its role in the twenties and the thirties

---

[26] *Ibid.*, 803-804.

[27] *Forbes*, February 15, 1967, p. 60.

[28] Chase National merged with Bank of Manhattan (a former Kuhn, Loeb bank) March 31, 1955, to become Chase Manhattan Bank. Directors of the Chase Manhattan Bank (1968) are David Rockefeller, Eugene R. Black, Roger M. Blough, John T. Connor, and C. Douglas

has been described.[29] There was a close connection between Chase and the Soviets in the pre-World War II days; for example the advisor to Reeve Schley (director and vice president of Chase National Bank) was Alexander Gumberg, reportedly a Bolshevik agent.[30] The Chase Bank also acted as an agent for the Soviets in the 1930s,[31] and in 1930 Amtorg accounts, according to the U.S. Treasury, were "all with the Chase Bank."[32] Today Chase Manhattan (the merged Chase National and Manhattan banks) is Moscow Narodny's correspondent in New York; hence the ties appear to continue.

The Chase Manhattan Bank is controlled by the Rockefeller interests. Nelson A. Rockefeller, governor of the State of New York, is also the prime founder of the International Basic Economy Corporation (IBEC), which in 1967 made an agreement with Tower International, Inc., headed by Cyrus Eaton, Jr., of Cleveland to further transfers of U.S. technology to the Soviet Union. As this agreement was reported, "The joint effort contemplated by International Basic Economy and Tower is seen as combining the investment skills and resources of the Rockefellers and the special entree to Soviet-bloc officialdom that Tower enjoys."[33]

U.S. CREDITS FOR FINLAND: ADMINISTRATIVE SCHIZOPHRENIA

While this study is limited chiefly to the technical and economic aspects

Dillon. Most if not all appear to be proponents of expanded trade with the U.S.S.R. For John T. Connor see U.S. Senate, *Export Expansion and Regulation*, Hearings before the Subcommittee on International Finance, 91st Congress, 1st session (Washington, 1969), pp. 183-85; for Dillon (former Secretary of the Treasury), see U.S. Senate, *Government Guarantees of Credit to Communist Countries*, Hearings before the Committee on Banking and Currency, 88th Congress, 1st session, November 1963 (Washington, 1964), pp. 74-109.

[29] See Sutton, I, pp. 90, 207-9, 226, 262, 277-78, 289-91. The links between Western financial houses providing financial assistance to the Soviet Union might be worth exploring. For example, Equitable Trust signed an agreement in London on March 7, 1923, to act for Gosbank (U.S. State Dept. Decimal File 316-126-295); a director of Equitable Trust was Otto Kahn, who was a director of Kuhn, Loeb, which has been prominent in financing of Russian business. Directors of Guaranty Trust included Thomas W. Lamont (of Morgan interests) and W. Averell Harriman, who also had other business connections with the U.S.S.R. The evidence appears to suggest (although the author has not explored the topic) that a comparatively small group of bankers and financiers has been consistently associated with Soviet financing. At least these are the names that turn up in the fifty-year history; it may simply be that more information is on record concerning their financial houses. (A study of the financial links between the West and the Soviet Union would be a fascinating and worthwhile topic for a doctoral dissertation.)

[30] *Guide to the Manuscripts of the State Historical Society of Wisconsin* (Madison: Wisconsin State Historical Society, 1957), p. 57. On Gumberg, see Robert Bruce Lockhart, *British Agent* (New York and London: G. Putnam's Sons, 1933), p. 220.

[31] *Congressional Record, House*, vol. 77, pt. 6, 73d Congress, 1st session, June 15, 1933, p. 6227.

[32] U.S. Senate, *Morgenthau Diary (China)*, Committee on the Judiciary, (Washington, 1965), p. 70.

[33] *New York Times*, January 16, 1967.

of transfers, it may be instructive to examine in more detail a sample case
of U.S. Government assistance to the U.S.S.R.

Credits from the United States were used to modernize and expand the
wood products and paper industries of Finland after World War II; and the
output of these industries was sent to the U.S.S.R. as reparations. There is
a divergence between contemporary accounts of U.S. intentions and actions
as recorded in the State Department files (at least in the declassified portions).
While it was denied that there was any intent to grant U.S. credits to enable
Finland to make Soviet reparations, in practice the United States advanced
credits for precisely that purpose in a case that affords a well-documented example
of foreign government assistance to the U.S.S.R.

In 1945 the *New York Times* noted that it was unlikely the United States
would grant a Finnish request for a $150 million loan; such a grant was deemed
undesirable as it would be used to develop industry to pay Soviet reparations.[34]
Two weeks later, however, the Export-Import Bank granted a $5 million cotton
credit and a $35 million general credit.[35] In the following month (January 1946)
Secretary of State James Byrnes telegraphed American Chargé Hulley in Finland
concerning the manner in which he should inform the Finnish authorities of
the Bank actions:

> You should carefully emphasize that the credit has no political implications but
> has been granted entirely on the basis of economic considerations, and within
> the framework of our policy which you have repeatedly stressed to Finns that
> we do not propose to contribute directly or indirectly to reparations payment
> by Finland; that the purpose of credit is to facilitate the resumption of U.S.–Finnish
> trade.[36]

Later in the year there was a series of communications from the State Department
to Finland advising that further loans could not be given or even considered.
In one telegram (August 9, 1946) Hamilton, U.S. minister in Finland, indicated
that the Finnish Government had been informed it would be a mistake for
a Finnish mission to go to the United States with too optimistic a feeling,
as the Export-Import Bank had many demands upon it.[37] This was followed
by an urgent telegram (Acheson to Hamilton): "Further credit Eximbank out
of question at this time" and "visit of mission to U.S. most undesirable and
should be indefinitely postponed,"[38] and by another (Hamilton to Acheson):
"[I have] strongly advised Finnish Government against mission to U.S.A. also

[34] *New York Times,* December 1, 1945, 7:3.
[35] U.S. State Dept. Decimal File 860d.51/1-1446: telegram.
[36] *Ibid.*
[37] *Ibid.,* 860d.51/8-946: telegram. Hamilton, August 9, 1946.
[38] *Ibid.,* Acheson to Hamilton, August 12, 1946.

advised against Graesbeck [head of the Finnish financial mission] proceeding to U.S.A. in private capacity."[39]

These telegrams, however, were followed by a grant of a $20 million long-term credit, a $12 million short-term credit, and a $5 million credit for industrial goods.[40] And contrary to the published assertions, the credits granted to Finland were in large part specifically for equipment that was virtually certain to be used to manufacture reparations goods for the Soviet Union. For example, the $20 million long-term credit of January 1948 was for

> machinery, equipment and materials required for recovery of export production in the lumber, pulp and paper industry. These materials include wood-working machinery, hydroelectric equipment, iron and steel, spare parts for trucks, lead, coal, and petroleum products.[41]

There is no question that the State Department was informed that these credits would be used to modernize and expand the pulp industries. A Memorandum of Conversation dated December 12, 1946, concerning the discussion between the Finnish delegation headed by Graesbeck and two State Department officials (Havlik and Cleveland)[42] raised a question about the low level of Finnish exports of chemical pulp and commented, "Mr. Graesbeck's explanation of ... the run-down state of the machine equipment was not entirely satisfactory."[43] However, the meeting culminated in a suggestion that the Finns go to the Export-Import Bank. The consensus of the U.S. participants, after the departure of the Finnish delegation, was that a "small" loan of $20 to $25 million should be granted. One month later a $20 million loan was granted for the purchase of industrial machinery and equipment for the lumber and pulp and paper industries.

The U.S. export figures to Finland for the years 1945-48 reflect these credits and their use to purchase equipment for the manufacture of Soviet reparations. Sweden had provided credits for Finnish reconstruction in 1944 and 1945 to the amount of Kr150 million; Sweden's share of total Finnish imports was 51.3 percent in 1945 and only 10.0 percent in 1946 as the credits ran out.[44] On the other hand, the U.S. share of total Finnish imports was zero in 1945 (when no financing was available) and 19.4 percent in 1946 as financing became available under the Export-Import Bank credits.[45] Out of $59 million in 1947, just under $11 million was U.S. machinery and just under $5 million steel products—both categories required for the Finnish industrialization plan needed

[39] U.S. State Dept. Decimal File 860d.51/8-1446: telegram. Hamilton to Acheson, August 14, 1946.
[40] See Table 5-1.
[41] *New York Times*, January 23, 1947, 13:3.
[42] U.S. State Dept. Decimal File 860d.51/12-1246.
[43] *Ibid.*
[44] Urho Toivola, *The Finland Year Book 1947* (Helsinki, 1947), p. 261.
[45] *Ibid.*

to meet Soviet reparations demands. In the following year (1948) U.S. exports to Finland declined to $36 million but the proportion of machinery increased by almost 40 percent to over $14 million, including $5.5 million of industrial machinery. Thus American machinery, financed by the Export-Import Bank, was acquired by Finland to manufacture reparations for the Soviet Union.[46] (See Table 5-1.)

Table 5-1 CREDITS GRANTED TO FINLAND BY THE UNITED STATES, 1945-47

Date	Government agency in the United States	Amount authorized	Details
December 1945	Export-Import Bank	$5.0 million	Cotton credit
December 1945	Export-Import Bank	$35.0 million	General credit
January 1947	Export-Import Bank	$37.0 million	$20 million long term $12 million short term $5 million credit for industrial goods
February 1947	Export-Import Bank	$2.5 million	Credit
May 1947	Foreign Liquidation	$10.0 million	Credit to purchase surplus property overseas
September 1947	War Asset Administration	$10.0 million	Credit to purchase surplus in U.S.
Total 1945-47		$99.5 million	

Source: *New York Times*, December 1, 1945, 7:3; January 23, 1947, 13:3.

In the 1960s direct government-to-government financing came to the fore-front. Germany advanced $400 million to the Soviet Union to purchase oil pipeline at 6 percent over 12 years coupled with assistance to pump natural gas into Germany. Italy financed about $400 million of the U.S.–VAZ automobile plant.[47] The largest single such transaction was made in early 1970 under the Pompidou Government in France; this agreement provided a credit of $810 million to the U.S.S.R. to finance five years' purchases of French machinery and equipment; the credits were for seven to eight and a half years, but interest rates were not announced.[48]

---

[46] The large proportion of Finnish output accounted for by reparations in the lumber, pulp, and paper fields, and in shipbuilding, may be found in Toivola, *Ibid.*, pp. 187-209.

[47] *Washington Post*, March 14, 1970, pp. A1, A15.

[48] *Ibid.* The interest rate is of some significance. This was an era of world investment opportunities at 8 percent; previous French credits were granted at 5.95 percent and it was reported the Soviets were pressing to bring even this low rate down. If Pompidou had granted lower rates (or even 5.95 percent in the light of world conditions in 1970) there would indeed have been widespread criticism. It does appear on the basis of the skimpy evidence publicly available, however, that the French, British, German, and Italian (and perhaps the U.S.) governments have been willing to grant more favorable terms to the U.S.S.R. than to their own citizens.

CHAPTER SIX

Patterns of Indirect Technical Assistance
to the Soviet Union

There are several reasonably well-defined patterns of indirect transfer of technology to the Soviet Union apart from the direct transfers that are the subject of the bulk of this three-volume series. These important indirect transfers pose particular problems for enforcement of export control laws; indeed the existence of indirect transfers has been cited as a prime reason for the difficulty of reaching inter-allied agreement on export control. This difficulty in turn is urged by proponents of more assistance to the U.S.S.R. as a reason for further abandonment of control.

Flows of technology may be broadly categorized as follows:

A. Technology originating in the United States and transferred

1. directly from the United States to the Soviet Union, as in the "Transfermatic Case"

2. indirectly from the United States to an East European communist country, then retransferred to the U.S.S.R. either as technical assistance under COMECON[1] specialization agreements or in the form of equipment manufactured in Eastern Europe and supplied to the U.S.S.R.

3. indirectly from the United States to Europe and then to the U.S.S.R.

4. as direct assistance to an East European plant making equipment for the Soviet Union, i.e., contributing to their operative efficiency for technological exports to U.S.S.R.

B. Technology originating in Europe and Japan and transferred

1. directly to the U.S.S.R., as in the Burmeister & Wain technical-assistance agreement of 1959

2. indirectly through East Europe, as were M.A.N. (West Germany) engines built under license in Poland and exported in Polish ships to the U.S.S.R.

3. as European assistance to East European countries contributing to their capability to supply technology to the U.S.S.R.

---

[1] COMECON is the Council for Mutual Economic Assistance. An excellent review of its structure and function is M. Kaser, *Comecon: Integration Problems of the Planned Economies*, 2d edition (London: Oxford University Press, 1967).

It is these indirect flows that are briefly considered in this chapter.

DIRECT TRANSFERS OF TECHNOLOGY
ORIGINATING IN THE UNITED STATES AND EUROPE

An excellent example of technology originating in the United States and directly transferred to the Soviet Union may be found in the "Transfermatic Case" of 1960-61. This case involved the proposed U.S. sale to the Soviet Union of two Transfermatic machines valued at $5.3 million. The units involved are multi-stage transfer machines for complete process machining of an engine—milling, boring, broaching, drilling, etc. Although the initial Department of Defense position was against granting the license on the grounds it would make a significant contribution to Soviet technology, in the final analysis U.S. Defense Secretary Robert McNamara decided on the basis of his own knowledge of such equipment that the application could go forward. Similar cases decided at about the same time involved Bryant Automatic grinders equipped with high-frequency grinding spindles, and automatic bore grinders for use in the manufacture of internal combustion engines. All these cases embodied a technology significantly advanced beyond that in the Soviet Union at 1960.[2]

More typical than these major transactions decided at a high political level are the smaller exports of U.S. technology. One of thousands of possible examples involved the December 4, 1961 licensing for shipment to the U.S.S.R. of eight flame detectors and industrial instruments. The shipments reportedly were for use in a plant to produce titanium dioxide. The rationale for export of such flame detectors was that industrial instruments of this type could be readily obtained by the Soviet Union from Western Europe.[3]

An example of direct transfer of technology from Europe to the Soviet Union is embodied in the Burmeister & Wain technical-assistance agreement of 1959 to transfer large marine diesel engine technology to the U.S.S.R. Thus the large marine diesels produced at the Bryansk plant in the Soviet Union are of Burmeister & Wain design. Burmeister & Wain technology is also transferred to the Soviet Union indirectly, through East European communist countries. For example, Polish marine diesel engines are based largely on the designs of Sulzer in Switzerland and Burmeister & Wain in Denmark, both of which firms have technical licensing agreements with Polish organizations.

---

[2] See p. 224 for more data.

[3] U.S. House of Representatives, *Investigation and Study of the Administration, Operation and Enforcement of the Export Control Act of 1949, and Related Acts,* Hearings before the Select Committee on Export Control, 87th Congress, 1st session (Washington, 1962), pt. I, p. 411.

TECHNICAL COOPERATION AGREEMENTS
WITH SOCIALIST COUNTRIES

Numerous agreements aimed at strengthening technical cooperation among socialist countries and with European countries were made by the Soviet Union in the decades of the 1950s and the 1960s and provided vehicles for transfer of Western technology. These included agreements with Yugoslavia (April 26, 1955),[4] East Germany (April 26, 1956),[5] Finland (July 17, 1954),[6] Hungary (June 28, 1956),[7] United Kingdom (May 24, 1959),[8] (December 1, 1959),[9] and (January 9, 1961).[10]

Article I of such treaties is exemplified by the Soviet-Yugoslav agreement of 1955:

> The Government of the Federal People's Republic of Yugoslavia and the Government of the Union of Soviet Socialist Republics shall strive to develop scientific and technical cooperation between the two countries by exchanging the experience and technical achievements of the two Contracting States in industry, mining, construction, transport, agriculture, and other fields of economic activity, in the interest of each Contracting State.[11]

Article II usually specifies the manner by which the transfer shall be effected, i.e., through the "reciprocal communication of technical documentation and the exchange of relevant information, including patents and licenses, in accordance with the provisions in force in each of the Contracting States."[12]

The transfer in the Yugoslav case was to be conducted by the exchange of experts, students, and researchers and by the provision of documents and materials. The final articles in the treaty specify the technical details of funding, location of commissions, and similar matters.

The basic agreement was established with the creation of COMECON (Council for Mutual Economic Assistance, formed in January 1949), but it was not implemented for a number of years. Its purpose is to exchange economic experience, extend technical assistance, and generally render mutual economic assistance among socialist countries; it also provides for the bilateral technical-assistance agreements, or specialization agreements, among socialist countries

---

[4] United Nations, *Treaty Series*, vol. 378, no. 5423 (1960).
[5] *Ibid.*, vol. 259, no. 3692 (1957).
[6] *Ibid.*, vol. 240, no. 3403 (1956).
[7] *Ibid.*, vol. 259, no. 3700 (1957).
[8] *Ibid.*, vol. 374, no. 5344 (1960).
[9] *Ibid.*, vol. 351, no. 5032 (1960).
[10] *Ibid.*, vol. 404, no. 5810 (1961).
[11] *Ibid.*, vol. 378, no. 5423 (1960).
[12] Ibid.

(Table 6-1). These agreements provide the organizational structure for transfer of Western technology indirectly to the Soviet Union from Eastern Europe.

The specialization agreements made under COMECON and the resultant bilateral agreements (as reported in Western sources) are surprising in that, with the exception of agricultural and raw materials which comprise the bulk of Soviet exports, the listed specializations for production by the Soviet Union often are in sectors where this study has revealed a definite technical lag on the part of the Soviet Union.

The listed specializations do include all technologies mastered by Soviet engineers and those in which there has been a degree of indigenous progress, i.e., blast furnaces, open-hearth steel, heavy-section rolling mills, steam turbines over 100,000 kw, large generators, power plants, and heavy tractors.[13] Although in greater part based on foreign technology, these are sectors where the Soviet Union in the early 1960s was standing on its own feet.

On the other hand, the specialization agreements involve some technical areas where the Soviets are decidedly weak and backward. For example, very large long-distance pipe lines, synthetic rubber, large-capacity cement mills, printing industry equipment, synthetic fiber production equipment, heavy diesel and electric locomotives, passenger automobiles, and specialized ships all are areas where the Soviet Union is backward and requires continuing dependence on imported technology.[14]

Production of both synthetic rubber and plastics is retarded in the Soviet Union. The bulk of synthetic rubber capacity at 1960 was either the prewar SK-B or the Dupont Nairit process; similarly, plastics were few in number, poor in quality, and utilized a great deal of imported equipment or Soviet copies of foreign equipment. In neither of these industrial processes has the Soviet Union any new or worthwhile production equipment for export.

Ships are listed as a Soviet COMECON specialty, although three-quarters of the Soviet mercantile fleet and four-fifths of its marine propulsion units have been built in foreign yards. Large marine and locomotive diesels are also listed, although the Soviets lag badly in both. Equipment for the printing industry and synthetic fiber industries is currently imported, and Lavsan and Nitron fibers use British equipment.

Forging equipment is a known area of Soviet backwardness. Cement factories of large capacities are bought abroad. In 1970 steel sheet rolling mill and finishing equipment was at the U.S. 1930 level. Passenger cars were the subject of the so-called "Fiat agreement" in 1966.

---

[13] Not all shown on Table 6-1; see Heinz Kohler, *Economic Integration in the Soviet Bloc*, (New York: Praeger, 1965), pp. 138-40.

[14] *Ibid.*, pp. 138-40. For evidence see the following: long-distance pipelines, p. 130; synthetic rubber, p. 153; cement mills, p. 170; printing equipment, p. 329; synthetic fiber equipment, p. 178; locomotives, p. 248; passenger automobiles, p. 191; and specialized ships, p. 282. Compare with Table 6-1.

Table 6-1   COMECON SPECIALIZATION FOR HEAVY INDUSTRIAL EQUIPMENT

	U.S.S.R.	Bulgaria	Czechoslovakia	DDR	Hungary	Poland	Rumania
Oil drilling equipment	X	X					X
Oil refinery equipment	X						X
Rolling mill equipment	Heavy section iron rolling mill trains, heavy rolling mill trains		Heavy section iron rolling mill trains, wire-rod mill trains[a]	Continuous and semicontinuous wire-rod mill trains, leaf-metal and tube rolling mills[b]	Wire-rod mill trains	Light section mill trains, small rolling mill trains	
Coal industry equipment	Single-bucket excavators and shovel excavators for open-pit mining[c]		Multi-bucket excavators, stackers, over-burden trans-porter bridges[d]			Coal combine equipment, open-pit lignite, coking plants	
Lignite industry equipment				Multi-bucket excavators for open-pit mining, briquette factories[e]			
Cement factory equipment	Furnace capacity of over 1,000-2,000 t/day		Furnace capacity up to 800 t/day	Furnace capacity of 1,000-2,000 t/day			Furnace capacity of 400-450 t/day
Sugar factory equipment			X	X		X	
Aluminum production equipment					X		
Forging and pressing equipment	X		Heavy	Light		Heavy	

	Specialized, such as turret head lathes, long planing machines[f]	Specialized, for making ball bearings, lathes, drills	Highly mechanized automatic, precision, such as duplicating milling machines[g]	Specialized, such as open front vertical drills	Specialized, such as complete wheel set machining lathes, horizontal presses[h]	Specialized, such as knee and column type milling machines
Heavy machine tools						
Gas pipes	Very large, long-distance	Large, long-distance	Small, long-distance			
Marine diesels		Large	Large, 4,000-5,000 hp		4,000-5,000 hp ship diesel engines	
Diesel engines (excl. marine diesels)				X		
Blast furnaces	X	X			X	
Complete factories for reinforced concrete					X	

X = Specialization in all equipment in category

a Medium and fine sheet metal rolling mills

b Rolling mill trains, light section iron rolling mill trains and drawing die mill trains

c Coking plants, coal combines, coal cutting machines

d As well as soft coal mining equipment

e Burden transporter bridges, stackers, conveyor bridges, rotary bucket excavators with a cutting power of 80 kg/cm

f Machine tools for ball bearings

g Honing machines, thread grinding machines, gear hobbing machines, pipe cutters, pipe thread cutters, ball and roller bearings machine tools, lathes

h Up to 250 tons, cold pressure automatics, horizontal face plate lathes, roll grinding machines, toothed-wheel grinding machines for ball bearings

i Transverse planing machines, long planing machines with wide bench

Source: H. Köhler, *Economic Integration in the Soviet Bloc* (New York: Praeger, 1965).

It is interesting to note, therefore, that most of the categories claimed for Soviet specialization fall into one or the other of the two extremes—that which the Soviet Union has mastered and technically does reasonably well and that where it is decidedly backward and behind other bloc members, who themselves turn westward for technology.

The asserted existence of a COMECON category of Soviet specialization in sectors where the Soviet Union is ill equipped for specialization is confirmed by trade figures for the Soviet Union with East European countries. Table 6-2 expresses machinery and equipment as a percentage of total trade between the U.S.S.R. and various East European communist countries; the category of machinery and equipment of course comprises the most important category of products included in specialization agreements. With all East European social-ist countries taken as a group, just over 42 percent of their total exports to the Soviet Union comprise machinery and equipment. On an overall basis, only 13 percent of Soviet exports to these countries comprises machinery and equipment; this 13 percent also includes exports to relatively backward countries, such as Bulgaria. In other words, East European countries in general are three times more important as shippers of machinery and equipment to the U.S.S.R. than is the U.S.S.R. as a shipper of equipment to those countries. This certainly suggests a relative technical backwardness in the Soviet Union in machinery and equipment. This pattern is highlighted by exports of the most important equipment producers: 62 percent of East German exports to the U.S.S.R. com-prise machinery and equipment, over 58 percent of Hungarian exports are of this nature, and almost 45 percent of Czech exports.

Although the COMECON specialization and technical-assistance features relate to documentation and engineering assistance, not to physical movements of machinery, these trade figures do support the assertion of Soviet backwardness, as trade figures must broadly parallel relative technical capabilities. It would be unlikely that the Soviet Union is a major importer of machinery and at the same time provides extensive technical assistance for that machinery; such might apply in one or two special cases (e.g., in the provision of documentation for a specific machine), but not over the broad range of technology indicated. In any event, we know from other sources that the listed Soviet technical speciali-zations which are in fact East European technical specializations, involve areas where these East European countries are receiving technical assistance from Western firms. For example, ship equipment is the subject of "hundreds" of technical-assistance agreements between Western firms and East European coun-tries;[15] these firms are major builders on Soviet account although "specialized ships" are listed as a Soviet category under COMECON.

This question will now be examined in more detail.

---

[15]   John D. Harbron, *Communist Ships and Shipping* (London, 1962), p. 108.

Table 6-2 MACHINERY AND EQUIPMENT AS PERCENTAGE OF TOTAL
SOVIET TRADE WITH EAST EUROPEAN SOCIALIST COUNTRIES IN 1960

Country	Percentage of machinery and equipment in total exports to the U.S.S.R.	Percentage of machinery and equipment in total imports from the U.S.S.R.
All Socialist countries of Eastern Europe	42.36	13.52
East Germany	62.19	3.59
Hungary	58.39	22.57
Czechoslovakia	44.97	9.5
Poland	31.32	11.31
Bulgaria	16.36	13.52
Rumania	8.33	22.13
Yugoslavia	14.58	26.00

Source: P. I. Kumykin, ed., *50 Let sovetskoi vneshnei torgovli* (Moscow, 1967), pp. 108-38.

TECHNICAL ASSISTANCE FROM CZECHOSLOVAKIA TO THE SOVIET UNION

In December 1947 a scientific and technical cooperation agreement was signed between the U.S.S.R. and Czechoslovakia. It has been renewed at annual intervals with changes in the direction and focus of the technical cooperation. The agreement provides for extensive exchange of both personnel and documents. During 1956, for example, Czechoslovakia granted documentation to the Soviet Union on processes for leatherworking and shoemaking machinery, glass blocks, measuring and medical instruments, piping insulation, turbine blades, railroad wagons, locomotives, heavy diesel engines, and automobile engines:

> Over 100 Soviet experts acquainted themselves in Czechoslovakia with the production of sanitary equipment. Groups of experts from 16 Union Republics visited Czechoslovakia in order to study the manufacture of different kinds of footwear, artificial fibers, building structures, pumps, compressors, etc.[16]

In turn the Soviet Union passed over documentation for production of raw rubber, aluminum, phenol, steel works, coke and chemical plants, an aluminum wide-sheet mill, a plant for manufacture of penicillin and streptomycin, and high-voltage cables.[17]

In 1957 the Soviet Union assisted in the construction of an atomic reactor

[16] *Czechoslovak Economic Bulletin* (Prague), February 1957, pp. 17-19.
[17] *Ibid.*, p. 18.

and a cyclotron and Czechoslovakia in turn passed to the Soviet Union documentation for mine, metallurgical, machine tool, and other equipment:

> The Czechoslovak factories and research institutes will acquaint Soviet experts with the technology of production, for example, of turbines for high heads, high-pressure pumps, the production of heat-treated steel, diesel engines, equipment for the manufacture of artificial leather and with the application of light ferroconcrete constructional units.[18]

Some interesting observations may be made about the exchange. There is little question that Czechoslovak diesels, electric locomotives, and other equipment sent to the Soviet Union are of top quality. Skoda diesels compete in the world market against Western-made diesel engines. On the other hand, some of the Soviet grants seem out of place. In 1957, for example, the Soviet Union sent instructions for the manufacture of calculating machines and steel tubes—two of the most backward fields in the U.S.S.R. To be sure, it also gave assistance in open-hearth furnaces and coke ovens—areas in which Soviets have made design progress based on classical Western processes.[19]

The Skoda Works at Pilsen provides an excellent example of indirect U.S. assistance via an East European communist country to the Soviet Union. The Skoda plant is the most important single industrial unit in Czechoslovakia and a prominent manufacturer of diesel engines, armaments, and heavy industrial equipment. Czechoslovakia itself is the fourth largest world producer of diesel engines, of which 80 percent are exported, the largest buyer being the Soviet Union.

Under terms of the 1956 scientific and technical cooperation agreement with the Soviet Union, Skoda sends technical assistance to the Soviet Union in the field of diesel engines and specialized machine tools for making ball bearings, lathes, and drills, together with heavy equipment for forging and pressing. This type of equipment is a specialty of the Skoda plant, which also has an agreement with the Simmons Machine Tool Corporation of Albany, New York. Simmons is an old, established machine tool company specializing in the design of large automatic and numerically controlled special-purpose machines. Under the agreement Simmons equipment is built by Skoda in Czechoslovakia and marketed under both the Simmons name and specification in the United States and also as a joint Simmons-Skoda line. Included in the Simmons-Skoda line are such machine tools as heavy-duty lathes (40-inch to 13-foot-diameter swing), vertical boring mills (53-inch- to 60-foot-diameter swing), horizontal boring mills (five-, six-, eight-, and ten-inch bar diameter), rotary tables from 78.74 by 78.74 inches to 14.9 by 18 feet, planer-type milling

[18] Ibid., p. 19.
[19] See p. 123 below.

machines, and roll and punch shaft grinders.[20] In 1961 an electronic computer valued at $68,600 was exported to the Skoda Works in Pilsen in Czechoslovakia for use in payroll processing and stock control.

Thus it may be seen that a prominent East European communist organization supplying both armaments and specialized heavy equipment to the Soviet Union is able to take direct advantage of the most advanced U.S. technology. Thus, indirectly, advanced U.S. technology is made available to the Soviet Union.

The nature of Czechoslovak exports to the U.S.S.R. indicates the technical assistance provided. In 1957 the Czechs installed a large turbocompressor refrigerator plant at Stalingrad. The plant is one of the most modern in the world with a capacity to supply 30 ice rinks.[21] In the same year the following were shipped: several small rolling mills; two rotary cement kilns with a capacity of 500 tons every 24 hours; Tesla BS 242 electron microscopes; and 40 cooling plants. One of the most interesting contracts in 1958 was to supply the U.S.S.R. with 55 complete automatic cement packing plants, each unit capable of filling 1000 bags of 50 kg every hour.[22] Between 1945 and 1960 Czechoslovakia supplied the U.S.S.R. with equipment for 21 complete sugar mills.[23] In 1959, 20 pig slaughtering lines, 60 diesel electric shunting locomotives, seven vessels for a pressure of 320 atmospheres, another 140 refrigerator units, and similar equipment were sent.[24]

SPECIALIZED ASSISTANCE FROM YUGOSLAVIA

Much of Yugoslav trade with the Soviet Union (Table 6-3) is in specialized metal commodities and fabricated metal units, partly restricted under export control laws for direct sale to the U.S.S.R. by Western countries. The most prominent Yugoslav example is that of copper. During the decade of the fifties copper was on export control lists for the U.S.S.R.; Yugoslavia, a one-time exporter of copper to the United States, then became a net importer of U.S. copper and channeled its own copper production to the Soviet Union in the form of copper products and wire.

A letter to Congress from Frederick G. Dutton, an assistant secretary in the Department of State (dated July 30, 1962), indicated that during 1957 and 1958 Yugoslavia made a number of exports to the Soviet Union of items prohibited under the Battle Act, Title 1. These shipments included semifinished copper

---

[20] *Thomas' Register*, 59th edition (1969), vol. VII, p. 988; the agreement is reported in European League for Economic Cooperation, *Economic Industrial, Scientific and Technical Cooperation Between the Countries of Eastern and Western Europe* (Brussels, 1967), p. 43.
[21] *Czechoslovak Foreign Trade* (Prague), no. 2, 1957.
[22] *Ibid.*, no. 6, 1958.
[23] *Ibid.*, no. 1, 1959.
[24] *Ibid.*, no. 4, 1959.

products valued at $5.3 million, cable valued at $1 million, electric motors and generators valued at $355,600, machine tools valued at $175,400, and a small quantity of lubricating oil. On January 9, 1959, the President directed continuation of U.S. assistance to Yugoslavia despite these breaches in the CoCom limitations.[25]

Table 6-3   COMMODITIES SUPPLIED BY YUGOSLAVIA TO THE
              U.S.S.R., DURING JANUARY 1960-SEPTEMBER 1961

	January-December 1960		January-September 1961	
Commodity	Weight, kilograms	Value, thousands $ ·	Weight, kilograms	Value, thousands $ ·
Copper rods	153,709	206.0	27,686	26.0
Copper plates	—	—	129,234	127.0
Copper tubes and piles	—	—	12,847	16.0
Tubes, pipes, plates, and sheets of copper alloys	—	—	28,929	23.0
Castings and forgings of copper alloys	6,267,978	7,445.0	4,885,762	5,213.0
Welding electrodes	998,000	245.0	1,471,946	364.0
Electric transformers	1,707,130	1,191.0	507,333	1,191.0
Power cables	12,524,760	6,273.0	10,501,015	4,800.0
Installation material	40,818	101.0	73,195	563.0
Installation wire for power current	1,537,577	1,306.0	516,283	563.0
Winding wire	695,183	858.0	372,899	423.0
Low-tension cable	3,450,044	1,711.0	1,491,037	665.0
Other electric equipment	13,223	71.0	—	—

Source: *Statistika Spoljne Trgovine SFR Jugoslavije za 1960 godinu*
·$1 = 300 dinars.

POLISH ASSISTANCE IN SHIPBUILDING

The COMECON technical agreements provide for Polish specialization in shipbuilding, marine diesel engines, and auxiliary-ship plant technologies. This technology is subsequently sent to the U.S.S.R. as finished products of Polish industry, i.e., ships and engines, as well as in the form of technical documents and prototypes.[26]

[25] U.S. House of Representatives, *op. cit.* n.3, 2d session, pt. 3 (Washington, 1962), p. 662.
[26] See chapter 21 for Polish ships supplied to U.S.S.R.; see also U.S. Naval Institute *Proceedings*, (Annapolis, Md.), January 1970.
  For example, "... the Polish auxiliary industry which supplies equipment for shipbuilding, actively participates in the works concerning unification and specialization of the production shipbuilding equipment, which are carried out in the Engineering Commission of COMECON." *Polish Technical Review* (New York), no. 2, August 1964, p. 21.

Table 6-4   WESTERN LICENSE AGREEMENTS FOR SHIPBUILDING
TECHNOLOGY WITH POLISH SHIPBUILDERS (IN FORCE AS OF 1964)

Polish company	Western licensee	Technology
Marine Equipment Plant (at Rumia)	Burmeister & Wain (Denmark)	Heat exchangers for marine power plants
Marine Equipment Plant (at Rumia)	Sulzer (Switzerland)	Silencers for main and auxiliary engines
Marine Equipment Plant (at Rumia)	Fiat (Italy)	Oil, water, and air coolers for Cegielski marine engines
ZAWO (at Slupsk)	Gustav F. Gerdts (West Germany)	Automatic steam traps for marine boilers
Hydroster Works	Baader (West Germany)	Fish processing plants
Gdynia Yards	C. Plath (West Germany)	Electronavigation equipment
Gdynia Yards	AEC (U.K.)	Gyropilots
Cegielski	Sulzer (Switzerland)	Electric power generators
Zgoda	Sulzer (Switzerland)	BH-22, BAH-22
	IMO (Sweden)	Vertical and horizontal screw pumps
	A/B Separator (Sweden)	Oil separators

Source: Polish Technical Review, no. 2, 1964, pp. 15-21; no. 3, 1967, pp. 9-11.

The first Polish oceangoing ship was built in 1948—the year of the takeover by the Polish Workers' Party—and since then the industry has expanded at a very rapid rate. In 1964, for example, there were no fewer than 90 plants in Poland making shipbuilding equipment, and Poland has been the leading foreign supplier of ships to the Soviet Union. It is, then, an important channel for indirect technical transfer of Western technology to the U.S.S.R.

Polish shipyards are a major supplier of ships for the Soviet merchant marine; in fact, three-quarters of Polish exports to the U.S.S.R. consist of rolling stock and ships,[27] and the level of ship purchases has been maintained over a period of many years. In general, Poland sells twice as much machinery to the U.S.S.R. as she purchases from the U.S.S.R.

Main diesel engines produced by Polish marine engine builders in 1960 were of two types: Burmeister & Wain, produced by Cegielski, the largest Polish engine builder, and Sulzer-type diesels produced by Zgoda. Referring to the Sulzer RD engines, the *Polish Technical Review* states:

---

[27] Alfred Zauberman, *Industrial Progress in Poland, Czechoslovakia, and East Germany, 1937-1962* (New York: Oxford University Press, 1964), p. 301.

The RD engines are of comparatively new construction; however exploitation has already confirmed their high value. The best proof ... is the fact that the Sulzer firm took in 1963 the first place in world production of engines of this class. The exploitation results of RD engines produced with great care by H. Cegielski show that they equal the generally known and valued Swiss products.[28]

In addition, a wide range of other marine equipment, including all major shipboard mechanical equipment items, has been produced for Polish companies under foreign licensing arrangements; some of the more important agreements are summarized in Table 6-4. This Western technology has been transferred to the U.S.S.R. in two ways: as components of finished ships and as the export of component parts of Polish manufacture. Soviet use of this equipment is exemplified by Soviet ships on the Haiphong supply run to North Vietnam in the mid to late 1960s. Further, in the same period Polish-built ships were leased to Red China or used directly by the Polish Government to assist North Vietnam.

EAST GERMAN TECHNICAL ASSISTANCE TO THE U.S.S.R.

H. Mendershausen has cited the following examples of Western exports to East Germany that are utilized in Soviet end products[29]: copper sheet and tubes, special steel valves, measuring instruments, plastic sheet, nickel wire, bronze alloy used in mobile and stationary liquid-oxygen plants for Soviet missile sites at Karaganda, ball bearings from Switzerland for hammer crushers for use in Soviet cement plants; aluminum-plated metal and glass for electronic tubes from the U.S.A.; germanium from West Germany for machinery; crankshafts and valve springs from West Germany for marine diesel engines; and electrical parts for Soviet electrical equipment.

Mendershausen concludes that machinery imports from the West in great part equip East German production facilities and so make possible the highly developed East German metal fabricating industry and its extensive export programs. For example:

The machinery-building divisions of this industry are the mainstay of East Germany's export trade. Heavy and general machinery, vehicles, and ships bulk large in export to the Soviet Union and the bloc countries.[30]

The Krupp concern of Essen has concluded several agreements with East European countries which significantly increase their ability to produce machinery

[28] *Polish Technical Review*, no. 2, August 1964, p. 22.
[29] Horst Mendershausen, *Dependence of East Germany on Western Imports* (Santa Monica: RAND Corp., July 17, 1959), Report no. RM-2414, pp. 36-39.
[30] *Ibid.*, p. 31.

for Soviet trade. One agreement with Hungary was for a $12 million plant to produce machine tools and truck engines in Budapest; the output from this plant is marketed throughout Eastern Europe. Another agreement provided for manufacture of machines from semifinished iron and steel in Poland; Krupp furnished the machinery but retained its ownership and sent technicians. Compensation in this case is in the form of part of the plant's production.[31]

AN EXAMPLE OF INDIRECT TRANSFER
OF A TECHNOLOGY: MARINE DIESELS

The East European shipbuilding yards are major suppliers of ships to the Soviet Union. These yards are also recipients of significant technical assistance—in all major ships' components—from West European countries. Thus indirectly the Soviet Union again is a recipient of European technical assistance. Marine diesel engines may be taken as an example to illustrate this process of transfer.[32] (See Figure 6-1.)

The Burmeister & Wain company of Copenhagen, manufacturer of marine diesels, has a technical-assistance agreement with the U.S.S.R. to build B & W marine diesels at Bryansk.[33] The company also has a technical-assistance agreement with Polish shipbuilding organizations for Burmeister & Wain engines.[34] Thus Stocznia Gdanska, most of whose output goes to the U.S.S.R., produces the B & W model 63-VT2BF-140 under license; a total of 355,000 hp was produced in 1968.[35] The two other Polish engine builders, Cegielski and Z.U.T. Zgoda, have technical-assistance agreements with Sulzer of Switzerland to produce Swiss Sulzer diesels up to 15,000 bhp (Cegielski) and 3000 bhp (Zgoda).[36] These agreements, concluded in 1956, are for production of the RSAD type, now the RD-76.[37] Cegielski also has a technical-assistance agreement with Fiat of Italy.[38]

Ships built in East Germany have marine diesels built either by VEB Diesel-Motoren-Werke Rostock or VEB Maschinenbau Halberstadt; both plants have technical-assistance agreements with M.A.N. of West Germany[39] to produce the M.A.N. model K6Z 57/80 marine diesel.

The four marine engine builders in Yugoslavia also have agreements with

[31] European League for Economic Cooperation, *op. cit.* n.21, pp. 44-45.
[32] The Soviets provide the Poles with hard currency to purchase ship equipment of this type on their behalf.
[33] *East-West Commerce* (London), VI, 2 (February 10, 1959).
[34] *Ibid.*, VI, 9 (September 28, 1959).
[35] *International Shipping and Shipbuilding Directory*, 1968, (80th edition; London: Benn Brothers), p. 455.
[36] *Ibid.*
[37] Harbron, *op. cit.* n. 16, p. 112.
[38] *Ibid.*, p. 109.
[39] *Ibid.*, p. 199.

Figure 6-1   INDIRECT TECHNICAL ASSISTANCE TO THE U.S.S.R. VIA EASTERN
EUROPE: THE CASE OF MARINE DIESEL ENGINES

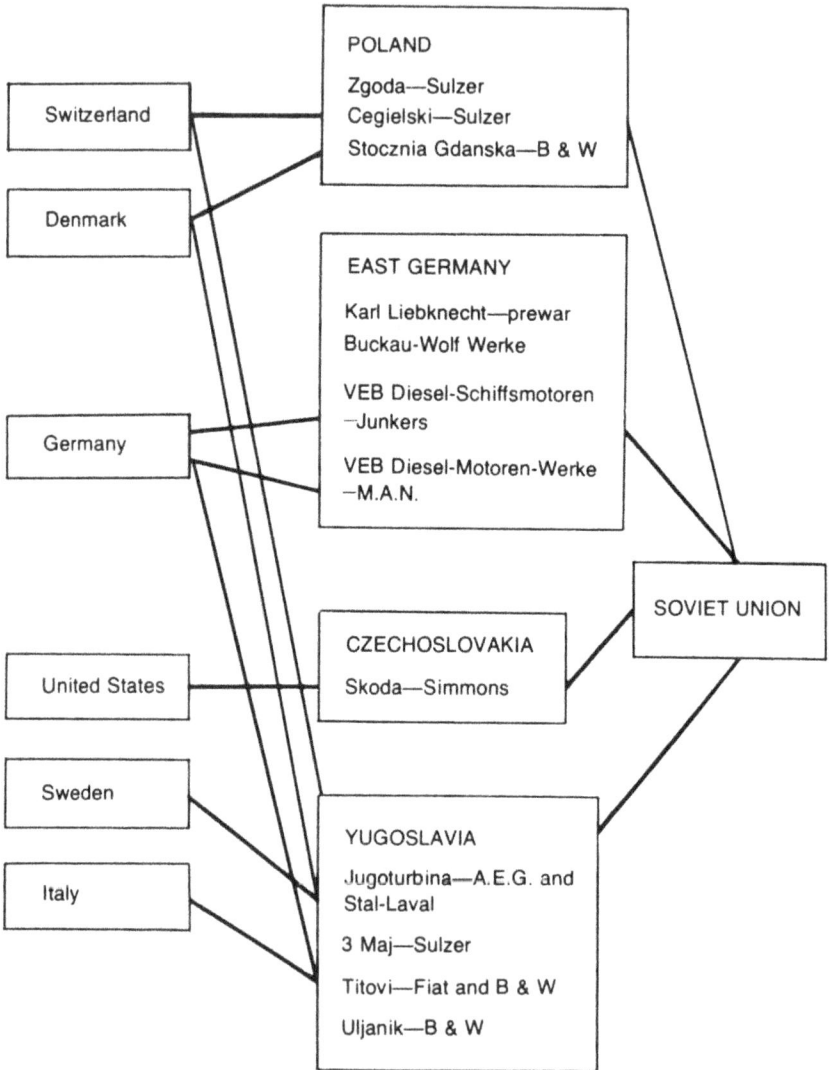

Sources: John D. Harbron, *Communist Ships and Shipping* (London, 1962); *International Shipping and Shipbuilding Directory, 1968* (80th edition; London: Benn Brothers).

Western countries. Titovi Zavodi Litostroj manufactures B & W and Fiat engines under license; "Uljanik" Brodogradiliste I Tvornica Dizel Potora at Pula manufactures B & W marine engines under license; the 3 Maj plant manufactures Sulzer marine diesels under license;[40] and the Jugoturbina plant manufactures Sulzer and A.E.G. turbines under license. These plants provide the total Yugoslav marine-engine building capacity, and are the source of engines for Yugoslav ships built on Soviet account.

It is particularly interesting that B & W (which provides technical assistance for the Bryansk plant in the U.S.S.R. and in the Yugoslav, Polish, and Finnish plants building engines on Soviet account) depends on U.S. technology for its engine-designing facilities. In 1967 Burmeister & Wain installed extensive computer facilities in its electronic data processing department for "extensive calculations for shipbuilding and design and construction of diesel engines."[41] This equipment comprised a Univac 1107 system with central processing and two Univac 1004 computers. Thus diesel engines for Soviet ships are designed with the aid of American computer equipment.[42]

---

[40] *International Shipping and Shipbuilding* ..., *op. cit.* n. 35, p. 458.
[41] *Shipping World and Shipbuilder* (London), July 20, 1967, p. 1249.
[42] See p. 318.

CHAPTER SEVEN

Western Equipment and Soviet Foreign Aid

On the assumption that Soviet construction work abroad will throw light on
Soviet engineering and technology without the screen of censorship, attention
should now be given to the most important of Soviet foreign aid projects—the
Bhilai steel plant in India and the Aswan Dam in Egypt. Both projects were
heralded as triumphs of Soviet engineering, and without question each has been
a key factor in the economic development of the recipient country. Indeed,
Aswan will have a fundamental influence on Egypt unparalleled in that country's
thousands of years of recorded history.

Both projects had higher priority than any but military projects. The Soviet
engineers and equipment utilized were the finest that could be obtained in the
U.S.S.R.; in both cases the Soviets preferred to undertake construction using
only Soviet equipment, and in the case of Aswan this was written into the
first Soviet-Egyptian agreement. In Bhilai and Aswan, then, we have not only
two prominent examples of modern Soviet engineering but also reasonably free
access to uncensored information on Soviet construction methods and their results.[1]

THE BHILAI STEEL PROJECT IN INDIA[2]

In January 1945 the Indian Government appointed a panel of iron and steel
industry experts to consider expansion of the Indian steel industry. The recommendations of the panel included construction of a major integrated plant at Bhilai
in Madhya Pradesh. Construction started in 1955 with $130 million of financing
from the U.S.S.R. to be repaid by India in 12 annual installments at 2.5 percent
annual interest; capacity was planned as 1.3 million tons of ingot steel annually
with possible expansion to 2.5 million tons.

A significant feature of the Bhilai project was that 90 percent of the erection
work was done by Indians under the supervision of Soviet engineers. In June

---

[1] The best available technical description is a special supplement of *Indian Construction News*
(Calcutta), VIII, 10 (October 1959).

[2] *Ibid.,* pp. 46-49.

92

1959 about 60,000 Indians were employed under 700 Soviet engineers and 854 Indian engineers.

All civil engineering work at Bhilai was handled by private contractors, the leading company being Hindustan Construction Co., Ltd., which had a contract for more than 80 percent of the excavation and concrete work, in addition to installation of underground communications. The company supplied from its own equipment resources the central batching plant, shovels, scrapers, bulldozers, cranes, and dump trucks. Photographs in *Indian Construction News*[3] indicate clearly the American origins of this equipment—Le Tourneau-Westinghouse, Northwest, Euclid division of General Motors, and so on.

An article by N. B. Lobotsky, Deputy Chief Engineer at Bhilai, comments: "Civil work is of paramount importance in constructing a steel works, and very often it is progress of civil work which determines a further success of various kinds of erection and special work."[4] Thus although Bhilai was designed by Gipromez (and is therefore a typical American layout),[5] Indian companies undertook the basic civil engineering, including the massive excavation needed for iron and steel works and the placement of 600,000 cubic meters of concrete in foundations and construction of concrete buildings.

In short, the excavation and concrete work—those project phases which later, at Aswan, were to cause the Soviets acute embarrassment—were undertaken at Bhilai by private Indian contractors. Ultimately the problem was similarly resolved at Aswan: 93 percent of excavation was handled by Egyptian contractor Osman Ahmed Osman, although originally it had been planned as 100 percent Soviet work.[6]

The Bhilai installation consists of three large standard blast furnaces, six large open hearths, and a merchant rolling mill. It utilizes the very simplest of iron and steel manufacturing techniques, producing only a narrow range of mild-carbon steel products. Its output may be described simply as production of the maximum tonnage of a limited range of the simplest steel shapes. Capacity is 770,000 tons of steel products annually comprising the following:[7]

Rails	110,000 tons
Heavy structurals	284,000
Sleeper bars	90,000
Rounds & squares	121,000
Flats	15,000
Billets	150,000
	770,000 tons

[3] *Ibid.*, p. 40.
[4] *Ibid.*, pp. 42-43.
[5] See above, p. 128 (below).
[6] Supplement, *Indian Construction News, op. cit.* n.1, p. 26.
[7] William A. Johnson, *The Steel Industry of India* (Cambridge, Mass.: Harvard University Press, 1966), p. 157. Johnson also points out that the ability to roll heavy sections for long rolling periods means little downtime and reflects favorably in output figures. The actual capacity

The plant produces mild-carbon steel shapes only—it does not produce flat-rolled products, wire, or alloy or tool steels, all of which require extensive finishing facilities including pickling, annealing, cold-rolling and other equipment, facilities in which the Soviet Union is noticeably backward.

Furthermore, even for this limited product range there are numerous restrictions imposed by the equipment; one of the most far-reaching in terms of Indian development is the small range of rolled sizes. The Bhilai mill can be compared (Table 7-1) with the Monterrey mill in Mexico, a small plant producing only 240,000 tons of steel products a year, but roughly in the same categories, and supplying a similar market in an underdeveloped country. Monterrey, however, produces a far greater range of sizes and offers a greater choice of products, although its smaller mill is confined basically to the types of steel products produced by Bhilai. The notable point is that although Bhilai has three times greater capacity than Monterrey, the Mexican mill can supply a greater range of sizes for every finished product, and this applies particularly to angles and flats.

Table 7-1   COMPARISON OF PRODUCTS FROM BHILAI MILL (INDIA)
AND MONTERREY MILL (MEXICO)

Type of steel product	BHILAI		MONTERREY	
	No. of sizes	Range of sizes	No. of sizes	Range of sizes
Rails	8	24 – 105 lb/yd	11	12 – 112 lb/yd
Beams	10	100x50 – 600x210 mm	13	76 - 381x152mm
Channels	8	41x32 – 400x100 mm	10	76x35-300x60mm
Angles	34	40x40x5 – 80x80x12 mm	128	19x19x3 – 152x102x25mm
Flats	27	50x8 – 100x20	227	12x3 - 355x51mm
Rods	3	6, 8, 10 mm	11	6 – 38 mm
Rounds and squares	16	20 – 63 mm	51	6 – 101 mm

Sources: Bhilai mill: Hindustan Steel, Ltd., "List of Products from Bhilai Steel Plant," supplied by Bhilai Steel Plant, Public Relations Dept., January 1969.
Monterrey mill: Cia. Fundidora de Fierro y Acero de Monterrey, S.A., *Manual para constructores* (Monterrey, Mexico, 1959).

This interpretation of Bhilai's limited capabilities is shared by W. A. Johnson, who comments: "Bhilai rolls the simplest of products, heavy sections, which require less reprocessing than the lighter sections rolled by Durgapur and the flat-rolled products by Rourkela."[8]

of the plant is well in excess of rated capacity; i.e., there is a built-in excess capacity, enabling the plant to fulfill its targets with ease.
[8]   See Table 7-2.

Table 7-2 LOCATION OF TRAINING FOR ENGINEERS AND SKILLED WORKERS FOR THE BHILAI PROJECT

	Soviet Union	Private Indian firms			Indian Government works		Total
		Tata Iron and Steel Co., Ltd.	Indian Iron and Steel Co., Ltd.	Other firms	Mysore Iron and Steel Works	Bhilai	
Junior engineers	109	—	—	—	—	2	111
Graduate trainees	188	—	—	—	—	35	223
Operative trainees	231	108	16	—	45	190	590
Skilled worker trainees	29	52	4	670	40	234	1029
Artisan trainees	—	—	—	—	—	50	50
Vacation trainees	—	—	—	—	—	10	10
Total (numbers)	557	160	20	670	85	521	2013
Total (percent)	26.67	42.23			30.10		

Source: *Indian Construction News* (Calcutta), October 1959; based on table on page 114.

Training of engineers and skilled workers for Bhilai was divided between the U.S.S.R. (about 26 percent, mainly engineers), Bhilai itself (about 25 percent, mainly operatives), and private and Indian Government firms (the remainder).[9] (See Table 7-2.)

Therefore, Bhilai may be described as a steel mill producing a very limited range of the simplest of steel products, with a typical American layout. Further, the civil engineering work and some of the training during construction were handled by private Indian contractors.

THE ROLE OF EGYPTIAN CONTRACTORS
AND FOREIGN EQUIPMENT IN BUILDING THE ASWAN DAM

Construction of the Aswan High Dam was financed by the Soviet Union between 1958 and 1963 to the extent of $552 million at 2.5 percent interest. This loan was disbursed as follows:[10]

December 27, 1958	$100 million repayable over ten years for construction of the first stage of dam
August 27, 1960	$225 million repayable over ten years for the second stage of dam construction
Summer 1962	$170 million for additional construction work
June 18, 1963	$57 million for the hydroelectric power equipment
Total	$552 million

A series of international disputes, combined with Gamal Nasser's persistent determination to build the dam, led to the initial 1958 Soviet offer, which was promptly accepted by Egypt. The original German design, drawn up by Hochtief-Dortmund in the early 1950s, was inherited by the Soviets and studied in Moscow. Major changes were proposed in May 1959. These changes were considered by an international consultant board previously appointed by the Egyptian Government; this board in turn strongly advised against two of three Soviet proposals. The Soviets ignored further advice from the international board —as their contract gave them every right to do—and proceeded to plan and build according to their own ideas.

There is little question that the Soviet design changes made sense, although as finally built the dam looks little different from the original German elevation

[9] This chapter is limited to chiefly the examination of two projects; but our hypothesis might well be tested with respect to all overseas Soviet projects, although these were not numerous before 1960. For example, it is reported that the Soviet-built hotel at Inya Lake (Burma) has Otis elevators and Westinghouse air conditioning; see Victor Lasky, *The Ugly Russian* (New York: Trident 1965), pp. 21-2.

[10] B. R. Stokke, *Soviet and Eastern European Trade and Aid in Africa* (New York: Praeger, 1967), p. 83.

design. The main Soviet changes involved work methods and shifting the axis of the dam about 600 yards south; in fact, the sluicing method of moving sand suggested by the Soviets (and rejected by the international board) worked well in practice.

The Soviet engineers insisted that Aswan should be an example of state enterprise and therefore initially refused to subcontract to private Egyptian companies. Also, rather than adhere to the ten-year schedule planned by Hochtief-Dortmund, the Soviets reduced the construction schedule time to eight years.

The first years of work involved only the operational sequence of drill, blast, dig, load, and dump. The equipment needed for this sequence included drills, excavators, and dump trucks, and these items the Soviets supplied immediately in quantity.[11] Equipment problems began almost at once; by mid-1961 only 900,000 cubic yards of rock excavation was completed, instead of a planned three million yards. Soviet trucks broke down, Soviet-made tires were slashed by the granite rock, and while the old-fashioned Ulanshev excavators held up (except for the bucket teeth) the Soviet drills did not—so the Aswan Dam project headed into a major construction crisis.[12]

After a great deal of government-level discussion the excavation and concrete contracts were let to two private Egyptian companies: General Enterprises Engineering Company, run by Osman Ahmed Osman, and the Misr group.[13] The Misr contract covered the concrete work on the tunnels and the power station. The Osman contract, granted to Arab Contractors, Ltd., was of fundamental importance. Only one million yards of the 14 million cubic yards to be moved had been excavated by the Soviets; the Osman company handled the other 13 million yards under this contract. In other words, 93 percent of the Aswan Dam rock excavation was handled by a private Egyptian company, not by the Soviet construction force.[14]

Studies by Osman's Egyptian engineers pinpointed the Soviet dump trucks, only 77 percent as efficient as Western models, as the key to the problem. Subsequently, 54 British Aveling-Barford 35-ton dump trucks were hastily imported to supplement the 100 Soviet 25-ton dump trucks already at work. There was continual friction between Soviet and Egyptian engineers,[15] but the

[11] Construction equipment supplied by the U.S.S.R. included 16 electric excavators (4 to 5 cubic meters shovel capacity), 90 small excavators, 160 dump trucks of 25 to 30 tons capacity, 1600 drilling machines of various sizes, 75 bulldozers, 150 trucks, 140 passenger cars, 100 buses, 80 cranes of various capacities, 80 movable air compressors, 15 tugboats, 13 Hooper barges of 200 to 500 tons' capacity, and 11 sets of equipment for hydraulic movement of sand. *The High Dam, Miracle of XXth Century* (Ministry of the High Dam, Cairo Information Department: January 9, 1964), pp. 16-17.

[12] T. Little, *High Dam at Aswan: The Subjugation of the Nile* (London: Methuen, 1965).

[13] Arab Contractors, Ltd., with the Aswan Dam contract is a subsidiary of General Enterprises Engineering; the latter is partially financed by the government but operates as a privately owned company.

[14] Little, *op. cit.* n.12, pp. 100-4.

[15] *Ibid.*, p. 111.

private contractors held to their schedule. In the face of Soviet objections, overruled by Nasser, Soviet equipment was supplemented by foreign compressors, Atlas Copco (Sweden) drills (with Swedish engineers to supervise the drilling work), and two Ruston-Bucyrus excavators. A British engineer from Dunlop of the United Kingdom was brought in to find a solution for the shredding Soviet truck tires, and workmen were set to chipping away sharp rock edges. At one point late in 1963, "the U.A.R. Government begged Aveling-Barford to give them extraordinary priority by allowing more dump trucks, then at sea and bound for another destination, to be diverted to Egypt."[16] At the final ceremony, however, this British and Swedish equipment was hidden away from inquisitive eyes.[17]

There is no question that injection of private Egyptian companies using imported Western equipment into the Aswan Dam project turned a crisis into a schedule met on time.[18] A similar problem had been avoided at Bhilai in India by using imported Euclid dump trucks operated by the Hindustan Construction Company from the start of construction.

OTHER SOVIET PROJECTS IN THE UNDERDEVELOPED WORLD

It is notable that the Soviet Union has not undertaken to construct large-scale industrial projects elsewhere. Such socialist-sponsored projects have been handled by East European nations, although sometimes the financing has been provided by the U.S.S.R. in a three-way arrangement.

In Syria, the largest communist project under way at the end of the 1950s was a petroleum refinery constructed by Czechoslovakia at Homs. Built at a cost of $15 million financed on long-term credits, and having a capacity of one million tons, the plant has Czech equipment and supervision although some Russian engineers supervised parts of the construction.[19] East Germans and Bulgarians erected other projects in Syria in the 1950s while Soviet material assistance appears to have been confined largely to armaments.

In the Far East, although large Soviet offers of assistance were made in 1958 to Indonesia, the only two completed bloc projects in 1958 were a Czechoslovak tire factory and an East German sugar plant.[20]

---

[16] *Ibid.*

[17] *Ibid.*, p. 213.

[18] "The violent overhaul that the project needed was led by an Egyptian, Osman Ahmed Osman, forty-eight, the prime contractor and a master at getting big projects done under primitive conditions. Over the objections of the Russians, Osman supplemented their faulty equipment with better British and Swedish gear ... Osman became the hero of Aswan." *Fortune,* January 1967, p. 130.

[19] U.S. Dept. of State, *The Sino-Soviet Economic Offensive in the Less Developed Countries* (Washington, 1958), p. 55.

[20] *Ibid.*, p. 79.

In general, at the end of the fifties there had been large Soviet offers,[21] but except for Aswan and Bhilai, actual assistance had been confined mainly to military supplies.

Thus Soviet construction under its technical-assistance programs appears to generate more propaganda than transfer of indigenous Soviet technology. Bhilai had all civil engineering handled by Indian firms, and much training was handled at Bhilai or by private Indian Government firms. The chief Soviet contribution was in supplying equipment for a simple integrated facility with restricted rolling capabilities, and that based on typical American layouts. At Aswan the Soviets started excavation, but after 7 percent of the work was completed the civil engineering was contracted to two private Egyptian companies utilizing imported Swedish and British equipment.

These two large-scale projects, both of which received the highest nonmilitary priority, confirm the general conclusions of this study concerning weaknesses in Soviet engineering and technology.

---

[21] Raymond F. Mikesell and Jack N. Behrman, *Financing Free World Trade with the Sino-Soviet Bloc* (Princeton: Princeton University Press, 1958), p. 158. See Appendix Table II for a list of such offers from January 1953 to 1958.

Part II

Technical Transfers and Their
Role in Soviet Industry

CHAPTER EIGHT

Western Origins of Mining
and Excavating Equipment

Four fields of mining and excavating activity have been selected for consideration in this chapter: underground coal mining, the most important mining activity in the Soviet Union; iron ore beneficiation, important because of the nature of Russian iron ores; peat excavation, a typically Soviet industry; and the development of earth excavating equipment.

At the end of the 1920s imported German mining machinery was largely replaced by imported American machinery and still later by duplicates of this American machinery, in some cases manufactured in the U.S.S.R. under technical-assistance agreements with U.S. manufacturers. This practice has extended historically and in terms of equipment beyond the four mining activities considered in this chapter. A typical example, which also reflects the U.S. origins after 1930, may be found in production of dredges. By July 1932, some 22 new American Yuba-type dredges were sent to various placer gold fields in the Soviet Union;[1] these included three of 13.5-foot capacity, twelve of 7.5-foot capacity, and seven of 3.5-cubic foot capacity. The larger dredges were capable of handling 566 tons of sand per hour and were used in the Lena, Alden, and other Siberian fields. Steam and electric thawing apparatus was installed by American engineers hired from Alaskan gold mines, and five American-design cyanide plants were built in Siberia. U.S. hydraulic nozzles, steam shovels, cranes, scrapers, heated sluices, and other equipment also were imported.

Beginning in 1930 attempts were made to manufacture such equipment in the Soviet Union. In an earlier agreement with the Union Construction Company, an American firm, drawings and specifications had been supplied for gold dredges, and a similar agreement was made in 1932 with the Yuba Manufacturing Company, also American, for platinum dredges. A section of the Krasnyi Putilovets plant was set aside for the manufacture of the large Yuba dredge and three or four smaller dredges a year were manufactured at Votkinsk and Irkutsk. The production program of Soviet plants called only for duplication

---

[1] *Far Eastern Review* (Manila, Shanghai) April 1933, p. 168.

of U.S. and German equipment. For example, the production program of the Irkutsk plant in 1933 called not only for American-type dredges and power excavators, but also for 60 Black model ore crushers, 20 Simons model ore crushers, 2000 Koppel ore cars, and 2000 Anaconda ore cars.

These imports and Russian domestic copies were supplemented by heavy equipment imports under the Lend Lease program (see Table 8-1) and the October 1945 "pipeline" agreement.

Table 8-1   LEND LEASE EXPORTS OF MINING AND EXCAVATING
EQUIPMENT TO THE U.S.S.R.

Lend Lease category no.	Description	Total exports (arrived, after losses)
V-4	Crushing, screening, and mixing machinery	$8,048,000
V-49	Mining and quarrying machinery	1,763,000
V-50	Earth, rock boring, and drilling equipment	8,983,000
V-51	Well and blast-hole drilling machinery	9,023,000
V-52	Excavating and dredging machinery	31,050,000
V-59B	Mine locomotives	1,133,000
Total		$60,000,000

Source: U.S. Dept. of State, *Report on War Aid Furnished by the United States to the U.S.S.R.* (Washington: Office of Foreign Liquidation, 1945).

In 1945 300 Russian coal mining engineers were sent to locate and dismantle equipment in the German brown coal region. This equipment was transferred to the Moscow brown coal mining basin. Some equipment went elsewhere; for example, eight single-bucket excavators were sent to Tashkent.[2] Excavating equipment totaling 200,000 to 220,000 cubic meters daily capacity was removed to the U.S.S.R., as was coal mining equipment with a daily capacity of 40,000 to 45,000 tons and briquette-making capacity of 16,000 to 18,000 tons daily.[3]

Major imports of mining equipment have continued since World War II. One major U.S. mining equipment manufacturer, Joy Manufacturing Company of Pittsburgh, received a Lend Lease contract from the U.S. Government in 1944 to supply 600 long wall coal cutters for the Donbas mines and has continued to sell equipment for the coal and potash mining sectors since that time.[4] In

[2] Robert Slusser, ed., *Soviet Economic Policy in Postwar Germany* (New York: Research Program on the U.S.S.R., 1953) p. 84.

[3] *Ibid.*, p. 85.

[4] U.S. Senate, *East-West Trade*. A Compilation of Views of Businessmen, Bankers and Academic Experts; Committee on Foreign Relations, 88th Congress, 2d session, November 1964 (Washington, 1964), p. 81. The company name is omitted in the testimony but the facts suggest it was the Joy Manufacturing Company.

1963 the company received a $10 million contract—the eighth—for 30 continuous miners for potash mining,[5] and the following year it received another $5.5 million contract for combines, loading equipment, and self-propelled trolleys for potash mining.[6] Company representatives subsequently made an interesting statement before Congress concerning Soviet copying of their equipment designs:

> The Russians have copied our machines, but apparently there is not high enough priority on coal mining machinery in Russia to make a real effort in copying even for their use within the U.S.S.R. We know this because they continue to buy from us machines of which we know they have made copies.[7]

Recent Soviet technical manuals have descriptions and photographs of these "Soviet-Joys." For example, the self-propelled trolley VSD-10 manufactured at the Voronezh mining equipment plant from 1966 onward is a copy of the Joy self-propelled trolley.[8]

Where other countries have the preferred technology the Soviets are aware of it. For example, Canada is the traditional world leader in asbestos milling and processing equipment; Soviet mills were provided technical assistance by Canadian companies in the 1920s and 1930s[9] and in more recent times Canadian firms have continued to keep Soviet asbestos mills abreast of Western technology. In 1964, for example, Lynn MacLeod Engineering Supplies, Ltd., of Canada supplied $7.8 million in asbestos processing equipment for the Urals asbestos mills with technical assistance and company technicians for installation of the equipment.[10] It is interesting to note that a U.S. embargo on one component was overcome quite simply: "...the company eventually decided to use a Canadian-built product made under a licensing agreement with a U.S. company."[11]

Therefore we can trace a history of import of foreign mining equipment—with U.S. equipment usually the preferred equipment—and only partially successful domestic duplication of this equipment. Lack of total success in duplication is of particular interest in those sectors which are of relatively greater importance in view of Russian resource conditions; peat recovery and iron ore beneficiation are two such sectors and are considered below.

[5] *Congressional Record, House of Representatives*, August 23, 1963.

[6] *Los Angeles Times*, September 14, 1964.

[7] U.S. Senate, *East-West Trade*, op. cit. n. 4, p. 82. A notation is added that copies of the companies' equipment were on exhibit at the permanent industrial exposition in Moscow.

[8] For the VSD-10 see *Gornye mashiny dlya dobychi rud* (Moscow, 1968), and compare to the Joy self-propelled trolley in A. S. Burchakov *et al.*, *Tekhnologiia, mekhanizatsiia i avtomatizatsiia proizvodstvennykh protsessov podzemnykh razrabotok* (Moscow, 1968), p. 329.

[9] See Sutton I, pp. 108-12; and Sutton II, pp. 184, 368.

[10] *Wall Street Journal*, February 19, 1964, 12:6.

[11] *Ibid.*

FOREIGN ORIGINS OF UNDERGROUND
MINING EQUIPMENT IN THE COAL INDUSTRY

The coal mining industry, by far the most important of all mining industries in the Soviet Union, is mechanically almost completely based on foreign technical developments. Fortunately, we have a series of excellent reports by the National Coal Board of the United Kingdom that describe this technical diffusion from the West,[12] although this was not the prime purpose of the reports. Furthermore, in the words of one NCB report: "It must be appreciated ... that the Report emphasizes what is best in Soviet mining technique and does not elaborate on much that was seen which was well below the standard of modern British practice."[13]

Of the 391 million tons of coal produced in the Soviet Union in 1955, about 319 million tons was hard coal mined underground, only 7.5 million tons was open-pit mined, and the balance was brown coal. A large number of power-loading machines were in operation in the late 1950s, and Table 8-2 gives the total number of such machines, mostly face power loaders based on the frame-jib design, held in stock and in use in Soviet coal mines in the late 1950s with their Western prototypes. The in-use number is about twice that utilized in British mines in 1956-57.

Underground mining equipment in the Soviet coal industry is based completely on foreign models.[14] The variations, described below, are essentially either simplifications of foreign models or models which omit ancillary equipment or functions forming part of the original foreign machine.

The most commonly seen coal face cutter loader in the Soviet Union is the Donbass 1. There were 1411 in stock in 1956, and according to Soviet literature this model was widely used in the late 1960s.[15] There are six variants of the Donbass, all manufactured at Gorlovka—the Donbass 1; a more powerful version, the Donbass 2; the Donbass 6; a Donbass thick-seam machine; and the Gornyak, the thin-seam version. The Donbass 7 variant has a picked drum "rather similar to that recently developed for the Meco-Moore."[16] The Donbass in all its variants is essentially the British Meco-Moore. The main difference

---

12 *Report by the Technical Mission of the* [U.K.] National Coal Board, *The Coal Industry of the U.S.S.R.*, pt. 1 (London, 1957); pt. 2 of this report consists of appendices.

13 *Ibid.*, pt. 1, p. i.

14 This conclusion is confirmed under current conditions (1969) by Vasiliy Strishkov of the U.S. Bureau of Mines, and is consistent with the National Coal Board reports: "The mining equipment and processes used in the Soviet mineral industry are standard—usually patterned on early American and West European models"; and "Studying, copying, and extensive application of Western technological progress and equipment in the Soviet mineral industry will be the main trend in the improvement of mineral industry technology." Letter to writer, May 6, 1969, from U.S. Bureau of Mines.

15 V. N. Khorin *et al.*, *Ugol'nyi kombain "Donbass-1G"* (Moscow, 1969).

16 U.K. National Coal Board, *op. cit.* n. 12, p. 26.

Table 8-2   POWER LOADING MACHINES IN SOVIET COAL MINES
(AS OF APRIL 1, 1956)

1	2	3	4	5
	Number of Machines		Percentage	
Type of machine	Held	In use	in use	Western prototypes
COAL FACE MACHINES				
Donbass 1	1411	954	83.61	Meco-Moore
Donbass 2	11	3	27.27	Meco-Moore (more powerful Donbass 1)
Donbass 6	6	2	33.33	Meco-Moore (thick-seam version)
Gornyak	414	265	64.01	Meco-Moore (thin-seam version)
UKT 1-2	177	112	63.28	Colmol (or) Korfmann
UKMG	142	66	46.68	U.K. multi-jib design
Shakhter	81	60	74.07	Meco-Moore variations
	2242	1462	60.75	
OTHER POWER LOADING MACHINES				
Heading loaders:				
PK-2m (brown coal)	191	116	60.73	Joy Continuous Miner
ShBM-1 (tunneler)	26	17	65.39	Soviet prototype
	217	133	61.20	
Dirt loading:				
UMP	620	401	64.68	—
PPM 2-3	493	312	63.29	Conway Shovel
EPM 1	1808	1303	72.07	Eimco – 21
PML 5	1075	858	79.81	Eimco – 40
PMU	49	21	42.88	U.K. gathering arm loader
	4045	2895	70.32	
Coal loading machines:				
All types	777	534	68.86	—
(including GNIZ-30)	49	38	77.55	—
	826	572	69.25	

Source: United Kingdom, National Coal Board, *The Coal Industry of the U.S.S.R.*, Report by the Technical Mission (London, 1957), p. 24. Column 5 added from text.

is that the Russian Donbass cuts one way only, and is then flitted back along the coal face in a new track, while the original Meco-Moore machine is turned at the end of each cut. The Meco-Moore was originally designed in 1930 by Mining Engineering Co., Ltd., of the United Kingdom. It was developed throughout the 1930s and received a stimulus in 1941 from increased wartime demand for coal. As of September 1956 some 155 Meco-Moore cutter loaders were in operation in the United Kingdom compared to 1224 Russian Donbass models based on a prototype Meco-Moore.[17]

In describing the less common coal face machines, the U.K. National Coal Board team reported that the UKMG cutter loader was "basically similar to our multijib design," with a slight difference in the cutter chains, and with no separate loading mechanism.[18] The same team reported with reference to the UKT 1 and 2 cutter loaders that "the general design of the machine is similar to the Colmol or Korfmann—and it loads coal in a similar manner—but it is single ended and there are no proposals in hand for making it double-ended."[19] Other cutter loaders under development were the K-26, described as similar to the Dosco,[20] and the A-2 plow of the Löbbehobel type with a support system similar to the Dowty Roofmaster.[21] Vasiliy Strishkov, a U.S. observer, comments on coal plows:

> In 1950, West Germany introduced a high-speed coal plough. But coal ploughs were not introduced in the Soviet Donets basin mines until 1962. It took 12 years for the U.S.S.R. to study, copy, and produce coal ploughs.[22]

Similar observations were made on other machines. The PK-2m brown coal cutter loader is described as similar to the Joy Continuous Miner (supporting the company's own observations) except that the cutter head swings horizontally, not vertically.[23] The most popular loaders are the rocker-arm type corresponding to the Eimco-21 and Eimco-40, with a smaller unit, the PPM-2, equivalent to the Conway Shovel. Of the PMU-1 the report noted: "This is railmounted, and the significant difference between it and British machines is that two conveyors are used."[24]

The winding systems in coal mine shafts use Ward-Leonard controls, the most modern being at Gorlovka, but no automatic winders, except one Ward-Leonard, have been seen.[25] A report of a French Cement Industry delegation noted that Ward-Leonard 250- to 300-kw controls are made at the Urals plant.[26]

---

[17] R. Shepherd and A. G. Withers, *Mechanized Cutting and Loading of Coal* (London: Odhams Press, 1960), p. 311.
[18] U.K. National Coal Board, *op. cit.* n. 12, p. 28.
[19] *Ibid.*, p. 29.
[20] *Ibid.*
[21] *Ibid.*, p. 30.
[22] Strishkov, *loc. cit.* n. 14.
[23] U.K. National Coal Board, *op. cit.* n. 12, pp. 32, 34, 41.
[24] *Ibid.*, p. 43. See also *Gornye ...*, *op. cit.* n. 8, for a Russian description of these machines with place and date of manufacture.
[25] U.K. National Coal Board, *op. cit.* n. 12, p. 58.
[26] *L'Industrie cimentière en U.S.S.R.*, Compte rendu de mission 9-28 avril 1960 (Paris, 1960), p. 33.

Flotation machines used in coal concentration plants are to a great extent based on French and U.S. designs and imports. As of 1964 there were 230 such machines operating in the U.S.S.R.[27] Of these, 104 were Fm-2.5 or FF-4 based on the French "Minemet," while eight were apparently Minemet Model NS-1500. These units are built in France by the firm of Minère et Meto, and in the U.S.S.R. at Novo-Irminskoi.[28] Another seven units were Airlift; the remaining 77 machines were Giprokoks Model 51-52 and KhGI-57—apparently also based on Minemet models.[29]

Plants manufacturing and repairing coal mining equipment were noted as modern and well equipped. In the case of the Prokopevsk Lamp Works, the NCB delegation noted "a large proportion of the equipment was seen to be of Continental or American manufacture."[30] Of the Rutchenkovsky Zavod the delegation said: "The majority of the machines installed are of American and Continental manufacture."[31]

In sum, in underground coal mining, the largest mining industry in the U.S.S.R., we find almost complete technical dependence on Western equipment —although a great deal of research and experimental work has been undertaken in Soviet research institutes.

BENEFICIATION OF IRON ORE

The Soviet Union has made considerable investment in upgrading facilities for iron ore, particularly to convert low-grade ores into blast-furnace charge. A brief summary of these developments suggests great dependence on Western, and in this case primarily German and American, practice. The 1959 report of the American Steel and Iron Delegation[32] concluded that "the equipment is standard—usually patterned after early American models."[33] In the late fifties there were 40 iron-ore beneficiation plants in the U.S.S.R., and the more advanced were visited by the delegation. Where magnetic separation can be used, "they have definitely settled on rotary kilns developed originally by the Lurgi company in Frankfurt."[34] The standard 150 by 11-foot kiln has a capacity

---

[27] N. G. Bedran, *Flotatsionnye mashiny dlia obogashchaeniia uglia* (Moscow, 1968), p. 5.
[28] *Ibid.*, pp. 57, 108-9.
[29] *Ibid.*, pp. 82-83.
[30] U.K. National Coal Board, *op. cit.* n. 12, p. 62
[31] *Ibid.*, p. 65. The close watch maintained on the U.S. coal mining industry is apparent in the Russian technical literature. See, for example, R. Yu. Poderni, *Ugol'naia promyshlennost' SSha* (Moscow, 1968), and K. K. Kuznetsov, *Rekonstruktsiia, mekhanizatsiia i avtomatizatsiia shakht za rubezhom* (Moscow, 1968).
[32] *Steel in the Soviet Union*, Report of the American Steel and Iron Ore Delegation's Visit to the Soviet Union May and June 1958 (New York: American Iron and Steel Institute, 1959).
[33] *Ibid.*, p. 58.
[34] *Ibid.*, p. 57.

of 1000 tons per day. For nonmagnetic ores, i.e., oxidized ores, the Soviets have decided on reduction roasting followed by separation. For this purpose two pilot Lurgi-type kilns served as pilot plants and it was planned in the late 1950s to build 50 similar kilns in the Krivoi Rog basin alone,[35] thus standardizing on Lurgi kilns for both magnetic and nonmagnetic ores.

For sintering iron ores, the German Lurgi-type machine is used as the standard. It is based on drawings for a 537-square-foot machine purchased from Lurgi and similar drawings for a 805-square-foot Lurgi machine from Czechoslovakia, the Czechs having passed on their purchased Lurgi drawings.[36]

Crushers for iron ore are patterned after American models; the 60-inch primary crushers, although strengthened, are "definitely patterned after an American model."[37] Cone crushers are of the Symons type with both long and short head varieties.[38] Most of the pumps for sand pumping "are patterned after a well-known American sand pump."[39] Internal drum filters "look very much like American types"; however in the late 1950s the Soviets intended to replace these with magnetic-type vacuum filters developed in Scandinavia.[40] The standard magnetic separator for wet work "is the American-type belt machine with a 55-inch belt."[41] The delegation report comments that at one of the plants the manager "took some pains" to point out the name plates on the machines (i.e., "made in the U.S.S.R."), but the report noted that "very few original developments in the concentrating equipment were seen."[42]

---

[35] *Ibid.*, p. 58.

[36] *Ibid.*, p. 109-10. No essential differences between the Soviet and the Lurgi sintering plants were seen. Sinter comprises about 60 percent of total furnace feed in the U.S.S.R. "In 1928 the Russians built a Swedish-type sintering plant equipped with movable pans (apparently what is known as the Holmberg system), and in 1931 the first continuous Dwight-Lloyd type plant was built in Kerch. Experiments showed that the continuous system had about 30 percent advantage over the Swedish system. Since that time all plants built in the Soviet Union were of the continuous Dwight-Lloyd type." *Ibid.*, p. 107.

[37] *Ibid.*, p. 58.

[38] *Ibid.*

[39] *Ibid.*

[40] *Ibid.*

[41] *Ibid.*, p. 59.

[42] *Ibid.* It should be remembered that the delegation visited only a few "advanced" plants. The position appears to have remained the same in 1963. Although the Indian Iron and Steel Delegation did not specifically mention origin of Russian processes, those processes described by that delegation are similar to those mentioned in the earlier American report. See National Productivity Council India, *Iron and Steel Industry in U.S.S.R. and Czechoslovakia* (New Delhi: National Productivity Council, 1963), pp. 44-45.
Other comments by the U.S. delegation include (at Magnitogorsk): "Plant equipment observed is based on original American models. The cone crusher is a 7-foot Nordberg ... Wet magnetic separators are all of the American Crockett belt type ... seldom used in new installations in the U.S.A." (p. 78). And (at the Kuznetsk concentrator): "The group was shown an automatic regulating and recording device for controlling the pulp density of the classifier. In design it appeared to be similar to one developed by Masco." "There are four magnetic separators for each section, all of them being of a modified Crockett belt type." "There are two filters per section. These are of the Dorrco internal drum type ... manufactured in East Germany." Two Lurgi kilns were being installed. American Iron and Steel Institute, *op. cit.* n. 32.

THE PEAT INDUSTRY IN RUSSIA

The Soviet Union has large deposits of peat and is the most important industrial user of fuel peat in the world. Six methods of production are used: elevator, scraper elevator, dredge-excavator, hydraulic (hydropeat), hydraulic-elevator, and milling.

The elevator and scraper elevator methods account for a small percentage of production. The dredge-excavator method was in use before the Revolution, as was the hydropeat method, developed by two Russian engineers. The hydraulic-elevator method combines the hydraulic method with an elevator installation. The milling method is undertaken with cultivators and milling machines towed behind tractors.[43]

Although the peat industry is primarily a Russian industry it has seen a good deal of transfer of technology. (See Table 8-3.) In the 1920s unsuccessful attempts were made to use foreign machines in bulk drying, and the Typermas machine was developed on Caterpillar tracks. For machines used in excavating large canals, foreign excavators and dredges manufactured by Marion, Weser-Hutte, and other foreign firms were the basis of Soviet excavators P-075, LK-0.5A, and E-505.[44]

Table 8-3   THE PEAT INDUSTRY METHOD OF EXTRACTION
(1913 TO 1950)

Method	(given as percentage of total)				(tonnage expressed in 1000 gross tons)			
	1913		1930		1940		1950	
	tons	%	tons	%	tons	%	tons	%
Hydropeat	—	—	1797	21.7	9050	28.2	9040	25.3
Hydroelevator	—	—	90	1.1	1240	3.9	1000	2.8
Milling	—	—	186	2.2	5130	16.0	8280	23.2
Excavator (bagger)	—	—	40	0.5	961	3.0	5960	16.7
Elevator	1537	92.2	4054	48.8	9649	30.1	7350	20.6
Cutting	131	7.8	2139	25.7	6025	18.8	4070	11.4
Percentage mechani- zation	—	0	—	25.5	—	51.1	—	68.0
Total production	1688	—	8306	—	32,055	—	35,700	—

Source: G. Kazakov, *The Soviet Peat Industry* (New York: Praeger, 1956), pp. 217-18.

[43] George Kazakov, *Soviet Peat Resources* (New York: Research Program on the U.S.S.R., 1953), pp. 140-47.
[44] George Kazakov, *The Soviet Peat Industry* (New York: Praeger, 1956).

The standard Instorf elevator installation has been used since 1927. The Soviet SE-3 scraper-elevator installation, first built in 1938, consists of a dragline excavator combined with parts and motors from the standard elevator machine.

Mechanization of the bagger operation was undertaken by use of Ekelund excavators and other foreign machines, such as the Wieland. This was followed by the development of Russian designs—the Pankartov and the Biryukov baggers which in turn were replaced by the Instorf excavator, which is the standard excavator.

After 1950 the TE.P-2 excavator was introduced. This is a single-row multibucket excavator mounted on Caterpillar tracks and with a processing unit patterned on a Jeffrey crusher used in the Canadian peat industry.

The hydropeat method uses a water jet to flush out the peat and incorporates equipment of foreign origin—for example, the Ludlow type water valves, and NF-14 pumps patterned after American pumps.[45]

In peat loading, the UKL machine for loading peat onto rail cars is modeled on the U.S. Joy loader. In milling peat, equipment of German origin is used in addition to Randall-type harrows.[46]

THE ORIGINS OF SOVIET EXCAVATORS

We know from the Gorton Papers at the Hoover Institution that in the early 1930s Soviet planners consulted American engineers on the most suitable types of Western excavators to be copied and then proceeded, with U.S. assistance, to study, copy, and produce these machines in series.[47]

In 1931, for example, the Machine Building Trust collected data from those organizations using draglines and finally settled on five models; specifications of these models were then circulated to U.S. engineers for comments on suitability and numbers needed for 1932 and 1933. By 1932 choice had settled on five specifications:[48]

Model I: 4-cu. yd. bucket (3 cu. meters); total weight 12-13 tons, boom length 26-36 (8-11 meters); dumping radius, 15-16 ft. (4.5 to 5 meters); 30-40 hp on crawlers.
Model II: 0.97-cu. yd. bucket (0.75 cu. meter); boom length, 21 ft. (6.5 meters); dumping radius, 36 ft. (8 meters); weight, 35 tons.
Model III: Shovel clam shell bucket and crane; weight, about 65 tons; crawlers boom 25 ft. (7.6 meters); bucket 1.5 cu. yd. (1.15 meters).
Model IV: Shovel clam shell bucket and crane; weight, 120 tons crawlers; boom, 46 ft. (14 meters); dumping radius, 53 ft. (10 meters).

[45] *Ibid.*, pp. 76-85.
[46] *Ibid.*, p. 108.
[47] Sutton II, pp. 294-95.
[48] Gorton Papers, Hoover Institution Special Collections.

Figure 8-1 DEVELOPMENT OF SOVIET TRACTORS AND
EQUIPMENT FROM THE CATERPILLAR D-7 TRACTOR

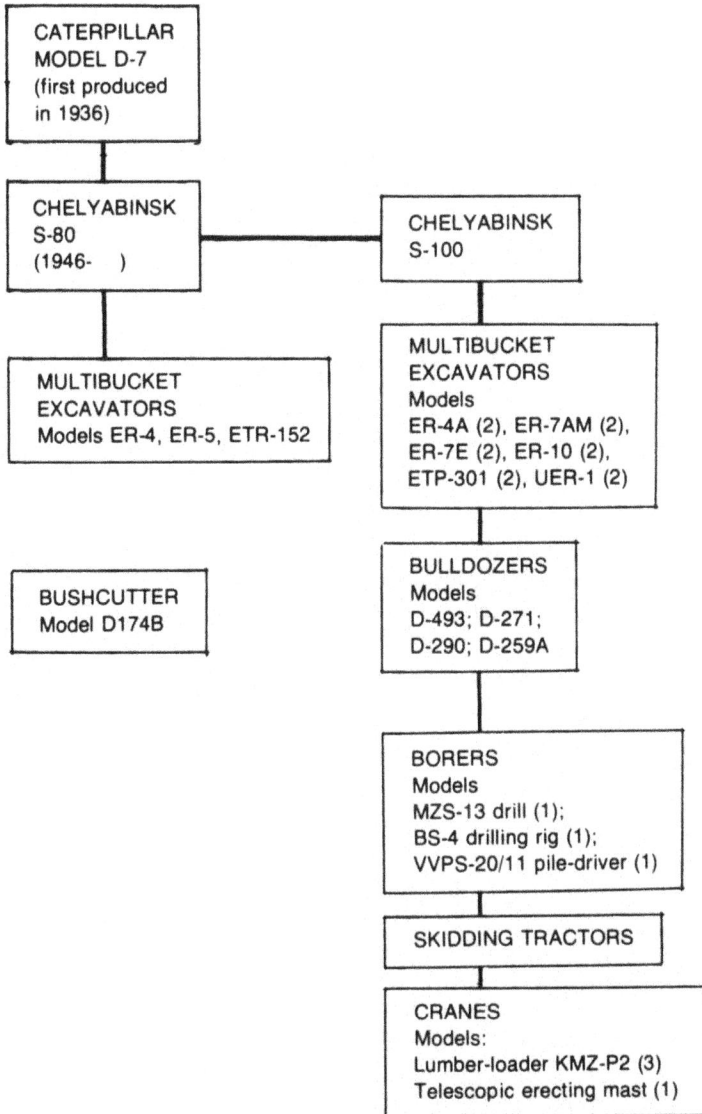

CATERPILLAR
MODEL D-7
(first produced
in 1936)

CHELYABINSK
S-80
(1946-   )

CHELYABINSK
S-100

MULTIBUCKET
EXCAVATORS
Models ER-4, ER-5, ETR-152

MULTIBUCKET
EXCAVATORS
Models
ER-4A (2), ER-7AM (2),
ER-7E (2), ER-10 (2),
ETP-301 (2), UER-1 (2)

BUSHCUTTER
Model D174B

BULLDOZERS
Models
D-493; D-271;
D-290; D-259A

BORERS
Models
MZS-13 drill (1);
BS-4 drilling rig (1);
VVPS-20/11 pile-driver (1)

SKIDDING TRACTORS

CRANES
Models:
Lumber-loader KMZ-P2 (3)
Telescopic erecting mast (1)

Sources: P.S.Neporozhnii, *Electrification and Power Construction in the U.S.S.R.* (Jerusalem: Israel Program for Scientific Translations, 1965), pp. 135-37; Ya. B. Lantsburg, *Spravochnik molodnogo mashinista keskavatora,* 2d edition (Moscow, 1968), p. 27.

Model IVa: Dragline for rocks, 3.2 cu. yd. (2.5 meters); weight, 120-130 tons; dumping radius, 36 ft. (11 meters).

These became the Soviet standard dragline excavators, and are based on the U.S. Marion and various German machines.

The Caterpillar D-7 tractor, first produced in the United States in 1936, became the Soviet S-80 in 1946 and the S-100 crawler tractor in the 1950s. The S-80 and the S-100 were then used as base models for a wide range of other Soviet equipment used in industries ranging from mining and lumber to construction. Figure 8-1 illustrates the origins of this equipment in relation to the Soviet S-80 and S-100 tractors. The ER-4, ER-5, and ETR-152 multibucket excavators were based on the S-80 tractor[49] and were replaced by another range of multibucket rotary excavators, the ER-4A, the ER-7AM, the ER-7E, the ER-10, the ETR-301, and the UER-1, all constructed on a C-100 tractor base. The two remaining models of multibucket rotary excavators are based on the T-74 tractor (the ETR-141) and the T-140 (the ETR-131).[50]

Bulldozers D-493, D-271, D-290 and D-259A—including most bulldozers produced in the U.S.S.R.—are based on the S-100 tractor base.[51] The MZS-13 drill, the BS-4 drilling rig, and the VVPS-20/11 pile driver are mounted on an S-100 tractor.[52] A telescopic erection mast is also mounted on a S-100 tractor chassis; and in the lumber industry numerous pieces of equipment, including the KMZ-P2 lumber loader, are based on the S-100.[53]

In sum, then, the range of mechanical handling equipment used in a wide range of industries is based on a single tractor chassis, the S-100 (earlier the S-80), derived from a prewar Caterpillar tractor model, the Caterpillar D-7.

[49] M. I. Kostin, *Ekskavatory: Spravochnik* (Moscow, 1959).

[50] Ya. B. Lantsburg, *Spravochnik molodnogo mashnista keskavatora* (Moscow, 1968), p. 27.

[51] M. D. Artamonov, *Tiagovye i dorozhnye mashiny na lesozagotovkakh* (Moscow, 1968), p. 303-6.

[52] P. S. Neporozhnii, *Electrification and Power Construction in the U.S.S.R.* Jerusalem: Israel Program for Scientific Translations, 1965), pp. 135-37.

[53] Alexis J. Pashin of Yale University has concluded on the basis of personal observation that "all the major equipment" in the logging industry "was either of foreign manufacture or copies, with some relatively slight modifications." This observation was made in 1958, but Pashin considers it holds good for 1968. Pashin also adds: "The same applies to the equipment we saw in the sawmills, plywood plants, and pulp and paper mills. All the major pieces of equipment were either of foreign make or obvious copies." Letter to writer, February 19, 1968.

CHAPTER NINE

Western Assistance
to the Nonferrous Metal Industries

CANADIAN ASSISTANCE FOR NICKEL PRODUCTION

The first Russian nickel plant started production in February 1934 at Ufa in the South Urals with a capacity of 3000 tons annually. The Ufa plant, based on oxide ores, uses methods similar to those in the nickel plants of New Caledonia and Germany. It also processes oxidized nickel ores. The second Russian nickel plant started operations in 1935 at Rezh, near Sverdlovsk; this plant is also based on oxide ores and uses a similar process to produce nickel matte, which is transferred to the Ufa plant.

A third nickel plant, also based on nickel oxide ores, began operating in the 1930s in the Orsk and Aktyubinsk raions. The Orsk plant has a capacity of 10,000 tons of nickel per year and utilizes four Dwight-Lloyd sinter strands,[1] with electrorefining "similar to Canadian and Norwegian practice."[2]

The Pechenga plant, formerly called Petsamo, processes one quarter of Soviet nickel. This plant was developed and built by Petsamon Nikkeli Oy, a subsidiary of International Nickel Company, and taken over by the Soviets; it has three electric furnaces with a capacity of 1800 tons of concentrate per day with electrorefining at Monchegorsk.

Norilsk (started in 1940) and Monchegorsk (started in 1950) are also based on sulfide ores and Canadian practice, i.e., concentration by flotation, smelting to matte in electric furnaces, converting, and separation by flotation and electrorefining. These plants refine about one half of Soviet nickel, using processes based on International Nickel patents, while electrorefining at Monchegorsk is similar to Canadian and Norwegian practice.[3]

---

[1] Germany, Wehrmacht, Oberkommando: Microfilm T 84-127-8116, Captured German Documents.

[2] J. R. Boldt, Jr., *The Winning of Nickel* (Princeton: D. Van Nostrand, 1967).

[3] U.S. Patent 2,419,973 of 1947; U.S. Patent 2,425,760 of 1947; and U.S. Patent 2,432,456 of 1947. The flotation separation of copper nickel ores is attributed in Soviet literature to I. N. Maslenitskii and L. A. Krichevskii, although it is clearly based on International Nickel patents. Compare the flow sheet in *Journal of Metals*, XII, 3 (March 1960); K. Sproule, *et al.*, "Treatment of Nickel-Copper Matte," and I. P. Bardin, *Metallurgiya SSSR (1917-1957)* (Moscow, 1958; Jerusalem: Israel Program for Scientific Translations, 1961).

THE COPPER MINING AND SMELTING INDUSTRY

The technical assistance provided by American engineers to the Soviet copper mining and smelting industry was described in a previous volume.[4] No new locations had been established by the early 1960s, when production of refined copper reached an estimated total of 416,000 tons per year.[5] This capacity was achieved by expanding the already large plants built by Arthur Wheeler Corporation, Southwestern Engineering Corporation, and German firms in the 1930s; the Sverdlovsk refinery is still the largest Soviet refinery, followed by the Balkash refinery.

Copper is a subsector for which the Soviets have released very little hard data; it is surmised that major problems exist within the industry. For example, the Soviets are processing both oxide and sulfide ores by the same techniques; consequently, the recovery rate from oxide ores doubtless has been very low. There is also evidence that the metal content of the ore is declining, probably reflecting inadequate exploration methods. The recovery rate may also be declining.

This deficiency apparently has been offset by metal imports. Between 1954 and 1959 the Soviet Union purchased almost 550,000 tons of unwrought copper and copper wire from Free World countries—about 20 percent of total supply. This purchase was apparently necessary despite 391,711 tons of copper under Lend Lease, i.e., about seven years' supply at estimated 1940 rates of production, and in addition to over one million miles of copper wire and cable.[6] Imports rose at the end of the fifties to 150,000 tons in 1958 and 125,000 tons in 1959, and remained at high levels in the 1960s.[7]

Export control at first limited the form in which copper could be imported, but after August 1954 CoCom removed restrictions on wire of 6 millimeters and less in diameter; in August 1958 CoCom removed embargo on all forms of copper. Soviet copper exports to satellite countries have been balanced by imports of goods from those countries containing an equivalent amount of copper.

ALUMINUM PRODUCTION IN THE U.S.S.R.

In contrast to the Free World practice of using only bauxite ores for the production of aluminum, the Soviets use both bauxite and nonbauxite (nepheline, alunite, and sillimanite) ores—probably because of geological conditions rather than by technical choice. The nonbauxite deposits are low grade but can be

---

[4] See Sutton II, chapter 4.
[5] Confidential source.
[6] U.S. Dept. of State, *Report on War Aid Furnished by the United States to the U.S.S.R.* (Washington: Office of Foreign Liquidation, 1945).
[7] *Vneshniaia torgovlia SSSR: Statisticheskii sbornik, 1918-1966* (Moscow, 1967).

openpit mined and are near power sources; the major factor militating against the use of nonbauxite deposits is the difficulty met in developing a usable technology. About 30 percent of Soviet aluminum is probably derived from nonbauxite ores which also yield byproducts for use in manufacture of cement and caustic soda. (See Table 9-1.)

Table 9-1   MINES, ALUMINA PLANTS, AND ALUMINUM PLANTS
IN THE U.S.S.R. (WITH ALUMINUM PLANT PRODUCTION)

Mine	Type of ore	Alumina plant	Aluminum plant	Annual plant production (1000 metric tons)
Goryachegorsk	Nepheline	Achinsk	Stalinsk	160
			Krasnoyarsk	n.a.
			Irkutsk	n.a.
Arkalyk	Bauxite	Pavlodar	Pavlodar	n.a.
Boksitogorsk	Bauxite	Boksitogorsk	Volkhov	25
			Nadvoitsy	20
			Kandalaksha	20
Kyakhta	Sillimanite	n.a.	Irkutsk	n.a.
Severouralsk	Bauxite	Krasnoturlinsk	Krasnoturlinsk	120
		Kamensk	Stalinsk,	60
			Zaporozhye	
			Yerevan	20
			Sumgait	60
			Stalingrad	100
Zaglik	Alunite	Kirovabad	Kirovabad	n.a.

Source: Confidential.

The conventional Western methods, i.e., Bayer and lime-soda sinter processes, are utilized for production of the 70 percent of alumina produced from bauxite. Development work on a process for producing alumina from nepheline goes back to at least 1929[8] but such a process was not in full use until the mid 1950s; up to 1955 all production of alumina was still from bauxite, in spite of claims that Volkhov utilized the nepheline process in 1932.[9]

The standard electrolytic method of reducing alumina to aluminum is used in Soviet plants, although there has been some discussion of a new electrothermal technique[10] at Irkutsk by which sillimanite is reduced directly to aluminum and silumin. It is likely that a percentage of equipment now in general use

[8] The Leningrad Institute of Applied Chemistry was working on the problem in 1929, apparently with help from American engineers. F. N. Stroikov, *"Alumina from Nepheline"* (mimeographed), is in the Stanford University Engineering Library. Presumably this translation was made for use by American engineers. See also Bardin, *op. cit.* n. 3, on the metallurgy of aluminum. A limited-edition review by Theodore Shabad, *The Soviet Aluminum Industry* (New York: American Metal Market, 1958), also has useful information.

[9] See Sutton II, pp. 57-60.

[10] *Izvestia*, December 20, 1960.

Table 9-2   ALUMINUM AND MAGNESIUM WORKS REMOVED
FROM GERMANY TO THE U.S.S.R., 1945

Name of German plant	Production	Annual capacity	Extent removed to U.S.S.R.
Aluminiumhutte Bitterfeld der I.G. Farbenindustrie A.G. (Aluminiumwerk GmbH), Bitterfeld	Aluminum metal	35,000 tons (1943)	100 percent
Aluminium-Schmelzwerk, Bitterfeld der Metall-Gesellschaft A.G., Bitterfeld	Aluminum metal and castings	not available	80 percent
Aluminiumwalzwerk, Bitterfeld	Rolled aluminum	35,000 tons (1943)	80 per cent
Aluminiumwalzwerk, Aken	Rolled aluminum	10,000 tons (1943)	Part
Leipziger Leichtmetall-Werk Rackwitz (Bernard Berghaus Co.), nr. Leipzig	Aluminum and magnesium metal	10,000 tons (1944)	Part
Leichtmetallhutte, Aken. (I.G. Farbenindustrie A.G.)	Magnesium metal	8,000 tons	Part
Leichtmetallhutte (Magnesiumwerk), Stassfurt	Magnesium metal	12,000 tons	Part
Magnesiumwerk und Elektronbetriebe der I.G. Farbenindustrie, Bitterfeld	Magnesium metal	5,500 tons	80 percent
Aluminiumwerke Carl Ziegmann, Fischbach	Aluminum metal	70,000 tons	Part
Aluminiumhutte Lautawerke, Lauta	Aluminum metal	100,000 tons	Part
Aluminium-Prazisionsgub A.G., Potsdam-Babelsberg	Rolled aluminum	—	Part
Aluminium-Schmelzwerk Lautawerk, Lauta	Aluminum foundry	—	Part
Havelschmelze Velten, Aluminium-Schmelzwerk	Aluminum foundry	—	Part
Veltner Leichtmetallgieberei GmbH, Velten	Aluminum foundry	—	Part

Sources: G. E. Harmssen, Am Abend der Demontage; Sechs Jahre Reparationspolitik, (Bremen: F. Trüjen, 1951); Great Britain, Ministry of Economic Warfare, Economic Survey of Germany (London: Foreign Office, n.d.).

is from Czechoslovakia; it was reported in the early sixties that the Czechs had "financed construction" of aluminum plants in the Soviet Union and received aluminum in exchange.[11]

In the production of more sophisticated aluminum metals, recourse is certainly to Western technology. For example, in 1969 the Glacier Metal Company (a

[11] Alfred Zauberman, Industrial Progress in Poland, Czechoslovakia, and East Germany, 1937-1962 (New York: Oxford University Press, 1964), p. 225

member of the Associated Engineering group in the United Kingdom) installed a Soviet plant under an $8.4 million contract for the production of tin-aluminum bimetal strip for automobile and tractor bearings.[12]

After World War II the Soviets removed fourteen German alumina and aluminum-metal rolling and casting plants totally or in part to the U.S.S.R.[13] (See Table 9-2.) The most important alumina plant was the Vereinigte Aluminium-Werke A.G. plant at Lauta; it used the Bayer process (100,000 annual metric tons) with a small capacity using the Goldschmidt process (8000 metric tons annual capacity).

REMOVAL OF THE GERMAN MAGNESIUM ALLOY INDUSTRY TO THE SOVIET UNION

During World War II almost all the German magnesium alloy industry was concentrated around Bitterfeld, near Leipzig in the Soviet Zone of Germany, where it was founded in the late nineteenth century by I. G. Farben. The capacity of this industry in 1943 was 31,500 tons per year.[14] Most of the magnesium smelting, casting, and rolling capacity was therefore in plants operated by I. G. Farbenindustrie, and most of it was removed to the U.S.S.R.[15]

The industry was not damaged in World War II, and was visited by various Combined Intelligence Objectives Subcommittee (CIOS) teams in June 1945; their reports give an accurate indication of the technical state of the industry as it was taken over by the Soviet forces. The Metallguss Gesellschaft at Leipzig, partly removed to the Soviet Union, was a foundry casting light metal alloys and producing high-grade magnesium-alloy castings for aircraft engines as a licensee of I.G. Farben. Production averaged 400 metric tons per month of aluminum castings and 150 tons per month of magnesium-alloy castings; four-fifths of the output went to parts for Junkers engines and the balance for BMW engines.[16]

The Leipziger Leichtmetall-Werk GmbH at Rackwitz, near Leipzig, was a fabricator of aluminum and magnesium alloys with a capability of producing 200 metric tons of magnesium-alloy sheet per month and 50 tons of magnesium-alloy extrusions per month. The extrusion shop had four large presses and the capability to draw duraluminum wire. Two I.G. Farben plants, one at Aken and the other at Stassfurt, each had the capability to produce 12,000 tons of

---

[12] *Wall Street Journal,* November 1, 1969, 14:4.

[13] G. E. Harmssen, *Am Abend der Demontage; Sechs Jahre Reparationspolitik* (Bremen: F. Trüjen, 1951).

[14] Great Britain, *Ministry of Economic Warfare, Economic Survey of Germany* (London: Foreign Office, n.d.), p. 90.

[15] Harmssen, *op. cit.* n. 13, pp. 94-95.

[16] Edward Johnson and Robert T. Wood, *The Magnesium Alloy Industry of Eastern Germany,* CIOS Report no. XXXIII-21, p. 6.

magnesium per year; both plants contained presses and extrusion equipment for aluminum tube.

The most important magnesium works was the I.G. Farben plant at Bitterfeld—also largely removed (80 percent) to the Soviet Union. The CIOS team reported on this plant as follows:

> 'For many years in Germany the I.G. Farbenindustrie plant at Bitterfeld had been the fountainhead of research and development work on magnesium alloys and by far the most important producer. It can be said that these works is the birthplace of the modern magnesium industry. Many of the techniques used in fabricating magnesium alloy and much of the physical, chemical and engineering data on magnesium and its alloys originated in Bitterfeld.[17]

There were two press buildings at Bitterfeld, each containing extrusion as well as forging presses. These major equipment items gave the Soviets a significant capability in magnesium forging. The older press building of Bitterfeld contained the following equipment:

a) 6000-ton Eumuco forging press

b) 3500-tons Schloemann extrusion press capable of extruding ingots up to 350 mm. in diameter

c) 1000-ton vertical tube extrusion press made by Hydraulic Duisberg

d) 300-ton forging press

e) 600-ton forging press

f) 5 small old extrusion presses

The new press building at Bitterfeld contained even more significant equipment:

a) A 5000-ton Eumuco extrusion press for ingots up to 450 mm in diameter

b) A double-acting air hammer made by Eumuco rated at 8000 meter-kilograms

c) Forging rolls by Eumuco for propellers

d) A 15,000-ton forging press made by Schloemann

e) A 30,000-ton forging press made by Schloemann[19]

This equipment can be used for the production of large magnesium and aluminum forgings, such as aircraft engine bearers and aircraft landing wheel forgings for use in the aircraft and space industries.

Massive use of this German technology generated some criticism in the 1950s. For instance, one Soviet metallurgist, B.S. Gulyanitskii, commented, ''After the end of the War, Soviet specialists had the opportunity to acquaint themselves in detail with German and Japanese magnesium industry.... Some

[17] *Ibid.*, p. 41.

[18] *Ibid.*

[19] *Ibid.*

workers of the magnesium industry showed a tendency to redesign the national magnesium industry, completely imitating German technology."[20]

Thus we may conclude that Soviet nickel and copper smelting and refining processes are derived from Canadian, American, and Norwegian practices.

About 70 percent of Soviet alumina is produced by the Bayer and lime soda processes, and about 30 percent by a Soviet process based on nepheline; major difficulties have accompanied the use of the latter process. There were extensive removals of aluminum rolling and magnesium rolling and fabricating equipment from Germany at the end of World War II, and since that time imports of equipment have originated in Czechoslovakia and in Free World countries.

[20] *Ibid.*

CHAPTER TEN

Western Assistance
to the Soviet Iron and Steel Industry

BLAST-FURNACE DESIGN AND OPERATION SINCE 1950

The U.S.S.R. relies heavily on blast furnaces to produce pig iron. Since Soviet industry generates comparatively little scrap, steel plant input is predominantly liquid pig iron from blast furnaces; by contrast, the United States practice uses pig iron and scrap in various proportions depending on location and relative prices.

M. Gardner Clark has discussed the development of blast-furnace design in the U.S.S.R.,[1] where until 1955 there were three basic furnace designs. The first, developed in about 1930 by the Freyn Company of Chicago, had a capacity of 930 to 1000 cubic meters and a nominal daily output of 1000 tons of pig iron. The second (1935-36) basic design was by Gipromez, with the earlier assistance of the McKee Corporation of Cleveland as consultants, and had a capacity of 1100 cubic meters. The third basic design of 1300 cubic meters came shortly thereafter and was worked out completely by Gipromez. During World War II there was a temporary reversal to a 600-cubic-meter design, and although a 1500-cubic-meter furnace was designed during that period by Gipromez, postwar construction continued in the three basic designs of the 1930s.

According to P. A. Shiryaev,[2] only one operating furnace in 1951 had a useful volume of 1370 cubic meters, i.e., the third, all-Gipromez, design. In other words, up to 1951 all Soviet blast furnaces except one were of the basic 1930 design, for which the McKee and Freyn firms acted as consultants.

In the late 1950s there was considerable discussion in Soviet engineering circles concerning larger furnaces with capacities of 1513, 1719, and 2286 cubic meters (the last designed by Giprostal), and Shiryaev has tables on the technical and economic efficiency of such designs.[3] According to the calculations

---

[1] M. Gardner Clark, *The Economics of Soviet Steel* (Cambridge, Mass.: Harvard University Press, 1956), p. 64-69.
[2] P. A. Shiryaev, "The Economic Advantages of Large Types of Blast Furnaces" in *Contemporary Problems of Metallurgy*, A. M. Samarin, ed., (New York: Consultants Bureau, 1960), p. 236.
[3] *Ibid.*

of Shiryaev and Ramm, there is little doubt that the large design (2286 cubic meters) is efficient in terms of cost. However, as was pointed out by American consultants in the 1930s, large-capacity blast furnaces have problems not reflected in the theoretical calculations; in particular, there are raw-material feed problems and physical problems connected with the ability of coke to withstand increased stack pressures. The Russians have built seven of the larger design, each producing 3000 tons of pig iron per day[4] although designed to produce 4000 tons per day.[5]

BLAST-FURNACE INNOVATIONS

Metallurgists have known since 1871 that raising blast furnace gas pressures substantially increases the rate of smelting. Application of top pressure began in both the United States and the U.S.S.R. during World War II, and widespread adoption of the technique came in both countries in the early 1950s. According to data in an article by V. G. Voskoboinikov, adoption started in the United States, but the U.S.S.R. quickly caught up, and by 1956, 51 furnaces with high top pressure were operating in the U.S.S.R. against only 28 in the United States.[6] Rapid adoption in the U.S.S.R. was undoubtedly due to the fact that output could be increased 5 to 10 percent with a comparatively small investment and simple equipment modifications; introduction was helped by a concentrated research effort.

Early studies in Belgium and at the U.S. Bureau of Mines noted two offsetting drawbacks to the use of oxygen in blast furnaces (as distinct from its use in open-hearth furnaces)—the cost of oxygen, and the detrimental effect on furnace linings. According to M. Gardner Clark, the Soviets repeated these tests in the 1940s, came to the same conclusions, and dropped this line of development. Later, in January 1963, the Voest Company of Austria received $10 million in lieu of patent rights for use of the Linz-Donawitz oxygen refinement process.

Direct reduction can be achieved by a number of comparatively recent processes—there are more than 30 variants—that circumvent the blast furnace. Their useful features are lower capital costs, lower minimum capacities, the ability to use noncoke fuels, and the ability to use low-grade ores. Although Germany had commercial direct-reduction operations before World War II, the process did not make headway until the 1950s.

The early German plants were moved to the U.S.S.R. in 1945, and the U.S.S.R. has since purchased further direct-reduction plants.

[4] *Wall Street Journal*, April 17, 1963, 14:3.
[5] N. G. Cordero, ed., *Iron and Steel Works of the World*, 3d edition (London: Quin Press, 1962), p. 771.
[6] V. G. Voskoboinikov and L. I. Slephushova, "Blast Furnace Operation at Increased Gas Pressures" in *Samarin, op. cit.* n. 2. p. 190.

Table 10-1 DISPOSAL OF 29 KRUPP-RENN DIRECT-REDUCTION PLANTS

Plant no.	Original location	Date built	Date moved to U.S.S.R.
1	Barbeck	1935	1945
2	Frankenstein	1935	1945
3	Watenstedt-Salzgitter	1941	1945
4	Czechoslovakia	1943	Still in place
5 to 29	Japan, Korea, and Manchuria	1935-45	All in Korea and Manchuria moved to U.S.S.R. in 1945-46

Source: *The Krupp-Renn Process, for Production of Iron Without Metallurgical Coke Using Fine-grained Fuel and for the Economical Processing of Low-grade High Silica Ores* (Essen, n.d.).

CONTINUOUS CASTING OF STEEL

Soviet attempts to apply continuous casting on a wide scale in an attempt to circumvent the blooming-mill stage demonstrate clearly both the political pressure for innovation in the Soviet Union and one of the pitfalls implicit in centrally decreed innovation.

Continuous casting of metals has been under development since Sir Henry Bessemer's original patent in 1858; by eliminating the need for the soaking pits and the blooming mill it offers the promise of large savings in capital costs and greater metal yields. The B. Atha Company in the United States produced file steel by continuous casting from about 1890 to 1910, but up to 1950, commercial applications of continuous casting were limited mainly to nonferrous metals, and particularly to aluminum. (All U.S. aluminum today is continuous-cast.) The first large-scale Western commercial steel installation was for alloy steels at Atlas Steel in Welland, Canada, in 1954, and by 1959 a total of 25 plants were operating on a development or commercial basis in at least 12 countries. In 1959 the U.S.S.R. had three development plants and probably three in production.[7] These were plants of the Junghans-Rossi type.[8]

The advantages of continuous casting are numerous if the process can be used on a production scale. Quality of cast slabs and blooms is good, although considerable difficulties have been encountered with continuous-cast rimming steels. The yield is excellent, with a ratio of liquid steel to slab of about 94 to 97 percent, compared with the conventional yield of 85 percent using a

[7] In 1963, one source stated only three plants were operating in the U.S.S.R. This is probably conservative, but see *Wall Street Journal*, April 17, 1963.
[8] *Institute of Metals Journal* (London), March 1958, p. 182; *Metal Progress* (Cleveland, O.), May 1959, p. 106.

blooming mill. Capital costs are decidedly lower, especially in small plants; both capital and operating costs for a blooming mill may be four times greater than with continuous casting.

In the early 1950s Soviet weaknesses in certain areas of iron and steel production became pressing. Rolled flat products (i.e., sheet and strip steel) comprised 20 percent of total rolled products in 1940[9] and increased to only 25 percent by 1955. By comparison, in the United States the 1940 ratio was over 45 percent, and in 1955 probably over 60 percent. A number of studies[10] have indicated that the percentage requirements of flat-rolled steel products increases with industrialization. In other words, the relative demand for sections (e.g., bars and structurals) declines, and the relative demand for sheet steel (for use in automobiles, appliances, galvanizing, pipe, and tinplate) increases as industrial development progresses. However, flat-rolled products require a much greater investment in processing and finishing facilities (pickling, annealing, cold rolling, skin pass mills, galvanizing, and tinning lines) than do section products. Apart from the magnitude of the investment involved, there are indications that the Soviets have not fully appreciated the technological gap they have to bridge between hot-rolled sections and flat cold-rolled products.[11]

The prospect of having to make substantial investments in rolling mill equipment and new techniques prompted a search for less expensive alternatives. Continuous casting was one promising alternative, which was recognized by Gipromez and other design bureaus; development work on the process began at the Central Research Institute for Ferrous Metallurgy in Moscow in 1938. The Krasny Oktyabr Works (1951), Novo Tula (1955), and Kirov (1956) continued this work. In 1956 continuous casting was presented to the Twentieth Congress of the CPSU as a possible means of leap-frogging Western technology: the lower capital costs would avoid heavy investment in blooming mills, sim-

---

[9] R. H. Jones, *The Roads to Russia* (Norman: University of Oklahoma Press, 1969), p. 20. Soviet production of steel was 20 million tons in 1940 and only 8.8 million tons in 1942; 2,589,766 tons of steel were sent between 1941 and 1945 under Lend Lease. Although this appears only a small fraction of Soviet output, Jones comments, "Appearances are deceiving. Most of the Lend Lease steel comprised specialty steels such as high-speed cold steel, cold-finished bars, hot-rolled aircraft steel, tinplate, steel wire, pipe and tubing, and hot-rolled sheets and plates. More than one-fifth of the Lend Lease steels included railroad rails and accessories. In other words, Russia imported specialty steels, freeing her mills from the expense and time involved in their production." Jones adds that the $13.2 million worth of equipment for their steel mills enabled the Soviets to increase the output of carbon steel ingots by 2.5 million tons per year.

[10] Various reports of the Economic Commission for Europe and Economic Commission for Latin America (United Nations).

[11] For example: "Of the cold-rolled sheets from rimming steel ingots at the Novosibirsk plant, 50 percent of the sheets were classified in the second grade ... due to ... small scabs ... measuring 0.5-3 mm wide and 200-300 mm long with a thickness of up to 0.2 mm." G. V. Gurskii, "The Continuous Casting of Steel" in *Samarin, op. cit.* n. 2, p. 285. No Western mill would classify this defect as a "second"; laminations of this magnitude are classified as scrap.

plified construction would reduce lead time required for development of more powerful blooming mills, and excellent yield offered the promise of increasing steel output per ruble of investment.[12] There is no doubt that by 1956 considerable progress had been made in solving problems connected with continuous casting of tonnage steels, but by Western engineering standards the process developed was not suitable for application in large plants. Western engineers were in general agreement that the process was then limited to alloy steels with a high hot strength. Inland Steel, for example, considered the process, and *Iron Age* reported: "In 1956 ... Inland decided in favor of conventional equipment and against continuous casting ... there was not sufficient time available to master all the problems."[13]

In 1956, then, continuous casting was under consideration in both the West and the U.S.S.R. for large-tonnage plants. Engineering opinion in the West was against adoption; on the other hand, the process was adopted in the Soviet Union.

Stal' reports that by 1961 ten installations had been brought into use, including pilot plants and single-strand units with limited capacity.[14] A rough estimate is that probably about one-half million tons was poured by continuous casting in the U.S.S.R. in 1961, with an absolute maximum of one million tons; directives of the party congress had called for 12 to 15 million tons to be poured by this method in 1961. By 1962 no Soviet plant was entirely dependent on continuous casting; i.e., the soaking-pit blooming-mill stage was retained in all steel plants. The cost to the Soviets in trying to meet the goals set by the party must have been considerable because of the investment in continuous casting plants, the continued demand for blooming mills and soaking pits which necessitated running two methods simultaneously in the same plant, and the lead time lost in blooming-mill development. In particular, it was known in 1956 that continuous casting was not suitable for rimming steels, which are preferred for reasons of quality in flat-rolled products, and for which Soviet production capacity is notably weak. By 1962 the problems connected with rimming steels had not been solved in either the U.S.S.R. or the United States.

---

[12] "Capital investment for the construction of continuous pouring installations is repaid in less than one year. With continuous pouring there is no need for blooming mills [or] the building of such costly premises of open-hearth plants as the mold yards and shops for ingot stripping. Continuous pouring of steel will become widespread in the sixth five year period. It was pointed out at the 20th Congress of the CPSU that if 12-15 million tons of steel are poured by the new method in 1960, which is fully feasible, this will yield an additional million tons of rolled stock (by cutting down losses and waste) and a saving of 2,000 million rubles." Lazar Roitburd, *Soviet Iron and Steel Industry* (Moscow: Foreign Languages Publishing House, 1956).

[13] *Iron Age*, May 18, 1961.

[14] S. K., "The Twenty-second Congress of the CPSU and the Soviet Iron and Steel Industry," *Stal'* (English version), no. 7, July 1961.

STEEL ROLLING TECHNIQUES IN THE SOVIET UNION

Although there was no attempt after World War II to remove complete iron and steel plants under reparations to the U.S.S.R., there was a great deal of selective removal—particularly of rolling mills and finishing equipment. The Hüttenwerk Salzgitter A.G. was dismantled between 1945 and 1950;[15] in fact, Alfred Zauberman estimates that four-fifths of East German metallurgical capacity was dismantled[16] (although this may have been restricted to specialized units). Plate rolling mills, tube facilities, coal washing plants, and special steel facilities in Manchuria were completely dismantled,[17] but blast furnaces were not removed and other facilities were only selectively removed.

Well after the war the U.S.S.R. was still turning out a large proportion of its limited production of steel sections on hand-bar mills; in 1956, for example, only 53 percent of rolled steel sections was produced on modern mills, leaving 47 percent to be produced on the old-type "in-train" hand mills. These figures indicate a considerable lag in technology. The hand-bar mill is very limited in both speed and capacity; continuous and semicontinuous mills have replaced "in-train" mills almost completely in the West. The only use for the hand-bar mill in the United States during the last 50 years or so has been possibly in limited rollings of special products; e.g., it is probably used for wrought iron. Even in Europe such mills are rare.

By far the weakest part of the Soviet iron and steel industry is in the production of flat-rolled products, i.e., hot- and cold-rolled sheet and strip as well as coated sheet and strip. For such production the choice of techniques is essentially between continuous or semicontinuous sheet and strip mills (including Steckel mills) and the obsolete hand-sheet mill or pack mill.[18] In 1960, the United States had 39 continuous wide hot-strip mills, all with extensive additional cold-rolling and finishing facilities; at the same time Japan had five, the United Kingdom four, and Mexico two wide strip mills. In 1960 the U.S.S.R. had only five continuous or Steckel-type mills.[19]

This lack of wide strip rolling facilities is reflected in the composition of Soviet steel output. The share of sheet steel in all rolled products was 25 percent

[15] *Germany, 1945-1954* (Cologne: Boas International Publishing Co. [1954?]), p. 493.
[16] Alfred Zauberman, *Industrial Progress in Poland, Czechoslovakia, and East Germany, 1937-1962* (New York: Oxford University Press, 1964), pp. 174, 187.
[17] Edwin W. Pauley, *Report on Japanese Assets in Manchuria to the President of the United States, July 1946* (Washington, 1946).
[18] The hand-sheet mill has a few uses in the West today; it is used in the United Kingdom and Belgium for blue planished sheets, and in the United States probably only for high-silicon electrical sheets.
[19] Based on Iron and Steel Institute, *Production of Wide Steel Strip* (London, 1960), p. 75.

in 1955, but of this only 23 percent came from continuous or semicontinuous mills.

Table 10-2 suggests a heavy dependence on Western technology in the five wide strip mills operating in the U.S.S.R. in 1960: three are of Western manufacture. The first Russian-built continuous sheet mill was installed not in Russia but at Nowa Huta in Poland.[20] The tinplate mill for this plant was supplied by U.S. firms "financed from American credit."[21] The reported operating troubles of the Russian-made mill[22] would suggest in the context of our study that the Soviets installed their first mill in Poland to avoid domestic production interruptions from an inadequately engineered mill.

Table 10-2   ORIGINS OF SOVIET CONTINUOUS WIDE STRIP MILLS
AS OF 1960

Mill	Type	Width, inches	Origin
1. Zaporozhtal	Continuous	60	U.S. (United)
2. Kuibyshev	Continuous	50	U.S. (United)
3. Magnitogorsk	Continuous	96	U.S.S.R. (Kramator)
4. Chelyabinsk	Semicontinuous	72	German (Steckel)
5. Voroshilov	Continuous	96 (?)	U.S.S.R. (?)

Source: Great Britain, Iron and Steel Institute, Production of Wide Steel Strip (London, 1960).

Note: There is also evidence of an old 50-inch German semicontinuous mill (from reparations) at Nizhni Tagil. A prototype Kramator reversing mill with furnace coilers is located at Lipetsk.

Thus it is concluded that there is a heavy Soviet dependence on Western technology in the production of flat-rolled steel from continuous and semicontinuous mills. It should be noted that the development, construction, and operation of this type of mill requires far greater technical sophistication than do the facilities for pig iron or steel production. "Shock" methods applied to wide strip mill scheduling would be chaotic, as shock methods cannot be applied to the more sophisticated technologies where tight control of specification is easily lost and a delicate balance must be maintained between the subsystems.

THE STEEL PIPE AND TUBE INDUSTRY

The two basic techniques in pipe and tube manufacturing are the seamless and welded tube processes. The earliest seamless techniques were variants of

---

[20] M. Gardner Clark, "Report on the Nowa Huta Iron and Steel Plant Named After Lenin, Near Cracow, Poland" (Ithaca: School of Industrial and Labor Relations, Cornell University, September 1957), mimeographed.

[21] Zauberman, op. cit. n. 16, p. 193.

[22] Clark, op. cit. n. 1.

the Mannesman skew rolling principle using a mandrel; present-day Stiefel mills, plug mills, and continuous seamless mills are based on Mannesman rolling principles and account for about 60 percent of Soviet tube production. The push-bench techniques, now obsolete, and the extrusion process for small-diameter special-alloy tubes are also of German origin.

The second main group of manufacturing techniques is a variant of the welded seam process, and accounts for the remaining 40 percent of Soviet tube output. The Fretz-Moon technique of continuous butt welding originated in the United States in the early 1920s; submerged electric-arc welding for large-diameter tubes and electric-resistance welding (ERW) were developed at a later date, although ERW did not come into widespread use until after World War II.

Most techniques in use in the world today conform to one of these two basic Western methods, one German and one American. An examination of Soviet methods indicates that all plants use one of these methods (except Lipetsk, which uses a spun-cast process of unknown origin). Moreover in 1962 Soviet pipe and tube plants not only were based on Western technology but to a great extent were using Western equipment. The Soviet heavy-machinery-building

Table 10-3 PROCESS USED IN SOVIET PIPE AND TUBE MILLS IN 1963

Plant	Process	Product
Taganrog	Pilger	Oil Pipe
Novomoskovsk	Pilger	Large-diameter oil pipe
Zhdanov	—	Seamless pipe and tube to 14 inches
Dnepropetrovsk	Stiefel	Seamless tubes
Dnepropetrovsk (Karl Liebknecht)	Pilger	—
Nikopol	Stiefel Mannesman }	Small-diameter tube
Pervouralsk	Stiefel Rockrite }	Tubes for oil and chemical industry
Chelyabinsk	Fretz-Moon }	Oil and gas pipes to 38 inches in diameter
	Stiefel	—
	Pilger	—
	Electric resistance	—
	Weld mill	—
Kamensk-Uralskiy	Draw bench type	Pipe to 75 mm diameter
Viksa	Electric weld mill	—
Lipetsk	Spun cast	—
Rustavi	Mannesman (U.S.-built)	—
Sumgait	Seamless mills	—
Novosibirsk	Electric weld mills	—

Source: Economic Commission for Europe, *The European Steel Pipe and Tube Industry* (Geneva, 1955); M. Gardner Clark, *The Economics of Soviet Steel* (Cambridge, Harvard University Press, 1956); M. G. Cordero, *Iron and Steel Works of the World*, 3d edition (London: Quin, 1962).

plants do not appear to have completely mastered the art of building tube-rolling machinery, or else it has been found more advantageous to import Western equipment. There has been a limited development of new techniques, in effect modifications of the basic methods, by TsKBMM, and "authors' certificates" have been awarded to some Soviet designers, but the scope of this work is not extensive.

Table 10-3 indicates the process used in 15 Soviet tube and pipe plants.

In 1960 the Soviet Union apparently could not produce a tube mill of any type capable of manufacturing steel tube greater than 400 mm in diameter.[23] This observation is confirmed by examination of the equipment contained in the most important Soviet tube mills. The Chelyabinsk tube mill, the largest in Europe with a production in excess of one million tons of tubes and pipes per year, has equipment completely of Western origin. Chelyabinsk has four Fretz-Moon mills for production of butt-welded tube between 3/8 and three inches in diameter; the strip heating furnaces in the Fretz-Moon mill were built from Salem Engineering drawings, and the leveling and uncoiling machines were made by Aetna Standard Company.[24] The Stiefel mill shop produces tubes between three and four inches in outside diameter using the standard Stiefel mill. The Pilger mill shop produces large-diameter seamless tubes from 12 to 22 inches in outside diameter; the piercer is a rotary-type Mannesman followed by two Pilger mills built by Eisenwerk Witkovice in Czechoslovakia. The worn rolls are built up by welding with Krupp welding rod.[25] A newer plant, completed in 1959, produces welded pipe up to 820 mm (32.3 inches) in diameter by the U.S. submerged-arc process, and is the first plant of its type in the Soviet Union.[26]

Another important Soviet tube mill is at Rustavi (all Soviet seamless tube capacity is located at either Nikopol or Rustavi). The report of the 1956 British Iron and Steel Delegation indicated that the Rustavi mill was "orthodox in design and layout and generally typical of works built about 30 years ago."[27] The Nikopol mill was originally installed by a U.S. firm in the 1930s.[28] In 1956 two Russian-built electric-resistance welding mills also were installed in Nikopol; these have piercers of the Mannesman type followed by plug or Stiefel mills.

[23] V. L. Agre,*Tekhnicheskii progress v chernoi metallurgii SSSR; Prokatnoe i trubnoe proizvodstvo* (Moscow, 1962). This is an excellent compendium of technicoeconomic information.

[24] *Iron and Steel Making in the U.S.S.R., with Special Reference to the Urals Region,* A Report to the British Iron and Steel Federation by a British Steel Delegation, (Rochester, Kent: Staples, 1956), p. 66.

[25] *Ibid.,* p. 67.

[26] *Ibid.,* p. 65.

[27] *The Russian Iron and Steel Industry,* A Report Prepared by a British Steel Mission to the U.S.S.R., Special Report No. 57 (London: Iron and Steel Institute, April 1956), p. 19. The reader should also see Yu. F. Shevakin, *Stany kholodnoi prokatki trub* (Moscow, 1966); and L. I. Spivakovskii, *Ekonomika trubnoi promyshlennosti SSSR* (Moscow, 1967).

[28] See Sutton II, p. 74.

SOVIET CONTRIBUTIONS TO METALLURGY

According to J. H. Westbrook, writing in 1961 after a visit to seven Soviet metallurgical laboratories,[29] the Soviets are more interested in exploiting the properties of compounds than in improving or understanding their nature. Says Westbrook:

> In the superalloy field, despite a large amount of research on nickel, cobalt, and iron-based superalloys, Soviet scientists are apparently without any unique advances or developments of their own. This observation is even more surprising in that they have had full knowledge of both the empirical and theoretical developments of the Western world. Most of their work is descriptive—it has not been (and, in most instances, *cannot* be) correlated with particular models of deformation or fracture.[30]

Westbrook then identifies three areas in which the Soviets have made unique contributions in the field of materials processing, although a decade later there is contradictory evidence as to whether the Soviets have been able to maintain their position in these fields:

1. friction welding
2. electroslag melting (for ingots of special alloys)
3. powder rolling

Westbrook also notes that laboratories in the early sixties were well supplied with equipment of foreign origin: "... they have a considerable amount of foreign-made equipment as well as Russian of foreign designs."[31] After pointing out that his delegation saw Russian-built copies of General Radio Variacs, Simpson meters, Du Mont oscilloscopes, and L & N recorders, Westbrook continues: "... they appear to concentrate on one design, their own or that of someone else, and then build and use large numbers of identical units."[32]

Soviet work in electroslag welding (where, unlike arc welding, the heat is obtained by passage of electric current through a bath of molten slag) came to fruition in about 1960 with the attainment of an ability to weld parts up to a thickness of 2⅜ inches using one electrode.[33] The process was immediately licensed to the Swedish firm Esab.[34] Russian work in friction welding by V. I. Vill led to publication of his textbook *Friction Welding of Metals* by the American Welding Society in 1962, although there is some question whether the Soviets have maintained any significant advance over current U.S. knowledge

[29] J. H. Westbrook, "High Temperature Materials in the Soviet Union," *Metal Progress* (Cleveland, O.), February 1962.
[30] *Ibid.*
[31] *Ibid.*
[32] *Ibid.*
[33] *Welding Journal* (London), February 1959, pp. 132-34.
[34] *East-West Commerce* VI, 3 (March 31, 1959), 8.

and methods.[35] Continued Soviet imports of furnaces for heat treating of metals from the 1930s through the 1960s also suggests that Russian work in metals processing has been somewhat uneven.[36]

Thus we may conclude, as have other observers,[37] that at the end of the 1960s Soviet technology in ferrous metallurgy industries is an adaptation of Western technology, although much Soviet work and effort have been devoted to developing this technology.

The classical blast furnace has been increased in volume and top pressure has been introduced. Sintering strands are Dwight-Lloyd to Lurgi drawings; coke ovens are modified Koppers-Becker[38]; and direct reduction is Krupp-Renn.

In steelmaking we find expansion in the size of the classical open-hearth furnaces with indigenous technological improvements. Oxygen convertor practice is Austrian and continuous casting Junghans-Rossi; blooming mills are basically United and Demag. Rolling techniques and finishing facilities in general are backward (except where modernized by imported equipment) and approximate the U.S. level of the 1930s.

---

[35] Appreciation is due E. Strickland for this information; see U.S. Patent 3,460,734 of August 12, 1969.

[36] A number of controlled-atmosphere heat-treating furnaces have been supplied from the United States and from Birlec, Ltd., in England; see *East-West Commerce*, IV, 9 (September 30, 1957), 14, and V, 11 (November 29, 1958), 3.

[37] Clark, *op. cit.* n. 1, p. 272: "We can say that the spectacular technical progress of the Soviet iron and steel industry in recent years has been almost exclusively in the realm of adoption, modification and improvement of inventions and innovations pioneered by the Western world."

[38] See pp. 141-43.

CHAPTER ELEVEN

Western Origins of Petroleum
and Allied Industries

THE TURBODRILL: AN INDIGENOUS DEVELOPMENT

In the field of oil well drilling the turbodrill is a distinct Soviet innovation and quite different in principle from the U.S. rotary drill. In the 1960s over 80 percent of Russian oil well drilling was undertaken by the turbodrill method, which utilizes a hydraulic drive at the bottom of the drill hole in contrast to mechanical transmission through a string of steel pipes used in the rotary process.[1] It appears, however, that the method has not proved completely satisfactory: in 1960 it was recommended that development work be resumed on rotary drilling, a recommendation no doubt dictated by overheating problems with turbodrills as geological conditions necessitated ever deeper holes.

Russian turbodrills were tested by Dresser Industries of Texas specialists, who concluded that the drills did not offer any advantage over prevailing U.S. rotary techniques. Robert W. Campbell, whose work on the economics of the turbodrill is by far the most exhaustive, concluded:

> There is no denying that the turbodrill did make a very great contribution to the improvement of Soviet drilling performance, and the conclusion of our critique is not that the turbodrill was a mistake. Rather it is that the turbodrill could have made an even greater aid to improved drilling performance if the designers of this technology had better understood the correct economic criteria for design decisions.[2]

The interesting point is that while the Soviet Union was converted to the rotary technique in the 1920s by American companies,[3] a decision was made in the 1930s to convert to the indigenous turbodrill, and to a lesser extent to the electrodrill[4] (rarely used outside the U.S.S.R.). This decision, defective

---

[1] The best technicoeconomic discussion of Soviet drilling practice in English is Robert W. Campbell, *The Economics of Soviet Oil and Gas* (Baltimore: Johns Hopkins Press, 1968); see especially the appendix to chapter 5, "Economics of the Turbodrill."

[2] *Ibid.*, p. 120.

[3] Sutton I: *Western Technology . . . 1917 to 1930*, pp. 23-25.

[4] The electrodrill in a Russian development similar to the turbodrill and dating back to the 1920s; in the 1960s it accounted for no more than 1 percent of total Soviet drilling footage.

on economic grounds (*vid.* Campbell), left the Soviets with major technical problems in the face of increasing deep-drilling requirements.

On the other hand, the work that has been done in the U.S.S.R. on rock bits, both core and cone types, follows American practice. For example in 1940 the Carter Oil Company in the United States began work on cone bits, first on a four-cone version and then on a three-cone version. Testing was started by Carter in 1948 and the technology was licensed to The Hughes Tool Company in 1956 although no tool based on the Carter principle has been made commercially.[5] The Soviets started experimenting with a two-cone bit in 1950 that had a "striking resemblance" to Carter's tools and methods.[6] The first Soviet bit No. DV-5 had a diameter of ten and three-quarter inches in working position and less than six inches collapsed, and "the Soviet method of lowering, connecting, disconnecting, and raising the retractable bits closely followed the Carter technique."[7]

U.S. ORIGINS OF REFINERY PROCESSES

Refinery capacity was expanded during World War II with significant assistance from Lend Lease.[8] Initial Russian requests for refinery equipment, handled by President Roosevelt and Harry Hopkins, included "crude distillation, cracking and stabilization plants; an aviation lubricating oil plant; a high-octane gasoline unit; and gasoline absorption plants."[9] These facilities were approved by September 1942 and required $41 million in equipment plus the services of 15 U.S. engineers.[10] Russian representatives inspected the ten "newest" refineries in the United States, and a program was established for training Russian engineers and operators in the use and maintenance of the equipment.[11]

At least 150,000 tons of equipment was sent under the program to build four new refineries, two with catalytic cracking and alkylation equipment; equipment for the production of 100-octane aviation gasoline was later added to

[5] *Petroleum Week* (Chicago), August 14, 1959, p. 25. Comparative diagrams in the text of this article.

[6] *Ibid.*

[7] *Ibid.*, p. 29. For details of the continuing Soviet interest in U.S. rotary drilling technology and bits, see N. N. Kalmykov, *Burovaia tekhnika i tekhnologiia za rubezhom* (Moscow, 1968).

[8] Sutton I, pp. 35-40, and Sutton II, pp. 81-90, for data concerning pervasive U.S. assistance in 1928-44.

[9] U.S. Dept. of the Interior, *A History of the Petroleum Administration for War, 1941-1945* (Washington, 1946), p. 269.

[10] U.S. Dept. of State, *Report on War Aid Furnished by the United States to the U.S.S.R.* (Washington: Office of Foreign Liquidation, 1945), p. 16. The figure of $41 million is too low; final figures were probably closer to $100 million for refineries. See U.S. Dept. of the Interior, *op. cit.* n. 8, p. 270, and add subsequent shipments under the "pipeline agreement."

[11] U.S. Dept. of the Interior, *op. cit.* n. 9, p. 270-71.

the other two refineries.[12] In all, U.S. assistance was provided for seven refineries between 1942 and 1946. Between $14 and $15 million worth of equipment was shipped for refineries at Guriev, Orsk, Kuibyshev, and Krasnovodsk, with an unknown amount of equipment for refineries at Syzran, Sterlitamak (Novo Ufa), and Moscow.[13] These American acquisitions became the basis for Soviet construction.

The Soviets have standardized the design of domestic-built refineries, and new capacity comprises completely integrated units with attendant secondary facilities. The Type A standard refinery has an annual crude oil charge of about 2.8 million tons and the more common Type B has an annual crude oil charge of 6.6 million tons; these are multiples of the smaller Type A unit. (See Table 11-1.) One refinery, that at Omsk, consists of three Type B standard units. Design also includes standardized process schemes dependent on the specification of the available crude oil:

Type I: For crude oil under 1.9 percent sulfur, producing fuel and lubricating oils—atmospheric and vacuum primary distillation, thermal cracking, catalytic cracking, catlytic reforming, lubricating oil production, and asphalt production.

Type II: For crude oil with less than 1.9 percent sulfur, producing fuel only—atmospheric and vacuum primary distillation, thermal cracking, catalytic cracking, and catalytic reforming.

Type III: For crude oil with over 2.0 percent sulfur—atmospheric distillation.[14]

The 1960 U.S. Oil Delegation was able to acquire sufficient data to construct flow diagrams and so isolate the standard process schemas described above. The basic flow sheets are those of Lend Lease installations known to have U.S. equipment, e.g., Novo Kuibyshev (Type A), Novo Ufa (Type A), Novo Baku (Type B), and Syzran (Type B). Further, R.E. Ebel has described Novo Ufa as "U.S. wartime design,"[15] and according to the Petroleum Administration for War Kuibyshev and Syzran were destinations for U.S. Lend Lease instal-

---

[12] *Ibid.,* and U.S. Dept. of State, *op. cit.* n. 10, p. 16, appendixes A and B "Pipeline Agreement." There was a significant amount of other petroleum assistance both in export of petroleum products and in oil field equipment.

[13] U.S. Dept. of the Interior, *op. cit.* n.9, p. 270. The figures given in this source for Syzran, Sterlitsmak, and Moscow are incomplete; they do not take account of shipments under the "pipeline agreement" of October 1945. A rather interesting example of the attempt to imitate American practice is the reprinting in book form of the standards of the American Petroleum Institute, particularly those relating to pumps, compressors, tubes, and casing. See *Rukovodstvo po trubam neftianogo sortamenta i ikh soedineniiam, primeniaemym za rubezhom (Spravochnoe posobie)* (Moscow: Standardy Amerikanskogo Neftianogo Instituta, 1969).

[14] *Impact of Oil Exports from the Soviet Bloc,* A Report of the National Petroleum Council, vol. II, October 4, 1962 (Washington, 1962), pp. 143-44. Also see *Chemische Technik* (Berlin), XIII, 7-8 (July-August 1961), 473-76.

[15] Robert E. Ebel, *The Petroleum Industry of the Soviet Union* (New York: American Petroleum Institute, June 1961), p. 118.

lation.[16] Thus we can trace domestic Soviet refinery construction to U.S. design and technology.

Table 11-1 MAJOR SOVIET REFINERIES BUILT BETWEEN 1945 AND 1960

Refinery	Year of probable start	Year of finish	Final capacity (million metric tons	Origin of refinery
Novo Baku	1948	1952-53	7.1 (increment 1950-60)	Type B standard
Kuibyshev No. 2	1947	1950	25.0	U.S. Lend Lease (Houdry)
Novo Ufa	1948	1951	12.5	U.S. Lend Lease (Houdry)
Chernilovsk	1950	1955	12.5	n.a.
Syzran	pre-1946	1950	7.0	U.S. Lend Lease
Salavat	pre-1946	1954	3.2	n.a.
Novo Ishimbay	1953	1955	2.6	Type A standard
Novo Gorki	1951	1958	2.6	Type A standard
Omsk	1949	1955	18.9	3 of Type B standard
Stalingrad	1946	1957	6.6	Type B standard
Perm	1951	1958	6.6	Type B standard
Fergana	1949	1958	6.6	Type B standard
Novo Yaroslavl	1953	1960	6.6	Type B standard
Ryazan	1952	1960	6.6	Type B standard
Angarak	1954	1960	12.6	2 of Type B standard
Kritovo	1958	1960	2.6	Type A standard
Pavlodar	1958	1960	6.6	Type B standard
Polotsk	1958	1960	6.6	Type B standard
TOTAL			149.7	

Source: Impact of Oil Exports from the Soviet Bloc; A Report of the National Petroleum Council (Washington, D.C., 1962), vol. 2, p. 150.

Just after World War II part of the German Leuna-Merseburg brown-coal synthetic gasoline plant was installed at Dzerzhinsk (Gorki) to produce avgas and nitrogen.[17] In 1953 East German companies supplied equipment for a synthetic gasoline plant, at Lake Baikal, producing 20,000 barrels per day.[18] In 1956 two refineries in the Arctic Circle near the Taimyr Peninsula installed U.S. equipment.[19]

A considerable quantity of oil processing equipment has been imported by the U.S.S.R. since World War II from Czechoslovakia, including sufficient

[16] U.S. Dept. of the Interior, op. cit. n. 9, p. 270.
[17] Petroleum Refiner (Houston), vol. 35, no. 9, p. 421. See p. 139 below.
[18] Ibid.
[19] Ibid.

capacity for several refineries, presumably for the standard Soviet Types A and B. Until June 1957 Czechoslovakia had manufactured and shipped the following units:[20]

Four cracking plants	1,460,000 tons/yr.
Two AVT plants	4,380,000 tons/yr.
Four GFU plants	1,460,000 tons/yr.
Five thermal cracking units	1,825,000 tons/yr.
Eleven AVT plants	12,045,000 tons/yr.

Moves to upgrade early U.S. technology were made in the first part of the 1960s. In 1963 Harold Wilson, the British prime minister, reported that the U.S.S.R. wanted to purchase a complete oil refinery in the United Kingdom and was prepared to pay $280 million for the installation.[21] In 1966 a contract was let to a French company, Société Gexa, for a gasoline plant; no further data were given except that the contract was valued at $13 million.[22] Presumably this acquisition will become the basis for further domestic construction in the refinery sector.

DEVELOPMENT OF NATURAL GAS UTILIZATION

The Soviet Union has rich resources of natural gas located some distance from consuming centers; this focuses attention on the development of a transmission system to move gas to the larger cities, and particularly to the industrial areas. Although writers do not agree on the exact figures, it is apparent that the length of pipelines in operation increased from about 4000 kilometers in the mid 1950s to about 40,000 by 1966.[23] Campbell has said: "In the Soviet Union the length of the city distribution network is only about two-thirds of the transmission system, whereas in the United States it is about double the length of the transmission system."[24] This implies, as Campbell points out, a low domestic utilization of natural gas.

Two factors of interest for this study are the diameter of the pipeline, as

---

[20] *Czechoslovak Foreign Trade* (Prague), June 1957.
[21] *Wall Street Journal,* June 14, 1963, 2:3.
[22] *Wall Street Journal,* June 27, 1966, 9:3.
[23] There is a discussion of this question in Campbell, *op. cit.* n. 1, chapters 7 and 10. Also see, J. Chapelle and S. Ketchian, *URSS, seconde producteur de petrole du monde* (Paris: Publications de l'Institut Français du Pétrole Collection, Science et Technique du Pétrole No. 4, 1963), pp. 258-63, for details on pipelines, maps, and listing of gas deposits. An incisive first-hand description of the situation in 1961 is contained in American Gas Association, Inc., "*U.S.S.R. Natural Gas Industry,*" the report of the 1961 U.S. delegation to the Soviet natural gas industry. There is more information on city distribution methods in National District Heating Association, *District Heating in the Union of Soviet Socialist Republics* (Pittsburgh, 1967).
[24] Campbell, *op. cit.* n. 1, p. 208.

the Soviets have definite restrictions on size of pipe rolled,[25] and the use of compressors. The longest lines have been built with imported pipe. The first line, Saratov-Moscow (843 kilometers), completed in 1946, had U.S. Lend Lease assistance; the 1951 Dachava-Kiev-Moscow line was built with 20-inch (720-mm) pipe supplied by A. O. Smith in the United States[26] and as of 1962 it was the only pressure-welded line in the Soviet Union. The Moscow-Stavropol line (1020 mm) utilized pipe purchased from Phoenix-Rheinrohr in West Germany,[27] and Swedish welding rods.

The inability to produce requisite sizes of compressors has been a major drawback and has forced reliance on either imported compressors or the use of field pressure, thus reducing the effectiveness of transmission systems. The first line, Saratov-Moscow, with daily capacity of 80 million cubic feet, was equipped with 24 U.S. compressors of 1000 hp installed in six booster stations.[28] Campbell points out that lines have operated without compressors and cites the intention to install seven million kilowatts of compressor capacity on 26,000 km of line built between 1959 and 1965 (actually there was only one million kilowatts of compressors in the 28,500-kilometer system as of January 1, 1964).[29] The problems facing the Soviets in the field of compressors, and particularly in securing the desired mix of compressor types, are described by Campbell; suffice to note for our purpose that the original standard compressor 10GK-1 is a copy of the U.S. unit supplied for the Saratov-Moscow line,[30] and other mechanical units appear to be based on American types. For example, the 1961 American Gas Association Delegation reported a turbine unit in one new station: "The machine is very similar, except for its combustion system, to our Westinghouse W-52 PM- 5000 hp units"; and then the report adds the comparative data for the two units.[31] Further, while commenting on possible use of gas turbines, one Russian reportedly stated

> ... he would like to obtain information on gas turbine experience from a maintenance and operating standpoint in the United States. The only gas turbine with which they have had any extensive experience was a Brown-Boveri.[32]

The overall conclusion of the American Gas Association Delegation was: "In general it can be stated that the techniques of recovery, transportation, and utilization of natural gas in the U.S.S.R. are far behind those in the United States."[33] This conclusion was confirmed in 1970 when an agreement was

[25] See chapter 10.
[26] American Gas Association, Inc., op. cit. n. 23, p. 10.
[27] Ibid., pp. 12-13.
[28] The Oil Weekly (Houston), November 5, 1945, p. 5.
[29] Campbell, op. cit. n. 1, p. 154.
[30] Ibid.
[31] American Gas Association Inc., op. cit. n. 23, p. 28.
[32] Ibid., p. 25.
[33] Ibid., p. ii.

signed with the Mannesmann-Thyssen concern of Essen, Germany, to supply 1.2 million metric tons of 52-inch-diameter pipeline for a total value of $327 million to carry natural gas from Siberia to Germany. Production of 52-inch-diameter pipe was not possible in the U.S.S.R. in 1970.[34]

THE GERMAN HYDROGENATION PLANTS

Soviet removals from the German petroleum industry after World War II were concentrated on a relatively few German plants for the production of liquid fuels and lubricating oils by the hydrogenation of brown coal. In general, liquid fuel plants were only partly removed.

The largest unit, a hydrogenation plant near Szczecin, Poland, with a capacity of 600,000 tons per year, was removed to the U.S.S.R.[35] The only unit in Germany reported as completely removed was the Brabag (Braunkohle-Benzin A.G.) at Magdeburg-Rothensee,[36] with a capacity of 220,000 tons per year including 120,000 tons of aviation fuel.[37] A smaller plant, Mineralölwerk Lutzkendorf (Wintershall A.G.), was 80 percent removed;[38] this plant was a producer of primary products from petroleum residues and tars, with a capacity of less than 50,000 tons per year.[39] The dozen or so other synthetic plants, although not greatly damaged by Allied bombing,[40] were only partially removed.[41]

In Austria the oil fields were not dismantled, but they were operated on Soviet account until the 1950s.[42]

REMOVAL OF THE GERMAN BROWN COAL BRIQUETTING INDUSTRY

Germany has large deposits of brown coal which requires drying and briquetting before use. The raw material is disintegrated by rollers, pressed to remove water, and passed through driers into briquetting machines. Since the coal itself

[34] *San Jose Mercury* (San Jose, Calif.), February 2, 1970.

[35] Alfred Zauberman, *Industrial Progress in Poland, Czechoslovakia, and East Germany, 1937-1962* (New York: Oxford University Press, 1964), p. 154.

[36] G. E. Harmssen, *Am Abend der Demontage: Sechs Jahre Reparationspolitik* (Bremen: F. Trüjen, 1951), p. 94, no. 3.

[37] CIOS XXXII-107, *I.G. Farbenindustrie A. G. Works, Leuna*, p. 137M.

[38] Harmssen, *op. cit.* n. 36, no. 9.

[39] CIOS, *op. cit.* n. 37.

[40] U.S. Strategic Bombing Survey, *Oil, Chemicals and Rubber Division, Team 46, Plant Report No. 2: Braunkohle Benzin A. G.*, Zeitz, Germany; Braunkohle Benzin A.G., Boehlen, Germany; Wintershall A.G., Luetzkendorf, Germany (July 24, 1945).

[41] Harmssen, *op. cit.* n. 36, pp. 94-106.

[42] *Germany, 1945-1954* (Cologne: Boas International Publishing Company, [1954?]), p. 476.

contains a substantial quantity of bitumen, cementing material is not required.[43] German production of brown coal briquettes in 1938 was over 44 million metric tons—about 98 percent of the world's total production.

Russia possesses similar large deposits of brown coal in an area to the south of Moscow. The German brown coal briquetting plants were therefore of considerable interest, and 27 major plants from the Soviet Zone of Germany were removed to the U.S.S.R. (See Table 11-2.)

Table 11-2 LOCATION AND CAPACITY OF MAJOR GERMAN BRIQUETTING
PLANTS COMPLETELY REMOVED TO THE U.S.S.R. IN 1944-46

German owner	Location of plant	Number in Harmssen	1937 production (000 metric tons)
Eintracht-Braunkohlenwerke A.G.	Werminghoff	16	790
Deutsche Erdöl	Regis-Breitingen	17	1200
Babina-Braunkohlenverwertung (Hermann-Mine)	Muskau	18	76
Ilse Bergbau A.G.	Hoyerswerda (Erika, Anna-Mathilde, and Renate-Eva plants)	22 60 61	2772
Bergwitzer Braunkohlenwerke	Bergwitz	34	230
Concordia	Nachterstedt	35	
Riebechsche Montanwerke	Deuben Profen Paul	36 37 38	2013
Braunkohlen- und Brikettindustrie A.G. (Bubiag)	Mückenberg	39	1659
Eintracht Braunkohlenwerke A.G.	Welzow	57-58	800
Hallesche Pfännerschaft	Senftenberg	59	267
	Total 1937 Production		9,807

Source: G. E. Harmssen, Am Abend der Demontage; Sechs Jahre Reparationspolitik, (Bremen: F. Trüjen, 1951), p. 78 et seq.

Of these 27 plants, fourteen, with an annual briquetting capacity of almost 10 million tons, were completely removed to the Soviet Union and another ten, with a capacity of 6.3 million tons, were partly removed.[44] In all, briquetting capacity of over 16 million tons was all or partly removed and the remainder put into SAGs to produce brown coal briquettes which were partly exported to the West

[43] U.S. Department of War, Coal Mining Industry of Germany, W.D. Pamphlet no. 31-204 (Washington, September 7, 1944), pp. 155-57.
[44] A.G. Sächsische Werke (SPD # 15, Espenhain); Deutsche Erdöl A.G. (SPD # 19, Zipsendorf); Deutsche Erdöl A.G. (SPD # 20, Gross-Zossen); A.G. Sächsische Werke (SPD # 21, Hirschfelde); Werchen-Weiszenfelser Braunkohlen A.G. (SPD # 40, Zeitz); Riebecksche Montanwerke (SPD # 42, Kupferhammer, Oberroblingen); Mitteldeutscher Stahlwerke (SPD # 43, Lauchhammer); Deutsche Grube A.G. (SPD # 44, Bitterfeld); Michel-Werke (SPD # 46, Witznitz); Senftenberger Kohlenwerke A.G. (SPD # 62, Meurostolln).

in 1946-48 and partly exchanged for reparations equipment for the Soviet Union.

Other plants with similar processes in Poland, i.e., Oberschlesesche Hydrier-werke A.G. at Blachownia, I.G. Farben Heydebreck works at Kedzierzynia, and Anorgana (New Rokita) at Brzeg Dolny, also were partly dismantled and shipped to the U.S.S.R.[45]

A typical Lurgi standard low-temperature carbonization plant was that of A. G. Sächsische Werke at Espenhain,[46] where bomb damage was relatively light. Operations were easily restored, including the brown coal plant that was equipped to recover 5-6000 bbl/day of liquid hydrocarbons from coking brown coal. Built in 1936-40 and completely modern, the plant processed about six million tons a year of brown coal in a briquetting plant with 37 plunger-type presses—the largest in Germany. Briquets were then charged into a typical Lurgi "Schwelerie" (low-temperature carbonization plant), from which about 1.4 million tons of coke was produced annually.

The 1944 output of this plant was as follows:

Brown coal briquets	2,696,000 metric tons
Tar from Schwelerie	297,000 metric tons
Coke from Schwelerie	1,400,000 metric tons
Fuel oil	42,778 metric tons
Diesel oil	14,699 metric tons
Hard wax	6,541 metric tons
Soft wax	4,676 metric tons
Electrode coke	7,080 metric tons
25 percent crude phenols	32,000 metric tons
Sulfur	22,000 metric tons
Carbolic acid	9,600 metric tons

It can readily be seen that these plants were effective units for converting low-grade brown coal, first into useful fuels and then by subsequent processing into various chemicals.

KOPPERS-BECKER COKE OVEN TECHNOLOGY[47]

Construction of Soviet coke oven batteries before 1933 was undertaken by German, French, and American companies.[48] No coke ovens or byproduct recovery equipment, except for prototype items, have been purchased abroad

[45]   Zauberman, *op. cit.* n. 35, p. 232.

[46]   CIOS XXVIII-23, *A.G. Sächsische Werke, Espenhain.*

[47]   Readers interested in coke oven accessory equipment should compare the excellent detail in I. L. Nepomniashchii, *Koksovye mashiny, ikh konstruktsii i raschety* (Moscow, 1963), with any standard Western book on coke oven practice or, for a quick comparison, United States Steel Corp., *The Making, Shaping and Treating of Steel* (Pittsburgh, 1957), chapter 4.

[48]   Described in Sutton II, pp. 115-19.

since 1933; Soviet efforts have been concentrated on duplicating the best of foreign technology, particularly the Koppers-Becker system developed by Koppers Company, Inc., and its foreign licensees.

Soviet design organizations—particularly Giprokoks—have undertaken considerable work to improve Western coke oven systems. Giprokoks has been constantly at work since the early 1930s modifying and improving the original Koppers-Becker designs, and this work forms a distinct pattern based on the Koppers-Becker system with cross-over flues.

Table 11-3   DEVELOPMENT OF SOVIET COKE OVEN CONSTRUCTION, 1945-60

| Period | Coking chamber dimensions, in mm | | | Coal charge in metric tons or chamber volume in cubic meters |
	Width (average)	Height	Length	
1945	407 (16")	4,300 (14'-1¼")	13,120 (43'-½")	20.0 (716 cu.ft.)
1950	407 (16")	4,300 (14'-1¼")	13,830 (45'-4½")	21.2 (748 cu.ft.)
1956-1960	407 (16")	4,300 (14'-1¼")	14,080 (46'-2¼")	21.6 m³ (760 cu.ft.)
	450 (17¾")	5,000 (16'-5")	15,040 (49'-4⅛")	30 m³ (1060 cu.ft.)

Source: Walter Farr, "Development of Coke-Oven Techniques in the U.S.S.R.," *Gas Journal* (London), September 12, 1962, p. 313.

The first standardization of the Koppers-Becker system was the PKl, which was followed by a second standardization, the PK-2, again followed in 1942-47 by modifications and improvements of Koppers-Becker and Disticoque designs of the early 1930s. These comprised first the PK-42 produced in 1942, the PK-45 produced in 1945, and the PK-47 produced in 1947. The disadvantages of the Koppers-Becker design were isolated and analyzed, and from this work and ensuing modifications came the PK-2K system. The new system was first built on a large scale at Choku in 1947, and with recirculating flues at Krivorozhye in 1949; essentially, the PK-2K improved Koppers-Becker system is equipped with cross-over flues and double-rich gas flues, with recirculation of heating gases. This design turned out to be satisfactory and was adopted for widespread application in coke-oven batteries built in the 1950s and later. In 1955 the design, further modernized, resulted in the type PV R-46, of which the first operating battery was erected in 1959 at Dneprodzerzhinsk.

One of the major changes resulted from an evaluation of the dimensions of coke-oven chambers. World practice has been to accept an average width of about 18 inches (457 mm); the Soviet Union early adopted a standard of 16 inches (407 mm). (See Table 11-3.) The first battery of type PK-2K coke ovens at Khoku was built with 17¾-inch wide (450 mm) chambers, and during 1950-51 three further batteries were built with widths of 16 inches (407 mm), 17¾ inches (450 mm) and 20 inches (510 mm).[49] By the early 1960s Giprokoks was investigating the possibility of designing very large coke batteries, i.e., eight batteries with a capacity of up to seven million metric tons of coke per year.

Thus in coke oven practice we find the Soviets in the early 1930s obtained a cross section of Western technology which was installed in the Soviet Union by Western companies with Western equipment, and then proceeded to improve this Western technology. Improvements took the form of a consistent series of detailed experiments with coke ovens and analysis of operating results, and changes in oven design were developed on the basis of these results. However, the basic technology remains that of Koppers-Becker, with modifications to suit Soviet conditions.

[49] "Development of Coke Oven Techniques in the U.S.S.R.," *Gas Journal* (London), September 12, 1962, p. 311.

CHAPTER TWELVE

Western Assistance
to the Basic Chemical and Fertilizer Industry

The Soviet chemical industry in 1960 reflected a very rapid growth in production of basic chemicals. Outside these basic chemicals, however—i.e. in such products as resins, herbicides, mixed fertilizers, plastics, general organics and petro-chemicals—the overall production range was relatively small and the industry's progress had been insignificant.

Sulfuric acid is the most important of inorganic acids and probably the most important of all industrial chemicals; it enters into almost all industries. Its production in Russia increased from 121,000 tons in 1913 to just under 3,000,000 tons in 1953, 4,804,000 tons in 1958, and 8,518,000 tons in 1965. As has been indicated in an earlier volume,[1] the Soviets have utilized basic Western or Tsarist processes for the manufacture of sulfuric acid and have duplicated these processes in their own machine-building plants.

A recent Russian paper on sulfuric acid manufacture indicates that in the mid-1960s, 63 percent of sulfuric acid production was based on pyrites and carried out according to a standardized version of Western processes.[2] The Soviet process (utilizing fluidized bed roaster, electric precipitator, towers, and contact apparatus) is similar to contact processes in use in the West. No claim is made for Soviet innovation; rather the claim is made for the ''intensification of operating units'' based on Western processes. For example, ''in 1930 the Soviet Union bought a small unit design (24 tons a day) for sulfuric acid production by the contact process. During the exploitation of the unit, Soviet specialists made some improvements, as a result of which its capacity was increased to 46 tons per day.''[3] This scaling up of a process, similar to that noted in other industries, has been the sole form of Soviet innovation in sulfuric acid manufacture.

On the other hand, there is no indication that any great quantity of Western equipment has been imported for the Soviet chemical industry since World War II. In 1965 Nordac Limited of Uxbridge in the United Kingdom sold

[1] See Sutton II, pp. 109-12.
[2] United Nations Report E/CN.11/635, *Development Prospects of Basic Chemical and Allied Industries in Asia and the Far East* (New York, 1963), p. 518.
[3] *Ibid.*, p. 519.

a sulfuric acid concentration plant with a capacity of 24 tons per day of 78 percent sulfuric acid, but this contract appears to have been an exception.

In the production of the basic alkali—caustic soda—there has also been a rapid increase in Soviet production, from 55,000 tons in 1913 to 101,000 tons in 1933, to 448,000 tons in 1953, to 709,000 tons in 1958, and to 1,303,000 tons in 1965.[4] The traditional method of making caustic soda involves causticizing soda ash; this method has been replaced by a more modern method utilizing the action of an electric current on a brine solution, yielding chlorine as a byproduct. It is in the newer electrolyte process that we find Soviet dependence on the West: the Soviet electrolytic cell BGK-17 is an almost exact replica of the Hooker electrolytic cell.[5]

Although electrolyzer cells were on the embargo list in 1960, it appears that the Soviets were able to purchase sample cells and reproduce them in the Soviet Union. There is also a report that in 1960 a sodium hydroxide (caustic soda) plant was purchased in the West as well as a 24-ampere converting plant to be used in a chlorine unit.[6] Another source states that Krebs et Cie in France has supplied an electrolytic chlorine and caustic soda plant with a capacity of 200,000 tons per year.[7]

A substantial amount of standard equipment for producing alkali chemicals was obtained in Germany at the end of World War II. For example, the Deutsches Solvay Werke, an ammonia-soda works, was completely removed to the Soviet Union. Various producing plants with Billiter and mercury cells also were partly removed: the Bitterfeld North plant was 40 percent removed, the Wolfen plant was 40 percent removed, and the Goldschmidt plant was 80 percent removed to the Soviet Union.[8]

Therefore it may be seen that in the production of sulfuric acid, the large-tonnage commercial acid, and of caustic soda, the large-tonnage basic alkali, the Soviets have adopted and duplicated Western processes and in this manner achieved significant rates of increase in the output of basic chemical products.[9] However, as will be seen in following sections on the production of fertilizers and other types of chemicals outside this basic limited range (particularly in the organic chemicals), the Soviets have been forced to purchase capacity and

---

[4] G. Warren Nutter, *The Growth of Industrial Production in the Soviet Union* (Princeton: Princeton University Press, 1962), p. 423.

[5] Compare *50 [Piat' desiat] let sovetskaya khimicheskaya nauka i promyshlennost'* (Moscow, 1967), p. 168; and Charles L. Mantell, *Industrial Electro-Chemistry* (New York: McGraw Hill, 1940), p. 419.

[6] Samuel Pisar, *A New Look at Trade Policy Toward the Communist Bloc.* (Washington: Subcommittee on Foreign Economic Policy of the Joint Economic Committee, 1961).

[7] *Chemical Week* (New York), September 3, 1960, p. 42.

[8] CIOS XXXIII-31, *Investigation of Chemical Factories in the Leipzig Area;* and G. E. Harmssen, *Am Abend der Demontage: Sechs Jahre Reparationspolitik* (Bremen: F. Trüjen, 1951).

[9] *Chemistry and Industry* (London), February 13, 1960.

technology in the West on an increasing scale as the economy feels the adverse effects of its restricted range of chemical production.

Another aspect of Western purchases has been the acquisition of chemical apparatus obviously for experimental and prototype use: in 1960 the British company Griffin & George, Ltd., sold 13 gas liquid chromatographs for analysis—an area in which the Soviets lag badly. And a vacuum-insulated liquid-oxygen storage tank was sold by a British company in 1960.[10] Moreover there have been heavy imports of centrifuges and other laboratory apparatus.

Thus the chemical sector lags in both commercial development of new chemicals and manufacture of the intricate apparatus required to research and produce these new chemicals on a pilot basis. For technical advance in chemistry the Soviets look to the West.[11]

WESTERN PURCHASE
FOR KRUSHCHEV'S CHEMICAL PLAN

In the late 1950s, as we have seen, the Soviets lagged in all areas of chemical production outside the basics previously described. This lag inspired a massive purchasing campaign in the West between 1958 and 1967. In the three years 1959 to 1961 alone, the Soviet Union purchased at least 50 complete chemical plants or equipment for these plants from non-Soviet sources.[12] Indeed the American trade journal *Chemical Week* commented, with perhaps more accuracy than we then realized, that the Soviet Union "behaves as if it had no chemical industry at all."[13] Not only was the U.S.S.R.'s industry producing little beyond basic heavy chemicals but, of greater consequence, it did not have the technical means of achieving substantial technical modernization and expansion of product range.

According to the general pattern of this "turn-key" purchase program, the Soviets supplied buildings—largely of prestressed concrete of a standard design —and associated power stations, together with unskilled labor and Russian engineer-trainees. The Western firm supplied designs and specifications according to exacting Soviet requirements, and process technology, engineering capability, equipment, and startup and training programs. These contracts were package deals that provided even more than the typical Western "turn-key" contract. Such contracts, unusual in the West except perhaps in underdeveloped areas

---

[10] Pisar, *op. cit.* n. 6.

[11] The reader should consult *50 let . . ., op. cit.* n. 5, the official Soviet summary of 50 years of chemical production in the U.S.S.R., with two factors in mind: (a) the extraordinary degree of omission, i.e., nonstatement of simple facts, and (b) mentally insert the factor of unstated Western assistance.

[12] *Chemical Week,* March 11, 1961, p. 53. For a list see *Chemical Week,* September 3, 1960, pp. 42-44.

[13] *Chemical Week,* March 11, 1961, p. 54.

lacking elementary skills and facilities, were very attractive and highly profitable to Western firms: although the Russians are hard bargainers, their plight was well known in Western business circles.

The overall extent of equipment acquisition for the chemical industry may be judged from the following figures relating to Soviet purchases of chemical equipment from West European countries between 1960 and 1963, three key years in the campaign:

West Germany	$93 million
United Kingdom	$123 million
Italy	$72 million
France	$61 million
Holland	$20 million[14]

In the first stage of this program the Soviets placed sizable orders in West Germany under the 1958 trade agreement for plants to be constructed between 1958 and 1960. The larger plants under this program included an agglomerating plant from Lurgi A.G. with a hearth area of 75 square meters for sintering lead concentrates; a plant with a capacity of 6000 metric tons per year and valued at about $5 million, for the production of paraxylol and dimethyl-terelphtalate; three plants by Lurgi for the manufacture of detergents from petroleum products; and three plants for whale oil extraction.[15] Between 1961 and 1963 additional plants were supplied for the manufacture of polypropylene, di-isocyanates, and phosphorus[16] and sodium sulfate; plants for the hydraulic refining of benzene, dimazine, and atrazine; and two plants for the manufacture of foils from viniplant.[17] Further plants included an acetylene-from-natural-gas factory using the BASF process, with a capacity of 35,000 tons per year; a plant to manufacture phthalic anhydride; and a 5000-ton-per-year plant for the manufacture of highly dispersed Aerosil.[18]

Between 1961 and 1963 Italian companies, in particular Montecatini, supplied plants for the manufacture of acetylene and ethylene from natural gas. They also supplied plants for titanium oxide (20,000 tons per year) and maleic anhydride ammonia, and probably other units.[19]

Complete chemical plants supplied from the United Kingdom included numerous units apart from those in textiles, synthetic fibers, rubber, plastics, and fertilizers discussed elsewhere.[20]

A particular lag filled by British companies may be noted in pesticides.

[14] *Chemical Week,* March 21, 1964, p. 27.
[15] *British Chemical Engineering* (London), August 1958, p. 452.
[16] *Economist* (London), April 1, 1961, p. 54.
[17] See p. 163.
[18] *Chemical Week,* September 3, 1960, p. 42.
[19] *Economist* (London), April 1, 1961, p. 54.
[20] For Western plants for these industries, see relevant chapters.

In 1961 a British consortium, Wycon Services (a joint Fison's Pest Control and Constructors John Brown unit), contracted for two chemical plants in Ufa, Bashkir ASSR, at a cost of $6 million. One plant, based on Fison's Harston works, was designed to produce MCPA, a hormone weed killer. It was to have the capacity to produce enough weed killer for 11 million acres of cereal.[21] The other plant was to produce DMEU (dimethylol ethyleneurea), a resin used in the manufacture of drip-dry fabrics; this unit, with a capacity of 12,000 tons per year of resin, was fully automatic and based on Whiffen & Sons, Ltd., technology.[22] In 1964 the same consortium established a third plant, one for the production of TRA weed killer with a capacity of 200 long tons per year.[23]

In January 1967 Sturtevant Engineering of Manchester received a contract for $1.5 million to build yet another plant to produce agricultural pesticides with complete technical assistance.[24] A few weeks later Thomas Swan & Son of Consett, Durham, was asked to tender a bid for a complete plant for a "chemical used in road building."[25] A unit for the production of two and one-half tons per hour of glaubers salts was supplied by Kestner.[26]

In 1964 a British company—Power Gas Corporation, Ltd.—was building a $14 million plant for the manufacture of acetic acid in the U.S.S.R.[27] In December 1958 Hydrotherm Engineering, Ltd., of London contracted to supply equipment including an automatic heating and cooling plant (with heat generators, circulating pumps, and control equipment) to be used in the manufacture of synthetic resins.[28]

Two plants for the production of sodium sulfate, an input for the paper and pulp industries, were erected by British companies. The first, built in 1958-59, utilized the Kestner centrifugal atomization system, and the Kestner Evaporator & Engineering Company, Ltd., supplied a large spray-drying plant, all motors, a drier, and conveyer equipment for a plant to manufacture 5000 pounds of sodium sulfate per hour.[29] Of the second plant, built by Simon-Carves, Ltd., in 1962-63, little is known except that Darchem Engineering, Ltd., supplied 180 feet of 54-inch-diameter mild-steel gas main lined with stainless steel to Simon-Carves for installation in the project.[30] Also in the early 1960s, Constructors John Brown, Ltd., this time jointly with another British company, Marchon

[21] *Economist* (London), April 1, 1961, p. 54.
[22] *Ibid.*, see also *Chemistry and Industry*, March 18, 1961, p. 349.
[23] *Business Week*, May 30, 1964, p. 52.
[24] *The Times* (London), January 11, 1967.
[25] *The Times* (London), January 20, 1967.
[26] *Chemical Week*, September 3, 1960, p. 42.
[27] *Chemical Week*, November 14, 1964, p. 23. Power Gas Corp., Ltd., has a long history of activity in the Soviet Union; see Sutton II, pp. 103, 288, 369.
[28] *British Chemical Engineering*, December 1958, p. 690.
[29] *Chemistry and Industry*, February 7, 1959, p. 202.
[30] *Chemistry and Industry*, May 12, 1962, p. 869.

Products, Ltd., designed, equipped, and started up two plants for the manufacture of raw materials for detergents under a $15 million contract.[31]

Numerous complete plants have been supplied from other European countries. Belgium has provided a plant for the production of acetylene from natural gas and another for ammonia synthesis.[32] France has supplied numerous plants, including one for the production of acetic anhydride (20,000 tons per year), one for the production of phosphoric acid (60,000 tons per year), one for the production of titanium dioxide (20,000 tons per year), and another for the production of detergents.[33]

A number of plants have come from unknown origins (i.e., reported but without data concerning Western origins). In 1960 for example, a plant was supplied for the production of synthetic glycerin (20,000 tons per year); another for ethyl urea (1000 tons per year); one for the production of synthetic fatty acids (5000 tons per year); one for the production of sodium tripolyphosphate; one for the production of carbon black (in addition to another supplied by Japan); and two for the production of germanium.[34]

The United States has not been a major supplier of chemical plants; however, it has supplied several for fertilizer and phosphoric acid production.[35] It was reported in 1965, for example, that the Food Machinery Corporation of San Jose, California, was to build, maintain, repair, and operate a carbon disulfide plant in the U.S.S.R. This chemical is used for the manufacture of viscose rayon, ammonium thiocyanate, formaldehyde resins, xanthates, and carbon tetrachloride.[36]

The Soviet Union appears to be backward in both the development and the utilization of pharmaceutical drugs. The U.S. Delegation on Hospital Systems Planning, which visited the Soviet Union between June 26 and July 16, 1965, recorded the impression: "Although the important pharmaceutical agents are available for the treatment of patients, hospital pharmacy is not nearly as significant an endeavor as it is in the United States."[37]

An earlier visitor to the Soviet Union had reported to the State Department as follows: "Most of the antibiotics research is applied rather than fundamental ... development (or redevelopment) of products already produced by the West."[38] George Brown of the Sloan-Kettering Institute for Cancer Research in New York also commented that "it was Soviet practice to get the

[31] *Chemistry and Industry*, October 15, 1960, p. 1310.
[32] *Chemical Week*, September 3, 1960, p. 42.
[33] *Ibid.*
[34] *Ibid.*
[35] *Ibid.*
[36] *Los Angeles Times*, January 18, 23, and 30, 1965.
[37] U.S. Dept. of Health, Education and Welfare, *Hospital Services in the U.S.S.R.*, Report of the U.S. Delegation on Hospital Systems Planning, Public Health Service, June 26-July 16, 1965 (Washington, November 1966), p. 36.
[38] *Chemical Week*, October 3, 1959.

production facts concerning pharmaceutical drugs from U.S. patents and literature and then to develop these same drugs through experimentation.''

The Austrian company Grill & Grossman supplied a $154,000 penicillin production plant in 1960,[39] and there has been continuing import of medical instruments and supplies.

PROGRAM FOR EXPANSION OF FERTILIZER PRODUCTION

Up to 1960, Russian output of fertilizers was mostly in the form of low-quality straight fertilizers;[40] there was no production of concentrated and mixed fertilizers such as are used in the West, and the use of liquid-nitrogen fertilizers was limited to the irrigated cotton-growing areas of Central Asia. In the early 1960s and particularly after the disastrous 1962 harvests resulting from Khrushchev's New Land plan, a program was begun to step up the production of fertilizers. Logically it made more sense to spend foreign exchange on fertilizer plants than on imported wheat.

Part of the expansion program was the purchase from the Joy Manufacturing Company of Pittsburgh of mining equipment (for potash mining)[41] valued at $10 million. This was supplemented by the purchase of a modern large-scale fertilizer production plant in the West. As Ivan Volovchenko, the Soviet minister of agriculture, put it: ''We are scouring Europe for machinery capable of providing a quick start to the chemicalization of our agriculture, especially by the production of fertilizers.''[42]

The program actually was initiated in about 1961 when Werkspoor N.V. of Holland (see Table 12-1) concluded a contract to build three plants for the production of urea (carbamide); part of the equipment for these plants came from the United Kingdom—Power-Gas Corporation, Ltd., supplied three installations for the crystallization of high-purity urea, each with a capacity of 100 tons per day, by the Krystal process.[43]

Also in 1961 a Belgium firm, Société Belge, was awarded a contract to provide technology for two ammonia synthesis plants with the equipment to

---

[39] *Chemical Week.* September 3, 1960, p. 42.
[40] The only removal of a fertilizer plant from Germany to the U.S.S.R. in 1945-46 was the Pierteritz phosphate plant reported dismantled in 1945; see *Germany, 1945-1954* (Cologne: Boas International Publishing Company, [1954?]), p. 376.
[41] See chapter 8.
[42] *Wall Street Journal,* November 7, 1963, 1:6.
[43] *Chemistry and Industry,* June 3, 1961, p. 754. These processes turn up in Soviet technical literature; see for example, D.S. Petrenko, *Proizvodstvo sul'fata ammoniia* (Moscow, 1966). The Simon-Carves vacuum evaporator is described on p. 43, the Power-Gas ''Krystal'' crystallizator on p. 44. Another aspect of the Soviet response is current publication of technical material on foreign mixed-feed apparatus; for example, see A.S. Danilin, *Proizvodstvo kombikormov za rubezhom* (Moscow, 1968).

Table 12-1 FOREIGN PURCHASES OF FERTILIZER PLANTS AFTER 1960

Name of firm supplying plant	Type of produced fertilizer	Year of contract	Annual capacity (metric tons)
Union Chimique-Chemische Bedrijven (Belgium)	Phosphoric acid	1964	620,500
Union Chimique-Chemische Bedrijven	Sodium tripoly phosphate	1962	365,000
COMECON (Kingisepp)	Phosphate fertilizer	1964	1,700,000
Société Belge	Ammonia synthesis	1961	two plants
Werkspoor N.V. (Holland)	Urea (carbamide)	1961	three plants (total 658,800)
Mitsui (Japan)	Urea	1964	—
Montecatini (Italy)	Ammonia	1964	—
Woodall-Duckham Construction Co., Ltd. (U.K.)			
Newton Chambers & Co., Ltd. (U.K.)	Chemical fertilizer	1964	ten plants
Occidental Petroleum Corporation (U.S.)			

Sources: *Chemical Week*, October 24 and November 14, 1964; *New York Times*, September 27, 1964; *Wall Street Journal*, October 18, 1963.

be supplied by another Belgian firm.[44] Under the 1960 trade agreement with Italy several plants were supplied for the production of ammonia.[45]

Then in 1964 a contract was awarded to Union Chimique-Chemische Bedrijven of Brussels for a 620,500 ton per year plant for the production of phosphoric acid, and another plant to be built near Kuibyshev with an annual capacity of 365,000 tons of sodium tripoly phosphate.[46]

A joint development with a Soviet "satellite" was reported in the Kingisepp area, under which the mining and production equipment was provided by the satellite in return for fertilizer; this program had a starting capacity of 850,000 tons per year and projected expansion to 1.7 million tons per year.[47] Other such plants were built by Mitsui of Japan and Montecatini of Italy, although the largest was an announced series of ten fertilizer plants arranged by the Occidental Petroleum Corporation[48] and built by Woodall-Duckham Construction Company, Ltd., and Newton Chambers & Company, Ltd., of the United Kingdom.[49]

The chemical sector provides an excellent illustration of the link between

[44] *Chemical Week*, October 24, 1964.
[45] *Ibid.*
[46] *Ibid.*
[47] *Ibid.*
[48] *Ibid.*
[49] *Ibid.*

Soviet planning and Western technology and equipment. In 1960 the Soviets had achieved considerable rates of increase in chemical production by the duplication of standard Western equipment and processes in a few basic chemicals—particularly sulfuric acid and caustic soda. Figures reflecting these impressive increases tended to obscure the extremely limited range of chemical products. When practical demand forced manufacture of a wider range of chemicals the Soviets turned to the West for process technology, complete plants, and equipment.

In 1959-60 orders for more than 50 complete chemical plants were placed in the West and the trade journals catalogued these acquisitions;[50] this process continued throughout the 1960s with the expenditure of several billions on Western chemical equipment to provide everything from penicillin to germanium processing for transistors and to fulfill a massive program for the production of mixed and concentrated fertilizers.

The interesting phase of the acquisition has yet to come. Many of the processes acquired during the 1960s are complex units requiring a great deal of highly sophisticated technical skill in construction and operation. While automation will solve the operating problem it may not be easy to duplicate the plants as has been done with the Solvay process in caustic soda and the Herreshoff-Bauer system in the manufacture of sulfuric acid.[51]

[50] *Chemical Week,* September 3, 1960, p. 42.
[51] See Sutton II, pp. 110-12.

CHAPTER THIRTEEN

Western Assistance
to the Rubber and Plastics Industries

SYNTHETIC RUBBERS INTRODUCED AFTER 1945

It was demonstrated in the second volume of this series that although the Soviets had an early start in synthetic rubber production with the Russian-developed, sodium-polymerized SK-B butadiene, this lead was not maintained, and during World War II U.S. plants and technology were imported under the Lend Lease program to supplement the low-quality and limited-use SK-B.[1] Apart from a small production of Thiokol, the only Soviet synthetic rubber until the import of Lend Lease plants and technology was a butadiene type polymerized by sodium.

There was a significant change in the structure of Soviet synthetic rubber production in the 15 years between the end of the war and 1960. By 1959 only 55 percent of synthetic rubber was polymerized with sodium from alcohol (SK-B), while chloroprene-using Lend Lease technology and equipment (Dupont-Neoprene) constituted only about 7 percent of the total; the bulk of the remaining 38 percent came from the introduction of copolymers or styrene-butadiene types (SK-S), and a small production of nitrile (SK-N) with pilot production of other types. There was no commercial production in the Soviet Union of butyl and polyisobutylene types in 1960.[2]

In terms of tonnage, the Soviet Union produced about 323,000 tons of synthetic rubber in 1960. Of this total, 177,327 tons was the original SK-B type based on alcohol, of very low quality and providing products of low wearing abilities; 104,975 tons was of styrene-butadiene copolymer including the oil-extended types; 23,256 tons was Dupont-Neoprene (now called Nairit); and the balance comprised small-scale pilot production of 8075 tons of nitrile (SK-N) and 8798 tons of other types. By contrast, 99,000 tons of butyl and 38,000 tons of nitrile rubber alone were produced in the United States in 1960.

In brief, the increment in Soviet production of synthetic rubber between

---

[1] See Sutton II, pp. 122-26.
[2] See Table 13-1.

153

1945 and 1960 consisted almost completely of copolymers; i.e., it was of the styrene-butadiene type, in the amount of 104,975 tons. This copolymer was developed by I.G. Farbenindustrie A.G., and was produced in Germany from 1935 onward as Buna-S. Buna-S accounted for 90 percent of German synthetic rubber production in World War II and was introduced into the United States under the government construction program of 1942. It was not produced in the U.S.S.R. during the war.

At the end of World War II the Soviets removed as reparations two large I.G. Farben synthetic rubber plants from Germany—the Buna-Werke-Schkopau A.G. and the Chemische Werke Hüls GmbH. The combined capacity of these plants was just over 100,000 tons of styrene-butadiene copolymers; so a reasonable presumption is that the Soviet copolymer capacity came from the Schkopau and Hüls plants. Sumgait and Yaroslavl seem the logical relocation sites in the U.S.S.R. on both technical grounds (the raw material base is butane from oil) and intelligence grounds (these are sites known to have received such plants in the early postwar period.)[3]

The remaining increment in production came from the Dupont chloroprene type. (See Table 13-1.) Part of the chloroprene capacity came from Manchurian removals. A new plant opened in 1944 to produce 750 tons per year—the Manchurian Synthetic Rubber Company at Kirin—was largely removed under the supervision of two Soviet officials, Major Sherishetsky and Major Diement. Removals were concentrated on the gas generators; the reaction equipment; the distillation, polymerization, and catalyst preparation equipment; and the rolling equipment.[4]

Thus in the period 1945 to 1960 the increment in Soviet synthetic rubber capacity came from Buna-S plants transferred from Germany under reparations, from Lend Lease capacity, or to a small extent from Manchuria. No new Soviet types were developed and placed in full production, although a close watch was kept and research work undertaken on new Western developments.[5]

Given this inability to produce modern synthetic rubbers, reliance was placed both on import of Western synthetics and on plants to produce new types.

[3] CIOS no. XXII-22, *Synthetic Rubber Plant, Buna Werke-Schkopau A.G.*, and compare to *50 [Piat' desiat] let sovetskaya khimicheskaya nauka i promyshlennost'* (Moscow, 1967), p. 346. Also see CIOS no. XXII-21 *Synthetic Rubber Plant,Chemische Werke-Hüls;* and *Germany, 1945-1954* (Cologne: Boas International Publishing Company), p. 37: "Hüls suffered much more than other companies from dismantling." Further, see *Chemistry and Industry* (London), May 16, 1959, p. 628, for an article of Russian origin that states that the chief type produced after World War II was the butadiene-styrene by continuous emulsion polymerization.

[4] Edwin W. Pauley, *Report on Japanese Assets in Manchuria to the President of the United States, July 1946* (Washington, 1946), p. 188.

[5] The general impression of Soviet backwardness in the rubber industry is confirmed by Edward Lane, Chairman of Seiberling Rubber Company, Akron, Ohio, who, after a trip to the U.S.S.R., stated he found industrial methods "very backward and far below ours." *Los Angeles Times,* July 20, 1964.

Table 13-1   SYNTHETIC RUBBER PRODUCTION TECHNOLOGY IN THE SOVIET UNION IN 1960
(BY TYPE OF RUBBER AND PLANT)

Plant	Sodium polymerized butadiene (SK-B)	Styrene-butadiene copolymers (SK-S)	Nitrile (SK-N)	Chloroprene (neoprene)	Butyl and Polyiso-butylene	Others (including silicones)
Kazan	Yes	—	—	—	—	—
Krasnoyarsk	Yes	—	—	—	—	—
Sumgait	—	Yes	Yes	—	—	—
Voronezh	Yes	Yes	—	—	—	—
Yaroslavl	Yes	Yes	Yes	—	—	—
Yerelfremov	Yes	—	—	—	—	—
Yerevan	—	—	—	Yes	—	—
Process used	1. Original Soviet SK-B 2. U.S. wartime standard	I.G. Farbenindustrie (Buna)	Pilot production	Dupont (Neoprene or NAIRIT)	—	Pilot production
Percent produced by type	54.9	32.5	2.5	7.2	0.0	2.6
Quantity produced by type (metric tons)	177,327	104,975	8,075	23,256	0.0	8,798

Source: G. F. Borisovich, *Ekonomika promyshlennosti sinteticheskogo kauchuka* (Moscow: Khimiya, 1968). p. 37, for distribution by type. Tonnage calculated by author. For process and plants, see text.

Butyl rubber was deleted from U.S. export control in 1959,[6] allowing exports
to the U.S.S.R., and a butyl plant utilizing Western equipment[7] came into
pilot production in the 1965-66 period.[8]

In 1960 the Glasgow firm of John Dalglish & Sons, Ltd., implemented
a "package deal" under which the firm supplied and erected in a new synthetic
rubber plant in Siberia a series of machines for de-watering, drying, baling,
wrapping, and packaging of synthetic rubber. This plant had a capacity of
70,000 tons of synthetic rubber per year.[9]

In 1961 the new synthetic rubber plants at Kursk and Ryzan received equipment installed and supplied by Von Kohorn International of White Plains, New
York.[10]

In 1964 a Japanese consortium supplied a plant valued at $5.6 million to
produce 8000 metric tons annually of rubber antioxidants; the consortium included
the Fujinagata Shipbuilding Company, Kansai Catalyst, and Japan Chemical
Machine Manufacturing Company.[11]

The Pirelli Company of Italy signed two contracts in 1968 with the Soviet
organization Tekhmashimport of Moscow. The first contract with the Soviet
organization was for supplying a plant, valued at over 800 million lire, for
the manufacture of rubber latex thread. The second contract was to supply
Russia with two complete plants for the manufacture of rubber latex gloves
for surgical and industrial use; the amount of the transaction was about 750
million lire.[12] Pirelli was building about a dozen other plants in Eastern Europe
and the Soviet Union in the late 1960s for such products as rubber tires, elastic
yarns, and synthetic leather. In addition, a contract was concluded in 1967
for a $50 million plant to produce rubber parts for the Fiat 124 to be produced
in the U.S.S.R., and negotiations were in progress for another plant to make
tires for Soviet-Fiats.[13]

PRODUCTION OF CALCIUM CARBIDE AND ACETYLENE

Acetylene, a major input for synthetic rubber in the U.S.S.R., historically
is produced from calcium carbide. Prewar Soviet calcium carbide capacity was

[6] U.S. House of Representatives, *Investigation and Study of the Administration, Operations,
and Enforcement of the Export Control Act of 1949, and Related Acts,* Hearings before the
Select Committee on Export Control, 87th Congress, 1st session (October and December 1961),
pt. I, p. 333. Butyl, silicone, and nitrile rubbers were removed from embargo in the third
quarter of 1959. Letter from Office of Export Control to writer, January 29, 1970.
[7] Confidential source.
[8] G. F. Borisovich, *Ekonomika promyshlennosti sinteticheskogo kauchuka* (Moscow, 1968), pp.
32, 37.
[9] *Chemistry and Industry,* December 19, 1959, p. 1609.
[10] *Chemical Week* (New York), March 11, 1961, p. 53.
[11] *Chemical Week,* November 14, 1964, p. 23.
[12] Communication from the Embassy of Italy, Washington D.C.
[13] *Business Week* (New York), July 13, 1968, p. 62. See also p. 200.

from Miguet-Perrou system furnaces installed in the 1930s[14] and having an annual capacity of about 80,000 metric tons.

A considerable addition to this capacity was made from reparations equipment removed from Germany and Manchuria. The I.G. Farben Buna-Werke at Schkopau, near Merseberg, produced its own calcium carbide by the electric furnace process for conversion into acetylene, in turn converted into acetaldehyde and butadiene.[15] Capacity was 298,255 metric tons in 1943[16] and the plant was largely removed to the Soviet Union.[17] Other calcium carbide capacity was removed from the Piesteritz works of Bayrische Stickstoffwerke A.G.,[18] which had a 1943 capacity of 155,570 metric tons[19]; the Mückenberg works of Elektrochemische Werke Dr Wacker GmbH using the Wacker dry process[20] with a 1943 capacity of 99,015 metric tons;[21] and a small plant at Spremberg, the Lanza GmbH, with a 1943 capacity of 22,550 metric tons.[22]

In Manchuria, at the Manchu Electrochemical Company, Ltd., in Kirin, the Soviets removed all the equipment from two plants including transformers and all auxiliary machinery, leaving only the electric furnace shells;[23] calcium carbide capacity of these plants was about 81,000 metric tons per year. The removal operation was supervised by Red Army Majors Sherishefsky and Diement, using Japanese technical assistance and local labor.[24]

About 500,000 metric tons of calcium carbide was made in the Soviet Union in 1960—the same as in 1953—and the major end use was the manufacture of acetylene; thus a large proportion of carbide capacity, and so ability to make synthetic rubber, can be traced to foreign origins. Even if reparations removals consisted only of machinery removals, excluding the furnaces, these machines would form the essential core of building efforts in the immediate postwar period.

As of 1953 there were numerous widely dispersed plants making calcium carbide—at Kirov, Yerevan, Kirovakan, Pipetsk, Voroshilovgrad, Leningrad, Kirovgrad, and Zaporozhe.[25] About one-half of the 1953 output of 500,000 tons was for synthetic rubber production, of which about one-third was made from calcium carbide.

---

[14] See Sutton II, p. 156.
[15] CIOS no. XXVIII-13, *Synthetic Rubber Plant, Buna Werke-Schkopau A.G.*
[16] BIOS, *The Acetylene Industry and Acetylene Chemistry in Germany during the period 1939-45*, Survey Report no. 30, pp. 10-11.
[17] G.E. Harmssen, *Am Abend der Demontage: Sechs Jahre Reparationspolitik* (Bremen: F. Trüjen, 1951), p. 106, no. 36.
[18] *Ibid.*, p. 106, no. 35.
[19] *Ibid.*, p. 106, no. 70.
[20] BIOS, *op. cit.* n. 16.
[21] *Ibid.*
[22] Pauley, *op. cit.* n. 4, appendix 10.
[23] Pauley, *op. cit.* n. 4.
[24] *Ibid.*
[25] S. A. Miller, *Acetylene: Its Properties, Manufacture and Uses* (New York: Academic Press, 1965).

Acetylene has in more recent times been made from hydrocarbons rather than calcium carbide; in the United States in 1958 some 40 percent of acetylene was made from hydrocarbons and other Western countries were moving toward this ratio. For example, in 1958 Italy produced 35 percent from hydrocarbons; France and West Germany, 34 percent; and Japan, 20 percent.[26] The Soviet Union and East Germany continued to produce 100 percent of their acetylene from calcium carbide, reflecting relative technical backwardness compared to the more advanced capitalist nations. (See Table 13-2.)

Table 13-2   PRODUCTION OF ACETYLENE FROM CARBIDE
              AND HYDROCARBONS, 1958

| | (000 metric tons) | | | Percentage of total carbide |
Country	From carbide	From hydrocarbons	Total	
U.S.A.	230	150	380	60
Italy	82	45	127	65
France	115	37	152	76
West Germany	255	80	335	76
Japan	250	60	310	80
East Germany	266	—	266	100
U.S.S.R.	170	—	170	100

Source: D.W.F. Hardie, *Acetylene, Manufacture and Uses* (London: Oxford University Press, 1965), p. 46.

Further, backwardness in acetylene manufacturing technology has been isolated as the main reason for the generally retarded nature of the Soviet organic chemicals industry.[27] Although there has been a great deal of research into various acetylene chemistry fields the knowledge has not been exploited, and in 1960 a U.S. Commerce Department report predicted that "Soviet progress in plastics, drugs, synthetic rubber, adhesives, and chemical intermediates will be retarded."[28]

In 1960 one-half of Soviet acetylene was being utilized for welding and cutting—compared with only 20 percent in the United States; the balance in both countries was used for the manufacture of organic chemicals. In other words, quite apart from the inability to utilize improved methods of production of acetylene, the end uses of the product itself were not changed. Thus market pressures making for technical change in the acetylene industry apparently were absent.

[26]   D. W. F. Hardie, *Acetylene, Manufacture and Uses* (London: Oxford University Press, 1965), p. 46.
[27]   *Chemical and Engineering News*, November 28, 1960, p. 26.
[28]   *Ibid.*, quoting U.S. Dept. of Commerce report.

Evidently a pilot plant built in 1958 using the Russian Grinenko process[29] was unsuccessful, because in 1964 three plants were under construction by Western firms, all using Western processes. One of these plants, with a 35,000-ton capacity for the production of acetylene from hydrocarbons, was using the BASF process (formerly known as the Sachsse method); another in Angarsh, Siberia, was to use the SBA process of Société Belge de l'Azote; and the third plant, also with a capacity of 35,000 tons, was built in the Urals by the Italian firm Montecatini and using the Montecatini process.[30]

Consequently, by briefly examining the interlocking nature of chemical processes—even in only one field of organic chemistry, i.e., synthetic rubbers and one of its inputs—we can perceive two weaknesses in the Soviet system. First there is a technical weakness, i.e., an inability to convert promising research into practical working commercial systems; second, there is an economic weakness, i.e., the lack of economic forces or pressures to bring about technical change.

It is unlikely that these weaknesses stem from lack of effort or ability in research. In October 1963 a group from the Confederation of British Industry visited the Synthetic Rubber Institute in Leningrad.[31] The group concluded that it was an institute of "high calibre," the staff was competent, and the research was "well organized"; further, "the equipment is modern and lavish with clean and well planned laboratories."

The Institute has an interesting history. Founded in the 1920s by S. V. Lebedev,[32] it handled the original successful research and pilot production of sodium-butadiene synthetic rubber. Its function has expanded over the years and by 1961 the institute was housed in a new building of 5500 square meters and had established several pilot plants, some able to supply several hundred tons of rubber for large-scale evaluation. A total of 940 persons worked at the institute itself and another 900 at the pilot plants. It was noted that there was a "wealth of standard equipment" including, for example, five spectrometers—one of which was British (Hilger) and one German.

The main purpose of the institute in 1963 was (a) to find synthetic rubbers to replace natural rubbers in all applications and (b) to produce rubbers with special properties. The materials under investigation in 1963 included stereorubbers, ethylene, propylene copolymers, butadiene acrylonitrile, silicone, and

[29] S. A. Miller, *op. cit.* n. 25, p. 474.
[30] *Ibid.* Also see Kirk-Othmer, *Encyclopedia of Chemical Technology* (New York: Wiley, 1968), vol. I, pp. 186-88. The SBA process is reported as the SBA-Kellogg process, but the Kellogg company (in the U.S.) denies having built a plant in Siberia in 1964; letter to writer, April 17, 1969. The process referred to is probably one developed by Société Belge de l'Azote et des Produits Chimiques du Marly of Liège, Belgium.
[31] Confederation of British Industry, "Synthetic Rubber Institute, Leningrad, 18th October 1963"; typescript of manuscript sent to writer.
[32] Sutton I, p. 122.

polyurethane rubbers. Work was also in progress on a variety of antioxidants, including Ionol (I.C.I.) and Santowhite (Monsanto Chemical Company) as well as some Soviet developments.[33]

Thus in 1963 the Synthetic Rubber Institute had a long operating history, excellent research facilities, and capable staffing. Yet despite these observations and despite early work in the field and the successes which fructified in the original SK-B, there has been a significant lag in Soviet development of synthetic rubbers.

WESTERN ASSISTANCE FOR RUBBER TIRE PRODUCTION

The manufacture of almost all motor vehicle tire production can be traced directly to equipment of Western origin and, if we take account of the Soviet practice of working plants on a three-shift continuous basis, it is possible that all rubber tires in the Soviet Union have been produced on Western-origin equipment. As of 1960 the tire production capacity of equipment known to have been supplied by Western firms was about 24 million tires annually. Soviet civilian production in 1960 was about 16 million tires; closing of obsolete capacity and production of tires for military use constituted the difference.

Table 13-3 provides an approximate statement of equipment origins for tire production. A more precise statement relating foreign equipment to individual

Table 13-3   SOVIET TIRE OUTPUT IN RELATION TO WESTERN EQUIPMENT SUPPLY

Years	Foreign firms supplying equipment or complete tire plants	Source	Approximate annual capacity of this equipment supply
1931-7	Seiberling Rubber Co., Inc.[a] Francis Shaw & Co., Ltd.	U.S. U.K. }	3,000,000 tires
1944-5	Ford Motor Co.[b]	U.S.	1,000,000 truck tires
1945-6	Deka-Werke (German reparations)[c]	Germany	300,000 truck tires
1946	Manchu Rubber Co. – (Manchurian reparations)[d]	Manchuria	30,000 truck tires
1957	United Kingdom 'Rustyfa' consortium (Dnepropetrovsk)[e]	U.K.	15,000,000 tractor truck and equipment tires
1957	Chatillon Tire Cord	Italy	—
1959-1960	Simon Handling Engineers, Ltd., Krasnoyarsk[f]	U.K.	2,000,000 tractor, truck and equipment tires
1968	Pirelli Co.[g]	Italy	—

Sources: [a] Sutton I: Western Technology . . . 1917 to 1930; [b] Sutton II Western Technology . . . 1930 to 1945; [c] See p. 31; [d] Calculated as 75 percent of the Manchu plant capacity; [e] Anglo-Soviet Trade, supplement to Manchester Guardian, December 7, 1960, p. 12; [f] Mechanical Handling (London), January 1964; [g] Business Week, July 13, 1968 p. 62.

[33] Confederation of British Industry, op. cit. n. 31.

plants cannot be made, as Soviet censorship has carefully eliminated from published reports data concerning tire sizes produced at each plant (an indicator by which equipment could be traced back to its Western origins) or any statement concerning location of foreign-purchased equipment.

The first Russian rubber tire plant was installed by the Seiberling Rubber Company at Yaroslavl[34] and a second plant was installed by Francis Shaw & Company, Ltd., of the United Kingdom in the early 1930s.[35] During World War II a Ford Motor Company tire plant was transferred to the U.S.S.R. and became the Moscow rubber tire plant.[36] Bought by Lend Lease for $10 million in 1942, it included a power plant for steam and electricity, and was capable of producing one million military tires per year; most of the plant had been shipped by autumn 1944. Some American engineers went to Russia in February 1944 to give technical advice, but in October 1945 the plant still lacked necessary utilities—water, steam, electricity, and compressed air.[37] The Deka-Werke, a producer of truck tires, was transferred to the U.S.S.R. from Germany under the reparations agreements,[38] and the adjustable-size tire-forming machines—about 75 percent of capacity—with autoclaves and calendars were removed from the Manchu Rubber Company in Manchuria and transferred to the U.S.S.R. in 1946.[39]

Soviet tire output in 1949 was 5,680,000 automobile and truck tires—about the capacity of the above-named plants.

In the mid to late 1950s several major contracts were let to foreign firms to supply complete, highly advanced tire manufacturing plants. The largest of these contracts was to a consortium of six British firms, known as Rustyfa,[40] and involved a total contract of $40 million.

The first inquiries to British firms for a new, modern tire factory came in April 1956; concurrent approaches were also made to firms in France, Germany, and the United States. A five-man British mission from the Rustyfa consortium flew to Moscow in March 1957 to complete negotiations. (One firm in the consortium, Francis Shaw and Company of Manchester, had already equipped a Russian tire factory in the thirties.) Dunlop Advisory Service acted as consulting engineers, and undertook the engineering survey and plans for the factory.[41]

---

34 Sutton I, p. 223.
35 *Economist* (London), April 13, 1957, p. 171.
36 Sutton II, p. 184.
37 Robert H. Jones, *The Roads to Russia* (Norman: University of Oklahoma Press, 1969,) p. 223.
38 Harmssen, *op. cit.* n. 17.
39 Pauley, *op. cit.* n. 4, appendix 10, Plant Inspection Report 2-C-2.
40 Other members were Crompton Parkinson, Lancashire Dynamo Holdings, David Bridge, Ltd., Mather & Platt, Francis Shaw, Ltd., Simon Handling. George King and Heenan & Froude were subcontractors; see Peter Zentner, *East-West Trade: A Practical Guide to Selling in Eastern Europe* (London: Max Parrish, 1967), p. 80.
41 *Economist* (London), April 13, 1957, p. 171.

The Rustyfa plant at Dnepropetrovsk, with its annual capacity of 15 million tires, is one of the largest tire factories in Europe. The advanced nature of the equipment supplied for the plant is typified by the monitoring equipment supplied. In 1957 the British Iron and Steel Research Association (BISRA) announced the development of an advanced system of recording plant performance; in 1957 Digital Engineering Company, Ltd., a firm licensed to build and sell the system, was awarded a contract to supply the BISRA monitoring equipment for the Dnepropetrovsk plant. This equipment comprised 500 monitoring or "detection points," with a centralized counting apparatus and printers for recording information. Many of the geared motors and mechanical handling equipment came from Lancashire Dynamo and Crypto, Ltd., whose Willesden works made the largest single shipment in its history—298 crated items—in April 1960 to the Russian plant.[42]

TECHNICAL ASSISTANCE TO THE PLASTICS INDUSTRIES

The Russian plastics and resins industry is even more backward than the synthetic rubber industry. It was reported in 1960 by Russian engineers that the Soviet Union did not have, "and badly needed high-speed, continuous process production equipment,[43] that there was no production of polyvinyl chlorides and foam plastics (among other types), and that there was only small-scale pilot production of such products as plastic laminates and glass fiber products.[44]

This admission by a Soviet plastics delegation to the United States confirmed reports from an earlier American delegation to the U.S.S.R. While avoiding overt criticism of the plants visited and indeed any overall conclusions concerning technical capacity in the plastics industry, individual observations and comments in the U.S. report suggest that the Soviets were noticeably backward in all areas except thermosetting plastics for industrial use. The report stated that the U.S. delegates were "surprised" that there apparently was no production of such plastics as polyethylene and noted particularly the considerable number of "plants they were not able to see," such as a caprolactum-nylon plant,[45] a butanol plant,[46] or "any petrochemical operations."[47]

Equipment in the plastics products plants visited constituted a mixture of imported machines (the polyvinyl chloride—PVC—compounding equipment at Vladimir Chemical, the compression molding shop at Karacharovo, the urea

---

[42] *Electrical Review* (London), April 15, 1960, p. 747.
[43] *Engineering News-Record* (New York), 164 (January 21, 1960), 56.
[44] *Ibid.*
[45] *Report on visit of U.S.A. Plastics Industry Exchange Delegation to U.S.S.R.*, Society of the Plastics Industry, Inc., June 2 to June 28, 1958 (New York, 1958), p. 2.
[46] *Ibid.*, p. 59.
[47] *Ibid.*, p. 61.

resin shop at Carbolit) and Russian-made equipment (the presses at Leningrad Laminated Plastics, Carbolit, and Karacharovo). Some of the usual comments about "copying" were made, although this report contains fewer observations concerning equipment origins than do similar reports from other industries.

Backwardness in plastics was solved in the usual manner, i.e., by the purchase of complete plants from the West. In 1959 the West German firm Badische Anilin licensed production of its process for the manufacture of polyethylene to the U.S.S.R.,[48] and German firms are reported to have sold numerous other plants,[49] including a polyester glass fiber unit (5000 tons per year); a styrene and copolymer unit (5000 tons per year); high- and low-pressure polyethylene plants by Salzgitter Industriebau GmbH (each of 24,000 tons per year); a polypropylene unit (10,000 tons per year); a polyvinyl pyrrolidone unit (180 tons per year); a melamine plant (10,000 tons per year); two plastics foam plants (3000 tons per year each); a PVC sheet plant; a PVC cable plant (40,000 kg/hr capacity); a polyethylene sheet plant and a processing unit (about $1.5 million together); and two plants for the manufacture of polyethylene pipe.[50]

In the early 1960s a group of six plants was contracted to British companies. The Simon-Carves, Ltd., firm, a member of the Simon Engineering Group, received a contract in 1963 valued at $56 million to design, equip, and start up four polyethylene plants; two had a capacity of 48,000 tons each and two a capacity of 24,000 tons each, with completion due in 1966.[51] Financing of $36 million was on five-year terms and arranged by Lazard Brothers & Company, an affiliate of Lazard Freres, the investment bankers of New York.[52] The total capacity of the four plants equaled total British polyethylene capacity in 1964.

Two gas separator plants to provide ethylene for two of the Simon-Carves polyethylene plants were ordered from Humphries and Glasgow, a U.K. engineering firm; these plants had an annual capacity of 120,000 tons of ethylene, the raw stock for polyethylene. The contract was valued at $16.8 million[53] and used the I.C.I. high-pressure process. Part of the contract was subcontracted to English Electric, Tube Investments, and Taylor Controls.[54]

In 1961 Sterling Moulding Materials, Ltd., of Cheshire shipped $12.1 million worth of equipment for Russia's first polystyrene molding powder plant, a facility with a capacity of 10,000 long tons per year. The company supplied technical assistance, installation services, and startup of operations for the Soviet Union.[55]

---

[48] Horst Mendershausen, *Dependence of East Germany on Western Imports* (Santa Monica: RAND Corp.), RAND RM-2414, July 17, 1959, p. 39.

[49] See p. 147 above.

[50] *Chemical Week*, September 3, 1960, p. 40.

[51] *Wall Street Journal*, April 30, 1963.

[52] *Ibid.*

[53] See *The Times* (London), February 1, 1965, for Russian complaints concerning these plants.

[54] *Economist* (London), May 4, 1963, p. 456.

[55] *Chemical Week*, March 11, 1961, p. 53.

Another British firm supplied $210,000 worth of plastics mixing equipment —FKM 300 DK Lodige-Morton mixers made by Morton Machine Company, Ltd., for PVC and PVA (polyvinyl acetate) powders.[56] Other chemical-plant orders placed in the United Kingdom included a styrene and polystyrene unit (20,000 tons per year) supplied by P.G. Engineering and BX Plastics; a cellulose acetate plant (3000 tons per year) supplied by Industrial Plastics and East Anglia Plastics; and a styrene foam plant.[57]

In 1965 a French firm, Speichim, contracted to build a plastics plant in the U.S.S.R. using technology licensed from Stauffer & Company, the U.S. chemicals manufacturer. The process was for the production of vinyl chloride by cracking ethylene dichloride, and was transferred for a flat fee plus royalties.[58] A unit for manufacture of polyethylene cloth also was purchased in France.[59]

In 1964 a Japanese consortium installed a polyvinyl chloride plant at a contract price of $14 million with an annual capacity of 60,000 metric tons of PVC. The consortium included Toho Bussan, a subsidiary of Mitsui; Kureha Chemical for process technology; and Chiyoda Chemical for engineering work.[60] The Sekisui Chemical Company had earlier supplied a plant to manufacture polyvinyl pipe (1200 tons per year) and polyvinyl fittings (1200 tons per year).[61]

In 1969 Berner Industries of New Castle, Pennsylvania, supplied equipment for a plastics plant,[62] supplementing an earlier installation for plastic pipe by Omni Products Corp.;[63] the Japanese Mitsui group reportedly was negotiating another contract for an ethylene plant of 450,000 tons' capacity to use Lummus technology[64] (Lummus is an American firm). Valued at $50 million, the plant was scheduled for construction in Siberia.

We may conclude that while SK-B synthetic rubber is an original Soviet development, no internal engineering ability was developed to break away from exclusive use of this limited-use rubber. Thus Soviet chloroprene rubber today is Dupont, the styrene-butadiene copolymers are I.G. Farben; a plant for butyl rubber was supplied by Western companies, as was equipment for the production of other synthetics and rubber antioxidants, and for the processing of finished synthetic rubber.

---

[56] *Chemistry and Industry*, April 4, 1959, p. 464.
[57] *Chemical Week*, March 11, 1961.
[58] *Wall Street Journal*, July 22, 1965, 10:4.
[59] *Chemical Week*, March 11, 1961.
[60] *Chemical Week*, November 14, 1964, p. 23.
[61] *Ibid*.
[62] *Business Week*, September 20, 1969.
[63] *Chemical Week*, November 14, 1964, p. 23.
[64] *Wall Street Journal*, July 9, 1969. Installations of unreported origin include another PVC plant and a 3000-ton per year plant for tetrafluorethylene; see *Chemical Week*, November 14, 1964.

The Soviet production of acetylene, an input for synthetic rubber, was restricted in the 1950s to the calcium carbide process at a time when the Western world was moving into production of acetylene from hydrocarbons. The Soviets then bought three acetylene-from-hydrocarbon plants in the West, each utilizing a different process.

Rubber tire output has been traced to Western production equipment. Similarly, in plastics the Soviets have purchased production capacity for polyethylene, ethylene, polystyrene, and polyvinyl chloride—key plastics in the modern world. No indigenous large-scale plastics production has been traced, only pilot operations.

CHAPTER FOURTEEN

Western Assistance
to the Glass and Cement Industries

WESTERN ASSISTANCE TO THE GLASS INDUSTRY

The glass industry provides one of the earliest examples of Soviet duplication of Western equipment after significant import of similar equipment. In 1929 the Lissitchansk glass factory installed 80 Fourcault sheet glassmaking machines.[1] The following April, in 1930, the Gusev glass plant in Moscow, with a capacity of 10,000 tons of window glass per year, installed ten new Fourcault sheet glassmaking machines, of which two were imported from Belgium but eight were Soviet-made copies of earlier imports.[2]

Fourcault machines were built from 1929 onward at the Moscow machine building plant, and an attempt was made to supply the equipment demands of the glass industry completely from domestic production.[3] However, the Soviet glass industry appears to have had more than the normal share of problems, whether equipped with foreign or domestic machinery. The Dagestanskii Ogni plant, equipped by a U.K. firm with Fourcault machines and with four Owens bottle-making machines capable of producing 20 million bottles per year, was able to produce only one and one-half million bottles per year, and this production was at a cost 11 times greater than estimated with 60 to 70 percent rejects.[4] In 1930, to help overcome technical problems, Steklostroi employed an American mechanical engineer, C. E. Adler, a specialist in the design of machinery for glass factories.[5]

Even as late as 1957, however, the industry journal *Steklo i keramika* (New York) was reporting numerous problems in the glass and ceramic industries. In the late 1950s the industry was reported to be greatly in arrears and with little innovative ability. These observations were coupled with recommendations that Western technology be adopted. One report specifically mentioned the Dagestanskii Ogni works and indicated that there the only design change from the

---

[1] *Die Chemische Fabrik* (Weinheim, Ger.), II, 52 (December 25, 1929), 541. See also Sutton I, p. 222, for equipment in the Bely Bychok Plate Glass Works built in 1927.
[2] *Economic Review of the Soviet Union* (New York), V, 8 (April 15, 1930), 162.
[3] *Glass and Ceramics* (Washington, D.C.), 1957, p. 379.
[4] Society of Glass Technology *Journal* (London), 1928, p. 198.
[5] Amtorg, *Economic Review of the Soviet Union* (New York), V, 3-4 (February 15, 1930), 57.

original machines had been a change in the bearings and belt drive—this being presented as "modern technology."

After World War II major plant facilities from the German glass industry, particularly the optical grinding and optical instrument industries, were transferred to the Soviet Union. These transfers included the famous optical plants at Jena with subsidiary plants at Berlin and Perna in Saxony. These plants were essentially the only optical glass and instrument manufacturers in Germany and in the year October 1943 to October 1944 produced a total of 1700 metric tons of clear transparent optical glass and 28 metric tons of colored filter glass.

The Karl Zeiss plant at Jena, 94 percent transported to the U.S.S.R.,[6] was modern and particularly well equipped, with over 100 diamond saws; two of these were 420 mm in diameter and capable of running at 900 rpm, giving a surface speed of 20 meters per second.[7] Zeiss manufactured many lines of optical and scientific instruments including optical comparators and projectors, micrometers, and lenses and prisms.[8] The main plant was reassembled at Monino, near Moscow,[9] and utilized Zeiss experts Eitzenberger, Buschbeck, and Faulstich to develop detector, remote control, and recording gear. Other optical glass and optical instrument firms removed to the U.S.S.R. included the Zeiss-Ikon A.G. works at Dresden; Elektro-Optik GmbH at Teltow, Berlin (100 percent removal); and a number of camera manufacturers.[10]

However, the transfer of the Zeiss and similar works did not guarantee transfer of German technical expertise. In 1930 the Moscow planetarium had been equippped by Zeiss,[11] and in 1965, twenty years after the Zeiss plants had been removed to Moscow, the rebuilt Zeiss plant in Jena provided a two-meter-diameter mirror for solar, planetary, and satellite observations at the Shemakinskaya observatory.[12] The backwardness in optical, and particularly spectroscopic, instruments was confirmed by Soviet academician S. L. Mandel'shtam: "The design and production of these important instruments lags behind our needs and world quality standards. We are forced to buy abroad, and these are among the most expensive instruments."[13]

Laboratory glass exemplifies this technical backwardness. Up to about 1930 only one type of laboratory glass was used: type "No. 23" developed by V.

---

[6] G. E. Harmssen, *Am Abend der Demontage; Sechs Jahre Reparationspolitik* (Bremen: F. Trüjen, 1951), p. 105.

[7] CIOS no. XXVII-23, *Optical Grinding and Centering Equipment Used by Karl Zeiss, Jena, 1946.*

[8] *Machine Tools*, (Washington: U.S. Foreign Economic Administration, Interagency Committee on German Industrial and Economic Disarmament, July 1945), p. 48.

[9] Werner Keller, *Ost Minus West=Null* (Munich: Droemersche Verlagsanstatt, 1960), pp. 283, 357, 365.

[10] Harmssen, *op. cit.* n. 6, p. 105.

[11] Amtorg, *Economic Review of the Soviet Union*, V, 1 (January 1, 1930), 10.

[12] *Kommunist* (Yerevan), November 3, 1965, p. 1.

[13] U.S. Senate, *Soviet Space Programs, 1962-65; Goals and Purposes, Achievements, Plans, and International Implications*, Staff Report, Committee on Aeronautical and Space Sciences, 89th Congress, 2d session (Washington: U.S. Government Printing Office, 1966), p. 351.

Ye. Tishchenko in 1899 and used continuously from 1900 to the present day. Although having certain disadvantages as well as advantages over standard foreign laboratory glasses (Jena 1920 and Pyrex), its chemical endurance is such as to merit its continued use. After 1930 manufacture of four other types was added to No.23; these types were Pyrex, No.846, Neutral, and Improved White.[14] These five varieties provided enough flexibility for laboratory requirements until the 1950s, when a few additional standard types were manufactured; however, the varieties manufactured in 1968 mainly consist of the old, established types including the original No. 23, Jena 20 (German), and Pyrex and Superpyrex (U.S.), plus imported glass from Czechoslovakia (Simax, Sial, Neutral, and Palex).[15]

In 1963 a British research delegation that was able to visit the three-year-old Glass Research Institute in Moscow particularly noted one laboratory that "carries out pilot plant work on glass manufacture on a scale that is equaled by only two or three laboratories in the whole of the Western world." This laboratory contained four small glass-melting tanks, but the major equipment was a large furnace capable of melting 70 tons of glass per day for a new experimental centrifugal spinner for the production of cone or back section of a cathode-ray tube for television receivers. The delegation concluded that this machine had many novel features and "seems to be an advance on other machines of this type in use in the Western world;"[16] apparently, however, it never reached development stage.

Manufacture of window glass, the largest tonnage glass product, exemplifies the present pervasive utilization of Western technology. The Fourcault process, imported in the U.S.S.R. in the 1920s soon after it was developed in Belgium, is the basis for standard Soviet glassmaking equipment. In this process the glass is drawn vertically in a continuous manner through a partially submerged "boat" with a narrow slot in the center over asbestos-covered rolls. The Soviet VVS machine is a replica of the Fourcault process (Figures 14-1 and 14-2), even utilizing direct translations of the integral parts of the process—for example, the "boat" is termed *lodochka* (a literal translation). Although the Colburn glassmaking process is known and described in Soviet texts,[17] it is not known whether the process has been utilized in practice.[18]

---

[14]   *The Glass Industry* (New York), XXVI, 5 (May 1945), 228.

[15]   *Spravochnik khimika* (Moscow) vol.V, 1968, pp. 333-34.

[16]   *Visit to Glass Research Institute Moscow on 12th October, 1963,* Report by Confederation of British Industry, London, appendix E4. Unfortunately, no further trace of this machine has been found in the literature. See chapter 23 for technical assistance to the television industry; in 1967 the Soviets bought from France a pilot plant for manufacture of television tubes; *The Times* (London), February 1, 1967. Several months later Corning Glass in New York was reportedly negotiating for supply of glass, on which it holds patents, for color TV tubes to be used in this system; *Wall Street Journal,* May 23, 1967, 10:3.

[17]   For example, I. I. Kitaigorodskii, *Tekhnologiia stekla* (Moscow, 1967), p. 336.

[18]   This text also describes Soviet utilization of other Western glassmaking processes—for example, the Danner tube-making principle; *ibid.,* p. 418.

Figure 14-1 THE FOURCAULT PROCESS FOR SHEET GLASS MANUFACTURE

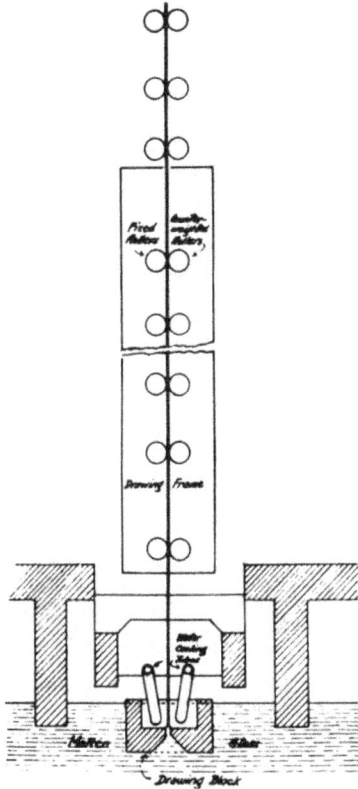

Source: Glass Industry, August 1928, p. 175.

In early 1967 the Soviet Union concluded a licensing agreement with Pilkington Brothers, Ltd., of Lancashire, England, to produce float glass in the Soviet Union. This is a new and revolutionary method of producing flat glass with a surface that does not need grinding after solidifying. By floating molten glass on a bed of liquid tin and making use of the solidification at different temperatures there is no requirement for rollers (as in the Fourcault process), which create imperfections requiring grinding. The agreement included supply of equipment by the Pilkington firm to a value of $4.2 million, sufficient to equip a plant to produce 50 million square feet of flat glass per year.[19]

---

[19] *Wall Street Journal*, March 30, 1967, 16:3.

Figure 14-2   SOVIET VVS MACHINE FOR SHEET GLASS MANUFACTURE

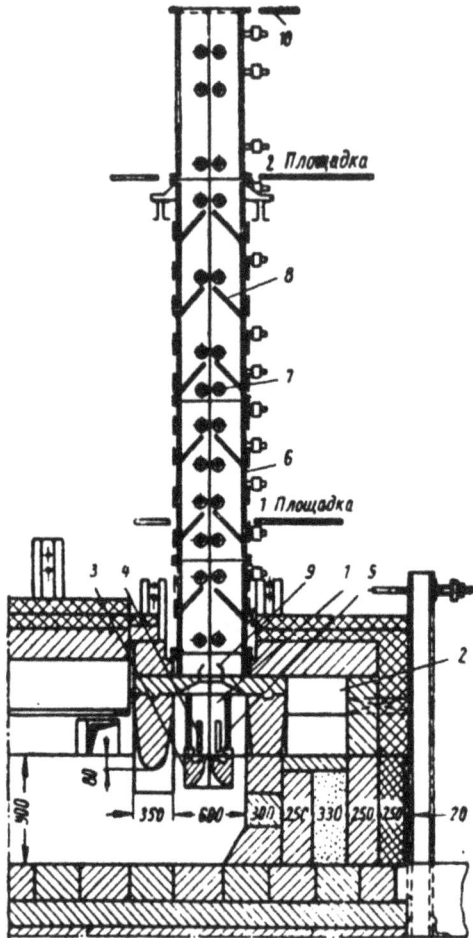

Source: I. I. Kitaigorodskii, *Tekhnologiia stekla* (Moscow, 1967), p. 319.

WESTERN ASSISTANCE TO THE CEMENT INDUSTRY

By and large the Soviets did not attempt to transport cement kilns to the Soviet Union under reparations, except for removals from Manchuria. (See Table 14-1.) The reduction in Manchurian cement capacity due to Soviet removals was approximately 890,000 metric tons with a replacement value of $17.8 million.

Table 14-1   MANCHURIAN CEMENT PLANTS REMOVED TO THE U.S.S.R.

Name	Soviet removal or destruction	Metric tons capacity	Notes
Harbin	none	110,000	Chicom territory
Mutanchiang	large	100,000	Chicom territory; Soviets removed equipment
Changtu	large	140,000	Chicom territory; Soviets removed equipment
Anshan	small	200,000	Some repairs needed
Miaoling	large	90,000	Equipment removed by Soviet Army
Dairen	none	210,000	Under Soviet control
Kirin	large	260,000	Soviet Army removed almost all equipment
Chinhsi	small	150,000	50,000 metric tons capacity remaining
Fushun	small	210,000	80,000 metric tons capacity remaining
Liaoyang	small	180,000	90,000 metric tons capacity remaining
Penchihu	small	250,000	100,000 metric tons capacity remaining
Kungyuan	large	170,000	Soviets removed all equipment
Antung	large	130,000	Chicom territory; Soviets removed all equipment
Total		2,200,000 metric tons	

Source: Edwin W. Pauley, *Report on Japanese Assets in Manchuria to the President of the United States, July 1946* (Washington, 1946).

The Pauley Mission commented on the removals from six plants in the Fall of 1945 as follows:

> The six plants which suffered major removals by the Soviets were the most recently constructed and equipped with the newest machinery. The equipment which seemed to be particularly desired was the crushing, grinding, and pulverizing equipment, electric motors, generators, laboratory and testing equipment, and inter-plant haulage equipment. In one plant (Kirin) an attempt was made to cut the rotary kilns into sections and remove them. Fabricated fixtures were not ordinarily removed but they were usually badly damaged. Severe and wholly unnecessary damage to auxiliary equipment and buildings was characteristic of almost all stripped plants inspected by the Pauley Mission. There was a general appearance of complete devastation, probably due to the haste with which the Soviets were compelled to operate.... The nature of the removals has been such that restoration to former capacity of the plants affected will require almost complete rebuilding of the entire facilities.[20]

[20] Edwin W. Pauley, *Report on Japanese Assets in Manchuria to the President of the United States, July 1946* (Washington, 1946), pp. 217-18.

Equipment removals varied greatly and, as Table 14-1 reveals, extended even to plants under Chinese Communist control. At Fushun, Soviet removals were limited to office supplies and equipment, testing equipment, automotive vehicles, a considerable number of cement bags, and some cement; similarly, at the Anshan plant only some equipment was removed. At Kungyuan, however, a complete removal job was undertaken; railroad tracks were laid into the center of the 170,000-metric-ton capacity cement plant to facilitate loading of equipment onto rail cars, and parts of the buildings were destroyed to remove machinery. This was a portland cement plant with a typical dry process; the American engineer (N.M. Taylor) who inspected the plant for the Pauley Mission reported that the rock crushers, belt conveyers, and overhead cranes were removed completely; the drive mechanism from two 70-meter kilns was removed, as was the drive mechanism from five (of eight) ball-reduction mills. The coal pulverization plant, four bagging machines, and the steam turbine generator were also removed.

At Penchihu only the steam turbine generators and about one quarter of the electrical control equipment were removed; while equipment at the Kirin plant, a 220,000-ton-per-year portland cement producer, was almost completely removed, including a gyratory crusher, two hammer crushers, three material dryers, five clinker mills, three cold dryers, one coal mill, two rotary kilns (only the blowers were taken, the kilns were not removed), two waste heat boilers, two turbogenerators, 38 transformers, 107 electric motors, and 18 machine tools.

Of a total of 2.2 million tons capacity affected by Soviet removals, about 890,000 tons was completely removed to the U.S.S.R.; the balance suffered selective equipment removals.

In East Germany only one cement plant was removed—Zementwerk at Niedersachswerfen.[21] The great prize in Germany was the Magdeburg works of Krupp-Gruson A.G., before the war one of the world's leading manufacturers of heavy machinery and structural steel fabrication; its principal products included heavy machinery for crushing and grinding and complete cement manufacturing plants. According to the U.S. Strategic Bombing Survey, only about 10 percent of the equipment in this plant was destroyed and another 10 percent damaged.[22] Consequently, the Soviets received an advanced and almost complete plant for production of complete cement plants. The immediate task of the plant was to provide a cement-making capacity of six million metric tons per year for the Soviet Union.

Although the Soviets have standardized domestic production of cement plants they have continued to buy advanced technology on the world market. In 1959–60

---

[21]   Harmssen, *op. cit.* n. 6, p. 107.
[22]   U.S. Strategic Bombing Survey, *Friedrich Krupp Grusonwerke, Magdeburg, Germany*, January 1947.

the largest cement plant in the world was built in Siberia by the French company Société Fives-Lille-Cail of Paris. The company provided a complete cement manufacturing installation including two 19-by-575-foot kilns. Construction of the plant was supervised by French engineers with startup and performance tests conducted by the Fives-Lille-Cail company. The production capacity is 33,000 barrels of Type I portland cement per day from an unusual mixture of limestone and nepheline residues. The technology in this plant was certainly the most advanced in the world at the time the plant was built. For example, the grinding department, the largest in the world, produced two grades of portland cement in mills 10 feet 5 inches in diameter and 46 feet long, each unit weighing 260 tons, loaded with upwards of 170 tons of grinding media and designed to run at 19 rpm through 2500-hp helical reducers. The storage and bagging facilities reflected the plant's size and included 20 silos with a total storage capacity of 80,000 tons, i.e., 16 days kiln production.[23]

In general, a large number of Soviet cement kilns have been manufactured abroad, although there is domestic production of standard designs.[24] The extent of internal use of foreign designs may be broadly gauged from a report of the French cement industry delegation to the U.S.S.R. in 1960.[25]

The description of cement plants visited by that delegation suggests they contain a considerable quantity of Western-manufactured equipment and Western equipment copied in the Soviet Union. It was reported that the Vorovskoi plant, built in 1911 and modernized in 1930 and 1945, with a current production of 325,000 tons, uses four Smidth (Copenhagen) furnaces; the crusher equipment was Krupp and Smidth with one crusher from the "Urals plant" (probably Uralmash).

At the Sebriakov plant near Stalingrad, with its annual production of one million tons of cement considered one of the most modern plants in the Soviet Union, it was noted that the crushing plant used 12 Wilfley-type pumps, with furnaces by Tellman in East Germany; the power station equipment was from Tempella in West Germany, and three turbo-alternators came from Skoda in Czechoslovakia. The crushing equipment was built in the Urals.

At the Novorossisk plant, founded in 1880 and expanded over the years, the delegation noted a considerable quantity of equipment of Western origin. The Novorossisk combinat comprises four plants: the October, with a capacity of one million tons per year; the Proletariat, with a capacity of 1,150,000 tons per year; the October Victory, with a capacity of 300,000 tons; and the First of May, also with a capacity of 350,000 tons. The Proletariat plant was not visited by the delegation, but it reported concentrators with Smidth Folax

[23] *Rock Products* (Louisville. Ky.). May 1959, pp. 128-31. See also E. I. Khodorov, *Pechi tsementnoi promyshlennosti* (Leningrad, 1968), p. 90.

[24] E. I. Khodorov, *op. cit.* n. 23, pp. 82-83.

[25] *L'Industrie cimentière en U.R.S.S.*, Compte rendu de mission 9-28 avril 1960 (Paris, 1960).

equipment. The October Victory plant was not visited. Equipment at the October was reported to be five Krupp crushers, five crushers manufactured in the Urals, and five Dorr-type silos of 500 cubic meters; the furnaces were identified as Tellman (Magdeburg). The First of May plant had four Lepol-type firing units, two standard Polysius (East Germany) granulators, and one large Polysius granulator; the plant uses a dry process of the Lepol type with equipment furnished by Polysius at Dessau and Magdeburg; the bagging machinery is from Smidth.

In the Soviet glass industry, the large-tonnage window glass sector is based on the Belgian Fourcault process with recent addition, with British equipment and technical assistance, of a Pilkington Brothers, Ltd., float glass unit. Glass tubing manufacture uses the Danner process, and laboratory glass production appears to consist of a limited range of types including a number of U.S. and Czechoslovakian glasses, and, notably, the Russian No.23 Tishchenko formula developed in 1899. Optical glassmaking is technically backward.

The cement industry utilizes a significant proportion of foreign equipment. The most advanced mills (for example, in Siberia and Sebriakov) utilize extensive foreign equipment in the kiln and crusher sections. Soviet domestic production of cement plants is of the standard type with no observable departures from world practice.

CHAPTER FIFTEEN

Western Technical Assistance to the Textile, Synthetic Fiber, and Pulp and Paper Industries

TEXTILES AND CHEMICAL FIBERS

Western assistance to the textile industry in the 1920s has been described in the first volume of this series.[1] In addition to the technical assistance in the period 1929-1931 provided by Lockwood Greene, a U.S. firm, and French technical assistance for the manufacture of viscose, there was a large supply of U.S., British, and German machinery for textile plants. The Kirovsky combine received textile equipment from the United States valued at $800,000 in 1930,[2] the Krasnaya Shelk textile plant received U.S. equipment in 1928,[3] and the large textile combine at Ivanovo-Voznesensk received 100,000 spindles, mostly from the U.K. firm of Tweedales and Smalley of Manchester, with warping machines from Schlafhorst of München Gladbach in Germany.[4] The Schlafhorst company also supplied warping machines for the Shuya Melange textile mill in 1932.

Some textile mills were also directed by foreign engineers. For example, in 1930 Samuel Fox was hired as a mechanic at $510.00 per month with a group of other American mechanics and sent to Baku to erect and start operation of a textile plant equipped with machinery from the United States. Fox directed the installation of equipment and later became director of the mill.[5]

Textile plants from East Germany were removed to the Soviet Union in 1945-46. Two large artificial silk spinning operations in Saxony (the Pirna and Sehma plants of Fr. Küttner A.G.) were completely removed to the U.S.S.R.,[6] and two Brandenburg units, the Premnitz plant of Agea and the Kurmärkische Zellwoll-AG plant at Wittenberge, both artificial silk producers, were removed, the former about 50 percent and the latter about 80 percent. Regular spinning mills appear to have been only partly dismantled; eight plants

---

[1] See Sutton I, pp. 231-33.
[2] Amtorg, *Economic Review of the Soviet Union* (New York, II, 11 (June 1, 1930), 224.
[3] *Ibid.*, V, 16-17 (September 1, 1930), 351.
[4] U.S. State Dept. Decimal File 861.5017/1c/684.
[5] U.S. State Dept. Decimal File 861.5017/Living Conditions/144, March 25, 1930.
[6] All data in this section from G. E. Harmssen, *Am Abend der Demontage: Sechs Jahre Reparationspolitik* (Bremen: F. Trüjen, 1951), p. 109.

in Saxony, three in Thuringia, and one in Mecklenburg were partly removed to the U.S.S.R. Of the nine weaving mills removed from Saxony, only one, the Mechanische Weberei at Grimma, was completely removed. Similarly, only six finishing operations were affected by dismantling—none was reported completely removed.

In 1954 an upgrading process began, and a large contract was granted Platt Brothers of the United Kingdom for the supply of $19.6 million worth of machinery to equip plants in the cotton, worsted, spinning, weaving, and finishing sections of the industry; numerous textile machine firms in Yorkshire and Lancashire participated in supply.[7] In 1958-59 Courtaulds, Ltd., supplied machinery and technical assistance for several rayon and cellulose acetate plants;[8] Fawcett Preston & Company of Bromborough, Cheshire, secured an order for nine pulp-steeping presses and two fiber-baling presses to be incorporated in this rayon plant;[9] and Kestner Evaporator & Engineering Company, Ltd., supplied Keebush equipment to Courtaulds for installation in the plants.[10]

In 1959 a plant for the production of rayon was supplied by Vickers-Armstrongs (Engineers), Ltd., and Highpolymer and Petrochemical Engineering Company, Ltd., for a total value of $7 million,[11] with $1 million worth of instrumentation supplied by Honeywell Controls, Ltd., a subsidiary of the U.S. firm.[12] A few years later, in 1966, Bentley Engineering Group (a subsidiary of Sears Holdings, Ltd.) received an order valued at $14 million for knitting machinery to equip two new knitting mills.[13]

Italian companies also have been prominent suppliers of textile machinery since World War II. In 1959 Châtillon supplied equipment for a high-tensile-strength cord fiber plant.[14] Further textile mill equipment was supplied under a contract with Sniaviscosa,[15] and in 1967 a contract was awarded the Sant'Andrea company of the Bombrini Parodi Delfino group and the Nuova San Giorgio firm of the IRI Finmeccanica group for machinery to equip a 50,000-spindle mill for the production of mixed woolen and synthetic yarns.[16]

A/B Karlstads Mekaniska Werkstad of Sweden received an order in 1959 for the "design and complete installation and equipment for a viscose rayon factory" (annual capacity of 200,000 tons of prehydraulized sulfate viscose rayon), and machinery was supplied by several Swedish factories.[17]

In 1958 a significant international arrangement to supply three synthetic

[7] New York Times, May 20, 1954, 3:6.
[8] Chemistry and Industry (London), August 2, 1958.
[9] East-West Commerce (London), VI, 12 (December 8, 1959), 6.
[10] Chemistry and Industry, December 2, 1961, p. 1968.
[11] Chemistry and Industry, May 9, 1959, p. 609.
[12] Electrical Review (London), 167 (August 1960), 308.
[13] Wall Street Journal, August 19, 1966, 11:6.
[14] Problems of Economics (New York), III, 4 (August 1960), 23.
[15] Ibid.
[16] Communication from Italian Embassy, Washington D.C.
[17] East-West Commerce, VI, 9, (September 28, 1959), 4.

fiber (probably rayon) plants to the U.S.S.R. was headed by Von Kohorn International Corporation of New York. Under this arrangement equipment was supplied by the U.K. firms of Baker Perkins and the A.P.V. Company, while Von Kohorn was "responsible for technical advice connected with the engineering and machinery part of the contract."[18]

Over $30 million worth of machinery was acquired in the United States in 1960 from a consortium of 40 U.S. textile equipment manufacturers. This, the largest single order received from the U.S.S.R. since the end of World War II, provided equipment for a 50,000-spindle mill at Kalinin, to spin, weave, and finish cotton, worsted, and man-made-fiber fabrics. This order was in addition to $6-7 million worth of similar equipment previously shipped by Intertex Corporation, a trading firm representing the 40 U.S. textile machinery manufacturers. Of the total $30 million, $20 million was paid in cash.[19]

Some of the principal equipment—to give an idea of the magnitude of the arrangements—included the following[20]:

Crompton & Knowles	630 type W-3 looms
Saco-Lowell	VersaMatic drawing frames
	S.J. spinning frames (MagneDraft)
	Saco-Lowell worsted frames
Whiting Machine Works	20,000 American system worsted spindles
Rodney Hunt	One continuous peroxide bleaching range

The 1962 report of an Indian textile delegation[21] covered nine of the larger textile mills with spinning departments. These were reported as old installations—"some of them 150 years and a few about 30 years old." They clearly represented the two eras of textile mill construction, the first under the Tsars and the second in the late 1920s and early 1930s by British and German companies. This imported equipment was supplemented by domestic duplicates of foreign equipment; neither the Indian nor the U.S. delegation noted indigenous innovation.

Duplication of Western Textile Equipment

In the late 1920s the Soviets started to copy Western textile equipment, and by 1928 the Shunsk mechanical plant at Ivanovo-Voznesensk produced its one thousandth automatic loom of the "Northrup type."[22]

---

18 *Chemistry and Industry*, June 21, 1958, p. 763.
19 *American Machinist* (New York), January 11, 1960, p. 84.
20 *Textile World* (New York), February 1960, p. 4.
21 *Textile Industry in the U.S.S.R. and Czechoslovakia* (New Delhi: National Productivity Council, November 1962), Report no. 19.
22 Amtorg, *Economic Review of the Soviet Union*, III, 9 (April 15, 1928), 161.

In 1958 the U.S. Cotton Delegation visited the Tashkent textile machine construction plant, perhaps the largest manufacturer of roving frames, spinning frames, and twisters in the U.S.S.R. After noting that in the machine shop "there were many U.S.-made lathes and shapers in operation," the delegation reported that the plant expected to go into production of a "new apron-type long draft roving ... an improved Platt design which the staff had modified."[23]

The Indian delegation[24] noted that the blowroom lines in all Russian mills had the following equipment: porcupine opener, Crighton opener, double porcupine opener, and Scutchner with Kirschner beater. Carding machines were of the "ordinary" type with one mill using "Shirley type of cards." The only nonconventional (i.e., non-Western) equipment noted was used in the grinding of flats: "Flats are ground once in three months on Russian-made single flat-grinding machines. Their flat grinder is different in design and manufacture from the types common in our country."

In the drawing process "there was nothing particularly striking" and the mills used the "conventional" process, except that one mill used Saco-Lowell combers with heavy laps. Russian ring frames were "ordinary and conventional models"[25] with conversion to the Blaus-Roth type. In doubling, the Roto-Coner type machine was "generally used," and for multiple and winding a "similar type of English and Japanese double diner is used."[26]

In 1947 a shuttleless loom similar to the shuttleless loom weaving machine produced by Sulzer of Winterthur, Switzerland, was developed by Leonytev of the Moscow Textile Institute.[27] The U.S. delegation also noted winders of the Leesonia type[28] and "imperfect copies" of the Franklin Process package dyeing equipment.[29]

WESTERN DEVELOPMENT OF SOVIET SYNTHETIC FIBER CAPACITY

Soviet production of synthetic fibers is well behind that of the Western world. In 1965, of a total production of 407,300 metric tons of chemical and synthetic fibers, only 77,900 tons was synthetics; the bulk of the Soviet production

[23] U.S. Dept. of Agriculture, *Cotton in the Soviet Union*, Report of a Technical Study Group, Foreign Agricultural Service (Washington: U.S.G.P.O., June 1959), p. 5.

[24] *Ibid.*

[25] *Ibid.*, p. 58.

[26] *Ibid.*, p. 59.

[27] *Encyclopedia of Textiles* (Englewood Cliffs, N.J.: Prentice-Hall, 1960), p. 242.

[28] U.S. Dept. of Agriculture, *op. cit.* n. 23, p. 6. See Russian literature for more detail; for example see A. M. Liberman, *Organizatsiia i planirovanie predpriiatii tekstil'noi promyshlennosti* (Moscow, 1969), p. 167, for manufacture of Barber-Coleman winders.

[29] U.S. Dept. of Agriculture, *op. cit.* n. 23, p. 10.

was viscose fiber, which accounted for just under 75 percent of all chemical and synthetic fiber production in 1965.[30]

Although no breakdown by type of synthetic fiber has been traced in Soviet literature, it is estimated that the Soviets produced the following quantities of synthetic fibers in 1965:

Nylon	65,575 metric tons
Polyester	7,331
Acrylics	2,851
Polyvinyl chloride	1,629

77,386 metric tons

This is a significant increase from the approximately 13,500 tons produced in 1956 (all Nylon 6), but still far below the U.S. production totals. In 1954, for example, the United States produced over 132,000 tons of synthetic fibers, just under twice the Soviet 1965 production.

Most Western observers comment on the extensive and potentially valuable research on synthetic fibers undertaken in the U.S.S.R. Writing in 1960, I.V. Maistrenko of the Institute for the Study of the U.S.S.R.,[32] described the work of VNIIV (All-Union Artificial Fiber Research Institute) while pointing out Soviet weaknesses in the engineering aspects of synthetic fiber production. E. M. Buras, Jr., in a detailed two-part summary of Soviet synthetic fibers in 1961, concluded that "if its fiber industry lags in growth, the cause will not be any lack of research and development capacity."[33]

In 1960 the Soviets were publishing papers on synthetics at the same rate as U.S. authors; Buras points out that "if we were to list references on synthetic fiber research, about 400 authors in all would have to be cited."[34] This activity was accompanied by cooperation with Czechoslovakia on 81 projects at 112 laboratories in the U.S.S.R. and Czechoslovakia. Further, Buras has outlined areas of research which the U.S. had hardly investigated and where the Soviets were deeply involved—particularly "elementorganic" polymers with possible military applications.[35]

---

[30] The Soviets have not always distinguished between synthetics and chemical fibers; a distinction has been maintained where possible throughout this section.

[31] These figures were calculated as follows (the Soviets have not published production figures for each synthetic): total for all "chemical" fibers (including synthetics) is given in *Narodnoe khoziaistvo SSSR, v 1968g.: Statisticheskii ezhegodnik* (Moscow, 1969), p. 253; the percentage of each type is given in *50 [Piat'desiat] let sovetskaya khimicheskaya nauka i promyshlennost'* (Moscow, 1967), p. 366.

[32] *Industrial and Engineering Chemistry* (Washington, D.C.), February 1960, pp. 44A-48A.

[33] *Chemical and Engineering News*, July 31, 1961, p. 134.

[34] *Ibid.*, August 7, 1961, p. 83.

[35] *Ibid.*

Finally, a report by two U.S. Army research scientists[36] concluded that by the end of the 1950s the Soviets had made independent advances in synthetic fibers; indeed, they had produced three synthetics with no counterpart in the West, and were cooperating with satellite countries in this research. Much Soviet research was being directed to military applications of fibers, and the authors point out:

> A possible threat from Soviet textile research lies, not in the development of slightly improved counterparts of nylon, Orlon, etc., but in the possibility of a real breakthrough emanating from extensive work in this field of new and unusual fibers.[37]

Three new research achievements reportedly were "Enant," a Nylon 7 represented as a new fiber made from cheap raw materials; "Ftorlon," a process which was said to have better mechanical properties than the Western "Teflon"; and "Vinitron," which was described simply as a "superior" product.[38]

Yet despite this obviously ambitious and viable research program, we find that all Soviet large-scale production facilities for synthetics have derived in greater or lesser degree from the West.[39]

Origins of Nylon 6 (Kapron) and Nylon 66 (Anid) Technology

The synthetic fiber nylon, made from benzene, hydrogen, and oxygen with no vegetable or animal fibers, originated with basic work in the 1920s at Dupont in the United States. Nylon 6 was developed and patented by Paul Schlack in Germany[40] and is known in Germany as "Perlon," while Nylon 66 was selected from among many possible nylons and established on a commercial scale in the United States in 1938; this nylon requires commercial quantities of two intermediates, hexamethylene diamine and adipic acid, the latter—as we shall see later—proving a problem for the Soviets.

Although considerable progress was made in the United States before World War II and in Germany during the war, the Soviet Union had no capacity for producing synthetic fibers (i.e., completely man-made fibers) at the end of World War II. The first Soviet synthetic fiber plant was brought into production

---

[36] R. C. Laible and L. I. Weiner, "Russian and Satellite Research and Development in the Field of Synthetic Fibers," *Textile Research Journal* (New York), 30, 4 (April 1960).

[37] *Ibid.*, p. 247.

[38] *Ibid.*

[39] This contrast has been noted in Western trade journals. For example, an editorial entitled "The Soviet Puzzle," *Skinners Silk and Rayon Record* (London), 37, 7 (July 1962), asks, "But why is there apparently such a gap between research and commercial development?"

[40] U.S. Patent No. 2,242,321 of May 6, 1941 (assigned to I. G. Farbenindustrie A. G.). The Soviets make a claim for Nylon 6 (Kapron) as a Soviet development in 1944; see *Bol'shaia Sovetskaia Entsiklopediia*, 2d edition (Moscow, 1949), vol. 9, p. 14.

at Klin in 1948[41] for the production of Kapron, i.e., Nylon 6. Large-scale production of Perlon (also Nylon 6) started in Poland at Landsberg (Gorzow) in 1941 with an annual production of 8.7 million pounds of Nylon 6 and one million pounds of Nylon 66.[42] This plant was owned by I. G. Farben, assignee of the Schlack patents, and used intermediates from the Leuna works. According to A. Zauberman,[43] the Landsberg plant was dismantled and shipped to the U.S.S.R. in 1944; it is probable that the first Soviet Kapron (i.e., Perlon or Nylon 6) plant at Klin was the rebuilt Landsberg plant. In fact, the Soviets may have acquired more than the Landsberg plant. For example, one excellent source comments:

> Much of the work on the production and spinning of synthetic polymers was done in Eastern Germany, in works which were either not seen at all or which could be only very superficially examined before they were taken over by the Russian forces. This may explain the scantiness of the available information about the spinning of polyurethane fibres ... vinylidene chloride copolymers ... [and] acrylonitrile polymers.[44]

Two other plants at Kiev and Riga (in former Latvia), both producing Kapron, were brought into production in the 1950s, and in 1956 Soviet production of Nylon 6 was 25 million pounds—which may be compared with U.S. production of 265 million pounds of all synthetic fibers in 1954. In 1960 Nylon 6 was the only synthetic fiber in full-scale production in the Soviet Union.

During the 1950s and 1960s a number of plants were built using the Schlack process of melt spinning and cold drawing the fiber from the condensation polymer of ε-caprolactum; these included Chernigov in the Ukraine, Mogilev in Soviet Armenia, the Engel plant in Saratov, Darnitsa in Kiev, and the Kalinin plant.

Kapron production was stressed over other synthetics for two reasons, according to A. L. Borisov:[45] first, there was an improvement in caprolactum production (the raw material for nylon), and second, the Kapron plants required relatively lower capital investment. In the fifties there was criticism in the technical literature concerning the substandard caprolactum supplied by Soviet plants; this quality problem was overcome by the supply of equipment from Germany for two

[41] E. P. Ivanova, *Ekonomika promyshlennosti khimicheskikh volokon* (Moscow, 1968), p. 30. The Soviets include synthetics within the "chemical fiber group"; the statistics in Ivanova are far more detailed for the United States and Europe than for the U.S.S.R., for which data are expressed as percentages computed from an undisclosed base.

[42] *Encyclopedia of Chemical Technology*, 2d edition (New York: John Wiley, 1963), vol. 16, p. 47.

[43] A. Zauberman, *Industrial Progress in Poland, Czechoslovakia, and East Germany, 1937-1962* (New York: Oxford University Press, 1964), p. 267.

[44] A. R. Urquhart, *The German Rayon Industry During the Period 1939-1945* (London, 1952). BIOS Subcommittee Survey Report no. 33, pp. 25-26.

[45] Soviet State Committee on Chemistry, quoted in *Chemical and Engineering News*, July 21, 1961, p. 131.

10,000-ton-per-year caprolactum (from aniline) plants, a caprolactum distillation plant, two caprolactum continuous polymerization plants, and a 10,000-ton adiponitrile-hexamethyl-enediamine plant.[46] This equipment—the core of the caprolactum manufacturing process—was installed at Soviet plants at Kirovakan (for the Kapron plant at Razdan), the Gubakha plant, and the Lisichansk plant in Kiev.

Continuing Soviet technical problems with the production of caprolactum were again eased in 1964 by the purchase of two caprolactum plants from a British-Dutch consortium. Two Japanese firms, Ube Industries, Ltd., and the Nissho Trading Company, were also competing for an order finally awarded by Tekhmashimport to a group including Simon-Carves of the United Kingdom and the Dutch State Mines for a bid of $25 million. Capacity of the caprolactum plants was 50,000 tons each per year.[47]

Therefore it may be seen that the enormous increase in Nylon 6 (Kapron) production in the U.S.S.R. has been dependent on supply from West Germany and the United Kingdom of key equipment and technical assistance for the manufacture of its essential raw material caprolactum.

Little practical success has been achieved in producing other nylons, although much research has been undertaken. Pilot plant production of Anid (Nylon 66) as made by Dupont and British Nylon Spinners was started in 1956 and small-scale production started at Kursk after Krupp installed German nylon spinning equipment. Part of the problem encountered in this production appears to have been a shortage of adipic acid; this lack was only partly offset by blending the available supply of hexamethylene adipamide salt with caprolactum (from the German and British plants) and hexamethylene azelaamide to form a mixed-fiber Anid G-669 and H-669. Another fiber, Enant (or Nylon 7), has been produced in small quantities only.

Other synthetic fibers produced in commercial quantities are Lavsan, Nitron, and Kanekalon.

Krupp Construction of the Stalinogorsk-Kursk Lavsan Complex

Between 1958 and 1961, under a $14 million contract, Krupp of West Germany built a polyester fiber (polyethylene terephthalate) complex of three plants in the Soviet Union.[48] The fiber produced by this complex is known in the U.S.S.R. as Lavsan. Its patents are held by Imperial Chemical Industries, and it is known as Terylene in the United Kingdom and Dacron in the United

---

[46] *Ibid.*

[47] *New York Times,* September 13, 1964. In 1967 it was reported that the Soviets were seeking six additional caprolactum plants in Germany; *Wall Street Journal,* April 14, 1967, 4:4.

[48] *East-West Commerce,* V. 6 (June 16, 1958), 3; *Chemical and Engineering News,* July 31, 1961, p. 132. It was reported in 1967 that the Soviets were purchasing six polyester plants, with total capacity of 60,000 tons per year, in Czechoslovakia; *Wall Street Journal,* April 14, 1967, 4:4.

States. The first unit built by Krupp was at Novo Kuibyshev to convert petroleum stock into *p*-xylol, which is shipped to a second Krupp-built plant at Stalinogorsk for conversion into dimethyl terephthalate. This stock in turn is shipped to the third Krupp-built plant at Kursk, where the raw material is spun into Lavsan polyester fiber. The project has capacity to produce six million pounds of Lavsan annually.[49]

Polyspinners, Ltd., Construction of the Siberian Lavsan Plant

Imperial Chemical Industries, in a continuing association going back into the 1930s, has made available to the Soviet Union polyethylene manufacturing technology and information on manufacture of polyester fibers and petrochemicals.[50] In May 1964 the company headed a consortium known as Polyspinners, Ltd., which signed a contract worth $140 million—probably the largest British contract with the U.S.S.R. since the Bolshevik Revolution and itself part of a larger agreement. The Polyspinners consortium was required to build a combine in Siberia for the production of a polyester fiber developed from terephthalic acid and ethylene glycol, i.e., Terylene or Dacron. The contract was guaranteed by the British Government under its Export Credit Guarantee Program, and bank credit provided for a 12- to 15-year loan to assist the Soviets in paying for the complex. Utilizing British engineers as supervisors, the combine was built at Irkutsk in Siberia with Russian operating engineers trained at ICI plants in the United Kingdom.[51] The chief construction companies were John Brown & Company, Ltd., of Scotland and Stone Platt of England; numerous other British companies made up the consortium, some of which were the following:[52]

Baker Perkins Chemical Machinery, Ltd.	Loadcell weighing equipment
Gardners (Gloucester)	Large drum blenders
Sigmund Pulsometer Pumps	Pumps
Sharples (Camberley)	Centrifuges
Hydrotherm Engineering, Ltd.	High-temperature heating systems
W. P. Butterfield, Ltd. (Engineering)	Stainless and mild-steel pressure vessels
Lawrence Scott and Electro-motors	Electrical machines and control gear
Aiton & Co., Ltd.	Agitators
Gibbons Bros., Ltd.	Shell and tube-heat exchangers
English Electric Co.	Electric motors and switchgear
Dunford & Elliott Process Engineering, Ltd.	Rotary louvre pryers
Petrocarbon Developments	High-purity nitrogen plant

[49] *Chemical and Engineering News*, July 31, 1961.
[50] *Ibid.*
[51] *New York Times*, May 17, 1964.
[52] P. Zentner, *East-West Trade: A Practical Guide to Selling in Eastern Europe* (London: Max Parrish, 1967), p. 78.

Purchase of Japanese Kanekalon and Acrylonitrile Plants

The Soviet-Japanese trade agreement of March 1959 included provision for Soviet purchase of technology and a production plant for Kanekalon, a Japanese-developed synthetic fiber based on acryl and blended with 60 percent polyvinyl acetate and 40 percent acrylonitrile. For a total purchase price of $30 million the Soviets received patent rights, engineering data, and plant equipment to produce 30 tons of Kanekalon and 15 tons of acrylonitrile daily. This amount was apportioned three-quarters to the Kanekalon and one-quarter to the acrylonitrile, the former being supplied by Kanegafuchi Chemical Company and the latter by Toyo Koatsu Industries. Machinery came from several Japanese companies: filament spinning equipment from Kawasaki Aircraft; instrumentation from Yokogawa Electric; and electric motors from Tachikawa and Toshiba. It is notable that the capacity of the plant was large by Japanese standards; payment terms provided for 20 percent down and the balance over five years.[53] The agreement included the necessary training of Russian engineers and technicians in Japan.[54]

Several years later, in 1965, it was reported that the Asahi Chemical Company in Tokyo had sold the Soviets "the world's largest acrylonitrile monomer manufacturing plant," at a cost of $25 million.[55]

The other half of the Soviet acrylic fiber capacity has come from Courtaulds, Ltd., in the United Kingdom. In April 1959 Courtaulds concluded a $28 million contract for the construction of a complete acrylic fiber plant and related supply of process technology and technical assistance. This single plant doubled Soviet 1960 acrylic fiber production.[56]

WESTERN ASSISTANCE TO THE PULP AND PAPER INDUSTRY

In 1930 the Soviet Union had a shortage of paper and wood pulp and both were imported in substantial quantities; pulp and papermaking machinery was not produced in the Soviet Union until after 1932.[57] The large pulp and paper plants built in the Soviet Union before 1930 were with complete American equipment and technical assistance. The Balakhna plant, with a capacity of 88,200 tons of pulp and 145,000 tons of paper including 133,000 tons of newsprint, started operation in 1928; a second section was activated in 1930. All equipment—General Electric control units and Bagley Sewall papermaking

[53] *The Oriental Economist* (Tokyo), October 1960, p. 555.
[54] *Chemical and Engineering News*, July 31, 1961.
[55] *Los Angeles Times*, August 31, 1965.
[56] *Chemical and Engineering News*, July 31, 1961. See also R. W. Moncrieff, *Man-Made Fibres* (New York: Wiley, 1963), p. 695.
[57] *Za Industrializatsiiu* (Moscow), February 21, 1931.

equipment—was imported. The Siaz plant started operating in 1930 with a capacity of 144,000 tons of pulp per year, again with completely imported equipment, part from Norway and part from the United States, including Thorne bleaching towers.[58] The Kondopoga plant started its first section in 1930, and foreign technical assistance and equipment for this plant was so extensive that American foremen supervised the mill as late as October 1933.[59]

Plants built in the Soviet Union after 1933 and before World War II used domestic duplicates of foreign equipment, particularly the Fourdrinier machine; some outside assistance was given during the Lend Lease era, when $367,000 worth of pulp and paper industry machinery was shipped to the Soviet Union.

Table 15-1   ORIGIN OF SOVIET PAPER, BOARD
                    AND PULP CAPACITY AS OF 1958

	Metric Tons		
Origin	*Paper*	*Board*	*Pulp*
Russia (pre-1917)	247,800	8,200	91,000
Soviet Union (1917-58)	509,720	26,500	977,750
Manchuria (reparations)	13,000	—	33,000
Baltic States (occupation)	110,500	—	252,000
Finland (occupation)	119,700	45,000	417,000
South Sakhalin (occupation) (Karafuto)	1,277,000	—	2,492,000
Total (1958)	2,277,720	79,700	4,262,750

Source: Pulp, Paper and Board Bills: Union of Soviet Socialist Republics, (New York: American Paper and Pulp Association, April 1959), p. 6.
Note: Excludes East German reparations and Lend Lease equipment.

Although these mills provided sizable additions to Russian pulp and paper capacity before and during World War II, the extraordinary increment of capacity came after Soviet occupation of Finland, the Baltic States, and Karafuto (South Sakhalin), with lesser increments provided by equipment removals from Manchuria and East Germany. In 1958 Soviet sulfite, sulfate, and mechanical pulp capacity totaled 4,262,750 metric tons, of which 91,000 metric tons was prerevolutionary capacity and 894,750 metric tons built in the Soviet period. The balance, i.e., 75 percent of capacity, was from Finnish, Baltic, and Karafuto mills.

A total of 252,000 metric tons of pulp capacity and 110,500 metric tons of paper capacity was added by mills in Lithuania, Latvia, and Estonia. In Lithuania the Soviets gained the 70,000-ton sulfite pulp mill at Klaipeda; in

[58] Amtorg, *Economic Review of the Soviet Union,* V, 10 (May 1930), 210.
[59] U.S. State Dept. Decimal File, 861.5017/Living Conditions/726.

Latvia the Sloka mill, founded in 1886, provides a capacity of 60,000 tons of sulfite pulp and 50,000 tons of paper. Two smaller pulp mills have contributed another 25,000 tons to Soviet capacity. In Estonia the Soviets have the use of four mills: the Tallin mill, founded in 1890, with an annual capacity for 3000 tons of paper and 77,000 tons of mechanical and sulfite pulp; the Kero mill, another large mill with a capacity for 40,000 tons of sulfate pulp and 16,000 tons of paper; and the Turi and Koil mills, each with a capacity for 8000 tons of paper (the Turi mill also has a 5000-ton sulfite pulp capacity).

Former Finnish mills are the Enso (30,000 tons board and 80,000 tons sulfite pulp capacity), and the Kexholm, on Lake Ladoga, with a capacity of 100,000 tons of bleached and unbleached pulp; the Sovietskii, Vyborg, Lyaskelya, Pitkyaranta, Kharlu, and Souyarvi also are former Finnish mills making Finland's contribution to Soviet pulp and paper capacity 417,000 and 119,700 metric tons, respectively. The Souyarvi mill has a 15,000-ton board capacity, making a total of 45,000 tons (with the Enso board capacity) obtained from Finland.

Over one-half ot the total Japanese production of pulp wood between 1935 and 1945 was from Karafuto, the Japanese half of the Sakhalin peninsula.[60] These wood pulp facilities, mainly chemical pulp processes—sulfite pulp and kraft pulp—were ceded to the Soviet Union at the end of World War II and included nearly all Japanese productive facilities in these types. The significant contribution of these former Japanese facilities to Soviet pulp and paper capacity is indicated in Table 15-2. No less than 1.40 million tons capacity of sulfite pulp, 1.09 million tons of mechanical pulp, and 1.27 million tons of paper capacity were transferred to the Soviet Union.

The Manchurian pulp and paper industry was removed on a selective basis to the Soviet Union. One plant, the Manchurian soya bean stem pulp mill, was removed completely, and according to T. A. Rendricks, a U.S. Army inspection officer, "This plant was more completely stripped than any I have seen to date."[61] The mill produced a high-grade pulp from reeds growing on the banks of the Liao, Yalu, and Sungari rivers as well as a staple fiber from soya bean stalks by a company-developed process. Capacity was 15,000 tons of kraft pulp and 10,000 tons of paper per year, and equipment consisted of shredders, cooking and reagents tanks, separators, mixers, and storage tanks.[62] "Absolutely everything was removed by the Soviets except built-in installations, namely cooking tanks, reagent tanks, drying furnaces, separation tanks, and

[60]   Based on R. Seidl, *The Wood Pulp Industry of Japan* (Tokyo: SCAP [Supreme Command Allied Forces in Pacific] General Headquarters, Natural Resources Section, September 1946), Report no. 56.
[61]   Edwin W. Pauley, *Report on Japanese Assets in Manchuria to the President of the United States*, (Washington, July 1946).
[62]   *Ibid.*

Table 15-2   JAPANESE PULP AND PAPER MILLS ON SAKHALIN
(KARAFUTO) TAKEN OVER BY THE SOVIET UNION
IN 1945

			CAPACITY IN METRIC TONS				
			PULP			MECHANICAL	
Mill	Location	Built	Sulfite	Sulfate	Mechanical	Paper	Board
Korsakov	Otomari	1914	140,000	—	—	—	—
Yuzhno Sakhalinsk	Toyohara	1917	280,000	—	—	25.000 kraft	—
Dolinsk	Ochiai	1917	280,000	—	—	264,000 kraft	—
Kholmsk	Maoka	1919	—	—	—	240,000	—
Tomari	Tomarioru	1915	140,000	—	140,000 (rayon)	20,000	—
Chekhov	Noda	1922	140,000	—	—	59,000	—
Uglegorsk	Esutoru	1925	140,000	—	268,000	388,000	—
Makarov	Shirutoru	1927	280,000	—	204,000	281,000	—
Poronaisk	Shikuka	1935	200,000	—	280,000 (rayon)	—	—
TOTALS			1,600,000	—	892,000	1,277,000	—

Source: *Pulp, Paper and Board Mills: Union of Soviet Socialist Republics,* American
Paper and Pulp Association, April 1959; *Note:* Excludes East German reparations and
Lend Lease equipment.

bases for heavy lathes," according to Rendricks. Dismantling began on September 28, 1945, and the last shipment was made on November 15, 1945.[63]

The Nippon-Manshu pulp manufacturing plant at Tunghua, with an annual pulp capacity of 18,000 metric tons, also was completely removed to the Soviet Union,[64] as was the Yaluchiang paper mill at Antung with a capacity of 3000 tons of printing paper per year.[65]

Other plants were selectively removed. The Shinseimei paper plant at Chinchow lost five carloads of paper felts, conveyer belts, and electric motors,[66] while the Kanegafuchi Paper Company lost only 10 percent of capacity[67] and the Chihua Paper Company was not disturbed at all.[68]

Removals from Germany in this industrial sector consisted only of paper plants. The most important removal was the Leipziger Chromo- und Kunstdruckpapierfabrik vorm. Gustav Najork in Leipzig. About 27 plants in Saxony and

[63] *Ibid.*
[64] *Ibid.*, p. 231.
[65] *Ibid.*, p. 231.
[66] *Ibid.*, p. 227.
[67] *Ibid.*, p. 231.
[68] *Ibid.*

another dozen in Thuringia, Brandenburg, and Mecklenburg were also removed to the Soviet Union.

Considerable equipment has been supplied from Finland for the woodworking and paper-manufacturing industries. For example, in the 1956 trade agreement it was agreed that Finland would supply three paperboard-making machines and four papermaking machines, in addition to two plants for the manufacture of sulfate cellulose. This was in addition to a large quantity of pumps and fittings. The Tampella firm, as part of this agreement, received an order from the Soviet Union "for machinery for a semicellulose plant and a cardboard factory with a daily capacity of 200 tons for delivery in 1959. The cellulose plant will use reeds as raw material."[69] In 1962 the Tampella firm built another corrugated cardboard mill in the Soviet Union with a capacity of 300,000 tons per annum.[70] It was also reported:

A/B Defibrator, Stockholm, has obtained an order from the Soviet Union for Kr32 million (£2,200,000) worth of machinery and equipment for making hardboard. Delivery is to take place by the end of 1958. The company has previously sold fiberboard machinery to the Soviet Union.[71]

In 1958 the West German firm of Himmelheber contracted to install in the U.S.S.R. several plants based on the Behr process of manufacture of fiberboard; these were of 50,100 tons daily capacity.[72]

By combining the capacity originating in Japan, Manchuria, Finland, and the Baltic States we arrive at the conclusion that only between one-quarter and one-third of Soviet pulp, board, and paper capacity in 1960 was actually built by the Soviets, either with or without foreign technical assistance. In 1960 only 22.4 percent of papermaking capacity had been built in the Soviet era in the Soviet Union; another 10.9 percent had been built in Russia before the Revolution; the balance (66.7 percent) came from postwar Soviet acquisition of facilities in the Baltic States, Finland, and Japanese Karafuto. (See Table 15-3.)

In pulp-making capacity, we find that only 22.9 percent was built in the Soviet Union during the Soviet era, and only 2.1 percent of 1960 capacity originated in prerevolutionary Russia; no less than 75 percent of pulp-making capacity came from Soviet acquisitions in Finland, the Baltic States, and Karafuto.

[69] *East-West Commerce*, IV, 12 (December 9, 1957), 4.
[70] *Fortune*, August 1963, p. 80.
[71] *East-West Commerce*, IV, 6 (June 28, 1957), 11.
[72] U.S. Dept. of Agriculture, *Forestry and Forest Industry in the U.S.S.R.*, Report of a Technical Study Group (Washington, March 1961), p. 56. Also see pp. 56-57 for use of Western equipment in the manufacture of fiberboard.
      Alexis J. Panshin of Yale University concluded on the basis of his 1958 tour that in the sawmill, plywood, and pulp and paper plants, "all the major pieces of equipment were either of foreign make or obvious copies." Letter to author, February 19, 1968.

Table 15-3   ORIGINS OF SOVIET PAPER, BOARD, AND
                              PAPER CAPACITY IN 1960

	Percentage Built in Soviet era	Percentage Built in Tsarist era	Percentage from occupation	Total
Paper	22.4	10.9	66.7	100.0
Board	33.3	10.2	56.5	100.0
Pulp	22.9	2.1	75.0	100.0

Source: Table 15-1.

In board-making capacity, about one-third had been built in the Soviet Union, primarily with Western technical assistance, and 10.2 percent was inherited by the Soviets from prerevolutionary mills. Over one-half, i.e., 56.5 percent, of board-making capacity came from Soviet acquisitions in Finland and the Baltic States.

Therefore it may be seen that as of 1960 a relatively small portion of Soviet capacity in this industry had been built in the U.S.S.R. during the Soviet era—and even this with extensive foreign technical assistance.

The 1960s saw the beginning of the construction of a gigantic wood-processing combine at Bratsk in Siberia. The capacity of this combine increased by a factor of two Soviet rayon pulp output, and by 300,000 tons (or six times) the amount of paper-board production. The combine has associated sawmills, a furniture plant, a hard-board mill and various wood chemistry plants.[73] The rayon cellulose plant utilizes equipment from the EMW firm of Karlstadt, Sweden; the carton manufacturing equipment was installed by Tampella of Finland.[74] The central instrumentation for the pulp plant was provided by A/B Max Sievert of Stockholm, Sweden; this company supplied installations as built by Leeds and Northrup and the Foxboro Company (Sievert is the manufacturing licensee and agent in Sweden for the Leeds and Northrup Company).[75] The wood pulp plant near Irkutsk has equipment from Rauma Repola Oy of Finland.[76]

Thus it can be seen that the Soviet pulp and paper industry and the textile industry utilize large proportions of imported machinery. No innovation was noted in textile production in the fifties and sixties by expert delegations from the United States and India, and Russian-made equipment then consisted of duplicates of Western equipment—primarily U.S., U.K., and German. This duplication apparently was not altogether successful, as large new installations were made in the 1960s by Italian and American companies.

[73] *Metsalehti* (Helsinki), March 3, 1959.
[74] *Chemical Week*, (New York), September 24, 1966, p. 39.
[75] Letter to author from Leeds and Northrup Company, Philadelphia, August 14, 1967.
[76] *Chemical Week*, September 24, 1966, p. 39.

It seems clear that all developments and equipment in synthetic fiber have originated in the West, despite significant Soviet research efforts in this field. Production of Nylon 6, particularly the production of caprolactum, is dependent on Western equipment and processes from the United Kingdom, Germany, and Japan. Lavsan utilizes German and Czechoslovak machinery; the largest Lavsan unit was built by a British consortium (Polyspinners, Ltd.). Acryl fiber technology and capacity is from Japan and the United Kingdom.

In pulp and paper we find an unusual situation in that as of 1960 two-thirds of the Soviet paper capacity, over one-half of board capacity, and three-quarters of pulp capacity originated in countries occupied by Soviet forces in the forties—the Baltic States, parts of Finland, and particularly Japanese Karafuto. The new Siberian wood processing combines are heavily dependent on Swedish, Finnish, and, indirectly, American technology and equipment. There has been no significant innovation in this group of industries.

CHAPTER SIXTEEN

Western Assistance to the Motor Vehicle and Agricultural Equipment Industries

THE MOTOR VEHICLE INDUSTRY

The Soviet motor vehicle manufacturing industry has a history of production of a very limited range of utilitarian vehicles in a few large plants built with considerable Western technical assistance and equipment. These few plants manufacture most of their own components but export some components to vehicle assembly plants in other areas of the Soviet Union.

There is a high degree of integration between military and civilian models, partly because military and civilian vehicles require a large proportion of similar parts and partly because of the need to maintain unification of military and civilian design to assist model changeover in case of war. This unification of military and civilian automobile design has been described by A. N. Lagovskii:

> The fewer design changes between the old and the new type of product, the easier and more rapidly the enterprise will shift to new production. If, for example, chassis, motors, and other parts of a motor vehicle of a civilian model are used for a military motor vehicle, of course the shift to the mass production of the military motor vehicle will occur considerably faster and more easily than if the design of all the main parts were different.[1]

To achieve unification, precise standards are imposed on Soviet civilian vehicles to enable their conversion in wartime, and as Lagovskii points out, part of current "civilian" production of tractors and motor vehicles may be used directly as military vehicles.[2]

Quite apart from the "unification of design" aspect described by Lagovskii, the Soviets produce both military and civilian vehicles in the same plants, continuing a practice begun in the early 1930s. Accordingly, claims that U.S. technical assistance to the Soviet automobile industry has no military potential, are not founded on substance.[3]

[1] A. N. Lagovskii, *Strategiia i ekonomika*, 2d edition (Moscow, 1961), p. 192.
[2] *Ibid.*, pp. 192-93.
[3] U.S. House of Representatives, Committee on Banking and Currency, *The Fiat-Soviet Auto Plant and Communist Economic Reforms*, 89th Congress, 2d session (Washington, 1967), p. 42. See chapter 27 for military vehicle production. The installation is commonly known as the Fiat-Soviet auto plant, although the Fiat technical component is negligible compared with that of U.S. equipment supplies.

191

Western assistance to this industry may best be described by examining motor vehicle plants separately in approximate order of size and by outlining the Western contribution to the technical design and production facilities of each.

Table 16-1 lists in descending order of size the major Soviet motor vehicle plants planned or in operation as of 1971, together with approximate output and the main features of Western origin; Table 27-1 (see p. 384) identifies the civilian and military models produced by these plants.

Table 16-1   WESTERN ORIGINS OF AUTOMOBILE AND TRUCK PLANTS
IN THE SOVIET UNION AS OF 1971

Plant	Model Designation	Approximate Annual Output	Summary of Western technical assistance
Volgograd (Togliatti)	VAZ	600,000 (1974 projected)	Three-quarters of equipment [a] from United States; Fiat technical assistance in construction and operation
Moscow Small Auto	MZMA	300,000	Original Ford Motor Co. equipment (1930), replaced by German Opel (1945) and Renault (1966)
Gorki	GAZ	220,000	Ford Motor Co. (1930); Renault (1970); Gleason Works (1970)
Kama	(KAZ?)	100,000 [b] (projected)	Design and engineering by Renault (France). Equipment from a consortium of U.S. firms: licenses applied for (1971) by Satra Corp., Swindell-Dressler, Ex-Cell-O Corp., Cross Company, and (unconfirmed) Giffels Associates, Inc.
im. Likhachev	ZIL	100,000	U.S. equipment (mostly prewar)
Urals (Miass)	URAL	55,000	A. J. Brandt, Inc. (1930 plant moved from Moscow in 1941)
Odessa } assembly Lvov } plants	OdAZ LAZ	21,500	General Motors (1945)
Minsk	MAZ	14,400	German technical assistance (1945-46)
Yaroslavl	YaAZ	8,000	Hercules Motor Co. (1930)

Sources: See Sutton II, Chapter 11; *Kratkii avtomobil'nyi spravochnik,* 5th edition (Moscow, 1968); *Automotive Industries* (Philadelphia), January 1,1958; U.S. House of Representatives, Committee on Banking and Currency, *The Fiat-Soviet Auto Plant and Communist Economic Reforms,* 89th Congress, 2d sess. (Washington, 1967); Leo Heiman, "In the Soviet Arsenal," *Ordnance,* January-February 1968 (Washington: American Ordnance Association, 1968); U.S. Senate, Committee on Foreign Relations, *East-West Trade: A Compilation of Views of Businessmen, Bankers, and Academic Experts,* 88th Congress, 2d sess., November 1964 (Washington, 1964); *Metalworking News,* August 16, 1971.

[a] *Forbes* (October 1, 1966) states three-quarters; the figure may be somewhat less, but is certainly over one-half.

[b] Will be the largest plant in the world (covering 36 sq. mi.), and its output of heavy trucks will be greater than that of all U.S. manufacturers combined. Financing by Chase Manhattan Bank and the Export-Import Bank.

Lend Lease provided a significant contribution to the Russian vehicle stock in World War II and provided the basic designs for postwar domestic production. Vehicles supplied under Lend Lease included 43,728 Jeeps and 3510 Jeep-Amphibians; truck shipments included 25,564 vehicles of three-quarter ton, 218,664 of one and one-half ton, 182,938 of two and one-half ton, 586 of two and one-half ton amphibian, and 814 of five ton. In addition, 2784 special-purpose trucks, 792 Mack ten-ton cargo trucks, 1938 tractor trailers, and 2000 spare engines were sent.[4]

The report of the British delegation visiting the Central Automobile and Engine Research Institute in 1963 suggests that at that time there was a continued reliance on the West, but for design and equipment rather than assembled vehicles. The delegation reported:

> The first installation which we were shown was two single-cylinder engines on which combustion chamber research was carried out; these were old U.S. Universal crankcases, presumably supplied on Lend Lease during the War, and which had obviously not been used for some time. The lack of up-to-date instrumentation was noticeable, the only instrument other than normal thermometers and pressure gauges being an original type Farnborough indicator.[5]

The delegation found no evidence that the extensive staff at the institute, although obviously capable, was doing any large amount of development work. The numerous questions asked of the delegation related to Western experience —for example, on the V-6 versus the in-line six layout—and this, to the delegation, suggested an absence of worthwhile indigenous development work.

German Automotive Plants
Removed to the Soviet Union

During the latter part of World War II much of the German automotive industry moved eastward into the area later to be occupied by the Soviet Union, while the second largest auto manufacturer in Germany, Auto-Union A.G., with six prewar plants dating back to 1932, was already located in the Chemnitz and Zwickau areas. Before the war the six Auto-Union plants had produced and assembled the Wanderer automobile, the Audi automobile, Horch army cars and bodies, DKW motorcycles, and automobile motors and various equipment for the automobile industry. It is noteworthy that Auto-Union and Opel, also partly located in the Soviet Zone, were more self-contained than other German vehicle manufacturers and met most of their own requirements for components and accessories. Although Auto-Union was the only German automobile

---

[4] U.S. Dept. of State, *Report on War Aid Furnished by the United States to the U.S.S.R.* (Washington: Office of Foreign Liquidation, 1945), p. 19.

[5] Confederation of British Industry, "Visit to the Central Research Automobile and Engine Institute, 12th October 1963"; typescript supplied to the writer.

producer to produce automobiles during the war, the firm did make a sizable percentage of tanks and army vehicles (Table 16-2) and in 1944 was the only producer of engines (HL 230) for Tiger and Panther tanks.

Table 16-2   MODELS PRODUCED BY AUTO-UNION A.G. IN 1945
               AS PERCENTAGE OF TOTAL GERMAN PRODUCTION

Model	Maximum monthly production	Percentage of total German production of this model
Full-track truck (R.S.O.)	600	50
1½-ton Steyr truck	750	40
3-ton half-truck	400	50
Steyr motor	1650	45
Steyr gear-box	1300	40
3-ton half-track motor (HL 42)	1500	60
Tank engine (HL 230) for Tiger & Panther	800	50
Army automobile	1000	30
Light motorcycle (RT 125)	600	100
Heavy motorcycle (NZ 250)	1650	100

Source: U.S. Strategic Bombing Survey, *Auto-Union A.G., Chemnitz and Zwickau, Germany*, January 1947 edition, (Washington: Munitions Division, 1947), Report No. 84, p. 5. Date of Survey: June 10-12, 1945.

The Siegmar works near Chemnitz, which manufactured tank engines, was heavily damaged during the later phases of the war. But because all equipment except twenty machine tools, i.e., 4 percent of the total machine-tool stock, was repaired within ten weeks the plant was in full operation at the end of the war. It is also noteworthy that the one-and-one-half-ton Steyr truck, produced at a rate of 750 per month at the Horch plant of Auto-Union, was specially designed for Russian winter conditions in early 1942 as a result of the difficulties experienced with the German standard army truck in the 1941-42 winter campaign.[6]

When the Russians occupied Saxony in 1945, one of their first measures was to completely dismantle the Auto-Union plants and remove them to the Soviet Union.[7] When one considers that in these key plants they had acquired complete facilities to produce tank engines at a rate of 750 per month as well as a truck specially designed for Russian conditions, it is not surprising that

[6]   U.S. Strategic Bombing Survey, *Auto-Union A.G., Chemnitz and Zwickau, Germany*, 2d edition (Washington: Munitions Division, 1947), Report no. 84. (Dates of survey: June 10-12, 1945).
[7]   G. E. Harmssen, *Am Abend der Demontage; Sechs Jahre Reparationspolitik* (Bremen: F. Trüjen, 1951), pp. 101-2; see also *Germany, 1945-1954*, (Cologne: Boas International Publishing Co., [1954?]).

Soviet armored personnel carriers to this day bear a distinct resemblance to German World War II armored personnel vehicles.[8]

Full information is not available on the movement of the Leipzig plant owned by Bussing-National Automobil A.G., a manufacturer of armored cars, or of the firm's dispersal plants in the Saxony area; however, it was reported that the Bussing-National Chemnitz plant was 30 percent removed to the Soviet Union.[9] Three BMW (Bayerische Motorenwerke A.G.) plants were dismantled by the Russians and reportedly were completely shipped to the Soviet Union[10] (see Table 16-3). And the Adam Opel A.G. truck plant at Brandenburg, with a 1944 production of 20,000 three-ton Opel trucks and a capability to produce its own parts (with the exception of sheet metal, rear axle gears, and brake cylinders) was completely removed to the Soviet Union.[11]

In the Soviet sector of Berlin, the Ambi-Budd Presswerk A.G., a subsidiary of the U.S. Budd Company, was the largest single body producer in Germany before World War II. This plant completely escaped bomb damage. Although its equipment was dismantled for transportation (including tools and pressing machines for German passenger automobiles such as the Ford Taunus, the Hanomag 1.3 litre, and the Adler Trumpf-junior), it was not removed to Russia. Instead, "The machines, tools and pressed parts, carefully packed and numbered ... lay for years on the grounds of the works under the guard of a small section of Russian soldiers."[12] Apparently the Soviets had no requirement for equipment to manufacture automobile bodies and no reason to invest in transportation of the 300 specialized machine tools to the Soviet Union. Ultimately, the Ford Company at Cologne negotiated the return of the tools for the Taunus model to the Rhine plant of the Ford Motor Company, and Hanomag succeeded in doing the same for its own equipment.[13]

Other German automotive producers were completely or partly removed to the Soviet Union, including Vomag Betriebs A.G. of Plauen in Saxony, a manufacturer of trucks and diesel engines, and the Auto-Räder plant at Ronneburg in Thuringia, with 550 machine tools for the production of wheels for automobiles and military vehicles. The Bastert Chemnitz plant, a manufacturer of cylinders, was completely removed to the Soviet Union; the Auto-Bark motor plant at Dresden was completely removed; and the truck producer Phanomen-Werke at Zittau was partly removed to the Soviet Union.[14]

[8] *Ordnance* (American Ordnance Association, Washington) January-February 1968, pp. 372-73.
[9] Harmssen, *op. cit.* n.7, pp. 101-2, no. 31.
[10] Harmssen, *op. cit.*, pp. 101-2, nos. 78,79, and 80. However, *Germany, 1945-1954 (op. cit.* n. 7, p. 216) reports that the BMW plant was later reconstructed sufficiently to build vehicles for the Red Army.
[11] Harmssen, *op. cit.* n. 7, pp. 101-2, no. 105.
[12] *Germany, 1945-1954, op. cit.* n. 7, p. 216.
[13] *Ibid.*
[14] Harmssen, *op. cit.* n. 7.

Table 16-3　SUMMARY OF GERMAN AUTOMOBILE PLANTS MOVED TO
THE SOVIET UNION IN 1944-50

Name of plant in Germany	Percentage removed from Germany to the U.S.S.R.	Output, 1939-45
Auto-Union A.G. Chemnitz Plant No. 1	95 ⎫	Caterpillar trucks (RSO)-5650
Auto-Union A.G. Chemnitz Plant No. 2	100 ⎬	1½-ton truck – 2000 HL 230 tank engine – 4519
Auto-Union A.G. Siegmar-Schönau plant	100 ⎭	HL 230 tank engine – 4519
Auto-Union A.G. Audi plant	100	One-half-ton truck – 7787
Auto-Union A.G. Horch plant at Zwickau	100	Steyr motor – 30,000 Steyr gear box – 24,500
Auto-Union A.G. Zschopau plant	100	Army motorcycles
Auto-Union A.G. Scharfenstein plant	100 ⎫	Parts and electrical equipment
Auto-Union A.G. Burkhardtsdorf branch plant (Fa. Max Pfau & Gustav Frisch)	100 ⎭	
Bussing-National Automobil A.G. press plant, Chemnitz	30	Armored cars
BMW (Bayerische Motorenwerke A.G.), Dürerhof (Eisenach plant)	100 reported	
BMW Diedorf plant	but possibly	Army vehicles
BMW Treffurt plant	less	
Adam Opel A.G. truck plant, Brandenburg	100	Trucks

Sources: G. E. Harmssen, Am Abend der Demontage; Sechs Jahre Reparationspolitik (Bremen: F. Trüjen, 1951), pp. 101-2; Germany, 1945-1954 (Cologne: Boas International Publishing Co. [1954?], pp. 216, 422; U.S. Strategic Bombing Survey, Aircraft Division Industry Report, 2d edition (Washington, 1947), Report no. 4.

In Austria the automobile plants at Graz and Steyr were almost completely dismantled and removed.[15] These plants produced three models of the Steyr Type A one and one-half ton truck. These, complete with an eight-cylinder V-type engine, were produced at the rate of 50 to 60 per day. The Ford plant in Budapest, Hungary, was not removed but operated on Soviet account.[16]

Some of these removals can be traced directly to Russian locations through subsequent production. These aspects will now be considered in more detail.

[15]　F. Nemschak, Ten Years of Austrian Economic Development, 1945-1955 (Vienna: Association of Austrian Industrialists, 1955).
[16]　U.S. Foreign Economic Administration, U.S. Technical Industrial Disarmament Committee to Study the Post-Surrender Treatment of the German Automotive Industry (TIDC Project no. 12, Washington, July 1945), p. 23.

Origins of the Moskvich Passenger Automobile

The Moscow Small Car plant, built by the Ford Motor Company as an assembly plant for parts manufactured in the United States and later at the Ford-built Gorki plant, was brought into production in 1940 but produced only a few model KIM-10 light cars before World War II. In 1947 the plant reopened producing a single model, the Moskvich 401, through 1956. That model was replaced by the Moskvich 402. The 407 came into production in 1958 and in turn was replaced by the 408 in 1964.

The 1947 Moskvich 401 was, in effect, the 1939 German Opel Kadett with a few minor differences.[17] *Product Engineering*[18] concluded that the Moskvich 401 "bears a more than striking appearance to the prewar German Opel Kadett"—the instrument panel "is identical to the 1939 car," the four-cylinder engine has the "same piston displacement, bore, stroke, and compression ratio," and the same single-plate dry clutch, four-speed gear box, Dubonnet system front-wheel suspension, and four-wheel hydraulic brakes (derived from early Chevrolet models).

Differences from the original Opel were a Russian-made carburetor (K-25A), which "closely resembles a Carter down draft unit"; the electrical system, "similar in appearance to the Bosch design"; and a six-volt "Dutch-made battery."[19] The only apparently unique, noncopied feature was a device for facilitating brake adjustment.[20]

In 1963 the Moscow Small Car plant was visited by a delegation from the Confederation of British Industry, which reported an annual production of 80,000 cars produced by 15,000 workers in a plant of 160,000 square meters. Forge and press work was done in-plant, but castings were bought from supplier organizations. The delegation noted: "The layout of the plant and the tooling are not greatly different from Western European plants, but space, ventilation, and lighting are well below U.S. standards."[21]

In October 1966 an agreement was made with the French state-owned automobile manufacturers Renault and Peugeot to place French technical assistance and automobile know-how at the disposal of the Moskvich plant. As a result of this $50 million agreement, the plant increased its output capability

---

[17] A. F. Andzonov, *Avtomobil' Moskvich* (Moscow, 1950).
[18] New York, November 1953, pp. 184-85.
[19] The domestic Moskvich had a 3-CT-60 battery; *Product Engineering* probably examined an export version. The Soviets typically use foreign batteries, radios, and tires on export versions, and sometimes foreign engines as well (Rover and Perkins diesels).
[20] The *Product Engineering* article has a photograph of the Moskvich; also see *Kratkii avtomobil'nyi spravochnik*, 5th edition (Moscow, 1968), pp. 41-45.
[21] Confederation of British Industry, "Visit to the Moskvitch Car Manufacturing Plant, 10th October 1963"; typescript supplied to the writer.

from 90,000 to 300,000 automobiles annually; and the Renault company retooled the plant to produce modern compact automobiles[22] by installing two new production lines.[23]

The Ford-Gorki Plant

Vehicles produced by the Gorki plant, originally built by the Ford Motor Company and originally a producer of the Ford Model A and 1934 model Ford, continued to manifest their American lineage after World War II, and the plant's original U.S. equipment continues in use to the present day.[24] Production of two trucks and the Pobeda M-20 passenger vehicle started in 1946. The first postwar trucks (GAZ 51 and GAZ 63) were almost exact duplications of U.S. Army World War II vehicles; indeed, the unusual hood design and the hubcap design on the front wheels, for example, were precise replicas. Parts were also made at Gorki for the GAZ 93 and shipped to Odessa to be assembled; GAZ 93 was a dump truck with the same engine and chassis as the GAZ 51.

The Pobeda, produced between 1946 and 1955, had obvious similarities to the U.S. Army world war passenger vehicle, and had an M-20 engine remarkably similar in construction to a Jeep engine. The GAZ 69 and GAZ 69A, produced at Gorki between 1953 and 1956 when production was shifted to Ul'yanovsk, are described by the C.I.A. as "Jeep-like vehicles" and indeed bear a resemblance to the U.S. Army Jeep.[25] The 1956 model change introduced the Volga—described as a replica of the 1954 Mercury;[26] those cars, fitted with automatic transmissions, received a single-stage torque convertor with features like those in early U.S. models.[27]

The Moscow Plant im. Likhachev

The Moscow plant im. Likhachev is the old AMO plant originally built in 1917, rebuilt by A. J. Brandt, Inc., in 1929-30[28] and expanded over the

[22] *Wall Street Journal,* October 17, 1966; and *Minneapolis Tribune,* October 1, 1966. Other interesting information concerning the negotiations and Soviet demands is contained in *Le Monde* (Paris), June 2, 1966, and *L'Express* (Paris), October 1966, pp. 10-16.
[23] *The Times* (London), February 1, 1967.
[24] U.S. Senate, Committee on Foreign Relations, *East-West Trade: A Compilation of Views of Businessmen, Bankers, and Academic Experts,* 88th Congress, 2d session, November 1964, p. 79.
[25] *The Fiat-Soviet Auto Plant..., op. cit.* n. 3.
[26] *Wall Street Journal.* May 6, 1966.
[27] *Automotive Industries* (Philadelphia). June 1, 1958, p. 61.
[28] Sutton I. pp. 248-49.

intervening years. Over time its name has been changed from AMO to the Stalin plant and then to im. Likhachev. The plant contains key equipment supplied under Lend Lease. For example, the crankshaft lathes currently in use were supplied by a U.S. firm in October 1944.[29] One or two copies of these lines were then duplicated by the Soviets in 1948-49.[30]

In the late 1950s it was reported that "Likhachjov [*sic*] does its own design and redesign and in general follows American principles in design and manufacture"; the same source suggested that the Soviet engineers were quite frank about copying, and that design lagged about three to five years behind the United States. The plant's bicycle production techniques were described as "American with Russian overtones";[31] the plant had developed the "American Tocco process" for brazing[32] and many American machines were in use, particularly in the forging shops.[33]

The Urals plant at Miass (known as Urals ZIS or ZIL) was built in 1944 and largely tooled with the A. J. Brandt equipment evacuated from the Moscow ZIS (now ZIL) plant. The plant started production with the Urals-5 light truck, utilizing an engine with specifications of the 1920 Fordson; this suggests that the original Ford Motor Company equipment supplied in the late 1920s was being used, probably supplemented by Lend Lease equipment.

Smaller plants at Ul'yanovsk and Irkutsk assemble the GAZ 69 from parts made in Moscow, although in 1960 Ul'yanovsk began its own parts production and Irkutsk and Odessa handled assembly of other vehicles—including the GAZ 51 at Irkutsk and trucks with large bodies for farm and commercial use at Odessa. Other assembly plants are Kutaisi (KAZ-150 four-ton truck), the Zhdanov bus works at Pavlovsk (PAZ-651 bus and PAZ-653 ambulance), and the Mytishchi machine works (building trucks on ZIS-150 and GAZ 51 chassis).

The Odessa Truck Assembly Plant

The Odessa truck assembly plant almost certainly originated from two Lend Lease truck assembly plants shipped from the United States to Odessa via Iran in 1945.[34]

Nearly half of the Lend Lease trucks supplied to the Soviet Union were shipped through the Persian corridor route in parts, assembled at two truck

[29] *East-West Trade ...., op. cit.* n. 24. p. 79. Contract No. W-33-008 Ord 586, Requisition R-30048-30048A1.
[30] *Ibid.*
[31] *Product Engineering*, July 14, 1958.
[32] *Ibid.*
[33] *Automotive Industries*, January 1, 1958.
[34] This is inferred from evidence presented in this section; the writer does not have positive identification.

assembly plants in Iran, and forwarded by road as complete vehicles with Russian drivers to the U.S.S.R. About 409,000 trucks were thus sent to the U.S.S.R., equal to seven and a half months of U.S. production at the peak wartime period. The two Truck Assembly Plants (TAPs), at Andimeshk and Khorramshahr, were designed by General Motors and consisted of bolted structural framework on poured concrete floors; they were equipped with cranes, tractors, trailers, and battery chargers. Their output was 50 trucks each per eight-hour shift or about 168,000 vehicles per year from both plants if operated on a three-shift basis—as they would be in the U.S.S.R. Under authorization of November 1944,[35] these two plants were dismantled and shipped to Odessa.[36]

Between 1948 and 1955 the Odessa assembly plant turned out the GAZ 93 dump truck with a GAZ 51 six-cylinder gasoline engine of 70 horsepower, followed by a modified version model GAZ 93S. Since 1960 Odessa has been a major trailer manufacturing plant.[37] The GAZ 93 and 93A have a basic resemblance to the Lend Lease U.S. Army two-and-one-half-ton cargo trucks.

U.S. and Italian Assistance to Volgograd (VAZ)[38]

The Volgograd automobile plant, built between 1968 and 1971, has a capacity of 600,000 automobiles per year, three times more than the Ford-built Gorki plant which was the largest auto plant in the U.S.S.R. until Volgograd came into production.

Although the plant is described in contemporary Western literature as the "Togliatti plant" and the "Fiat-Soviet auto plant," and indeed does produce a version of the Fiat 124 saloon, the core of the technology is American, and three-quarters of the equipment,[39] including the key transfer lines and automatics, came from the United States. What is remarkable is that a plant with such obvious military potential[40] could have been equipped from the United States in the middle of the Vietnamese war, which has been largely supplied by the Soviets. Had there not been strong Congressional objections, it is likely that even the financing would have come from the United States Export-Import Bank.

---

[35] Memorandum 28, November 1944, AG 400.3295, HQ Amet.

[36] T. H. Vail Motter, *The Persian Corridor and Aid to Russia*, (Washington: Department of the Army, Office of the Chief of Military History, 1952), pp. 281, 432, and 494.

[37] Trailers OdAZ Models 885, 784, 794, 832, 795, 935, 822, and 857 B for cattle and the refrigerated trailer Model 826. See *Kratkii ...*, *op. cit.* n. 20, pp. 307-50.

[38] The best summary of this project, the largest single unit of assistance in the 50 years since the Bolshevik Revolution, is *Fiat-Soviet Auto Plant ...*, *op. cit.* n. 3. This document also reprints many of the more informative journal articles written while the contract was in negotiating stages. The Italian economic daily *24 Ore*, May 5 and May 7, 1966, also has details.

[39] See note to Table 16-1.

[40] See chapter 27.

The construction contract, awarded to Fiat S.p.a., included an engineering fee of $65 million;[41] in 1970 at peak construction, 1000 Italian engineers and technicians were employed on building the Volgograd plant.[42]

The agreement between Fiat and the Soviet Government includes:

> The supply of drawing and engineering data for two automobile models, substantially similar to the Fiat types of current production, but with the modifications required by the particular climatic and road conditions of the country;
>
> The supply of a complete manufacturing plant project, with the definition of the machine tools, toolings, control apparatus, etc;
>
> The supply of the necessary know-how, personnel training, plant start-up assistance, and other similar services.[43]

About three-quarters of the production equipment in Volgograd, including all key machine tools and transfer lines, came from the United States. Although the tooling and fixtures were designed by Fiat, over $50 million worth of special equipment came from U.S. suppliers. This included:

a) foundry machines and heat-treating equipment, mainly flask and core molding machines to produce cast iron and aluminum parts and continuous heat-treating furnaces;

b) transfer lines for engine parts, including four lines for pistons, lathes, and grinding machines for engine crankshafts, and boring and honing machines for cylinder linings and shaft housings;

c) transfer lines and machines for other components, including transfer lines for machining of differential carriers and housing, automatic lathes, machine tools for production of gears, transmission sliding sleeves, splined shafts, and hubs;

d) machines for body parts, including body panel presses, sheet straighteners, parts for painting installations, and upholstery processing equipment;

e) materials handling, maintenance, and inspection equipment consisting of overhead twin rail Webb-type conveyers, assembly and storage lines, special tool sharpeners for automatic machines, and inspection devices including surface roughness measuring instruments for paint, fabric, and plastic materials.

Some of the equipment was on current U.S. Export Control and CoCom lists requiring clearance and changing of control regulations.

U.S. equipment was a necessity (despite talk of possible European supply and the fact that the Soviets had made elementary automatic production lines

---

[41] *Ibid.*, p. 21.
[42] *The Times* (London), February 1, 1967.
[43] Letter from Fiat S.p.a. to writer, May 31, 1967.

as far back as 1940[44]) because U.S. equipment has proved to be far more efficient and productive than European, and Soviet automatic lines have been plagued with problems and deficiencies.[45] Fiat plants in Italy are themselves largely equipped with U.S. equipment—a measure of the necessity of U.S. equipment for the VAZ plant.

Table 16-4   EXPORT OF U.S. MACHINERY
                   FOR THE VOLGOGRAD AUTOMOBILE PLANT

Year and quarter	Description of industrial machinery		Approved licenses (Million)
1968			
2d quarter	Gear manufacturing and testing	$9.2	
	Molding and casting line		$15.6
	foundry equipment	2.9	
	Crankshaft grinding machinery	2.3	
3d quarter	Automatic piston machinery	5.1	
	Automatic crankshaft grinders	2.3	10.8
	Industrial furnaces	1.3	
4th quarter	Valve grinding line	2.0	
	Metal cutting machinery	1.6	6.4
	Grinding and honing machinery	0.8	
1969			
1st quarter	Not specified	32.8	32.8
Total			$65.6 million

Source: U.S. Dept. of Commerce, *Export Control* (Quarterly Reports), 1968, 1969.

Some of the leading U.S. machine tool firms participated in supplying the equipment enumerated in Table 16-4: TRW, Inc., of Cleveland supplied steering linkages; U.S. Industries, Inc., supplied a "major portion" of the presses; Gleason Works of Rochester, New York, supplied gear cutting and heat-treating equipment; New Britain Machine Company supplied automatic lathes.[46]

Further equipment was supplied by U.S. subsidiary companies in Europe and some came directly from European firms (for example, Hawker-Siddeley Dynamics of the United Kingdom sold six industrial robots.)[47] In all, approximately 75 percent of the production equipment came from the United States

[44]   U.S. Senate, *Export of Strategic Materials to the U.S.S.R. and Other Soviet Bloc Countries*, Hearing Before the Subcommittee to Investigate the Administration of the Internal Security Act and Other Internal Security Laws. 87th Congress, 1st session, Part 1, October 23, 1961. "Appraisal of Soviet Mechanization and Automation" in testimony by J. A. Gwyer, p. 84.
[45]   *Ibid.*
[46]   *Forbes,* October 1, 1966.
[47]   *Schenectady Gazette,* August 6, 1969.

and about 25 percent from Italy and other countries in Europe, including U.S. subsidiary companies.[48]

In the late 1960s Soviet planners decided to build what will be the largest truck factory in the world on the Kama River. This plant will have an annual output of 100,000 multi-axle trucks, trailers, and off-the-road vehicles. It was evident from the outset that, given the absence of internal Soviet technology in the automotive industry, the design, engineering work, and key equipment for such a facility would have to come from the West. In late 1971 the plant was under construction with design and engineering work by Renault of France. A license had been issued for equipment to be supplied by a consortium of American firms: Satra Corporation of New York, Swindell-Dressler, Ex-Cell-O Corporation, Cross Company, and according to *Metalworking News* (August 16, 1971) Giffels Associates, Inc., of Detroit.[49]

TRACTORS AND AGRICULTURAL MACHINERY

A report by a technical study group of the U.S. Department of Agriculture summarized the Russian agricultural machinery position in 1959 as follows: "Machinery from the U.S.A. has been used as a pattern for Russian machinery for many years. This is evident from the designs of older machines in particular, and a few of the new machines."[50]

This official statement parallels the findings of this study for the period to 1960, although the writer was unable to find any new designs that could not be traced to some foreign, but not necessarily American, origin. (The study group was interested in U.S. machinery—not European equipment.)

Soviet tractors produced before World War II came from three plants established in the early 1930s with major U.S. technical and equipment assistance.[51] The Stalingrad tractor plant was completely built in the United States, shipped to Stalingrad, and then installed in a building also purchased in the United States. This unit, together with the Kharkov and Chelyabinsk plants, comprised the Soviet tractor industry at that time, and a considerable part of the Soviet tank industry as well. Equipment from Kharkov was evacuated and installed behind the Urals to form the Altai tractor plant which opened in 1943.

---

[48]   There are varying reports on the percentage of U.S. equipment. See *Los Angeles Times*, August 11, 1966, and note to Table 16-1. The figures may be approximately summarized as follows: all key equipment, three-quarters of the production equipment and one-half of all equipment used in the plant and supporting operations.

[49]   See p. 192.

[50]   U.S. Dept. of Agriculture, Agricultural Research Service, *Farm Mechanization in the Soviet Union*. Report of a Technical Study Group (Washington, November 1959), p. 1.

[51]   Sutton II, pp. 185-91.

Three postwar tractor plants were in operation by 1950, and thereafter there was no further construction. The Vladimir opened in 1944, the Lipetsk in 1947, and the Minsk plant and the Kharkov assembly plant in 1950. This was the basic structure of the Soviet tractor industry in 1960. In brief, additions to tractor capacity between 1917 and 1960 can be identified in two phases:

Phase I, 1930-33: Stalingrad (1930), Kharkov (1931), Chelyabinsk (1933); U.S. equipment and design with U.S. models.

Phase II, 1943-50: Altai (1943), Vladimir (1944), Lipetsk (1947), Minsk (1950), and Kharkov tractor assembly plant (1950); U.S. and German equipment, with U.S. (and one German) models.

These plants produced a limited range of tractors with a heavy emphasis on crawler models rather than the rubber-tired tractors more commonly used in the United States. The 1959 USDA technical delegation[52] estimated that 50 percent of the current output was in crawler models as contrasted to only 4 percent in the United States; the military implications of such a mix is obvious. These crawler models, including the heavy industrial tractors S-80 and S-100, are produced in the older plants built in Phase I in the 1930s.

In 1960 the Stalingrad plant produced the DT-54 and the DT-57 crawlers at a rate of about 110 per day.[53] Kharkov produced the DT-54 at a rate of 80 per day[54] in addition to 80 DT-20 wheeled tractors and 20 self-propelled chassis DSSH-14 using the same single-cylinder engine. Chelyabinsk concentrated on the production of S-80 and S-100 industrial models, used not only as tractors but as bulldozers and as mobile base for a wide range of equipment including cranes, excavators, and logging equipment.

The postwar tractor plants concentrated on agricultural tractors. The Altai, with prewar U.S. equipment evacuated in 1943 from Kharkov, produced 40 of the DT-54 crawlers per day; Vladimir produced 60 wheeled models per day, first the DT-24 model and after 1959 the DT-28. Lipetsk produced about 55 of the crawler KDT-35 model per day, and Minsk produced about 100 of the MTZ-5 Belarus and seven Belarus models daily.[55]

In general, the Soviet Union in 1960 produced about one-half—a very high proportion—of its tractors in crawler models and concentrated this production in two or three types, almost all production being C-100 industrial tractors or DT-54 and DT-20 agricultural tractors. The remaining models were produced in limited numbers only.

[52]   U.S. Dept. of Agriculture, *op. cit.* n. 50, p. 24.
[53]   *Ibid.*
[54]   *SAE Journal* (New York), February 1959.
[55]   *Ibid.*

The S-80 and S-100 (Caterpillar) Crawler Tractors

In 1951 two Soviet S-80 Stalinets diesel crawler tractors were captured by the United States Army in the Korean War and shipped to the United States, where they were sent to the Caterpillar Tractor Company for technical inspection and investigation. The S-80 was identified as almost identical to Caterpillar designs built in Peoria, Illinois, between February 1942 and March 1943. As 85 percent of machines in this period were sold to the U.S. Government, it is a reasonable supposition that the originals were Lend Lease tractors. The Caterpillar Company investigation concluded the following on the S-80:

> It looked like a Caterpillar tractor. It smelled like a Caterpillar tractor. It sounded like a Caterpillar tractor. It made horsepower like a Caterpillar tractor.[56]

The Caterpillar investigation provided two clearcut conclusions. First, the Soviet copy was well engineered; in fact according to Davies, "We feel this machine is the best engineered of any foreign-made tractors we know anything about."[57] The design had been completely changed over to the metric system—no small task—and the machine had been "completely reengineered" to conform to Soviet shop practice, manufacturing standard and domestically available machines and materials. Although it was concluded that the machine was roughly finished and probably noisy, Caterpillar investigators expressed a healthy respect for Soviet engineering abilities. They commented: "The whole machine bristles with engineering ingenuity."

The second major conclusion was that the Soviet engineers "were clever in not trying to improve the Caterpillar design.... By sticking to Caterpillar's design, they were able to come up with a good performing, reliable machine without the usual development bugs.[58]

Figure 16-1 illustrates some of the technical similarities of the Caterpillar D-7 and the Chelyabinsk S-80.

The metallurgical composition of the S-80 component parts varies from the original—mainly in the substitution of more readily available manganese and chrome for U.S. molybdenum specifications, and in different heat-treatment practices which probably reflect Soviet equipment and process availabilities. However, according to observers the end result is not significantly different—except that the Russian product generally has a rougher finish (except where finish is needed for functional purposes)—and tolerances are held as

---

[56] Lecture by J. M. Davies, director of research for Caterpillar Tractor Company, to the Society of Automotive Engineers Earthmoving Conference at Peoria, Illinois, April 10, 1952.

[57] *Ibid.*

[58] *Ibid.*

Figure 16-1   Comparison of Caterpillar D-7 and Chelyabinsk S-80

(a) TRANSMISSION CASE AND DRAWBAR

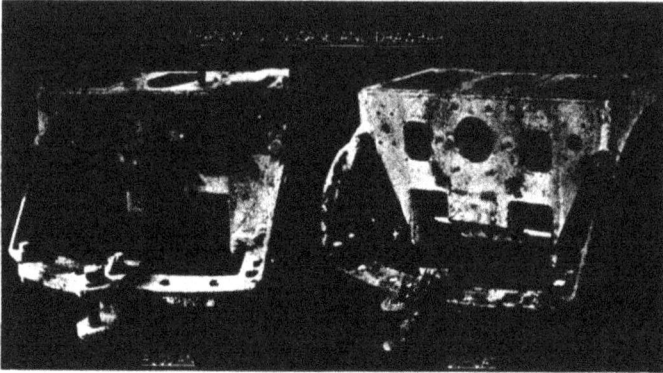

This comparison exemplifies differences in manufacturing practices; where Caterpillar used forgings, the Soviets used castings—no doubt reflecting lack of forging machines.

(b) TRANSMISSION GEAR

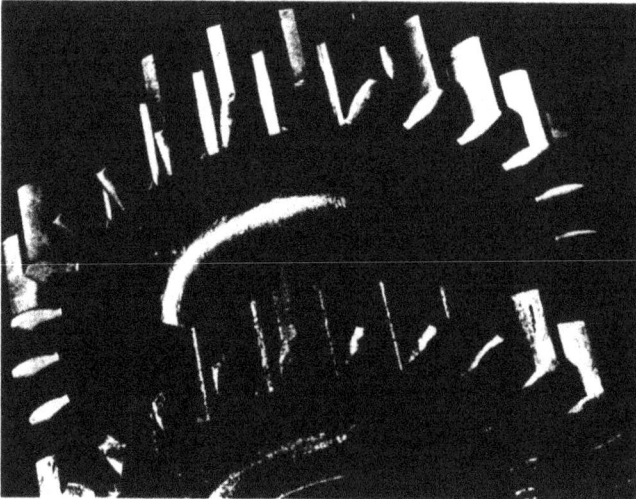

The Soviet gear has the same number of teeth but due to rough finish has more error in tooth spacing. Russian gear teeth are hand-finished, not machined-finished.

Figure 16-1 (cont.)

(c) TRANSMISSION SHIFT AND FORK

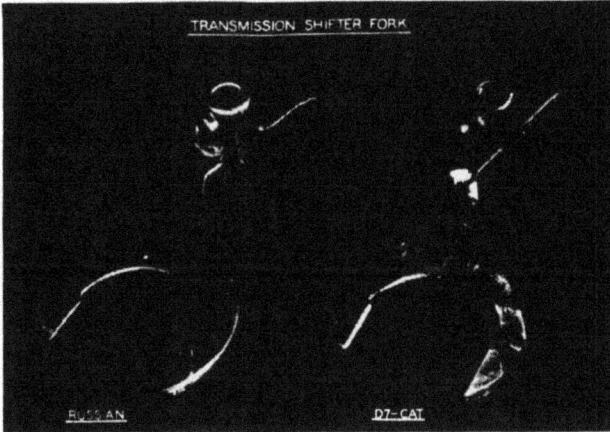

Possibly because the Soviet forging dies were newer, the transmission fork is a better job; Caterpillar does a little more machining.

(d) PISTON

The Russian alloy in the piston has both silicon and copper; Caterpillar has no silicon. The casting methods differ slightly.

Figure 16-1 (cont.)

(e) WATER PUMP IDLER

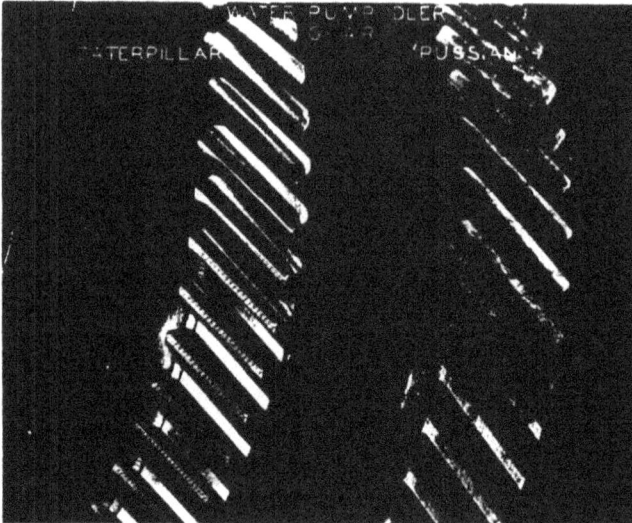

Again the Soviet finish is rough, and this may affect life of the gear.

(f) SOVIET S-80 TRACTOR

(Photographs 16 a-f courtesy of Caterpillar Co.)

Further comparisons of this nature are contained in *Product Engineering*, (New York), October 1952; and *SAE Journal*, (Society of Automotive Engineers, New York), June 1952; these compare other parts of the tractor, but in general their conclusions support the findings indicated in this text.

close as, or even closer than, on the American counterpart.[59] Comparison of metallurgical specifications of Russian and American tractor parts from the Caterpillar D-7 tractor in Table 16-5 illustrates this point.

Table 16-5   COMPARATIVE METALLURGICAL SPECIFICATIONS
IN SOVIET S-80 AND CATERPILLAR D-7 TRACTORS

Part	Material	Hardness	Heat Treatment	Miscellaneous
Soviet S-80				
Fuel pump plunger	AISI 52100	Rockwell A79-82	Oilp-quenched and tempered	—
Fuel pump barrel	AISI 52100	Rockwell A79-28	Oil-quenched and tempered	—
Track pin bushing	Approx. AISI 1020	Case: Rockwell C64 Core: Rockwell C32	Carburized, quenched, and tempered	Cracks in case
Flywheel clutch plant (center)	Gray iron, high emanganese	Approx. Brinell 230-250	None	Pearlitic cast iron
Final drive gear	AISI 1045	Case: Rockwell C56 Core: Rockwell C20	Induction-hardened one tooth at a time	Prior structure quenched and tempered; Residual tensile strength
Final drive pinion	2.7% Ni 0.85% Cr	Tip of tooth: Rockwell C60-64 Core: Rockwell C22-25	Carburized, quenched and tempered	About 1% C in case
Transmission gear	2.5% Mi 1.04 Cr	Tip of tooth: Rockwell C61-65	Carburized, quenched, and tempered	About 1.25% in case
Caterpillar D-7				
Fuel pump plunger	AISI 52100	Rockwell A79-82	Oil quenched and tempered	—
Fuel pump barrel	AISI 52100	Rockwell A79-82	Oil quenched and tempered	—
Track pin bushing	AISI 1020	About same	Carburized, quenched, and tempered	Bushings sometimes sometimes crack due to soft core
Flywheel clutch plant (center)	Cast iron (0.6%C.) (0.6%Cu)	Brinell 230-250	None	Pearlitic matrix
Final drive gear	AISI 1045	Case: Rockwell C56 Core: Rockwell C18	Induction-hardened and tempered	High compressive stress in rim
Final drive pinion	0.55%Ni 0.50%Cr 0.20%Mo	Rockwell C59-64	Carburized, quenched,and tempered	
Transmission gear	0.55%Ni 0.50%Cr 0.20%Mo	Rockwell C59-62	Carburized, quenched, and tempered	Depth of carburized case is less

Source: Caterpillar Company

59 *Product Engineering,* October 1952, pp. 154-59.

The parts for which Russian standards were higher are probably accounted for by the fact that the tractors examined were military tractors made to more exacting specifications; for example, on the track pins the Russian pin has a much better uniformity of hardening that the D-7 pin, and the Russian track link is considerably lighter.[60]

Soviet copies are not, then, precise replicas—they are more accurately described as "metric imitations." Two principles are balanced in the imitation process: (1) to copy the original Western model as precisely as possible, to avoid costs of research and development and by close copying to avoid the pitfalls ironed out in the original debugging of Western development models; and (2) to convert the model to Soviet metric practice and shop practice—not always consistent with the first principle.

Thus, the Caterpillar Company research engineers reported:

> Not a single Russian part is interchangeable with the Caterpillar part from which it was copied. Metric dimensioning is not the only reason, however, because even the internal parts of the Caterpillar fuel pump (made to metric dimensions originally) are not interchangeable with the Russian parts.[61]

In effect, then, the Russian tractor S-80 was a very ingeniously reengineered copy of the Caterpillar tractor D-7. The question logically arises: Why spend so much effort and engineering time on a complete reengineering job? The answer has to lie in some extraordinary defect in the Soviet industrial system; if it pays to reengineer a U.S. tractor to metric dimensions with the numerous problems involved rather than design a new tractor for Russian operating conditions, then something more than cost of research and development is involved.

Wheel-Track Tractors in the Soviet Union

The first mass-produced wheel tractor in the Soviet Union was based on the International Harvester Farmall.[62] It was produced first in Leningrad, and after 1944 at the Vladimir factory, with a 22-hp four-cylinder kerosene engine. In 1953 this wheel tractor model was supplemented by the Belarus, produced at the Minsk tractor plant; this is a 40-belt horsepower diesel-engined wheel tractor similar to the Fordson Major manufactured by Ford Motor Company, Ltd., at Dagenham in England. Finally, in the early 1950s the Soviets produced the DT-20 Row Crop tractor and the ABC-SH-16 self-propelled chassis, both with the same one-cylinder diesel engine and built at the Kharkov tractor works.

---

[60]   *Ibid.*, p. 159.
[61]   *Product Engineering*, October 1959, p. 155.
[62]   See V. V. Korobov, *Traktory avtomobili i sel'skokhozyaistvennye dvigateli* (Moscow, 1950), p. 10.

The self-propelled chassis and the single-cylinder engine are based on a design originated by the German firm of Heinrich Lanz A.G. of Mannheim, West Germany. Before World War II this firm produced the well-known Lanz single-cylinder two-stroke hot-bulb type engine, which was of great simplicity, able to perform well on low-grade fuels, and therefore suitable for use in relatively underdeveloped countries. In the late 1950s the total daily production of the Lanz engine and associated equipment was approximately 545 per day.[63]

Origins of Other Farm Machinery and Equipment

Soviet agricultural machinery and equipment is dependent almost entirely on foreign prototypes. As late as 1963 a U.S. Department of Agriculture report commented as follows:

As soon as feasible the U.S.S.R. buys prototypes of new foreign machines and places them at one of ... 29 machine test stations. If the machine or parts of it have desirable characteristics, production is recommended.[64]

In 1958 a U.S. technical study group sent to the Soviet Union to observe soil conservation[65] noted that the Soviet laboratories in the soil science field had instruments and equipment similar to those in American laboratories. Furthermore, methods of application of fertilizer had been copied from American equipment. For example:

We observed a large number of anhydrous ammonia applicators, for injecting ammonia gas into soils, at the Middle Asian Scientific Research Institute on Mechanization and Electrification of Irrigated Agriculture near Tashkent. These seemed to be copies of ours; in fact, a Schelm Bros. machine made in East Peoria, Ill., was alongside several Soviet machines. Also exhibited at the Institute

[63] *SAE Journal*, February 1959, p. 51.
[64] U.S. Dept. of Agriculture, *Soviet Agriculture Today*, Report of the 1963 Agriculture Exchange Delegation, Foreign Agricultural Economic Report No. 131 (Washington, December 1963), p. 35. There is some confusion on the part of executive departments concerning this copying. For example, the following statement was made to Congress in 1961: "MR. LIPSCOMB. Does the Department of Commerce feel that Russia has developed a great deal of their agricultural equipment from prototypes obtained both legally and illegally from the United States? MR. BEHRMAN. No, sir. I don't think that the evidence we have indicates that the equipment that they themselves produce copies—that they produce copies of equipment which we have supplied." U.S. House of Representatives, Select Committee on Export Control, *Investigation and Study of the Administration, Operation, and Enforcement of the Export Control Act of 1949, and Related Acts*(H.R. 403), 87th Congress, 1st session, October 25, 26, and 30, and December 5, 6, 7, and 8, 1961; p. 403.
[65] U.S. Dept. of Agriculture, Soil Conservation Service, *Soil and Water Use in the Soviet Union*, Report of a Technical Study Group, (Washington, 1958), p. 23.

for Mechanization and Electrification was a crude version of the two-wheel, tractor-drawn broadcast-type spreader such as is widely used in the United States.[66]

Drainage research equipment also appears to have been developed from U.S. models; the conclusion of the delegation was: "Most of [the machines] appear to be adaptions of American or European types."[67] These observations relate to a back-hoe ditcher, a wheel-type trencher, and a tile laying machine (copied from a similar machine made in the Netherlands by the Barth Company), a pool ditcher, a mole drain device, a ditch cleaner, brush cutters, and a virgin peatland plow.[68]

Other agricultural equipment also appears to have been copied from U.S. equipment; for example, the fertilizer spreader No. BB-35 is a close replica of the New Idea, an American model, and the corn drill model SUK-24 is very similar to U.S. models of such equipment. Examination of a single agricultural machine—the cotton picker—will bring out this process of duplication in greater detail.[69]

The Rust Cotton-Picking Machine

The Rust cotton-picking machine, developed and patented by John Rust, an American agrarian socialist, was the first spindle picker, and in the long run the most successful; in fact, the Rust principle has been preserved essentially in its original form in machines currently made by four U.S. companies. The first Rust patent was filed in 1928. By 1936 ten machines had been built in the United States, and two of them were sold to Amtorg.[70] Whereas Rust in the United States was forced to abandon production by 1942 because of insufficient financing and lack of durability in the machine, the Soviets on the other hand went ahead—they adopted the Rust principle and started to produce cotton pickers utilizing this principle in large quantities.[71]

---

[66] *Ibid.*, p. 30.

[67] *Ibid.*, p. 36.

[68] *Ibid.*

[69] This duplication may be found even in minor equipment items. For example, compare various seed drills and their feedwheel mechanisms; *Encyclopedia Britannica* 17: "Planting Machinery," (Chicago: William Benton, 1958) p. 1011; and V. N. Barzifkin, *Mekhanizatsiia sel' skokhoziaistvennogo proizvodstva* (Moscow, 1946), p. 103.

[70] J. H. Street, *The New Revolution in the Cotton Economy* (Chapel Hill, N.C., 1957). On p. 128 Street quotes from *Survey Graphic* (July 1936) as follows: "John Rust made a trip there [to the U.S.S.R.] to supervise their introduction in the belief that they [the cotton pickers] would be used 'to lighten man's burden rather than to make a profit at the expense of the workers.'"

[71] *Strana Sovetov za 50 let: Sbornik statisticheskikh materialov* (Moscow, 1967), p. 156. A good source of technical detail concerning the Soviet cotton picker is I. I. Gurevich, *Khlopkouborochnaya mashina KhVS-1, 2M: Rukovodstvo po ekspluatatsii* (Tashkent, 1963). There is a translation: U.S. Dept. of Commerce TT 66-51114/1966.

By 1940 the Soviets had a park of 800 cotton pickers based on the Rust principle, whereas the United States, where Rust had initiated, developed, and built the original machines, had none in commercial production and only a few in use on a custom picking basis. Only in 1942 did International Harvester announce it was ready to go into commercial production of machines based on the principle, producing 12 in 1941 and 1942, 15 in 1943, 25 in 1944, and 75 annually in 1945-47. In 1945 Allis-Chalmers started work using a modified Rust principle, but by 1949 only 49 Allis-Chalmers pickers had been manufactured. By 1953 cotton pickers designed on the Rust principle were produced not only by International Harvester and Allis-Chalmers but also by Ben Pearson, J. I. Case, and Massey-Harris-Ferguson. Deere attempted to develop the Berry spindle picker between 1943 and 1946, but abandoned the effort.

In 1953, then, about 15,000 pickers were available in the United States while the Soviet Union had about 5000 cotton pickers in operation.[72]

In summarizing this discussion of the Soviet automotive sector, it may be said that the Soviet Union was as dependent on Western automobile manufacturing technology in 1970 as it was in 1917. In 1968-70 U.S. companies installed over $65 million worth of equipment in the 600,000-autos-per-year VAZ plant; in 1917 the Baltic and AMO plants, large units for the times, were also equipped with the latest American equipment.[73] Therefore there has been no innovation of indigenous Soviet automobile or truck technology.

The Stalinetz S-80 and S-100, both heavy tractors that provide the chassis for other Soviet equipment, were found to be replicas of the Caterpillar D-7. Other agricultural equipment, including farm implements and cotton pickers, is based on American models, although there are a few examples of British (Fordson Major), German (Lanz tractor engine), and Dutch (Barth tile laying machine) origins.

---

[72] *Strana Sovetov* ..., *op. cit.* n. 71.
[73] Sutton I, pp. 243-44.

CHAPTER SEVENTEEN

Western Origins of Soviet Prime Movers

This chapter examines the Western origins of some of the common Soviet prime movers—diesel engines for marine and truck use and internal combustion engines, together with steam boilers and steam and gas turbines.

Fortunately, complete and reasonably accurate Soviet data are available on marine prime movers (diesel, steam, and gas turbine engines) used in marine propulsion systems. These data, derived from a detailed descriptive listing of the 5551 ships in the Soviet merchant marine as of July 1967,[1] were subjected to an exhaustive analysis to determine the types and origins of marine engines used in Soviet merchant ships. (See Table 17-1.)

Two characteristics were examined: first, diesel, and steam engines by type and system, i.e., by their technical characteristics; and second, the origin and date of construction of these engines in order to arrive at an understanding of the manner in which the Soviet merchant marine had been acquired, i.e., the rate of addition of different types of engines, changes in foreign supply sources, and the extent to which the Soviets may possibly have divested themselves of foreign assistance.

Table 17-1 lists marine diesels (if more than four units of a single type were identified) in use in the Soviet merchant marine in 1967. The table does not include steam turbines, reciprocating steam engines, diesel-electric engines, or gas turbine engines; steam turbines and gas turbines are discussed later in the chapter. The table does include about 80 percent of the marine propulsion units in use.

The most striking characteristic is the absence of diesel units of Soviet design. Although a few (reference numbers 6, 10, 11, 12, 14, and 35) are listed as of probable foreign origin and three units (reference numbers 9, 26, and 43) are not identified, there is evidence to suggest that these units are of Sulzer or M.A.N. design except for reference number 43, which is probably of Fiat design. Early technical-assistance agreements in the 1920s with the Sulzer and M.A.N. firms resulted in several "Soviet" diesels manufactured

---

[1] Registr Soyuza SSR, *Registrovaya kniga morskikh sudov soyuza SSR 1964-1965* (Moscow, 1966), plus annual supplements.

Table 17-1   TECHNICAL CHARACTERISTICS
OF SOVIET MARINE DIESELS IN USE IN 1967*

			Specification of marine diesels in use in 1967			
Reference number	Engine design	Country of origin	Number of cylinders	Cylinder diameter (mm.)	Piston stroke (mm.)	Rated bhp
1	Buckau-Wolf	G.D.R.	8	240	360	300
2	Buckau-Wolf	G.D.R.	6	320	480	400
3	Buckau-Wolf	G.D.R.	8	320	480	550
4	Skoda	Czechoslovakia	8	430		2500
5	Görlitzer	G.D.R.	6	175	240	200
6	M.A.N.(probable)	Germany	6	300	500	600
7	Alco	U.S.A.	6	318	3300	1000
8	Burmeister & Wain	Denmark	5	500	1100	2900
9	Not identified	—	6	180	220	150
10	Sulzer (probable)	Switzerland	6	250	340	300
11	M.A.N. (probable)	Germany	8	300	500	800
12	M.A.N. (probable)	Germany	4	300	500	400
13	M.A.N.	Germany	6	570	800	4000
14	M.A.N. (probable)	Germany	12	150	180	300
15	Sulzer	Switzerland	6	760	1550	9600
16	Burmeister & Wain	Denmark	5	620	1400	600
17	M.A.N.	Germany	7	700	1200	6000
18	Görlitzer	G.D.R.	8	365	550	2000
19	Burmeister & Wain	Denmark	8	740	1600	13000
20	Sulzer	Switzerland	5	720	1250	4500
21	Sulzer	Switzerland	8	480	700	3000
22	Lang	Hungary	8	216	310	200
23	Lang	Hungary	8	315	450	1000
24	Burmeister & Wain	Denmark	9	500	1100	5200
25	M.A.N.	Germany	6	520	900	1900
26	Not identified	-	12	180	200	150
27	Burmeister & Wain	Denmark	7	740	1600	11000
28	M.A.N.	Germany	6	700	1200	5800
29	Sulzer	Switzerland	6	560	1000	2400
30	M.A.N.	Germany	5	520	700	4500
31	Burmeister & Wain	Denmark	8	350	620	2260
32	Burmeister & Wain	Denmark	9	900	1550	19800
33	Sulzer	Switzerland	6	500	900	2000
34	Polar	Sweden	6	340	570	1550
35	M.A.N. (probable)	Germany	6	150	180	150
36	Mash.Kiel A.G.	Germany	8	290	420	640
37	Götaverken	Sweden	7	760	1500	8750
38	Burmeister & Wain	Denmark	6	740	1600	9760
39	Fiat	Italy	8	750	1320	8000
40	M.A.N.	Germany	9	720	1200	8150
41	M.A.N.	Germany	6	600	1050	5600
42	Polar	Sweden	5	345	580	1260
43	Not identified	Italy	6	540	960	2000
44	Sulzer	Switzerland	7	760	1550	9100

Source: Calculated from Registr Soyuza SSR, *Registrovaya kniga morskikh sudov soyuza SSR 1964-1965* (Moscow, 1966).

* Includes all units for which more than four engines of a single type were identified.

in the 1930s and 1940s.[2] No purely Soviet marine diesels have been traced in this period,[3] so the units mentioned are probably either M.A.N. or Sulzer. These companies have manufactured units with similar technical characteristics.

Positive identification of foreign origin for the other units in Table 17-1 has been made, and agreements or sales have been traced from the Western company either to the Soviet Union or to an East European country manufacturing the design under foreign license and then in turn selling the unit to the Soviet Union.

The two most common designs are those of M.A.N. (Maschinenfabrik Augsberg-Nurnberg A.G.) of Augsburg, Germany, and Burmeister & Wain of Copenhagen, Denmark. The latter company has supplied technical assistance and designs for large marine diesels, while M.A.N. units are normally less than 4500 hp. Sulzer in Switzerland, the former Buckau-Wolf at Magdeburg in Germany, Skoda in Czechoslovakia, and Nydqvist & Holm (Polar) in Sweden are other commonly found marine diesel designs.

Table 17-2 indicates the number of each of these marine diesel designs in use in the Soviet merchant marine in relation to geographic origin. One noticeable disclosure is that, of the 4248 marine diesels in use in 1967, an extraordinarily large number (2289 or 54 percent) were manufactured in Czechoslovakia and that 82 were manufactured at the prerevolutionary Russky Disel plant in Leningrad. Another common design is that of Görlitzer in East Germany, comprising 239 marine diesels in two models.

Table 17-2   ORIGINS OF SOVIET MARINE DIESELS,
BY NUMBER OF EACH DESIGN, 1967

Reference number in Table 17-1	Built outside U.S.S.R.	Built inside U.S.S.R.	Total
1	1,413	—	1,413
2	519	6	525
3	351	—	351
4	170	82	252
5	202	—	202
6	2	147	149
7	—	142	142
8	76	25	101
9	—	96	96
10	41	47	88
11	—	80	80
12	—	68	68
13	66	—	66
14	—	64	64

[2]   See Sutton 1, pp. 35, 332.
[3]   Ibid.

Table 17-2 (cont.)

Reference number in Table 17-1	Built outside U.S.S.R.	Built inside U.S.S.R.	Total
15	61	—	61
16	51	—	51
17	39	—	39
18	37	—	37
19	36	—	36
20	36	—	36
21	42	—	42
22	35	—	35
23	31	—	31
24	5	24	29
25	24	—	24
26	—	23	23
27	10	12	22
28	21	—	21
29	21	—	21
30	17	—	17
31	18	—	18
32	13	—	13
33	11	—	11
34	11	—	11
35	1	9	10
36	10	—	1C
37	10	—	10
38	5	5	10
39	7	—	7
40	6	—	6
41	7	—	7
42	5	—	5
43	4	—	4
44	4	—	4
TOTAL	3418	830	4248

Source: Calculated from Registr Soyuza SSR, *Registrovaya kniga morskikh sudov soyuza SSR 1964-1965* (Moscow, 1966).

Burmeister & Wain of Denmark has been a prominent supplier of diesel marine engines, and under an agreement signed in 1959 the Soviet Union now manufactures Burmeister & Wain diesels at Bryansk in the Ukraine. Thus numerous Burmeister & Wain designs figure into Table 17-2, either as units imported from Denmark (reference numbers 8, 16, 19, 24, 27, 31, 32, and 38) or as units manufactured at the Burmeister & Wain plant in Copenhagen and, under license, at Bryansk in the Soviet Union (for example, reference numbers 8, 24, 27, and 38).

The most prominent feature of Table 17-2, however, is the relatively small number (830, or 19.5 percent) of marine diesels actually manufactured inside the Soviet Union.

Table 17-3 lists the origins of these Soviet marine diesels according to aggregate horsepower. This listing provides a more accurate reflection of the importance of each type of unit for the Soviet merchant marine.

In general terms, four-fifths (79.3 percent) of the aggregate diesel generated horsepower was built outside the Soviet Union. Of a total of 4,633,890 hp, some 3,672,890 hp was built outside the Soviet Union and only 961,000 hp was built inside the Soviet Union, and even that portion required foreign technical assistance.

Table 17-3   ORIGINS OF SOVIET MARINE DIESELS AS OF 1967, BY AGGREGATE HORSEPOWER FOR EACH DESIGN

		Aggregate horsepower built			
No.	Reference number from Tables 17-1 and 17-2	Outside U.S.S.R.	Inside U.S.S.R.	Total	Percentage of this design built outside the U.S.S.R.
1	4	425,000	205,000	630,000	67.5
2	1	423,900	—	423,900	100.0
3	8	220,400	72,500	292,900	75.2
4	13	264,000	—	264,000	100.0
5	32	257,400	—	257,400	100.0
6	27	110,000	132,000	242,000	45.5
7	17	234,000	—	234,000	100.0
8	2	207,600	2,400	210,000	98.8
9	3	193,050	—	193,050	100.0
10	20	162,000	—	162,000	100.0
11	24	26,000	124,800	150,800	17.2
12	7	—	142,000	142,000	0.0
13	21	126,000	—	126,000	100.0
14	28	121,800	—	121,800	100.0
15	38	49,500	99,000	99,000	50.0
16	6	1,200	88,200	89,400	1.3
17	37	87,500	—	87,500	100.0
18	30	76,500	—	76,500	100.0
19	18	74,000	—	74,000	100.0
20	11	—	64,000	64,000	0.0
21	15	58,560	—	58,560	100.0
22	39	56,000	—	56,000	100.0
23	29	50,400	—	50,400	100.0
24	40	48,900	—	48,900	100.0
25	19	46,800	—	46,800	100.0
26	25	45,600	—	45,600	100.0
27	16	41,400	—	41,400	100.0
28	5	40,400	—	40,400	100.0

Table 17-3 (cont.)

No.	Reference number from Tables 17-1 and 17-2	Aggregate horsepower built			Percentage of this design built outside the U.S.S.R.
		Outside U.S.S.R.	Inside U.S.S.R.	Total	
29	31	40,080	—	40,080	100.0
30	41	39,200	—	39,200	100.0
31	44	36,400	—	36,400	100.0
32	23	31,000	—	31,000	100.0
33	12	—	27,200	27,200	0.0
34	10	11,400	15,000	26,400	43.2
35	33	22,000	—	22,000	100.0
36	14	—	19,200	19,200	0.0
37	34	17,050	—	17,050	100.0
38	9	—	14,400	14,400	0.0
39	43	8,000	—	8,000	100.0
40	22	7,000	—	7,000	100.0
41	36	6,400	—	6,400	100.0
42	42	6,300	—	6,300	100.0
43	26	—	3,450	3,450	0.0
44	35	150	1,350	1,500	10.0
		3,672,590	961,000	4,633,890	79.3 percent

Source: Calculated from Registr Soyuza SSR, *Registrovaya kniga morskikh sudov soyuza SSR 1964-1965* (Moscow, 1966).

The most important design, Skoda of Czechoslovakia, contributes 630,000 hp to the Soviet merchant fleet. The next design in terms of contribution to aggregate horsepower is that of Buckau-Wolf, contributing 423,900 hp; this is numerically the most common unit. Other prominent designs are Burmeister & Wain (the 2900 hp unit) with 292,900 hp, M.A.N. of Germany with 264,000 hp, and Burmeister & Wain (the 11,000-hp unit), which contributes some 242,000 hp to the total.

The last column in Table 17-3 indicates the percentage of each design built outside the Soviet Union. While it is obvious from the table that a comparatively small amount (20 percent) of aggregate horsepower was built inside the Soviet Union, it may not be so readily obvious that this domestic construction is also concentrated into a few designs. For example, the 1000-hp unit, originally an American Locomotive design sent to the Soviet Union under Lend Lease, contributes 142,000 hp. It is today built only inside the Soviet Union, whereas other types, particularly Burmeister & Wain designs, are both built in the Soviet Union and imported.

Table 17-4 shows quite clearly the fact that units of large horsepower are not built in the Soviet Union. This table lists construction inside and outside the Soviet Union in terms of rated horsepower category. It is notable that the units of 9000-12,000 hp, partly built in the Soviet Union and partly imported, are the Burmeister & Wain design built with technical assistance under terms of the 1959 agreement. Otherwise, units built in the Soviet Union are of much smaller capacity.

Table 17-4   PERCENTAGE OF SOVIET MARINE DIESELS BUILT
OUTSIDE THE SOVIET UNION AS OF 1967
(BY RATED HORSEPOWER CATEGORY)

Horsepower rating category	Built outside U.S.S.R. (in bhp)	Built inside U.S.S.R. (in bhp)	Total bhp	Percentage built outside U.S.S.R.	Category as a percentage of total aggregate horsepower
Less than 1,000	891,000	235,200	1,126,300	79.1	24.3
1-1,999	99,950	142,000	241,950	41.3	5.2
2-2,999	839,880	277,500	1,117,880	75.2	23.9
3-3,999	126,000	—	126,000	100.0	2.7
4-4,999	502,500	—	502,500	100.0	10.8
5-5,999	187,000	124,800	311,800	59.9	6.7
6-6,999	275,400	—	275,400	100.0	5.9
7-7,999	—	—	—	—	—
8-8,999	192,400	—	192,400	100.0	4.1
9-9,999	144,460	49,500	193,500	74.2	4.2
10-10,999	—	—	—	—	—
11-11,999	110,000	132,000	242,000	45.5	5.2
12-12,999	—	—	—	—	—
13-13,999	46,800	—	46,800	100.0	1.0
14-14,999	—	—	—	—	—
15-15,999	—	—	—	—	—
16-16,999	—	—	—	—	—
17-17,999	—	—	—	—	—
18-18,999	—	—	—	—	—
19-19,999	257,400	—	257,400	100.0	5.5
Totals	3,672,890	961,000	4,633,890	79.3	99.5

Source: Calculated from Registr Soyuza SSR, *Registrovaya kniga morskikh sudov soyuza SSR 1964-1965* (Moscow, 1966).

Note: This table includes all marine diesels where more than 20 of a single model were manufactured or imported. It does not include reciprocating steam engines, steam turbines, gas turbines, or diesel-electric drives.

We may conclude concerning marine diesels that the Soviet Union is still heavily dependent on Western technology. The significant increment in size of unit built after 1960 is due mainly to the Burmeister & Wain technical-assistance agreement, although East Germany and Czechoslovakia have also contributed significantly to Soviet construction of marine diesels. The technical lag is extraordinary when compared to the gigantic increment since World War II in the Soviet mercantile fleet.

FOREIGN TECHNICAL ASSISTANCE
TO SOVIET MARINE ENGINE CONSTRUCTION

The Soviet marine diesels actually manufactured in the Soviet Union have received a considerable amount of foreign technical assistance. Technical-assistance agreements were made with both M.A.N. and Sulzer in the 1920s,[4] and the Soviet Union has continued since that time to receive M.A.N. and Sulzer technology in addition to new assistance agreements with Burmeister & Wain of Denmark and Skoda of Czechoslovakia in the fifties and sixties.

An agreement was signed in early 1959 in Copenhagen by Niels Munck, managing director of Burmeister & Wain, and Mikoyan, who visited the company on his way back to Moscow from a visit to the United States.[5] The Danish company also has a licensing agreement with the Polish engine builders Stocznia Gdanska, and part of that organization's annual production of 350,000 bhp of B & W designs goes to the Soviet Union.[6]

Under the 1956 Scientific and Technical Cooperation agreement between the U.S.S.R. and Czechoslovakia, the Skoda works sends technical documentation and technical assistance to the U.S.S.R. on the latest marine diesel designs. Skoda is also a major direct supplier of diesel engines to the U.S.S.R.[7]

The available evidence strongly indicates that all Russky Disel (Leningrad) marine engines are made under the technical-assistance agreement with Skoda of Czechoslovakia while all diesels at Bryansk are built under the B & W agreement. Under the COMECON specialization agreements, Czechoslovakia undertakes development and production of large marine diesels while the Soviet Union is not listed for that responsibility—nor indeed for any development or production of marine diesels of any size.[8] Agreements and trade between the two countries confirm this. The 1956 Scientific and Technical Corporation required Czechoslovakia to send technical documentation for the manufacture of the latest designs in diesel engines to the U.S.S.R. Further, Czechoslovakia is not only the fourth largest producer of diesel engines in the world—far larger

---

4 *Ibid.*
5 *East-West Commerce,* VI, 2 (February 1959), 3.
6 See chapter 6.
7 See chapter 6 for more information on these indirect transfers.
8 See Frederic L. Pryor, *The Communist Foreign Trade System* (London: George Allen & Unwin, 1963), Appendix E.

Table 17-5   UTILIZATION OF DIESEL ENGINES IN SOVIET VEHICLES

Diesel engine model	YaAZ-M204A	YaAZ-M204B	YaAZ-M206A	YaAZ-M206B	YaAZ-M206D
Soviet vehicle model	ZIL-152 MAZ-200 MAZ-200G MAZ-205 MAZ-501	MAZ-200B MAZ-502	KrAZ-219 KrAZ-221 KrAZ-222	KrAZ-214	ZIL-127 YaAZ-210E YaAZ-218 (1957) YaAZ-210 (1951-58) YaAZ-210G (1951-58)

Source: *Kratkii avtomobil'nyi spravochnik*, 5th edition (Moscow, 1968) p. 409.

Table 17-6   ORIGINS OF TRUCK DIESEL ENGINES IN THE SOVIET UNION UP TO 1960

Basic engine Model number	Type	Weight, kg	Number of cylinders	Displacement	Cylinder diameter, mm	Piston Stroke	Horsepower	rpm	Western origin
YaAZ-M206D	In-line	960	6	6.97	108.0	127.0	180	2,000	GMCModel (U.S.)
YaAZ-M206A	V	890	6	6.97	108.0	127.0	180(215)	2,000	GMC Model (U.S.)
YaAZ-M204A	V	800	4	4.65	108.0	127.0	120	2,000	GMC Model (U.S.)
D-12A	V	1,400	12	38.80	150.0	180.0	300	1,500	Not known

Source: *Kratkii avtomobil'nyi spravochnik*, 5th edition (Moscow, 1968).

than the U.S.S.R.—but also exports 80 percent of all its diesels, and the U.S.S.R. is the largest buyer.[9]

DIESEL ENGINES FOR TRUCK USE

The range of diesel engines for truck use in the Soviet Union is very limited. Between 1945 and the mid-1960s, when new models YaMZ-236 and YaMZ-238 replaced earlier engines,[10] only four commonly used models were identified.

Three models widely used in trucks and buses were based on General Motors engines: the YaAZ-M206D, a six-cylinder in-line 180-hp engine; the YaAZ-M206A, a V-type version of the same engine; and a four-cylinder V type developing 120 hp mainly for use in the MAZ-200 truck produced from 1947 to 1966 at Minsk. These three basic models, produced at Yaroslavl,[11] have been utilized for at least a dozen Soviet truck and bus models. (See Table 17-5.)

The only other engine that has been produced is the D-12 type used in the MAZ-525, MAZ-530, and BelAZ-540 dump trucks. This engine has a 300-hp rating, compared to the 120-180-hp range of the YaAZ series (see Table 17-6). Its origin is not known, although the Soviets received the Kloeckner-Humboldt-Deutz diesel engine plant in 1946 under U.S. Operation RAP,[12] and Deutz prewar diesels had similar specifications.

The new model truck diesels introduced in the late 1960s (YaMZ-236 and YaMZ-238) bear considerable resemblance to the U.S. Cummins engine. The YaMZ-236 has a layout similar in many respects to the Cummins 90° V6-200, while the YaMZ-238 resembles the Cummins 90° V8-265.[13]

A backwardness in truck diesel engines is reflected in Soviet use of European diesel engines in the few Soviet automobiles assembled in Belgium and sold on the European market. The Volga automobile was offered with an optional Rover U.K. diesel engine in 1965; the Moskvich was offered by the Soviets, also in 1965, with a Perkins U.K. 99 diesel engine.[14] In 1968 Soviet trucks sold in Europe also utilized diesel engines supplied by Perkins.

In 1960-61 the Soviets attempted to purchase in the United States over $40 million worth of specialized equipment for the manufacture of truck engine blocks.[15] This generated a great deal of controversy in Congress, and ultimately

---

[9] *Czechoslovak Economic Bulletin* (Prague). no. 306 (March 1956). 25.

[10] *Ekspluatsionnye kachestva dvigatelei YaMZ-236 and YaMZ-238* (Moscow. 1968).

[11] See Sutton II for assistance to this plant.

[12] See chapter 2.

[13] No confirmation can be obtained from the company on this point. but compare G. D. Chernyshev. *Dvigateli YaMZ-236, YaMZ-238* (Moscow. 1968), pp. 5, 16, with D.S.D. Williams. *British Diesel Engine Catalogue*. 6th edition (London, 1965). p. 57.

[14] S. d'Angelo, ed., *World Car Catalogue* (New York: Herald Books. 1965). pp. 228, 356.

[15] U.S. House of Representatives. Select Committee on Export Control. *Investigation and Study of the Administration, Operations, and Enforcement of the Export Control Act of 1949, and Related Acts (H.R. 403)*. 87th Congress, 1st session, October, December 1961 pt. 1, p. 220.

the sale involved only two transfermatic machines to produce V-8 engine blocks; one unit was valued at $3.4 million and one at $1.9 million, for a total of $5.3 million. The units were required by the Soviets to produce 225-hp truck engines.

DIESEL-ELECTRIC PRIME MOVERS

The most important Soviet diesel-electric prime mover is the 2 D 100 unit utilized in more than 1000 type TE 3 diesel-electric locomotives and more than 50 merchant vessels.[16] The 2 D 100 power plant is a two-stroke, opposed piston model with ten cylinders developing 2000 hp at 850 rpm. Design work started in 1950; the first locomotive with the unit was produced in 1953 and the first ship in 1954.

The opposed piston principle was developed by Fairbanks-Morse in the United States, and the Soviet 2 D 100 is a copy of Fairbanks Morse Model 38D 8-1/8 series, although the cylinder diameter of the Soviet version is 207 mm compared with 206.37 mm in the Fairbanks Morse original.[17]

Since no other diesel-electric unit has been identified in current production, the possibility exists that this unit is used in the Soviet icebreakers of the "Ledokol" series for which no engine data are given in the Soviet Register, and also in numerous Soviet naval units propelled by diesel-electric propulsion units.

INTERNAL COMBUSTION ENGINES

About 95 percent of Soviet internal combustion engine production in 1959 was represented by two engines, an in-line six-cylinder in the GAZ 51 truck series and another in-line six-cylinder in the ZIL 150 series.[18] Most of the remaining production was taken up by heavier truck engines. Table 17-7 summarizes the origins of the major truck and automobile gasoline engines in operation up to 1960.

The original Moskvitch 401, a four-cylinder in-line engine, was a copy of the 1939 German Opel engine. Two subsequent versions, the MZMZ 407 and the MZMA 408, were modified versions of the original Moskvitch 401

---

[16] For merchant ships see Registr Soyuza SSR, *op. cit.* n. 1; for locomotives see K. A. Shishkin *et al., Teplovoz TE-3* (Moscow,1969).

[17] Fairbanks Morse, Power Systems Division, *Fairbanks Morse 38D8 1/8 Series Opposed Piston Diesel and Gas Engines* (Beloit, Wis., n.d.), Bulletin 3800D8-S3.

[18] Barney K. Schwalberg, *Manpower Utilization in the Soviet Automobile Industry*, Supplementary Report (Washington: U.S. Department of Commerce, Bureau of the Census, June 1959), p. 16.

Table 17-7   ORIGINS OF AUTOMOBILE AND TRUCK INTERNAL COMBUSTION ENGINES IN THE SOVIET UNION UP TO 1960

Basic engine model number	Type	Weight, kg	Number of cylinders	Displacement, litres	Cylinder diameter, mm	Piston stroke	Horsepower	rpm	Western Origin
401	in-line	112	4	1.07	67.5	75.0	26.0	4,000	Opel
MZMA 407	in-line	123	4	1.36	76.0	75.0	45.0	4,500	modified
MZMA 408	in-line	123	4	1.36	76.0	75.0	50.0	4,750	
GAZ 20	in-line	153	4	2.12	82.0	100.0	52.0	3,600	World War II Ford/Willys
GAZ 69	in-line		4	2.12	82.0	100.0	52.0	3,600	¼-ton truck (Jeep)
GAZ 21A	in-line	146	4	2.445	92.0	92.0	75.0	4,000	Improved GAZ 20
UAZ 451	in-line	145	4	2.445	92.0	92.0	70.0	4,000	(WW II Jeep)
UAZ 450	in-line		4	2.43	88.0	100.0	62.0	3,800	
GAZ 13	V		8	5.52	100.0	88.0	195.0	4,200	Ford Motor Co.
ZIL 111	V	312	8	5.98	100.0	95.0	200.0	4,200	Ford Motor Co. plant
GAZ 51	in-line	235	6	3.48	82.0	110.0	70.0	2,800	
ZIL 158B	in-line	400	6	5.55	101.6	114.3	109.0	2,800	
Ural 353A	in-line	380	6	5.55	101.6	114.3	95.0	2,600	
ZIL 150	in-line		6	5.55	101.6	114.3	90.0	—	1934 Fordson engine;
ZIL 164A	in-line	380	6	5.55	101.6	114.3	100.0	2,800	Hercules Motor Co.
ZIL 157K	in-line	380	6	5.55	101.6	114.3	110.0	2,800	equipment
KAZ 606A	in-line	380	6	5.55	101.6	114.3	104.0	2,600	
GAZ 53	V	215	8	4.25	92.0	80.0	115.0	3,200	Ford Motor Co. plant

Source: *Kratkii avtomobil'nyi spravochnik*, 5th edition (Moscow, 1968).

and the latter was used in the Moskvitch automobile as late as the mid-1960s.

The GAZ 20 is the four-cylinder U.S. Jeep engine and used in both the civilian and military versions of the GAZ 20 and the GAZ 69. Its closest U.S. counterpart is the World War II Ford/Willys one-quarter-ton Jeep engine, and the Soviets presumably based their design on Lend Lease supplies and equipment.

The GAZ 21A and UAZ 451 are improved versions of the original Jeep engine, with somewhat larger displacement (2.445 instead of 2.12 litres) and a higher horsepower rating (70-75 hp instead of 52 hp). The GAZ 51, the GAZ 53 with a V-8 engine of U.S. type, and all other GAZ engines, are built in the Ford-designed and -built Gorki plant,[19] which received a considerable quantity of new U.S. machinery during and after World War II.

The 5.55-litre displacement engine used in the ZIL-158B, the Ural 353A, the more common ZIL 150, the ZIL 164A, the ZIL 157K and the KAZ 606A has the same engine characteristics as the prewar Fordson tractor engine produced at Yaroslavl with equipment installed by the Hercules Engine Company in 1934.[20]

FRENCH ORIGINS OF MARINE GAS TURBINES

Soviet marine gas turbines are based on French turbines imported in 1959. Table 17-8 lists all gas turbine-powered Soviet ships built up to 1967 and the origin of their gas generators and turbines. The typical plant consists of four free-piston gas generators, 340 by 904 mm, manufactured by S.I.G.M.A. at Venissieux,[21] and a gas turbine geared to the shaft manufactured by Société Alsthom of Belfort, France.[22] The hulls were built and the French turbines installed at the Baltic Yards in Leningrad.

WESTERN ORIGINS OF SOVIET STEAM TURBINES

Analysis of the Soviet register of shipping suggests that no steam turbines for merchant marine use were manufactured in the Soviet Union before 1959.[23]

---

[19] See Sutton I and II.

[20] *Ibid.*

[21] S.I.G.M.A. is Société Industrielle Générale de Mécanique Appliquée, a subsidiary of Organisation Bossard et Michel S.A.

[22] Alsthom is Société Générale de Constructions Electriques et Mécaniques Alsthom, a subsidiary of Française Thomson-Houston-Hotchkiss-Brandt S.A. Cie and affiliated with Thomson Electric Company of New York.

[23] This statement should be modified by the observation that Soviet Navy ships use steam turbines; hence the Soviets probably had a capability for manufacturing marine steam turbines before 1959. The statement here applies only to the merchant marine.

Table 17-8   ORIGINS OF SOVIET MARINE GAS TURBINES
AS OF 1967

Soviet register number	Name of Ship	Date Launched	Gas Turbine manufacturer
2126	*Pavlin Vinogradov*	1960	S.I.G.M.A. France (1960)
4465	*Umbales*	1962	S.I.G.M.A. France (1959)
4859	*Johann Mahmastal*	1965	S.I.G.M.A. France (1959)
2197	*Pechorales*	1964	S.I.G.M.A. France (1959)
4345	*Teodor Nette*	1963	S.I.G.M.A. France (1959)

Sources: *Lloyd's Register of Shipping, 1969-70*, (London, 1969); *Registr Soyuza SSR, Registrovaya kniga morskikh sudov soyuza SSR 1964-1965*, (Moscow, 1966).
Note: These five ships constituted the total Soviet fleet of gas turbine-powered ships to 1967

In 1964 the Soviet mercantile fleet had 45 ships powered by steam turbines. The acquisitions of these turbines fall into three distinct periods: stage one, that of foreign purchases only; stage two, that of foreign purchases concurrent with limited domestic production of steam turbines; and stage three, that of domestic manufacture of steam turbines without foreign imports.

Stage one extended from 1953 through 1956. In 1953 the Soviets installed German boilers in a Dutch ship with turbines built in 1919, possibly as a test bed for further work. Then in 1955 six steam turbines for marine use were ordered in France and two more in East Germany. Of the French turbines, one came from Schneider et Cie at Le Creusot (France), one from a subsidiary of this company (Société des Forges at Ateliers du Creusot), and four from Ateliers et Chantiers de Bethune located at Nantes on the western coast of Brittany. The turbines supplied by Schneider et Cie at Le Creusot were undoubtedly of Westinghouse design, inasmuch as Schneider has a licensing agreement with the Westinghouse Electrical Corporation in the United States and both companies jointly own a French development company, Société de Développement Westinghouse-Schneider of Paris.

In 1959 the Soviets produced the first domestic (at least nonmilitary) marine steam turbine, which was installed in a 12,000-ton ship (Soviet Register Number 1602); this was followed by construction of four turbines in 1959, seven in 1960, six in 1961, five in 1962, and eight in 1963. However in 1959, when the first Soviet merchant marine steam turbine was produced, four turbines were purchased abroad and installed in ships later added to the Soviet mercantile fleet. One turbine came from Italy and was installed in the *Giuseppe Garibaldi;* this was a geared turbine manufactured by the Ansaldo shipyards in Genoa,

Italy. This company is licensed to manufacture De Laval geared turbines (De Laval is an American corporation). Another De Laval turbine was installed in the *Trud* (Soviet Register Number 4393). This was a geared turbine manufactured by De Lavals Angturbin in Stockholm, Sweden, and also manufactured under license from the De Laval Company in the United States. Two additional steam turbines were purchased in Japan. One, from the shipbuilding company Hitachi, is a Kawasaki turbine with water tube boilers. The second turbine was purchased in 1960, and is a geared unit manufactured by Ishikawajima Harima in Tokyo; this company has a licensing agreement with Foster Wheeler in the United States for manufacturing water tube boilers for marine use.

Thus, between 1958 and 1961 the Soviets purchased four steam turbines abroad and manufactured another five or six steam turbines within the Soviet Union. Undoubtedly the initial Soviet steam turbines were compared with imported turbines concerning operating characteristics.

Up to 1962 we find that the Soviets manufactured an average of five or six steam turbines per year and since that time all units have been manufactured domestically. The Western predecessors of these domestic steam turbines are not known; they may be Metropolitan-Vickers (a subsidiary of Westinghouse) under an old agreement, or General Electric, or possibly even Sulzer.

A similar three-stage development process appears to be under way in marine gas turbines; several gas turbines were purchased in France in 1960 and presumably by the end of the decade of the sixties the Soviets will have started to manufacture, within the Soviet Union, marine gas turbines according to this design.

ORIGINS OF MARINE BOILERS INSTALLED
BETWEEN 1945 AND 1960

Between 1945 and 1960 a total of 447 marine boilers of three types (water tube, fire tube, and combined) were installed in Soviet merchant ships. Of this total, only 76 (or 17.0 percent) were manufactured in the Soviet Union. The remainder were imported: 181 (or 40.5 percent of the total) from Finland, 116 (or 25.9 percent) from the East European communist countries of East Germany and Poland, and the rest from non-Finnish sources in the Free World, including 46 (or 10.3 percent) from Sweden.

There are several noteworthy observations concerning these boilers. The large percentage imported, i.e. 83 percent, suggests there was a major Soviet weakness in this area. The 17 percent Soviet-manufactured boilers also are of a standard type; between 1949 and 1954 only one type of marine boiler was manufactured, i.e., of a 174-square-meter heating surface with a working pressure of 15.0 kg/cm^2. Between 1955 and 1960 this standard model was replaced by another of 180-square-meter heating surface with the same working pressure. During this period of 15 years the Soviet Union manufactured only a single standard boiler model at any one time. The flexibility required in practice was attained by imports from Eastern Europe and the Free World;[24] larger sizes of marine boilers with greater working pressures were imported in a variety of models from Finland, Poland, East and West Germany, Sweden, Italy, Denmark, Norway, Belgium, the United Kingdom, and Holland. (See Table 17-9.)

Table 17-9   ORIGINS OF MARINE BOILERS INSTALLED
                  IN THE SOVIET UNION BETWEEN 1945 AND 1960

Size of boiler; m² of heating surface	Finland	U.S.S.R.	Poland	East Germany	Sweden	Other Free World countries	Total
718	—	—	—	—	—	2 (Italy)	2
495	—	—	2	—	—	—	2
390	—	—	—	4	—	—	4
386	—	—	—	2	—	—	2
287	—	—	1	—	—	—	1
286	—	—	—	2	—	—	2
260	—	—	—	—	3	—	3
254-6	—	—	69	2	—	1 (Denmark) 2 (Norway) 4 (FRG)	78
245	—	—	4	—	—	3 (U.K.)	7
235-8	—	—	—	—	32	—	32
213-9	—	—	—	—	11	1 (Belgium)	12
204	—	—	8	—	—	—	8
186	—	—	—	16	—	—	16
180	—	35	—	—	—	—	35
174	—	41	—	—	—	—	41
170	4	—	—	4	—	6 (Holland) 4 (FRG)	18
163-5	17	—	—	—	—	2 (FRG)	19
150	1	—	—	—	—	—	1
140	128	—	—	—	—	1 (FRG)	129
136	—	—	—	2	—	—	2
125	—	—	—	—	—	2 (Norway)	2
103	31	—	—	—	—	—	31
	181	76	84	32	46	28	447
Percentage of Total	40.5	17.0	18.8	7.1	10.3	6.2	99.9

Sources: Registr Soyuza SSR, *Registrovaya kniga morskikh sudov soyuza SSR 1964-1965* (Moscow, 1966). See chapter 28 for diagram based on these data.

---

[24] See diagram, p. 407.

The most significant conclusion is that a detailed examination of one important class of prime movers—marine diesels, for which we have complete and accurate data does not produce evidence of useful Soviet innovation. Four-fifths of these units, whether measured in terms of units or aggregate horsepower, were built abroad and those built inside the U.S.S.R. had considerable, if not complete, dependence on foreign designs and for the most part technical assistance in the form of drawings and sample engines.

The evidence produced for truck diesels, internal combustion engines, and gas turbines suggests a similar heavy dependence on foreign technology—no indigenous Soviet work forms the basis for large-scale production of these propulsion systems. In boilers we find long-term manufacture of a single model of 174 to 180 cubic meters for marine use (boilers are of course manufactured in other models for nonmarine uses), with flexibility obtained by boilers from outside the U.S.S.R.

CHAPTER EIGHTEEN

Western Assistance to Soviet Atomic Energy

SOVIET THEORETICAL WORK BEFORE WORLD WAR II

Russian aptitude for theoretical work in mathematics and physics is well exemplified in the fields of high-energy physics and atomic theory. As a result of the work of Petr Kapitsa and other physicists in the decade of the twenties, Soviet research paralleled Western research in the 1930s. A series of institutes was established, of which the Nuclear Physics Laboratory at the Leningrad Technical Institute under Igor Kurchatov was preeminent. Two cyclotrons were established under Kurchatov (at the same time as scientists at the University of California at Berkeley pioneered the cyclotron), but two other cyclotrons were left unfinished until the end of the war.

According to A. Kramish, Soviet scientists had made several major discoveries by 1940 and "the Russians are justified in claiming priority for the discovery of spontaneous fission."[1] Work was undertaken on methods for quantity production of fissionable materials, i.e., uranium-235 and heavy water, and methods later used by the United States in the Manhattan Project were under active discussion and even partly published in the U.S.S.R. before World War II.

The Nazi attack of June 1941 brought this promising theoretical work to a halt, and for some years thereafter Russian activity was limited to monitoring Western progress, particularly the extraordinary progress in the United States. There is no question that Soviet scientists were at least on a par with Western scientists in 1940, and in some areas of theory they could have been slightly ahead.

The wartime monitoring process comprised espionage, not only in the United States and Canada,[2] but also in Germany.[3] It was later asserted in scientific circles in the United States that scientific "secrets" could not be effectively retained, and official U.S. policy, as announced by President Truman in October 1945, was to retain the engineering and industrial techniques but not the scientific

---

[1] M. J. Ruggles and A. Kramish, *The Soviet Union and the Atom: The Early Years* (Santa Monica: RAND Corp., 1956), Report no. RM-1711. Arnold Kramish has also published *Atomic Energy in the Soviet Union* (Stanford, 1959); this is in great part a reproduction of the material in RAND report no. RM-1711 and companion studies.

data within the United States; hence the preparation of the 1945 Smyth Report, which was of some assistance to Soviet work.[4]

German wartime efforts in the same field, from the scientific viewpoint, were on a level with those of the United States. The Weinberg-Nordheim report[5] concluded that German wartime researchers "were on the right track and their thinking and developments paralleled ours to a surprising extent. According to this report the Germans knew the correct lattice dimensions for a P-9U system as well as the required quantity (four tons) of P-9. Their uranium metal "was about as pure as ours," their theory of the chain reaction "was in no wise inferior to ours, in some respects it was superior," and the only nonengineering "secrets" they might not have had was an understanding of the Xeon-135 poisoning problem and possibly of the properties of plutonium-240.[6] It was primarily lack of heavy water that accounted for inability of the Germans to achieve a chain reaction; however, their total effort was on a much smaller scale than the American effort. The report concludes:

> We must proceed, therefore, on the basis that anyone knowing what is in the German reports can establish a chain reaction provided he has sufficient materials. The Smyth report will give additional very helpful hints. The time when others can establish a chain reaction is therefore no longer a matter of scientific research but mostly a matter of procurement.[7]

Given vigorous Soviet atomic espionage, the high level of prewar Soviet scientific work, the American inability to retain scientific secrets, and the availability of German atomic work, scientists, and equipment to the Soviet Union (both through espionage and as a result of postwar capture of German reports), the Soviets had adequate *theoretical* knowledge of atomic weapons manufacture in 1945.

What was perhaps as important as the access to atomic bomb research,

[2] See U.S. Congress, Joint Committee on Atomic Energy, *Soviet Atomic Espionage*, 82d Congress, 1st session, April 1951; and *The Report of the Royal Commission to Investigate the Facts Relating to and the Circumstances Surrounding the Communication, by Public Officials and Other Persons in Positions of Trust, of Secret and Confidential Information to Agents of a Foreign Power; June 27, 1946* (Ottawa, 1946).

[3] A. Kramish, *The Soviet Union and the Atom: The "Secret" Phase* (Santa Monica: RAND Corp., 1957) Report no. RM-1896, p. 17 fn.

[4] U.S. Senate, *Nuclear Scientist Defects to United States*, Subcommittee to Investigate the Administration of the Internal Security Act and Other Internal Security Laws of the Committee on the Judiciary, 89th Congress, 1st session (Washington, 1964).

[5] U.S. Atomic Energy Commission, *Memorandum on the State of Knowledge in Nuclear Science Reached by the Germans in 1945*, by A. M. Weinberg and L. W. Nordheim (Oak Ridge, Tenn: Technical Information Service, November 8, 1945), German Series no. G-371.

[6] Weinberg and Nordheim pointed out their limited access to German reports, but were able to establish these major propositions.

[7] AEC *Memorandum, op. cit.* n. 5, p. 3.

the Soviets had access *on an exclusive basis* to German hydrogen bomb work. David Irving notes a series of experiments on thermonuclear fusion at the German Army explosives research establishment at Kummersdorf; the results of these experiments were captured by Soviet forces and the only document to fall into Western hands, according to Irving, was a "six-page report among the *Alsos* collection ... entitled 'Experiments on the Initiation of Nuclear Reactions by Means of Exploding Substances.' "[8]

Therefore, as the Weinberg-Nordheim report concludes, the important restriction to Soviet atomic development at 1945 was not the scientific method of "making an atomic bomb" but the materials and equipment with which to undertake the program; i.e., it was "mostly a matter of procurement."[9]

CONTRIBUTION OF THE ATOMIC SPIES TO SOVIET WORK

The Soviets made persistent efforts during World War II to penetrate Western work in atomic energy. General L. R. Groves indicates that the major atomic espionage was carried on by Soviet, not German, agents,[10] and such espionage has undoubtedly continued since that time. There is a correlation between the work of the known Soviet agents—Fuchs, Greenglass, May, and Pontecorvo—and subsequent Soviet developments in the atomic energy and weapons field.

Klaus Fuchs, a theoretical physicist, was a member of the inner group in the development of the atomic bomb in World War II; his work in England concerned the gaseous diffusion process used in the Oak Ridge plant. In the United States, Fuchs was intimately associated with both groups (SAM and the Kellex Corporation) working on gaseous diffusion.[11] According to Karl Cohen, former director of the Atomic Energy Commission, Fuchs " ... had intimate and detailed knowledge of all phases of the design of the K-25 plant, including methods of fabricating the barrier, the assembly of the diffuser, and the planned production rate."[12] At Los Alamos, Fuchs took part in making the first atomic bomb and in the weapons work involved.

By contrast, both May and Pontecorvo understood the operating problems

---

8 David Irving, *The Virus House* (London: William Kimber, 1967), pp. 193-95; p. 194 has a photograph of p. 1 of the 1944 German Army report on initial work on an H-bomb. The full report is probably at Oak Ridge, Tennessee.

9 AEC *Memorandum, op. cit.* n. 5, p. 3.

10 Leslie R. Groves, *Now It Can Be Told* (New York: Harper and Row, 1962), p. 141.

11 U.S. Congress, Joint Committee on Atomic Energy, *Soviet Atomic Espionage*, 82d Congress, 1st session, April 1951 (Washington, 1951).

12 Letter, Cohen to Joint Committee on Atomic Energy, in *ibid.*, p. 23. Fuchs also was working on uranium hexafluoride and the control problems of gaseous diffusion plants.

of plutonium piles and both worked on the Hanford reactor, which was copied by the Soviet Union in developing the first Soviet reactor.[13]

Nunn May worked in 1942 at the Cavendish Laboratories in Cambridge, England, and in January 1943 went to Canada where he was senior member of the Nuclear Physics Division. Espionage, for which he was sentenced to ten years in prison, consisted of supplying the Soviets with samples of uranium-235 and uranium-233. May admittedly also passed on to the Soviets information that was still classified in 1946.[14]

Prior to his defection to Russia in 1950, physicist Bruno Pontecorvo worked as senior principal scientific officer at the British Harwell Laboratory. The most significant knowledge possessed by Pontecorvo concerned the Hanford reactor and the nuclear aspects of the Canadian NRX heavy-water pile at Chalk River, Ontario—at that time the most advanced reactor of its type in the world.[15]

David Greenglass, the fourth atomic spy, was a machinist assigned to the Los Alamos weapons laboratory, where he worked on high-explosive lens molds: "Greenglass testified that he conveyed to Russia a diagram of the atomic bomb, along with a detailed explanation and related materials in writing."[16]

In sum, the Soviets gained a great deal of useful information and technical know-how from espionage sources; by themselves these data were of limited use, but combined with other sources they comprised a package with significant potential.

THE GERMAN CONTRIBUTION
TO SOVIET ATOMIC ENERGY PROJECTS[17]

The widespread impression that the Soviets did not gain useful materials, equipment, or information from the German atomic research program is erroneous.[18] (See Table 18-1.)

---

[13] *Ibid.:* May p. 2, Pontecorvo p. 2. See also p. 242 below.

[14] *Ibid.*, p. 2.

[15] *Ibid.*, p. 1.

[16] *Ibid.*, p. 3.

[17] For the status of the German atomic energy projects in 1945 and also for a measure of the technology and facilities removed to the Soviet Union, see the G Series of reports at the Atomic Energy Commission, Oak Ridge, Tennessee. Some 394 reports are listed in Atomic Energy Commission TID-3030, *German Reports on Atomic Energy.* See also BIOS Final Report 675, *Production of Thorium and Uranium in Germany.*

[18] For example, see G. A. Modelski, *Atomic Energy in the Communist Bloc,* (Melbourne, 1959), p. 36. Modelski concludes: "... the Russians may have picked up some useful material and information, as well as some trained men, but the sum total cannot have been very large. German research had not progressed very far during the war and by 1944, far from having a pile working, German scientists merely envisaged the possibility that one might be made to work."

Table 18-1   SUMMARY OF GERMAN ATOMIC ENERGY PROJECTS
                REMOVED TO THE U.S.S.R. IN 1945

Material or project	Location and plant	Status at 1945
Uranium metal reduction	DEGUSSA, Frankfurt plant (moved to Berlin in 1944)	Peak annual production 5,000 kg (1942); removed to U.S.S.R.
	DEGUSSA, Berlin-Grünau plant	Peak production of 376 kg (1945); removed to U.S.S.R.
Stocks of uranium metal and oxides at Oranienburg plant Uranium metal refinery	Auer A.G.	Removed to U.S.S.R.
Heavy water	Stocks at Leuna in Silesia	Probably removed to U.S.S.R.
Separation processes	von Ardenne magnetic separator	Removed with von Ardenne to U.S.S.R.
	Groth centrifuge	
Linear accelerator	Berlin	Removed to U.S.S.R.

Source: David Irving, *The Virus House* (London: William Kimber, 1967).

In 1945 the bulk of German uranium ore, the balance of 1200 tons removed by the German Army from Belgium in 1940, was moved to a salt mine near Stassfurt in what was to become the Soviet Zone. A British-American mission attached itself in 1945 to a U.S. infantry division and under ''Operation Harborage'' seized the mine and the 1100 tons of Belgian ore located nearby. This uranium ore was removed to the American Zone of Germany.[19]

Uranium metal was produced in Germany in World Warr II at two plants operated by DEGUSSA (German Gold and Silver Extraction Corporation). Uranium oxide supplied by Auer A.G. in Berlin was reduced by DEGUSSA at its Frankfurt plant, and by the end of 1940 the company was producing a maximum of one ton of uranium metal per month. In the United States, by way of comparison, almost no uranium metal was available until the end of 1942; when the first chain reaction took place at Chicago, the DEGUSSA plant in Frankfurt had manufactured over seven tons of uranium metal.[20]

Work began in 1942 on a second uranium production plant identical to the DEGUSSA plant but at Grünau, Berlin. In January 1945 the DEGUSSA Frankfurt plant was removed to the Auer location near Berlin, where the uranium metal was being refined. The Soviets occupied Oranienburg and the Auer works, and so obtained several tons of pure uranium oxide and, more importantly, the two DEGUSSA uranium smelting plants and the Auer refining plant. In addition they captured five tons of uranium metal powder, a quantity of uranium

[19] See Irving, *op. cit.* n. 8; also see S. Goodsmit, *ALSOS* (New York: Schuman, 1947).
[20] Irving, *op. cit.* n. 8, pp. 75-76.

cubes, and about 25 tons of unrefined uranium oxide and uranates. This became the uranium stockpile for the early Soviet atomic bomb program.[21]

Unlike the American program, for which the ultrapure graphite necessary for use as a moderator was produced by several firms, the German atomic project was not able to use graphite as a moderator and thus came to be dependent on the use of heavy water. Part of the Norwegian heavy water plant, captured by the Germans and then destroyed by British Commandos, was duplicated by I. G. Farben at Leuna. The Leuna plant was later subjected to heavy bombing, but the surviving drums of heavy water were transported to the I. G. Farben plant at Myrow in Silesia and presumably captured there and removed to the Soviet Union.[22]

By the time the war ended the Germans had seven isotope separation processes under consideration, excluding the gaseous diffusion process used in the United States, and at least two of these had been brought to the equipment stage. Manfred von Ardenne had developed a magnetic isotope separator similar in concept to the magnetic process that was then used at Oak Ridge in the United States and later built at von Ardenne's Berlin laboratories. Also, a prototype centrifuge with an operating speed of 50,000 revolutions per minute was built by Groth; although the early models failed, it seems that this centrifuge process had practical possibilities for isotope separation. In 1945, von Ardenne's laboratory at Berlin, complete with a Van de Graaf machine, a cyclotron, and the prototype electromagnetic isotope separation equipment, was removed with von Ardenne himself to the Soviet Union.

The Germans also built several subcritical piles. The first German pile was at the Kaiser Wilhelm Institute of Biology and Virus Research in Berlin. This was a heavy-water pile, and according to the American intelligence mission which inspected it in July 1945 after much of the equipment had been removed to the Soviet Union, it appeared to have been excellently equipped when compared to the primitive setup that Enrico Fermi used at Columbia University in the United States.

The Kaiser Wilhelm Institute was stripped of all its equipment, including a high-voltage linear accelerator, and moved to the Russian atomic project at Obninchoye.[23]

Another pile, built at Leipzig, was destroyed in a 1942 explosion, and a third pile was located at Haigerloch. In the late summer of 1944 all uranium pile research was removed to Stadtilm in Thuringia in what was to be the Soviet Zone. Later, in 1945, some pile research was moved south.

It is interesting to note, then, that while in 1944 and early 1945 rocket development projects under Werner von Braun moved westward into the future

---

[21] *Ibid.*, p. 263.
[22] *Ibid.*, pp. 157, 178, 191-92.
[23] *Ibid.*, p. 264.

U.S. and British zones, the movement of atomic energy projects (metal reduction, uranium ore, and pile research) was eastward into the future Soviet Zone, and there most of it remained when the war ended.

Finally, the Soviets rounded up the uranium project scientists and most went, under good contracts, to the Soviet Union. Among these men were von Ardenne, an expert in the separation process and something of an equipment genius, and Nikolaus Riehl, an expert in the processing and refining of uranium metal; both worked for about ten years on the Soviet atomic project.[24]

The German nuclear scientists were settled at Sukhumi and remained there from 1945 until some time after 1955. The sanatoriums along the Black Sea coast were converted into nuclear research institutes where the German groups were installed and projects started. For example, Heinz Barwich was the leader of 18 scientists working on theoretical questions concerning control problems in the diffusion process of isotope separation.[25] Associated in this work was Yuri Krutkov, who was technically known as a "prisoner-engineer" and had been released from a prison camp for this purpose. Another group at Sukhumi was the von Ardenne team working with R. A. Demirkhanov on instrumentation for nuclear energy and later on ion sources and mass spectrography. Although the Sukhumi laboratories are today of secondary importance, they formed the key section for the development of atomic energy in the Soviet Union in the forties and fifties and employed many German engineers. Some of the personnel have since returned to Germany, but others are still in Sukhumi.

Methods for the mass production of uranium-235 were developed at Sukhumi. The Soviets undertook duplication of both the barrier method (already established in the United States) and the centrifuge method of isotope separation. Doctor Zuehlke specialized in the barrier question. The manufacture of metallic barriers was divided into two groups: those working on flat barriers and those working on tube barriers. Max Steenbeck, another German scientist, was one who concentrated for a number of years on the ultracentrifuge method for separating uranium gas.[26]

In summary, at the end of World War II the Soviets obtained from Germany not only scientists and expert technicians (the Germans were then on the threshold of achieving a chain reaction) but facilities for ore processing, reduction, and refining of uranium metal and oxides, two working isotope separation processes and operating equipment, advanced laboratories and equipment, and several

---

[24] *Ibid.*, p. 263. Irving also lists about a dozen other Germans, key members of the German atomic energy project, who went to the Soviet Union.

[25] See Dr. Barwich testimony to U.S. Senate, *Nuclear Scientist Defects* ..., *op. cit.* n. 4, pp. 10 *et seq.*

[26] See *ibid.*, for usefulness of U.S. reports to German work in the U.S.S.R. Also see U.S. Senate, Committee on the Judiciary, *Scope of Soviet Activity in the United States*, Hearings Before the Subcommittee to Investigate the Administration of the Internal Security Act and other Internal Security Laws, 84th Congress, 2d session, (Washington, 1956), pt. 21.

subcritical piles. In addition they located and removed small stocks of heavy water, uranium metal, and uranium oxides.

The Soviets failed to obtain from the Germans any information on the gaseous diffusion separation process, the use of graphite as a moderator, or knowledge of a chain reaction in practice. Nor did they obtain any operational atomic weapons technology, although they did acquire useful German research work. These technologies could only have come from the United States or from Great Britain (for the gaseous diffusion process).

Probably the most accurate estimate of Soviet capability in atomic development at the end of World War II was made in November 1945 by Major General L. R. Groves, testifying before the Senate Special Committee on Atomic Energy. General Groves was director of the Manhattan Project during World War II, and at that time was more knowledgeable than any other person concerning the industrial and technical features of production of atomic materials and atomic bombs. He made a statement relative to the Soviet Union as follows:

> I testified before the House Committee in response to a direct question on that point, that one nation could catch up and produce a bomb, if they did it in complete secrecy, probably within from 15 to 20 years—more likely the latter. If they did it without secrecy and with a great deal of help from the United States and from England and Switzerland—and I say Switzerland because she is a manufacturer of precision machinery—it would be done in five to seven years, probably seven.[27]

Under questioning from the committee, General Groves elaborated on the assistance that would be needed. This would have to include engineering developments, i.e., the design and manufacture of and the specifications for metallurgical processes. Groves commented on the fact that at the Hanford Engineering Works, the Dupont Company had over 10,000 subcontractors, "each of them supplying a different material ... they were supplying subassemblies."[28] At least 50 percent of these 10,000 subcontractors required some special "know-how." With all the technical resources of American industry it had taken 18 months to build this kind of equipment, and according to General Groves, in 1945 such resources could have been obtained only in the United States, England, and Switzerland, with possibly some parts in Sweden. Switzerland was isolated by General Groves because it has been a center of high-grade machine tools of special design: "You find a great many [Swiss machine tools] in this country [i.e., the U.S.A.]

[27] U.S. Senate, Special Committee on Atomic Energy, *Hearings* Pursuant to S. Res. 179, Creating a Special Commission and Investigating Problems Related to the Development, Use and Control of Atomic Energy, 79th Congress, 1st session, November and December 1945 (Washington, 1946), pts. 1-3; *idib.*, 2d session, January and February 1946 (Washington, 1946), pts. 4, 5.

[28] *Ibid.*, pts. 1-3, p. 67.

particularly in any plant that has been in operation for a number of years and has accumulated a number of special Swiss machines.''[29]

It is quite clear that in 1945 the Soviets with outside help of a detailed nature, would have required five to seven years to reproduce the American achievement, and that such assistance could only come from one of three countries—the United States, England, or Switzerland. General Groves's testimony is entirely consistent with evidence provided in this study concerning Soviet technical backwardness.

INDUSTRIAL ASPECTS OF THE SOVIET ATOMIC PROGRAM

The conclusion of the Weinberg-Nordheim report is supported by Klaus Fuchs's statement that he could do no more than explain to the Soviets the principle upon which a bomb was based: '' ... it was up to the Russians to produce their own industrial equipment.''[30] Neither could any other of the atomic spies provide more than information on scientific and technical principles. The key question after taking atomic espionage into account, then, is this: Where did the Soviets get the industrial ability to manufacture an atomic bomb? This achievement is infinitely more important than transfer of scientific information; it is also more difficult to assess.

Klaus Fuchs indicated that he had been "astonished" when the Soviets "succeeded in making and detonating a bomb so rapidly," and he added that although scientifically they were sufficiently advanced, he "could not have believed that commercially and industrially they had developed so quickly."[31]

Certainly the overall conclusions of this study and General Groves's expressed views raise similar questions about Soviet industrial ability. In 1945-46 the U.S.S.R. was technologically backward and heavily dependent on the West. Even though priority there is traditionally given to military objectives, the extraordinary effort required—one that strained even American technical resources—was far beyond purely Soviet industrial abilities in the 1940s and 1950s.

It is therefore suggested, in line with the Weinberg-Nordheim report and the comments of Klaus Fuchs, that the essential question to be answered about Soviet atomic weapons development, and about the Soviet atomic energy program in general, is what was the source of the industrial capability to manufacture atomic materials, including atomic weapons. The argument, outlined below, is that the technical capability came by various routes from the West.

The basic raw material for atomic reactors is uranium ore converted into uranium metal—the metal being the raw material for pile operation.

[29] *Ibid.,* p. 69.
[30] Allan Moorehead, *The Traitors,* (London: Hamish Hamilton, 1952), p. 141.
[31] *Ibid.*

In January 1943 the Soviet Purchasing Commission requested eight tons each of uranium oxide and uranyl nitrate salts.[32] A. Kramish indicates that if this was processed into metal it would yield "just about the right amount of material necessary to duplicate the United States experiments at Chicago."[33]

In March 1943 two licenses were granted to the S. W. Shattuck Chemical Company of Denver, Colorado, for shipments to the Soviet Union: one was for 200 pounds of urano-uranic oxide and 220 pounds of uranium nitrate, and one for 500 pounds each of urano-uranic oxide and uranium nitrate. Granting of these licenses was followed in April 1943 by a license for 25 pounds of uranium metal and in November 1943 by a license for 1000 grams of heavy water. These licenses were granted by the Lend Lease administration to the Soviet Purchasing Commission in the United States. General Groves comments:

> There was a great deal of pressure being brought to bear on Lend Lease apparently to give the Russians everything they could think of. There was a great deal of pressure brought to give them this uranium material.[34]

However, it seems unlikely that the Soviets obtained sufficient reactor materials from U.S. sources. Soviet requisition No. R-12045 of February 4, 1943, for uranium oxide was not filled, and so far as the allowed 25 pounds of uranium metal is concerned, General Groves comments:

> We didn't stop [the] shipment for a very good reason. We were anxious to know if anybody in this country knew how to make uranium metal. . . . We were willing that the Russians have 25 pounds ... it would be worth more than that to us to find out how to make uranium metal.[35]

Later, on March 31, 1944, Lieutenant General L. G. Rudenko wrote to Secretary of War Stimson to the effect that the Soviet Union was "in most urgent need of the following materials for its war industry," i.e., eight tons of uranium nitrate, eight tons of urano-uranic acid, and 25 pounds of uranium metal. Again, these quantities were sufficient to duplicate U.S. work.[36]

The only Soviet receipt of uranium metal from the United States was two pounds of inferior material. However, in June 1948 the Canadian Radium & Uranium Corporation of New York City did ship to the Soviet Union 500 pounds of black uranium oxide and 500 pounds of uranium nitrate—and the

---

[32] U.S. Congress, *Soviet Atomic Espionage, op. cit.* n. 11, pp. 184-92.
[33] Kramish, RAND Report RM-1896, *op. cit.* n. 3., p. 63.
[34] U.S. House of Representatives, Committee on Un-American Activities, *Hearings Regarding Shipment of Atomic Materials to the Soviet Union*. 81st Congress, 1st and 2d sessions, December 1949-March 1950 (Washington, 1950), p. 940.
[35] *Ibid.*, p. 942.
[36] *Ibid.*, p. 1044.

Atomic Energy Commission did not become aware of this shipment for five years.[37]

Of far greater value than uranium metal or oxides supplied from the United States and Canada was the Soviet capture of the Auer A.G. plant at Oranienburg, just outside Berlin, together with German uranium metal and oxides. The Auer plant produced uranium metal for the German atomic program.[38]

SOVIET URANIUM MINING IN SAXONY: WISMUTH A.G.

German uranium ore was mined in Saxony. As soon as American forces evacuated the Saxony area of East Germany, Soviet geologists prospected the old mines around Oberschlema. Subsequently, a corporation named Wismuth A.G. was formed to reopen the mines and develop the uranium content. The chief German adviser used by the Soviets for this project was a Nazi named Schmidt, a former mine inspector and an expert on the Saxony mines. Released from a Soviet concentration camp for this purpose, Schmidt was provided with an excellent salary and privileges on the understanding that the mines were to come into active production.

By 1951 there were ten producing groups of mines within the Wismuth corporation comprising a total of between 65 and 70 individual uranium mines. (See Figure 18-1.) In addition there were subsidiary organizations for the construction of mining equipment, a warehouse for technical equipment, a uranium processing point at Aue, and auxiliary units for equipment of repair, lumber, assay, and other mining operations. Electrical equipment, compressors, and electric pumps were supplied by former East German companies.[39]

A German mining engineer, Hans Scherbel, has described the working conditions for the 300,000 Germans who worked around the clock in these mines: "The equipment was incredibly primitive. The shaft had no elevator. You had to climb 250 feet down on ladders. The miners had to make this climb twice daily."[40] Concerning construction of a new shaft at the Filzteich pond at Schneeberg to mine a pocket of high-grade ore, Scherbel comments that the operation was conducted "in a manner that can only be described as criminal.

---

[37] *Ibid.,* p. 969.

[38] Irving, *The Virus House,* p. 250, says the plant was bombed "and completely destroyed." Reference to the U.S. Strategic Bombing Surveys suggests that few of these "completely destroyed" plants were in fact put out of action for long. Reference to the bombing records would determine the state of the plant as occupied by the Soviet forces.

[39] See Nikolai Grishin, "The Saxony Uranium Mining Operation (Vismut)" in Robert Slusser, ed., *Soviet Economic Policy in Postwar Germany* (New York: Research Program on the U.S.S.R., 1953), p. 127. This is an excellent description of the Soviet uranium mining operations in Saxony as of 1950.

[40] "The Secret Mines of Russia's Germany," *Life,* XXIX, 13 (September 25, 1950), 83.

Figure 18-1 THE SOVIET URANIUM MINES IN SAXONY

```
12°30'              13°              13°30'              14°
                                              • Dresden
51°     GERMANY                       • Freital   • Niedersedlitz 51°
                                                   • Pirna
                   • Frankenberg    • Freiberg
              • Chemnitz
  • Glauchau
                   • Zschopau
• Zwickau    • Stollberg            • Sayda
                                 •Olbernhau
   Niederschlema          • Marienberg
Schneeberg• •Oberschlema
Neu Stadtel •   • Aue      • Annaberg
        • Schwarzenberg              CZECHOSLOVAKIA
50°30'   • Eibenstock
Johanngeorgenstadt

        • Jachymov
```

THE SAXONY
URANIUM MINING AREA

0 ———————————— 25
MILES

0 ———————————— 25
KILOMETERS

Source: Robert Slusser, ed., *Soviet Economic Policy in Postwar Germany* (New York: Research Program on the U.S.S.R., 1953), p. 137. Map data are from annex 1, pp. 154-55.

A diagonal shaft had been driven from the surface downward under the pond ... floods periodically swept through the shafts below.''[41]

The reopening of the mines was successful, and output increased from 135 tons of ore in 1946 to about 900 tons in 1948; the output stabilized at this figure, and after processing was shipped to the U.S.S.R.

THE FIRST SOVIET REACTOR

The feasibility of a nuclear chain reaction was demonstrated at the University of Chicago in 1942; the Soviets had no need, therefore, to duplicate initial American work. The first Soviet reactor had the same functions as the fourth U.S. reactor at Hanford, i.e., to test materials and produce limited quantities of fissionable material. A. Kramish has pointed up the technical similarities between the first Soviet PSR reactor and the Hanford reactor, concluding that

[41] *Ibid.*

a reactor physicist would deduce that "the Soviet reactor was practically a carbon copy of the American 305 reactor built at Hanford during the first phases of the Manhattan Project."[42] (See Table 18-2.)

Table 18-2	COMPARATIVE CHARACTERISTICS OF THE AMERICAN HANFORD AND SOVIET PSR REACTORS	
	Hanford 305	First Soviet reactor (PSR)
Start-up date	1944	1947
Power	10 watts	10 watts
Diameter	18-20 feet	19 feet
Lattice Spacing	8½ inches	8 inches
Loading	27 tons of uranium	25-50 tons of uranium*
Rod diameter	1.448 inches	1.2 to 1.6 inches

Source: A. Kramish, *The Soviet Union and the Atom: The "Secret" Phase*, RAND Report RM-1896, p. 64.

*Soviet estimate.

Kramish also points out that the Soviet PSR reactor was completed many years before the declassification of data on the Hanford 305 reactor and observes that "the similarity of construction is interesting. Is it coincidental, or were details on the 305 reactor obtained through espionage?"[43]

The first Soviet power reactor (VAM-1), as distinct from a materials testing reactor, began operation in June 1954, and was promptly claimed as the world's first atomic power station.[44] This was not an altogether accurate statement; the first nuclear reactor to generate electric power was operated in the United States in 1951. The first full-scale power reactor was the Calder Hall unit in England, which began operation in October 1956 with a reactor generating ten times more power than the 5-MWe net capacity of the Soviet 1954 reactor. The first authentic industrial reactor, the Shippingport pressurized water reactor, was built in the United States in 1958.

The original 5-MWe Soviet power reactor VAM-1 was the only Soviet power reactor from 1954 until 1964. In that year two more power reactors came into operation, the AMB-1 graphite water reactor of 100 MWe and the VVPR-1 pressured water dual-purpose reactor of 210 MWe. Therefore, although they had an extensive program employing 31,400 persons, the Soviets in 1965 had only three power reactors in operation generating a total of 315 MWe. By way of comparison, France in 1965 had five power reactors generating 350 MWe and the United Kingdom was far ahead with nine reactors generating

[42] Kramish, RAND Report RM-1896, *op. cit.* n 3, p. 64.
[43] *Ibid.*, p. 65.
[44] For a brief description see G. Ostroumov, *Pervaia v mire* (Moscow, 1956).

1395 MWe. Germany and Italy had no reactors at all in 1960, but Germany by 1965 had one reactor generating 50 MWe and Italy had three generating 607 MWe. This comparative development is of some interest in view of the early Soviet start in generation of electric power by use of atomic energy and the claims made for atomic energy in the early 1950s by Soviet scientists. (See Table 18-3.)

Table 18-3   COMPARATIVE DEVELOPMENT
                           OF ATOMIC POWER REACTORS

| | Net installed capacity | | | | Manpower employed in |
| | 1960 | | 1965 | | |
Country	Plants	MWe	Plants	MWe	nuclear energy at 1965
Soviet Union	1	5	3	315	31,400
France	3	85	5	350	37,500
Germany	—	—	1	15	9,676
Italy	—	—	3	607	3,500
United Kingdom	3	373	9	1395	38,632

Source: John W. Shartall, Atomic Handbook (London: Morgan, 1965), pp. 9, 13-14.

The position was even more distinctive at the end of 1969, when a map in Pravda[45] pinpointed only four operating atomic power reactors in the Soviet Union, with none under construction. This total obviously includes the original three brought into production between 1954 and 1964 together with the Siberian dual-purpose reactor brought into production sometime after 1965. This may be compared with developments in the United States, where in June 1969 a total of 13 power reactors were in operation and another 79 were on order or under construction.[46]

It appears that Soviet atomic energy development has been held back by lagging development of instrumentation and computers. The history of atomic reactors and digital computers is intertwined. Development for both began at about the same time during World War II and considerable support was given to computer development by early atomic energy researchers; the AVIDAC at Argonne, the ORACLE at Oak Ridge, and the MANIAC I at Los Alamos were products of this early cooperation.[47] By 1959, "over 300 nuclear reactor codes had been programmed in the United States for digital computers,"[48] including such major problem areas as burn-up, age diffusion equations, and kinetic responses of reactors. Soviet backwardness in computer technology is noted elsewhere.[49]

[45] Pravda, November 14, 1969.
[46] Business Week, June 14, 1969.
[47] Ward C. Sangren, Digital Computers and Nuclear Reactor Calculations (New York: John Wiley & Sons, 1960), p. 3.
[48] Ibid., p. 10.
[49] See p. 318 below.

The 1963 U.S. atomic energy delegation to the Soviet Union had an unparalleled opportunity to see Soviet atomic development at first hand; the delegation report substantiates the evidence of Soviet technical weakness in atomic energy.[50]

For example, the delegation reported: "Equipment in the hot cells, such as viewing devices and manipulators, was not as good as that found in equivalent U.S. installations."[51] The delegation also reported: "An example of Soviet instrumentation was a transistorized television camera in a radiation cell. This was the only piece of completely transistorized equipment that the delegation saw during the trip."[52]

Only one project, the 70-GeV proton synchrotron then under construction at Serpukhov, appeared to strike the delegation as outstanding:[53]

> The delegation formed a generally favorable impression of the project and personnel. The plant layout appeared to be sound, and factory-made equipment looked as if it were of high quality, e.g., canned rotor pumps. Standard field construction, however, was of a poorer caliber. For example, the masonry work was not done as carefully as might be expected. The few examples of stainless-steel welding seen, however, looked competently done.
>
> On the whole, the project seems well conceived and is being executed with adequate competence.[54]

Inasmuch as the Serpukhov operation was singled out for comment, a brief study was undertaken of the origins of the Serpukhov equipment.

CERN ASSISTANCE FOR THE SERPUKHOV PROTON SYNCHROTRON

The European Center for Nuclear Research (CERN) was established in Geneva, Switzerland, in 1954 to provide for nuclear research collaboration among European countries. On July 4, 1967, an agreement was signed in Moscow relating to scientific and technical cooperation between CERN and the Soviet Union for construction and operation of a 70-GeV proton synchrotron at Serpukhov. It was to be capable of the highest energy acceleration in the world. Discussions concerning the possibilities of such collaboration had been initiated

---

[50] Further evidence for the 1950s is in Medford Evans, *The Secret War for the A-Bomb* (Chicago: Henry Regnery Company, 1953)

[51] *Atomic Energy in the Soviet Union*, Trip Report of the U.S. Atomic Energy Delegation, May 1963 (Oak Ridge, Tenn.: AEC Division of Technical Information, n.d.), p. 25.

[52] *Ibid.*, p. 7.

[53] *Ibid.*, pp. 54-55. Concerning the preinjector for the 70-BeV machine, the delegation observed: "This was perhaps the most interesting and surprising piece of equipment of the tour."

[54] *Ibid.*, p. 65.

by Victor F. Weisskopf while he was director general of CERN in the mid-1960s.[55]

The main features of the technical-assistance agreement were as follows:[56]

1. CERN provides a fast-ejection system for the Serpukhov accelerator which becomes the property of Serpukhov; "CERN will be responsible for the design, construction, testing, and installation of the system (including its magnets, their vacuum tanks, and the associated supplies and controls), and for commissioning the vast ejected proton beam at the accelerator."

2. CERN provides radio-frequency particle separators which will be used at Serpukhov, "and will be responsible for the design, construction, testing, and installation of these items of beam line equipment and for commissioning at the accelerator."

   The Soviets for their part agreed to make available necessary technical information to build the extraction system and the separators, and also to establish at Serpukhov the buildings and supplies of electricity, cooling water, etc., and generally provide services such as workshops and stores. Also the U.S.S.R. has the responsibility to operate the accelerator and provide the beams which are necessary for the program.

3. CERN has the right to propose a succession of electronics experiments to be incorporated in the experimental program and the 70-GeV machine.

4. CERN Institute for High-Energy Physics in Switzerland will collaborate in bubble-chamber physics, and Soviet scientists will join teams working at CERN "in preparation for the start of bubble-chamber physics at Serpukhov."

In October 1966 the French Government agreed to send to Serpukhov a large hydrogen bubble chamber (with a volume of 6000 litres) developed at the Saclay Laboratory in France. Under the agreement, French scientists were to participate in the bubble-chamber experiments with Soviet scientists.[57] This provision is interesting in light of the comment of the U.S. delegation report that "only one specific item of experimental equipment was mentioned, namely, a large hydrogen bubble chamber."[58] The report did not state the origin of the bubble chamber.

Two factors bring Western assistance to Serpukhov into focus: first, the technical complexity and cost of these machines increase with size; and second, because of its technical complexity the Soviets would have been unable to build the Serpukhov unit without CERN assistance. Indeed the Soviets started

[55] *CERN Courier* (Geneva), VII 7 (July 1967), 23. V. F. Weisskopf was among the small group of physicists who in 1939 made the historic and voluntary agreement to restrict publication of information concerning nuclear developments. At present (1969) Weisskopf is chairman of the High-Energy Physics Advisory Panel of the Atomic Energy Commission.

[56] *CERN Courier*, VII, 7 (July 1967), 23.

[57] *Ibid.*, p. 122.

[58] *Atomic Energy in the Soviet Union, op. cit.* n. 51, p. 77.

excavation for a 6-GeV machine at Erevan in 1960 and only completed it in 1967, a little before the 70-GeV Serpukhov unit started. At that time the most powerful accelerator in the United States was the 15-GeV proton synchrotron at the Argonne National Laboratories in Chicago; the CERN machine of 24 GeV started in 1959, and then the largest Soviet installation, at Dubna, was rated 10 GeV.

Therefore Western techniques and instrumentation enabled the Soviets to claim the most powerful high-energy accelerator in the world.[59] Although such machines are generally regarded as basic research units, it has been argued by physicists in the high-energy field that accelerators do have a technical spillover effect of some magnitude. For example, R. R. Wilson in the 1968 Richtmyer Lecture acknowledged the assistance given by the accelerator to the nuclear power industry and noted also,

> ... the kind of unexpected but immediately practical developments that accompany any intensive technological activity ... the high-power transmitting tube ... fast pumps ... high-vacuum techniques ... particle counters ... flip-flop circuits.[60]

In a survey of Soviet technology the field of atomic energy poses a paradox of some magnitude.

General Groves's opinion in 1945 was that the Soviet Union would require 15 to 20 years to construct an atomic bomb. This view is supported by such diverse sources as Klaus Fuchs and this study. The Soviet Union in fact required four years to achieve a ''nuclear explosion.''

Today we find that while the Soviet Union has some first-class scientists—the physicist Lev Artsimovich is one whose name comes to mind—it is obviously weak in converting nuclear science into practical systems. We see the evidence in restricted development of power reactors, Western observations of Soviet project instrumentation, assistance required for the Serpukhov proton synchrotron, and the backwardness in computer technology.

Given this relative technical backwardness both in 1945 and today, the paradox is in the Soviet Union's ability to achieve an advanced nuclear weapons capability. This is not an economic question of how resources were shifted but a question of engineering capability. It is therefore suggested as a working hypothesis that even in nuclear weaponry, in the development of controlled thermonuclear reactions and all fields of nuclear science and technology requiring extensive computer backup and instrumentation, there has been a large—and yet unrecorded—transfer of equipment and technology from the West.[61]

[59] The existence of the Serpukhov machine also gave U.S. scientists a useful means to prod Congress into appropriating $250 million for the 200-GeV unit under construction at Weston, Illinois, in 1970.

[60] *CERN Courier*, VIII, 7 (July 1968), 156-57.

[61] This chapter is restricted by the limited open data available on most aspects of atomic energy. It should be viewed as little more than a preliminary to the study of the transfer of Western assistance to the Soviet nuclear program.

CHAPTER NINETEEN

Western Origins
of Soviet Railroad Locomotives

While there is little question that the Soviet railroad system has made gigantic strides since the early 1930s, there was still a high degree of technical dependence on the West at the end of the 1960s.[1]

As of 1960 more than 31,000 steam locomotives were still in use in the Soviet Union. This was considered undesirable (despite the excellent working characteristics of the locomotives), and efforts were directed to the electrification of high-density lines and the use of diesel-electric locomotives on low-density lines. Gas turbines and diesel-hydraulic locomotives were in an experimental stage. The 1960 U.S. Railroad Delegation concluded on the basis of its observations that this motive equipment "showed no radical departure from familiar designs but is rather an adaptation or copy of designs of engines and components found in the United States and Western Europe—without regard for patent considerations."[2]

Special-purpose cars were rarely used, customers being enjoined to conform their requirements to standard box, flat, tank, gondola, or refrigerator cars. Although many of these were two-axle units, they were being replaced by four-axle units. As far as signals and communications are concerned, the 1960 delegation commented: "Observations confirmed that the systems in service in the United States during the years from about 1930 to 1945 have been reproduced and manufactured for use on the Soviet railroads."[3]

A number of wagon and locomotive construction and repair plants were removed from Saxony and Thuringia to the U.S.S.R. in 1945-46. The wagon

---

[1] See Sutton I and II for data concerning early Western technical transfers.

[2] Association of American Railroads, *Railroads of the U.S.S.R.*, Report on the Visit of the United States Railroad Exchange Delegation to the Soviet Union during June 1960 (Washington, n.d.), p. 9. The wide use of foreign locomotives as late as 1962 may be gauged from an observation by J. N. Westwood, on leaving Sebastopol: "As the train moved out through the suburbs it was easy to fancy that this was not Russia but Czechoslovakia, for it was only after several miles that I saw a Russian-built locomotive. Not only were the passenger trains Skoda-hauled but switching and local freight were in the care of new Czech-built 750-hp diesel switchers (class ChME2)." *Trains* (Milwaukee, Wis.), July 1962, p. 44.

[3] *Railroads . . .*, *op. cit.* n. 2, p. 11. See Sutton II, pp. 205-6, for assistance of Union Switch and Signal Company (Subsidiary of Westinghouse Electric) in the 1930s.

248

construction plants at Stassfurt and near Halle were partly removed to the U.S.S.R.; also in Saxony, the Gotha wagon-building plant was about 60 percent removed and the Ilmenau works was completely removed. In Thuringia the Wurzen plant was partly removed; Waggon- und Maschinenbau A.G. (Wumag) at Görlitz was also partly removed and Waggon- und Maschinenfabrik A.G. at Bautzen was about 50 percent removed to the U.S.S.R.[4] However, the more important present-day Russian locomotive and car construction plants are enlarged Tsarist plants or units built in the 1930s rather than transferred German plants.

AMERICAN ORIGINS OF DIESEL-ELECTRIC LOCOMOTIVES

By 1960 the Soviet locomotive construction industry had produced three basic diesel-electric locomotive models in addition to several prototypes (Table 19-1). The three basic production models were based on U.S. locomotives—on American Locomotive Company (Alco), General Electric, and Fairbanks-Morse designs. During World War II a considerable number of U.S. diesel-electric locomotives were shipped to the U.S.S.R. under the Lend Lease program. These locomotives ultimately became prototypes for postwar Soviet models; they included the Alco (Soviet Type Da) and the standard Baldwin (Soviet Db).[5]

Table 19-1   DIESEL-ELECTRIC LOCOMOTIVES
IN THE SOVIET UNION FROM 1944 to 1965

Soviet class	Weight, tons	Dates in use	Western origins
		Foreign construction	
Da	—	1943	Alco
Db	—	1943	Baldwin Locomotive
	Soviet construction based on foreign basic design		
TE-1	124	1947	Alco-Da class
TE-2	85	1950-56	Modified TE-1(Alco-Da)
TE-3 (standard)	126	1956-	Fairbanks-Morse engine

Source: J. N. Westwood, *Russian Locomotive Types,* (Bristol: W. Norman, 1960).

The Soviet TE-1, for which production started in 1947 and continued until 1950, was based on an imported Alco-G.E. diesel-electric road switcher that

[4] G. E. Harmssen, *Am Abend der Demontage; Sechs Jahre Reparationspolitik* (Bremen: F. Trüjen, 1951).
[5] U.S. Dept. of State, *Report on War Aid Furnished by the United States to the U.S.S.R.* (Washington: Office of Foreign Liquidation, 1945).

was first delivered to U.S. customers in 1941. Although designed primarily for road service, it was similar in basic design to a yard-switching locomotive. The 1000-hp diesel engine operated at 740 rpm, and was turbocharged by the Buchi system; the electrical equipment for the engine was built entirely by General Electric, and included the main traction generator, auxiliary generator, and four G.E. 731 traction motors with Type P control equipment and Westinghouse air-brake equipment.[6] The Soviet-built version of this Alco model (i.e., the Da type) had three truck bogies (like the Alco unit delivered under Lend Lease) and a D-50 six-cylinder four-stroke diesel engine of 1000 hp. About 300 such TE-1 models were still in service in 1960.[7]

The TE-1 was followed by the TE-2, which first appeared in 1948 with series production from 1951 to 1956. About 1100 were still operating in 1960. The D-50 diesel engine and generators were the same as in the earlier TE-1.

In 1950 design started on a more powerful locomotive—the TE-3 freight (and TE-7 passenger version)—with a prototype appearing in 1953 and series production started in 1956. This locomotive had a 2000-hp ten-cylinder engine (the 2D 100) based on the Fairbanks-Morse opposing piston design. Today the TE-3 and the TE-7 are the standard Soviet freight and passenger diesel electric locomotives.[8]

The TE-3 locomotive unit has been described by an American railroad delegation as containing

> . . . a 2000-hp opposed piston type normally aspirated diesel engine with ten cylinders operating at 850 rpm. This engine appears to be very similar to the Fairbanks-Morse diesel engine used in the United States.[9]

It is normally used as a two-unit consist providing a total of 4000 hp with a passenger service modification (the TE-7).

We may conclude, then, that in the 1960s Soviet diesel-electric locomotives were based on U.S. models of the 1940s; there had been no major improvement in design in Soviet models over their earlier American predecessors.

Soviet hydraulic-electric locomotives are of Austrian and German origin. In 1956 the U.S.S.R. imported some Voith (Austrian) 200-hp switchers, and in 1957 some 400-hp units (Soviet class MG-2) with Voith transmission and Jenbach mechanical units and engine. These were supplemented in 1962 with further imports of German 4000-hp Henschel Werke units with Maybach engine

[6] The Alco-G.E. road switchers are described in *Railway Mechanical Engineer* (Philadelphia), February 1942, pp. 62-66.
[7] *Railroads . . . , op. cit.* n. 2.
[8] For technical details of Soviet diesel-electric locomotives see K.A. Shishkin *et al., Teplovoz TE-3* (Moscow, 1969), which contains numerous construction diagrams and details. For electrical equipment on the 2TE-10L, TEM-2, and TE-3 see *Elektricheskoe oborudovanie teplovozov* (Moscow, 1968).
[9] *Railroads . . . , op. cit.* n. 2, p. 47.

and Maybach-Mekydro transmission. Soviet production began in 1962 at Kaluga with 4000-hp units obviously based on these Austrian and German prototypes. Other experimental hydraulic-electric units, the TGM-10 (1200 hp) and the T-106 (4000 hp) were built at Bryansk and Lugansk, respectively.[10]

The Soviet gas turbine that was in the experimental stage in 1960 used the body of the TE-3 2000-hp diesel-electric,[11] whereas gas turbine locomotives in the United States are specially designed overall as gas turbine locomotives. It would be reasonable to surmise that the Soviet unit was merely a test bed for an engine rather than the prototype of a gas turbine locomotive.

Table 19-2   ORIGINS OF ELECTRIC LOCOMOTIVES IN USE IN
THE SOVIET UNION, EARLY 1960's

Class	Rated output	Weight, tons	Year first built	Builder of mechanical equipment	Builder of electrical equipment
			Foreign Construction		
NO	2490 kw	132	1954	Skoda (Czechoslovakia)	Skoda
chS1	2285	85	1957	Skoda (Czechoslovakia)	Skoda
F(T)	4550	138	1959	Schneider-Alsthom, SFAC (France)	S.W.; Jeumont
FP(TP)	4550	131	1960	Schneider-Alsthom, SFAC (France)	S.W.; Alsthom; Jeumont
K	4730	138	1961	Krupp (Germany)	Siemens-Schukert
chS2	3430	120	1961	Skoda (Czechoslovakia)	Skoda
			Domestic Construction		
VL 22m	2340	132	1947	Tbilisi	Tbilisi
VL 23	3070	138	1952	Novocherkassk	Novocherkassk
VL-8 (N8)	4065	180	1953	Novocherkassk	Novocherkassk
VL-60 (N60)	4065	138	1959	Novocherkassk	Novocherkassk
VL-10 (T8)	5070	184	1961	Tbilisi	Tbilisi
VL-62 (NO-VL 61)	4065	138	1961	Novocherkassk	Novocherkassk
VL-80 (N80)	6050	184	1961	Novocherkassk	Novocherkassk

Source: Adapted from *Worlds Railways*, 1964-65, (London: Odhams Press, 1965), p. 240.

[10] W. M. Keller, "What We Saw in Russia," *Railway Age* (Chicago), July 11, 1966, p. 15. "Q. Are their hydraulic locomotives on the order of the Krauss-Maffei or do they have their own design? Keller: They're similar to the Krauss-Maffei."
[11] *Trains*, July 1960, p. 27.

FOREIGN PROTOTYPES OF ELECTRIC LOCOMOTIVES

From the beginning of the 1930s to the present, Soviet electric-locomotive manufacture and prototype design has been based almost completely on Western models acquired from all countries making advanced designs. According to J. N. Westwood,[12] however, the Soviets have had considerable technical problems with domestic locomotives based on such foreign designs and therefore the railroad sector continues to be heavily dependent on COMECON and Western technical assistance.

The most common electric locomotives in 1960 were the VL-22 and VL-22m of which almost 2400 were in operation. These can be traced directly to the General Electric S class imported in 1932, according to Westwood: "It is possible to trace elements of the present VL-23 design back to the American engines delivered 32 years ago, and in outward appearance type S is almost indistinguishable from the later VL-22m."[13] Also, about 150 types VL-19 and VL-19m, based on a Soviet design of the early 1930s and built after World War II, were still in operation in the early 1960s.

The other standard electric locomotive of the period 1945 to 1960 was the N class, the prototype of which was produced at Novocherkassk in 1953; the locomotive was mass-produced at Novocherkassk after 1955 and at Tbilisi after 1958. About 310 were in operation by 1960.[14] These locomotives, although acceptable to Soviet customers, were backward by Western standards; an AARR report, for example, isolated obsolescent use of tape insulation on the traction motors:

> While a few traction motors of comparable nature may possibly still be in use in America, none with this type of insulation had been built for railroad use for twenty-five years or more.[15]

The wide application of outdated practices in 1960 may be noted from the observation that standardized traction motors—the latest DP type—are used in Classes VL-22, VL-22m, VL-19, and NO electric locomotives, as in all the main locomotive classes. Moreover, import of foreign component parts for electric locomotives (for example, mercury rectifiers from Japan under the

---

[12] J. N. Westwood, *Soviet Railways Today* (New York: Citadel Press, 1964), pp. 46-59, has an excellent description of electric locomotive development, its origins and current problems. Westwood considers that production of the basic N-60 and N-80 models was premature: "The fundamental problem of railway electrification in the U.S.S.R. is that at a time when more and more line is rapidly being electrified, there are no completely satisfactory locomotives in operation." (p. 58).

[13] *Ibid., p. 46.*

[14] Association of American Railroads, *A Report on Diesel Locomotive Design and Maintenance on Soviet Railways,* (Chicago: AAR Research Center, September 1966), p. 80.

[15] *Ibid.,* p. 74.

1956 trade agreement) supports the argument that the Soviets lag in domestic abilities.

One advantage of import of electric locomotives for line haul use is that imports are of greater technical sophistication and give better performance than domestically produced models. Westwood gives the power-to-weight ratio for several Soviet and foreign locomotives. The Soviet N 60, for example, has a ratio of 28.1 kw of power per ton of weight compared with 32.6 for the imported French T class electric locomotives; similarly, the Soviet VL-23 has a ratio of 22.8 compared to the Czech ChS2 with a ratio of 33.0. Thus Soviet electrics are decidedly heavier for their power output.[16] Imports also provide the basis for further Soviet technical development and, through comparative performances, afford us a measurement of domestic technical lag.

---

[16]   J. N. Westwood, "Russian Railroading Revisited," *Trains*, July 1962, p. 46. See also Novocherkasskii elektrovozostroitel'nyi zavod, *Elektrovoz VL 60 k* (Moscow: Transport, 1969).

CHAPTER TWENTY

Western Origins of Aircraft
and Space Technology

AIRCRAFT DESIGN AND ENGINE TECHNOLOGY

During World War II the Soviets produced 115,596 aircraft and Lend Lease delivered to the U.S.S.R. an additional 14,018.[1] The Russian-produced aircraft were mainly obsolete prewar types and most were one-engine wood and canvas models with inferior engines. Domestic production was assisted, however, by a high degree of production specialization. The only Soviet dive bomber, the Stormovik (IL-2), was in production at three plants; each plant produced about the same number of IL-2s but no other aircraft. Fighter production was concentrated on the YAK-3, the YAK-2 and YAK-6 being advanced trainer versions. The YAK was produced in six widely scattered plants producing only YAK aircraft at rates of between 65 and 400 per month.

Two-engined bomber production included the PK-2 (based on the French Potez), at two plants, and the IL-4 at three plants, only one of which (Komsomolsk) produced other aircraft. The LI-2 (or Douglas DC-3) transport was produced only at Tashkent, and the PO-2 (or De Havilland Tiger Moth) was

[1] R. H. Jones, *The Roads to Russia* (Norman: University of Oklahoma Press, 1969). According to U.S. Dept. of State, *Report on War Aid Furnished by the United States to the U.S.S.R.* (Washington: Office of Foreign Liquidation, 1945), Lend Lease deliveries of aircraft to the Soviet Union from June 22, 1941, to September 20, 1945, were as follows:

Fighter planes	Quantity delivered	Bombers	Quantity delivered	Cargo planes	Quantity delivered
P-40	2,097	A-20 (light)	2,908	C-46	1
P-39	4,746	B-25 (medium)	862	C-47	707
P-47	195	B-24 (heavy)	1 (force-landed in Siberia)	O-52 Observation	19
				Advanced Trainers	82
P-63	2,400			PBN Navy Patrol planes	137
				PBY-64	48

254

produced only at Kazan. Training aircraft (YAK-6s) were produced at three locations and the UT-2 advanced single-engined trainer at two locations.

Thus Soviet aircraft production was concentrated on a comparatively few simple types, each for a single function only. Most plants concentrated on the production of a single model, although several plants were usually involved with the production of the important types.

Lend Lease was of great assistance in the development of the Soviet aircraft industry. For example, Henry Wallace after his visit to the important Komsomolsk aircraft plant commented as follows:

> The aircraft factory in [Komsomolsk], where Stormovik bombers were being built, owed both its existence and its production to the United States. All the machine tools and all the aluminum came from America.... It looks like the old Boeing plant at Seattle.[2]

However, according to General G. A. Tokaev:[3]

> The aircraft industry was lagging well behind the West owing to constant political interference, political purges, and the general low level of technical efficiency. Consequently, at the end of World War II the Soviets had not produced a single jet engine or guided missile.

Work in 1945 and 1946 involved nothing sensational from the design viewpoint and in effect consisted in mastering the German aircraft industry that was developed from 1941 to 1943. The years immediately after 1946, however, were to show a remarkable expansion in the industry, an expansion achieved by utilizing German and some British technical assistance in an expert manner. Technical assistance from the West entered through two main channels—first from the United Kingdom and particularly through transfer of the Rolls-Royce Nene, Derwent, and Tay engine technologies; and second (and a much larger flow) from Germany via the transfer of the wartime German aircraft industry to the Soviet Union.

The postwar Soviet aviation and space industries have their roots in German World War II aircraft and rocket developments. In 1945 the Germans had a large and relatively undamaged aircraft and rocket manufacturing industry that had been dispersed under threat of continued Allied bombing toward the eastern regions of Germany—that area later occupied by the Soviets (Figure 20-1). Over two-thirds of this productive capacity fell intact into Soviet hands[4] and

---

[2] Quoted by Werner Keller, *Ost minus West =Null* (Munich: Droemersche Verlagsanstalt, 1960), p. 265.
[3] G. A. Tokaev, *Soviet Imperialism* (New York: Philosophical Library, 1956), p. 56.
[4] The writer has calculated the capacity in terms of 1944-45 output as 68 percent of the assembly capacity, although this figure varies by type of aircraft produced.

Figure 20-1 LOCATION OF THE GERMAN AEROENGINE PLANTS AT THE END OF WORLD WAR II.

Source: U.S. Strategic Bombing Survey, Aircraft Industry Survey, Figure VII-2, based on data from the German Air Ministry.

was largely, but in some cases not immediately, transported to the U.S.S.R. These transfers included development and experimental work, but most important they also included complete production lines for aircraft engines, equipment, and the V-2 missile. Consequently in both aircraft and rocket industries we can trace Soviet developments directly to German wartime research and development work and production methods.

Accurate information concerning this transferred productive capacity and technology comes as a result of an unusual sequence of events which itself is still subject to debate. In 1945 American and British armies swept 200 miles into what is now the Soviet Zone and met the Soviet armies on the Elbe-Mulde river line rather than on the zonal frontiers earlier agreed upon. Very little, if any, machinery was removed by the West before this area was surrendered to the Soviet armies, although dozens of CIOS, BIOS, FIAT, U.S. Army, and U.S. Navy teams had scoured the factories in the occupied areas assessing German technical developments.[5] The intelligence results were published in several hundred detailed technical reports. As some Allied teams were examining German plants only days before the Soviets took over, we have accurate, detailed accounts of the equipment and technical information that came under Soviet authority.

The technical information flowed first to the Central Institute of Aerohydrodynamics (TsAGI) and then to design institutes in Moscow, where it was allocated to various Soviet design teams working closely with deported German engineers and technicians. German technology was converted into experimental work, and after choice of design production was carried out at associated production units. The Mikulin design team at Plant No. 300, for example, worked on the Mikulin turbojet and was associated for production purposes with the Tushino Plant No. 500, Moscow Aircraft Engine Production Plant No. 45 (which produced the Rolls-Royce Nene engine from 1948 to 1956), Kharkov Plant No. 75, and a plant associated with the Gorki automobile plant and known as Plant No. 466. In this way, Soviet-German experimental and design teams were located at specific factories, but the design reproduction and experimental stages normally were kept apart from the production process.

These flows of technology will be examined as follows: (a) the flow of aircraft engine technology and production facilities from Germany and the United Kingdom, (b) airframe manufacturing and design capacity, which came almost entirely from Germany (although B-29 bomber technology came from the United States), and (c) space technology, which, again, came largely from Germany.

---

[5] Reports were issued later by CIOS (Combined Intelligence Objectives Committee), BIOS (British Intelligence Objectives Committee), and FIAT (Field Information Agency Technical).

The German Aircraft Engine Industry
In The Soviet Zone

The capacity of the German aircraft engine industry was more than adequate for the German aircraft program in the first years of the war, and its production schedules were maintained almost until the end in 1945. The basic design, development, and production companies were Junkers, Daimler-Benz, and BMW. These companies licensed production to additional firms, particularly in the case of Junkers and Daimler-Benz; BMW licensed only to Klockner in Hamburg. The largest single unit in the German Air Ministry expansion program was the Ostmark plant in Vienna, Austria, which covered an area of 3,000,000 square feet. This plant, although begun in 1941, did not produce engines until May 1943 and by the end of the war it had produced only 3000 engines in all.[6]

Daimler-Benz operated 10 aircraft engine plants (see Table 20-1). The largest plant was Genshagen near Berlin, which had produced a total of 30,000 aircraft engines by the end of World War II and in December 1944 was operating at a rate of 700 engines per month. In 1945 part of the principal plant at Genshagen was moved to a gypsum mine in Heidelburg to set up what was called the Goldfischwerke.[7] In all, 2500 machine tools were moved to the Goldfisch works. The Soviets acquired the greater part of both the Genshagen main plant in Berlin and the Goldfisch underground plant at Heidelburg; according to G. E. Harmssen, all of the machine tools at Genshagen were removed to the U.S.S.R. and 80 percent of the Goldfisch underground plant was removed to the U.S.S.R. at the end of 1945, under U.S. Operation RAP.[8] Total production of all Daimler-Benz plants in 1944 was 28,669 aircraft engines; since 16,794 of these were produced in plants located in the future Soviet Zone, it is clear that the Soviets gained control of the greater part of aircraft engine production of Types 603, 605, and 610.[9]

Daimler-Benz produced only reciprocating aircraft engines; gas turbines were produced by Junkers and BMW. The BMW 003 gas turbine was actually in production in 1945 and a total of 450 had already been built when the war ended.[10] Production facilities established for the 003 were much greater than

---

[6]   U.S. Strategic Bombing Survey, *Aircraft Division Industry Report*. 2d edition (Washington, January 1947), Report no. 4, p. 96.

[7]   *Ibid.*, p. 28.

[8]   G. E. Harmssen, *Am Abend der Demontage: Sechs Jahre Reparationspolitik* (Bremen: F. Trüjen 1951), p. 102; and Germany, Office of Military Government, (U.S. Zone), Economics Division, *A Year of Potsdam: The German Economy Since the Surrender* (n.p.: OMGUS, 1946), p. 36.

[9]   For further information see BIOS Report no. 35: *Report on Visit to Daimler Benz, at Stuttgart-Unterturkheim.*

[10]   CIOS Report no. XXX-80: *Bavarian Motor Works-A Production Survey.*

the production total indicates, however; the German program envisaged a production of 2500 per month by September 1945 from Harz Mountain area occupied by the Soviets.[11] These plants, built underground at Eisenach and Zuhlsdorf, were removed to the Soviet Union.[12] Moreover the Munich plant of BMW, with a production of 500 engines at the end of 1944, was removed to the Soviet Union under Operation RAP.[13]

Similarly, the Junkers turbojet was of special interest to the Soviets. By March 1945 approximately 6000 of these engines had been built, although the German Air Ministry was beginning to favor production of the BMW 003 for technical reasons. The Junkers 004 was in production at three centers in 1945—at Mäldenstein across the river from Dessau in the Soviet Zone (not examined by either the British or the American intelligence teams), at Kothen about 20 miles southwest of Dessau, and at Nordhausen in the V-1 and V-2 factories. Junkers was also producing the 012 engine with a similar layout to the 004, and an 11-stage axial compressor and a thrust of seven thousand pounds. The 022—a propeller version of the 012—was in the project stage and designed to attain 500 miles per hour.[14]

Table 20-1   REMOVAL OF MAIN
GERMAN AIRCRAFT ENGINE PLANTS IN 1945-46

Type of engine	Location produced	Total production 1939 - 1944	Total production Dec 1944	Disposal of plant in 1945
Daimler-Benz (603)	Stettin	3582	250	Probably removed to U.S.S.R.
Daimler-Benz (601,603,606)	Berlin, Marienfelde	—	65	Not known
Daimler-Benz (601,605,606,610)	Bussing (Brunswick)	13,805	—	Not removed to U.S.S.R.
Daimler-Benz (601,605)	Henschel (Kassel)	13,119	600	Not removed to U.S.S.R.
Daimler-Benz (605)	Manfred Weiss (Budapest)	1,189	—	Probably removed to U.S.S.R.
Daimler-Benz (605)	Steyr	1,885	65	Probably removed to U.S.S.R.
Daimler-Benz (603)	Prague	311	76	Probably removed to U.S.S.R.
Daimler-Benz (603)	Austria (Ostmark)	2,890	77	Probably removed to U.S.S.R.
Daimler-Benz (601,605,606,610)	Genshagen	30,833	700	100 percent removed to U.S.S.R.

[11] *Ibid.*, p. 62.
[12] Harmssen, *op. cit.* n. 8, no. 78.
[13] *Op. cit.* n. 8. p. 36.
[14] CIOS Report no. XXXl-66: *Notes on Aircraft Gas Turbine Engine Developments at Junkers, Dessau and Associated Factories.*

Table 20-1 (cont.)

Type of engine	Location produced	Total production 1939 - 1944	Total production Dec 1944	Disposal of plant in 1945
Daimler-Benz (601,605,606,610)	Goldfisch underground (Heidelburg)			80 percent removed at end of 1946
BMW (801)	Allaco- Munich*	17,529	526	82 percent removed at end 1946
BMW (801)	Klockner (Hamburg)	4,206	150	Not removed to U.S.S.R.
BMW (801)	Spandau (Berlin)	5,695	326	Probably removed
BMW (132)	Eisenach	4,099 ⎫	plan 2500 month by September '45	100 percent removed to U.S.S.R.
BMW (323)	Zuhlsdorf	3,227 ⎭		100 percent removed to U.S.S.R.
Junkers (004,012)	Mäldestein (Dessau)	—	—	100 percent removed to U.S.S.R.
Junkers (004)	Kothen	—	—	100 percent removed to U.S.S.R.
Junkers (004)	Nordhausen	—	—	100 percent removed to U.S.S.R.
Junkers (003)	Magdeburg	—	—	100 percent removed to U.S.S.R.

Sources: U.S. Strategic Bombing Survey, *Aircraft Division: Industry Report*, Number 84 (January 1947), Table VII-1; *A Year of Potsdam* (n.p.: Office of Military Government for Germany [U.S. Zone], Economics Division, 1947) p. 36; G. E. Harmssen, *Am Abend der Demontage; Sechs Jahre Reparationspolitik* (Bremen: F. Trüjen, 1951), p. 102.
Note: BMW Argus and Franck plants excluded.

The Junkers company had extensive engine manufacturing facilities in the Soviet Zone. The Dessau aircraft design and production plant produced the regular Junkers engines and design work on the 012. There was also a Junkers engine plant at Magdeburg, and a great deal of development work on the 003 gas turbine was handled by underground shops there. The Junkers company also operated the rear portion of Tunnel No. 2 at the Nordhausen underground facilities.[15]

[15] CIOS Report no. XXXI-36: C. L. Fay, *Junkers Aircraft and Engines Facilities*, May 1945.

TRANSFER OF GERMAN TECHNICIANS
AND TECHNOLOGY TO THE U.S.S.R.

Continuing the pattern established with the absorption of Junkers technology after the Treaty of Rapallo in 1922, the main channel of aircraft engine production facilities for the U.S.S.R. was from East Germany to Aircraft Plant No. 1 at Kuibyshev. This plant was established essentially with Junkers facilities transferred from Germany and using Junkers engineers, designers, foremen, and test pilots. The central function of the plant was to convert the promising German jet technology into the first Soviet jet fighters and bombers.

The aircraft industry was not removed immediately to the Soviet Union, however. Soviet designers like Tupolev and Gurevitch first visited German aircraft factories and examined prototypes and production methods. The Junkers company organized for this purpose an exhibition of German secret aircraft projects and arranged for tours of inspection of the industry.[16] Equipment was then removed under the program of OKBs (Osoboye Konstruktorskoye Byuro); for example, OKB No. 1 was at the Dessau plant of Junkers.

Nor were the German technical personnel immediately removed to the Soviet Union.[17] The bulk of the German engineers and scientists were moved by train to Russia on the night of October 22-23, 1946—in what was probably the largest mass movement of scientific brains in the history of the civilized world.[18] Engineers and scientists were not given contracts or other written agreements; they were divided into small groups of about 15 persons, and about 30 Russian engineers were attached to each German nucleus for study and work. The Russian groups were changed with some rapidity, and each project was handled by stages—the draft stage, the technical project stage, and finally the presentation stage. Whenever a project was almost complete it was canceled by the Soviets and the related drawings, papers, biographies, and technical material were turned over. Duplicate work was undertaken by separate all-Russian groups some distance from the location of the original German pilot groups; in addition German groups were put in competition one with another.[19]

Often the complete working environment of the German specialists was removed to the U.S.S.R., according to Keller:[20]

Engineers and draftsmen found the same desks lying ready for them which they

---

[16] *Flying* (New York), 51, 5, (November 1952), 15.
[17] V. L. Sokolov, "Soviet Use of German Science and Technology, 1945-1946" (New York: Research Program on the U.S.S.R., 1955; Mimeographed Series no. 73) argues that the removal program was carried out hastily; this is not completely in accord with other evidence.
[18] *Aviation Week* (New York), 62, 14 (May 9, 1955).
[19] *Ibid.*
[20] W. Keller, *op. cit.* n. 2, p. 336.

had used in Dessau, Oranienburg, Halle, or Leipzig. They were able to find their old drawings and tracings, technical reports, neatly tied up with labels bearing cyrillic lettering.

Most German designers and engineers in the aeroengine industry were sent to Kuibyshev.[21] They came largely from the Junkers and BMW plants; no less than 800 engineers and technicians came from these two companies alone in 1946.[22] Among the members of the BMW contingent was Kurt Schell, former head of the BMW rocket laboratory, and engineers Winter, Kaul, Schenk, Tietze, Weiner, and Muller.[23] The Junkers group led by Walter Baade was the most important. Not only was Dr. Baade formerly chief engineer of Junkers; he had previously worked for ten years in American aeronautical plants and so was fully familiar with American methods of aircraft construction. With Dr. Baade was a group of engineers including Freundel, Haseloff, Wocke, Elli, Lilo, Rentel, Hoch, Beer, Antoni, Reuss, Heisig, and Hartmann. The Junkers engine team in the Soviet Union was headed by Dr. Scheibe, who designed the Junkers P1 turbine; he was assisted by engine designers Gerlach and Pohl, who at Dessau had been in charge of the engine testing department. Also in this group were Steudel and Boettger and a large number of personnel from the turbojet department, including engineers, foremen, and skilled workers.[24] Another prominent designer, Ernst Heinkel, worked in the Soviet Union at the Kalinin Experimental Station.[25]

The Junkers plant itself was rebuilt at Kuibyshev, "almost exactly" as it had stood in Leipzig.[26]

Development Of The First Soviet Jet Engine

The use of German engineers to develop Soviet jet engines fell into three stages. The first stage included the reproduction of the Junkers 004 and the BMW 003 jet engines removed to the Soviet Union with their production equipment. The 004 became the Soviet RD-10, and the BMW 003 was produced as the Soviet RD-20 on a stop-gap basis until more advanced designs came along.[27] (See Table 20-2).

[21] Ibid.
[22] Aviation Week, 66, 14 (April 8, 1957), 53.
[23] Aeronautics, (London), April 1952, p. 46.
[24] Ibid.
[25] Ibid.
[26] Flying, 51, 5 (November 1952).
[27] Aviation Week, April 8, 1957, p. 54.

Table 20-2   ORIGINS AND UTILIZATION OF SOVIET JET ENGINES

Engine	Thrust, lb	Weight, lb	Max. rpm	Compressor	Used on	Western origins
RD-10	2,200	1,650	8,700	Axial	MIG-9 YAK-17	Junkers 004
RD-20	2,250	1,375	10,000	Axial		BMW 003
RD-45F	5,000	1,612	12,500	Centrifugal	MIG-15 IL-28	Rolls-Royce Nene
RD-500	3,600	1,280	14,700	Centrifugal	YAK-23	Rolls-Royce Derwent
VK-1 (Klimov)	6,000	1,930	—	Centrifugal	IL-28	Rolls-Royce Tay
VKIA	7,590	1,960	—	Centrifugal	IL-20 MIG-15 MIG-17	Rolls-Royce Tay
VK-2	5,950	—	—	Centrifugal	MIG-15	Rolls-Royce Tay
VK-2JA	6,850	—	—	Centrifugal	MIG-17	Rolls-Royce Tay
VK-2R	7,500	2,650	—	Centrifugal	—	Rolls-Royce Tay
VK-5	8,690	—	—	Axial	MIG-19 YAK-25	—
AM-2 (Mikulin)	6,000	4,250	—	Axial	—	Junkers 022
AM-3	19,000	5,000	—	Axial	Badger Bison	Brandner
AM-5						
MIK-205	10,000	3,000	—	Axial	—	(Junkers-BMW team)
MIK-205R	13,000	3,900	—	Axial	—	(Junkers-BMW team)
AM-9						
M-209	14,850	5,500	—	Axial	TU-104	(Junkers-BMW team)
	22,000				Fishpot	(Junkers-BMW team)

Sources: Text; *Aero/Space Engineering*, October 1959, pp. 45-50; H. Hooftman, *Russian Aircraft* (Fallbrook, Calif.: Aero Publishers, 1965); W. Keller, *Ost Minus West = Null* (Munich: Droemersche Verlagsanstalt, 1960), pp. 341-42, 348-49; C. L. Fay, *Junkers Aircraft and Engine Facilities*, CIOS No. XXXI - 36, p. 7.

The first project given to the German design groups was a Soviet specification for a 3000-hp jet engine; essentially this was a development of the Junkers 012 turbojet, which was at the design stage in Germany at the end of World War II. By 1947 the Junkers 012 had been developed as a 12-burner assembly, but operating inefficiencies and two blade failures canceled development of this engine in 1948.[28] The next project specification given to the German designers was for a 6000-hp turboprop to attain a speed of 560 miles per hour at sea level. Essentially, this engine was developed from the Junkers 022 turboprop engine, with the same general design and characteristics as the 012 but

[28] *Ibid.*

modified to provide geared turbine drive to contrarotation propellers.[29] By 1949 the Brandner design teams had essentially met the Soviets' specification and immediately set to work on yet another detailed specification—a power plant with 12,000 hp in contrast to the 6000 hp developed by the Junkers 022. The first (unsuccessful) attempt at this specification was to couple two Junkers 002 power plants together.

Finally, the Type K turboprop was developed by the Junkers-BMW Team as a 14-stage compressor and five-stage turbine engine; it was a logical development from the German engines under development in the latter stages of World War II. The Type K engines produced by the mid-1950s power the Soviet four-engine bombers (TU-20 Bear) with four MK-12M turboprop engines of 12,000-hp capacity, and the civilian version, the Rossiya.

The AM series (after Mikulin) developed from the work of a Junkers-BMW team in the U.S.S.R. under engineer Brandner. The most powerful end result of this design, the AM-3, was seen in 1958 by an American engineer whose comment was "The engine is not an outstanding power plant, being of simple design of very large diameter and developing about 15,000 pounds thrust with 8 compression stages."[30] It is currently used in the TU-104 "Camel," which was developed from the TU-16 ("Badger").

Rolls-Royce Nene And Derwent Turbojets

In 1946 the Soviets bought 55 Rolls-Royce centrifugal compressor-type turbojets—25 Nenes and 30 Derwents. These Rolls-Royce engines, simple and well suited to Soviet mass production methods, introduced the Soviets to the use of a centrifugal turbojet; Russian turbojets up to that time were of the axial-flow type based on German designs.

Two versions of the Rolls-Royce engines were produced at Engine Plant No. 45 near Moscow beginning in 1948 and continuing at least until 1956. The plant was toured in 1956 by U.S. Air Force General Nathan Twining, who noted that it contained machine tools from various countries including the United States and Germany, and had 3000 workers engaged in producing the Rolls-Royce Nene.[31]

The American counterpart in 1951 to this Rolls-Royce engine was the Pratt & Whitney J-42 Turbo-wasp, based on the Nene but not then in quantity production.[32] Thus when the Korean war broke out in 1950 the Russians had thousands of improved Nene engines in service powering MIG-15s, whereas the U.S.

[29] CIOS XXXI-36, *op. cit.* n. 15, p. 7.
[30] *Ordnance*, May-June 1958, p. 1084.
[31] *Aviation Week*, July 2, 1956, p. 29.
[32] *Aviation Week*, June 11, 1951, p. 16. See also *The Times* (London) April 28, 1953, p. 9c.

Air Force had only a few hundred F-86A Sabres with comparable engines. The Soviets had also been able to solve certain turbine blade problems that were still puzzling Rolls-Royce and Pratt & Whitney engineers.[33]

By 1951 the Soviets had two versions of the original Rolls-Royce Nene in production quantities. The first version, the RD-45 that powered an early MIG-15, was a direct copy of the original Nene and delivered 5000 pounds of thrust. The second version of the RD-45 delivered 6000 pounds of static thrust at sea level and 6750 pounds of thrust with water injection.

Significant improvements were made by the Russians in the original design:

> Principally the changes involved the combustion chambers, which have 15 percent greater area, and the turbine blades which are longer and of wider chord. Comparison with the earlier Nene dimensions shows the blade is one-half inch longer and one-fourth inch wider in chord. Blade profile is still similar.
>
> Tailpipe area is reported 30 percent greater than that of the original Nene. The scale-up of internal gas passages was accomplished, however, with no increase in the 50-in. overall diameter of the original Nene.
>
> Other refinements [are]: an additional ring of perforations just aft of the primary zone of the combustion chambers for increased dilution of air; insertion of reinforcement rings in the liner perforation in the hot zone of the combustion chambers; increased gage of metal used in hot zone and liner; improved duplex fuel nozzle.
>
> The refined Soviet engine weighs about 2000 lb as compared to 1715 lb for the original Nene. Specific fuel consumption is given as 1.14 lb fuel/lb thrust/hr. The engine analyzed did not incorporate afterburning. It was noted that tailpipe diameter and length were sufficient to utilize a short afterburner which would boost total thrust a calculated 1000 lb additional.[34]

The turbine blades in the Soviet RD-45 engines were made of a stainless steel alloy of the Nimonic 80 type while the burner liner and swirl vanes were made of Nimonic 75. Parts of the Nene sold to Russia in 1948 were fabricated from Nimonic alloys—"Nimonic" being the registered trademark of Henry Wiggin and Company of Birmingham, England. Both Nimonic 75 and Nimonic 80 were developed by Mond Nickel about 1940, and their specifications had been earlier published by the Ministry of Supply in the United Kingdom. There are considerable difficulties in the production of Nimonic alloys, and such difficulties could be surmounted only with the practical know-how accumulated by Wiggin.[35]

Several engines from captured MIG-15s were evaluated by the United States Air Force, and reports were prepared by engineers of Pratt & Whitney Aircraft

---

[33] *Aviation Week*, March 12, 1956, p. 264.
[34] *The Aeroplane* (London), August 1, 1952, p. 163.
[35] *Ibid*.

Division of United Aircraft Corporation, the Wright Patterson Air Force Base, and Cornell Aeronautical Laboratory.[36]

The RD-45 (Nene) was produced not only in Moscow but also at Magadan from 1951, and at Khabarovsk, at Ufa Plant No. 21, and at Kiev Plant No. 43 from 1951 until sometime after 1958.

Soviet Acquisition Of Four-Engine Aircraft

During World War II the United States was unwilling to send heavy four-engine bombers to the Soviet Union under Lend Lease. Although in April 1944 General John R. Deane recommended U.S. approval of Russian requests for heavy bombers, the War Department refused on the grounds that the Soviets could not train a bombing force prior to the spring of 1945 and that certain special equipment for such bombers was in short supply.[37]

The official Lend Lease report on war aid therefore lists Russian acquisition of only one four-engine bomber (a B-24 that force-landed in Siberia), although the Soviets were in fact able to acquire four others. One of these was acquired in July 1944 when a U.S. bomber ran low on fuel after a raid against Mukden in Manchuria and landed at Vladivostok; two others—B-29s—landed at Vladivostok during the war, both having run short of fuel while on bombing raids over Japan; the fourth, a B-17 Flying Fortress, crash-landed in Siberia in December 1944 and its crew was rescued by Red Army forces. The Soviets retained all four aircraft.[38]

The Soviets then started work on the Tu-4 four-engine bomber and the Tu-70 civilian transport, and in 1946 Amtorg attempted to purchase from the Boeing Aircraft Company a quantity of B-29 tires, wheels, and brake assemblies. The attempt was unsuccessful, but nevertheless when in 1947 the Soviets produced the Tupolev Tu-70 it was immediately identified as a virtual copy of the B-29. The similarity was described in *Boeing Magazine:*[39]

> The famed Boeing 117 airfoil that the Tu-70 is sporting is an exact replica of the Boeing B-29 wing. Along with the wing are the *Superfortress* nacelles: outline, cooling air intake, auxiliary air scoop, cowl flaps and inboard and outboard fairings. The cabin cooling air inlet in the wing leading edge between the body and the inboard nacelle is the same. The trailing edge extension on the flap between the inboard nacelle and the side of the fuselage are also identical, according to the evidence provided by the photographs.

---

[36] For a summary of these examinations see *Product Engineering* (New York), August 1952, pp. 194-95.

[37] Jones, *op. cit.* n. 1.

[38] *Boeing Magazine* (Seattle), February 1948; *Flying*, 42, 6 (June 1948) 28; *New York Times*, December 24, 1944, 12:3.

[39] *Boeing Magazine*, February 1958.

The Tupolev Tu-70 uses the Twenty-nine's main landing-gear structure as well as its fairings and doors. The nose gear also appears to be that of the *Superfortress*, with the upper trunnion located closer to the body contour of the Tu-70 than on the Boeing bomber.

The tail surfaces of the Russian transport also come direct from the Boeing engineering department. On comparison it is apparent that the vertical tail and the dorsal outline as well as the leading edge of the rudder are the same on the two planes. The rudder of the Tu-70 appears to end at what would be the top of the tail gunner's doghouse on the *Superfortress*. The shape of the stabilizer and the elevator is the same on the two ships, and the transport also uses the inverted camber of the B-29's tail.

Propellers of the Tupolev Tu-70 appear to be original B-29 props, less cuffs. The hubs are characteristic of the Hamilton-Standard design. Boeing engineers also report that the drift meter installation of the Russian transport looks like that of the *Superfortress*, and the pitot head type and location match.

Tupolev did, however, design a new fuselage for the transport. It sits higher on the wing of the Tu-70 than does the fuselage of the B-29, and the fuselage is larger in diameter and a little longer (119 feet as compared to 99 feet). While the transport has a new fuselage, it retains the bomber nose, including the bombardier's plate-glass window.

An interesting question, not discussed in the late forties, was the manner by which the Soviets were able to advance from their inability to produce four-engine bombers to their ability to produce a workmanlike design requiring an extensive period of research and flight testing. Even if the designs were available, jigs and dies to put the plane into quantity production also were required. The 18-cylinder Wright engines for the B-29 had been extremely difficult to manufacture even in the United States, and had required several years to reach the desired standard of reliability. Further, the Soviets had no apparent experience in the production of four-engine bombers; the wartime Tupolev PE-8 was generally considered not to be a successful design. Moreover we know from Douglas Aircraft files that in 1940 the Soviets had enormous difficulties in putting the much simpler DC-3 twin-engine transport plane into production and repeatedly came back to the Douglas Aircraft Company for aluminum sections, parts, and technical advice.[40] There is an unknown element of some magnitude (also found in other technical areas, such as atomic energy) concerning the ability of the Soviets to produce in the brief span of three years between 1944 and 1947 a usable copy of the complex B-29 U.S. four-engine bomber.[41]

[40] See Sutton II: *Western Technology . . 1930 to 1945*, p. 234.
[41] A possible explanation appears in the German intelligence material. It will be remembered that Vice President Henry A. Wallace on his visit to Komsomolsk Aircraft Factory No. 126 in 1944 commented that the plant looked like the Boeing Plant in Seattle (above, p. 255). The German intelligence report on Komsomolsk Plant No. 126 indicates that in October 1943 the plant was producing the Boeing B-17, and makes the notation that it was receiving materials from the United States.
Another German intelligence report lists no fewer than 371 four-engine aircraft from the

The German Contribution
To The Aircraft Manufacturing Industry

The major design units of the German wartime aircraft industry were removed to Podberezhye, about 90 miles north of Moscow,[42] and included most elements from Junkers, Siebel, Heinkel, and Messerschmidt. Professor Walter Baade of Junkers continued development of the Ju-287K (as the EF-125) after moving to Podberezhye and followed this with the T-140 and T-150 bombers—jets capable of carrying an atomic bomb and, according to one report, out-performing the U.S. B-47.[43] There were 11 major Junkers plants in the Soviet Zone and six of these are known to have been completely removed to the U.S.S.R., including the main Otto Mader works two miles east of Dessau (where Professor Baade had been located) in addition to the Aschersleben, Bernburg, Leopoldshall, and Schönebeck plants.[44] We know the condition of some of these plants at the end of World War II. Aschersleben was a fuselage building plant in process of changing over to the production of the He-162; its instrument storeroom was "virtually intact" and was placed under military guard by the U.S. Army until the Soviets were able to take it over.[45] Bernburg was intact. Leopoldshall had been "badly damaged."[46] The condition of the Schönebeck plant is not known.

In 1944, the outstanding German rocket designer Sanger was working the Sanger-Bredt project to develop a long-range rocket aircraft. Former Russian General G. A. Tokaev recalls that in 1947 he was summoned by Stalin to a Moscow conference concerning the project:

United States in stock in the Soviet Union at November 1944. (This contrasted to the five presumed to be in the Soviet Union at that time). This stock allegedly consisted of 119 B-17 Flying Fortresses, 129 Consolidated B-24 Liberators, 81 C-56 Lockheed Lodestar, and 42 C-54 Douglas Skymasters.

The German intelligence reports, if correct, would go far to explain the production capability question outlined above. If indeed the Soviets were producing B-17 bombers during World War II at Komsomolsk, then this would be with U.S. Lend Lease assistance, and such assistance might well have given the Soviets sufficient production background and experience to produce B-29 bombers by 1947. However, if the German data are correct, the official U.S. reports are erroneous.

According to Anthony Kubek (quoting Isaac Don Levine), the Soviets obtained blueprints of the B-36 from the United States; see Kubek's How the Far East Was Lost, (Chicago: Regnery, 1963), p. 46.

[42]   Keller, op. cit. n. 2, p. 336.

[43]   Sokolov, op. cit. n. 17, p. 31. Methods used to get Baade to the U.S.S.R. are described in Flying 51,5 (November 1952), 15. This article also describes the German development of the Type 150 for the U.S.S.R. ˉAlso see Irmgard Grottrup, Rocket Wife (London: Andre Deutsch, 1959).

[44]   Harmssen, op. cit. n. 8.

[45]   CIOS XXX1-36, op. cit. n. 15, p. 7-13.

[46]   Ibid.

A thorough examination of the Sanger Project would prove invaluable, partly because it might enable us to produce a super-plane, but far more importantly because of the experience such research would give our scientists in solving related problems and preparing a base for future activities. In other words, by mastering Sanger's theories our experts would be able to begin where he had left off.[47]

A group of Soviets was already working on the concept, as was a group of Germans under Dr. Lange. Stalin then signed a draft decree (reprinted in Tokaev's book) instructing a commission to "direct and coordinate work" in piloted and rocket planes "and the Sanger project"; for this purpose "a commission" was sent to Germany.[48] Despite such high-level efforts, however, Professor Sanger was never captured by the Soviets.

A particular gap in Soviet technology in 1945 was in modern fighter aircraft. Dr. Siegfried Gunther and Professor Benz, both developers of German fighter aircraft, were moved to the U.S.S.R. Gunther had been chief designer for Heinkel and a designer of jet fighters since the late 1930s, while Benz designed the German HE 162-Volksjager jet fighter that achieved over 500 mph in 1944.

Among the Soviet acquisitions in Saxony was the Siebel works at Halle, where the experimental rocket-powered research aircraft DFS 346 (equivalent of the Bell X-1 and X-2 and the Douglas X-3) was in final assembly; this work was continued at Halle on behalf of the Russians until October 1948, when it was moved to the OKB-2 combine at Podberezhye with workers from the Junkers, Heinkel, and Siebel plants.[49] Flight testing of the versions built in the U.S.S.R. was begun in early 1948 using a Lend Lease North American Mitchell B-25 bomber and later a Boeing B-29 Superfortress as mother aircraft. The first test pilots were German, later replaced by Russian pilots.[50]

The MIG-15 used in Korea was powered by various versions of the Rolls-Royce Nene engines (see Table 20-2) and came from the same source as the U.S. F-86 fighters—German World War II aircraft.[51] Armament was the German Rheinmetal-Borsig feed for a MK-108 gun, but in general the MIG-15 had far less equipment than the comparable U.S. plane.

The aircraft manufacturing facilities removed from Germany contained unique equipment. Two German Wotan presses of 15,000 tons were removed and

[47] G. A. Tokaev, *Stalin Means War* (London: Weidenfeld and Nicolson, 1951), p. 100 See also *Flying*, 53, 4 (October 1953), 22, 61.

[48] Tokaev, *op. cit.* n. 47, p. 158.

[49] *Interavia* (Geneva), VIII, 5 (1953), 256-57. This article has much detail, including drawings of the Germano-Russian DFS-346. See *Flying*, 46, 1 (January 1950) for details of Soviet development of Me-163 and similar plants into mass production facilities.

[50] *Interavia*, VIII, 5 (1953).

[51] For details see *Aviation Week*, July 7, 1952, pp. 10-15; for welding techniques see *Aviation Week*, November 2, 1953, pp. 46-47, and for structural details see *The Aeroplane*, August 1, 1952, pp. 160-62. Also see M. Gurevich, "How I Designed the Mig 15," *Aero Digest*, (Washington, D.C.), July 1951, pp. 17-19.

at least four copies were made and others developed from these presses.[52] Aircraft equipment plants included the former Nitsche plant at Leipzig, used in the U.S.S.R. to manufacture curve potentiometers, and the Karl Zeiss plant, used for position finders, wind-tunnel parts, and various precision instruments. It was estimated that in 1954 this segment of German industry supplied between 65 and 75 percent of Soviet radar equipment and precision instruments.[53]

In sum, about two-thirds of the German aircraft industry with its top designers and many technicians and engineers established the postwar Soviet aircraft industry. Attention was focused first on designs for military use and these then were adapted, sometimes rather crudely, for civilian use; in fact some Russian civilian aircraft have complete military subassemblies.[54]

Gradually, by the 1960s, the Soviets attained some design independence, but whether the resulting aircraft were successful or not—at least in economic terms—is doubtful. The MIG-21s sold to India were plagued with maintenance and structural problems.[55] It was reported that a Scandinavian Airlines delegation that examined the Tu-104 concluded that a Western commercial line could not afford to fly them if given away "for free" because of high operating costs.[56] In the mid-1960s we find evidence of a pattern that was also established in other industries—a report of a joint French-Soviet project to build an airliner, the fuselage to be supplied by the French and the engines by the Soviets.[57]

THE SOVIET SPACE PROGRAM

Historically, the Russians have had a great interest in rockets. Pyrotechnic rockets were manufactured in the seventeenth and eighteenth centuries, and Russian literature on rockets dates from that period. Signal rockets were used by the Russian Army as early as 1717. Russian theoretical development stems from the work of K. E. Tsiolkovskii, whose papers, beginning in 1903, investigated atmospheric resistance, rocket motion, and similar problems. This work was continued in the Soviet Union during the twenties and thirties (meanwhile close observation was kept on the work of Robert H. Goddard in the United States and Hermann Oberth in Germany). In 1928 Tsiolkovskii wrote that the value of his contribution had been in theoretical calculations, however, and that nothing had been achieved in practical rocket engineering. Some years later, in 1936, V. F. Glushke designed and made a prototype rocket engine,

---

[52] *American Aviation*, (Washington, D.C.), 19, 1 (June 6, 1955).
[53] *Ibid*.
[54] *Aviation Week*, April 2, 1956, p. 31.
[55] *Aviation Week*, November 4, 1963, pp. 33-34.
[56] Hans Heymann, Jr., *The Soviet Role in International Aviation*, RAND Report no. RM-2213 (Santa Monica, December 4, 1957), p. 6.
[57] *New York Times*, October 16, 1966.

the ORM-65; this rocket used nitric acid and kerosene as a propellant. The Russians later developed the ZhRD R-3395, an aircraft jato rocket using nitric acid and aniline as a propellant (during the early 1930s Dupont had provided technical assistance and equipment for the construction of large nitric acid plants).[58] And during World War II, Soviet rockets used "Russian cordite," which was 56.5 percent nitrocellulose; the nitrocellulose was manufactured under a technical-assistance agreement made in 1930 with the Hercules Powder Company of the United States. Finally, under Lend Lease, 3000 rocket launchers and large quantities of propellants were shipped from the West to the U.S.S.R.

German Rocket Technology At The End of World War II

The major assistance to Soviet rocket ambitions undoubtedly came from Germany at the end of World War II. This assistance may be summarized as follows:

1. The testing sites at Blizna and Peenemunde were captured intact (except for Peenemunde documents) and removed to the U.S.S.R.
2. Extensive production facilities for the V-1 and V-2 at Nordhausen and Prague were removed to the U.S.S.R.
3. The reliability tests from some 6900 German V-2s were available to the Soviets—a major prize.
4. A total of 6000 German technicians (but not the top theoretical men) were transported to Russia and most were not released until 1957-58.

The German weapons program was in an advanced state of development in 1945. About 32,050 of the V-1 "flying bomb" weapons had been produced in the Volkswagen plant at Fallersleben and at the underground Central Works (Mittelwerke) at Nordhausen.[59] In addition, 6900 V-2 rockets had been produced—6400 at the underground Mittelwerke at Nordhausen and 500 at Peenemunde.[60] Rocket fuel facilities had been developed in the Soviet Zone: liquid oxygen plants at Schmeidebach in Thuringia and at Nordhausen, and a hydrogen peroxide plant at Peenemunde.[61]

The Germans undertook two and one-half years of experimental work and statistical flight and reliability evaluation on the V-2 before the end of the war. There were 264 developmental launchings from Peenemunde alone.[62] In

[58] See Sutton II, pp. 100-101.
[59] U.S. Strategic Bombing Survey, *op. cit.* n. 6, p. 114a.
[60] *Ibid.*, p. 120a.
[61] *Ibid.*, p. 121
[62] D. K. Huzel. *Peenemunde to Canaveral* (Englewood Cliffs, N. J.: Prentice Hall, 1962), pp. 128-29.

February 1945 it was decided to abandon Peenemunde, and the base was left intact; papers and personnel were removed after some deliberation:

> To whom, the Russians or the Americans, would fall this treasure of engineering research and knowledge? It was more than just a question of who would catch us first, because we still had some element of choice. We had, in point of fact, already exercised this choice by moving West away from the Russians.[63]

Thus it was that 400 top Peenemunde people were at Garmisch-Partenkirchen at the end of the war. Of these about 118 later went on to the U.S. rocket program. The data, hidden in the Harz Mountains, were transferred to the Aberdeen Proving Grounds.[64]

Mittelwerke at Nordhausen was visited in June 1945 by U.S. Strategic Bombing Survey teams who reported that the enormous underground plant could manufacture V-ls and V-2s as well as Junkers 87 bombers. Twenty-seven tunnels—a large proportion of the plant—were used to manufacture V-2s. The plant was well equipped with machine tools and with "a very well set up assembly line for the rocket power unit."[65] Its output at the end of the war was about 400 V-2s per month, and its potential output was projected at 900 to 1000 per month. The team commented: "Jigs and fixtures developed for the fabrication of fuselages and tail units were excellently conceived, consisting of copper-lined jigs permitting stilus spot welding of the steel sheets and parts used in this design."[66] The Nordhausen plant was removed completely to the U.S.S.R.

The United States and Britain were less successful in gaining access to German rocket testing sites in Poland. The Sanders Mission reached the Blizna test station only after considerable delays in Moscow,[67] and when they got there they found equipment had been removed "in such a methodical way as to suggest strongly to the mission's leader that the evacuation was made with a view to the equipment being reerected elsewhere."[68]

The Sanders Mission accumulated one and one-half tons of rocket parts and readied them for shipment to the West. The parts included:

> a complete steel burner unit; the framework for a radio compartment; a rear fin significantly providing for a wireless aerial; and numerous radio and servo-mechanical components. Of great importance was the finding of a forward fuel

[63] *Ibid.*, p. 150
[64] *Ibid.*, p. 222.
[65] U.S. Strategic Bombing Survey, *Inspection Visits to Various Targets: Special Report* (Washington, 1947), p. 13.
[66] *Ibid.*
[67] D. Irving, *The Mare's Nest* (London: William Kimber, 1964), p. 278.
[68] *Ibid.*, p. 285.

tank, whose capacity was estimated at 175 cubic feet, sufficient to contain 3900 kilogrammes of alcohol.[69]

Unfortunately, when the mission reached home it was found that the rocket fragments had been intercepted by the Soviets:

> The rocket specimens which they had crated up in Blizna for shipment to London and the United States were last seen in Moscow; the crates were indeed duly freighted to the Air Ministry in London, but were found to contain several tons of old and highly familiar aircraft parts when they were opened. The rocket specimens themselves had vanished into the maw of the Soviet war machine.[70]

Many German rocket technicians (as distinct from the top theoreticians in German rocketry) went or were taken to the Soviet Union. The most senior was Helmut Groettrup, who had been an aide to the director of electronics at Peenemunde; 200 other former Peenemunde technicians are reported to have been transferred as well.[71] Among those from other sites were Waldemar Wolf, chief of ballistics for Krupp; engineer Peter Lertes; and Hans Hock, an Austrian specialist in computers. Most of these persons went in the October 22-23 haul of 92 trainloads comprising 6000 German specialists and 20,000 members of their families. Askania technicians, specialists in rocket-tracking devices, and electronics people from Lorenz, Siemens, and Telefunken were among the deportees, as were experts from the Walter Raketentriebwerke in Prague.

The Balance Sheet On German Rocket Technology

It is possible to make a reasonably accurate estimate of what the Soviets did—and did not—gain from German World War II rocket work. Their prize was considerable in material terms: the Blizna site in Poland (subject of the abortive Sanders Mission), the Peenemunde facilities (but not the documents),

---

[69] *Ibid.*
[70] *Ibid.* This is inconsistent with Ambassador W. Averell Harriman's report to the State Department in Washington. Harriman stated that after a "firm but friendly letter to the Deputy Chief of the Red Army General Staff [pointed out] that neglect to consider U.S. Army proposals was giving the impression that the Red Army did not want to cooperate; the Red Army made more favorable and quicker decisions, one of which was that when Anglo-American technical experts were finally allowed to visit German experimental rocket installations in liberated Poland, they were given the most complete collaboration and attention." U.S. State Department Decimal File 711. 61/9-2944: Telegram, September 29/44.
[71] For material on these transfers see A. Lee, *The Soviet Air and Rocket Forces* (New York: Praeger, 1959), pp. 229-40; Albert Parry, *Russia's Rockets and Missiles* (London: Macmillan and Company, 1960), pp. 113-31; and V. L. Sokolov, "Soviet Use of German Science and Technology, 1945-1946" (New York: Research Program on the U.S.S.R., 1955), Mimeographed Series no. 72.

the main production facilities at Nordhausen, all Berlin production facilities, and various rocket manufacturing plants in Germany and Prague went completely to the Soviets. In terms of physical facilities, the West got the documents from Peenemunde and the Nordhausen area together with only a sample selection of rockets from Nordhausen. But as far as personnel was concerned, the best went west. The von Braun group was determined to go west; only Groettrup and several thousand technicians went east.

In sum, the Soviets got production facilities and the technical level of personnel. The West got the theoretical work in the documents and the top-level German scientists and theoretical workers.

With true Bolshevik determination the Soviets concentrated talent and resources into a rocket program; the result was *Sputnik*—which came to fruition in 1957, just at a time when it was essential for strategic reasons for the U.S.S.R. to convince the world of its prowess and technical ability. The nations of the West, too, had integrated their acquired top-notch theoreticians and wealth of documentary material into developmental programs—but with less zeal. They had undertaken the British tests at Cuxhaven and the U.S. work at White Sands, but the real propaganda prize had slipped from their grasp.

It is impossible to say which side received "the most." In the long run, however, because of the indigenous strength of the Western industrial systems it is probable that the West gained less from the German work.

German Origins Of Soviet Rockets And Missiles

It is not surprising in view of these technical acquisitions that the postwar rocket and missile industry in the Soviet Union had strong roots in and orientation toward German developments.

The most important Soviet missile developments have taken place with respect to intermediate- and intercontinental-range missiles. In essential features these have been developed from the German V-2, and up to 1959 the developments were attained with German assistance. (See Tables 20-3 and 20-4.)

Although the original V-2 had only 28,400 pounds of thrust, this was improved to 78,000 pounds in the Soviet T-1. Then by grouping the T-1 and T-14A rockets that had been developed in a German-Soviet effort into two- and three-stage versions, the Soviets formed the T-3, T-3A T-3B, and T-4 missiles. The T-3 three-stage ballistic missile became operational in 1960 and was designed to carry a thermonuclear warhead and to travel 5000 miles.

In addition the Soviets adapted the German Rheinbote and R-4/M air-to-air rockets as well as the antiaircraft Wasserfall rocket.[72] The German air-surface

---

[72] *Aviation Week*, January 14, 1952, pp. 37-41.

Table 20-3   SOVIET ROCKETS AND THEIR GERMAN V-2 ORIGINS

Liquid fuel models, with thrust in lb		Stages	Western origin
V-2	28,400	Single stage	Captured German V-2
R-10,	41,500	Single stage	Improved V-2 ⎫ Developed
T-1,	78,000	Single stage	Improved R-10 ⎬ from V-2
T-1A,	99,000	Single stage	Improved T-1 ⎭
T-2.	78,000	Two stage	R-10(V-2) plus R-14A
	268,000		(German-Soviet effort)
T-3.	78,000	Three stage	R-10(V-2) plus R-14A
	268,000		
	440,000		
T-3A.	78,000	Three stage	R-10(V-2) plus R-14-A
	268,000		
	520,000		
T-4.	52,800	Two stage	V-2 plus two R-10
	180,000		(German Sanger concept)
Golem-1,	120,000	n.a.	n.a.
Golem-2,	242,000	n.a.	n.a.

Sources: Alfred J. Zaehringer, *Soviet Space Technology*, (New York: Harper & Brothers, 1961), p. 75; U.S. Senate, Committee on Aeronautical and Space Sciences, *Soviet Space Programs, 1962-65; Goals and Purposes, Achievements, Plans, and International Implications*, Staff Report, 89th Congress, 2d session (Washington, December 1966).

Table 20-4   SOVIET MISSILES
AND THEIR GERMAN ORIGINS, IN 1960

Soviet missile	Description	German origin
M-100	air-to-air; early version unguided, later infrared guidance	Developed in U.S.S.R. under Boris von Schlippe
M-1	2-stage surface to air; liquid-fueled	Developed from Walther-KHW-109-509 (or the Rheintochter)
T-44	Boost glide bomber	Sanger-Bredt antipodal bomber
Golem-1	Underwater to surface	German A-12 underwater

Sources: RAND Corp. Report T-33: Volursus, *The Secret Weapons of the Soviet Union* (Santa Monica, February 1964), pp. 3-4; *Missiles and Rockets* (Washington, D.C.), July 20, 1959, pp. 172-6.

rockets HS-293 and FX 1400 also were taken over.[73] By early 1954 some German technicians had been separated from Soviet rocket work, and return of the main group started in 1958. Even today, however, East Germany supplies the U.S.S.R. with rocket fuel, electrical equipment, and guidance and control equipment, although this role probably is not decisive.

Asher Lee sums up the transfer of German rocket and missile technology:

> ... the whole range of Luftwaffe and German Army radio-guided missiles and equipment fell into Russian hands. There were the two Henschel radar-guided bombs, the Hs-293 and the larger FX-1400 ... the U.S.S.R. also acquired samples of German antiaircraft radio-guided missiles like the X-4, the Hs-298 air-to-air projectile with a range of about a mile and a half, the Rheintochter which was fitted with a radar proximity fuze, and the very promising Schmetterling which even in 1945 had an operational ceiling of over 45,000 feet and a planned radius of action of about twenty miles. It could be ground- or air-launched and was one of the most advanced of the German small-calibre radio-guided defensive rockets; of these various projectiles the Henschel-293 bomb and the defensive Schmetterling and Hs-298 (the V-3) are undergoing development at Omsk and Irkutsk ... Soon they may be going into production at factories near Riga, Leningrad, Kiev, Khabarovsk, Voronezh, and elsewhere.

Other plants in the same areas produced improved radar based on the Wurzburg System; the airborne Lichenstein and Naxos systems were reported in large-scale production in the 1950s.

U.S.-Soviet Technical Cooperation In Space

In 1955 as German technicians began returning home, the United States started to make approaches to the Soviet Union on the question of technical cooperation in space;[74] indeed, in the ten-year period between December 1959 and 1969, the United States made 18 individual initiatives. Any acceptance by the Soviets would of course have supplemented their gains from German assistance.

In December 1959 NASA Administrator T. Keith Glennan offered assistance in tracking Soviet manned flights; on March 7, 1962, President Kennedy proposed an exchange of information from tracking and data acquisition stations, and on September 20, 1963, the President proposed joint exploration of the moon, an offer later repeated by President Johnson. There was no Soviet response

---

[73]   Parry, *op. cit.* n 71, p. 119; see Chapter 8, "The German Role in Russian Rockets." See also A. Lee in *Air University Quarterly Review* (Montgomery, Ala.), Spring 1952, p. 14.

[74]   U.S.-Senate, Committee on Aeronautical and Space Sciences, *NASA Authorization for Fiscal Year 1970*, (Hearings, 91st Congress, 1st session, May 1969 (Washington, 1969), pt. II, p. 635.

to these offers. There followed a series of proposals from NASA itself: on December 8, 1964, the administration proposed an exchange of teams to visit deep-space tracking and data acquisition facilities; on May 3, 1965, NASA suggested joint communications tests via the *Soviet Molniya I*; on August 25, 1965, NASA, at the request of President Johnson, asked the Soviet Academy of Sciences to send a high-level representative to the launching of *Gemini VI*, and on November 16 of the same year NASA inquired once again about joint *Molniya I* communications tests. Four more U.S. offers were made in 1966: in January NASA inquired about cooperation on Venus probes; on March 24 and May 23 Administrator James Webb suggested that the Soviets propose subjects for discussion; and in September Ambassador Arthur Goldberg again raised the question of tracking coverage by the United States for Soviet missiles. None of these suggestions was taken up. The U.S. emphasis on assistance in tracking coverage is interesting because this constitutes a Soviet weak area.

The unwillingness of the Soviets to cooperate is exemplified by their response to the U.S. National Academy of Sciences proposal in March 1967 that the Soviets provide *Luna 13* soil meter experiment data in advance of normal world reporting "in return for comparable data from future flights in the Surveyor series."[75] The Soviet data were indeed forwarded—but only after they had been reported at the International Committee of Space Research (COSPAR) meeting in London.

Further offers were made in March, April, June, October (twice), and December 1967 with no Soviet response.

Similar efforts elsewhere have met with the same negative results. For example, COSPAR, aware of the possibilities of planet contamination, noted that an "extremely costly effort has been made by the United States to ensure that its probes do not contaminate the planets." COSPAR has "repeatedly" made efforts to obtain similar information from the Soviets "so that the adequacy of Soviet techniques can be exposed to the judgment of the world scientific community."[76] Over the entire ten-year period the Soviets have provided only generalized assurances, and while there was general agreement that Soviet rocket stages had impacted the planets, "no assurances of any kind have been forthcoming regarding sterilization or diversion from the planets."[77]

The only agreement for an exchange of information came in June 1962 after President Kennedy's initiatives; there were limited projects then that appear to have achieved mediocre success. An agreement to exchange meteorological information was made but "to date [1969] the Soviet data have not been operationally useful to us."[78] No exchange of data on magnetic field mapping took

---

[75] *Ibid.*
[76] *Ibid.*
[77] *Ibid.*
[78] *Ibid.*

place between 1962 and 1969, and although arrangements have been made for exchange of ground-based data "these have not been completely successful either."[79] Cooperative communications using the U.S. passive satellite *Echo II* were completed in February 1964: "The Soviets received communications only, declining to transmit. Technical difficulties of this experiment limited the results received." In space biology and medicine, a U.S. team spent two years putting together material, while the Soviet side has failed to respond.

A direct Washington-Moscow bilateral circuit for the exchange of meteorological information went into effect in September 1964. Without interruption since September 1966, the United States has transmitted to Moscow cloud analyses for one-half the world and selected cloud photographs. Although the Soviets launched a total of seven weather satellites between 1964 and 1969 "there have been numerous interruptions in the transmission for data, at one time for a period of four months."[80] Further, because of insufficient coverage by Soviet satellites, the Soviet data have been limited, often of marginal quality and received after the period of maximum usefulness. It is probable in the light of these results that the Soviet space program is far less technically advanced than has been generally believed, and fear of disclosing this backwardness inhibits the Soviets from taking advantage of superior U.S. technology.

We may conclude that although the Soviets produced large quantities of aircraft during World War II these were for the most part elementary wooden models with inferior piston engines.[81] No jet engines or advanced reciprocal engines had been produced by the end of the war, and Russian aircraft plants were heavily dependent on Lend Lease supplies, equipment, and technology.

During 1945-47 about two-thirds of the extensive German wartime aircraft and missile industry was transferred to the Soviet Union, including designers, engineers, plans, models, equipment, and complete production lines. The most important categories were Junkers and BMW jet engines, with production lines and teams of German engineers used in the late 1940s and 1950s to advance this jet engine technology. This was supplemented by the purchase of 55 Rolls-Royce engines in 1947 which became the prototypes for another group of Soviet jet engines. Soviet jets and turboprops in the early sixties were descendants of these German and British engines.

Although some aircraft are direct copies of Western machines (for example, the Tu-4 bomber and the Tu-70 civilian version in many ways duplicate the Boeing B-29), some design independence is recognizable from the mid-1950s

---

[79] *Ibid.*
[80] *Ibid..*
[81] Sutton II, Chapter 14.

onward, although this is not of an advanced nature and dependence is still a factor.[82]

Soviet rockets and missiles can be clearly traced to German V-2 technology and transferred production capabilities; this observation applies also to air-to-air and underwater missile weapons.

[82] A popular but reasonably accurate account of Soviet backwardness in space and aviation in 1958 is Lloyd Mallan, *Russia and the Big Red Lie* (New York: Fawcett, 1959). This is based on a 14,000-mile, almost unrestricted trip to interview 38 Soviet scientists. Mallan's conclusions, amply supported by photographs, are generally consistent with the material presented here. Some of the more interesting items: the Remington Rand UNIVAC computer was used to illustrate an article in *Red Star* on Soviet computers (with captions translated into Russian) (p. 16); Soviet computers had such primitive characteristics as cooling by air blowing over the tubes (pp. 17, 20, and 24); calculations for the Lunik trajectory were done by use of a hand calculator made in Germany, not a computer (p. 26); the major equipment at a Soviet tracking station was an aerial camera that could be purchased at a war surplus store in the United States for $80 (p. 30); primitive cross-hair techniques were in use (p. 34); there was a General Electric radio telescope at Byurakan Observatory (p. 44); Mallan saw Soviet copies of the U.S. Navy space suit (p. 56-57) and the nose-cone spring release from the Viking rocket (p. 86); German rocket launchers were used (p. 95); there were copies of the C-123, Convair, B-29 (pp.112-120); numerous B-29 parts were used on the Tu-104, which had no servomechanisms and thus required brute force to fly; there were no radarscopes on the IL-18 (despite its radome nose, presumably false, p. 121); the ZIL-111 had a Cadillac gold V on the radiator, and the Moskvitch proved to be a copy of the West German Ford Taunus (p. 135).

CHAPTER TWENTY-ONE

Western Construction
of the Soviet Merchant Marine

SHIPYARD FACILITIES IN THE SOVIET UNION

Soviet shipyard facilities, in 1944 mostly Tsarist yards, were supplemented after World War II by reparations equipment from Germany (see Table 21-1) and import of shipbuilding equipment from the West, particularly from Finland, the United Kingdom, and Germany.

Table 21-1   SHIPYARDS REMOVED FROM GERMANY
               TO THE U.S.S.R. IN 1945-46

Name of yard	Location	Extent removed to U.S.S.R.
Deutsche Schiffs-und Maschinenbau A.G. (Deschimag)	Bremen	Complete [a]
Deutsche Schiffs-und Maschinenbau A.G. (Valentin)	Bremen	Complete [a]
Schiffswerft und Maschinenfabrik	Dresden-Laubegast	Part only [b]
Schiffswerft Uebigau	Dresden-Uebigau	Part only [b]
Schiffswerft Rosslau	Saxony-Anhalt	Complete [b]
Neptunwerft Rostock	Rostock	Part only [b]

Sources: [a] Germany, Office of Military Government (U.S. Zone), Economics Division, *A Year of Potsdam* . . . (n.p.: OMGUS, 1947), p. 36; [b] G. E. Harmssen, *Am Abend der Demontage; Sechs Jahre Reparationspolitik* (Bremen: F. Trüjen, 1951), pp. 101-2.

Shipyards at Bremen in the U.S. Zone of Germany were completely removed to the U.S.S.R. on a priority basis under U.S. Operation RAP.[1] The German submarine yards at Bremen and Stettin, including the torpedo and fire-control manufacturing plants, were also completely dismantled and shipped to the U.S.S.R., together with engine manufacturing plants and some "4000 submarine experts and construction supervisors."[2]

[1] See p. 26.
[2] U.S. Naval Institute, *Proceedings* (Annapolis, Md.), October 1945, p. 1225.

This is of great significance, as the German submarine of 1945 was quite different from the submarine of 1943; the later units were streamlined, with revolutionary engines enabling a tripling of underwater speed.[3] These German facilities became the nucleus of Soviet postwar construction of submarines and naval ships.

In 1954 this German equipment was supplemented by extensive purchases of shipbuilding equipment in the United Kingdom and Belgium. Under the January 1954 Soviet-Belgian trade agreement a total of $100 million in ships, floating cranes, and marine boilers was to be supplied from Belgium during the years 1955-57.[4] Large orders also were placed in the United Kingdom for shipbuilding equipment. For example,

> Soviet orders are being placed for shipbuilding equipment, Messrs Fielding and Platt having recently secured a £2¼ million contract for hydraulic equipment, including joggling presses and large forging and flanging presses.[5]

Moreover, Finnish deliveries to the Soviet Union for the latter half of the decade of the 1950s contained, among other equipment, five floating docks and 25 floating cranes and electric bridge cranes.[6]

These equipment deliveries were in addition to the extensive use of foreign shipyards—and this particularly applies to Finland and Poland—to build up the Soviet merchant marine. Many yards in Western Europe have since about 1951 had a large proportion of their tonnage on Soviet account, and a few yards have produced almost entirely for the Soviet Union. For example, in 1954 in the Netherlands the De Schelde, Kononklijke Mij N.V. yards in Flushing produced 100 percent of their output on Soviet account. In Belgium in 1954 the shipyard Boel et Fils S.A. produced 20 percent of its output on Soviet account. In Finland in the same year the two major yards Wärtsilä-Koncernen A/B (Sandvikens Skeppsdocka) and Wärtsilä-Koncernen A/B (Crichton-Vulcan) produced 50 and 64 percent, respectively, of their output on Soviet account. In the same year in Sweden Oskarshamns Varv A/B at Oskarhamn built 25 percent of its output on Soviet account. And in the same year in the United Kingdom the yards of William Gray and Company, Ltd., at West Hartlepool produced 20 percent of their output on Soviet account.

In addition, foreign government-owned yards have produced ships on Soviet account. For example the Howaltdwerke in Kiel, Germany, is owned by the German Government and has been a major source for Soviet ships.[7]

---

[3] *Ibid.*

[4] Raymond F. Mikesell and Jack N. Behrman, *Financing Free World Trade with the Sino-Soviet Bloc* (Princeton: Princeton University Press, 1958), Appendix.

[5] *The Motor Ship* (London), XXXIV, 408 (March 1954), 549.

[6] U.N., *Treaty Series*, vol. 240 (1956), p. 202.

[7] Gunnar Adler-Karlsson, *Western Economic Warfare, 1947-1967* (Stockholm: Almquist and Wikesell, 1968), p. 94. *Merchant Ships: World Built* (Southampton: Adlard Coles, annual).

CONSTRUCTION OF THE SOVIET MERCHANT MARINE

The total tonnage in the Soviet merchant fleet at July 1967 was 11,788,625 gross registered tons. Of this total, only 34.4 percent (4,058,427 gross registered tons) was built in the Soviet Union; the balance of 7,730,198 gross registered tons was built outside the Soviet Union.[8]

The largest single supplier of shipping to the Soviet Union has been Poland, a country that was not even a shipbuilder before 1950. During the period 1950-66 Poland supplied 379 ships totaling 1,454,314 gross registered tons, to the Soviet merchant marine. Table 21-2 illustrates the number of Polish ships built on Soviet account in each year during that period and gives their gross tonnage. It may be observed that the average size of these ships increased quite significantly at the beginning of the 1960s, when "hundreds" of technical-assistance agree-

Table 21-2   MERCHANT SHIPS BUILT IN POLAND
ON SOVIET ACCOUNT FROM 1950 to 1966

Year	Number of Ships built	Gross registered tonnage	Average size built, GRT
1950	1	1946	1946
1951	—	—	—
1952	21	36,036	1716
1953	28	46,657	1666
1954	24	43,240	1800
1955	31	46,470	1499
1956	35	61,295	1751
1957	30	53,985	1799
1958	29	61,876	2133
1959	19	86,887	4573
1960	19	122,053	6424
1961	12	52,808	4400
1962	21	134,991	6428
1963	31	167,806	5413
1964	24	159,228	6634
1965	23	175,191	7617
1966	31	203,845	6576
Totals	379	1,454,314	

Source: Registr Soyuza SSR, Registrovaya kniga morskikh sudov soyuza SSR 1964-1965 (Moscow, 1966).

[8] Calculated from Registr Soyuza SSR, Registrovaya kniga morskikh sudov soyuza SSR 1964-1965 (Moscow, 1966). The reader should also examine Soviet Merchant Ships 1945-1968 (Havant, England: K. Mason, 1969), for detailed material. It should be noted, however, that that survey includes only about 2500 ships, whereas this section is based on the Soviet Register at July 1, 1967, i.e., it considers a total of 5551 ships.

ments between Polish shipyards and West European manufacturers of ship-building equipment came into operation;[9] from an average gross tonnage of about 1600 tons in the early 1950s, the average Soviet ship built in Polish yards in the mid-1960s was between 6500 and 7500 tons.

The largest Free World suppliers of ships to the Soviet fleet have been Japan and West Germany. In 1955-56 West Germany supplied 32 ships with an average tonnage of about 3000 gross registered tons. Thereafter orders dribbled down to one and two ships per year until 1964, when seven ships of 4700 tons each were delivered, and 1965-66, when eight ships of an average of 16,000 tons were delivered from West Germany to the Soviet Union. Japanese orders have been concentrated in the years 1962 to 1966 and comprise numerous 22-23,000-ton tankers.

Among socialist countries, Yugoslavia is a prominent supplier of ships to the Soviet Union; in 1965 Yugoslavia built 11 ships of two types (11,000 tons and 15,000 tons) and in the following year supplied another ten ships (also 11,000 and 15,000 tons). Most of these Yugoslav ships have Burmeister & Wain diesel engines.[10]

Construction in Soviet shipyards has concentrated on standard ships. One such standard ship is the *Leninskii Komsomol*,[11] a dry cargo ship of 12,000 gross registered tons and generally comparable to the U.S. "Mariner" class; i.e., it is a conventional design ship of a type known throughout the world. This type of vessel has also been ordered on Soviet account in Japan, Yugoslavia, Finland, and Poland.

Another standard dry cargo freighter is the 12,500-dwt class built at Nikolaev with engines based on Burmeister & Wain design; this "Poltava" class became well known in 1961 as a missile carrier to Cuba.

SOVIET OIL TANKERS AND WESTERN DIESEL ENGINES

The Soviet merchant marine is heavily dependent not only on Western ship-yards but on foreign marine diesel engine technology.[12] A quantitative expression of additions to the Soviet tanker fleet in 1964-65, i.e., those tankers under construction at the very end of the period under consideration, illustrates the point.[13] In those years a total of 541,201 gross registered tons of tankers was added and the construction origin of this segment was as follows:

[9] John D. Harbron, *Communist Ships and Shipping* (London, 1962), p. 196. The Soviets have also made hard currency available to the Poles for purchase of Western equipment for ships built in Poland on Soviet account. *Ibid.*, p. 109.
[10] See A. Sutton, "Soviet Merchant Marine," U.S. Naval Institute, *Proceedings*, January 1970, for Western construction of merchant ships on Soviet account.
[11] Registr Soyuza SSR, *op. cit.* n. 8, no. 1602.
[12] See chapter 17.
[13] This is the segment of the fleet contained in Supplement No. 1 to the Soviet Register. Registr Soyuza SSR, *op. cit.* n. 8.

Hulls built in U.S.S.R.		236,358 gross tons	(or 43.6 percent)
Hulls built in Eastern Europe:			
Yugoslavia	167,803		
Poland	13,218	184,881 gross tons	(or 34.1 percent)
Bulgaria	3,860		
Hulls built in Free World:			
Finland	13,439		
Japan	75,390	119,962 gross tons	(or 22.2 percent)
Italy	31,133		
			99.9 percent

In general these vessels had main engines manufactured in the country of hull construction; therefore the geographic distribution of engine construction is about the same in percentage terms. However, almost all the Soviet-built propulsion units (229,530 tons) were steam turbines. If we consider only that portion of tanker fleet additions equipped with diesel propulsion units, the distribution is as follows:

Main diesel units built in U.S.S.R.	1.7 percent	(5,372 gross tons)
Main diesel units built in Eastern Europe	59.8 percent	(186,337 gross tons)
Main diesel units built in Free World	38.4 percent	(119,962 gross tons)
	99.9 percent	(311, 617 gross tons)

If we make a further analysis and examine diesel engines by country of *design* (not construction) origin (most East European manufacturers have technical-assistance agreements with Western diesel engine manufacturers; all Yugoslav diesels in this segment, for example, have Burmeister & Wain main diesels), then the percentages are:

Main diesels designed in U.S.S.R.	1.7 percent	(5,372 gross tons)
Main diesels designed in Eastern Europe	1.7 percent	(5,318 gross tons)
Main diesels designed in Free World	96.5 percent	(300,981 gross tons)
	99.9 percent	(311,671 gross tons)

The most numerous class of Soviet tankers in a fleet of 300 such vessels[14] is the "Kostroma" class of 8229 gross registered tons. Between 1953 and 1961 about 58 were built in this class, which is a close copy of the U.S. wartime T-2 tanker;[15] about 17 of these have Skoda engines imported from Czechoslovakia and the remainder have a similar engine which is manufactured at Russky Diesel in Leningrad. According to J. D. Harbron,[16] the "Kostroma"

[14]   *Ibid.*, at July 1967. See Statistical Note to this chapter for detailed data on 242 (out of 300) tankers built after World War II.

[15]   Harbron, *op. cit.* n. 9, p. 151.

[16]   *Ibid.*, p. 154.

class in the early sixties was fully occupied in supplying oil to Cuba and in Soviet naval supply work.

The remaining tankers can be divided for analysis into three groups—large tankers in excess of 13,000 tons, medium tankers of about 3300 gross registered tons, and small tankers of less than 1772 tons. Analysis of these three classes is contained in the Statistical Note to this chapter (see pp. 295-302) and includes a breakdown by foreign and Soviet domestic production.

About two-thirds of large tankers in the Soviet tanker fleet as of July 1967 had been built outside the Soviet Union; of a total of 129 such tankers, only 25 had been built in the Soviet Union and all these were powered by steam turbine rather than diesel engines. Soviet construction falls into two classes: one class, of 21,255 gross registered tons, includes seven vessels built between 1959 and 1963, and the other class, of 32,484 gross registered tons, includes the remaining 18 tankers built between 1963 and 1966. All other Soviet tankers over 13,000 tons were built abroad. Italy built six of 20,000 and 31,000 gross registered tons; Holland built two of 16,349 gross registered tons; Poland built seven of a standard class of 13,363 gross registered tons; Yugoslavia built 15 of a standard tonnage (15,255 tons); Japan built 20 tankers of between 22,000 and 25,000 tons; and the remaining two tankers were a Polish-built standard vessel with East German engines and a Yugoslav-built tanker of 17,861 tons with a Swedish engine. This comprised the total Soviet tanker fleet in excess of 13,000 tons—and 67.5 percent in tonnage terms had been built abroad.

There were 76 tankers in a medium category (3300 and 3820 gross registered tons). Of these only 15 were completely built in the Soviet Union; however, the class does contain one unusual characteristic—a group of 22 tankers with Soviet diesel engines but built in Bulgaria. The largest group was built in Finland—28 of 3300 tons with hulls from Finnish shipyards and Danish engines. The remaining vessels in this group constituted a few built in Finland with Finnish engines, three built in Finland with Swedish engines, and two tankers built completely in Japan.

The last group of tankers comprised 89 vessels, all of less than 1772 gross registered tons, 70.8 percent built outside the Soviet Union. The largest group built inside the Soviet Union comprised 20 small tankers of between 756 and 802 gross registered tons, for use in the Caspian Sea. Another group of nine tankers of 1775 gross registered tons had hulls built in the Soviet Union but Czechoslovak Skoda engines. The largest group of small tankers built outside the Soviet Union comprised 33 tankers of between 260 and 305 gross registered tons, with both hulls and engines built in East Germany. A group of thirteen tankers of 1117 tons was built in Finland on Soviet account in 1954-55 and powered with Swedish engines.

Therefore it may be seen that as of July 1967 about two-thirds of Soviet tankers had been built outside the Soviet Union, and the foreign-built segment included almost all tankers in excess of 13,000 tons. Even two-thirds of the smaller tankers, including those for use in the Caspian Sea and for coastal use, were built abroad rather than in the Soviet Union. Further, a number of the tankers built in the Soviet Union had engines manufactured abroad, imported into the U.S.S.R., and then installed in hulls built in Soviet yards.

MODERNIZATION AND EXPANSION
OF THE SOVIET FISHING FLEET

Between 1945 and the late 1960s the Soviet fishing fleet was modernized and greatly expanded; between 1945 and 1961 about 3500 modern large and medium trawlers and refrigerator ships were added to the fleet.[17] The program started in the early fifties when orders were placed for prototype fishing vessels in the Netherlands, Sweden, Finland, Denmark, Japan, and, more significantly, in the United Kingdom and Germany.

The Soviets' first step in 1954 was a $20 million order for 20 modern fishing trawlers, placed with the United Kingdom firm of Brooke-Marine, Ltd., of Lowestoft.[18] In this connection, a U.S. Congressional report[19] notes:

> From the specifications they received, the British engineers learned that the Russians were still designing their trawlers pretty much as they were designed 20 years earlier. They seemed to have no knowledge of what went into the making of a modern fishing trawler....[20]

The series of 20 Brooke-Marine trawlers embodied the latest in world technology, and "after they were turned over to Russia, the new trawlers were distributed as prototypes among the shipyards of the U.S.S.R., Poland, and East Germany, and large-scale production of large, efficient, oceangoing fishing vessels was launched in earnest in the Soviet bloc."[21]

The first vessel in the class—the side-set trawler *Pioner*—was launched and delivered in 1956. Its equipment was of the most advanced type: Donkin & Co., Ltd., of Newcastle-on-Tyne supplied a partially balanced streamlined rudder actuated by means of electrohydraulic steering gear; an electrically driven windlass, installed by Clarke-Chapman & Co., Ltd., was capable of lifting two improved Hall stockless bower anchors from 260 feet at a rate of 30 feet

---

[17] U.S. Senate, Committee on Commerce, *The Postwar Expansion of Russia's Fishing Industry*, Report by the Fisheries Research Institute, 88th Congress, 2d Session, January 1964 (Seattle: University of Washington, 1964), p. 6.

[18] *Commercial Fisheries Review* (Washington, D.C.), 16, 5 (May 1, 1954), 68.

[19] U.S. Senate, *op. cit.* n. 17, p. 7.

[20] *Ibid.*

[21] *Ibid.* For details of equipment on Soviet trawlers see Yu. Kostyunin, *Rybolovnye traly* (Moscow, 1968).

per minute; the ventilating-heating system was by R.B. Stirling & Co., Ltd.; and the insulation, of "very high standard throughout," was by Darlington Co., Ltd.

The most up-to-date navigation aids were installed by Brooke-Marine, Ltd.—a Redifon radio apparatus, Pye sound reproduction system, Bendix echosounding gear, a Revometer, Browne standard and steering compasses, and an eight-way batteryless telephone communication system by Telephone Manufacturing Co., Ltd. The refrigeration plant was built by L. Sterne & Co., Ltd., of Glasgow with automatic controls by Malone Instrument Co., Ltd., and the fish meal plant by Farrar Boilerworks, Ltd. The main engine was a four-stroke, eight-cylinder diesel-type KSSDM by Mirrlees, Bickerton & Day, Ltd., developing 950 shp at 255 rpm. The whole ship was specially strengthened for ice work.[22]

In all, 20 ships were built to this specification by Brooke-Marine, Ltd., for the Soviet Union. (See Table 21-3.)

In 1954 the Scottish shipbuilder John Lewis & Sons, Ltd., of Aberdeen designed an advanced fishing vessel, the *Fairtry*, which was hailed in the trade

Table 21-3   TRAWLERS SUPPLIED BY BROOKE-MARINE, LTD
TO THE U.S.S.R. IN 1956-59

Soviet register	No.	Name	Gross registered tons	Date supplied
2855	PT-200	Pioner	684	1955
2856	PT-201	Akula	684	1956
2857	PT-202	Muksun	685	1956
2858	PT-203	Karas	684	1956
2859	PT-205	Sokol	684	1956
2860	PT-207	Sever	684	1957
2861	PT-208	Vostok	685	1957
2862	PT-209	Ug	685	1957
2863	PT-210	Zapad	685	1957
2864	PT-211	Tunets	685	1957
2865	PT-212	Rion	685	1957
2866	PT-213	Stavrida	685	1957
2867	PT-214	Shongui	685	1957
2868	PT-215	Kotlas	685	1957
2869	PT-216	Okun	685	1957
33	—	Adler	685	1958
2158	—	Pelamide	685	1958

Source: Registr Soyuza SSR, *Registrovaya kniga morskikh sudov soyuza SSR 1964-1965* (Moscow, 1966).

[22] Data from *The Shipbuilder and Marine Engine-Builder* (London), February 1956, p. 1179.

literature as one of the most interesting ships to have been built in recent years[23] and subsequently became the basis of the Soviet "Pushkin" class. The *Fairtry* resulted from experimental work that had been going on since 1947. It was the largest trawler built to that time and the first specially designed and constructed for stern trawling and for complete processing of the catch on board. The *Fairtry* had a gross registered tonnage of 2605 with a main propulsion unit built by Lewis Doxford—a four-cylinder oil engine capable of developing 1900 bhp.[24]

This advanced design was used by the Russians for their main postwar class of trawlers. The Soviets placed an order in the Howaldtwerke shipyards in Kiel, West Germany, for 24 trawlers based on the *Fairtry* design, and these trawlers of 2500 gross tons were built on Soviet account between 1955 and 1958.[25] The 24 German-built prototypes became the basis for the Soviet "Pushkin" class of stern trawlers, first launched in the spring of 1955, and the other 23 German-built units followed in the next several years.

After being tested in operation the "Pushkin" class became the prototype for a Soviet-built version—the "Maiakovskii" class; the "Maiakovskii" vessels of 3170 gross registered tons were of the same overall dimensions as the "Pushkin" class. Two years later work began in Poland on a modified version of the same trawler, the "Leskov" class of 2890 gross registered tons and of similar dimensions to the "Pushkins" and the *Fairtry*.

There is also an East German version of the *Fairtry* known as the "Tropik" class, of 2400 gross registered tons; the first craft in this series, launched in East Germany in July 1962, was specially built for operation by the Soviets in tropic areas.

Table 21-4   ORIGINS OF SOVIET STERN TRAWLERS AS OF 1965

Soviet trawler class	Design based on	Original prototype order	Number of copies
"Pushkin" 2,470 GRT	U.K. *'Fairtry'*; prototype built in W. Germany	24	—
"Maiakovskii" 3,170 GRT	U.K. *'Fairtry'*	—	60
"Leskov" 2,890 GRT	Polish modification of U.K. *'Fairtry'*	20	—
"Tropik" 2,600 GRT	East German version of U.K. *'Fairtry'*	—	65 (to 1965)

Sources: *Commercial Fisheries Review* (Washington), May 1, 1954; and author's calculations based on Soviet sources.

---

[23] *The Shipbuilder and Marine Engine-Builder*, September 1954, p. 541.
[24] *Ibid.*, pp. 541-44.
[25] *Commercial Fisheries Review*, 16, 5 (May 1, 1954), 69.

Therefore the numerous Soviet stern trawlers are based on a single British vessel, the most advanced of its type when first produced in 1954. (See Table 21-4.)

FISH FACTORY SHIPS, MOTHER SHIPS, AND REFRIGERATED FISH TRANSPORTS

In 1959 an order for 11 "Severod Vinsk" class mother ships was placed with the Polish Government shipyards in Gdansk. The ships were delivered between 1959 and 1962 with a gross registered tonnage of 11,500; their function is to serve as supply and base ships for Soviet trawler fleets.

The "Zakharov" class, based on the "Severod Vinsk" design, performs the functions of processing fish as well as the service functions of a mother ship; it is also equipped to manufacture fish meal and oil from wastes obtained during the canning operations. It was built at the Admiralty yards at Leningrad between 1960 and 1963. The "Zakharov" class ships have a daily canning capacity of 1600 cases, and one version receives fish from an accompanying fleet of medium fishing trawlers (SRTs) or from 12 motor boats carried on board (the motor boats are of a special Japanese Kawasaki design for catching king crabs with angle nets).

There are also about a dozen classes of refrigerator transport vessels, some of which have equipment for quick-freezing fish.

Table 21-5   ORIGINS OF REFRIGERATOR FISH CARRIERS AND
PRODUCTION REGRIGERATOR TRANSPORTS

Class	Built	GRT
"Bratsk"	East Germany	2,500
"Tavriia"	Soviet Union	3230
"Pervomaisk"	Denmark	3300
"Sevastopol"	Soviet Union	5525
"Skryplev"	Denmark	4700

Sources: Commercial Fisheries Review (Washington, D.C.), Nov. 1964 supplement, pp. 11-12; Registr Soyuza SSR, *Registrovaya kniga morskikh sudov soyuza SSR 1964-1965* (Moscow, 1966).

These refrigerated transport vessels have been built partly in the Soviet Union and partly abroad on Soviet account. (See Table 21-5.) The "Bratsk" class of refrigerated vessels, built in East Germany with a gross registered tonnage of about 2500 to carry a crew of 91 with a 40-day cruising capacity, was built after 1960 for the Soviet merchant fleet. The vessels have equipment installed in the East German yards of Stralsund Volkswerft, comprising freezing and refrigeration plant with two freezer machines, four air-blast freezing tunnels, packing departments, refrigerating machines, and refrigerating holds. Capacity is about 1800 cubic meters, permitting storage of about 800 tons of frozen fish.

Another class, built completely in the Soviet Union, is the "Tavriia" class (3230 gross registered tons), which performs the same function as the "Bratsk" class. Another is the "Pervomaisk" class built in Denmark on Soviet account and with Danish engines; these vessels are of about the same tonnage as the "Tavriia" class and about the same overall length, and there is in general a distinct similarity between this Danish class and the "Tavriia" class.

The largest class of refrigerator vessels is the Soviet-built "Sevastopol" of 5525 gross registered tons and about 430 feet in overall length, with a capacity to handle 100 metric tons of fish per day with equipment consisting of eight air-blast freezing tunnels each 39 feet long and related storage of five holds of 5400 cubic meters each; total capacity is 2700 metric tons of fish.

Finally, there is the "Skryplev" class, designated as refrigerator transports but actually factory ships with a capability of freezing fish and preparing fish meal and oil. These ships of 4700 gross registered tons and overall length of about 300 feet were built in Denmark in the early 1950s.

SOVIET OCEANOGRAPHIC AND RESEARCH VESSELS

In 1967 there were approximately 71 research and oceanographic vessels in the Soviet fleet. The origin of about one-half of these vessels has been traced. None of those traced originated in the Soviet Union.[27]

Several research ships have been built in East Germany on Soviet account. For example, the *Okeanograf* was built in East Germany in 1956 and has Buckau-Wolf diesel engines; the *Poliarnik,* built in East Germany in 1952, also has Buckau-Wolf engines; the *Akademik S Vavilov,* built in East Germany in 1949, has a 350-hp Buckau-Wolf diesel engine; the *Zemchug* of 422 tons, built in East Germany in 1950, also has a Buckau-Wolf 300-hp engine; similarly, the *Topseda* of 239 tons, built in East Germany in 1950, has a Buckau-Wolf 300-hp engine.

Some research vessels have been built in Finland. For example the *Professor Rudovits* of 626 tons was built in Finland in 1950, and has Finnish engines. The *Zaria*, built in Finland in 1952, has an East German 300-hp engine.

Holland built a large 12,000-ton research vessel, the *Ob*, in 1953 with a 7000-hp diesel-electric engine made by Schelde-Zulzer.

China built several research vessels for the Soviet Union in the mid-1950s and fitted them with East German Buckau-Wolf engines. For example, the *Pervenets* (442 gross registered tons) was built in 1956 in China. Some prewar

---

[26] *Commercial Fisheries Review,* 26, 11A (November 1964), Supplement.

[27] A list of these vessels is in U.N., Food and Agricultural Organization, *Research Craft Conference* (Seattle, 1968), pt. 2.

vessels also appear to have been converted for oceanographic use; for example the *Vitiaz* (5710 gross registered tons), built in Germany in 1939 with a Krupp reversible two-cycle engine of 3600-hp, was converted sometime in the 1950s for oceanographic use.

Finally, in 1966 Poland agreed to build ten advanced oceanographic research vessels for the Soviet Union. These are ice-strengthened to the highest classification in the Soviet Registry, 282 feet long, 45-foot beam and 15-foot draft with a displacement of 3735 metric tons, and propelled by two Sulzer diesels each of 2400 hp with variable-pitch propellers.[28]

Perhaps the most notable feature of Soviet oceanographic vessels is their navigation and echosounding equipment. This appears to have originated in large part in the West, although we have data for only about 20 of the approximately 70 ships in the Soviet oceanographic research fleet. For example the *Vitiaz*, the converted 1939 German 5700-ton vessel, has the following equipment:

Navigation: 2 gyrocompasses (Course 3 and Course 4)
3 magnetic compasses (2 track, 1 main)
1 Gauss-25 hydraulic log
1 electromechanical log
2 radiolocators (Don and Neptun)
1 Kelvin-Hughes navigation log
2 radio direction finders (Millard)
2 long-distance meteorological stations

Echosounders: 2 Kelvin-Hughes (10,000-meter)
2 Kelvin-Hughes (4500-meter range)
1 Kingfisher fishlocator

The *Ob*, built in Holland in 1953, similarly has Western equipment:

Navigation: 4 gyrocompasses
2 magnetic compasses
1 Gauss-25 log
2 Zarnitsa and Neptun radar

Echosounders: 2 Kelvin-Hughes (MS 26)
2 Nippon Electric L-5, 2000-meter range

Vessels built in East Germany on Soviet account also have been fitted with Western equipment. For example, the *Zemchug* has Nippon Electric echosounders; the *Akademik Vavilov* has echosounders made by Kelvin-Hughes and Nippon Electric; the *Poliarnik* has Nippon Electric echosounders; the *Sevastopol* has echosounders made by Hughes (type MS 26) and Nippon Electric.

So far as navigation equipment is concerned, we find similar use of Western equipment. For example, the *Okeanograf* built in East Germany in 1956 has a Thomson-type manual mechanical sounding instrument; the *Akademik Vavilov*,

[28] *Undersea Technology* (Washington, D.C.), May 1967, p. 67.

built in East Germany, has a Nippon Electric navigation sounder; the *Professor Rudovits* has a Lyth magnetic compass.

Therefore we may conclude that Soviet oceanographic research vessels are heavily dependent on Western sources, particularly for their instrumentation, even though this instrumentation has been indirectly acquired through East European socialist countries.

So far as underwater sea laboratories are concerned the Soviets are somewhat backward. An article in the U.S. Naval Institute *Proceedings* on the Russian sea lab[29] reviews the Russian *Sadeo-2* and concludes:

> Quite noticeable under various Soviet programs revealed to the West, is that living or working depths have been no more than 100 feet.... One can only speculate on the apparent Soviet backwardness in this field.

By contrast, the United States had vessels operating to a depth of 36,000 feet at that time (1969).

WESTERN ORIGINS OF SOVIET ICEBREAKERS

Before World War II the Soviet Union had only two or three icebreakers (built in Europe between World War I and the mid-1920s). Three modern icebreakers were transferred to the Soviet Union in the early 1940s under Lend Lease. Secretary of the Navy James Forrestal attempted to have these icebreakers returned in 1946, and in a memorandum to the State Department requesting institution of recovery proceedings Secretary Forrestal commented:

Of particular importance are the three CRs or icebreakers identified as:

U.S. Name	U.S.S.R Name
Northwind	*Severny Veter*
Southwind	*Admiral Makarof*
Westwind	*Severny Polus*

> These are high-powered icebreakers of the most modern design, sister ships (except in armament) of the two now in commission in the U.S. Coast Guard and of two others under construction and completing for the Navy. The importance of an adequate number of high-capacity icebreakers in supporting any operations in the frigid zones cannot be overemphasized. Three-sevenths of the total war production of this type are held by the U.S.S.R.[30]

The Soviet Register of 1966 lists icebreakers with characteristics similar

---

[29] U.S. Naval Institute, *Proceedings*, July 1969, pp. 113-15.
[30] U.S. State Dept. Decimal File 861.24/5-646.

to these Lend Lease vessels. Soviet Register No. 38, for example, is the *Admiral Makarov* (U.S. *Southwind*); however, this icebreaker is listed as built in the Soviet Union in 1941 with an engine built in the Soviet Union in 1939.[31]

In the early 1950s the Soviets contracted with the Wärtsilä Kon. Sandvikens shipyards in Finland for a series of 3000- and 9000-ton icebreakers with diesel-electric engines manufactured by Wärtsilä Kon. Crichton-Vulcan at Abo in Finland. These icebreakers are listed in Table 21-6.

Table 21-6   ICEBREAKERS BUILT IN FINLAND
                  ON SOVIET ACCOUNT FROM 1955 TO 1959

Name	Year built	Gross registered tons
Kapitan Belusov	1955	3710
Kapitan Voronin	1955	3419
Kapitan Melekhov	1956	3377
Murtaya	1958	2720
Moskva	1959	9165

Sources: *Lloyd's Register of Shipping,* 1965; *Registr Soyuza SSR, Registrovaya kniga sudov soyuza SSR 1964-1965* (Moscow, 1966); A. C. Hardy, *Merchant Ships: World Built* (Southampton: Adlard Coles, 1960).

Then in 1960 the Soviets produced the *Lenin,* an atomic icebreaker that was followed by a series of ten icebreakers adopted from earlier Finnish designs. The *Lenin* was launched in December 1957 as the world's first atomic icebreaker. Its reactors were reported as three and one-half times larger than the first Soviet reactor, which generated 5000 kw in June 1954. The main turbines were manufactured at the Kirov plant in Leningrad, the electric motors at the Electrosila plant, also in Leningrad; and the main generators were manufactured at KHEMZ in Kharkov, a plant originally designed and built by the General Electric Company. All together, some 500 Soviet plants contributed to the construction of the *Lenin.*[32]

In 1958 an equally large icebreaker, the *Moskva,* was supplied by Finland to the Soviet Union; this icebreaker has Siemens-Schuckert propulsion machinery and the same company made most of the electrical equipment.[33] When it was launched in January 1959 at Helsinki, the *Moskva* was the largest icebreaker built in Finland for the Soviets, with eight Sulzer engines generating 22,000 hp.

Between 1961 and 1967, the Soviets launched a series of ten standard ice-breakers named *Ledokol-1* to *Ledokol-10.*[34] This series has diesel-electric motors

[31] *Jane's Fighting Ships,* 1969-1970, lists the "Wind" class as returned to the United States in 1951.
[32] U.S. Naval Institute, *Proceedings,* November 1959, p. 142.
[33] American Society of Naval Engineers, *Journal* (Washington, D.C.), May 1959, p. 337.
[34] These are listed in the Soviet Register under different names; for example *Ledokol-1* is the *Vasily Pronchishchev.*

and is remarkably similar in dimensions to the series of icebreakers built for the Soviet Union in Finland in the 1950s.

Table 21-7   COMPARISON OF SOVIET "LEDOKOL" CLASS AND
EARLIER ICEBREAKERS SUPPLIED FROM FINLAND

Characteristic	Soviet "Ledokol" class	Finnish "Karhu" class
Overall length, feet	222.1	224.0
Breadth, feet	59.25	55.7
Depth, feet	27.23	28.10
Draught, feet	19.1	19.0
Propulsion	Diesel-electric	Diesel-electric (7500 shp)
Displacement, tons	—	3,370

Source: Lloyd's Register of Shipping, 1965; Registr Soyuza SSR, Registrovaya kniga sudov soyuza SSR 1964-1965 (Moscow, 1966); A. C. Hardy, Merchant Ships, World Built (Southampton: Adlard Coles, 1960).

It is a reasonable assumption that the Soviet series of standard icebreakers is based on the earlier Finnish designs. (See Table 21-7.)

Thus in icebreakers, a class of ship where the Soviets have requirements considerably greater than any country except perhaps Canada, apart from the single atomic icebreaker *Lenin* there is a dependence on designs originating in Finnish shipyards or on icebreakers built in Finland and the United States.

Construction of the Soviet merchant fleet constitutes a sector for which precise and accurate information is available—more so than for any other sector. The problem has been to distill the information into a succinct and meaningful pattern.

In broad terms, up to July 1967 65.6 percent of the Soviet merchant fleet was built completely (hulls plus engines) outside the Soviet Union. In terms of propulsion units, the most common engine is the marine diesel—and of these, just under 80 percent were built outside the U.S.S.R., but even those built in Soviet plants were derived from foreign designs, particularly Burmeister & Wain of Denmark and Skoda of Czechoslovakia.

Marine tonnage built inside the U.S.S.R. is of standard types, often based on Western prototypes, as in the cases of icebreakers, the "Kostroma" class tanker, and the "Pioner" class fishing trawler. In other cases, e.g., in oceano-graphic vessels, equipment is largely of Western origin and construction. Apart from the *Lenin* atomic icebreaker there is no vessel in the Soviet merchant marine that represents indigenous Soviet innovation.

Table 21-8A   ORIGINS OF MAIN ENGINES IN SOVIET MERCHANT SHIPS ADDED TO FLEET BEFORE 1930

	1929	1928	1927	1926	1925	1924	1923	1922	1921	1920	PRE-1920	Total
Germany	1	3	4	—	4	3	4	2	6	4	6	37
United States	—	—	—	—	—	—	—	—	1	1	25	27
Holland	—	—	—	1	—	—	1	1	3	—	7	13
Denmark	—	—	—	1	—	—	—	—	—	—	—	1
U.S.S.R.	1	4	1	—	—	—	—	—	—	—	3	9
Finland	—	—	—	—	—	—	—	—	—	—	2	2
United Kingdom	1	—	—	1	—	—	1	—	—	2	17	22
Sweden	1	—	1	1	—	—	—	—	—	—	1	4
Japan	—	—	—	—	—	—	—	—	—	—	5	5
France	—	—	1	—	—	—	—	—	—	—	—	1
Others	—	—	—	—	—	—	—	—	1	1	5	7
Totals	4	7	7	4	4	3	6	3	11	8	71	128

Source: Calculated from Registr Soyuza SSR, *Registrovaya kniga morskikh sudov soyuza SSR 1964-1965* (Moscow, 1966).

Table 21-8B

ORIGINS OF MAIN ENGINES IN SOVIET
MERCHANT SHIPS ADDED TO FLEET BETWEEN 1930 AND 1940

	1930	1931	1932	1933	1934	1935	1936	1937	1938	1939	1940	Total
United Kingdom	—	—	1	—	1	—	—	—	1	1	—	7
Germany	7	4	2	—	—	3	3	4	3	17	2	44
Norway	—	4	—	—	1	—	1	—	1	—	—	1
U.S.S.R.	3	1	6	5	1	3	2	3	2	—	—	29
Denmark	—	—	1	1	—	—	—	2	—	—	—	7
Holland	—	—	—	—	—	—	—	—	—	—	—	1
Finland	—	—	1	1	—	1	1	1	2	—	—	4
Japan	—	—	—	—	—	—	—	—	—	—	—	2
Sweden	—	—	—	—	—	—	—	—	—	—	—	1
United States	—	—	—	—	—	—	—	—	—	1	—	1
TOTALS	10	10	10	7	2	7	10	10	9	20	2	97

Source: Calculated from Registr Soyuza SSR, *Registrovaya kniga morskikh sudov soyuza SSR 1964-1965* (Moscow, 1966).

Table 21-8C   ORIGINS OF MAIN ENGINES IN SOVIET
MERCHANT SHIPS ADDED TO FLEET BETWEEN
1941 AND 1945

	1941	1942	1943	1944	1945	Total
United States	1	13	48	14	2	78
Germany	5	3	14	7	—	29
Norway	2	3	2	—	—	7
Sweden	—	—	1	—	—	1
United Kingdom	—	1	—	—	1	2
Finland	1	—	—	1	6	8
Hungary	—	1	—	—	—	1
Denmark	—	—	—	1	—	1
Holland	—	—	—	1	—	1
Others	—	—	—	1	—	1
Totals	9	21	65	25	9	129

Source: Calculated from Registr Soyuza SSR, *Registrovaya kniga morskikh sudov soyuza SSR 1964-1965* (Moscow, 1966).

Table 21-8D   CONSTRUCTION OF THE SOVIET TANKER FLEET
FROM 1951 TO 1967

	Hull and engine built in U.S.S.R.	Hull and/or engine built outside U.S.S.R.	Total added to tanker fleet	Percentage built outside U.S.S.R.
1951	8,229	1,113	9,342	11.9
1952	8,229	14,618	22,847	65.0
1953	24,687	16,570	41,257	40.1
1954	77,798	4,468	82,266	5.4
1955	65,077	20,721	85,798	24.1
1956	60,337	46,820	107,157	43.7
1957	59,532	54,109	113,641	47.6
1958	18,556	35,502	54,058	65.7
1959	90,066	24,663	114,729	21.5
1960	93,707	105,827	199,534	53.0
1961	31,074	56,397	87,471	64.5
1962	42,510	178,879	221,389	80.8
1963	87,693	179,055	266,748	67.1
1964	164,205	328,265	492,470	66.6
1965	132,872	242,201	375,073	64.6
1966	234,235	145,857	380,092	38.4
1967	—	41,833	41,833	100.0
Totals	1,198,807	1,496,898	2,695,705	55.6 percent average

Source: Calculated from Registr Soyuza SSR, *Registrovaya kniga morskikh sudov soyuza SSR 1964-1965 (Moscow, 1966).*

Table 21-8E   FOREIGN CONSTRUCTION OF MARINE
DIESEL ENGINES FOR THE SOVIET TANKER FLEET,
1951-JULY 1967

	Total installed in Soviet tankers	Foreign	Percentage foreign-built
1951	2	1	50
1952	7	6	86
1953	16	13	81
1954	14	4	28
1955	17	8	47
1956	25	14	56
1957	33	19	58
1958	17	9	53
1959	16	4	25
1960	15	3	20
1961	11	6	54
1962	21	18	86
1963	16	11	68
1964	22	19	86
1965	21	18	86
1966	22	12	55
1967	7	4	57
Totals	281	169	60

Source: Calculated from Registr Soyuza SSR, *Registrovaya kniga morskikh sudov soyuza SSR 1964-1965* (Moscow, 1966).

Table 21-8F   DESIGN ORIGINS OF MARINE DIESELS USED IN THE SOVIET TANKER FLEET, 1951- JULY 1967

Model	Specification	Total	1951	1952	1953	1954	1955	1956	1957	1958	1959	1960	1961	1962	1963	1964	1965	1966	1967
Manufactured in U.S.S.R.																			
Russki Diesel	8 x 300/500	53	—	1	—	1	2	6	9	8	4	6	4	3	4	3	1	1	1
	8 x 430/610	47	1	1	3	9	7	4	5	0	8	6	1	—	1	—	2	2	—
Bryansk	6 x 250/340	5	—	—	—	—	—	1	—	—	—	—	—	—	—	—	2	2	—
	5 x 500/1100	8	—	—	—	—	—	—	—	—	—	—	—	—	—	—	—	5	2
Total Manufactured in U.S.S.R.		113	1	1	3	10	9	11	14	8	12	12	5	3	5	3	3	10	3
Manufactured outside U.S.S.R.																			
Polar (Nydqvist & Holm)	6 x 300/500	2	1	1	—	—	—	—	—	—	—	—	—	—	—	—	—	—	—
Polar	6 x 345/580	2	1	1	—	—	—	—	—	—	—	—	—	—	—	—	—	—	—
	8 x 500/700	1	—	—	—	—	—	1	—	—	—	—	—	—	—	—	—	—	—
Skoda	8 x 430/610	25	—	—	1	—	3	5	6	3	—	—	4	—	3	5	2	2	1
Burmeister & Wain	5 x 500/1100	33	—	1	—	—	—	—	—	—	4	2	—	8	4	—	8	7	—
	6 x 740/1600	1	—	1	—	—	—	—	—	—	—	—	—	—	—	—	—	—	—
	8 x 740/1600 (Yugoslav license)	15	—	—	—	—	—	—	—	—	—	—	—	—	—	7	8	—	—
Deutz (?) E. Gern.	6 x 240/360	2	—	—	—	—	—	—	—	—	—	—	—	—	—	—	—	1	1
	8 x 240/360	35	—	—	8	—	3	8	13	3	—	—	—	—	—	—	—	—	—
Sulzer (Span. lic)	5 x 480/700	4	—	—	—	—	—	—	—	—	—	—	1	3	—	—	—	—	—
Sulzer (Jap. lic)	9 x 900/1550	18	—	—	—	—	—	—	—	—	—	—	—	5	4	7	2	—	—
	6 x 480/700	2	—	—	—	—	—	—	—	—	—	—	—	—	—	—	2	—	—
	6 x 760/1550	8	—	—	—	—	—	—	—	—	—	—	—	2	2	—	—	—	2
Atlas	6 x 340/570	12	—	3	3	4	2	—	—	—	—	—	—	—	—	—	—	—	—
Fiat (Italy)	9 x 900/1600	6	—	—	—	—	—	—	—	—	—	—	—	—	—	1	8	1	—
Stork (Holland)	8 x 750/1600	2	—	—	—	—	—	—	—	—	—	—	1	—	—	1	—	1	—
	6 x 360/480	1	—	—	—	—	—	—	—	—	—	—	—	1	—	—	—	—	—
Total manufactured outside U.S.S.R.		169	1	6	13	4	8	14	19	9	4	3	6	18	11	19	18	12	4
Total marine diesels in tanker fleet at July 1967		281	2	7	16	14	17	25	33	17	16	15	11	21	16	22	21	22	7

Source: Calculated from Registr Soyuza SSR, *Registrovaya kniga morskikh sudov soyuza SSR 1964-1965* (Moscow, 1966).

Table 21-8G   CONSTRUCTION OF SMALL TANKERS (1772 GRT AND LESS), 1951-67

	1951	1952	1953	1954	1955	1956	1957	1958	1959	1960	1961	1962	1963	1964	1965	1966	1967
U.S.S.R. hull and Czechoslovakia engines 1,772 tons	—	—	—	—	—	—	—	—	—	—	—	—	—	3	2	4	—
U.S.S.R. 756-802 tons	—	—	—	—	—	—	—	—	—	5	—	—	—	—	2	2	—
Finland 1,081 tons	—	—	1	—	—	—	6	—	4	—	—	—	1	—	—	—	—
Sweden 1,145 tons	1	2	1	—	—	—	—	—	—	—	—	—	—	—	—	—	—
Finland hull Sweden engine 1,117 tons	—	3	3	4	3	—	—	—	—	—	—	—	—	—	—	—	—
G.D.R. hull and engines 260-305 tons	—	—	8	—	3	7	—	3	—	—	—	—	—	—	—	—	—
Bulgaria hull G.D.R. engine	—	—	—	—	—	—	12	—	2	—	—	—	—	—	—	2	1
Poland hull Spain engine 1,333 tons	—	—	—	—	—	—	—	—	—	—	—	1	3	—	—	—	—
Total	1	5	13	4	6	7	18	3	6	5	1	3	1	3	4	8	1
Foreign-built	1	5	13	4	6	7	12	3	—	5	1	3	0	0	0	2	1
Percentage	100	100	100	100	100	100	66	100	—	100	100	100	0	0	0	25	100

Source: Calculated from Registr Soyuza SSR, Registrovaya kniga morskikh sudov soyuza SSR 1964-1965 (Moscow, 1966).

Table 21-8H

CONSTRUCTION OF MEDIUM CLASS TANKERS
(3300-3820 GRT), 1954-67

GRT		1954	1955	1956	1957	1958	1959	1960	1961	1962	1963	1964	1965	1966	1967	TOTAL
3737	Soviet-built 8 x 300/500	1	2	3	1	—	—	—	—	—	—	—	—	—	—	7
3821	Soviet-built 8 x 300/500	—	—	—	3	4	1	—	—	—	—	—	—	—	—	8
	Bulgarian hull USSR engine 8 x 300/500	—	—	—	—	—	3	3	2	3	4	4	1	1	1	22
	Soviet hull Danish engine	—	—	—	—	—	1	—	—	—	—	—	—	—	—	1
3300	Finnish hull Danish engine	—	—	—	—	3	3	2	3	6	4	4	3	—	—	28
3360	Finnish hull Finnish engine	—	—	—	—	—	—	—	—	—	—	1	1	—	1	3
3259	Finnish hull Swedish engine	—	—	1	—	—	—	—	—	1	—	—	1	—	—	3
3470-90	Japanese hull Japanese engine	—	—	—	—	—	—	—	—	—	—	—	2	—	—	2
3120	Swedish hull Danish engine	—	—	—	—	—	—	—	1	1	—	—	—	—	—	2
	Total	1	2	4	4	7	8	5	6	11	8	9	8	1	2	76
	Foreign-built hulls & engines	—	—	1	—	3	3	2	4	8	4	5	7	—	1	38(50%)

Source: Calculated from Registr Soyuza SSR, *Registrovaya kniga morskikh sudov soyuza SSR 1964-1965* (Moscow, 1966).

Table 21-8I   CONSTRUCTION OF LARGE TANKERS
(13,000 TONS AND OVER), 1959-67

	1959	1960	1961	1962	1963	1964	1965	1966	1967
U.S.S.R. hulls, steam turbines 21,255 GRT	1	2	1	2	1	—	—	—	—
U.S.S.R. hulls, steam turbines 32484	—	—	—	—	2	5	4	7	—
Italy (hull & engine) 20,659 GRT	—	1	—	—	—	—	—	—	—
31,295 GRT	—	—	—	—	1	3	1	—	—
Holland (hull & engine) 16,349 GRT	—	1	—	—	—	—	—	1	2
Poland (hull & engine) 13,363	—	—	—	2	2	—	—	—	—
Yugoslavia 15,255	—	—	—	—	—	—	8	7	—
Japan (hull & engine) 22-5,000	—	2	—	5	4	7	2	—	—
Poland hull; GDR engine 13,218	—	—	—	—	—	—	1	—	—
Yugoslavia hull; Sweden engine 17,861 GRT	—	—	1	—	—	—	—	—	—
Total	1	6	3	9	10	15	16	15	2
Foreign-built	0	4	2	7	7	10	12	8	2
Percentage	0	66	66	77	70	66	80	53	100

Total (1964-1965): 77 / 52 / 67.5

Source: Calculated from Registr Soyuza SSR, *Registrovaya Kniga morskikh sudov soyuza SSR 1964-1965* (Moscow, 1966).

CHAPTER TWENTY-TWO

Western Assistance to the
Machine Tool Industry

The Soviet Union is a major volume producer of machine tools. In 1964 the industry's production was about three-quarters, by value, of U.S. production of machine tools, slightly greater than the production of West Germany and equivalent to the combined machine tool output of Great Britain, Japan, and France.[1]

Historically, the increase of machine tool output has been significant. In 1928 the Soviet Union produced only 2000 metal cutting tools, and this output increased to 38,400 in 1945, 156,000 in 1960, and about 200,000 in 1967.[2] However, output does not tell the whole story; this flood of machine tools is by and large of simple construction with numerous quality defects. One observer has described the Soviet machine tool industry as follows:

> ... the bulk of current models turned out by the Soviet industry approach in make-up, speeds, rate of feed, etc., the U.S. models made during the late 1930s and during World War II. Since then the United States has made considerable advance in machine tool technology.[3]

Problems in machine tool quality are described in several sources. J. A. Gwyer in particular has listed excerpts from Soviet literature on problems of quality and reliability in the industry.[4] Lack of high-quality raw materials, reliability services, accurate instrumentation, trained Soviet technicians, and similar factors have led to major problems in quality control.

Another commentator, P. H. Ponta, a member of the U.S. Machine Tool Delegation to the Soviet Union in 1965, reported that although in general Russian

---

[1] Data in *American Machinist* (New York), January 18, 1965, p. 133.
[2] *Strana Sovetov za 50 let; Sbornik statisticheskikh materialov* (Moscow, 1967), p. 83.
[3] J. A. Gwyer, "Soviet Machine Tools," *Ordnance*, (Washington, D.C.), November-December 1958, p. 419.
[4] J. A. Gwyer, "Soviet Quality and Reliability Programs at the Crossroads," *R.S.Q.C. Conference Transactions 1968*, March 26, 1968. Also see Appendixes I, II, and III to U.S. Senate, Committee on the Judiciary, *Export of Strategic Materials to the U.S.S.R. and Other Soviet Bloc Countries*, Hearing Before the Subcommittee to Investigate the Administration of the Internal Security Act and Other Internal Security Laws, 87th Congress, 1st session, Part I, October 23, 1961 (Washington, 1961).

303

technical ability was "impressive," he found poor quality of workmanship, very bad material handling, and an extreme neglect of cleanliness and order. He suggested that the answer to the question of how the large output of Soviet machine tools can be absorbed lay in the fact that Soviet tools had a shorter average life than those made elsewhere, and this information, coupled with what is known about the scarcity of spare parts, implies earlier replacement than would be normal in the West. An article in *Stanki i instrument* (Moscow) in 1965 also points out considerable problems involved in manufacturing machine tools and suggests ways in which these problems can be overcome.[5]

Soviet imports today are not quantitatively as significant as domestic production, although they have been in the past.[6] Lend Lease was a major supplier, providing over $465 million worth of machine tools in addition to about the same amount of related engines, industrial equipment, electrical equipment, and machinery not normally included under the category of machine tools.[7] The major machine tool-related categories sent to the U.S.S.R. under Lend Lease included:

Machine tools, rolling mills, drawing machines	$404,697,000
Welding machinery, testing and measuring machinery, metal working machinery	15,199,000
Cemented carbide cutting tools, metal cutting tools	45,042,000

In 1965 the U.S.S.R. imported 6503 machine tools. Of these, 2249 came from Czechoslovakia, where the largest heavy machine tool manufacturer is the former Skoda company (which has a technical-assistance agreement with Simmons Machine Tool, an old, established machine tool manufacturer of New York.[8] However, the relatively small quantity belies the value of these more recent imports. The average unit value of Soviet imports of machine tools is twice that of exports.[9] By importing prototypes of advanced machines from the West the Soviets can, with little effort, keep abreast of world developments in this field. Thus, although the Soviets may lag by a few years at any one time, the effect over the long run is to keep Soviet machine tools more or less on an equivalent basis to current world technology.

---

[5] *American Machinist*, July 19, 1965.

[6] "It is a fact that some 300,000 of the very finest high-output machine tools were purchased abroad from 1929 to 1940, tools manufactured by the best companies all over the world." G. Anisimov, "The Motive Forces of Technological Progress in the U.S.S.R. at Its Present Stage of Development," *Problems of Economics*, (New York), III, 1 (May 1960), 18.

[7] U.S. Dept. of State, *Report on War Aid Furnished by the United States to the U.S.S.R.* (Washington: Office of Foreign Liquidation, 1945).

[8] See p. 84 below.

[9] *Vneshniaia torgovlia SSSR za 1965 god* (Moscow, 1966).

SOVIET ACQUISITIONS IN GERMANY

The prize machine-building plant removed by the Soviets from Germany was in the British Zone—the Dusseldorf plant of Schiess-Defries. It was the most important German manufacturer of heavy machine tools; the firm was noted for "crankshaft turning equipment, tool and cutter grinders, horizontal borers, gear cutters, gun boring equipment, universal milling machines, plane milling machines, heavy lathes, slotting machines, forging machines, equipment for railway shops, and special machine tools of the largest size."[10]

Two important tool manufacturers in the U.S. Zone were also removed to the U.S.S.R.—Hahn & Tessky and the Esslingen firm of Bohner & Koehle, manufacturers of aircraft presses.[11]

Toward the end of World War II, the greater part of German industry was moved eastward to avoid its being bombed. Accordingly, when the war ended there was a concentration of machine tool and equipment manufacturers in the provinces of Saxony, Thuringia, Mecklenburg, and Brandenburg, all later to be occupied by the Soviet forces. The greater number of the 636 machine tool companies in the area had equipment removed to the Soviet Union.[12] Unlike other industrial sectors, removals seem to have been complete: probably over three-quarters of the companies were 100 percent stripped of their equipment and the remainder were 80 or 90 percent stripped.

Fortunately (for the purposes of this study), a number of the larger machine tool manufacturing units, particularly those in Leipzig, were visited by CIOS (Combined Intelligence Objectives Subcommittee) teams just before the Soviet occupation; consequently, we have an accurate record of their condition and equipment capability at the time of the Soviet occupation.

One of the largest machine tool plants on the continent, Pittler Werkzeug-maschinenfabrik A.G. in Leipzig, was completely removed to the Soviet Union. This plant was earlier visited by both CIOS and U.S. Strategic Bombing Survey teams. The manufacturing program as of May 1945 consisted primarily in the production of turret lathes and automatic lathes, and the CIOS team reported

---

[10] U.S. Foreign Economic Administration, *U.S. Technical Industrial Disarmament Committee on the German Machine Tool Industry* (T.I.D.C. Project no. 11; Washington, 1945), p. 43. One observer suggested an interesting reason for the removal of this important plant from the British Zone to the Soviet Union: "This company *was* Germany's greatest producer of large type machine tools such as planers, lathes, and boring mills. They were [i.e., the company's plant was] completely dismantled, including machine tools and buildings, by the Russians. I learned from an authoritative source that this action was induced and approved by the British representative then in charge, who was the principal competitor of the Scheiss Company." F. H. Higgins Collection, Item I, Memorandum to Director, Industry Division, p. 5 (Hoover Institution Special Collections, Stanford University).

[11] Germany, Office of Military Government (U.S.Zone), Economics Division, *A Year of Potsdam: The German Economy Since the Surrender* (n.p.: OMGUS, 1946).

[12] G. E. Harmssen, *Am Abend der Demontage; Sechs Jahre Reparationspolitik* (Bremen: F. Trüjen, 1951), pp. 95-102.

that the Pittler plant was "very modern" and "only slightly damaged by bomb-ing"; the treating department was reported to be excellent and the stockrooms well filled with finished parts. The manufacturing methods appeared to be efficient, and the smaller turret lathes built in large quantities were assembled on a conveyer system.[13] Unfortunately the survey teams gave no estimate as to productive capacity, but they did indicate that, with materials on hand, 800 machines could be completed within a six-month period, which suggests a minimum capacity of 1600 machines per year.

Another company visited by a CIOS team was Kirschner A.G.– later completely removed to the Soviet Union. Kirschner was "one of the largest manufacturers of woodworking machinery on the continent."[14] The company produced a comprehensive range of woodworking equipment, including horizontal log-band mills and high-speed vertical saw frames for saw mills, as well as equipment for wood pattern shops such as band saws and a special coal-cutting machine.

Another machine tool plant removed completely to the Soviet Union was that of Werkzeugmaschinenfabrik Arno Krebs of Leipzig. This company man-ufactured plane and universal knee and milling machines in the following ranges: working surface of table from 8-1/2 by 26 inches up to 12 by 47-1/4 inches, longitudinal travel from 13 to 36 inches, cross travel from 4-3/4 to 13-1/2 inches, vertical travel from 11-1/2 to 19-1/2 inches. In addition, two types of hand-lever milling machines were manufactured.

The Köllmann-Werkzeugfabrik GmbH of Leipzig was 75 percent removed to the Soviet Union. This was not strictly a machine tool plant, but specialized in the manufacture of all types and sizes of gears up to 36 inches in diameter. It was a modern plant in excellent condition, with a machine shop containing 25 Gleason bevel gear generators, 27 gear grinders, and batteries of gear shapers, hobbing machines, and milling and grinding machines, together with a large number of other machines for manufacturing gears. There was also an excellent heat-treatment department with electric furnaces. The CIOS team commented: "The excellence of this particular plant has to be seen to be appreciated."[15]

The Köllmann-Werke A.G., Zahnräder- und Getriebebau of Leipzig was 75 percent removed to the Soviet Union. This company was a manufacturer of gears, with a modern plant built in 1935. In commenting on it the CIOS team reported: "The plant is in excellent condition, has a large number of Maag gear grinders, as well as other first-class equipment to manufacture precision-type aircraft gears."[16]

---

[13] See CIOS Report no. XXVIII-10; Andress. *et al., Machine Tool Targets,* Leipzig, pp.5-6, for lists of standard turret lathes, high-speed turret lathes, single-spindle automatic screw machines, and single-spindle and multispindle automatic machines manufactured by Pittler in 1945.

[14] *Ibid.*

[15] *Ibid.*

[16] *Ibid.,* p. 13.

Other companies moved included August Meiselbach, which was 95 percent removed to the Soviet Union; Meiselbach was a manufacturer of stocks and dies for use in public utilities.

Kleim und Ungerer of Leipzig, which manufactured sheet feeders for the printing trade, had 83 percent of its equipment removed to the Soviet Union. The plant contained a single-spindle automatic feeder, a drilling machine, and a stock of small turned parts. During the war it produced test machines for Junkers aeromotors and various parts in subassemblies for elevating antiaircraft guns.

A woodworking machine tool company completely removed to the U.S.S.R. was Deutsche Holzbearbeitungsmaschinenfabrik Jacob & Eichorn, a small firm manufacturing woodworking machines such as circular saws, band saws, planing machines, and jointing machines.

Conrad Modrach of Gera, a manufacturer of commercial shears, croppers, presses, and bending machines, was completely removed to the U.S.S.R., as was G. Weissken, also of Gera, a manufacturer of tool and cutter grinders and small lathes.

An overall indicator of the magnitude of plant removals in the machine tool industry is contained in Table 22-1, which lists eight plants removed to the U.S.S.R. (and approximate extent of removals) together with their ranking by the Foreign Economic Administration in 1944. Only those classified as of outstanding importance are included.

Table 22-1   GERMAN MACHINE TOOL MANUFACTURERS OF
"OUTSTANDING IMPORTANCE"*
REMOVED TO THE SOVIET UNION IN 1945-46

Percentage removed	Name of manufacturer	Location	Main product
100	Hille-Werke A.G.	Dresden (Soviet Zone)	Relieving lathes, multispindle drilling machines, thread millers, jog borers, diamond and fine borers, honing machines, drilling machines, radial drills.
50	Magdeburger Werkzeugmaschinenfabrik A.G.	Magdeburg (Soviet Zone)	Auto multicut lathes, turret lathes, gun-boring equipment, machinery for aircraft and propeller construction (Junkers plant)
100	Werkzeugmaschinenfabrik Hermann Pfauter	Chemnitz (Soviet Zone)	Tool and cutter grinders, gear cutters, gear hobbers, thread hobbers, long-cut milling machines, thread milling machines
Not known	Billeter & Kluntz	Aschersleben (Soviet Zone)	Surface grinders, ball and face grinders, planers, openside planers

Table 22-1 (cont.)

Percentage removed	Name of manufacturer	Location	Main product
Not known	Franz Braun A.G.	Zerbst (Anhalt) (Soviet Zone)	Lathes, frontal lathes, planing machines, drill presses, thermoplastic molding presses
100	Pittler Werkzeug-maschinenfabrik A.G.	Leipzig (Soviet Zone)	Single-spindle bar autos, multispindle bar autos, multispindle auto machines, turret lathes, die heads, hydraulic pumps, automatic screw machines
100	E. Reinecker A.G.	Chemnitz (Soviet Zone)	Relieving lathes, crankshaft, grinding machines, universal grinders, internal grinders, spline grinders, gear grinders, thread grinders, tool and cutter grinders, surface grinders, ball and face grinders, gear cutters, thread millers, tooth round-ing machines, jog borers, plant milling machines, tap and twist drill making, small tools, measuring instrument horizontal milling machines
100	Schiess-Defries	Düsseldorf (British Zone)	See text

Source: U. S. Foreign Economic Administration, U. S. Technical Industrial Disarmament Committee on the German Machine Tool Industry, Study of Interagency Committee on the Treatment of the German Machine Tool Industry from the Standpoint of International Security (Washington, 1945), TIDC Project no. 11.

· These are firms identified by the FEA as "of outstanding importance either by volume of output or by monopoly of production of a significant item."

IMPORTS AND EXPORTS OF MACHINE TOOLS FROM 1946 TO 1966

An examination of imports and exports of metal-cutting tools (specifically forges, presses, and the subgroup of mechanical and hydraulic presses) is sugges-tive of limited Soviet machine tool capabilities.

Firstly, imports of the major category of metal-cutting tools (Soviet foreign trade classification Group 100) have significantly increased in absolute terms since 1946. The year 1946 reflects heavy "pipeline" Lend Lease imports and is therefore abnormal; imports valued at less than 20 million rubles a year in the late 1940s, when the Soviets were absorbing Lend Lease and German reparations machine tools, are replaced by annual imports of 70–80 million rubles in the early 1960s. In specialized fields such as forges and presses we find proportionately greater import.

On the other hand, exports over the long run show a fairly consistent trend and average less than half of Soviet imports. In forges and presses we find that exports are minute (between one-sixth and one-eighth of imports), with none at all in the category of hydraulic presses. These figures reflect the overall composition of Soviet machine tool exports (simple lathes and shapers to under-developed countries—Cuba, India, China, Mongolia, and the newer African nations) and imports (sophisticated equipment for prototype use and specialized production machinery from advanced countries—U.K., West Germany, Japan, and U.S.A.). (See Table 22-2.) The exception to this rule is trade with East Germany and Czechoslovakia, which comprises large imports and exports.

Table 22-2

SOVIET IMPORTS AND EXPORTS OF
MACHINE TOOLS FROM 1946 TO 1966
(in million rubles)

Year	Metal cutting tools Stanki metallorezhushchie (Group 100)		Forge and press equipment Kuznechno-pressovoe oborudovanie (Groups 101-103)		Mechanical and hydraulic presses (Subgroups 10103-10123)	
	Imports	Exports	Imports	Exports	Imports	Exports
1946	40.3	0.4	4.9	0	2.3	—
1947	16.3	1.3	3.9	—	1.8	—
1948	5.8	3.1	2.4	0.3	1.5	—
1949	5.5	10.1	1.6	0.6	0.5	—
1950	13.7	19.2	2.0	0.8	0.8	—
1951	12.8	17.5	4.6	2.0	2.8	—
1952	13.5	22.7	4.3	2.9	2.7	—
1953	27.3	27.9	13.6	3.9	5.4	—
1954	25.4	13.8	14.8	2.3	7.4	—
1955	21.9	6.5	21.0	1.5	13.7	—
1956	25.8	7.8	24.3	1.1	17.0	—
1957	28.9	7.0	25.9	1.6	16.7	—
1958	38.9	13.9	31.4	2.3	21.3	—
1959	41.5	16.7	32.4	2.6	21.5	—
1960	56.7	12.9	34.4	4.7	19.2	—
1961	62.5	17.2	37.5	5.0	22.1	—
1962	73.1	25.1	42.1	5.7	24.3	—
1963	78.5	25.7	43.0	5.3	24.1	—
1964	86.7	27.6	49.0	3.3	20.6	—
1965	83.1	39.5	36.2	4.7	18.3	—
1966	76.2	57.2	32.2	7.4	13.7	—

Source: Vneshniaia torgovlia SSSR: Statisticheskii sbornik, 1918-1966 (Moscow, 1967), pp. 76-79 (exports), 98-101 (imports).

DUPLICATION OF WESTERN MACHINE TOOLS

Prewar practice continued after the war—much of Soviet machine tool design was derived from Western origins. In 1953 it was reported by an Austrian engineer who had returned from the U.S.S.R. after working in the Sverdlovsk machine tool plant (where he had access to the plant records) that in 1953 the Soviet Union was still operating "a good deal" with Lend Lease tools.[17] It was noted that the latest model U.S. and European machine tools were acquired despite export control laws, and these were sent to "copying offices" and there stripped, analyzed, and tested, and "exact duplicates [were] made."[18] About 30 to 35 such copying offices existed in 1953 at various machine tool plants, each specializing in a particular type of foreign machine tool. For example, all foreign lathe models went to Plant No. 115 at Novosibirsk, all foreign shaper models went to Plant No. 64 at Gorki, and all foreign hydraulic press models went to Plant No. 101 at Kurgan. In February 1953, Plant 101 was working on a 150-ton hydraulic press originally made by Merklinger in Germany.[19]

Thus in 1957 it was reported that the Leningrad large jig borer had been copied from the Hydroptic SIP (optical coordinate jig borer) and an American trade journal commented: "The machine . . . so closely resembles its West European counterpart that even the Sverdlov plant manager calls it the Leningrad SIP."[20] The Sverdlov Plant im. Lenini also specialized in Keller-type copying machines.[21]

Consideration of the foreign origin factor in machine tool production brings the Soviet achievement of gigantic runs of machine tools into focus. This point can be illustrated by a consecutive reading of statements by three independent observers concerning one Soviet machine tool plant—Ordzhonikidze in Moscow. Each statement is by itself an accurate but incomplete description of the plant; taken together, however, the statements point to a significant deduction.

The first description of the plant is by a highly qualified U.S. observer utilizing Soviet literature:

> Machine-Tool Manufacturing Plant im. S. Ordzhonikidze (Stankostroitel'nyy zavod im. Ordzhonikidze)—hence referred to as the Moscow Plant im. S. Ordzhonikidze. The plant, one of the largest in the U.S.S.R., specialized in the production of: automatic transfer lines, unit machine tools, radial drills, boring machines, assortment of automatic and semiautomatic lathes. The equipment installed in this plant is not modern by any means. As of 1 January 1956, 23.7 percent of metal-cutting machine tools was less than ten years old, 71.3 percent ten to twenty years old, and 8.1 percent more than twenty years old. Only 1.5 percent of all installed metal-cutting machine tools were represented by automatic and semiautomatic machines. Presses constituted 1.1 percent of all machine tools. During the 1951-55 period, the plant built 18 automatic transfer machines, in 1957 seven machines, and planned for 1958 an output of 16 machines.[22]

---

[17] *Iron Age* (Middletown, N.Y.), December 17, 1953.
[18] *Ibid.*
[19] *Ibid.*
[20] *American Machinist*, February 25, 1957, p. 179.
[21] *Ibid.*, p. 181.
[22] J. Gwyer, private communication to author.

The second description is recorded by an American visitor to the plant:

Ordzhonikidze specializes in making boring equipment. Most of the manufacturing equipment in the plant was foreign-made and has not been modernized, although in some areas the operations looked quite good. Here we saw many American machine tools such as Gardner grinders, different types of Cincinnati machines, King vertical lathes, Gray planers, and many other familiar types. Some were of fairly new vintage. Although many machines in this plant appeared to be old they were still in very good condition, all were running.[23]

The third report, also by an on-the-spot observer, confirms the predominance of foreign equipment:

In the plant itself, most of the items are imported—some are prewar and others wartime acquisitions. Very few of the machines we saw in this plant seemed to be postwar. Among those noted were two Butler planers and a whole battery of medium-sized Billeter & Klonz machines. There was a Kendall & Gent miller; a small Cincinnati (British-built); a Beliot-Gray planer-miller (this one one of the few postwar machines); a fairly elderly large Giddings & Lewis floorplate horizontal boring machine; Milwaukee millers; a Girards radial and a Wotan grinder.[24]

There is some reference to Russian-built machines: "In the turret lathe section we noticed quite a few copies of Warner & Swazey machines, but we did not see any Russian-built copying lathes."[25]

The first statement establishes the age of the equipment; the second and third statements identify its Western origins and make it clear that in this plant at least, production, including production of automatic transfer machines, is based on equipment imported from the West. *In other words, the machines that build the machines originated in the West.*

By their own admission, the Soviets imported 300,000 top-flight foreign machine tools between 1930 and 1940.[26] Add to this the large quantities received under the Nazi-Soviet pact, Lend Lease, German reparations removals from the occupied countries, and continuing imports since World War II, and it becomes apparent that the military and industrial machine-building industries of the Soviet Union could well be relying heavily on imported equipment. This supposition is supported by the nature of many of the machine tools imported—larger specialized automatic mass-production units.

[23] Nevin L. Bean, "Address Before the Detroit Chapter of the National Society of Professional Engineers," Detroit, February 22, 1956 (Dearborn: Ford Motor Co., News Dept.) pp. 8-9.
[24] *American Machinist*, November 19, 1956.
[25] *Ibid.* The Russian-built machines included also a horizontal boring machine and large- and medium-size planers.
[26] See p. 304 n. 6 above.

The substitution of numerically controlled machine tools for hand-controlled machine tools was indisputably the most important metal-machining innovation in the period 1945 to 1960. In the United States numerically controlled tools became commercially available in the early 1950s, and by the end of the decade there were probably several thousand in commercial use. Apart from substantially improving quality of product and operating control, numerically controlled tools allow substantial savings in both capital and labor.

Their introduction into the Soviet Union has been very slow, however: only two prototypes had been produced there by 1960, and at that time it was projected that only several hundred would be in use by 1965.[27] It is then more than possible that the numerically controlled units displayed at various exhibitions abroad are "one-off" items built for the purpose. For example, J. O. Ellison examined one exhibit model, a Model 1062 shaft-turning lathe that was automated and tracer-controlled, and published his conclusion in the trade journal *American Machinist*.[28] He described this model as a hybrid variation of a family of lathes based on the 1K62. It was the hybrid nature of the model that led Ellison to the conclusion that it was a compromise and therefore not "very salable in the United States"; Ellison added that "the most lasting impression I have of the demonstration aside from the technical points is that the Russians were very good showmen."[29]

BALL BEARING MANUFACTURE CAPABILITY

Ball bearings, of course, constitute a vital part of almost all machines and of numerous other products, including military weapons systems.

It was previously indicated that ball bearing plants in the U.S.S.R. had been equipped from the United States. One U.S. firm, the Bryant Chucking Grinder Company of Springfield, Virginia, was a prominent supplier in the 1930s and 1940s, while Italian and Swedish firms also have contributed a large proportion of the Soviet ball bearing production capacity.[30] Soviet dependence on the West for ball bearing technology came to a peak in the years 1959-61. The Soviets required a capability for mass production, rather than laboratory or batch production, of miniature ball bearings—80 percent of whose end uses are in weapons systems. The only company in the world that could supply the required machine—the Centalign B—on a commercial basis was the Bryant Chucking Grinder Company. The Soviet Union had no mass-production capabil-

---

[27] U.S. Congress, Joint Economic Committee, *Dimensions of Soviet Economic Power*, Hearings, 87th Congress, 2d session, December 10 and 11, 1962, p. 137.

[28] November 20, 1959, pp. 98-100: "Russia Exhibits Automated Lathe."

[29] *Ibid.*, p. 98.

[30] See Sutton, I: *Western Technology ... 1917 to 1945*.

ity whatever, and its miniature ball bearings were either imported or made in small lots on Italian and other imported equipment.

In 1960 there were 66 Centalign machines in the United States. Twenty-five of these machines were operated by the Miniature Precision Bearing Company, Inc., the largest manufacturer of precision ball bearings; 85 percent of Miniature Precision's output went to military applications. In 1960 the U.S.S.R. entered an order with Bryant Chucking for 45 similar machines. Bryant did not immediately accept the order but consulted the Department of Commerce; the department indicated willingness to grant a license and Bryant therefore accepted the order. The Commerce Department's argument for granting a license turned on the following points: (a) the process achieved by the Centalign is only a single process among several required for ball bearing production; (b) the machine can be bought elsewhere; and (c) the Russians can make ball bearings.[31] The Department of Defense, however, entered a strong objection to the export of the machines on the following grounds:

> In the specific case of the granting of the export license for high-frequency grinders manufactured by Bryant Chucking Grinder, after receiving the request for DOD's opinion from the Department of Commerce, it was determined that all of the machines of this type currently available in the United States were being utilized for the production of bearings utilized in strategic components for military end items. It was also determined from information that was available to us that the Soviets did not produce a machine of this type or one that would be comparable in enabling the production of miniature ball bearings of the tolerances and precision required. A further consideration was whether machines of comparable capacity and size can be made available from Western Europe. In this connection, our investigation revealed that none was in production that would meet the specifications that had been established by the Russians for these machines. In the light of these considerations it was our opinion that the license should not be granted.[32]

The Inter-Departmental Advisory Committee on Export Control, which includes members from the Commerce and State departments as well as the CIA, overruled the Department of Defense opinion and "a decision was made to approve the granting of the license."[33] The Department of Defense made further protest and demanded proof as to the capability of either the U.S.S.R. or Western Europe to produce such machines. No such proof was forthcoming.

The following summarizes the various objections of the Department of Defense, as then outlined by the official concerned:

---

[31] This section is based on U.S. Senate, Committee on the Judiciary, *Export of Ball Bearing Machines to Russia*, Hearings, 87th Congress, 1st session (Washington, 1961). There are three parts to these Hearings; they provide a fascinating story of one Soviet attempt to acquire strategic equipment. See also the Soviet "machine tools Case of 1945"; a microfilm of documents on this case has been deposited at the Hoover Institution.

[32] U.S. Senate, *op. cit.* n. 31, pp. 267-68.

[33] *Ibid.*

In resumé, the following actions were known to me regarding the transaction of this export license:

(a) I expressed dissatisfaction and suggested that the Department of Defense not concur in the initial request of the Department of Commerce.

(b) The official member of the Department of Defense in this connection concurred and, at a series of meetings of the Advisory Committee on Export Control, spoke against the proposal that an export license be granted.

(c) The Deputy Assistant Secretary of Defense, Supply and Logistics, after reviewing some of the circumstances, requested that I do whatever was possible to stop the shipment of these machines.

(d) A letter was transmitted from the Office of the Secretary of Defense to the Secretary of Commerce, approximately November 1, 1960, saying it [*sic*] spoke to the Department of Defense and requesting a further review.

(e) At two meetings where the matter was reviewed, the Department of Defense maintained nonconcurrence in the shipment of the equipment.

As of this writing I am still convinced that it would be a tragic mistake to ship this equipment.[34]

The reference to a "tragic mistake" refers of course to the known fact that miniature ball bearings are an essential prerequisite for missile production. Granting the license would give the U.S.S.R. a miniature ball bearing production capability equal to two-thirds that of the United States.

The relevance of the case for our study is twofold. First, it illustrates clearly a manner by which the Soviets have acquired a substantial productive capability, even for difficult technologies, very quickly. Second, as the case was uncovered only by accident (an official of the Miniature Precision Ball Bearing Company brought the matter to the attention of Congress), it implies that much "technical leakage" in the sensitive areas of atomic energy and weapons systems may well have gone undetected.

COMPUTING, MEASURING, AND PRECISION INSTRUMENTS

The Soviet Union has always had considerable technical difficulties producing computing, measuring, and precision instruments. Initial production of elementary adding machines in the early thirties was poor in quality and suffered from numerous deficiencies; in particular, early models had parts of nontempered steel and gear teeth were wearing out after just two weeks of operation.[35] The most common Soviet calculating machines today are direct copies of Western models; for example, the "Felix," the subject of the above complaints and the first machine produced in the U.S.S.R., was still in production in 1969

---

[34] *Ibid.*

[35] *Za industrializatsiiu* (Moscow), August 7, 1930.

and is by far the most common Soviet machine. It is a copy of the Brunsviga 1892 model, apparently without even the modifications introduced into Western models in 1927.[36] The full keyboard calculator of the 1930s—the KSM—is a copy of the Monroe. Punched-card machinery is Hollerith, although at one time a technical-assistance agreement was made with Powers. Campbell suggests, with justification, that the postwar Riazan machine works is the German Astra-werke which was transferred to the U.S.S.R. Other German plants, including the Archimedes and the cash register plant at Glasshütte, were also moved to the U.S.S.R.[37]

In the 1960s, a continuing widespread use of the abacus in the Soviet Union made the Soviets worry about their image abroad—it hardly seemed consistent with the age of cosmonauts and atomic icebreakers. It was this concern that led to an agreement in 1966 with Olivetti of Italy to establish two office equipment plants in the U.S.S.R. under a $60 million contract, one for the production of typewriters and one for the production of calculators and other office machinery.[38]

Several of the most important precision instrument manufacturers in Germany were moved to Russia at the end of World War II. The Zeiss works at Jena, manufacturers of optical and scientific instruments including micrometers, optical comparators, angle measuring equipment, and gear testers, was moved completely to Minino, near Moscow. There with three top German experts, Dr. Eitzenberger, Dr. Buschbeck, and Dr. Faulstich, the new plant developed detector and remote-control equipment, including radio-controlled recording gear and rocket guidance equipment.[39] The Askaniawerke A.G. at Berlin-Friedeman, a very important manufacturer of scientific equipment including optical measuring components such as lenses and prisms, was also moved to Russia. The Siemens & Halske plant at Siemens Stadt in Berlin (with its electron microscopes) was removed, and its top staff members were given work in Russia. The three A.E.G. electron microscopes at the K.W. Institut in Berlin also were removed to Russia.[40]

In the 1960s technical acquisition in the precision instruments field continued

---

[36] See, for example, S. R. Ivanchenko, *Schetnye mashiny i ikh ekspluatatsiia* (Moscow, 1968), pp. 42, 68, for data concerning the Felix as produced in the 1960s. Compare to *Encyclopedia Britannica* (1958 edition), vol. IV, p. 552 and the Western Brunsviga. For further details see R. W. Campbell, "Mechanization of Cost Accounting in the Soviet Union," *American Slavic and East European Review* (Menasha, Wis.), February 1958. Campbell ascribes the early Soviet arithmometers to the 1874 Russian Odner machine produced in St. Petersburg during World War I; however the design of the Odner is different from the Felix, although based on the same principles.

[37] *Wall Street Journal*, December 16, 1966, 7:3. For data on the Soviet-Olivettis see K. A. Borob'ev, *Konstruktsiia, tekhnicheskoe obsluzhivanie i remont bukhgalterskoi mashiny "Askota" klassa 170* (Moscow, 1969).

[38] Werner Keller, *Ost minus West=Null* (Munich: Droemersche Verlagsanstalt, 1960), pp. 283, 357, 365.

[39] BIOS Final Report no. 485: R. G. Allen, *German Filtration Industry*, pp. 18-18a, 22.

[40] *New York Times*, September 13, 1964.

with foreign purchases. It was reported in 1964 that "recent Soviet purchases cover a vast range from office equipment to camera shutters."[41] The firm of Rank-Xerox sold $3.7 million worth of its equipment, and the Japanese company Copal Koki signed a contract to supply producing facilities and know-how for a "sophisticated electric eye camera shutter."[42] Thus there has been a steady flow of instruments and precision equipment into the Soviet Union through the means of trade. The exception to Soviet inability in the field appears to be the various Soviet medical stapling instruments licensed by the United States Surgical Company and patented in the United States.[43]

In the period 1929 to 1940 the Soviets purchased 300,000 foreign machine tools, while its own output was concentrated in simple drilling machines and bench lathes of a standard type based on Western prototypes. These were supplemented by almost $400 million worth of Lend Lease machine tools.

Twelve very large machine tool plants were removed from Germany at the end of World War II—including the important Schiess-Defries and Billeter & Kluntz (Aschersleben) plants. These acquisitions have been supplemented by continuing and substantial imports from the West, greater in both quantity and unit value than Soviet exports of machine tools to underdeveloped areas.

"Copying offices," each specializing in a particular type of machine tool, have widely duplicated Western imports. Apart from "one-off" items for exhibition and to impress foreign visitors, Soviet machine tools are duplicates of foreign models, with occasional slight variations to adapt them to special Soviet conditions. In numerically controlled machine tools—certainly the most important innovation in the period under discussion—only a few prototypes were produced in the U.S.S.R. by the early 1960s, compared to several thousand in use in the United States.

The "U.S. ball bearing case of 1961," which brought to light a Soviet attempt to import the equivalent of two-thirds the U.S. capacity for producing miniature ball bearings (mainly used in missiles), suggests not only that there is a major lag on the part of the Soviet machine tool industry but that the Soviets are in a position to acquire even the latest and most significant of Western innovations in this field.

In the allied fields of computing, measuring, and precision instruments a like phenomenon was observed: a general backwardness and dependence on

---

[41] Ibid.

[42] Ibid.

[43] For example, U.S. Patent 3,078,465 of February 26, 1963. Sales from this license appear to have been insignificant; in the six-month period ending September 30, 1963, the United States Surgical Company paid only $495.00 in license fees. Direct sales to the Instrument Specialties Company were a little better, but not much—five sales totaling $2,892.62 in six months. See Supplemental Registration Statement (Pursuant to Section 2 of the Foreign Agents Registration Act of 1938) as filed in Department of Justice, Washington, D.C.

the West for modern technology acquired by purchases from such firms as General Electric–Olivetti (Italy), Rank–Xerox (U.K.), and Japanese firms.

Thus it is concluded that Soviet innovation in the field of machine tools and allied industries is almost non-existent (only hybrid machine tools have been isolated as Soviet innovations). Technological advance is gained by importing prototypes for copying, or where problems have been encountered in domestic copying, batches of specialized production machines are imported (as evidenced, for example, in the attempted acquisition of Centalign-B and tape-controlled machines).

CHAPTER TWENTY-THREE

Western Origins of Electronics and Electrical Engineering Technology

SOVIET COMPUTER TECHNOLOGY IN THE 1960s

The first generation of computers, developed from U.S. work in World War II, was based on the vacuum tube, and by present-day standards is slow (with only 2500 operations per second), of very limited capacity, and relatively bulky with about 2000 components per cubic foot. The second-generation computer, based on the transistor rather than the bulky vacuum tube, entered the U.S. market during the 1950s. With this development, speed was increased by a factor of ten, to 25,000 operations per second, and the transistor developed by Bell Telephone in 1948 brought component density up to 5000 components per cubic foot. By 1960 about 5000 second-generation computers were in use in the United States and had completely replaced the first-generation computer. Indeed even some early second-generation units had been removed from service by 1959.

The third generation of computers, based on microcircuits, was introduced commercially in 1961 and again increased both speed and capacity by a factor of ten. The third-generation IBM 360 system has 30,000 components per cubic foot, can handle 375,000 operations per second, and reduces the cost per 100,000 computations from $1.38 in first-generation machines to about 3.5 cents.[1]

Such, then, is the nature of the computer revolution in the Western world. The computer in Soviet technology, on the other hand, was still a relatively insignificant factor in the late sixties, behind not only the United States but Western Europe and Japan. Even first-rate scientific institutions have lacked advanced machines. For example, the main atomic energy research institute in the U.S.S.R., directed by famed physicist Igor Kurchatov, used the first-generation computer at the Academy of Science for calculations on uranium

---

[1] *Fortune*, September 1966, p. 120. An excellent study of the Western origins of Soviet computers appeared after this manuscript was completed: Richard W. Judy, "The Case of Computer Technology" in Stanislaw Wasowski, ed., *East-West Trade and the Technology Gap* (New York: Praeger, 1970). Judy's study is longer and more detailed than the section included here. There is a substantial unity between his conclusions and those of the author; for example, Judy states, "Computer technology in the Soviet Union is virtually entirely imported from the West"; and "literally all significant technological innovations [in the field] have occurred in the West."

burnup—at a time when the comparable Argonne Laboratories in the United States had two second-generation computers.[2]

There are several reasons why the Soviets were late in starting computer production and why their computer technology has lagged behind that of the West. These factors have been discussed in some detail by Richard W. Judy.[3] By 1957 the party journal *Kommunist* pointed out that "a number of firms are engaged in the production of electronic digital computers in the U.S.A., England, the Federal Republic of Germany, and France," and went on to suggest that a socialist economy could utilize electronic computers with even greater effect than capitalist economies. It was suggested that current deficiencies in planning, caused by the large number of manual calculations required, could be overcome by the use of electronic computers capable of operating with an enormous input and handling this input at a high rate of speed. In particular, *Kommunist* urged, the use of computers should be extended from the scientific field into the planning and management of industry.[4]

But if the Soviet dispute over the use of cybernetics in general was resolved, Soviet progress in the field of computer technology remained notably weak. At the end of the 1950s the United States had about 5000 computers in use while the Soviet Union had an estimated 120—about the same number as West Germany. Judging from the general characteristics of these Soviet computers as reported by well-qualified observers, the technology was well behind that of the West and barely out of the first-generation stage even as late as the 1960s.

The only Soviet computer in line production in 1960 was the URAL-I. It was followed by the URAL-II and URAL-4 modifications of the original model. With a prototype appearing in 1953 and series production beginning in 1955, the URAL-I had an average speed of 100 operations per second, compared to 2500 operations per second on U.S. World War II machines and 15,000 for large U.S. machines in the middle to late 1950s. Occupying 40 square meters of floor space, URAL-I contained 800 tubes and 3000 germanium diodes[5]; the storage units included a magnetic drum of 1024 cells and a magnetic tape of up to 40,000 cells, considerably less than U.S. machines. URAL-II and URAL-4 incorporated slightly improved characteristics.[6]

In the late fifties the Soviets also had about 30 to 40 BESM-type computers that were used primarily for research and development, including work on rockets and missiles.[7] The original version of the BESM had 7000 tubes; the later

[2] G. A. Modelski, *Atomic Energy in the Communist Bloc* (Melbourne, 1959), p. 97. In 1964 the Soviet Academy of Sciences received an Elliott Automation (General Electric subsidiary) Model 503 computer.

[3] See Judy, *op. cit.* n. 1, pp. 66-71.

[4] *Kommunist* (Yerevan), no. 7, 1957, pp. 124-27.

[5] Willis H. Ware and Wade B. Holland, *Soviet Cybernetics Technology. I: Soviet Cybernetics, 1959-1962,* (Santa Monica: RAND Corp., June 1963), Report no. RM-3675-PR, p. 91.

[6] *Ibid.,* p. 92.

[7] *Electronics* (New York), December 10, 1957.

version had 3000 tubes and germanium diodes. This computer had some features common to U.S. computers.[8]

Table 23-1   COMPARATIVE DATA ON SOVIET
                    AND WESTERN COMPUTERS UP TO 1968

Name	Operational date	Average speed operations per second	Storage capacity
STRELA	1953	2000	None
BESM I	1953	7000-8000	1023 words
SETUN	1959	4000	81 words
URAL-I	1953	100	None
URAL-II	1960	5000	8192 words
BESM-6	1967	1 million	—
General Electric -Elliott, 503	Installed by G.E. in Moscow Academy of Sciences in 1964	—	2 million characters
English Electric System 4 (RCA technology)	Installed in U.S.S.R. in 1967	23.8 μ sec	7.25 million characters
International Computers, Ltd. (U.K.) Model 1905E	Installed in U.S.S.R. in 1968	1.8 μ sec	8 million characters

Sources: Soviet machines: Willis H. Ware and Wade B. Holland, Soviet Cybernetics Technology: Soviet Cybernetics, 1959-1962 (Santa Monica: RAND Corp., June 1963), RM-3675-PR; Western machines: Office Automation (New York, 1962).

One observer has rated the BESM as follows: "One of the most impressive achievements of Soviet technology.... It cannot, however, properly be considered as a machine competitive with the IBM-701 or the IBM-704."[9]

The URAL series was manufactured at the Penza computing machine plant,[10] which in 1959 was in series production of URAL-I and preparing to change over to URAL-II. Production methods then were reported to be the same as those in the United States.[11] On the other hand, Soviet computers were far less efficient; the STRELA, for instance, was reported to have only a ten-minute mean free time between errors, while U.S. machines in the fifties normally operated eight hours without error.[12]

A Soviet business data electronic tabulator, the TAT-102, designed primarily for mechanical accounting, statistical calculations, and planning, was developed in the late 1950s and is quite similar to the IBM 604 electronic data-processing

[8]   Ware and Holland, op. cit. n. 5, pp. 85-91.
[9]   Nevin L. Bean, "Address before the Detroit Chapter of the National Society of Professional Engineers," Detroit, February 22, 1956 (Dearborn: Ford Motor Co., News Dept.), p. 11.
[10] Ware and Holland, op. cit. n. 5, p. 83.
[11] Ibid., p. 84.
[12] Control Engineering (New York), V, 11 (November 1958), 77.

machine. A machinability computer, the VPRR, designed to determine operating conditions for metal cutting tools, also was developed; it closely resembles the Carboloy machine developed by General Electric Company in 1955.[13]

Software has been copied from U.S. equipment. For example Willis H. Ware comments:

> We were shown about 40 card punches. About half of these were 90-column machines and the other half 80-column machines; all were generally similar to United States designs.... We also saw a 500-card per minute sorter which closely resembled a corresponding American product. It has electromechanical sensing of the holes and a set of switches for suppressing specific row selections as in American sorters.[14]

Backwardness in computer technology[15] has led (as in other fields) to imports from the Western world. Imports of computers from the United States were, until very recently, heavily restricted by export control; in 1965 only $5,000 worth of electronic computers and parts were shipped from the United States to the Soviet Union, and only $2,000 worth in 1966. In 1967 such exports totaled $1,079,000, and this higher rate of export of electronic computers has been maintained since that time.[16]

Business relations between International Business Machines Corporation (IBM) and the Soviet Union go back into the 1930s. In August 1936 IBM was advised that in the future all its business would be handled directly with Uchetimport (Bureau for the Import of Calculating Machines and Typewriters) rather than through Amtorg, the Soviet representative agency in the United States. According to E. F. Schwerdt, the Moscow representative of IBM,[17] this rather unusual business arrangement was due to Soviet dissatisfaction with IBM leasing arrangements and to a desire to purchase rather than lease IBM equipment. To avoid losing the business IBM proposed an arrangement under which the Soviets would establish a separate corporation whose sole business would be the import of IBM machines for rent to Soviet organizations at the uniform rental fee (in other words, Uchetimport in effect became an IBM agency); 30 percent of the royalties were payable to IBM with a guaranteed minimum annual payment. IBM was willing to maintain a technical servicing staff in the U.S.S.R. to be paid by the Soviets.[18] The precise amount and nature of IBM computer sales to the Soviet Union since World War II is not known, but it is known that after World War II IBM sales to the Communist world

---

[13] *Control Engineering,* V, 5 (May 1958).
[14] Ware and Holland, *op. cit.* n. 5, p. 85.
[15] The BESM-6 machine was installed at Dubna in 1967 but is not in general use.
[16] U.S. Dept. of Commerce, *Export Control* (Washington, D.C., issued quarterly). These figures calculated from data contained in various issues for the years 1966-68.
[17] U.S. State Dept. Decimal File, 861.602/279.
[18] *Ibid.*

came "almost entirely from [IBM's] Western European plants," partly because the U.S. equipment operates on 60 cycles whereas Russian and European equipment operates on 50 cycles.[19]

The earliest Western computer sale that can be traced is a Model 802 National-Elliott sold by Elliott Automation, Ltd., of the United Kingdom in 1959.[20] (Elliott Automation is a subsidiary of General Electric.) By the end of the sixties Soviet purchases of computers had been stepped up in a manner reminiscent of the massive purchase of chemical plants in the early sixties. In the last days of 1969 it was estimated that Western computer sales to all of communist Europe, including the U.S.S.R., were running at $40 million annually and these were in great part from subsidiaries of American companies.[21] In 18 months during 1964-65 Elliott Automation delivered five Model 503 computers to the U.S.S.R., one for installation in the Moscow Academy of Sciences;[22] the Elliott 503 ranged in price from $179,000 to over $1 million, depending on size, and has a 131,000-word core capacity. By the end of 1969 General Electric–Elliott automation sales to communist countries were four times greater than in 1968 and this market accounted for no less than one-third of General Electric–Elliott's computer exports.[23] Another General Electric machine, this time a Model 400 made in France by Compagnie des Machines Bull, also was sold to the U.S.S.R.; and Olivetti–General Electric at Milan, Italy, was also a major supplier of G.E. computers to the U.S.S.R. In 1967 the Olivetti firm delivered $2.4 million worth of data-processing equipment systems to the U.S.S.R. in addition to the Model 400 and the Model 115 machines already sold.[24] The Model 115 is a G.E. information processing system, but has a wide range of applications. It can be used as a free-standing tabulating unit or as a peripheral subsystem to other G.E. units.

In sum, General Electric has sold through its European subsidiaries from 1959 to 1970 a range of its medium-capacity business and scientific computers, including the fastest of the 400 series, which can be used either individually or as a group.

Perhaps of greater significance are English Electric sales, which include third-generation microcircuit computers utilizing Radio Corporation of America technology. In 1967 English Electric sold to the U.S.S.R. its System Four machine with microcircuits. This machine incorporates RCA patents[25] and is similar to the RCA Spectra 70 series.

[19]   *Wall Street Journal*, May 10, 1966. Thomas J. Watson, chairman of IBM, was in Moscow in October 1970 with four IBM engineers to discuss the nature of continued IBM assistance to the U.S.S.R.
[20]   *Electrical Review*, (London), no. 165, p. 566.
[21]   *Business Week*, December 27, 1969, p. 59.
[22]   *Wall Street Journal*, June 18, 1965.
[23]   *Business Week*, December 27, 1969, p. 59.
[24]   *Wall Street Journal*, February 7, 1967, 14:3.
[25]   *The Times* (London), January 24, 1967.

The largest single supplier of computers to the U.S.S.R. has been International Computers and Tabulation, Ltd., of the United Kingdom, a firm whose technology is largely independent of U.S. patents. In November 1969, for example, five of the firm's 1900 series computers (valued at $12 million) were sold to the U.S.S.R.[26] These are large high-speed units with integrated circuits, and without question they are considerably in advance of anything the Soviets are able to manufacture in the computer field. These machines are certainly capable of utilization in solving military and space problems.

AUTOMATION AND CONTROL ENGINEERING

Given the Soviet backwardness in computer technology, it is pertinent to examine briefly the nature and extent of Soviet achievement in the important fields of automation and control engineering.

The Russian application of the word automation is much wider than in the West; in the U.S.S.R. it can include such elementary control systems as automatic level controls and water pumping stations. In the Western definition, automation designates only advanced mechanization (mainly cyclical operations), automatic control, regulation, and direction work, including self-optimizing operations and the concomitant utilization of computers.

The Moscow Congress of the International Federation of Automatic Control held in June and July 1960, provided an excellent opportunity for examination of the state of automation in the Soviet Union at that time. It was the first such congress, and it brought together 1111 delegates from 29 countries, with the U.S.S.R. being represented by 397 persons, the U.S.A. by 137, the United Kingdom by 78, and a large number in attendance from European socialist countries. In a period of four and one-half days some 275 papers were read.

The general impression gained by British and American delegates to the conference was that the papers presented and the visits made did not support the general understanding of Soviet achievements in space research and nuclear engineering. For example, Professor H. H. Rosenbrock commented as follows:

It was difficult at first to set this in perspective. The known Russian achievements in theory and in the guidance of rockets did not at first accord with the elementary state of automation in some of the factories that were seen and with the shortage and out-of-date design of tools such as analog and digital computers.[27]

[26] *Business Week*, December 27, 1969. The 1900 series has numerous models and the company has not announced the model numbers of the machines shipped; models vary greatly in speed and capacity.
[27] H.H. Rosenbrock, "A Report of Symposium on Automatic Control," Institution of Mechanical Engineers, (London), 1960.

Similarly, a British delegate, D. C. Rennie, made the following comment:

> The consensus ... from the British delegation was that we saw nothing to support the tremendous achievements of the U.S.S.R. in space research and nuclear engineering. It would appear that the U.S.S.R. has poured much of its resources into these fields.
>
> We did not see anything that would justify the opinion that the U.S.S.R. is ahead of the West. In endeavoring to gauge the potential of any organization, it is usual to examine carefully the base of the pyramid supporting the spearhead. In fact, the "base" appeared to be missing. For example, the computers we saw were far behind those in the West. The instrument engineering in the factories was inferior to comparable Western equipment. The equipment and components being developed in the Institute of Automation at Kiev, one of the largest and most important in the U.S.S.R., were far behind the latest techniques in Britain and the U.S.A. It must be stressed that these opinions are based only on what we saw. It is conceivable that much of their later developments were carefully withheld. The writer is of the opinion that this was unlikely. Conversation with individual Russian engineers gave a strong impression that they were being open.[28]

One of the key institutes in the field of automation is, as Rennie indicated, the Institute of Automation in Kiev, which employs some 2000 persons working in 40 laboratories in addition to experimental workshops and pilot plants. It was of this facility that Dr. H. H. Rosenbrock commented: "This, incidentally, was the first time in Russia that I saw a transistor; all the other equipment, amplifiers and so on, was valve equipment."[29]

The papers presented at the conference confirm the rather skeptical outlook brought back by Western delegates concerning the level of Soviet achievements in automatic control systems. One conference paper, by General Electric engineer E. W. Miller on the "Application of Automatic Control Systems in the Iron and Steel Industry," aroused considerable interest and the author was cross-examined by the Russian engineers present for more than an hour. A British delegate commented that from the discussion it was obvious that the Americans were far ahead of the Russians in this field.[30]

The paper that followed Miller's, one on a similar topic by a Russian engineer (V. I. Feigin on "Automation of a Reversing Mill"), also suggests a much lower level of technology in the U.S.S.R. For example, the system Miller described controlled 12 parameters whereas the Soviet system controlled three parameters. Although the Russian paper took an hour to present, a delegate

[28] Private, unpublished report by D. C. Rennie, London, Eng.: "Report on Moscow Congress of the International Federation of Automatic Control," June 27-July 7, 1960, p. 1. Typescript supplied by author.
[29] Rosenbrock, *op. cit.* n. 27, p. 55. The 1963 U.S. Atomic Energy Delegation observed only one piece of transistorized equipment during the whole visit.
[30] Rennie, *op. cit.* n. 28, p. 12.

commented that at the end there were no questions or comments from the floor. The next Russian paper, also on a similar topic, was canceled.

The following day, on June 28, 1960, a paper by D. A. Patient of Baird and Tatlock (on "Techniques for the Automation of Sampling and Chemical Analysis") induced considerable Russian cross-questioning. However, the subsequent paper by M. Brozgol, a Soviet engineer (on "The Automation of Electric Drives"), was described by the British delegate as being in "the widest terms." The same observer reported that Western delegates "found it extremely difficult to pin the Russians down to giving precise information in one or another particular field," and that "the author of [the 'Electric Drives'] paper stated in response to a direct question that if he had been reporting today, he 'would have mentioned things which had been developed more recently.' " When pressed for further information he was not prepared to give it.[31]

Attempts by Western conference delegates to visit particular plants were not successful. H. H. Rosenbrock commented:

> No visits were arranged during the conference to chemical plants or process plants in general. I tried hard while I was over there to visit a chemical plant; but obviously I was not persuasive.[32]

Another delegate, W. D. Elliott, commented: "Although I tried for five days I was not able to get to see a computer institute."[33]

It may be justifiably concluded, then, that Soviet automation and control engineering is not in an advanced state. This conclusion is entirely consistent with earlier conclusions concerning the elementary nature of Soviet computers in the 1960s and the necessity to purchase IBM, General Electric, and RCA technology to fill a sizable technological gap. Given the fundamental place of these technologies in weapons systems, this conclusion raises serious questions concerning the origins of Soviet military computers and control mechanisms. This question is discussed in chapter 27; at this point the hypothesis is put forward that Soviet military capabilities also are from the West.

THE NATURE OF GERMAN TRANSFERS
IN THE ELECTRICAL INDUSTRY

The technical nature of the transfers from the German electrical industry at the end of World War II provide a plausible explanation for current Soviet backwardness in control instrumentation and computers. The Germans did not

---

[31] *Ibid.*, p. 14.
[32] Rosenbrock, *op. cit.* n. 27, p. 55.
[33] *Ibid.*, p. 57.

work on computer technology—facilities for the production of industrial control instrumentation were not in evidence among the numerous plants and equipment shipped to the U.S.S.R. from Germany.

In prewar Germany the electrical equipment manufacturing industry was heavily concentrated in the Berlin area. Although there was a slight movement away from Berlin as a dispersal measure under the threat of Allied bombing, eastern Germany was by the end of World War II the most important location for the electrical industry. This is confirmed by several sources. In a report from Dr. Fritz Luschen to Albert Speer in March 1945, in the last days of World War II, it was reported that since 1943 the industry had been dispersed to a great extent to Silesia and other eastern areas, and the Soviet advance had led to "severe inroads on manufacturing space and development workshops."[34] It was pointed out by Dr. Luschen that although in February 1945 the reduction in floor space was only 7.8 percent, "this trifling percentage is no index of the significance of the loss, since the most important and specialized manufacturing development facilities of the entire electrical industry had been installed in the East."

Furthermore, large stocks of electrical equipment had been lost, including, for example, 100 repeater stations and radar equipment. The Luschen report goes on to indicate that Berlin therefore had increased in importance and at the end of the war included about 50 percent of the German electrical industry. This reasoning was shared by the U.S. Strategic Bombing Survey team:[35]

> A study of the electrical equipment industry in Germany would have been concentrated in the Berlin area had the region been available for investigation. This is inevitable since there is no other area in Germany which is comparable in size and importance within the province of electrical equipment. The Russian occupation forces in the area did not permit American personnel to enter their zone of occupation at the time the survey was made.

This concentration in Berlin and eastern Germany enabled the Soviets to acquire probably 80 percent of the 1944-45 German electrical industry. As we have already seen, this came about, paradoxically, because of the Allied advance to the Elbe. The Soviets occupied the whole of Berlin and removed the electrical plants from all Berlin zones;[36] then when the frontiers were adjusted on July 1, 1945, the Soviets occupied and proceeded to dismantle the electrical industry of Saxony, Thuringia, and Brandenburg, which had been evacuated by U.S. forces.

---

[34] U.S. Strategic Bombing Survey, *German Electrical Equipment Industry Report*, 2d edition (Washington, Equipment Division, 1947), Report no. 48.

[35] *Ibid.*, p. 8.

[36] *Ibid.*, p. 9: "Investigation of plants in the Berlin area at the present time [July 1945] would not yield satisfactory results, as key electrical equipment plants have been removed from Berlin by the Russians."

What did the Soviets acquire in East Germany? About 65 percent of the facilities removed were for the production of power and lighting equipment (about one-quarter), telephone, telegraph, and communications equipment facilities (just under one-third), and equipment for the manufacture of cable and wire (about one-tenth).[37] The remainder consisted of plants to manufacture radio tubes, radios,[38] household electrical goods and batteries, and military electronics facilities for such items as secret teleprinters and antiaircraft equipment.

A large number of wartime military electronic developments were made at the Reichspost Forschungsinstitut (whose director went to the U.S.S.R.), and these developments presumably were absorbed into Soviet capability, including television, infrared devices, radar, electrical coatings, acoustical fuses, and similar equipment.[39]

Thus although 80 percent of the German electrical and military electronics industries was removed, the Soviets did not gain computer or control instrumentation technologies developed after World War II.

WESTERN ASSISTANCE TO INSTRUMENTATION SYSTEMS

The computer is the heart of modern control instrumentation. There is no available evidence that direct Western assistance was provided for the early Soviet computers, STRELA, BESM, and URAL, although the components, tubes, diodes, and later transistor technologies came from Germany (the reparations removals) and from postwar purchases of electrical equipment. There is, however, a great deal of Western design influence, and some equipment is copied from American models.[40]

At the 1955 Russian exhibit of nuclear instrumentation in Paris it was noted that Russian instrumentation was second to the U.S. "qualitatively and quantitatively" and overall "several years behind the U.S. on techniques." The items exhibited were largely copies; only one photomultiplier was exhibited and the "RCA people say [it] is a copy of [an] early RCA multiplier" (complete

[37] *Ibid.* For figures on distribution of production from 1943, see *ibid.*, p. 14.

[38] See p. 334 below. Removal of at least one radio equipment plant was somewhat delayed: "Of a certain radio-valve plant the Russians seized 50 percent of all the machines and transferred them to Russia. Then they ordered the management to build new machinery in order to keep up production. When the new machines were built and run in, they were seized and taken to Russia. This happened once again and when the plant had reached full production again, it was transferred to Russia, lock, stock, and barrel, including management, engineers, foremen, key workers, and the families of the male and female workers." *Aeronautics* (London). July 1951, pp. 35-36.

[39] U.S. Strategic Bombing Survey, *op. cit.* n. 34, contains a summary of the German wartime military electronics developments; see pp. 67-72.

[40] See p. 319.

with the RCA pinched neck). The pocket dosimeters "seemed similar to Argonne design."[41]

At about the same time a review by a "top German scientist" based on interviews of German electronics engineers returning from the U.S.S.R. concluded that the engineers were returned because the Soviets had nothing more to learn from them; the Soviets were said to "always have working models of the latest U.S. equipment,"[42] and were at that time testing the latest U.S. Tacan navigation system. The Loran system was later copied as the Luga system.[43] Another observer, Dr. W. H. Brandt of Westinghouse, noted that Soviet coil winding techniques were parallel to those of the U.S. in World War II,[44] and that the Soviets apparently were having problems manufacturing transistors. The American trade journal *Control Engineering* reported a few years later (in 1958) a visit by a delegation in industrial instrument design:

> We saw many examples of dial-type laboratory precision resistance decades, Wheatstone bridges, Kelvin bridges, and precision potentiometers, as well as portable bridges and potentiometers. Designs were strongly reminiscent of American designs. A few of the dial-type instruments used switching contact designs normally associated with German precision apparatus.[45]

However, N. Cohn of Leeds & Northrup commented: "Not all units were copies, and the Russians were proud of design advances—from their point of view—of their own." He then added:"We saw an assembly for measuring 10 to 100 percent relative humidity using wet and dry bulb resistance thermometers and a self-balancing computing circuit, originally developed in this country in the 1920s."[46]

An exhibit of Russian electronic test equipment in New York in 1959 provided another opportunity for preliminary observations on this sector of the electronics industry.[47] Unfortunately no opportunity was given visitors to observe the instruments in operation; consequently it was not possible to compare specifications with performance. In microwave test equipment, the design appeared adequate but the specifications were "so much poorer than ours."[48] It was observed that many instruments were copies, but one unique item was shown—a compact calibrating signal generator packaged into a compact unit. David Packard noted that a couple of instruments were "without question" copies of instruments originally developed by Hewlett Packard Company.[49]

[41] *Nucleonics* (New York), September 1955, pp. 12-13.
[42] *Aviation Week*, (New York), April 16, 1956, p. 75.
[43] Institute for the Study of the U.S.S.R. *Bulletin* (Munich), V (December 1956), 13.
[44] *Aviation Week*, April 9, 1956, p. 68.
[45] *Control Engineering*, November 1958, pp. 65-80.
[46] *Ibid.*, p. 74.
[47] *Electronic Design* (New York), August 17, 1960, pp. 50-70.
[48] *Ibid.*
[49] *Ibid.*

This backwardness in electronics was still apparent in 1960. The American trade journal *Electronics* illustrated Soviet space components and their U.S. counterparts, and noted the bulky and obsolescent nature of Soviet components—without printed circuits and using conventional military-type cables and plugs for space work.[50] The journal cited an example of an ionization detector and amplifier used in the 1961 U.S. moon shot in one package six inches long and the comparable Soviet instruments in *Sputnik III*—two packages about two feet long.[51]

Where the Soviets are operating modern systems, the origins can be traced to the West. For example, in 1966 an instrument-landing system valued at $280,000 was installed at the Sheremetyevo Airport in Moscow—the international airport—by Standard Cables & Telephone, Ltd., a subsidiary of International Telephone and Telegraph Corporation (ITT) of New York.[52]

In 1967 Le Matériel Téléphonique S.A. of Paris, France, another subsidiary of ITT, was awarded a contract to equip an all-purpose telephone information center in Moscow. The contract was for the manufacture and supply of telephone switching apparatus to give callers information on weather, time, and cultural events. Although the system was large—employing 500 operators and using advanced microfilm techniques—it seems unusual that this kind of system would still be bought in the West.[53]

SOVIET RADIO AND TELEVISION RECEIVERS

In late 1953 the U.S. Air Force Technical Intelligence Center made an "intensive scrutiny" of two Soviet television sets, the Muscovite and the Leningrad, and concluded that Soviet circuitry and design trailed that of U.S. practice by about ten years. The Muscovite T-1 small 7-inch screen television introduced in 1948 as the first Soviet television set was a "direct copy of a 1939 German receiver." It was capable of picking up only the single Moscow channel, and its performance was described as "mediocre." The follow-on unit was the Leningrad T-2 built in East Germany to Soviet specifications for sale in the

[50] *Electronics*, November 25, 1960, p. 43.
[51] *Ibid.*
[52] *Wall Street Journal*, May 10, 1966. Thus the pilot on the first Soviet flight to the United States was able to claim: "Captain Boris Yegorov said that the efficiency of traffic flow around Moscow was a good deal better than it was around New York, which has been suffering exasperating traffic delays. 'In Moscow, everything is on time,' said the captain after his own flight had to circle New York for an hour and 35 minutes and had come within 10 minutes of having to turn back to Montreal." *San Jose Mercury* (San Jose, Calif.) August 28, 1968.
[53] *Wall Street Journal*, July 31, 1967, 7:2. However, Soviet telephone equipment appears to be of the 1920s era; for example see chart compiled by L. T. Barnakova, entitled *Oborudovanie gorodskikh telefonnykh stantsii* (Moscow, 1966).

U.S.S.R.; this set, with an 8-inch screen, could pick up only the Leningrad station with a performance rated as "fair."[54]

The first color television project is claimed by the Soviet engineer I. Adamian for 1925.[55] In March 1965, however, the Soviets made an agreement with France to utilize the French color television system SEKAM in the Soviet Union.[56] This system, with circuits covered by Radio Corporation of America patents,[57] is used in the Soviet color television receivers Rubin-401, Raduga-4, and Raduga-5.[58]

IMPORT OF POWER STATION EQUIPMENT

Although Soviet literature stresses the ban that was placed on imported equipment for electrical generation in 1934,[59] there has in fact been considerable import of complete power stations and equipment for power generation, particularly during and just after World War II. Robert Huhn Jones estimates that the $167 million worth of electrical-plant shipments under Lend Lease were roughly equal to the capacity of the Hoover Dam or the combined generating capacity of the states of New Jersey, Connecticut, and New York.[60] Up to 1944 these deliveries constituted 20 percent of the increment in Russian wartime power capacity and were in addition to substantial shipments from the United Kingdom and Canada—sufficient to produce 1,457,274 kw of power.[61] The program provided complete stations (this accounted for the high construction cost of $144 per kw):

> ...[Western firms are] shipping the Russians equipment down to and including wiring for the plant's lighting system, leaving out only such items as light bulbs, freight or passenger elevators, metal stairways, and the like. Powerwise we send the Russians everything a complete station requires.[62]

Between 1942 and 1946 the United Kingdom shipped eight complete power

[54] *Product Engineering,* (New York), 1953, pp. 200-1.
[55] *Nauka i zhizn'* (Moscow), no. 6, 1965, p. 7.
[56] *Ibid.*
[57] *Wall Street Journal.* March 23, 1965, 3:2.
[58] A. Bartosiak, *Sistema tsvetnogo televideniia SEKAM* (Moscow, 1968). Dependence on foreign transistors is implicit in such publications as V. F. Leont'ev, *Zarubezhnye transistory shirokogo primeneniia* (Moscow, 1969) and G. G. Sitnikov, *Tranzistornye televizory SShA i Yaponii* (Moscow, 1968).
[59] P.S. Neporozhnii, *Electrification and Power Construction in the U.S.S.R.* (Jerusalem: Israel Program for Scientific Translations, 1966), p. 76.
[60] Robert Huhn Jones, *The Roads to Russia* (Norman: University of Oklahoma Press, 1969), p. 225.
[61] *Ibid.* A few of the units shipped were old and inefficient, such as, for example, the Consolidated Edison plant from Long Beach, California, shipped in 1943. See also Sutton II, pp. 167-68.
[62] *Electrical World* (Manchester, Eng.), August 19, 1944, p. 102.

stations to the U.S.S.R. (four of 10,000-kw, two of 12,000-kw, and two of 25,000-kw capacity[63]), as well as a mixed power-district heating plant.[64] In 1954 two large contracts were concluded, one with R. A. Lister & Company, Ltd., for 90 diesel generating stations of 410 kw each, at a cost in excess of $4 million, and the other and still larger contract with the Brush Group of companies for diesel generating sets, turbines, and transformers valued in excess of $12 million.[65] Motors and alternators were supplied by Crompton Parkinson later in the same year,[66] and in 1958 a 1000-kw gas turbine (Mark TA) was supplied by Ruston and Hornsby for mobile generator use.[67] In addition, large quantities of control instrumentation have been supplied by British firms —for example, an order for 100 starters from Brookhirst Switchgear, Ltd., in 1946[68] and large quantities of power cable and wire from Crompton Parkinson and Aberdare Cables, Ltd.[69]

Other countries have supplied similar equipment. For example, in 1947 the Swedish subsidiary of General Electric supplied a complete power station for delivery in 1949-52 at a cost of $2 million.[70] In addition there was movement of electrical power generating equipment from Germany to the U.S.S.R. under reparations, e.g., the Gensdorf plant,[71] and the removal of the generators from Siemens-Halske works in Berlin to the Elektrosila plant in Leningrad.[72]

THE INCREASE IN ELECTRICAL GENERATING CAPACITY

The only Western delegation to have visited the Soviet Union and returned to give glowing reports of Soviet technical achievements—and also to predict that the Soviet Union would surpass the United States within a foreseeable time period—was the 1960 U.S. Senate power industry delegation.[73] This delegation report was significantly different from that of two other U.S. electrical industry delegations[74] and to some extent from that of the Canadian Electric Power Industry Delegation.[75]

[63] *Electrical Review* (London), vol. 140 (1947), 442.
[64] *Ibid.,* vol. 135 (1944), pp. 764-70.
[65] *Ibid.,* vol. 154, (1954), p. 480.
[66] *Ibid.,* vol. 155 (1954), p. 290.
[67] *Ibid.,* vol. 163 (1958), p. 22.
[68] *Ibid.,* vol. 139 (1946), p. 941.
[69] *Ibid.,* vol. 155 (1954), pp. 290, 330.
[70] *Ibid.,* vol. 140 (1947), p. 986.
[71] See p. 29.
[72] Keller, *Ost minus West=Null* (Munich, 1960), p. 283.
[73] U.S. Senate, Committees on Interior and Insular Affairs and Public Works, *Relative Water and Power Resource Development in the U.S.S.R. and the U.S.A.,* Report and Staff Studies, 86th Congress, 2d session, May 1960.
[74] A Report on U.S.S.R. Electric Developments, 1958-1959 (New York: Edison Electric Institute, 1960).
[75] *Report of Visit to U.S.S.R. by Delegation from Canadian Electric Utilities, May 14 to June 2, 1960* (Toronto: September 9, 1960).

The Senate delegation report suggested that the Soviet Union was catching up with the United States in the production of electric power; that in 1961 it was constructing large hydroelectric dams faster than the United States; and that it had not only caught up with the Western world in hydroelectric engineering but "... in fact they are actually preeminent in certain specific aspects of such development."[76] The Senate committee that heard the report therefore recommended a massive U.S. Federal program and a study of planning "on a national basis."[77] On the other hand, the Edison Electric Institute report noted in distinct contrast:

> The economic problems facing the Soviet Union ... are vast and complex. Even assuming the [electrification] goal is reached, however, it is worth remembering that in 1965 the United States should have a total capability of 245 million kilowatts, and the present 123-million-kilowatt gap between Russian and American electric power capability will have increased by some 10 million kilowatts.[78]

The Canadian delegation noted "good" power equipment, impressive plans and organization, and "outstanding" transmission and hydraulic generation, but "their achievements in thermal generation and atomic power generation were not particularly impressive."[79]

Electrification of Russia has of course been a prime goal of the Soviets.[80] However, progress has not been as substantial as planned and certainly not as substantial in absolute terms as in the United States. The United States in 1950 had a total generating capacity of 82.8 million kw, including 18.7 million kw, or about one-quarter of capacity, generated from hydropower sources. In 1958 this total had increased to 160.7 million kw (30.1 million kw in hydropower), and in 1967 to 269.0 million kw (48.0 million kw by hydropower). In comparison, the Soviet total in 1950, after installation of the Lend Lease power station and heavy equipment imports of the 1940s, was 19.6 million kw (of which 3.2 million was from hydropower sources); this increased to 53.4 million kw in 1958 (10.9 million kw from hydropower) and 131.7 million kw in 1967 (24.8 million from hydropower).

The total generating capacity in the United States increased by 77.9 million kw between 1950 and 1958, compared with an increment of 33.8 million in the U.S.S.R. in the same period. During the next decade, 1958 to 1967, the United States increased its total generating capacity by 108.3 million kw and the U.S.S.R. by 78.3 million kw.[81] (See Table 23-2.)

[76]   U.S. Senate, *op. cit.* n. 73, p. 1.
[77]   *Ibid.*, p. 7.
[78]   *A Report on U.S.S.R. Electric Power Developments, op. cit.* n. 74, p. 19.
[79]   *Report of Visit to U.S.S.R.* ..., *op. cit.* n. 74. Further information on methods of construction may be obtained from "Excerpts from a Contractor's Notebook," kindly supplied by Dan Mardian of Phoenix, Arizona, and deposited in the Hoover Institution Library.
[80]   See Sutton I, pp. 201-6.
[81]   See Table 23-2.

Table 23-2   COMPARATIVE INCREMENTS IN ELECTRICAL POWER
CAPACITY IN THE UNITED STATES
AND THE U.S.S.R., 1950-67

Capacity	Year	United States (million kw) Increments		U.S.S.R. (million kw) Increments		Gap U.S./U.S.S.R.
Total electric	1950	82.8	—	19.6	—	63.2
power generation	1958	160.7	77.9	53.4	33.8	107.3
capacity	1967	269.0	108.3	131.7	78.3	137.3
Hydroelectric	1950	18.7	—	3.2	—	15.5
power generation	1958	30.1	11.4	10.9	7.2	19.2
capacity	1967	48.0	17.9	24.8	13.9	23.2

Sources: U.S. Bureau of the Census, *Statistical Abstract of the United States*, 1969 (Washington, 1969), p. 511; *Narodnoe khoziaistvo SSR* 1967 (Moscow, 1968).

The gap between U.S. and U.S.S.R. generating capacity therefore increased between 1958 and 1967. The difference was 107.3 million kw in 1958, and this difference had increased to 137.3 million kw in 1967. The gap in hydroelectric power, where the Soviets have placed particular emphasis, increased from 19.2 million kw in 1958 to 23.2 million kw in 1967. Increasing the relative gap in generating capacity is not an effective way of "catching up" with the United States.

There are other indications that the position of the Soviets is worsening. At the end of the sixties the United States had more than 70 atomic generating stations on order while the Soviets, with only three or four such stations built and none reported under construction,[82] appeared to be having difficulties with their construction. There is no indication that in the generation of electricity by the use of steam (thermal) plants the Soviets have generated any above-normal efficiency operations. Claims are made concerning the size of turbogenerators and that, for example, in 1960 several 200,000-kw units had been installed. The first U.S. 200,000-kw unit was installed in 1929.[83] The reported fuel consumption in 1958 was 0.97 pound per kw-hr compared with 0.90 pound in the United States, and the Eddystone unit under construction in the United States in 1960 was planned for fuel consumption of 0.60 pound per hour.[84]

The Soviet emphasis has been on the production of standardized facilities using reinforced and prefabricated concrete units in the buildings. In this connection it should be noted that a great deal of General Electric and Metropolitan-Vickers technical assistance was provided for thermal units in the 1930-40 period, and in 1944 a U.S. consulting firm—Ebasco Services, Ltd., under instructions from Lend Lease—prepared a set of drawings and specifications for standardized designs using the metric system. These designs made "extensive" use of rein-

[82] See *Pravda*, November 1969.
[83] *A Report on U.S.S.R. Electric Power Developments, op. cit.* n. 74, p. 8.
[84] *Ibid.*

forced concrete adapted to Russian conditions.[85] In addition, a number of power stations were equipped from the United States, Canada, and Britain at the end of and just after World War II.[86]

Lags in Soviet computer technology are clearly apparent throughout the period under discussion and have been compensated for by imports from IBM, General Electric-Elliott, English Electric, and International Computers, Ltd. This computer lag has in turn resulted in a major weakness in automation and control engineering, even in fields such as iron and steel where the Soviets have undertaken extensive research work.

These lags fit the pattern of transfers from the German electrical equipment industry at the end of World War II. The factories transferred then were largely for the manufacture of power and communications equipment, not computers and control equipment. In the field of communications equipment, for example for aircraft landing systems and color television, the Soviets utilized Western technology in the late 1960s.

As the gap between U.S. and Soviet electrical generating capacity is increasing—the gloomy forecasts of a Senate subcommittee notwithstanding—it is considered that the Soviets are well behind the United States. In atomic generating stations the Soviets were considerably behind in the late sixties, with only three or four stations built compared with 70 built or under construction in the United States.

---

[85]   L. Elliott, "Steam Plant Designed for Russia under Lend-Lease," *Electrical World*, December 23, 1944, pp. 69-71.
[86]   For detailed information on current standard thermal stations, see P. S. Neporozhnii, *Spravochnik stroitelia teplov ykh elektrostantsii* (Moscow, 1969).

CHAPTER TWENTY FOUR

Western Assistance
to Consumer Goods Industries

Consumer goods, the neglected sector under Soviet planning, contains a great diversity of products and technologies too numerous to discuss in detail in a single volume. To illustrate the problems of the sector, however, this chapter provides an in-depth examination of a single food industry, sugar beet production and refining, followed by a more or less cursory description of Western assistance to other consumer goods industries.

Sugar production was chosen as a case study because in the Soviet Union beet sugar refining is an old, established industry, larger in its productive capacity than in any other country, and consequently an industry in which the Soviets have had both the opportunity and the incentive to develop an indigenous technology. There was prerevolutionary Russian innovation and development in the industry; indeed, the Russians claim, probably with justification, that the first beet sugar plants were established in Russia. Indigenous innovative activity was continued in the industry after the October Revolution, and in 1928 two refining processes were planned. Innovative activity thereafter appears to have virtually ceased—it is unlikely that the Soviets would conceal any development in this sector—and we find that by the late 1950s the two 1928 refining inventions were still under development and the industry itself was based on foreign technology, either imported or duplicated. These developments may profitably be considered in more detail.

The first beet sugar mill in Russia, and the first in the world, according to P. M. Silin, was founded in Tula Province in 1802.[1] In the same year

---

[1] P. M. Silin, *Tekhnologiya sveklosakharnogo i rafinadnogo proizvodstva* (Moscow, 1958); translated as *Technology of Beet-Sugar Production and Refining* (Jerusalem: Israel Program for Scientific Translations, 1964), OTS 63-11073, p. 4. All references are to the translated version, which is more readily available in the United States. The first beet sugar mill in the United States was built in 1838 at Northampton, Mass.; it failed. The first successful U.S. beet sugar factory was not established until 1870 at Alvarado, California; see R. A. McGinnis, ed., *Beet-Sugar Technology* (New York: Reinhold Publishing Corp., 1951). The accuracy of the claim to Russian priority in sugar extraction from beets depends on how completely the story is told. It is true (as indicated in Silin) that a beet sugar extraction plant was constructed in the early 1800s in Russia. However, this was done with the aid of government subsidies as part of a Russian Government program to introduce foreign farming skills into Russia. Tsar Alexander I sent recruiting officers to Germany, and there is little question

Ya. S. Esipov developed the lime method of juice purification, a method later adopted throughout the world, and there followed in 1834 Davydov's development of the diffusion method of sugar extraction from beets. In 1852, Ivan Fomenko introduced at the Balakleya sugar mill the method of boiling massecuite for sugar crystallization, and two years later engineer M. A. Tolpygin developed the method of purifying sugar in a centrifuge by using steam and thus began what became widely known abroad as "Russian sugar washing." As Silin commented in 1958: "This advanced Russian method is now used in all sugar mills of the U.S.S.R. and was adopted by the American beet sugar industry."[2]

In 1890 Shcheniovskii and Pointkovskii created a new design for a continuous separator. In 1907 Ovsyannikov developed continuous crystallization of sugar, and in 1910 he was the first to apply continuous saturation. This work suggests, then, a respectable history of technological development in the field. However, Silin, who lists these Russian inventions and innovations, fails to list any major innovation after 1917. It is unlikely that the opportunity would have been missed had such innovation existed, as glorifications of Soviet technology are found throughout Silin. Silin's sole specific claim for more recent Soviet achievement is contained in the following sentence: "No other country can compete with the U.S.S.R. as to the volume of published scientific and technical material on sugar production."[3]

The following section examines Soviet beet sugar processes stage by stage, with particular reference to the origin of processes in use in Soviet sugar beet plants at about 1960.

COMPARATIVE TECHNOLOGY IN BEET SUGAR PLANTS

The flow diagram of a U.S. beet sugar refining plant is not unlike that of a typical Soviet plant (Figure 24-1).[4] To bring out the comparison the major stages of the refining process are examined in detail. These are:

1) beet washing equipment,
2) the cell method of diffusion,
3) predefecation,
4) thickeners,
5) filter presses,
6) evaporators,
7) centrifugals, and
8) crystallizers.

that German experiments in the extraction of sugar from beets came to their attention. See W. Keller, *Ost minus West=Null*, (Munich: Droemersche Verlagsanstalt, 1960), pp. 160-61; McGinnis, pp. 1-2; and Silin, pp. 4-5.
[2] Silin, *op. cit.* n. 1, p. 4.
[3] *Ibid.*, p. 9.
[4] See, for example, McGinnis, *op. cit.* n. 1, p. 134.

Comparison of Soviet and Western sugar beet washing units suggests that Soviet designers not only adopted Western designs but attached a name of their own to a design that differs little, if at all, from the Western progenitor. The Dobrovolskii beet washing unit with a Baranov stone catcher is identical to the Dyer beet washer and sand trap.[5] Priority of invention in this case is clearly with Western inventors and Soviet units show few variations from pre-1940 U.S. units. (See Figures 24-2 and 24-3.)

Silin's description of the Dobrovolskii unit applies equally to the operation of the Dyer unit:

> The Dobrovolskii washing unit consists of three compartments, the first of which is the most important. The beets move along a perforated false bottom placed above the floor of the washer. Dirt passing through the screen accumulates on the solid bottom from where it is periodically removed through drain hatches (a). The arms are arranged spirally, closer to each other in the first half of compartment I than in the second. The increased number of arms increases agitation, intensifies rubbing of roots against one another and hence improves washing. Since water level is high and the arms are fully submerged, the water surface over the arms remains calm. This very important feature permits the straw to float up to the surface and to be removed through an overflow drain together with the dirty water (left side of section CD). [See Figure 24-3.] Thus the washer acts as an additional trash catcher.... Compartments II and III act as stone catchers. They are fitted out with revolving paddles mounted on a shaft placed above the shaft of compartment I. The paddles rake up the beets from compartment II and send them over the partition into compartment III.[6]

Beet lifting wheels (which follow the washing units) used in the Soviet Union are almost exact replicas of the Stearns-Roger beet feeders; the only difference is in the shape of the flumes.[7]

Diffusion is the initial process by which sugar in impure form is extracted from sugar beets. Soviet cell-type diffusers are clearly of Western design, although there is a claim to indigenous research work in rotary diffusers. Priority of invention for rotary diffusers is claimed for the Soviet engineer Mandryko (1928) who, together with engineer Karapuzov, carried out extensive investigations in the 1930s "of all types" of rotary diffusers at the im. Karl Leibknecht plant.[8] Another Soviet claim is that a rotary diffuser "appearing like a prototype of the present BMA tower diffuser," was tested as early as 1928 by Professor Sokolov.[9] Silin adds that "at present" (i.e., 1960) an improved model of a Sokolov diffuser is being tested and further developed. Another vertical diffuser,

[5] *Ibid.*, p. 132.
[6] Silin, *op. cit.* n. 1, p. 100.
[7] Compare Silin, *op. cit.* n. 1, p. 96, with McGinnis, *op. cit.* n. 1, p. 129.
[8] Silin, *op. cit.* n. 1, p. 174, quoting A. S. Epishin, *Sakharnaya promyshlennost'*, no. 8 (1953), 14.
[9] Silin, *op. cit.*, n. 1, p. 174.

Figure 24-1   FLOW SHEET OF TYPICAL SOVIET BEET SUGAR PLANT

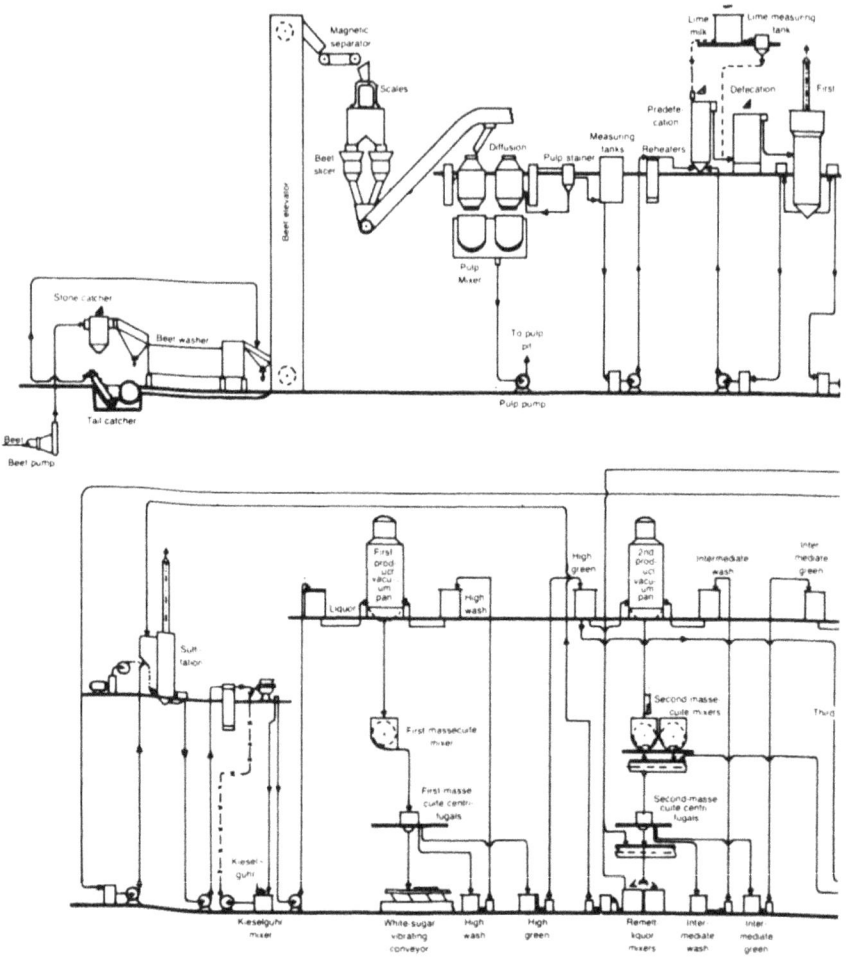

Source: P.M. Silin, *Technology of Beet-Sugar Production and Refining* (Jerusalem: Israel Program for Scientific Translations, 1964), appendix 1.

Figure 24-1 (cont.)

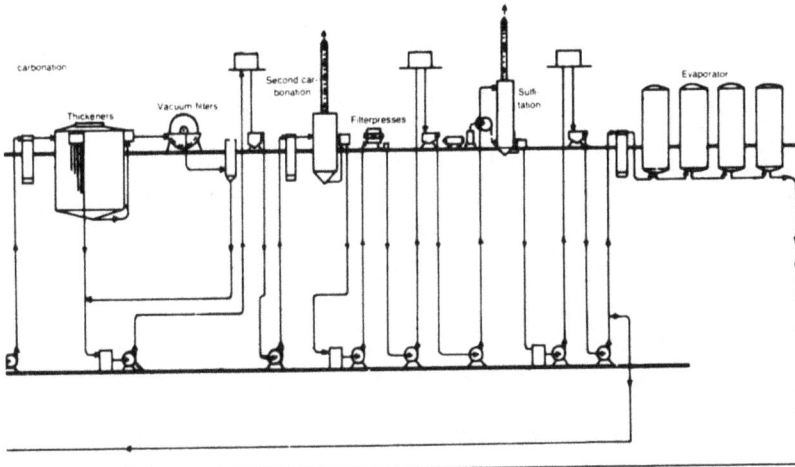

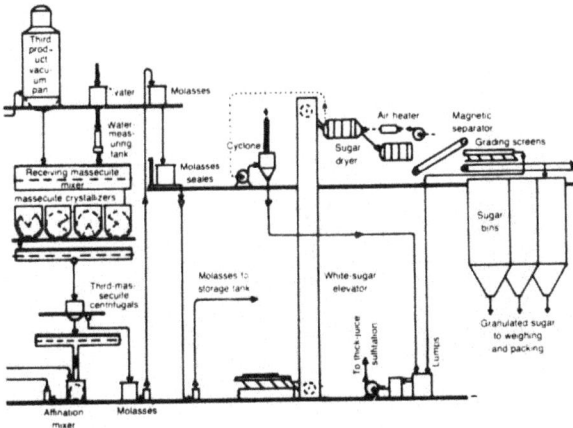

FLOWSHEET OF BEET-SUGAR PLANT

Figure 24-2

THE DYER BEET WASHER

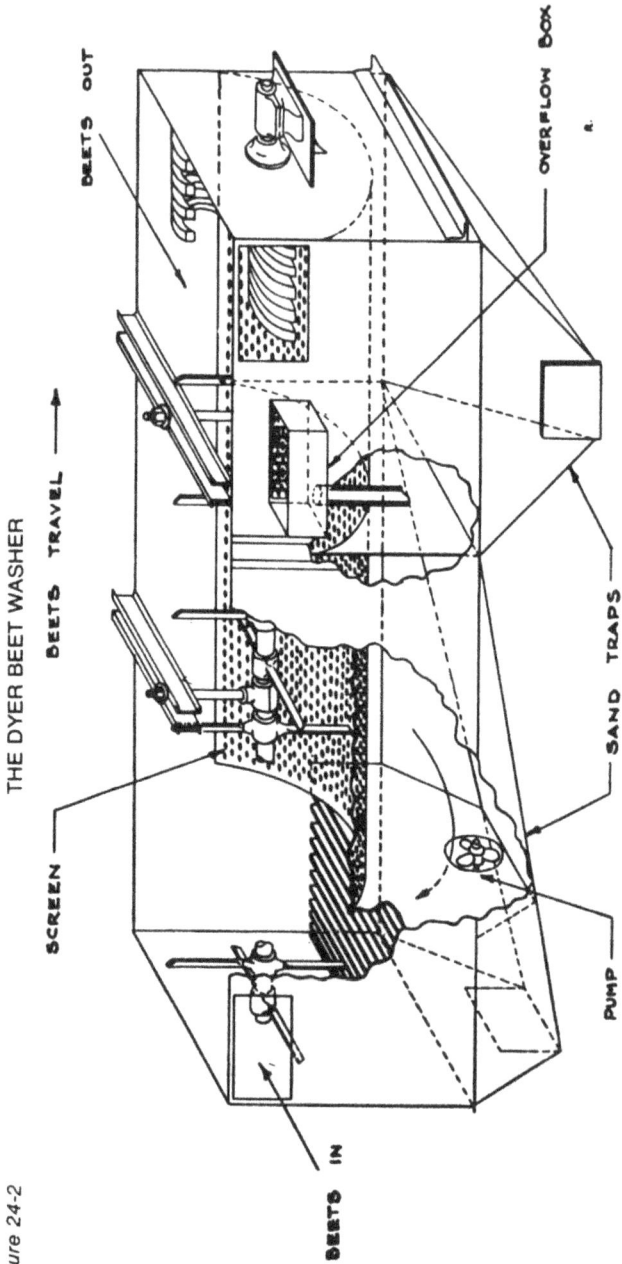

Source: R.A. McGinnis, ed., *Beet-Sugar Technology* (New York: Reinhold, 1951), p.132.

Figure 24-3   THE DOBROVOLSKII BEET WASHER UNIT

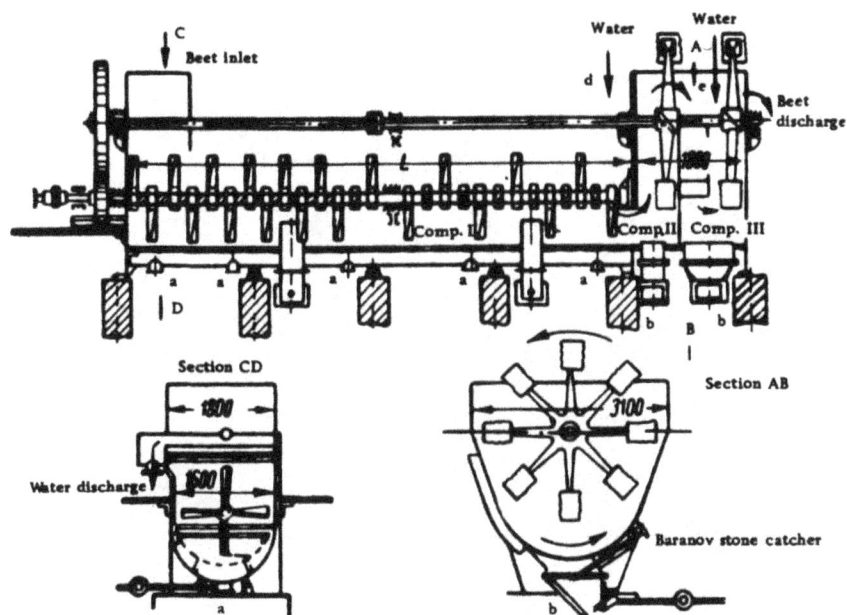

Source: Silin, p. 100.

developed by engineer Kundzhulyan,''was in operation at the Zherdevka sugar factory for a number of years.''[10]

There is no reason why these Soviet claims should not be accepted as accurate. It is probable that diffuser designs were developed and tested in Soviet factories from 1928 onward, but *what is striking is that no Soviet designs are in production or use today; neither is such a claim made.*[11] In fact the Sokolov model ''tested as early as 1928'' was still being tested in the 1960s.

The most common diffusion operation used in Soviet beet sugar factories is a duplicate of the Roberts cell. These cells are normally used in 12-cell batteries installed in two rows of six cells each. Figure 24-4 shows the cross-sectional elevation of a Robert cell, and Figure 24-5 shows the similar construction of a Soviet diffusion cell.

In the last two decades, world practice has been to utilize rotary continuous diffusers rather than cell-type diffusers and it was recently proposed to install approximately 200 continuous diffusers in the Soviet Union. The most common

[10] *Ibid.*, p. 175.
[11] *Ibid.*, p. 174.

Figure 24-4   CROSS SECTIONAL ELEVATION OF A ROBERTS CELL

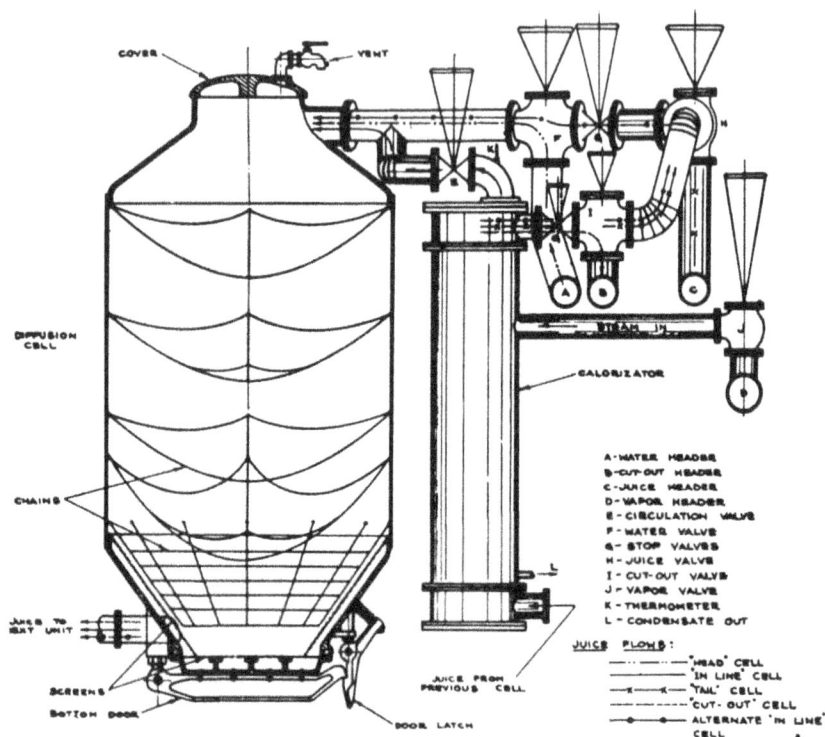

Source: McGinnis, p. 155.

type, the RT (Rotary Tirlemont), is in use in about 80 plants in the world, including ten in the Soviet Union. This process, developed by the Belgians, was first installed in the Tirlemont plant in Belgium.

Although the Soviets claim priority of invention for the rotary diffuser and also for the BMA diffuser (manufactured by Braunschweig Maschinenbau Anstalt), they appear to use rotary continuous diffusers only on an experimental basis (apart from the ten Belgium-type continuous diffusers already mentioned). It therefore appears that although work was done in the late 1920s and the 1930s on continuous diffusers, the Soviet sugar industry is today completely dependent on foreign models for this method of beet sugar extraction.

Equipment for the predefecation and first carbonation process in the Soviet Union is carried out in a vertical tank developed by the Central Scientific and Research Institute for the Sugar Industry (TsINS).[12] This is apparently of Soviet design and is widely used in Soviet sugar factories; however, Silin points

[12] *Ibid.*, p. 195.

Figure 24-5   SOVIET DIFFUSION CELL

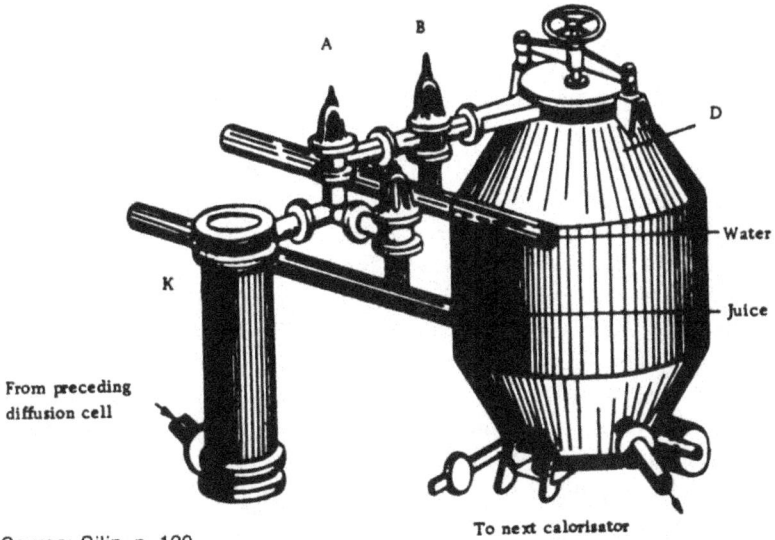

Source: Silin, p. 120.

Figure 24-6   Ts INS PREDEFECATION TANK

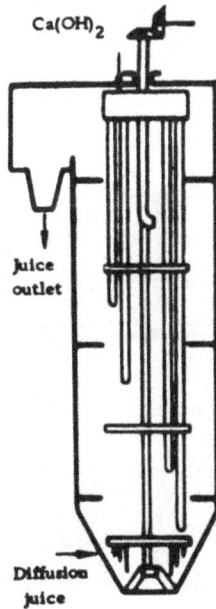

Source: Silin, p. 195.

out that foreign-made equipment, and particularly the Brieghel-Müller pre-predefecator, is easier to control and gives a more consistent alkalinity gradient. For example, he comments:

> In other predefecators, the milk of lime enters at a number of given points, creating each time a momentary excess of lime. These points tend to become centers of harmful overliming. The Brieghel-Müller apparatus is free of this defect.

It is notable (Figures 24-6 and 24-7) that the TsINS predefecation tank has the defect described and therefore by Silin's criterion would be inferior to the foreign Brieghel-Müller defecator.

As for the mud-thickening stage, Silin states that of the many types of mud thickeners available in the world, the Dorr-type multicompartment type is particularly widely used in the Soviet Union. It consists of a large cylindrical tank with a slightly conical bottom, filled with first combination juice. Four horizontal trays within the tank divide it into five compartments revolving on a central hollow shaft which carries arms acting as scrapers. Figure 24-8 illustrates the Dorr multifeed thickener while Figure 24-9 illustrates the multicompartment thickener made by the Rostov machine-building plant. Note that the Rostov thickener is an almost exact copy of the Dorr thickener unit. The only Soviet innovation claimed for this stage of refining is one by engineer Shugunov; this innovation apparently improved and speeded up the operation of the thickener by discharging the concentrated muds separately from each compartment and

Figure 24-7   BRIEGHEL-MÜLLER PREDEFECATOR

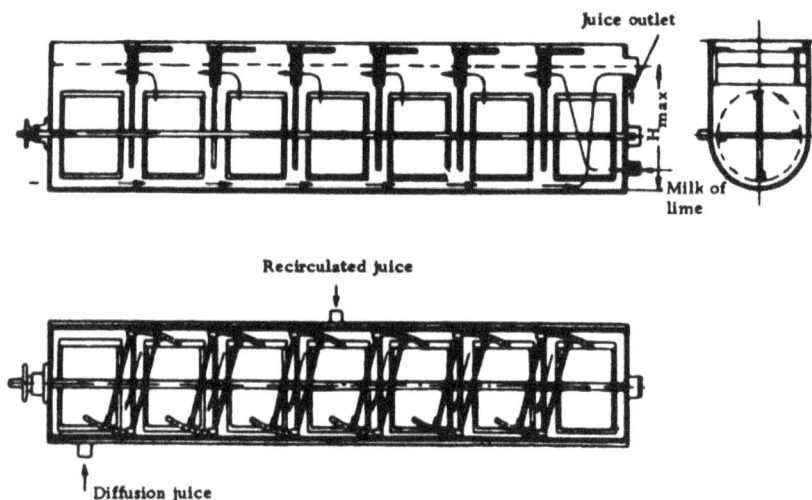

Source: Silin, p. 245.

Figure 24-8   DORR MULTIFEED THICKENER

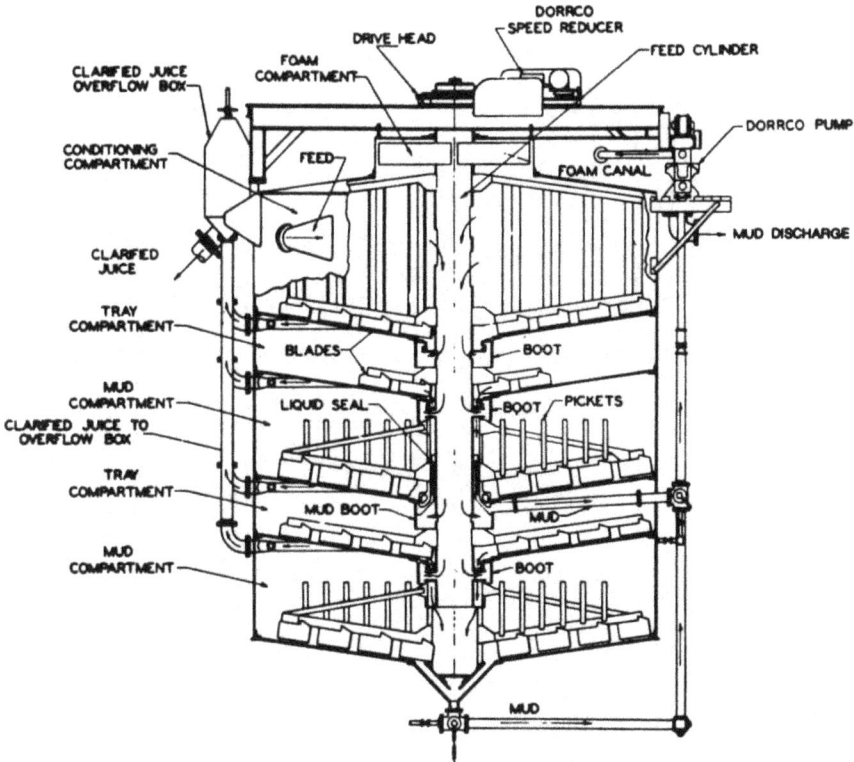

Source: McGinnis, p. 248.

by feeding each compartment with a suspension of exactly the same concentration.[13] The Dorr multifeed thickener has an arrangement similar to that claimed by Shugunov.

Filtration is required to separate the sediment from the liquid. This is done by using a filter press, and the common filter press in the Soviet Union is the Abraham type.[14] The Soviet filter press is of the standard type; i.e., the sides of the frames and the plates are fitted with lugs that support them on two guide bars. The carbonated juice with the precipitate is then pumped into the frames through ports connected with the extension holes. It is claimed that Soviet engineers, notably Gritsenko of the Kagarlyk sugar plant, have improved the operation of the Abraham filter press.

The next stage on the flow sheet is that of evaporation. The standard evaporator used in the Soviet Union is the single-pass TsINS evaporator, which

[13] *Ibid.*, p. 219.
[14] *Ibid.*, p. 211.

Figure 24-9   ROSTOV MACHINE-BUILDING PLANT
MULTICOMPARTMENT THICKENER

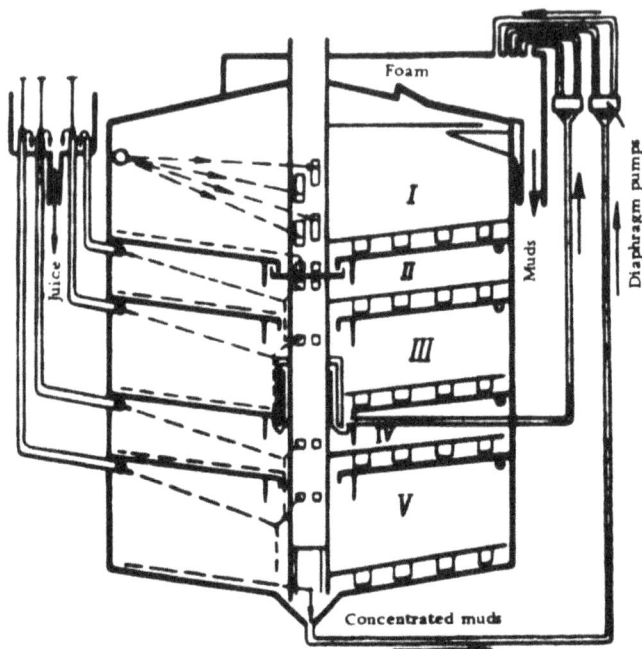

Source: Silin, p. 218.

is described by Silin as "similar to the Roberts evaporator, but [having] longer tubes."[15] Figures 24-10 and 24-11 show that the two units are of very similar construction; i.e., each is a closed cylindrical steel boiler with a steam chest at the bottom part of the boiler. In both units, vertical heating tubes are rolled into the holes of the perforated tube sheets and steam is introduced into the space between the tube sheets and so heats the vertical boiling tubes. The juice vapor rises to the top and is conducted outside the evaporator in both cases. It is quite clear that the Soviet single-pass evaporator is based on the Robert evaporator.

The production of white sugar consists in separating the sugar crystals from the mother liquor by centrifugal force. The most common type of centrifugal separator is the Weston type, which is also used in the Soviet Union.[16]

The final process in beet sugar refinement is that of crystallization, which is achieved by spinning of the second massecuite; the object of this process

---

[15] *Ibid.,* p. 274.
[16] *Ibid.,* p. 312-13.

Figure 24-10   ROBERTS-TYPE EVAPORATOR

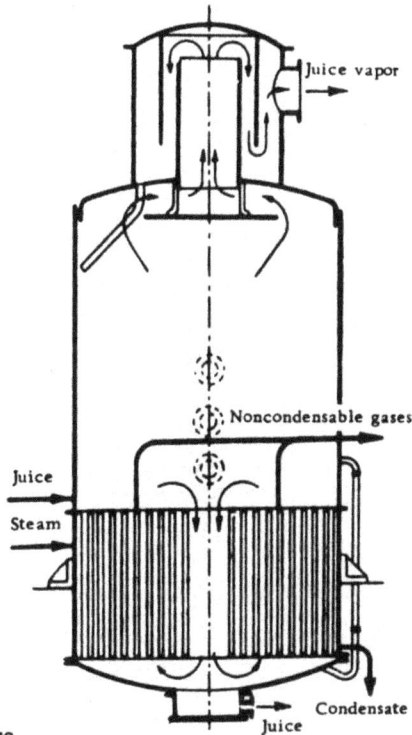

Juice vapor

Noncondensable gases

Juice

Steam

Condensate

Juice

Source: Silin, p. 273.

is to obtain the highest possible yield of sugar in the form of crystals. For crystallization, the second massecuite is mixed in a mixer crystallizer while its temperature is gradually lowered. The standard Western crystallizer is shown in Figure 24-12, and the Soviet mixer crystallizer is shown in Figure 24-13. The principle in both pieces of equipment is the same.

Thus it may be seen from comparison of individual pieces of equipment within sugar manufacturing plants in the Soviet Union with similar pieces of equipment in the West that, first, there is very little if any Soviet innovation; and second, by and large Soviet equipment more or less exactly replicates Western equipment. It is also obvious that much thought, preparation, and investigation have gone into examination of Western processes to choose the most suitable process and equipment for Soviet conditions.

Consistent with these findings concerning Soviet innovation in the beet sugar refining industry are the known major infusions of Western technical assistance and equipment for the industry. In the 1920s German firms reequipped and

Figure 24-11   SOVIET CONSTRUCTION EVAPORATOR

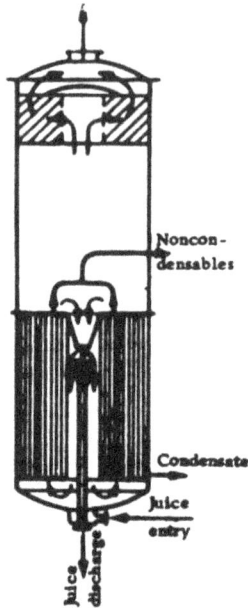

Source: Silin, p. 273.

Figure 24-12   CRYSTALLIZER BY SUGAR AND CHEMICAL MACHINERY, INC.

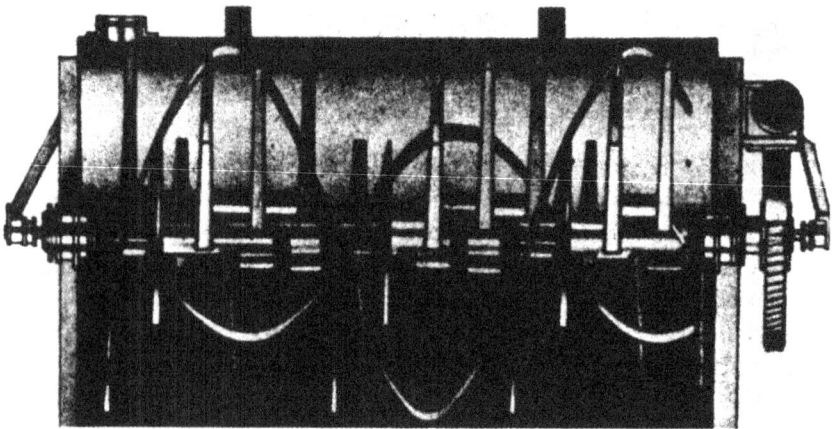

Source: McGinnis, p. 358.

Figure 24-13   SOVIET CRYSTALLIZER

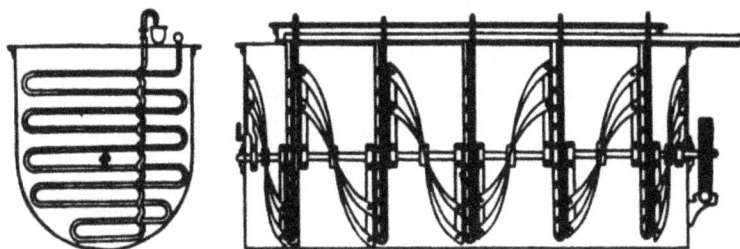

Source: Silin, p. 319.

brought back into operation the numerous Tsarist-era sugar plants.[17] This aid was supplemented in the early 1930s by technical assistance from the United States.[18] At the end of World War II a number of sugar plants were removed from Germany to the U.S.S.R., including 14 complete plants (for example, Zuckerfabrik Bach at Stöbnitz, Zuckerfabrik GmbH at Zörbig in Saxony-Anhalt, and the Vereinigte Zuckerfabriken GmbH at Malchin, Mecklenburg).[19]

In the postwar years sugar plants were built in Czechoslovakia on Soviet account—for example, two were shipped to the U.S.S.R. in 1955.[20] In the late 1950s and the 1960s extensive purchases were made in the United Kingdom and in Germany. What is more, an order for $4.2 million worth of sugar beet equipment was placed in 1959 with Booker Brothers, Ltd., McConnell & Company, and Vickers-Armstrongs (Engineers), Ltd.[21] This was followed in 1960 by an order to Vickers & Booker, Ltd., for two complete sugar plants to be located in Moscow and the Ukraine valued at $22.4 million and each capable of handling 5000 tons of sugar beet per day.[22] In 1961 Eimco (Great Britain), Ltd., supplied eight rotary vacuum filters, four five-compartment tray thickeners, and two filtration plants for $392,000.[23] Then in 1968 Vickers & Booker, Ltd., supplied a total of $23.8 million worth of beet sugar processing equipment to equip two complete plants—one of which was to be built by Vickers & Booker.

---

[17] See Sutton I, p. 235; and *Die Chemische Fabrik* (Weinheim, Ger.), I, 42 (October 17, 1928), 615.

[18] Amtorg, *Economic Review of the Soviet Union* (New York), IV, 23 (December 1, 1929), 428.

[19] G. E. Harmssen, Am Abend der Demontage; Sechs Jahre Reparationspolitik (Bremen: F. Trüjen, 1951).

[20] *Czechoslovak Economic Bulletin* (Prague), no. 293 (February 1, 1955).

[21] *East-West Commerce* (London), VI, 5 (June 4, 1959), 14.

[22] *Chemistry and Industry* (London), February 6, 1960, pp. 154-55. It is presumed that Vickers & Booker, Ltd., is a joint company formed by Booker Brothers and Vickers-Armstrongs (Engineers), Ltd.

[23] *Chemistry and Industry*, July 15, 1961, p. 1087.

WESTERN ASSISTANCE FOR FOOD-PACKING PLANTS

There has been consistent and substantial Western technical assistance for Soviet food-packing and canning operations since the 1920s. For example, in the 1930s at the Kamchatka salmon canneries it was reported,

> All the machinery "down to the nuts and bolts" was American and most of it had been made in Seattle. Makers included the Smith Cannery Machine Co. [and] the Troyer-Fox Co. (Continental Can subsidiary or affiliate), and the lighting installations had been made by Fairbanks-Morse.[25]

In the Kamchatka canneries at that time there were also about 14 Americans working in various positions to train Russians and supervise operations.[26] The American consulting engineer for the Kamchatka salmon canning industry was Alvin L. Erickson, who lived in Vladivostok for about three years in the early thirties, supervising the 15 central canneries that had been established since 1930. These were equipped with the "finest machinery and accessories": according to Erickson most were superior to the average West Coast or Alaskan cannery, " ... while some of them are in installation equal to any in the world."[27] Two of the canneries had been equipped with the latest vacuum-type machinery, each with four lines and a maximum capacity of 9000 cases per day. The industry also acquired 20 modern trawlers which were in charge of an English superintendent, and some German engineers were employed in installing new equipment.[28]

An even more comprehensive food processing contract was that received by the Chicago Kitchen Company, which supplied six architects for six months to design the Soviet community kitchens. This group prepared the detailed plans for 11 model community kitchens which were then duplicated by the Soviets.[29]

In the 1950s and 1960s the purchases of complete plants continued. It was reported in 1957, for example, that

> Mather & Platt, Ltd., Manchester, holds two contracts for the U.S.S.R. including canning lines for fresh peas and also canning lines to handle both fresh peas and runner beans. All these lines are complete, i.e., they start with viners, into

---

[24] *Wall Street Journal*, March 30, 1967, 20:6.

[25] U.S. State Dept. Decimal File 861.5017/Living Conditions/709, Report no. 689. See also /589 and 861.7186/1, Tokyo, August 31, 1933. The State Department in Washington made the notation, "The memorandum is not of great interest."

[26] U.S. State Dept. Decimal File 861.5017/Living Conditions/709.

[27] U.S. State Dept. Decimal File 861.5017/Living Conditions/701.

[28] *Ibid.*

[29] U.S. State Dept. Decimal File 861.5017/Living Conditions/371. This group had the rare privilege of working in OGPU installations.

which the complete peas plant is fed, and finish with packaging machinery which labels the cans, packs the required number into a case, and then seals the flaps of the case.[30]

A year later Yugoslavia concluded contracts with the U.S.S.R. to provide seven processing plants to manufacture tomato puree, the contract being valued at $440,000.[31] This continued an earlier contract for 12 complete tomato puree processing plants and was subsequently followed by a contract for yet another nine plants valued at $770,000.[32] It would not be unreasonable to suppose that Yugoslavia and Italy have provided the greater part of the Soviet tomato puree manufacturing capacity.

In 1967 the Italian firm of Carle & Montanari of Milan supplied equipment for a plant to be erected at Kuibyshev for the manufacture of 80 to 100 tons per day of chocolate and powdered cocoa, packed and ready for sale. The contract was valued at $10 million.[33] In the same year another Italian firm, S.p.a. Tecmo (Tecnica Moderna) signed a contract valued at $6.4 million to build and equip a plant at Stupino to produce cardboard packaging; the plant's capacity was to be 60,000 tons per year of containers for use in automatic food packing lines.[34]

However foreign assistance apparently is not always utilized industry-wide after it is attained. For example, the 1963 U.S. dairy delegation visited milk and dairy products processing plants, and one observer noted:

Based on about 27 years of milk plant experience in this country [i.e., the United States], I must say that [the Soviets'] processing equipment, in terms of bottle washers, holding tanks, clarifiers, pasteurizers, final bottling, and capping equipment, are many years behind that which we are permitted to use in this country.[35]

Considering that ten years earlier, in 1954, the Soviet Union purchased from U.D. Engineering Co., Ltd. (a United Kingdom firm and a subsidiary of the dairy chain United Dairies, Ltd.) milk bottling and processing equipment to a total of $3 million, the conditions encountered in 1963 by the U.S. dairy delegation are somewhat surprising.[36]

[30] *East-West Commerce*, IV, 4 (April 3, 1957), 11.
[31] *East-West Commerce*, V, 1, (January 3, 1958), 13.
[32] *Ibid*.
[33] Communication from Embassy of Italy, Washington, D.C.
[34] *Wall Street Journal*, November 14, 1967, 12:4.
[35] Unpublished report by George D. Scott, vice president of Ex-Cell-O Corp.: "Dairy Exchange Delegation to Russia, July 7, 1963-August 2, 1963"; typescript supplied by Dairy Society International, Washington, D.C. The delegation interpreter had the following parting words for Mr. Scott at the Moscow airport; "Mr. Scott, now that you have personally visited several of our great cities in the Soviet Union, and have learned the *truth*, I hope when you return to America, you will try to incite your people to a revolution against the tyranny of your capitalistic system." Report, p. 13.
[36] *The Times* (London), March 24, 1954, p. 4d. For further information see, V. P. Prityko and V. G. Lungren, *Mashiny i apparaty molochnoi promyshlennosti* (Moscow, 1968).

THE WEARING APPAREL INDUSTRY IN 1960

In the early 1960s the clothing industry of the Soviet Union, according to well-qualified U.S. observers, was very backward. In fact it might be concluded from reports of these observers that in terms of organization, methods, and equipment the industry had not advanced very much from Tsarist times.

In mid-1963 the United States sent a garment industry exchange group to the Soviet Union, and the report made by one member of that delegation, Alexander Lerner, President of Phoenix Clothes, Inc., of New York, is a perceptive account through the eyes of an expert observer.[37] After the delegation had visited several clothing factories, Lerner's general conclusion was:

> The production equipment, in my estimation, is very antiquated ... they are very backward in their supervision and pressing equipment. In their handling of production, they are as far back as 30 to 50 years.... [38]

The report then elaborates and supports this summary statement on a plant-by-plant basis. The delegation toured the Central Scientific Research Institute of the Sewing Industries and viewed films of new equipment in operation in the various factories. These films, however, did not show machines at work, and Lerner comments:

> After all this information was given to us, I was very anxious to see some of these machines in operation. We saw some of them at the different factories, but they did not accomplish in action what [I anticipated from what] I saw in the films. Many of the machines [shown in the films] I did not see at all.[39]

Similarly, the Indian Textile Delegation noted that although a great deal of development work was apparently under way in the research institutes they did not see models or systems actually in operation.[40]

The first factory visited by the American group was No. 16 in Moscow, founded before the Revolution. One of the Institute machines viewed was for pressing cuffs and collars by a hot-iron method using a spray of water and no steam—a method described in the report as "very obsolete." At this factory the sewing machinery as a whole was 20 to 40 years old, with perhaps 10 percent of it less than five years old. The second factory visited was No. 2 in Moscow, manufacturing men's suits and slacks. About 80 percent of the machinery here was 30 to 40 years old and the balance, less than five years

---

[37] Acknowledgement is due Mr. Alexander Lerner for his courtesy in making a copy of his report available. The complete report has been deposited in the Hoover Institution Archives.
[38] Lerner report, p. 1.
[39] Ibid., p. 3.
[40] Textile Industry in U.S.S.R. and Czechoslovakia, Report of Indian Productivity Team (New Delhi: National Productivity Council, November 1962), Report no. 19, pp. 42-43.

old, of Russian, German, and Hungarian manufacture. There was no steam pressing because "they had no way of making steam." The plant operated on a straight-line system:

> We visited their cutting rooms and [were] astounded to see their manner of cutting. They were using two-, three-, and four-suit markers.... Also, even though this wasn't heavy fabrics, they were only laying it up 14 double spread and less. They had a tremendous amount of cutters and spreaders for this operation. There were three spreaders to each table.

Lerner then mentions the low quality of Soviet clothes:

> I see now why the clothing is being delivered so badly [in] quality of workmanship. It is simply atrocious. Where they could use automation, they are using the most obsolete methods. I have been in the clothing business for over 35 years and I have never seen such pressing and finishing of garments.[41]

The next plant visited—the Kishinev—was more modern, an improvement over the Moscow plants with only 65 percent "antiquated" equipment and 35 percent less than five years old. The methods were better; while two-, three-, and four-suit markers were still in use, the cutting heights were greater—30 high, and slacks 50 layers high—and there were two, not three, spreaders per table. The Smitrnov-Lastochkin plant in Kiev had antiquated machinery—about 80 percent old and 20 percent more recent machines. The Ukraine factory, also in Kiev, had similar equipment and methods. Finally, the Volodarsky clothing factory in Leningrad was visited, and the systems, machines, and methods there were found to be similar to those of the plants previously toured.

On its return to Moscow for a promised look at the equipment making machines for clothing plants, the delegation was informed that the plant was closed. A visit to a Moscow woolen mill was substituted. This plant was over 100 years old but its machinery was installed after 1917; up to the mid-1950s it had used all American equipment; some of its more recent machines had been built in Tashkent. The delegation reported: "The looms are 10 years old and all German-made. They have ordered 50 percent of their new looms from Sweden."[42]

On the basis of this report by skilled observers it may be concluded that not only was the Soviet wearing apparel industry backward in 1961; it was heavily dependent for its current production on imported equipment.

The manufacture of boots and shoes is a consumer sector for which the Soviets apparently have been unable even to reproduce Western manufacturing equipment. In 1928 the Lenin shoe factory was equipped with foreign machines[43]

[41] *Ibid.,* p. 7.
[42] *Ibid.,* p. 18.
[43] Amtorg, *Economic Review of the Soviet Union* III, 6 (March 15, 1928), 104.

that had been supplied in addition to the concession arrangements previously described.[44] In the early 1930s foreigners apparently acted as supervisors of such plants. For example, in 1932 Max Korr, an American, was under a 300-rubles-per-month contract as superintendent of a shoe factory in Grozny making boots for the Red Army.[45]

More recently, in 1968, 20 complete shoe production lines for plants in Leningrad, Moscow, and Kiev were purchased for $5.6 million from British United Shoe Machinery Company of London (a subsidiary of United Shoe Machinery Corporation of the United States). This order included 2100 machines to produce shoes by the cemented-sole process, and the equipment was installed by British engineers.[46]

In addition, large orders for shoes have been placed abroad. In January 1967 the Lotus Company of the United Kingdom received an order for $2.8 million worth of men's and women's shoes;[47] a few weeks later the Cooperative Wholesale Society reported the largest single order it had ever received from the U.S.S.R.—80,000 pairs of women's shoes, which was 50 percent more than the previous year's order.[48] The British Shoe Corporation also announced a $490,000 order for 100,000 pairs of women's shoes.[49] Simultaneously, Japanese firms sold to the U.S.S.R. 1.2 million square feet of "Clarino"—a Japanese-developed "breathing synthetic material."[50]

[44] See Sutton I, p. 231.
[45] U.S. State Dept. Decimal File 861.5017/Living Conditions/505.
[46] *Wall Street Journal*, March 12, 1968, 27:5.
[47] *The Times* (London), January 8, 1967.
[48] *The Times* (London), January 20, 1967.
[49] *Ibid.*
[50] *The Times* (London), January 11, 1967.

PART III

Implications and Conclusions
of the Study

CHAPTER TWENTY-FIVE

Innovation in the Soviet Union

The purpose of this chapter is to summarize verifiable Soviet innovation and to determine the degree of indigenous innovation that has taken place in the Soviet Union relative to the import of foreign innovation. Hopefully this summary will throw some light on the organic capability of the Soviet society to innovate. We may first usefully sum up the innovations found to be truly of Soviet origin.

The first volume of this series isolated several unsuccessful attempts by the Soviets to develop their own technologies. Tractor production in the mid-1920s provides an excellent example.[1] Although these attempts failed, there is no question that considerable effort and resources were placed behind such innovative experiments.

In the period covered by the second volume,[2] the years 1930 to 1945, rather surprisingly we do not find continuation of early efforts; rather we see an abandonment of domestic innovation, but not of basic research effort, and the substitution of wholehearted adoption of foreign techniques. This policy led to the widespread practice of copying and duplication, so that by 1945 Soviet industry was a more or less haphazard copy of Western, predominantly American, technology. The major exceptions to this rule were to be found in Ramzin's "once-through" boiler (which, however, had been abandoned by 1945), the turbodrill, and several machine gun and weapons designs. The weapons designs originated with copies of Western guns, but by 1945 the Soviet stress on the military sector had provided some indigenous Soviet military capability—although Soviet technology was still woefully backward in areas such as fire control and radar. The U.S.S.R. was able to concentrate effort in this field by virtue of free import of Western advances in the general industrial sectors, thus releasing scarce design and engineering talent resources for military work.

In the period covered by this volume (1945-65) we find several groups of indigenous innovations, although obviously the hypothesis that there has been an absence of self-generated innovation is generally supported.

Two questions now arise: what is the nature of these groups of indigenous

---

[1] See Sutton I, pp. 133-35.
[2] Sutton II.

Soviet innovation? Why have they appeared in only a few fields, and not generally throughout the industrial structure?

SOVIET INVENTION IN THE WORLD MARKET

Table 25-1 contains a list (from an official Soviet source) of *all* Soviet foreign licensing agreements in force at January 1967.

Table 25-1   COMPLETE LISTING OF SOVIET PATENT
AND LICENSE AGREEMENTS IN FORCE OUTSIDE
THE U.S.S.R. AS OF JANUARY 1967

Country	Number of Agreements	Description of Soviet Invention Transferred
United States	17	16 agreements for suture instruments
		1 agreement for procedures for producing liquid cores and mold mixtures
Canada	1	Prosthesis of the forearm with bioelectrical control
United Kingdom	3	Computing device for calculating the number of sheets in a stack of paper (sheet counting machine)
		Prosthesis of the forearm with bioelectrical control
		Machine for wire cell bundling at iron and steel plants
Denmark	1	Liquid core and mold mixtures; procedure for producing cores and molds thereof
Italy	5	Universal system of industrial pneumoautomatic elements
		Optimalizing pneumatic controller
		Liquid core and mold mixtures; procedure for producing cores and molds thereof
		Electrodes for arc welding and building up of gray and high-strength cast iron
		Mill for cold rolling of tubes
Norway	1	Liquid core and mold mixtures; procedure for producing cores and molds thereof
France	18	Continuous steel casting plant
		Electro-pulse machine tool for processing to size of conducting materials, model 4733
		Device for automatic control of electrode rod gap
		Device for automatic selection and adjustment of optimal electrode rod gap, model 3P
		Rotary unipolar pulse generators
		High-frequency unipolar pulse generator
		Carbon-graphite material for measuring electrodes, grade
		Machine tool for processing shaped articles made of graphite-containing materials, measuring electrodes predominantly, model MA-459

Table 25-1 (cont.)

Country	Number of Agreements	Description of Soviet Invention Transferred
		Method for electroslag welding and metal buildup and the device for carrying out the above method (apparatus A-372 and A-501)
		Liquid core and mold mixtures; procedures for producing cores and molds thereof
		Method of producing the drug Luteneurin
		Universal system of industrial pneumoautomatic elements
		Optimalizing pneumatic controller
		Evaporative cooling plant for open hearth and heating furnaces
		Powder-cored wires
		Laminated material for resistors and high-precision potentiometer
		Electroslag remelting of metals and alloys in water-cooled mold and equipment for its realization
		Method of continuous neutralization of grease and oil in soap-alkaline medium
Federal Republic of Germany	5	Electrodes for arc welding and surfacing of gray and high-strength iron
		Powder wires agreements for 3 turbodrills
Switzerland	1	Method of dimecarbine production
Sweden	3	Method for electroslag welding and metal build-up and the device for carrying out the above method (apparatus A-372 and A-501)
		Liquid core and mold mixtures; procedure for producing cores and molds thereof
		Method for production of hydrogen peroxide with concentration up to 45 percent by weight
Japan	6	Continuous steel casting plant
		Method for preparation of fine-granulated components for the manufacture of the artificial building material silicalcite
		Electrodes for cold welding and buildup welding of gray iron
		Electroslag remelting of metals and alloys in water-cooled mold and equipment for its realization
		Digger shield for tunneling in weak ground, 3.6-meter diameter
		Mechanized composite mining units (Tula for complete mechanization of coal mining operations)

Source: Letter from Litsenzintorg (Licensintorg), Moscow, February 18, 1967.

In brief, this listing presents the sum total of Soviet invention that had the proven potential of competing in the world technical marketplace as of January 1967. It is not a list of adopted invention, i.e., innovation, but only of that Soviet invention which had possibilities of commercial adoption in the face of competing world technical developments. It is therefore an accurate comparative guide to the originality of Soviet invention, particularly as Party injunctions have been to sell Soviet technology abroad wherever possible. Table 25-2 summarizes the information contained in Table 25-1 on a country-by-country basis and indicates the degree of duplication of licensing agreements and the narrowness of the technical areas covered.

Table 25-2   SUMMARY OF SOVIET FOREIGN LICENSING AGREEMENTS AS OF 1967

Country	Number of agreements	Technologies			
		Suture instruments and apparatus	Liquid cores and molds	Welding techniques	Other
United Kingdom	3	—	1	—	2
Denmark	1	—	1	—	0
Italy	5	—	1	1	3
Canada	2	1	—	—	1
Norway	1	—	1	—	0
U.S.A.	17	16	1	—	0
France	18	0	2	4	12
F.R.G.	5	—	—	1	4
Switzerland	1	—	—	—	1
Sweden	3	—	1	1	1
Japan	6	—	—	2	4
	62	17	8	9	28

Source: Derived from Table 25-1.

The country having the largest number of agreements was France, with 18. The United States was second with 17, and of these 17, 16 were with U.S. Surgical, Inc., for suture instruments and one was for a core and mold mixture process with Heppenstal.[3]

As we have pointed out, these 62 licensing agreements constitute Soviet inventions that had potential on the world market at 1967. They do not constitute innovations, as the existence of a licensing agreement does not necessarily imply a technology's application in practice. Apart from the small number of such licensing agreements, analysis discloses some rather remarkable features. Of the 62 total, 17 were for medical suture instruments (there are duplicates, as

[3] Examination of Soviet technico-economic literature suggests there was a remarkable lack of substantive innovation—or even invention—in the late 1960s. See, for example, the numerous reports in the monthly Biulletin' tekhnikoekonomicheskoi informatsii (Moscow), and various appeals in Pravda for a higher technical level of invention and innovation. Pure scientific discovery was somewhat more satisfactory but hardly reflected the proportion of Soviet resources it absorbed.

the same machine may be licensed to more than one country) and another nine licenses were in the field of welding metals. Thus more than one-third of the agreements related to the extremely narrow and specialized aims of joining together either human tissue or metals. The next largest category is licensing in seven countries of a process for producing liquid core and mold mixtures.

In sum, a close look at these 62 licensing agreements reveals a remarkable paucity of Soviet invention to compete with the hundreds of thousands of processes licensed on the world market.

INDIGENOUS INNOVATION IN WEAPONS TECHNOLOGY

Soviet innovation presents a paradox: an extraordinary lack of effective indigenous innovation in industrial sectors is offset—so far as can be determined within the limits of open information—by effective innovation in the weapons sectors, although some weapons development is akin to "scaling-up" innovation (see pp. 362-64).

As far back as the 1930s some indigenous innovation was achieved in such weapons as machine guns and tanks.[4] Such development has become much more noticeable in recent years. A recent weapons innovation in which Russian engineers appear to have conquered a problem unsolved in the U.S. Navy is that of ship-borne radar. Although the U.S. Navy has done a great deal of work in radar control of ship-launched or shore-launched missiles, it remained for the Soviet Styx missile, in the fall of 1967, to sink the Israeli destroyer *Elath* at a distance of more than 12 miles with three shots, thus demonstrating dramatically the effectiveness of a radar-guided surface-launched anti-ship missile. The U.S. Navy had abandoned research because ship-borne radar in such a missile must lock onto a target ship and deliver guidance commands; these commands tend to be swamped by "sea clutter," i.e., spurious signals reflected from the water when radar operates at a flat angle. Obviously, Russian technicians were able to overcome the problem.[5]

We may deduce from this and similar examples that weapons innovation can be successfully achieved by a centralized bureaucracy. This is because weapons innovation is predicated upon well-defined objectives. Military planners, unlike economic planners, can estimate fairly accurately what the next technological stage will be for a given weapon and can define a technical objective for that weapon in clear terms. Work toward such a preordained objective can proceed along well-established lines. Moreover, military technology developed toward a specific objective can be pretested to determine whether it fulfills its objective.

[4] See Sutton II, pp. 240-45.
[5] *Business Week.* November 29, 1969, p. 32.

By contrast, economic innovation has no such clearcut technical objectives, and it does not lend itself to such pretesting. Effective innovation in industrial sectors results from the positive interaction of a myriad of complex forces; it can be realistically tested only in a market situation wherein the market itself determines its success or failure. Soviet central planning cannot anticipate key variables because it lacks the information network of a free market. Moreover the system provides little incentive to explore the unknown: central planning necessarily places its emphasis on known technology, not on revolutionary technology. Therefore innovation in the nonmilitary sectors is likely to be imported from market economies.

Thus the Soviets can achieve adequate weapons innovation—given the existence of a reasonably effective back-up industrial structure—while failing miserably in the economic area of industrial innovation.

Western creation of a viable Soviet industrial structure is therefore also a Western guarantee of a viable Soviet weapons system. This Western economic support ensures that weapons systems may be developed and brought into production because the output of the industrial sector is the input of the military sector, which, unlike the industrial sector, has a proved capacity for self-generated innovation.

SCALING-UP INNOVATION

Review and analysis of Soviet technical achievements outside those offered for export and weapons systems leads to the conclusion that many such other achievements are better described as technical progress attained by means of scaling up Western technologies. This conclusion may be best explained by considering in broad outline the categories in which the Soviets have made indigenous achievements and the relationships between these superficially dissimilar technologies.

Soviet indigenous technical progress is concentrated in three industrial sectors: iron- and steelmaking (but not steel rolling), electricity generation and high-voltage transmission, and rocket technology. It may be noteworthy that each of these three technologies was at one time or another pushed by dominant party personalities: Stalin, as his name implies, favored the iron and steel industry; Lenin of course was the force for the electrification of Russia; and Khrushchev was a force behind the development of rocket and space technology.

Soviet work on blast furnaces has been toward the development of larger volume furnaces and the application of new techniques to the classic process. In open-hearth steelmaking the lines of technical progress are somewhat more complex. In the words of one commentator: "Many things have contributed to the good results obtained by the Soviets on their open hearths, but I feel that the hot-metal spout and the basic roof setup are unique, and probably very important."[6]

Soviet advances in electricity generation have impressed many observers. In 1960 a subcommittee of the U.S. Senate noted that the Soviet power program produced the largest hydroelectric stations in the world—yielding the greatest amounts of electricity from the largest generators connected by the longest transmission lines operating at the highest voltage.[7] It was also noted that while in 1960 the heaviest U.S. transmission lines were 345 kv, the Russians then operated 400-kv lines. These were being stepped up to 500 kv and plans called for use of alternating-current transmission up to 1000 kv and direct-current transmission at 800 kv. The subcommittee concluded:

> It is to the Russians' credit that, building on the experience in technology acquired, they have now caught up with the rest of the world in the general field of hydroelectric development. In fact they are actually pre-eminent in certain specific aspects of such development.[8]

In point of fact, this Senate assessment was somewhat overstated. It was based on only a few observations, in themselves accurate but not sufficiently extensive to warrant the broad conclusions reached.

In rocket technology the Soviets first absorbed the German technology and then, after about 1960, went ahead on their own with more powerful rockets, in effect a scaling up of the original German rockets.

There is a common denominator in each of these seemingly unrelated industrial sectors where the Soviets have made indigenous advance. In each case the Soviets started with a basic Western technology—indeed a classic technology—that was well established and had a strong technical literature. The blast furnace dates from the eighteenth century, and the open-hearth furnace from the nineteenth century. In electricity generation the Soviets adopted the Kaplan and Francis runner systems, and of course long-distance electricity transmission was started in the 1920s. In rockets the Russians have a strong historical interest, but in practical technology they started with the relatively advanced German technology of World War II, and above all they had the reliability trial data from 5700 German tests.

Therefore the essence of each case in which the Soviets have made indigenous advance is that they first acquired and mastered a known and classic technology. In each case the considerable power of the Communist Party chose the industrial

---

[6] K. C. McCutcheon, "Open Hearth Shops of the U.S.S.R." *Journal of Metals* (New York), November 1958, p. 725.

[7] U.S. Senate, Committees on Insular Affairs and Public Works, *Relative Water and Power Resource Development in the U.S.S.R. and the U.S.A.*, Report and Staff Studies, 86th Congress, 2d session (Washington, 1960), p. 2.

[8] *Ibid.*, p. 1.

sector for allocation of resources, and indigenous technical progress in each case has been in effect a logical scaling up of an original classic Western technology.[9]

In each case the process technology has a precise technical framework and is capable of expansion in size. For example, in blast furnaces Soviet designers concentrated on increase in cubic volume or on specific developments, such as high top pressure, to increase output from a given volume. The same applies to open-hearth steel furnaces, which at a very early date the Soviets expanded in size to 500 square meters. In electrical generators we find the Soviet effort concentrated on an increase in generation capacity, and in transmission lines we find effort concentrated on increase in voltage transmitted.

Not all Soviet scaling-up efforts are so logically conceived as those cited above. Sometimes they are neither technically nor economically practical; sometimes size for its own sake seems to be the desired goal. For example, Moscow has the tallest television tower in the world. With a full height of 1722 feet this structure comprises a prestressed concrete base 1260 feet high topped by a 462-foot antenna. Conic in profile, it is 196 feet in diameter at the base tapering to 26.5 feet at the top. Construction, which took ten years, was interrupted by a debate as to whether high winds would induce oscillations that would create a safety hazard. The tower is designed to withstand winds of 141 mph, although winds of that velocity occur only about once in 50 years in Moscow. In such a wind the tower will oscillate 32.8 to 36 feet, while it is designed for oscillations up to 42.6 feet.[10] What is the end result of this project? The tower increases television range in Moscow from 30 to 50 miles; hence the incremental benefit is an increase of 20 miles in range, a benefit that hardly seems to justify the costs and risks of the effort. On the other hand, Moscow *does* have the tallest TV tower in the world.

In a similar vein, at a 1960 chemical exhibition in Europe the Soviets introduced "what must have been the largest model of a chemical plant ever to appear at a European exhibition."[11] There was nothing novel about the plant itself; the model represented a well-established process for making synthetic rubber. But it was the largest model, and that constituted its novelty.

In each of the cases cited as representative of productive indigenous advance, there was an expansion in quantitative terms of a known classic technology. Consequently much Soviet advance actually falls within the category of technical progress acquired by the application of engineering and experimental resources to a given known technology. It is not innovation in the sense that innovation establishes new and formerly unknown technological horizons.

---

[9] "Scaling-up" innovation based on Western processes may be found in other sectors, e.g., in sulfuric acid production (1000-ton-per-day contact systems) and coke-oven batteries.
[10] *Engineering News-Record* (New York), December 1, 1966, p. 33.
[11] *British Chemical Engineering* (London), December 1960, p. 868.

AN OVERVIEW OF TECHNOLOGICAL ORIGINS

We may conclude with empirical justification that Soviet indigenous industrial innovation is limited to two types: (a) scaling up, and (b) the miscellaneous category exemplified by the suture, welding, and minor industrial applications licensed for world marketing in 1967 (see Table 25-1).

Obviously, so far as the Soviet economy is concerned, the more important of these types is scaling-up innovation, whereby the Soviets take a classic Western process and proceed by dint of investment, research, and development work to increase the size or capacity of the productive unit. The results of such technical scaling up may or may not meet the test of the Western marketplace; there is no recorded case of its export to the West. Only the second category has led to attempts to export to the West. The returns from these exports are infinitesimal compared with the resources and talent available within the Soviet Union.

It now remains to bring together the overall picture from 1917 to 1965. Table 25-3 identifies origins for technology in 14 major Soviet industrial sectors in each of the periods examined in the three volumes of this study. Where Soviet innovation is the main process in use, it is noted in capitalized italics. Table 25-3 then, is a final summary of the conclusions from the empirical examination of technology in the U.S.S.R. over the course of 50 years.

Of necessity it is a broad examination. There are indeed many thousands of industrial processes; Table 25-3 includes only the most important and, for purposes of further illustration, a select number of lesser importance. There is no question, for example, that drilling technology is fundamental to oil production or that pig iron production is fundamental to iron and steel production; however, of necessity, numerous less important processes for each industry are omitted.

Table 25-3   AN OVERVIEW OF TECHNOLOGICAL ORIGINS OF
MAIN SOVIET INDUSTRIAL PROCESSES
FROM 1917 TO 1965

No.	Industrial Process	1917-1930	1930-1945	1945-1965
	MINING			
1.	Underground equipment	German	U.S./ German	U.S./U.K./ German
2.	Excavation equipment	German U.S./U.K.	U.S.	U.S./U.K./ German
3.	Crushers	U.S.	U.S.	U.S.
4.	Ore beneficiation	—	U.S./ Swedish	U.S./German/ French
5.	Sintering	—	U.S.	U.S.
	OIL INDUSTRY			
6	Drilling	U.S.	*SOVIET*	*SOVIET*

Table 25-3 (cont.)

No.	Industrial Process	1917-1930	1930-1945	1945-1965
7	Pumping	U.S.	U.S.	U.S.
8.	Pipelines: pipe	U.S./ German	U.S.	German/ Japanese
9.	Piplines: compressors	U.S./U.K.	U.S.	U.S./Swiss
10.	Refining and cracking	U.S./ German/U.K.	U.S.	U.S./French/ German/ Czechoslovak

FERROUS METALLURGY

No.	Industrial Process	1917-1930	1930-1945	1945-1965
11.	Pig iron	Classic blast furnace	Scaling-up	*SOVIET*/U.S./ German
12.	Steelmaking	Classic open hearth	Scaling-up	Austrian/ *SOVIET*
13.	Steel rolling: blooming	U.S./ German	U.S./ German	U.S./ German
14.	Steel rolling: wide sheets	U.S.	U.S.	U.S.
15.	Steel rolling: tubes	U.S./ German	U.S./	U.S.
16.	Continuous casting	U.S./ German	U.S./ German	German/ *SOVIET*

NONFERROUS METALLURGY

No.	Industrial Process	1917-1930	1930-1945	1945-1965
17.	Nickel smelting and refining	—	Canadian	Canadian/Norwegian
18.	Aluminum smelting and refining	German/ U.S.	U.S./*SOVIET*	*SOVIET*/U.S./ Czechoslovak
19.	Copper smelting and refining	U.S.	U.S.	U.S.

CHEMICAL INDUSTRIES

No.	Industrial Process	1917-1930	1930-1945	1945-1965
20.	Basic acids	U.S./German/ Italian	U.S. German	U.K.
21.	Basic alkalis	Tsarist/ U.S.	U.S./German/ U.K./Tsarist/ Swedish	U.S./German
22.	Fertilizers	Swedish/U.S./ German	Swedish	U.S./Belgian/ Dutch/Italian/ U.K./Japanese
23.	Synthetic fiber intermediates	French	French German	U.K./German/ U.S.
24.	Agricultural pesticides	—	—	U.K.
25.	Synthetic rubber	Tsarist	*SOVIET*	German/ U.S./U.K.
26.	Rubber tires	U.S./ German	U.S./U.K.	U.S./U.K. Italian
27.	Glass	U.S./ German	Belgian/ U.S.	U.K.

Table 25-3 (cont.)

No.	Industrial Process	1917-1930	1930-1945	1945-1965
28.	Cement mills	Danish/ German	Danish/ German	Danish/French German
29.	Coke byproducts	Tsarist	U.S./German	Scaling-up
30.	Pharmaceuticals	German	German/U.S.	U.S./Austrian
	MACHINE BUILDING			
31.	General technical assistance	German/U.K.	U.S./German	(None)
32.	Machine tools	German/U.S.	U.S./German/ U.K.	U.S./German
33.	Ball bearings	Swedish/Italian/ German	Italian/U.S.	U.S./Italian
34.	Instrumentation	U.S./German	U.S./German	U.S./German
	ELECTRICAL EQUIPMENT			
35.	General technical assistance	U.S./German/ U.K./German	U.S./U.K./	(None)
36.	Heavy electrical equipment	U.S./U.K./ German	U.S./U.K.	U.S./scaling-up
37.	Low tension equipment	U.S./Swedish/ French	U.S./German	German
38.	Instruments	German/U.S.	U.S./German	U.S./German
	COMMUNICATIONS			
39.	telephone	Swedish/French/ U.S.	Not investigated	French
40.	telegraph	Danish/U.K.	Danish	Not investigated
41.	radio	U.S.	U.S.	Not investigated
42.	television	—	U.S.(black and white)	French (color)/ German
43.	Computers	—	—	U.S./U.K.
	PRIME MOVERS			
44.	Steam boilers	Latvian/ German	*SOVIET*/U.S.	U.S./U.K./ German
45.	Internal combustion	U.S.	U.S.	U.S./German
46.	Diesel engines	German	German/U.K.	German/Danish/ U.S./Swiss
47.	Gas turbines	—	—	French
	AGRICULTURAL EQUIPMENT			
48.	Tractors	U.S./German	U.S.	U.S./U.K./ German
49.	Cotton pickers	—	U.S.	U.S.
50.	Seeding equipment	Tsarist	U.S.	U.S./German

Table 25-3 (cont.)

No.	Industrial Process	1917-1930	1930-1945	1945-1965
	TRANSPORTATION INDUSTRIES			
51.	Automobile and trucks	Tsarist/U.S./ Italian	U.S.	U.S./German/ Italian/French
52.	Railroad locomotives:			
53.	steam	Tsarist/ German/U.K.	Tsarist/U.S./ U.K.	SOVIET/U.S./ German
54.	diesel-electric	U.S./German	German	U.S.
55.	electric	German/U.S.	U.S./German	French/U.S.
56.	hydraulic	—	—	Austrian/ German
	SHIPBUILDING			
57.	Hull construction	German	75 percent foreign-built	66 percent foreign-built
	Engine design:			
58.	diesel	German	German	Danish/German/ Swiss
59.	steam turbine	U.K./U.S.	U.K.	Not known
60.	gas turbine	—	—	French
61.	Trawlers	—	U.K./French/ German	U.K./German
62.	Oceanographic equipment	—	U.S./German	U.S./Japanese
	AIRCRAFT			
63.	Aircraft	German	U.S./Italian	SOVIET(?)
	Aircraft engines:			
64.	internal combustion	U.S./German	U.S./French	—
65.	turboprop	—	—	
66.	pure jet	—	—	U.K./German
67.	Helicopters	—	SOVIET/Italian	SOVIET(?)
68.	Landing and communication equipment	Not investigated	U.S.	U.K./U.S.
	MILITARY INDUSTRIES			
69.	Explosives	German	U.S.	
70.	Poison gas	German	U.S.	
71.	Tanks	French/U.K./ Italian	U.S./U.K./ SOVIET	Data
72.	Machine guns	Tsarist/U.K.	SOVIET/ Finnish	classified
73.	Submarines	German	German/U.K.	
74.	Destroyers	—	Italian/French	
	CONSUMER INDUSTRIES			
75.	Clothing industries	Tsarist/U.S./ German	U.K./German	U.K./German/ U.S.
76.	Boots and shoes	Austrian/ Danish	Not known	U.K.

Sources: Column 1 — Sutton I: *Western Technology ... 1917 to 1930;* Column 2 — Sutton II: *Western Technology . . . 1930 to 1945;* Column 3 — Sutton III: *Western Technology . . . 1945 to 1965.*

Notes: (1) Multi-country listings indicate several technical origins, listed in order of relative importance. (2) In a few cases, as for example in the origin of steam locomotives in the 1930 to 1965 period, there has been Soviet adaptation of basic foreign or Tsarist-era designs; these entries are noted *SOVIET* first and foreign sources second.

The first column in Table 25-3 relates to the period 1917 to 1930. There was no Soviet innovation in this period, although there were, as described in the first volume, several attempts in tractors and synthetic rubber to establish Soviet products.[12] It should be noted that in this period the oil drilling industry was converted almost completely to the American rotary drilling technique.

The second column in Table 25-3 relates to the period 1930 to 1945. In this period Soviet innovation was identified in five of the 75 major industrial processes listed. Although the turbodrill used in oil-well drilling reportedly has German origins, the Soviets undoubtedly have worked on it extensively and the drill introduced in the 1930s may aptly be called a Soviet development; it replaced the rotary technique introduced in the 1930s and by the 1950s was handling the greater part of Soviet drilling. However, overheating and other technical problems led the Soviets to consider a return to rotary drilling in the 1960s. Smelting of alumina from nepheline is a process conducted only in the U.S.S.R. The original flow diagram and equipment for this process were designed by an American company,[13] but there undoubtedly has been some Soviet work. Synthetic rubber, butadiene SK-B, is a result of prerevolutionary Russian research effort, and production was developed under the Soviets. The Ramzin "once-through" boiler appears to be a Soviet innovation, as is the development of some machine guns.

There is no clearcut example in the 1930-45 period of a technology started and brought to productive fruition under Soviet guidance; each of the five examples cited above (except possibly the Ramzin boiler) had its origins outside the Soviet era. On the other hand, the conversion from pilot plant (or equivalent) to series production was achieved in the Soviet economy.

The last period (1945 to 1965) is of particular interest in that we find that several of the five "Soviet" processes adopted between 1930 and 1945 were partly supplanted by Western processes. SK-B was supplemented by Western synthetic rubbers produced with Western equipment. The Ramzin "once-through" boiler was limited to small sizes and Western models were introduced in larger sizes. In turbodrills we find the onset of technical problems and reconsider-

[12] See Sutton I, pp. 133 ff.; Sutton II, pp. 122 ff.
[13] See Sutton II, pp. 57-58.

ation of a Western method—rotary drilling. Only in machine guns and alumina from nepheline do we find continuation of a Soviet process started in the second and continued into the third period. In both of these cases we find some earlier Western influence: American flow diagrams and assistance in the early thirties for alumina from nepheline and the use of Western patents in machine guns.

In sum, it is possible to trace only a single industrial process (the turbodrill) which started, came to development fruition, and went through pilot-plant stages and then to series production without replacement by a later Western process, under the Soviet regime. But the turbodrill cannot stand the test of the Western marketplace (it was tested with this possibility in mind by Dresser Industries of Texas, and rejected). Synthetic rubber work was started under the Tsars and is today about 50 percent supplanted by non-Soviet developed synthetics.

Table 25-3 shows the origins of 75 major technologies in three time periods, or a total of 225 time slots with each slot describing the origins of a technology at one of the three time periods. This matrix is summarized in Table 25-4.

In the period 1917 to 1930 no major applied technologies originated in the U.S.S.R. In the period 1930 to 1945 only two such processes originated in the U.S.S.R., but in another five areas the Soviets developed and applied some major technology and we find both Soviet and Western processes used. In the period 1945 to 1965 three processes were of Soviet origin and again five technical areas used both Soviet and Western processes.

With these data expressed as a percentage of the total 75 time slots included in Table 25-3, we find that in the period 1917 to 1930 the percentage of Soviet technology was zero, that in 1930 to 1945 ten percent of the technologies examined had all or some Soviet components, and that in the period 1945 to 1965 eleven percent of all those major technologies examined had all or some Soviet components. It should be emphasized that this is the most favorable interpretation possible of the empirical findings. It could be argued, with accuracy, that Soviet processes in the 1930 to 1945 period were later replaced by Western origin processes, and that where both Soviet and foreign technologies are used the Soviet process is either relatively inefficient (the turbodrill) or used to a relatively small extent (steam boilers).

Table 25-4   SUMMARY STATEMENT OF THE ORIGINS OF SOVIET TECHNOLOGY FROM 1917 TO 1965

Number of Major Technologies examined: 75 (in three time-slots)

Period	1 Determined as all Soviet origin	2 Percentage of total examined	3 Determined as of both Soviet and Western origins	4 Percentage of total examined	5 Total (column 1 and 3)	6 Percentage of total
1917 to 1930	0	0	0	0	0	0
1930 to 1945	2	3	5	7	7	10
1945 to 1965	3	4	5	7	8	11

Source: Table 25-3.

CHAPTER TWENTY-SIX

The Level of Technology
in the Soviet Union

Given the conclusions of the previous chapter concerning lack of self-generated indigenous innovation in the Soviet economy, it must logically follow that the general level of technology in the Soviet Union at any one time is consistently behind that of the more advanced Western economies. That observation has been made by numerous observers and indeed appears to be valid. This chapter examines the proposition in more detail with respect to selected major technologies.

A prime source of observations concerning technical lags is to be found in the reports of industrial delegations sent to the U.S.S.R. under the technical exchange programs of the last decade.[1] During that period the only delegation to report on Soviet technology in glowing terms was one unskilled in technology—a U.S. Senate subcommittee, which reported on Soviet hydroelectric power developments—and this report was in distinct contrast to the impressions recorded by U.S. and Canadian electric power industry delegations.

In 1960 the Soviet Union in all sectors (apart from the area of rockets and guided missiles and other armaments for which resources had been concentrated) was well behind, even decades behind, both Europe and the United States. On the other hand, the delegations seem to agree that in general the Russian grasp of theory is excellent. The problem is not one of deficient individual ability but rather of the system's inability to convert theory into practical industrial operations; i.e., there is an engineering weakness, not a scientific one.[2]

In some industrial sectors which have seen no great change in technology in this century, Soviet imports of foreign technology essentially reflect a domestic mechanical engineering inability rather than a lack of innovation *per se*. For example, in the manufacture of internal combustion and diesel engines the basic technology has remained the same; improvements have been in the methods of manufacturing engines and the efficiency of the finished product. Table 26-1

---

[1] A collection of these reports has been assembled and deposited in the Hoover Institution Library.

[2] There are many other factors that contribute to this inability, of course, including misallocation of capital and a bureaucratic inertia. But the proximal technological factor appears to be an engineering weakness.

lists imports of engine manufacturing technology by the Soviet Union from the West from 1917 to 1970; these imports have been supplemented by even more numerous purchases of industrial machines and equipment. In sum, Table 26-1 analyzes the Soviet engine manufacturing capability. Imports do not reflect any great changes in levels of Western technology, but the acquisition of additional capacity does reflect improved manufacturing methods and more efficient engines and therefore suggests a weakness in Russian industrial engineering.

This industrial weakness is effectively hidden from both Soviet and Western eyes by the protective GOST identification. In the case of marine diesels, where we can match GOST identification to Western models (Table 26-2), we find that there probably are no Soviet-designed marine diesels, or at least no GOST numbers appear for marine diesels that do not have a foreign origin. Therefore if any Soviet marine diesels exist they have not been recorded in recent Soviet technical literature.

Table 26-1   TRANSFER OF ENGINE MANUFACTURING TECHNOLOGY
(INTERNAL COMBUSTION AND DIESEL)
TO THE U.S.S.R. FROM 1925 TO 1970

Date	Agreement	Origin of Technology	Western technology transferred
1926	Sulzer	Switzerland	Diesel manufacture
1926	M.A.N. diesel engines	Germany	Licensing of diesel engines
1929	Fiat S.p.A.	Italy	Truck engine manufacture
1930	Hercules Motor Co.	U.S.A.	Truck engine manufacture
1930	A. J. Brandt Co.	U.S.A.	Truck engine manufacture
1930	Ford Motor Co.	U.S.A.	Truck and automobile engine manufacture
1936	Budd Company	U.S.A.	Automobile engine
1944	General Motors Corp.	U.S.A.	Truck engine assembly
1944	Caterpillar Tractor Co.[a]	U.S.A.	Tractor diesels, KD17-40
1946	Kloeckner-Humboldt-Deutz	Germany	Diesel truck engines
1946	B.M.W.	Germany	Diesel engines
1946	Daimler-Benz	Germany	Diesel engines
1946	Steyr-Daimler-Pusch	Austria	Truck plant
1956	Skoda	Czechoslovakia	Engine manufacture
1959	Burmeister & Wain	Denmark	Marine diesels
1961	Transfermatic	U.S.A.	V-8 truck engine manufacture (U.S.)
1961	Perkins	U.K.	Small diesels
1968	Fiat S.p.A.	U.S.A.[b]	Engine manufacture
1968	Renault/Peugeot	France	Engine manufacture
1970	Renault/U.S. consortium	France/U.S.A.	3- to 11-ton tractors, truck trailers, off-the-road vehicles

Sources: Sutton I: *Western Technology . . . 1917 to 1930*; Sutton II: *Western Technology . . . 1930 to 1945*; *Washington Post*, March 14, 1970; *Business Week*, April 18, 1970 and June 19, 1971; *Metalworking News* (New York), August 16, 1971; [a] Not by agreement with U.S. firm; [b] U.S. technology supplied indirectly.

Table 26-2   WESTERN MARINE DIESELS AND SOVIET *GOST* DESIGNATIONS

Soviet GOST identification	Western firm or model
6 ChSP 10.5/12.7	Cummins JMC 600
1Ɛ DN 13/2 x 18.4	Napier-Pielstik
6 ChN 15/19	Mercedes-Benz MB-846A
12 ChVN 17.5/20.5	Mercedes-Benz MB-820
20 ChVN 18.5/25	Mercedes-Benz MB-518
16 D V21.6/25/4	GMC 567 C
16 D VH 22.2/26/6	GMC 498
8 ChR 24/36	8 DV 136 Buckau-Wolf
18 Ch NV 20/45	VV 45-M.A.N.
6 Ch R 32/48	R 6 DV 148 Buckau-Wolf
6 D R 34/47	M 46 M-Polar-Atlas
12 Ch VRN 40/46	PC-SEMT Pielstik
8 ChN 38.1/45.7	KSDM 8 Mirrlees
6 ChRN 45/66	K6V 45/66 M.A.N.
6 DR 52/90	6 GZ 52/90 M.A.N.
6 DKR 55/100	D 55 Cegielski
DKRN 62/115	62 VTBF 115 B & W
DKRN 70/120	KZ 70/120S M.A.N.
DKRN 75/132	C 750S Fiat
DKRN 76/150	760/1500 VGSU Götaverken
DKRN 76/150	RSAD 76 Sulzer
DKRN 84/180	84 VTBF 180 B & W
DKRN 84/160	KZ 84/160 C M.A.N.
DKRN 85/170	850/1700 VGAU Götaverken
DKRN 90/155	RD 90 Sulzer
DKRN 90/160	C 900S Fiat

Source: V. A. Vansheidt, *Sudovye dvigateli vnutrennego sgoraniia* (Leningrad, 1962), pp. 538, 540.

In some processes we can determine the borderlines of the ''engineering gap'' quite clearly. For example, the Soviet Union purchased enormous synthetic fiber capacity in the West between 1956 and the late 1960s; indeed, almost all of its synthetic fiber capacity has been built by British, German, Dutch, Japanese, and Italian firms. However, the Soviets also pressed forward their own research in synthetic fibers, and a report published by the U.S. Army Quartermaster Research and Engineering Command disclosed that by 1960 the Soviets had developed at least 18 synthetic fibers, including three with no counterpart in the West. These three are Enant (a Nylon 7), Ftorlon (a fluorine with a copolymer), and Vinitron (a combination of nitrocellulose with chlorinated polyvinal chloride). Consequently, given the ability to purchase synthetic fiber capacity in the West, Soviet synthetic fiber research has been directed toward military uses—lightweight textile clothing highly resistant to chemicals and photodegradation, parachutes, ballistic applications, and so on. Thus the Russian

Nylon 7 (Enant), not produced in the Western world, has useful stress-strain properties and ultraviolet resistance. The Ftorlon, a fluorine-containing fiber, is reported to have good resistance to chemicals and a much higher strength than Teflon, the only such polymer available in the United States in fiber form. Vinitron is a new fiber that will not shrink in water and has good dye characteristics. This and similar Soviet work, including development of heat-resistant fibers from organosilica fibers,[3] suggests that in textiles at least there is no lack of ability up to the pilot-plant stage. Like observations can be made for other industries.

The weakness starts with the conversion from pilot-plant production to full-scale production. Therefore, in discussing levels of technology it is important to note that an industrial and engineering journal may report new Soviet technical developments and even pilot-plant or small-batch production; the important factor to determine is whether the process has been utilized on a continuous basis for large-scale production (not just series production) over a period of time (years, not months). It is in this area that we find substantive evidence of Soviet weakness and inability.

DIFFUSION OF TECHNOLOGY WITHIN A SECTOR

Given a reliance on foreign innovation, the extent and speed of domestic technological diffusion becomes of paramount importance. It was indicated earlier[4] that in the twenties, when a trust consisted only of one or two Tsarist-era plants, diffusion was not a major problem. A technical-assistance agreement was made with either the trust or a large and more technically advanced plant; foreign technique was then diffused among the relatively few plants, as often as not by foreign engineers. A single capable consulting engineer in a single plant might, depending on the process, provide considerable information and know-how in a matter of months; rarely did Soviet plants require more than a year to acquire a specific technology.

With the increase in the number of plants, however, a problem of diffusion has arisen. Information on foreign techniques is rapidly acquired and distributed; but foreign machinery and equipment cannot be purchased for all plants. A solution has been found in standardization and duplication,[5] but still there are institutional barriers to rapid diffusion.

These barriers may be exemplified in two areas of technology—numerically controlled machine tools and large presses. Numerically controlled machine tools are typical of the complex computer-based technologies for which the

---

[3] *The Hosiery Trade Journal* (Leicester, Eng.), February 1962, pp. 134-38.
[4] See Sutton I, p. 331.
[5] See Sutton II, pp. 291-99.

Soviets have not been able to achieve rapid diffusion. The advantages of acquiring the technologies are clear; the Soviet problem is one of inadequate inputs, i.e., computers and precision machinery:[6]

Innovation and Economic effects	Extent of Diffusion in U.S.S.R.	In U.S.A.
Substitution of numerically controlled for manually controlled machine tools in production of custom (unit)-built machines, machines produced in small batches, and in large-scale production requiring frequent changeovers of tooling and setups. Economic effects: a) Reduction of labor skill requirements b) Capital saving by 20 to 25 percent c) High flexibility in production d) Possibility of centralized planning and control of processes e) Substantially improved quality of products f) Possibility of producing products prohibitively expensive to produce by other methods.	Surprisingly slow progress. Though at least two prototype models, one point-to-point positioning and the other continuous-path, had been produced by 1959, the plan for 1960 called for only 180 units and that for 1959-65 for only several hundred. The relative meagerness of press discussions about actual experience in use suggests that use is still concentrated in the armaments sector.	NC machine tools represent the most important technological innovation in U.S. metalworking sector of the last decade. The industry started experimenting with the idea in late 1940s. The first NC machines became commercially available around 1954. At the time of the Chicago machine tool show in 1960, more than 60 firms were in the business. Since then the number of firms in the business of NC machine tools has grown steadily and most of the functional types of machine tools have been adapted to the system. As yet there are no statistics available on the number of the machines in use. Estimates vary from 1500 to as many as 3000 in the early 1960s.

In metal stamping we find two divergent rates of diffusion for technology relating to the same basic process; one technology has made substantial progress and the other has made very little. It is to be noted that Soviet large presses have evolved from German very heavy presses removed to the U.S.S.R. at the end of World War II. This technology amply supplies Soviet needs; hence it has been well diffused. On the other hand, automatic coil feed for sheet presses, although it is a development that goes back to the early 1920s, is largely a postwar innovation; here we find a Soviet deficiency based on inability to import units in sufficient numbers or to establish the technology within the U.S.S.R. This is a problem that could be overcome given sufficient direction of resources into developing Soviet versions of Western presses and feed equipment:[7]

---

[6]   U.S. Congress, Joint Economic Committee, *Dimensions of Soviet Economic Power*, Hearings, 87th Congress, 2d session, December 10 and 11, 1962 (Washington, 1962), p. 137.
[7]   *Ibid.*

Innovation and Economic effect	Extent of Diffusion in U.S.S.R.	In U.S.A.
Application of extra-heavy presses for stamping large sections of aircraft bodies and heavy machinery parts instead of riveting small stampings.	Substantial progress achieved in recent 2 or 3 years	For all practical purposes, the 35,000- and 50,000-ton presses manufactured by 1957 are considered more than adequate even today
Economic effects:		
a) Dramatic reduction of production cycle b) Marked metal savings c) Substantial improvements in quality of products d) Large labor savings		
Substitution of automatic coil and strip feed presses for sheet presses in mass-production industries.	Thus far very little if any progress made because of deficient supply of presses	In U.S.A., automatic strip-feeding presses have been used for more than 40 years. In recent years phenomenal progress has been made in adapting the presses to wider strips, thicker gauges, and greater speeds. At this time automotive and household appliance industries are using presses with automatic feeds of steel coils up to 90 inches wide and ¼ inch thick
Economic effects:		
a) Marked metal savings b) Large labor savings in stamping c) Cost savings in steel mills because steel rolls are cheaper to manufacture than steel sheets		

In casting operations, to take another example, the rate and extent of diffusion of technology have varied. In the substitution of mechanical sandslingers for hand sandpacking, common in the United States, diffusion in the U.S.S.R. is limited to establishments able to manufacture their own equipment. In the substitution of machine core making and molding for hand operations, there has been substantially greater productivity of machines in the United States, contrasted to "slow progress" in the Soviet Union; in 1957 the Soviet Union had only about 20,000 molding machines, most of which were "primitive pre-World War II type." In the application of carbon dioxide techniques and related processes there has been rapid diffusion in both the United States and the Soviet Union. In the introduction of resin-bonded shell molding and core making there was rapid introduction in the United States, which slowed down in 1960 owing to introduction of a competing hot-box method; in the Soviet Union there was "slow progress" owing to lack of equipment, thermoreactive resins, and fine-grained sand. In two innovations there was rapid progress in both the United States and the U.S.S.R.—pressure die-casting and semipermanent and permanent mold casting in ferrous and nonferrous industries.

In only one casting process has there been more rapid diffusion in the U.S.S.R. than in the United States—in investment casting, largely by the "lost-wax" method. The restriction in the United States is due to the high cost of small operations and low levels of mechanization possible. The U.S.S.R. probably produced three times more by this method in 1958 than did the United States.

On balance the U.S.S.R. has a slow rate of diffusion brought about by equipment deficiencies and lack of necessary input materials. This completely contradicts the claim that central planning, in contrast to a "chaotic" market system, can foresee and plan for new material requirements. The history of innovative diffusion in the Soviet Union suggests that the market system is infinitely better able to provide new inputs to answer demands for innovative diffusion.

COMPARATIVE LEVELS OF TECHNOLOGY

The evidence presented in this study suggests that, as a result of the need to import foreign technology plus slow rates of technological diffusion, the general level of technology in the Soviet Union should be below that of the United States and the Western world. Certainly Soviet technological levels cannot be above or even generally on a par with those of the Free World in areas where the Soviets rely on foreign innovation. Although there are technologies specially designed by Western firms for the U.S.S.R., and even some examples of new Western processes introduced first in the Soviet Union by Western companies, these do not constitute a general rule—they are exceptions. The rule is that new technology is introduced first in the Western country and then after a time lag is made available to the U.S.S.R.

One OECD study[8] contains a table listing Soviet statements concerning relative technological levels of the U.S.S.R. and the West between 1959 and 1963. These statements form a useful starting point for consideration of comparative levels of technology.

The first of the groups where leadership is claimed is "high-speed aviation, space rockets, long-range rockets, atomic energy." This claim is not generally consistent with the data in this study. By the end of the sixties the Soviets had fallen behind the United States in rocket technology, although the United States started its major program only in 1957 rather than 1945. In atomic energy there is no question that the Soviets lag.[9] They have maintained general equality in high-speed aviation, but their aircraft are technically inferior in many respects (e.g., control systems) and have relatively high operating costs.

Leadership is claimed in steam turbines for the electrical industry, when parity would be a more accurate claim.

The leadership claim in the "extraction of oil" definitely is not supportable: the Soviet Union is today importing oil technology from Europe and the United

---

[8] E. Zaleski *et al., Science Policy in the U.S.S.R.* (Paris, Organization for Economic Cooperation and Development, 1969), pp. 496-99.

[9] See p. 239.

States. Leadership is claimed in terms of "output per unit volume" of blast furnaces and open-hearth furnaces; this is acceptable,[10] and is a result of "scaling-up" innovation. Claims for priority in rolling mill technology are not acceptable, but a claim for electro-slag resmelting is acceptable on the basis of equality with the United States.[11]

A claimed priority in production of liquid paraffin is limited to pilot-plant production. The claim of leadership in automatic and semiautomatic welding machinery design is not supportable (in 1970)—although there has been some

Table 26-3   COMPARATIVE STATEMENTS ON SOVIET TECHNOLOGICAL LAGS AS OF 1970

Technology	OECD Report [a]	Western industrial delegation [b]	Sutton [c]
Coal mining—underground operations	—	Ten years behind [d]	Ten-year lag
Atomic energy	"Equal or in the lead"	"Competent," "lack of experimental equipment" [e]	10-to 15-year lag as of 1970
Blast furnaces	"Equal or in the lead" (1959)	No lag [f]	No lag
Steel rolling	"Equal or in the lead" (1959)	20- to 30-year lag	30-year lag
Ore beneficiation	"U.S.S.R. lagging" (1960)	"Patterned after early American models" [f]	20-year lag
Oil well drilling	"U.S.S.R. equal or in the lead" (1959)	—	Depth limitations
Pipeline compressors	—	"Far behind" [g]	20-year lag
Large-diameter pipe	—	"Far behind" [g]	20-year lag
Chemical engineering (all phases)	"U.S.S.R. lagging (1959)	—	Minimum 30-year lag

Sources: E. Zaleski *et al., Science Policy in the U.S.S.R.* (Paris: Organization for Economic Cooperation and Development, 1969); [b] See text pp. 372 and 373; [c] See text pp. 369-70; [d] Private letter from Vasiliiy Strishkov, former Russian coal mining engineer, now with U.S. Bureau of Mines, Washington, D.C.; [e] *Atomic Energy in the Soviet Union,* Trip Report of the U.S. Atomic Energy Delegation, May 1963 (Oak Ridge, Tenn.: AEC Division of Technical Information Extension, n.d.); [f] *Steel in the Soviet Union,* Report of the American Steel and Iron Ore Delegation's Visit to the Soviet Union, May and June 1958 (New York: American Iron and Steel Institute, 1959); [g] "USSR Natural Gas Industry," Report of the 1961 U.S. Delegation to the Soviet Natural Gas Industry (n.p.: American Gas Association, n.d.).

[10] See p. 123.
[11] See p. 131.

Soviet development in the field.[12] Claims of engineering priority in four types of textile machinery are not acceptable.

In brief, the Soviets' claims of technological leadership were not generally consistent with the technical data presented in this study or with the reports made by Western industrial delegations and by individual Western observers. Table 26-3 compares the assessment made by different observers for a number of major technologies. The last column is a general assessment, based on the information available, of Soviet lags.

There is little question that behind continuing efforts to establish a paper priority for Soviet technology, particularly before politically aware audiences, is an acute knowledge that the substance of the claims is fragile. Only a superficial examination of Soviet claims is needed to reject many as absurd or inadequate; almost any technology can be asserted as superior to all others if care is taken to choose carefully the parameters of comparison.

In general, the level of Soviet technology is substantially behind that of the West except in those areas (blast furnaces, open-hearth furnaces, coke ovens, electrical generators, turbines) where scaling-up innovation based on classic Western processes has been successful.

[12] See p. 131.

CHAPTER TWENTY-SEVEN

National Security and Technical Transfers

The major conclusions presented by this study are that Western technology has been, and continues to be, the most important factor in Soviet economic development. The technical transfers that have fostered this development have continued over a period of 50 years. These observations will now be related to the declared hostility of the U.S.S.R. to the West since 1917, a hostility such that the United States alone apparently requires annual defense expenditures in excess of $80 billion (1969) to counter the threat.

That the Soviets have openly and consistently advocated the overthrow of Western democratic systems from 1917 to the present time is a fundamental starting point for the development of our national security policies. Rationality suggests, therefore, that either our policy regarding technical transfers to the Soviet Union is in error or our inflated annual defense expenditure is unnecessary. Either there is no valid rationale for much of our trade with the Soviets, i.e., for the main vehicle of technical transfers, or there is no valid rationale for defense against the Soviets. The two policies are incompatible.

The factors to be considered in highlighting this policy conflict are, first, the direct supply of military goods from the West to the U.S.S.R.; second, the supply of technology and equipment for Soviet production of military goods; third, the strategic implications of the technical transfers as seen by both the Soviets and the West; and fourth, the failure of Western export control and the reasons for that failure. Finally, analysis of these factors should conclude with a brief discussion of the relationship between technical transfers and national security in the light of this empirical study.

We are faced initially with the problem that the term "strategic" has a limited definition in the West. All technology, goods, and trade are strategic in the full sense of the word. Western definitions have been restricted, with obvious consequences. It is proposed to outline first some of the direct military transfers (i.e., those which would be militarily "strategic" by any definition) and then some indirect transfers applicable to military ends (but not strategic in the Western definition), and then to examine the spectrum of transfers in light of a more accurate definition of the term "strategic."

DIRECT SUPPLY OF MILITARY GOODS TO THE U.S.S.R.

Earlier chapters have described direct supply of weapons and other military supplies to the U.S.S.R. Before 1930 this was primarily a German transfer. The Red Army and Air Force were trained by German officers, using German equipment, and arsenals and plants for the production of weapons were established with German technical assistance and finance.[1]

In the 1930s Soviet sources of supply widened to include Great Britain and the United States for the early predecessors of Soviet tanks. The United States, for example, supplied the early tractor plants which doubled as tank-producing plants,[2] in addition to cartridge lines,[3] a nitrocellulose plant,[4] and military electronics.[5]

Lend Lease of course was a significant provider of weapons to the U.S.S.R.,[6] and numerous items supplied under Lend Lease became prototypes for later standard Soviet military equipment. For example, the BTR-40 Soviet armored personnel carrier of the 1950s is an almost exact copy of the U.S. M3 A1 scout car.[7] Although the skills of German scientists were used after the war to develop military electronics, including missile guidance systems, much technology in this field as well came from the United States. The Soviet search radar, for example, was based on U.S. Navy type SJ radar sets powered by magnetron tubes and received under Lend Lease.[8] Gun-laying radar was based on the British Mark II, and RUS I and RUS II radar units of the 1950s were based on Lend Lease supplies.

More recently, capture of the U.S.S. *Pueblo* provided the Soviets with electronic equipment 15 years ahead of anything they possessed at the end of the 1960s,[9] and persistent espionage in the United States has provided a steady flow of new military technologies.[10] In the famous 1962 Cuban missile crisis the ships used by the Soviets were fitted with extra-large hatches to carry missiles and were powered by engines manufactured by Burmeister & Wain in Copenhagen, Denmark.[11]

Finally, in 1970 the South African Air Force reported a Russian submarine taking on fuel from the Soviet tanker *Elgava*,[12] a vessel built in Sweden in

---

[1]   See Sutton I: *Western Technology ... 1917 to 1930*.
[2]   See Sutton II: *Western Technology ... 1930 to 1945*.
[3]   *Ibid.*, pp. 237-38.
[4]   *Ibid.*, pp. 246-47.
[5]   *Ibid.*, p. 160-63.
[6]   See pp. 3-11.
[7]   *Ordnance*. (Washington, D.C.), January-February 1969, p. 396.
[8]   J. M. Carroll, *Secrets of Electronic Espionage* (New York: Dutton, 1966), pp. 143-44.
[9]   *Los Angeles Times*, February 8, 1968.
[10] For example, missile accelerometers: in Great Britain, the Lonsdale case revealed that the Soviets had been provided with the Decca Tracking System.
[11] *The Washington Post*, February 27, 1970, p. A14.
[12] *The Star* (Johannesburg), weekly air edition, February 20, 1971, p.1.

1961 and equipped with Danish engines. The South Africans also reported the Russian ship *Bakoeriani* in the Indian Ocean en route to East Africa with a naval patrol boat as deck cargo. The engines of the *Bakoeriani* are Burmeister & Wain models built at the Bryansk plant in the Soviet Union under the 1959 technical-assistance agreement between the Soviets and the Danish company.[13]

Thus by one means or another—and the greater part of the information on this topic is understandably classified—the Soviets have received a flow of Western technologies for direct military use from 1917 down to the present day.

TECHNOLOGY AND EQUIPMENT FOR
THE PRODUCTION OF MILITARY GOODS

It is generally known that an automobile or tractor plant may be used to produce tanks and armored cars, military trucks, and other military vehicles. Indeed, one of the major conclusions reached by a U.S. interagency committee formed to study the war-making potential of U.S. and German automotive industries was that the motor vehicle industry has enormous military potential: "The Committee recognized without dissent that [Germany's] motor vehicle industry was an important factor in her waging of war during the period just ended."[14] On the basis of its findings, the committee recommended that the manufacture of complete automobiles in Germany be prohibited, that the manufacture of certain parts and subassemblies be "specifically prohibited," and that Germany "should not be permitted to retain in her possession any types of vehicles of particular military application, such as track-laying vehicles, multiaxle vehicles, etc."

The committee further listed more than 300 "war products manufactured by the automotive industry" based on a survey of the U.S. automobile industry.[15] Therefore after reviewing the U.S. and German automobile industries the U.S. Government was fully apprised of the industries' clear military potential. For reasons unknown, these conclusions apparently have been ignored with respect to the Soviet automobile industry, although by virtue of its Western origins (if for no other reason) the Soviet automobile industry is essentially no different from the U.S. or the German industry. It has the same capabilities and potentials.[16]

---

[13] *Ibid.*, p. 5.

[14] U.S. Foreign Economic Administration, *U.S. Technical Industrial Disarmament Committee to Study the Post-Surrender Treatment of the German Automotive Industry* (Washington, 1945), T.I.D.C. Project no. 12.

[15] *Ibid.*

[16] Shortly before this book went to press, the conclusions of the postwar interagency committee were brought to the attention of the Department of Commerce with specific reference to issue of export licenses for the Kama truck plant under construction in the U.S.S.R. in 1971 (see p. 203). The answer of the department was as follows: "The contribution an established

Table 27-1   CIVILIAN AND MILITARY MODELS PRODUCED IN
SOVIET AUTOMOBILE PLANTS, 1945-70

Plants	Civilian models	Military Models
Moscow (ZIL)	ZIL 110, ZIL 111 passenger autos ZIL 127, ZIL 155 buses ZIL 150, four-ton truck ZIL 585, three-ton dump truck	ZIL 150 armored truck ZIL 151 armored truck ZIL 157 2.5-ton truck
Ural (Miass)	Ural-ZIS-150, four-ton truck Ural-ZIS-5,	Ural-375T (6x6 wheeled) Ural-375 (tracked) Ural-375/BM-24, rocket launcher
Moscow Small Car works (MZMA)	Moskvich passenger auto	Moskva 402, 4-wheel drive cross-country Moskvich
Gorki (GAZ)	Pobeda and Volga M-21 passenger cars GAZ-69, medical vehicle GAZ-69 parts for assembly at Irkutsk, Odessa and Ulyanovsk	M-72 (4-wheel drive cross-country Pobeda) GAZ-46, Soviet jeep GAZ-47, amphibian personnel carrier GAZ-56, 1½-ton military truck GAZ-62, 1-ton truck (4-wheel drive) GAZ-69A, scout car GAZ-69, command car GAZ-69, Shmel rocket carrier
Yaroslavl (YaAZ)	YaAZ-210, 12-ton truck YaAz-210E, 12-ton truck YaAz-210A, 12-ton truck YaAZ-210G and D tractor	Not known to be making military vehicles at this time
Minsk (MAZ)	MAZ-205, 5-ton truck MAZ-525, 25-ton dump truck MAZ-200, 7-ton truck MAZ-200B tractor	MAZ-57, ammunition carrier MAZ-63, gun tow MAZ-100, utility vehicle

Sources: Institute for Study of the U.S.S.R., *Bulletin* (Munich), III, 1 (January 1956); Leo Heimann, "In the Soviet Arsenal," *Ordnance* (Washington, D.C.), January-February 1968; *Kratkii avtomobil'nyi spravochnik*, 5th edition (Moscow, 1968).

automotive industry can make to the military potential of a country is recognized by the Department. This factor, along with other considerations, enters into the decision whether or not to issue any licenses authorizing exports of equipment to a plant such as Kama." Letter to writer from Rauer H. Meyer, director of the Office of Export Control, Department of Commerce, November 12, 1971.

The logical deduction from this official statement is that the findings of the interagency committee are known to and are accepted by the administration in Washington. Inasmuch as licenses for the Kama plant nevertheless have been issued (according to the same letter), we are forced to the conclusion that the administration is knowingly allowing the export to the Soviet Union of U.S. equipment with military potential. At the time of this writing, licenses for the Kama project had been issued to Satra Corporation, Cross Company, Ex-Cell-O Corporation, Swindell-Dressler, and (not confirmed) Giffel Associates, Inc., of Detroit.

The interagency committee's conclusions at the end of World War II concerning the military potential of the automobile industry are supported by data on the postwar output of the Soviet automobile manufacturing industry. Table 27-1 lists Soviet automobile manufacturing plants and their production of military vehicles in the 1960s. The Western construction of these plants has been discussed elsewhere in the study.

The vehicles produced at Gorki—to take one example from Table 27-1—are basically Ford Motor Company technology. The plant was erected by Ford in the early 1930s,[17] and additional foreign equipment has been installed since that time.[18] Among the numerous civilian and military models produced today by this Ford plant is the GAZ-69, in its civilian version a medical aid vehicle but in its military versions a one-ton military truck, a scout vehicle, a command car, and a rocket launcher. Examination of the construction details of the GAZ-69 vehicle confirm that it is a facsimile of American technology; the *Katalog detalei avtomobilei GAZ-69, GAZ-69A, YAZ-450, YAZ-450A, i YAZ-450D*[19] includes diagrams of the various parts of the GAZ-69, and these can be usefully compared to parts shown in American catalogs—particularly those of the Ford Motor Company. Comparison of the oil pump (p. 30), oil filter (p. 36), fuel pump (p. 46), carburetor (p. 48), mufflers (p. 57), and radiator (p. 66) will make the point. Variations are mainly in body construction. For example, pages 192-93 provide details of a door construction utilizing wood and a design more common in World War II German vehicles than in present-day American vehicles.

Thus individual parts and overall design of present-day Soviet military vehicles, including those used for weapons systems (e.g., the GAZ-69 Shmel rocket carrier) may be traced in the main to American automobile technology sent to the Soviet Union as normal trade for peaceful purposes.

The more recent U.S.–Volgograd (VAZ) technical-assistance contract of the late sixties for construction of the VAZ plant[20] affords an excellent illustration of the military capabilities of allegedly civilian units. The implications are clear despite the fact that only very limited data have been released. It is known that the engine to be produced by the U.S. equipment belongs to "the small and medium European size class (engine displacement, respectively, 73 and

---

[17] See Sutton I, pp. 246-49.

[18] As recently as spring of 1971 it was reported that the Gleason Company had been granted a license for supply of bevel gear production equipment for the Gorki plant. *Rochester Times-Union*, June 3, 1971.

[19] Moscow: Mashinostroenie, 1968.

[20] Although this agreement is commonly called the "Fiat deal", the Togliatti plant at Volgograd uses mainly (about three-fourths) American equipment; Volgograd is the Soviet name (i.e., presumably, VAZ), and the facility is more accurately called the "VAZ" or "U.S.-VAZ" plant.

85 cubic inches)."[21] This is approximately the 1500-cubic-centimeter class of engine.

Does such an engine have any military usefulness? This is an important question, since this single plant will have a capacity of 600,000 vehicles per year, or more than twice the 1968 Soviet production of automobiles.[22] In other words, by 1975 over one-half of the total Soviet automobile output will come from this single plant; three-quarters of the plant's equipment, and all of its key equipment, comes from the United States.

The military possibilities for such a small engine include use as the main engine on a special-purpose small military vehicle (like the American Jeep), or as a propulsive unit for a specially designed vehicle for carrying either personnel or weapons. The Soviet strategy is currently toward supply of wars of "national liberation." Small vehicles of the types mentioned constitute excellent means of transportation to replace the bicycle used in Vietnam.

Soviet interest in such small vehicles goes back to World War II. The GAZ-46 is the Soviet version of the U.S. Jeep, and we know that such a vehicle figures into Soviet strategic thinking. For example, General G. I. Prokovskii has commented on one advantage of the Jeep as a weapons carrier: "Even relatively powerful recoilless artillery systems can, at the present time [the late fifties], be mounted on light automobiles, without reducing the number of men who can be accommodated."[23]

It may be argued that a U.S. Jeep engine is more powerful than the engine to be built in the U.S.–VAZ plant; it is estimated that the U.S.–VAZ unit is about two-thirds as powerful as the Jeep engine. But it should be borne in mind that requirements may be quite different from those of the United States. In World War II, for example, the Soviets received about 6500 U.S. Airocobras and promptly discarded armor plate, machine guns, and instrumentation, thereby reducing the weight by 3000 pounds and significantly increasing the performance they desired.[24] If the Soviets can strip 20 percent of the weight from an airplane, could not the same ingenuity be applied to a land vehicle? Certainly the U.S.–VAZ engine offers opportunities to resourceful Russian military engineers.

However, Russian engineers have no particular need to be ingenious. A proven vehicle of excellent capabilities utilizing a 1500-cubic centimeter engine already exists—and the Soviets have all the performance and manufacturing data. During World War II the Germans developed the N.S.U. three-quarter

---

[21]   U.S. House of Representatives Committee on Banking and Currency, *The Fiat-Soviet Auto Plant and Communist Economic Reforms*, 89th Congress, 2d session (Washington, 1967).

[22]   *Ibid.*

[23]   Major General G. I. Pokrovskii, *Science and Technology in Contemporary War* (New York: Praeger, 1959), p. 122. Accompanying Figure 14 in Pokrovskii's book is a photograph of a U.S. Jeep with mounted artillery weapons and inscription "U.S. 106-mm recoilless weapon mounted on Willys Jeep."

[24]   *Aviation Week* (New York), July 7, 1952.

track vehicle which weighed 3100 pounds laden, including three men. The ground pressure was only 4.5 psi, and with a turning circle of 13 feet it was capable of 50 mph. The Germans found this tracked vehicle "invaluable in wooded country impassable to a vehicle of normal size."[25] The propulsion unit was a 1500-cc four-cylinder Opel engine developing 36 bp; this same engine later powered the Moskvitch 401 and the Moskvitch 402 (Moskva) military cross-country four-wheel drive version of the 401, produced at the MZMA in Moscow. In brief, there already exists a tested and usable military vehicle capable of transporting men or adaptable for weapons use and powered by a 1500-cc engine. Therefore the numerous statements by U.S. officials to the effect that the Volgograd plant would have no military capabilities would appear to be erroneous.[26]

In 1961 a dispute arose in U. S. Government circles over the "Transfermatic case"—a proposal to ship to the U.S.S.R. two U.S. transfer lines (with a total value of $5.3 million) for the production of automobile engines. In a statement dated February 23, 1961, representatives from the Department of Defense went on record against shipment of the transfer lines on the grounds that "the technology contained in these Transfermatic machines produced in the United States is the most advanced in the world," and

> So far as this department knows the U.S.S.R. has not installed this type of machinery. The receipt of this equipment by the U.S.S.R. will contribute to the Soviet military and economic warfare potential.[27]

However, this position was overturned by a new secretary of defense, Robert McNamara, in November 1961. McNamara explained his decision in response to an inquiry from a Congressional investigating committee:

> I concluded that the Defense Department should not oppose export licenses for the transfermatic machines in question....My decision was based solely on the merits of the case as I saw them, from the point of view of alternative sources and availability of comparable machinery, and was in no part dictated by political or other policy considerations.
>
> My decision in this case was based on my own knowledge of this type of machinery and of its alternative sources of supply....

---

[25] "Its dimensions and small turning circle make it possible to operate the vehicle in places, such as mountain tracks and forests, impossible for ordinary transport." *Automobile Engineer* (London), October-December 1945, p. 481.

[26] For example, Eugene V. Rostow, under secretary of state for political affairs, is quoted to the effect that the U.S. equipment for the plant "would not contribute in any way to Soviet military capability." U.S. House of Representatives, *op. cit.* n. 21, p. 42.

[27] U.S. House of Representatives, Select Committee on Export Control, *Investigation and Study of the Administration, Operation, and Enforcement of the Export Control Act of 1949, and Related Acts, (H.R. 403)*, Hearings, 87th Congress, 1st session, pt. 1, October 1961, p. 217.

As you know, the transfermatic machines were not be be used for the manufacture of military vehicles, but rather for the production of medium-priced or high-priced passenger cars.

Your letter asks whether I consulted with other knowledgeable persons before making my April decision on transfermatic machines. The answer is that I reviewed this case thoroughly myself. I did not consult formally with other automotive experts as I had had the benefit of recent and direct experience with the equipment concerned in private industry.[28]

These Transfermatic machines were in fact for the production of 225-hp truck engines;[29] they were considerably more powerful than the units supplied for the plant at Volgograd and certainly adaptable to military end use.

The final case to be cited in the automotive sector is unfolding as this book goes to press. In 1970, with a still relatively limited car-truck production capacity—and all of that derived from Western sources—the Soviets decided they were faced with an immediate requirement for a plant capable of producing 100,000 three-axle 8- to 11-ton trucks a year, the largest such plant in the world.

The initial Soviet approach was made to the Ford Motor Company, probably the only organization in the world capable of building such a unit with its own technical resources. There is no question that Ford was interested. A company delegation under the leadership of Henry Ford II went to the Soviet Union,[30] and at one point it appeared likely that Ford would build the plant for the Soviets on a nonparticipating basis. In May 1970, however, Secretary of Defense Melvin Laird questioned construction by an American company on the grounds that the trucks to be produced would have military end uses. Henry Ford commented at the time that Secretary Laird's contention was "not only highly misleading but appears to be a gratuitous attack upon my common sense and patriotism."[31] However no one advanced the argument that the proposed plant could not produce military trucks, and the participation of Ford Motor Company faded away.

In subsequent months the Soviets tried elsewhere. The Satra Corporation in New York, which has secured financing for the Soviets in other sectors, attempted to put together a consortium of U.S. bankers and manufacturers of

---

[28]   *Ibid.,* December 1961, p. 474.

[29]   *Ibid.,* October 1961, p. 217. William P. Bundy states the 225-hp figure but not the end use. In 1961 no Soviet passenger car had an engine anywhere close to 225 hp. For a similar and better documented example, see the final summary of the "ball bearing machines case" also of 1961: U.S. Senate, Committee on the Judiciary, *Export of Ball Bearing Machines to the U.S.S.R.,* Hearings, 87th Congress, 1st session (Washington, 1961). This is an extraordinary case—the committee called it "of life and death importance to America and the free world" (p. 1)—of an attempt to provide the Soviets with a capability for producing miniature ball bearings, almost all of which are used in missiles.

[30]   *Business Week,* April 18, 1970.

[31]   *U.S. News and World Report,* May 18, 1970.

truck and truck equipment.[32] In August 1970 spokesmen for Daimler-Benz in Germany, the largest truck builder in Europe, declared that the firm expected to conclude a contract to build a factory in the U.S.S.R. to produce 150,000 trucks a year in the 10- to 20-ton range.[33] In September 1970 it was the French Government-owned Renault firm which announced a contract for construction of the plant, which would be known as the "Kama" plant because of its location on the Kama River, and which would produce 150,000 diesel trucks annually. The French Government had assured financing of $127 million for seven years at 5.95 percent—an extremely attractive package.[34]

Mack Trucks, Inc., entered into some preliminary discussions in 1971 concerning the supply of technical assistance for the plant;[35] and in August 1971 the Department of Commerce granted an export license to the Swindell-Dressler Company of Pittsburgh for $162 million worth of equipment for the Kama foundry.[36] Another license, valued at $37 million, reportedly was granted at the same time to Giffels Associates, Inc., of Detroit,[37] although this report was still unconfirmed in late 1971.

The planned capacity of the Kama plant is greater than that of all U.S. heavy truck manufacturers combined. Three basic models are to be produced: a 260-hp tractor for a 20-ton semi-trailer; a 210-hp tractor for a 16-ton semi-trailer; and a 160-hp dump truck with a seven-ton capacity. All such civilian units have clear military utility. Moreover, always in the past the Soviets have used Western-built plants for military production as soon as the Western engineers have left for home—from the Ford-built Gorki plant onward. Given this consideration, it will be a trusting Western government indeed that accepts a Soviet commitment that this plant will not be used for military purposes.[38]

Chemical industries also are essential to modern warfare, and some of these

---

[32] *Business Week*, August 29, 1970.

[33] *Ibid.*

[34] The provision of such favorable financing by a French government under President Georges Pompidou raises intriguing questions. The reader is referred to Henry Coston, *M. Pompidou, qui êtes-vous?* (Lectures Françaises no. 147/148, July-August 1969), and *Entre Rothschild et Moscou* (Lectures Françaises no. 146, June 1969), both published in Paris. Coston's arguments can only be described as extraordinary and should be read with some skepticism. Still, they have empirical support and the writer has not (as yet) been able to detect error in this factual support. There may be alternative interpretations, but Coston's charges will have to be answered at some point.

[35] *Business Week*, June 19, 1971, pp. 84-90.

[36] *Metalworking News* (New York), August 16, 1971.

[37] *Ibid.*

[38] For illustration of this point, see U.S. Senate, Committee on the Judiciary, *Soviet Political Agreements and Results*, 88th Congress, 2d session (3d revision; Washington, 1964), vol. 1, p. viii: "The staff studied nearly a thousand treaties and agreements ..., both bilateral and multilateral, which the Soviets have entered into not only with the United States, but with countries all over the world. The staff found that in the 38 short years since the Soviet Union came into existence, its Government had broken its word to virtually every country to which it ever gave a signed promise."

industries contribute directly to any war effort. For example, fertilizer plants can be converted to the manufacture of explosives. Illustrative of the fundamental assistance given in this sector for the development of military industries was the 1930s agreement by the Hercules Powder Company, Inc., to "communicate the secrets of production" of cotton linter, "prepare a complete design of a nitrocellulose plant for the production of 5000 tons yearly," provide drawings (by which the plant could be duplicated), send engineers, supervise installation of equipment and startup, train Russian engineers in manufacture of nitrocellulose and allow a "detailed study of nitrocellulose production" in Hercules' U.S. plants.[39]

This agreement was the basis of the Soviet explosives industry. Yet it was described by the company in a letter to the State Department as "apparently with the view of developing the production of nitrocellulose for peacetime arts."[40] Inasmuch as this letter was sent after informal discussion with Robert F. Kelley of the State Department, it has to be assumed that the department granted approval for Hercules to go ahead on the basis of full information. It is beyond the bounds of common sense to assume that either the State Department or Hercules was convinced that the application of this assistance would be limited to "peacetime arts."

Even in 1963 several congressmen objected strongly to the export of potash mining machinery to the U.S.S.R. on the grounds that potash could be used for explosives. However, the Department of Commerce took the position that potash "is used almost exclusively in the manufacture of potassium fertilizers."[41] Incendiary bombs require sulfuric acid; a process for the concentration of sulfuric acid was sent to the U.S.S.R. in the 1960s. One process for the manufacture of tear gas (used by North Vietnamese forces in South Vietnam) requires carbon tetrachloride and benzene; both products were shipped from the United States to the U.S.S.R. in the late 1960s.[42] Herbicides have the same chemicals as riot-control gases, and herbicides are among the volume imports by the U.S.S.R. from the U.S.A. Both the Japanese anthrax bomb plant at Harbin and the German Tabun plant were removed to the U.S.S.R. at the end of World War II.[43] Since that time the West has given indirect assistance to the Soviet chemical and biological warfare plants. For example, biological warfare requires refrigeration, and technical assistance has been provided for refrigeration; gelatin or synthetic polymers are needed to encapsulate biological warfare particles, and gelatin encapsulating apparatus has been shipped from the United States.

Textiles, of course, are war materials. This was clearly recognized during World War II, and the military end uses for textiles have expanded since that

---

[39]   See Sutton II, p. 246.

[40]   Letter from Hercules Powder Company, Inc., to State Department, July 2, 1930.

[41]   U.S. Congress, House of Representatives, *Congressional Record*, 88th Congress, 1st session, 1963; vol. 109, pt. II.

[42]   U.S. Dept. of Commerce, *Export Control* (Washington, D.C.), 1st quarter 1969 and 2d quarter 1967.

[43]   Seymour M. Hersh, *Chemical and Biological Warfare* (Indianapolis: Bobbs-Merrill, 1968).

time. In 1943 the Pepperell Manufacturing Company, a major U.S. textile producer, described its wartime activities: the firm manufactured parachute cloth, airplane fabrics, and life rafts from nylon, uniforms from twill, and jungle hammocks from percale sheeting. Canton flannel was manufactured for shipment to the U.S.S.R. for use in leg and foot wrappings, oil filters, and gun patches. Pepperell even described sheets as "war supplies" and commented that cotton spindles are "weapons."[44]

Soviet uses of textiles are of course similar to our own, and indeed Yuri Krotkov comments that in the early 1960s women's nylon stockings disappeared suddenly from Moscow shops. Why? "Because Gosplan had used up all its reserves of nylon in supplying the defense plants."[45]

What is remarkable is the change in interpretation that has taken place over the last 20 years. In the 1940s automobile plants and textile plants manufactured "war supplies"; by the 1960s these plants could manufacture only "peace supplies." The problem really boils down to one of the Soviets' *intent*. Do they intend to use the technology to military ends? Some of the foregoing examples introduce an element of doubt. But if Soviet intent is in fact peaceful, then has the item no strategic implication? And might there not be circumstances under which peaceful intent could change?

One area in which we can precisely identify Soviet uses of Western-built products is that of shipping, since each vessel is unique and identifiable.

In the 1930s Western-built ships were used to transport political prisoners to Siberia. According to A. Dallin, the following ships were operated for that purpose by the NKVD: *Djurma* (built in Holland), *Minsk* (Germany), *Kiev* (Germany), *Igarka* (United Kingdom), *Komsomol* (United Kingdom), *Svirstroi* (United States), *Volkhovstroi* (United States), *Shatourstroi* (United States).[46] According to V. A. Kravchenko, the *Dalstroi* (Holland) also was used by the NKVD to transport political prisoners to concentration camps.[47] These vessels were all apparently intended for merchant duty when they were received.

Lest the reader argue that such movement was an internal matter and hence not relevant to military strategy, it should be stated that Western-built ships also have been used for overtly military purposes against the builders of the vessels. For instance, it is known that the Soviets have used about 100 vessels on the supply run from the Black Sea and Vladivostok to carry weapons, munitions, supplies, fertilizers, and so on to Haiphong (and earlier to the Cambodian port of Sihanoukville) to supply North Vietnamese actions in South Vietnam and Cambodia. The names of 96 of these vessels were obtained,[48] and Table

---

[44] Pepperell Manufacturing Company, *People of Peace at War* (Boston, 1943), p. 33.

[45] Yu. Krotkov, *The Angry Exile* (London: Heinemann, 1967), p. 92.

[46] A. D. J. Dallin and B. I. Nicolaevsky, *Forced Labor in Soviet Russia* (London: Hollis & Carter, 1947), pp. 128-29, 137.

[47] V. A. Kravchenko, *I Chose Justice* (New York: Scribners, 1950), pp. 290, 300.

[48] U.S. Senate, Committee on Banking and Currency, *Export Expansion and Regulation*, Hearings Before the Subcommittee on International Finance of the Committee on Banking and Currency, 91st Congress, 1st session (Washington, 1969).

27-2 lists the origins of their main engines. Of the 96 vessels, identification of main engines was possible in all but 12. Of the 75 diesel engines it was

Table 27-2   WESTERN ORIGINS OF MAIN ENGINES IN
                   SOVIET SHIPS (96) USED ON THE HAIPHONG SUPPLY RUN

	Engines manufactured	
	in U.S.S.R.	not in U.S.S.R.
DIESEL ENGINES:		
Manufactured in the U.S.S.R. to Soviet design	0	
Manufactured in U.S.S.R. under license and to foreign design:		
Skoda (at Russky Diesel)	5	
Burmeister & Wain (at Bryansk)	8	
Manufactured outside U.S.S.R. to foreign design:		
Skoda		5
M.A.N.		11
Fiat		2
Burmeister & Wain (in Copenhagen and elsewhere under license)		8
Sulzer (Switzerland)		13
Lang (Budapest)		4
Görlitz (G.D.R.)		10
Lend Lease (United States) [a]		7
Non-Lend Lease (United States) [a]		1
Krupp (Germany)		1
Total diesel engine	13	62
STEAM TURBINES AND RECIPROCATING STEAM ENGINES		
Manufactured in U.S.S.R. to Soviet design	0	
Manufactured in U.S.S.R. to foreign design	1 (possible)[b]	
Manufactured outside the U.S.S.R.		
Canada [a]		1
U.S.A. [a]		3
United Kingdom [a]		1
Sulzer (Switzerland)		2
ZUT (Switzerland)		1
Total steam turbines	1	8
Grand total: diesel engines 75		
steam turbines 9		
84		
not identified 12		
96		

Source: U.S. Naval Institute, Proceedings, January 1970.
[a] Manufacture unknown.
[b] Possibly Sulzer steam turbine.

determined that 62 had been built outside the U.S.S.R. and 13 inside the U.S.S.R. The 13 domestic diesels were of either Skoda or Burmeister & Wain design, and only one steam turbine is listed as of possible Soviet manufacture and design.

The Burmeister & Wain technical-assistance agreement with the Bryansk plant has produced engines for numerous ships used by the Soviets for military purposes. Table 27-3 lists some Haiphong run vessels with Burmeister & Wain engines built at Bryansk.

Table 27-3		HAIPHONG RUN SHIPS WITH ENGINES MADE UNDER THE BURMEISTER & WAIN TECHNICAL-ASSISTANCE AGREEMENT OF 1959			
Soviet Register no.		Name	Tonnage	Type	Engine *model no.* (Burmeister & Wain)
4776	1965	*Belgorod Dnestrovskiy*	11,011	—	B&W 774-VT2BF-160
5450	1967	*Berezovka*	10,996	Cargo	B&W 674-VT2BF-160
569	1964	*Bryanskiy Rabochiy*	11,089	Cargo	B&W 774-VT2BF-160
5492	1967	*Partizanskaya Slava*	10,881	Cargo	B&W 674-VT2BF-160
2127	1964	*Pavlovsk*	11,089	Cargo	B&W 774-VT2BF-160
2172	1963	*Perekop*	11,089	Cargo	B&W 774-VT2BF-160
2232	1963	*Polotsk**	9,500	Cargo	B&W 674-VT2BF-160
2268	1964	*Pridneprovsk*	11,089	Tanker	B&W 774-VT2BF-160

Sources: U.S. Naval Institute, *Proceedings*, January 1970.
**Lloyd's Register of Shipping*, 1970 (London) indicates built at Bryansk; Soviet Register indicates built in Denmark.

Quite apart from main engines, complete ships have been built in the West and utilized for military purposes. Table 27-4 gives a selected list of such ships known to have supplied material to North Vietnam, together with their Western origins.

Table 27-4		SHIPS KNOWN TO HAVE TRANSPORTED MATERIAL TO NORTH VIETNAM		
Reg.No.	Year of Construction	Name of ship	Place of construction	
			Hull	Engines
M26121	1960	*Kura*(4084 tons)	West Germany	West Germany
M11647	1936	*Arktika*(2900 tons)	United Kingdom	United Kingdom
M17082	1962	*Sinegorsk* (3330 tons)	Finland	Sweden
M3017	1961	*Ingur*(4084 tons)	West Germany	West Germany

The *Ristna*, which was reported off Ghana in 1966 with arms for internal revolts,[49] is powered by M.A.N. six-cylinder engines (570-mm bore and 800-mm stroke) built in Hamburg.[50] During the Cuban missile crisis of 1962 Soviet ballistic missiles were carried to Cuba in the "Poltava" class of dry-cargo carrier. These have an exceptionally long No. 4 hatch (13.5 meters) enabling transport of intermediate-range missiles. The class consists of a number of vessels with common construction characteristics; thus details of one vessel, the *Poltava*, will make the point clear. The *Poltava* (Soviet registration number M-22600) is an 11,000-ton dry-cargo ship with engines constructed by Burmeister & Wain of Copenhagen, Denmark. The engines are two-cycle supercharged, six-cylinder diesel marine type, with a cylinder diameter of 740 mm and a piston stroke of 1600 mm; some vessels of the "Poltava" class have engines made in the Soviet Union but based on the Burmeister & Wain engine. The *Polotsk*, for example, has a Danish engine, but the *Perekop* has a Soviet-built B&W engine of the same type.[51]

In brief, there is a direct, identifiable military utilization by the Soviets of technologies, equipment, and products supplied by Western governments under the assumption that these items were for peaceful use.

What is more, there is evidence that there has been a considerable "leakage" of Western equipment under export control.[52] This, of course, is a different proposition from export of peaceful goods where reliance is placed on Soviet intent not to use these goods for military purposes. Where products are defined as "strategic" and still find their way in quantity to the U.S.S.R., there is a problem of ineffective administration.

THE FAILURE OF WESTERN EXPORT CONTROLS

The United States in the Export Control Act of 1949 and the Battle Act of 1951, and other Western nations under equivalent legislation, have attempted to restrict exports of "strategic" goods to the Soviet Union. In the United States the export of purely military goods is administered by the State Department while the export of "strategic" goods is vested in the Department of Commerce, although the State Department has a major influence in this area also. The Department of Defense may register objection to export of a specific item, but has been overruled on sufficient occasions with regard to strategic goods

[49] *Current Digest of the Soviet Press*, XIX (March 19, 1967), 35.
[50] Registr Soyuza SSR, *Registrovaya kniga morskikh sudov soyuza SSR 1964-1965* (Moscow, 1966).
[51] *Ibid.*
[52] See chapter 7, "The Arms Runners," in J. B. Hutton, *The Traitor Trade* (New York: Obolensky, 1963). Hutton is a former Soviet agent who was employed in smuggling strategic goods. Since the book has an epilogue by W. Averell Harriman it is presumably authentic.

that its influence may be considered as greatly subordinate to that of the State and Commerce departments.

The provision of fast, large ships for Soviet supply of the North Vietnamese will indicate the type of problem arising where export control has failed. Two segments of the Soviet merchant marine were examined to determine the relationship between Western origins and maximum speed of Soviet ships. It was anticipated that because of the NATO limitations on the speed of merchant ships supplied to the U.S.S.R. (reflected in export-control laws) the average speed of NATO-supplied ships would be considerably less than ships either supplied by East European countries to the U.S.S.R. or built within the U.S.S.R. itself. The results of the analysis are as follows:

SEGMENT 1: AVERAGE SPEED OF SOVIET SHIPS USED
ON THE HAIPHONG SUPPLY RUN
(42 ships)
Merchant ships with engines manufactured in Free World   14.62 knots
Merchant ships with engines manufactured in Eastern Europe   13.25 knots
Merchant ships with engines manufactured in Soviet Union   12.23 knots
(all built after 1951, i.e., after implementation of Battle Act).

SEGMENT 2: AVERAGE SPEED OF SOVIET SHIPS ADDED
TO THE MERCHANT FLEET IN 1964-65
(392 ships)
Merchant ships with engines manufactured in Free World   14.93 knots
Merchant ships with engines manufactured in Eastern Europe   11.93 knots
Merchant ships with engines manufactured in Soviet Union   10.95 knots

The most obvious point to be made is that the average speed of Western-supplied ships used by the Soviets in the Haiphong run was 2.4 knots (i.e., about 20 percent) above that of Soviet domestic-built ships used on the run. This segment includes only those ships built after 1951 (i.e., after implementation of the Battle Act with its stated limitation of speed and tonnage of ships supplied to the U.S.S.R.).[53] The second segment (ships added in 1964-65) indicates that the gap in speed between Western- and Soviet-built ships is widening—that Western ships on the average are almost four knots, or 36 percent, faster than domestic-built ships. We may conclude that not only has this discrepancy gone unobserved among export control officials, but whatever export-control principle is utilized is being eroded over time.

Figures 27-1 and 27-2 suggest that the lax administration applies also to weight limitations. Hence the faster, larger Soviet ships are from the West and the slower, smaller ships are from Soviet shipyards.

It is relevant to point out that under the CoCom provisions each nation

---

[53] Gunnar Adler-Karlsson, *Western Economic Warfare, 1947-1967* (Stockholm: Almquist & Wiksell, 1968), p. 93.

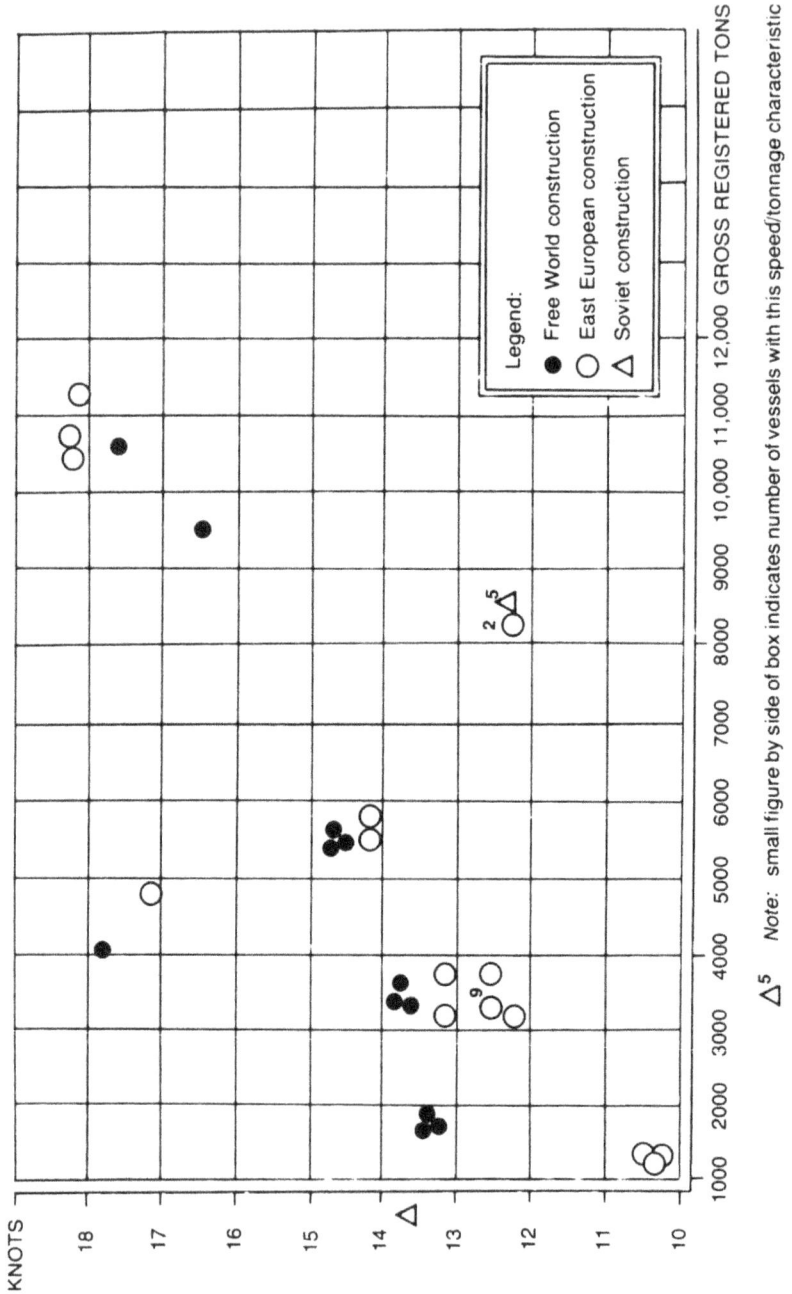

Figure 27-1

SOVIET SHIPS ON THE HAIPHONG RUN: CONSTRUCTION ORIGINS OF MAIN DIESEL ENGINES IN RELATION TO MAXIMUM SPEED AND TONNAGE

Legend:
● Free World construction
○ East European construction
△ Soviet construction

Note: small figure by side of box indicates number of vessels with this speed/tonnage characteristic

Figure 27-2

SOVIET SHIPS ON THE HAIPHONG RUN: DESIGN ORIGINS OF MAIN
DIESEL ENGINES IN RELATION TO MAXIMUM SPEED AND TONNAGE

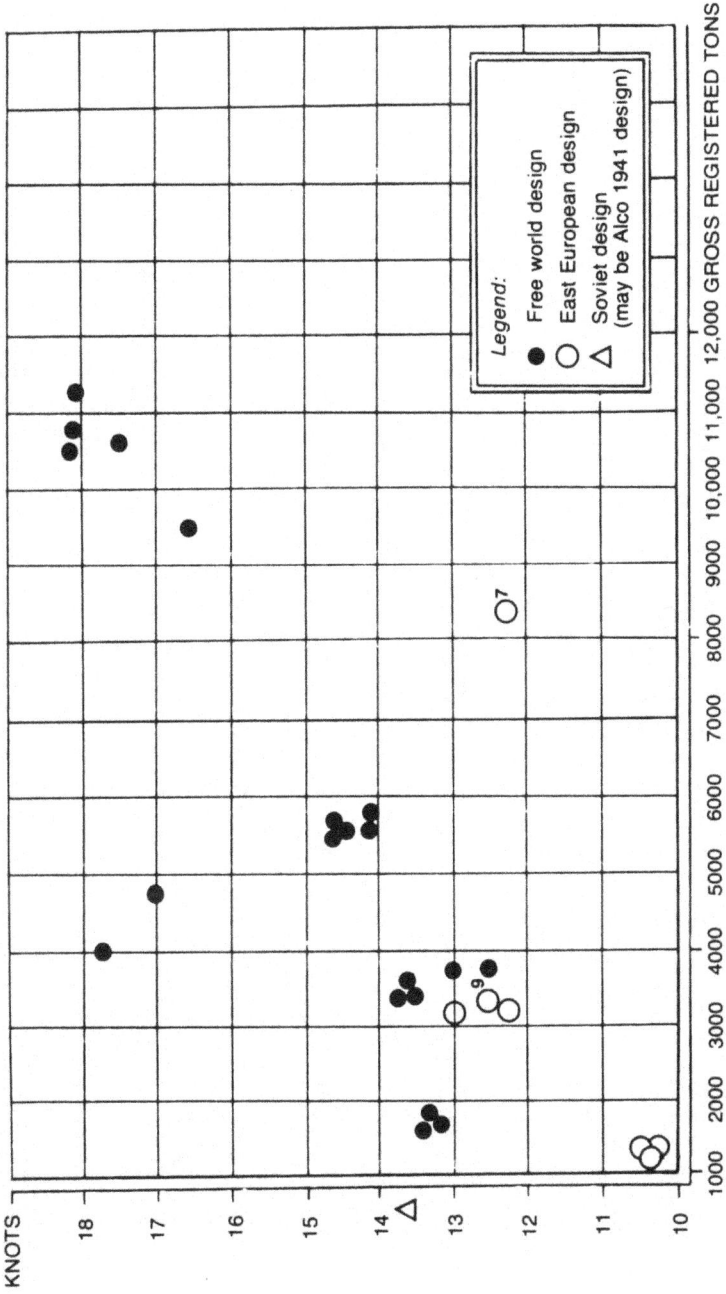

Legend:
● Free world design
○ East European design
△ Soviet design
   (may be Alco 1941 design)

○⁷ Note: small figure by side of box indicates number of vessels with this speed/tonnage characteristic

participating in the embargo of strategic materials submits its own views concerning whether or not specific items should be shipped. There is also a unanimity rule. In other words, no item is ever shipped to the U.S.S.R. unless all participating nations agree that it should be shipped. Objection by any nation would halt the shipment. Douglas Dillon, former under secretary of state, has pointed out: "I can recall no instance in which a country shipped a strategic item to the Soviet bloc against the disapproving vote of a participating member of CoCom."[54]

It must therefore be presumed that U.S. delegates participated in, and approved of, export of ships of high average speed as well as marine diesel engines, and of the Burmeister & Wain technical-assistance agreement of 1959 for Soviet manufacture of large marine diesels—all later used against the United States by the Soviets in supply of North Vietnam. In summary, the evidence suggests that the U.S. delegates to CoCom knowingly allowed export of ships above the NATO speed and weight limits that were later utilized against the United States. This possibility clearly demands further investigation.

RELEASE OF RESOURCES, INDIRECT
TRANSFERS, AND WESTERN SECURITY

The release of domestic resources is one of the most important effects of technical transfers from one country to another, and it may be the effect most difficult for the layman to appreciate. Whenever assistance is provided from outside the Soviet economic system internal resources are released, and by substitutions at the margin the Soviet Union is enabled to devote such released resources to political objectives of the system.

This substitution is of major importance to military objectives because while domestic resources are being devoted to military development the broader industrial base is being updated and fortified from abroad. The industrial base of any country is the prime determinant of its military strength and ultimately the determinant of success in military operations. The United States military does not produce its own weapons: research, development, and production are largely handled by private industry. It is the flexibility and efficiency of American private industry that is the basic resource on which the American military structure depends.

The Soviet military is equally dependent on Soviet industry. It has been estimated that between 70 and 75 percent of the annual Soviet military expenditure

[54] U.S. Senate Committee on the Judiciary, *Export of Strategic Materials to the U.S.S.R. and Other Bloc Countries*, Hearings Before the Subcommittee to Investigate the Administration of the Internal Security Act and Other Internal Security Laws, 87th Congress, 1st session, Part 1, October 23, 1961, p. 45.

goes to industry for the purchase of armaments.[55] The military has top priority, but its capabilities also reflect Soviet weaknesses brought about by the almost total absence of innovative effort. Flexibility and innovation for Soviet industry are imported from the West. Thus, ironically, the prime forces making for efficiency in Soviet military production are Western initiative and efficiency. This conclusion can be refuted only if it can be shown (a) that the transfers of innovation from the West do not take place and (b) that the Soviet military structure does not depend on the Soviet industrial structure for input materials.

Therefore, we cannot in the final analysis make any meaningful distinction between military and civilian goods. Every industrial plant directly or indirectly affords some military capability. It is the availability of Western technology that makes Soviet industry more efficient. The import of this technology releases resources for military efforts and also ensures that the Soviet industrial-military complex incorporates the latest of Western manufacturing techniques.

Nor can any meaningful distinction be made in the last analysis between technology exports to the U.S.S.R. and those to the other East European bloc countries. Recognition of political differences between Communist nations has led to Western policies based on such differences, and specifically to more favorable economic treatment of less hostile Communist countries. However, political differences among Communist nations have not led to any reduction in intra-bloc trade or transfers of technologies. Indeed, paradoxically, the Western reaction to polycentralism in the form of "more trade" has led to an increased transfer of Western technology to the Soviet Union. Processes and products embargoed for direct Soviet shipment are transferred to the Soviet Union indirectly through East European communist countries. There has been, then, an increase in transfer of technology to the U.S.S.R. as a result of the Western policies of the past two decades, policies based on erroneous assumptions concerning the extent to which polycentralism exists, and can exist, in the economic life of Eastern Europe.

As the acquisition of Western technology is a prime objective of all Communist nations, it must be further concluded that one effect on the West's response to its own interpretations of differing forms of communism in Eastern Europe has been to provide a more effective economic basis for fulfillment of Soviet foreign policy objectives. The international political objectives of Yugoslavia, for example, do not alter the fact that the Yugoslavs can and do supply the Soviets with such vitally needed items as advanced diesel engines, larger merchant ships, and copper electrical products. With their technical support to the U.S.S.R. the Yugoslavs are making a far more significant contribution to Soviet international aspirations than any possible purely political support would provide.

---

[55] Konstantin K. Krylov, "Soviet Military-Economic Complex," *Military Review* (Fort Leavenworth, Kans.), November 1971, p. 93.

A rational policy for any nation is one based on logical deduction from empirical observation. If a policy is based on erroneous information or on lack of facts, or if it is developed from accurate data by nonlogical, i.e., mystical, methods, the policy is not likely to achieve its objectives.

There is adequate reason to believe that Western policy toward the U.S.S.R. in the field of economic relations is based, first, on an inadequate observation of fact, and second, on invalid assumptions. In no other way can one explain the extraordinary statements made, for example, by State Department officials to Congress, by academic writers, and by 50 years of policies which prescribe first the establishment and then the continuing subsidy of a system that simultaneously calls forth massive armaments expenditures. Those countries which have been the prime technical subsidizers of the U.S.S.R. are also the countries with the largest expenditures on armaments against a presumably real threat from the Soviet Union.

The first requirement of a rational policy in economic relations between the Western world and any communist state is to determine the empirical facts governing both economic and strategic-military relations. These three volumes have established, from a precise technical examination, that the Soviet Union and its socialist allies are dependent on the Western world for technical and economic viability. At any time the West chooses to withdraw this technical and economic subsidy, the Soviet Union must either meet terms laid down by the West or effect within its own system the changes needed to achieve self-generated innovation. The major temporal and political demands of the second course suggest that the Soviet Union would come to terms. The West, then, has the option of taking major steps toward developing world peace.

To subsidize and support a system that is the object of massive military expenditures is both illogical and irrational. In other words, it calls into question not only the ability and the wisdom but indeed the basic common sense of the policymakers.

The choice therefore is clear: either the West should abandon massive armaments expenditures because the Soviet Union is not an enemy of the West, or it should abandon the technical transfers that make it possible for the Soviet Union to pose the threat to the Free World which is the *raison d'être* for such a large share of Western expenditures.[56]

---

[56] The numerous statements contrary to this conclusion do not stand up to penetrating analysis. For example, Assistant Secretary of State Nicholas de B. Katzenbach: "We should have no illusions. If we do not sell peaceful goods to the nations of Eastern Europe, others will. If we erect barriers to our trade with Eastern Europe, we will lose the trade and Eastern Europe will buy elsewhere. But we will not make any easier our task of stopping aggression in Vietnam nor in building security for the United States." U.S. House of Representatives, Committee on Banking and Currency, *To Amend the Export-Import Bank Act of 1945*, Hearings, 90th Congress, 1st session, April 1967, p. 64.

CHAPTER TWENTY-EIGHT

Economic Aspects of Technical Transfers

THE UNSTATED PREREQUISITE FOR CENTRAL PLANNING

The prolific literature on central economic planning published in this century contains no discussion—or even passing mention—of one apparently essential prerequisite: there must be systems not regulated strictly by central planning that are willing to provide technical services and productive units for the centrally planned system. A world of strictly centrally planned systems based on the Soviet model, or a single centrally planned world system, could not progress. It would choke on technical inertia. The Soviet state's dependence on the West was at least partly recognized by Lenin,[1] and it is effectively conceded by present-day Soviet leaders when they openly subscribe to advances in Western technology—not omitting, of course, politically necessary references to capitalism's "internal contradictions".

The outstanding achievement of central planning is its ability to realize substantial rates of growth through planned diversion of resources and efforts into chosen industrial sectors. Let us accept as a premise that over the course of 50 years Soviet growth rates in most sectors have been substantial. Iron and steel production is certainly one such sector: Russian pig-iron production was 4.2 million tons in 1913 and 70.3 million metric tons in 1966, while steel production was 4.3 million tons in 1913 and 96.9 million tons in 1966. Fertilizer production was 42,000 tons in 1913 and 6.9 million tons in 1966. Chemical fiber production was zero in 1913 and 458,000 tons in 1966.[2] Ship production totaled 1.75 million gross registered tons in 1914 and 11 million gross registered tons in 1967.[3]

In each case of exceptional rates of growth we find significant acquisition of Western technology at the start of the rise in growth; indeed, it is a matter of open record that increments in output were planned to be at least initially

---

[1] See for example, V. I. Lenin, *Selected Works*, J. Fineberg, ed. (New York: International Publishers, 1937), vol. 9, pp. 116-18.

[2] *Strana Sovetov za 50 let* (Moscow, 1967), p. 98.

[3] John D. Harbron, *Communist Ships and Shipping* (London, 1962), p. 140.

dependent on the West. The planned increment in production was achieved in a conscious manner, not by internal technical resources, but by the purchase of high-productivity advanced units in the West.

Could the Soviet system have attained high rates of growth in any single sector without outside injections of technology and capacity? The answer is: apparently not. At any rate, no example has been found of a sector in the Soviet economy achieving rapid rates of growth without technical injections from outside the system. The sector that has come closest to showing indigenous technical progress is the iron and steel industry, with Western technology first absorbed and then scaled up to provide massive increments in pig iron and raw steel output. However, with this sequence the sector's progress has been limited: full modern industrialization demands not only a balanced output of iron and raw steel but also of finished rolled products. Rolling is not subject to scaling-up innovation. One can quadruple the size of an open hearth or a blast furnace, but quadrupling the size of a blooming mill, and certainly a wide-strip mill, is technically impossible. The continuous casting process was seen as a way around the problems posed by the blooming mill, i.e., as a way to replace scaling up, but here, as we have seen, too-rapid introduction brought its own problems.

The logical conclusion, therefore, is that Soviet central planning absolutely demanded from the outset, and still demands, the existence of technically balanced systems from which it might leach new processes and purchase productive capacity. In the absence of such systems, it probably could not have made great technical progress.

THE FUNCTION OF IMPORTED TECHNOLOGY
IN THE SOVIET SYSTEM

The basic problem of the Soviet economy is, as we have seen, its essentially static nature. The system apparently lacks internal dynamic factors that make for indigenous technical progress other than that attained by duplication of an existing technology. On the other hand, true technical progress involves the steady substitution of ever more efficient ways of combining resources and is the most significant factor in increasing standards of living.

The function of imported technology in the U.S.S.R. is therefore to provide the missing dynamic element of technical progress, or more specifically, to supply innovation. This is achieved in several sequential steps. First, at an early stage in a sector's development the productive units themselves are imported, i.e., the machines, the boilers, the production lines. This is followed by a second stage, that of duplication or copying of the most useful of the imported units, according to a standardized design. Long runs of standard units without model change achieve the favorable growth rates noted. In certain sectors this may be followed by a third stage—adaptive innovation, i.e., scaling up. The Soviets have made excellent use of the scaling-up procedure in iron and steel and electricity generation. Such scaling up, however, cannot be applied in all sectors or in all basic technologies within a sector. As we have seen, it can be used in blast furnaces within limits, but not in rolling mills. It can be used in coke ovens within limits, but not in the production of precision machinery. It can be used in penicillin production, but not in radio-tube production. Thus the adaptive process of scaling up has significant limits.

So far as major indigenous innovation is concerned, we have seen that this is barely existent in the Soviet Union. There have been a few research achievements not found in the West (three synthetic fibers, for example), and some indigenous research has been placed into pilot production (as in the case of the Grinenko process). There is no case, however, of a large-scale productive unit based on self-generated indigenous Soviet technology. The Soviet technology that comes closest to this achievement is probably the turbodrill—but this technology is not comparable in its complexity to, say, automobile manufacturing, and in any case increasing demands for depth drilling have revealed turbodrill performance problems.

We can induce at least three contributions from technical transfer in addition to provision of technical modernization: the grant of economic flexibility (through release of resources), the grant of performance flexibility (because a standardized design is suitable for only a limited range of end uses), and the engineering contribution that inheres in foreign construction of large production units (those beyond available Soviet skills but not necessarily involving new technology).

Performance flexibility benefits may be noted in several of the sectors discussed in the study. One example can be seen with respect to marine boilers installed in Soviet ships between 1945 to 1960. All Soviet-made marine boilers are of one size and model. Flexibility for various requirements is achieved by importing boilers with nonstandard characteristics, e.g., unusual heating surfaces and working pressures. The existence of this phenomenon does not emerge from the trade and production statistics; its detection requires examination of the specifications for units produced and imported.

The engineering benefit, which is actually a variation of the flexibility contribution, is exemplified by the large number of complete plants bought abroad. It is also present in such acquisitions as refrigerator ships, where more complicated systems are purchased abroad and simpler systems are built inside the U.S.S.R.

THE SOVIET APPROACH TO IMPORT SUBSTITUTION

The Soviet approach to import substitution is of particular significance because in the Soviet Union the process results from more lengthy experience than in any other socialist economy. It appears to fall into three distinct stages: first, import of foreign equipment; second, a period of comparative testing during which both foreign and domestic copies are used side by side; and third, the elimination of imports and sole reliance on domestic-produced equipment.

Although this three-stage categorization is generally supported by the information presented here, it is possible to document the process fully in only one equipment area—steam turbines. Data are needed over a period of time (to cover the three stages hypothesized) to cover all units acquired, built, and installed and to determine their precise identification. The only source of such complete information available outside the U.S.S.R. is the Soviet Register of Shipping.[4] Of 5500 entries described in that source, 47 merchant ships are found to have steam turbines as propulsion units (there are many more in the Red Navy); these turbines are identified by type, origin, and date of installation.

When these data are plotted, it may be seen that installations fall into the three distinct periods postulated when viewed in terms of origins: first, a period from 1953 to 1957 with only foreign purchases (no domestic manufacture): second, a period from 1957 to 1960 with both foreign purchases and domestic production of steam turbines; and third, a period after 1960 with only domestic manufacture. Although import of steam turbines after 1960 would not invalidate the case (indeed, the Soviets would want to investigate any new Western design developments), in this case none appear to have been imported in the final period under consideration.

THE OUTPUT OF ENGINEERING SKILLS

A superficial conflict with the findings of this study is posed by the apparent numbers of engineers graduated in the U.S.S.R. compared to those in the U.S.A. A Soviet source gives the following statistics for engineering degrees granted in the U.S.S.R. and the U.S.A. in 1950 and 1965:[5]

U.S.S.R.	37,000 (1950)	170,000 (1965)
U.S.A.	61,000 (1950)	41,000 (1965)

According to these figures, output of engineers with degrees has increased four-fold in the period 1950 to 1965, while that of the United States has fallen by one-half in the same period. There is, of course, a relationship between numbers of engineers and level of technology.

If the Soviets had a vigorous indigenous technology, little further attention would be paid to this finding. However, the quantity production of engineers

---

[4] Registr Soyuza SSR, *Registrovaya kniga morskikh sudov soyuza SSR 1964-65* (Moscow, 1966).
[5] *Strana Sovetov ..., op. cit.* n. 2, p. 231.

since the 1930s appears to be inconsistent with the findings of this study. Some probing indicates a reconciliation. A Russian engineer is not the same as a Western engineer, particularly an American engineer. Not only is the Soviet engineer's training and experience much narrower; his level of skills is far lower. Indeed, a Soviet "engineer" may not have as high a level of technical ability as a master mechanic or ship superintendent in the United States. Moreover there is no question that top-level technical graduates are siphoned into military work and the balance go into industry; this diversion coupled with the generally lower skills requirements greatly reduces the effectiveness of the large reservoir of engineers.

This conclusion is supported by reports from at least two delegations to the Soviet Union. Appendix 9 of the 1963 Indian iron and steel industry delegation report[6] cites the engineering force and its utilization at the steel works called Zaporozhstal. Of a total of 16,829 workers, 1367 were classified as "engineers." These "engineers" were working in such locations as the telephone exchange (12), stores (8), instrument repair shop (58), water supply station (5), building repair facilities (20), and scrapyard (19). Obviously they were not engineers by any Western definition. In the West any one of the above-named operations (with the possible exception of instrument repair) can function without a single degree-qualified engineer.

Another example may be found in the report of a USDA forestry delegation.[7] That delegation inspected the Bozhenko furniture plant in Kiev and found that the 1600 employees included 104 technical people, of whom 64 had university degrees. Quite clearly if the 64 technical-degree holders in this small furniture plant are placed according to their abilities, their level of skills must be extraordinarily low. In the West such a plant with a comparable output could operate efficiently without a single technical-degree holder and rarely would there be need for more than two or three. The Bozhenko furniture plant as described by the U.S. delegation (and shown in photographs published in the report) suggests a management problem of major significance. The descriptions and photographs together depict a plant with abysmally low levels of efficiency when compared with Western plants. The factory painting facilities (a brick wall outside the plant), the intraplant "transport" (a man pushing an overloaded and wobbly trolley), and the general assembly shop could not be found in Europe or the United States: state factory inspectors would close the plant down as a hazard for its workers. If such an institution employs 64 degree holders, the logical questions must be: What are they doing? What is their training? What is their supposed purpose in the plant?

There are numerous reports of poor construction in the Soviet Union—and

[6] *Iron & Steel Industry in the U.S.S.R. and Czechoslovakia; Report of Indian Productivity Team,* (New Delhi: National Productivity Council, March 1963), p. 253.
[7] U.S. Dept. of Agriculture, Forestry Service, *Forestry and Forest Industry in the U.S.S.R.,* Report of a Technical Study Group (Washington, March 1961).

construction quality is a fair indicator of engineering ability. This may be exemplified by a report in 1966 to the effect that a French construction company was negotiating to build "earthquake-proof apartment buildings in the battered Soviet city of Tashkent. Some 30,000 apartments built [previously] by the company in Tashkent survived earthquakes there earlier this year."[8]

In 1960 two Soviet engineers named Zolotarov and Shteingauz claimed a world record in building dams on soft ground, mentioning specifically the dams at Svir and Tsimlyansk.[9] Given the very low ratio of dams built to hydroelectric power potential in the U.S.S.R. and the major engineering problems of building on soft ground (indeed, the initial engineering effort usually is to locate bedrock for dam construction), some kind of training problem seems obvious.

Equipment down-time is also an indicator of quality control and engineering skills in the manufacturing process, and the evidence points to Soviet deficiencies in this sphere. For example, in 1955 some Russian tractor models averaged more than one month out of service for repairs: the STZ-NATI required a total of 56 days in 1955 for overall repairs,[10] and the DT-54 a total of 59 days. If a tractor is out of commission almost two months in a year for technical reasons, it is clearly a faulty product.

We may justifiably conclude that the number of degreed engineers in the U.S.S.R. is not a reliable indicator of the nation's engineering capability, and that the equivalent U.S. figure should include at least master mechanics, shop superintendents, and a large proportion of skilled foremen.

USE OF IMPORTS TO FULFILL PLANNING OBJECTIVES

Where planning objectives of increased output cannot be achieved by duplication or by scaling-up innovation, resort has to be made to imports. Necessarily, the processes acquired in this manner are frequently those whose development abroad required large investments in capital and skill.

Examination of Soviet import statistics for the period 1946 to 1966 indicates that while total import values increased (692 million rubles in 1946 to 7122 million rubles in 1966, or a tenfold increase over two decades), the import of machinery and equipment remained consistently at one-third of the total (197 million rubles in 1946 and 2308 million rubles in 1966). However, analysis of the expenditure components reveals that planning objectives and directives have been reflected in significant increases in imports in the affected sectors. For example, the program to build a merchant fleet got under way in the early

---

[8] *New York Times,* October 11, 1966.

[9] T. L. Zolotarev and Y. O. Shteingauz, *Hydroelectric Power Plants and the Main Trends in Their Development* (Jerusalem: Israel Program for Scientific Translations, 1963), p. 146.

[10] *Problems of Agricultural Economy* (collection of articles) (Moscow, 1958); translation: Washington, D.C., 1960, p. 155.

50s and the import figures reflect the calculations given elsewhere—that since then over two-thirds of the Soviet merchant fleet has been built in the West. Similarly, Khrushchev's call for a massive increase in chemical production in 1957 was accompanied by an immediate increase in chemical equipment imports, a nearly tenfold increase in ten years (from 22 million rubles in 1957 to 100 million in 1959 and an average import of just over 200 million rubles in the mid to late sixties.)"[11]

Internal shortages are also reflected in changing import figures. For example, the agricultural problems of the early 1960s resulted in massive imports not only of foreign wheat but also of foreign fertilizers and agricultural equipment (from 14 million rubles in 1961 to 62 million rubles in 1966).

Table 28-1 SOVIET IMPORTS BY SOVIET TRANSPORT
CATEGORY FROM 1946 to 1966

Year	Total imports (million rubles)	Machines and equipment (Groups 10-19)	Ships and equipment (Group 192)	Chemical industry equipment (Group 150)	Agriculture equipment and fertilizers (Groups 181, 342)
1946	692.0	197.4	5.6	3.9	0.1
1947	670.3	119.1	3.9	1.5	0.2
1948	1106.6	99.0	5.4	0.9	0.1
1949	1340.3	193.4	23.6	1.9	1.7
1950	1310.3	281.7	25.8	1.7	6.2
1951	1791.7	372.0	33.9	6.4	0.4
1952	2255.5	486.2	71.6	9.3	0.2
1953	2492.1	684.8	106.7	18.3	0.3
1954	2863.6	875.4	201.7	23.0	0.5
1955	2754.5	832.8	237.5	22.1	6.4
1956	3251.4	805.8	273.8	19.3	6.1
1957	3544.0	846.4	215.5	22.1	13.0
1958	3914.6	958.1	214.7	45.5	10.7
1959	4565.9	1216.7	271.9	103.4	9.7
1960	5065.6	1507.7	340.4	167.0	8.6
1961	5344.9	1561.0	203.1	171.0	14.1
1962	5809.9	2020.6	332.9	141.8	24.8
1963	6352.9	2219.4	366.1	190.2	31.2
1964	6962.9	2398.5	483.9	186.4	53.1
1965	7252.5	2423.1	489.7	187.4	54.4
1966	7121.6	2308.4	493.7	208.0	62.8

Source: Vneshniaia torgovlia SSR: Statisticheskii sbornik, 1918-1966 (Moscow, 1967).

Imports provide, as has previously been noted, a degree of economic and technical flexibility to the Soviet Union; but in the cases noted above they provide more than flexibility—they provide the means for fulfilling key planning

[11] See Table 28-2.

objectives. The chemical industry plan, the synthetic fiber and rubber industry plans, and the automobile and merchant marine plans could not have been filled even by 10 percent if reliance had been solely on domestic abilities and resources.

These observations also provide a rational explanation for Soviet emphasis on domestic production of electricity, steel (simple construction sections rather than high-quality flat-rolled products), and building products such as cement and stone.[12] The perennial shortage of housing also suggests a diversion of construction material resources into other types of construction. Emphasis on the production of electricity, steel, and construction materials is consistent with massive import of foreign equipment and processes: the buildings to house imported process technology and equipment must be provided from domestic resources. Apart from the import of the steel-fabricated structure for the Stalingrad tractor plant in 1930 there is no known case of Soviet import of industrial building structures. These are built to a standard design in the U.S.S.R. from domestic materials.[13] The major inputs for industrial buildings are structural steel, plate steel, reinforcing rod, and cement. The planning emphasis on these products, then, is not founded in dogma but on practical construction demands. This also squares with observed Soviet postwar reparations practices; rather than removing fabricated steel structures (as the less experienced Western allies tried to do) the Soviets removed portable equipment and machinery of a high value-to-weight ratio. The building shell was erected in the U.S.S.R. and the equipment bedded down in its new location.[14]

THE "CATCHING-UP" HYPOTHESIS

An obvious benefit from the import of foreign technology is that it affords less developed countries the possibility of "catching-up" i.e., of establishing the basic means of production without enormous investment in research and development and long gestation periods. Presumably, when a nation attains a certain technological level of advancement it should be able to press ahead on its own.

This "catching-up" justification for basic technology import seems more logically applicable to ex-colonial areas, such as India, than to the Soviet Union.

[12] G. Warren Nutter, *The Growth of Industrial Production in the Soviet Union* (Princeton: Princeton University Press, 1962).

[13] See Sutton II: *Western Technology ... 1930 to 1945*, p. 251.

[14] See Edwin W. Pauley, *Report on Japanese Assets in Manchuria to the President of the United States, July 1946* (Washington, 1946), for excellent photographs of Soviet removal practice; the remaining portions of the plant are those needing duplication in the U.S.S.R., i.e., the building shell, equipment made of fabricated sheet steel, and machinery with a low value-to-weight ratio.

In the first place, there is a widespread misunderstanding concerning the state of technical development in Tsarist Russia. Whatever may have been the backward nature of the Tsarists' social and political system, their technology was reasonably well advanced for the time; indeed there is evidence that by 1916 Tsarist Russia had industrial units on a scale and utilizing a technology equal to that anywhere in the world.[15] Further, pre-Revolutionary indigenous Russian innovation was apparent in the beet sugar industry, in aluminum smelting (Bayer), in synthetic rubber (Ostrimilensky), and in automobiles and aircraft (Sikorsky). While a great many of the skilled workers, the management personnel, and the technicians either emigrated or returned to the villages after the revolution, the physical structure of the Russian economy was largely intact when the Bolsheviks came to power.

Moreover, various injections of foreign technology have enabled the Soviet Union to "catch up" in the 1920s, in the early thirties (mid-thirties for aircraft and oil refining), during World War II, at the end of the fifties, and in the massive plant acquisitions of the sixties. Thus a temporary need for "catching up" is not a likely explanation for the continued Soviet reliance on imported technology. A more plausible explanaton is that there is some inherent inadequacy in the system which stifles indigenous industrial development. The Soviet system is forever "catching up," by virtue of its institutional structure. Foreign technology converts this static system into a viable system.

A generally observed benefit of foreign technology import is that it enables the recipient country to avoid research and development costs. This saving may indeed be substantial, but it is minute compared with another factor, i.e., the avoidance of expenditures on innovations that fall by the wayside, the so-called wastes of competition. To allow the market to select the most efficient method, or the several most efficient methods for the manufacture of any given product, several hundreds may be taken partway to production (i.e., through pilot-plant stage) and several dozens actually placed into production. The market is the final test of efficiency. This process is vital to the dynamic progress of a market system, and for this reason the wastes of competition are not wastes at all: if it is necessary for purposes of efficiency to allow rejected processes to fall by the wayside, it is just as necessary to a viable economy that they be introduced into the market in the first place.

There is a cost incurred in the development of these fallen processes, however, and it is one that can be avoided by importing technologies after they have passed through the discipline of a market economy. The Soviets have been remarkably adept at selecting processes, after the initial shaking down to two or three that have ultimately been determined by the foreign market place to be the most efficient. They chose the Ford automobile in the late 1920s (not Cord, Maxwell, or any of the hundreds of others that have since fallen by

---

[15] See Sutton I: *Western Technology ... 1917 to 1930*, pp. 183-84.

the wayside). They chose the Douglas DC-3 within a year of its inception—an aircraft that proved to be the most efficient air transport of its time. They chose the Rust cotton picker. They have shown a remarkable ability to appreciate the market economy in operation, to acquire full knowledge of competing processes, and to step in as soon as a particular process has shown itself to have advantages not shared by others. A Western firm that has had its process or equipment chosen by the Soviets should use the fact as an advertising slogan—for Soviet choice has been so remarkably accurate that it is almost a badge of acceptability.

Finally, the Soviet Union (or any other importer of technology) can avoid the long gestation periods of modern technologies. The Soviets acquired the wide-strip mill within a few years of its introduction in the West. It would have taken decades to reproduce the technology within the U.S.S.R. They acquired the German jet and turboprop engines at a time when they had themselves hardly mastered the manufacture of piston engines. They obtained in the late fifties and early sixties numerous complete chemical plants far beyond their own technical abilities and certainly not then duplicable in the Soviet Union in the foreseeable future. Such gains in time are vital to the fulfillment of Soviet ideology, which requires a dynamic technical front.

The gestation advantage comes out most clearly in those technologies which involve a high degree of construction skill and cannot be imported. Atomic reactors, for example, require a lengthy construction period, cannot be legally exported from the West, and demand a high degree of construction skill. After a flashy start in the 1950s the Soviets had only four reactors in operation in November 1969 (the same number as in 1965), which is a far cry from the impressive predictions advanced in the 1950s for atomic power development in a socialist system.

The Soviet economy is always a few years behind the West, but under censorship conditions this has presented no great problem. By a combination of careful concealment and clever promotion,[16] the Soviets have had little difficulty in presenting to foreign observers the facade of a vigorous, sophisticated technology.

---

[16] "In the developing countries of Asia and Africa, Soviet aid places great stress on modern scientific symbols. A nuclear research lab is set up in Cairo, a fully automatic telephone exchange in Damascus, a technological institute in Rangoon—these tokens of advanced technology are intended to convey an image of Soviet progressiveness in human discovery and inventiveness in the application of science to peaceful progress." Hans Heymann, Jr., *The U.S.S.R. in the Technological Race* (Santa Monica: RAND Corp., 1959), Report no. P-1754, p. 6.

CHAPTER TWENTY-NINE

Conclusions

EMPIRICAL CONCLUSIONS: 1917 TO 1930

The first volume of this study concluded that the Soviets employed more than 350 foreign concessions during the 1920s. These concessions, introduced into the Soviet Union under Lenin's New Economic Policy, enabled foreign entrepreneurs to establish business operations in the Soviet Union without gaining property rights. The Soviet intent was to introduce foreign capital and skills, and the objective was to establish concessions in all sectors of the economy and thereby introduce Western techniques into the dormant postrevolutionary Russian economy. The foreign entrepreneur hoped to make a normal business profit in these operations.

Three types of concessions were isolated: Type I, pure concessions; Type II, mixed concessions; Type III, technical-assistance agreements. Information was acquired on about 70 percent of those actually placed in operation. It was found that concessions were employed within all sectors of the economy except one (furniture and fittings), although the largest single group of concessions was in raw materials development. In the Caucasus oil fields—then seen as the key to economic recovery by virtue of the foreign exchange that oil exports would generate—the International Barnsdall Corporation introduced American rotary drilling techniques and pumping technology. By the end of the 1920s 80 percent of Soviet oil drilling was conducted by the American rotary technique; there had been no rotary drilling at all in Russia at the time of the Revolution. International Barnsdall also introduced a technical revolution in oil pumping and electrification of oil fields. All refineries were built by foreign corporations, although only one, the Standard Oil lease at Batum, was under a concessionary arrangement—the remainder were built under contract. Numerous Type I and Type III technical-assistance concessions were granted in the coal, anthracite, and mining industries, including the largest concession, that of Lena Goldfields, Ltd., which operated some 13 distinct and widely separated industrial complexes by the late 1920s. In sectors such as iron and steel, and particularly in the machinery and electrical equipment manufacturing sectors, numerous agreements were made between trusts and larger individual Tsarist-era plants and Western companies to start up and reequip the plants with the latest in Western technology.

A.E.G., General Electric, and Metropolitan-Vickers were the major operators in the machinery sectors. Only in the agricultural sector was the concession a failure.

After information had been acquired on as many such concessions and technical-assistance agreements as possible, the economy was divided into 44 sectors and the impact of concessions and foreign technical assistance in each sector was analyzed. It was found that about two-thirds of the sectors received Type I and Type II concessions, while over four-fifths received technical-assistance agreements with foreign companies. A summary statement of this assistance, irrespective of the types of concession, revealed that all sectors except one, i.e., 43 sectors of a total of 44, had received some form of concession agreement. In other words, in only one sector was there no evidence of Western technological assistance received at some point during the 1920s. The agreements were made either with dominant trusts or with larger individual plants, but as each sector at the outset comprised only a few large units bequeathed by the Tsarist industrial structure, it was found that the skills transferred were easily diffused within a sector and then supplemented by imported equipment. Examination of reports by Western engineers concerning individual plants confirmed that restarting after the Revolution and technical progress during the decade were dependent on Western assistance.

It was therefore concluded that the technical transfer aspect of the New Economic Policy was successful. It enabled foreign entrepreneurs and firms to enter the Soviet Union. From a production of almost zero in 1922 there was a recovery to pre-World War I production figures by 1928. There is no question that the turn-around in Soviet economic fortunes in 1922 is to be linked to German technical assistance, particularly that forthcoming after the Treaty of Rapallo in April 1922 (although this assistance was foreseeable as early as 1917 when the Germans financed the Revolution).

It was also determined that the forerunners of Soviet trading companies abroad—i.e., the joint trading firms—were largely established with the assistance of sympathetic Western businessmen. After the initial contacts were made, these joint trading firms disappeared, to be replaced by Soviet-operated units such as Amtorg in the United States and Arcos in the United Kingdom.

It was concluded that for the period 1917 to 1930 Western assistance in various forms was the single most important factor first in the sheer survival of the Soviet regime and secondly in industrial progress to prerevolutionary levels.

EMPIRICAL CONCLUSIONS: 1930 TO 1945

Most of the 350 foreign concessions of the 1920s had been liquidated by 1930. Only those entrepreneurs with political significance for the Soviets received compensation, but for those few that did (for example, Hammer and Harriman), the compensation was reasonable.

The concession was replaced by the technical-assistance agreement, which together with imports of foreign equipment and its subsequent standardization and duplication, constituted the principal means of development during the period 1930 to 1945.

The general design and supervision of construction, and much of the supply of equipment for the gigantic plants built between 1929 and 1933 was provided by Albert Kahn, Inc., of Detroit, the then most famous of U.S. industrial architectural firm. No large unit of the construction program in those years was without foreign technical assistance, and because Soviet machine tool production then was limited to the most elementary types, all production equipment in these plants was foreign. Soviet sources indicate that 300,000 high-quality foreign machine tools were imported between 1929 and 1940. These machine tools were supplemented by complete industrial plants: for example, the Soviet Union received three tractor plants (which also doubled as tank producers), two giant machine-building plants (Kramatorsk and Uralmash), three major automobile plants, numerous oil refining units, aircraft plants, and tube mills.

Published data on the Soviet "Plans" neglect to mention a fundamental feature of the Soviet industrial structure in this period: the giant units were built by foreign companies at the very beginning of the 1930s, and the remainder of the decade was devoted to bringing these giants into full production and building satellite assembly and input-supply plants. In sectors such as oil refining and aircraft, where further construction was undertaken at the end of the decade, we find a dozen top U.S. companies (McKee, Lummus, Universal Oil Products, etc.) aiding in the oil-refining sector and other top U.S. aircraft builders in the aircraft sector (Douglas, Vultee, Curtiss-Wright, etc.).

Only relatively insignificant Soviet innovation occurred in this period: SK-B synthetic rubber, dropped in favor of more useful foreign types after World War II; the Ramzin once-through boiler, confined to small sizes; the turbodrill; and a few aircraft and machine gun designs.

The Nazi-Soviet pact and Lend Lease ensured a continued flow of Western equipment up to 1945.

In sum, the Soviet industrial structure in 1945 consisted of large units producing uninterrupted runs of standardized models copied from foreign designs and manufactured with foreign equipment. Where industrial equipment was of elementary construction (e.g., roasters and furnaces in the chemical industry, turret lathes in the machine tool industry, wooden aircraft, and small ships), the Soviets in 1945 were able to take a foreign design and move into production. One prominent example (covered in detail in this volume) was the Caterpillar D-7 tractor. The original, sent under Lend Lease in 1943, was copied in metric form and became the Soviet S-80 and S-100. It was then adapted for dozens of other military and industrial uses.

Thus in the period 1930 to 1945 the Soviets generally no longer required foreign engineers as operators inside the U.S.S.R. as they had in the concessions of the 1920s, but they still required foreign designs, foreign machines (the machines to produce machines), and complete foreign plants in new technical areas. By 1945 the Soviet Union had "caught up" at least twice; once in the 1930s (it could also be argued that the assistance of the 1920s constituted the first catching-up) with the construction of the First Five Year Plan by foreign companies, and again in 1945 as a result of the massive flow of Western technology under Lend Lease. While the technical skills demonstrated by the Tsarist craftsmen had not quite been achieved,[1] it may be said that in 1945 the nucleus of a skilled engineering force was once again available in Russia—for the first time since the Revolution.

EMPIRICAL CONCLUSIONS: 1945 TO 1965

In the immediate postwar period the Soviets transferred a large proportion of German industry to the Soviet Union—at least two-thirds of the German aircraft industry, the major part of the rocket production industry, probably two-thirds of the electrical industry, several automobile plants, several hundred large ships, and specialized plants to produce instruments, military equipment, armaments, and weapons systems. The stripping of East Germany was supplemented by a U.S. program (Operation RAP) to give the Soviets dismantled plants in the U.S. Zone. By the end of 1946 about 95 percent of dismantling in the U.S. Zone was for the U.S.S.R. (including the aircraft plants of Daimler-Benz, ball bearings facilities, and several munitions plants).

Manchuria and Rumania also supplied numerous plants. And as we have seen, Finnish reparations which supplemented the pulp and paper industries and ship construction were made possible by U.S. Export-Import Bank credits to Finland.

In the late 1950s all this industrial capacity had been absorbed and the Soviets turned their attention to the deficient chemical, computer, shipbuilding, and consumer industries, for which German acquisitions had been relatively slight.[2] A massive complete-plant purchasing program was begun in the late

---

[1] Tsarist-era technology was of a higher standard than is generally believed: it had achieved capability to produce aircraft, calculating machines, and locomotives. Foss Collection, Hoover Institution; see Sutton I, pp. 183-84.

[2] For typical articles that appeared in Western journals as the Soviets took steps to start a massive acquisition program to fill major technical gaps in the Soviet structure, see: Raymond Ewell, "Soviet Russia Poses a New Industrial Threat," *ASTM Bulletin*, no. 239 (July 1959), 43-44; W. Benton, "Are We Losing the Sheepskin War," *Democratic Digest*, July 1956; "From Revolution to Automation in 37 Years," *American Machinist*, November 19, 1956; G. Marceau, "Exceptionnelles possibilités du forage en U.R.S.S.," *Industrie du petrole*, 28 (November 1960), 47-49; "Soviet Scientists Emerge from Curtain to Crow about Progress," *Business Week*, September 14, 1957, pp. 30-32.

1950s—for example, the Soviets bought at least 50 complete chemical plants between 1959 and 1963 for chemicals not previously produced in the U.S.S.R. A gigantic ship-purchasing program was then instituted, so that by 1967 about two-thirds of the Soviet merchant fleet had been built in the West. More difficulty was met in the acquisition of computers and similar advanced technologies, but a gradual weakening of Western export control under persistent Western business and political pressures produced a situation by the end of the sixties whereby the Soviets were able to purchase almost the very largest and fastest of Western computers.

Soviet exports in the late sixties were still those of a backward, underdeveloped country. They consisted chiefly of raw materials and semimanufactured goods such as manganese, chrome, furs, foodstuffs, pig iron, glass blocks, and so on. When manufactured goods were exported they were simple machine tools and vehicles based on Western designs, and they were exported to underdeveloped areas. When foreign aid projects fell behind—although they had been given first priority on Soviet resources—they were brought back on schedule with the use of foreign equipment (e.g., British and Swedish equipment was used at the Aswan Dam). And while great efforts have been made to export to advanced Western markets Soviet goods with a technological component (i.e., watches, automobiles, tractors, and so on), a technical breakdown of these goods reveals in all cases examined either a Western origin or the substitution of Western parts where the products are assembled in the West.[3]

As a further indicator of Soviet technical backwardness, it may be noted that some Western firms selling to the Soviet Union have found "so many gaps in the control schemes proposed"[4] that a two-phase quotation format has been adopted: first a feasibility study is conducted (for which the Western company is paid), and then the actual quotation is determined for a complete system based on the feasibility study. In other words, technical inadequacy is such that the Soviets have not been able to specify exactly what is wanted. What this reflects is not a lack of scientific skill; it shows a lack of information on the technical constituents of a modern industrial system.

In the few areas where indigenous innovation was identified in the earlier period, we find a move back toward the use of Western technology. This is visible in the use of Western synthetic rubbers to replace SK-B, a renewed research effort on rotary drilling as a result of efficiency problems encountered in the use of the Soviet turbodrill, and instances of abandonment of the Ramzin boiler in favor of Western designs. The research and development effort has continued, but its results in practical engineering terms have been near zero. From the technical viewpoint the Soviet Union at 1970 is a copy—a rather imperfect copy—of the West. Generally, initial units are still built by Western

---

[3] For the example of watches, see *Business Week*, June 6, 1960, p. 74.
[4] *Control Engineering* (New York), November 1958, p. 80.

companies and subsequent units built by Soviet engineers are based on the original Western model, and imported equipment is used in key process and control areas.

ORIGINAL WESTERN INTENT FOR TECHNICAL TRANSFER

It may be unwise to attempt to read into an historical sequence of events as important as those described, any rational objective on the part of Western statesmen. Although the policies concerning trade and technical transfers appear vague and often confused, there is one fundamental observation to be made: throughout the period of 50 years from 1917 to 1970 there was a persistent, powerful, and not clearly identifiable force in the West making for continuance of the transfers. Surely the political power and influence of the Soviets was not sufficient alone to bring about such favorable Western policies. Indeed, in view of the aggressive nature of declared Soviet world objectives, such policies seem incomprehensible if the West's objective is to survive as an alliance of independent, non-communist nations. What, then, are the wellsprings of this phenomenon?

In the years 1917-20 a variant of the modern "bridge-building" argument was influential within policymaking circles. The Bolsheviks were outlaws, so the argument went, and had to be brought into the civilized world. For example, in 1918 a statement by Edwin Gay, a member of the U.S. War Trade Board and former Dean of the Harvard Business School, was paraphrased in the board minutes as follows:

> Mr. Gay stated the opinion that it was doubtful whether the policy of blockade and economic isolaton of these portions of Russia which were under Bolshevik control was the best policy for bringing about the establishment of a stable and proper Government in Russia. Mr. Gay suggested to the [War Trade] Board that if the people in the Bolshevik sections of Russia were given the opportunity to enjoy improved economic conditions, they would themselves bring about the establishment of a moderate and stable social order.[5]

At about the same time American businessmen were instrumental in aiding the formation of the Soviet Bureau, and several hundred firms had their names on file in the bureau when it was raided in 1918.[6] Hence there was Western business pressure through political channels to establish Soviet trade. No one appears to have foreseen the possibility of creating a powerful and threatening enemy to the Free World. There was widespread criticism of the Bolsheviks,

---

[5] Minutes of the U.S. War Trade Board, December 5, 1918, vol. V, pp. 43-44.
[6] New York [State] Legislature, Joint Legislative Committee to Investigate Seditious Activities (Lusk Committee), Albany, N.Y., 1919.

but this was not allowed to interfere with trade. In sum, there was no argument made against technical transfers while several influential political and business forces were working actively to open up trade.

The lack of clear policy formulation and foresight was compounded by the apparent efforts of some State Department officials in the 1930s to discourage collection of information on Soviet economic actions and problems. While the First Five Year Plan was under construction by Western companies, various internal State Department memoranda disputed the wisdom of collecting information on this construction.[7] For example, a detailed report from the U.S. Embassy in Tokyo in 1933 (a report containing precisely the kind of information used in this study) was described in Washington as "not of great interest."[8] It is therefore possible that no concerted effort to examine the roots of Soviet industrial development has ever been made within the U.S. State Department. Certainly internal State Department reports of the 1930s provide less information than the present study was able to develop. Such lack of ordered information would go far to account for many of the remarkably inaccurate statements made to Congress by officials of the State Department and its consultants in the 1950s and 1960s—statements sometimes so far removed from fact they might have been drawn from the pages of *Alice in Wonderland* rather than the testimony of senior U.S. Executive Department personnel and prominent academicians.[9]

In brief, a possibility exists that there has been no real and pervasive knowledge of these technical transfers—even at the most "informed" levels of Western governments. Further, it has to be hypothesized that the training of Western government officials is woefully deficient in the area of technology and development of economic systems, and that researchers have been either unable to visualize the possibility of Soviet technical dependence or unwilling, by reason of the bureaucratic aversion to "rocking the boat," to put forward research proposals to examine that possibility. This does not however explain why some of the outside consultants who were hired by all Western governments

---

[7] See U.S. State Dept. Decimal File, 861.50/Five Year Plan/50.

[8] U.S. State Dept. Decimal File, 861.5017/Living Conditions/709, Report no. 689, Tokyo, August 31, 1933.

[9] A former assistant chief of the division of research of the Department of State has formed equally harsh conclusions. Bryton Barron has listed four examples of highly strategic tools whose export to the U.S.S.R. was urged by officials of the Department of State:
"1. Boring mills essential to the manufacture of tanks, artillery, aircraft, and for the atomic reactors used in submarines.
"2. Vertical boring mills essential to the manufacture of jet engines.
"3. Dynamic balance machines used for balancing shafts on engines for jet airplanes and guided missiles.
"4. External cylindrical grinding machines which a Defense Department expert testified are essential in making engine parts, guided missiles, and radar."
Barron concludes: "It should be evident that we cannot trust the personnel of the Department to apply our agreements in the nation's interests any more than we can trust it to give us the full facts about our treaties and other international commitments." See Bryton Barron, *Inside the State Department* (New York: Comet Press, 1956).

in such profusion, have not systematically explored the possibility.[10] If it is argued, on the contrary, that Western Governments *are* aware of Soviet technical dependency, then how does one explain the national security problem, outlined in chapter 27?

An argument has been made that a policy of technical assistance to the U.S.S.R. before World War II was correct as it enabled the Soviets to withstand Hitler's attack of June 1941. This is *ex post facto* reasoning. The German Government financed the Bolshevik Revolution with the aim of removing an enemy (Tsarist Russia), but also with postwar trade and influence in mind. This German support was largely replaced in the late 1920s by American technical assistance, but until the mid-1930s the Germans were still arming the Soviets; it was only in 1939 that Hermann Goering began to protest the supply. Thus in the twenties and the early thirties it was not possible for anyone to foresee that Germany would attack the Soviet Union.

The Bolsheviks were assisted to power by a single Western government, Germany, and were maintained in power by all major Western governments. The result is that we have created and continue to maintain what appears to be a first-order threat to the survival of Western civilization. This was done because in the West the political pressures for trade were stronger than any countervailing argument.

This conclusion is supported by the observations that in both the 1930s and the 1960s the U.S. State Department pressed for the outright transfer of military technology to the U.S.S.R. over the protests of the War Department (in the thirties) and the Department of Defense (in the sixties). When in the 1930s the War Department pointed out that the proposed Dupont nitric acid plant had military potential, it was the State Department that allowed the Dupont contract to go ahead.[11] A Hercules Powder proposal to build a nitrocellulose plant was approved when the State Department accepted the argument that the explosives produced were intended for peacetime use.[12]

In the 1960s we have the extraordinary "ball bearing case" of 1961, which revealed that the U.S.S.R. was to receive 45 machines used to produce miniature ball bearings (in the United States almost all miniature ball bearings are used in missiles). That proposal was called a "tragic mistake" by the Department of Defense but supported by the State Department. In 1968 came the so-called "Fiat deal" under which the United States supplied three-quarters of the equipment for the Volgograd plant, the largest automobile plant in the U.S.S.R. This agreement ignored an earlier interagency committee finding that 330 military items can be produced by any civilian automobile industry and that the automobile industry is a key factor for war. It also ignores an argument particularly stressed

[10]   See p. x.
[11]   See Sutton, *Western Technology ... 1930 to 1945*, p. 101.
[12]   *Ibid.*, p. 113.

here—that any automobile plant can produce military vehicles. The supply of U.S. equipment for the Volgograd plant was diametrically opposed to any policy of denial of exports of stratetic goods to the Soviet Union, for under any definition of "strategic" the Volgograd plant has clear and significant military weapons capability. Yet the State Department was strongly in favor of the shipment of the plant equipment. The developing story of the Kama plant suggests history is repeating itself.

Under these conditions, where policy is so far removed from logical deduction, it would be imprudent to arrive at any conclusion concerning Western intentions. If logical intentions exist—and in chapter 27 it is suggested that our strategic policies are not logically derivable from observable fact—they are obscure indeed. The writer leans to the position that there is gross incompetence in the policymaking and research sections of the State Department. There is probably no simple, logical explanation for the fact that we have constructed and maintain a first-order threat to Western society.

IMPLICATIONS FOR THE SOVIET UNION

The Soviet Union has a fundamental problem. In blunt terms, the Soviet economy, centrally planned under the guidance of the Communist Party, does not constitute a viable economic system. The system cannot develop technically across a broad front without outside assistance; internal industrial capacity can be expanded only in those sectors suitable for scaling-up innovation and duplication of foreign techniques.

Quite clearly a modern economy cannot be self-maintained, however skilled its planners and technicians, if technical adoptions in basic industries are limited to processes that lend themselves to scaling up or duplication. Further, the more developed the economy the greater its complexity; consequently the planning problems associated with the acquisition of information must surely increase in geometric ratio.

Logically, then, a system that is strictly centrally planned is not efficient either for rapid balanced growth or for any growth at all once the economy is past the primitive stage. Beyond that stage, the chief function of central planning, so far as the economy is concerned, becomes the retention of political control with the ruling group. There are few economic functions, and certainly no technical functions, that cannot be performed in a more efficient manner by a market economy.

How have the Russian Party member, the Politburo, Stalin, Khrushchev, and Brezhnev looked upon Western technology in relation to Soviet technology? This is indeed a fascinating question. Party injunctions, for example in *Pravda*, suggest that on many levels there has been a deep and continuing concern with lagging Soviet technology. The general problem has long been recognized, ever since Lenin's time. But Lenin thought it curable;[13] the current Politburo must at least suspect it is incurable.

It is however unlikely that either the Party in Russia or the Communist parties in the West have fully probed the depths of the problem. First, their writings mirror a persistent confusion between science and technology, between invention and innovation.[14] Second, it is unlikely that most Marxists appreciate how important an indigenous innovative process is to a nation's self-sufficiency (in contrast to their clear understanding of the value of scientific endeavor and invention). Even breakaways from Marxist dogma still find it difficult to absorb the notion that virtually *all* widely applied (i.e., innovated) technology in the Soviet Union today may have originated in the outside world. Third, Russian designers and engineers may have succeeded in deceiving the Party and even themselves. By claiming as indigenous Russian work designs which in fact originated in the West, they may have obscured the realities of Soviet technology.

The dilemma facing the Soviets in 1970 is stark and overwhelming, and periodic reorganization and adjustments have not identified the basic cause. Indeed, each reorganization either stops short of the point where it may have lasting effect or leads to yet further problems. This is because the Party continues to demand absolute political control while a viable economy increasingly demands the adaptability, the originality, and the motivation that result from individual responsibility and initiative. Attempted solutions through use of computers may temporarily ease the problem, but ultimately they too will result in confusion because accurate information still has to be acquired and analyzed. The computer is only as useful as its human operators are capable and as its data input is sound. In any event, who will supply the computers?

Moreover a communist regime *cannot* yield political power; doctrine demands continuance of power in the hands of the Party. The economy demands diffusion

---

[13]   V. I. Lenin, *Selected Works*, J. Fineberg, ed., vol. IX (New York, International Publishers, 1937), pp. 116-118.

[14]   Another and more puzzling facet of the Soviet concept of what begets innovation is found in descriptions of the innovatory process in practice. For example, an article by G. B. Nagigin on innovation in the glass industry states: "Technical offices were established [in one factory] before the start of the competition. Leading engineers and technologists were on duty in these offices and gave practical assistance to innovators who turned to them for advice, consultation, etc. The technical offices are equipped with reference literature and other material needed by innovators and inventors. For example, there is a drawing board and the necessary instruments in the technical office of the Gushkovskii Works. The establishment of well-equipped technical offices, with qualified engineers on duty, naturally had a very favorable effect on the development of innovation and invention work in the factories." *Steklo i keramika* (New York), vol. XIV, no. 2. p. 66. A table is included in the article giving "results." We have to assume that this scheme to encourage competition was a serious attempt to induce the innovatory process—although one is tempted to dismiss it as naive in the extreme. It need only be said that anyone with the slightest knowledge of invention and innovation would con- clude that little that is worthwhile can be achieved by such a forced and artificial process.

of power. What will be the result? If Russian historical precedent is any indicator, then the outlook is gloomy indeed. The Russian Revoluton was a gigantic and violent upheaval. The first revolution achieved what had been attained by evolutionary means elsewhere, the substitution of relatively democratic control for autocracy. Then the briefly emergent democratic forces in Russia were caught between the autocracy of the right and the Bolsheviks of the left and were rendered impotent. A new absolutism took power. Today there is no question that a fundamental change has to come again; what is unknown is the form that change will take and whether it will be revolutionary or evolutionary.

It is also clear—and the writer makes this assertion only after considerable contemplation of the evidence—that whenever the Soviet economy has reached a crisis point, Western governments have come to its assistance. The financing of the Bolshevik Revolution by the German Foreign Ministry was followed by German assistance out of the abysmal trough of 1922. Examples of continuing Western assistance include the means to build the First Five Year Plan and the models for subsequent duplication; Nazi assistance in 1939-41 and U.S. assistance in 1941-45; the decline in export control in the fifties and sixties; and finally the French, German, and Italian credits of the sixties and the abandonment of controls over the shipment of advanced technology by the United States in 1969. All along, the survival of the Soviet Union has been in the hands of Western governments. History will record whether they made the correct decisions.

IMPLICATIONS FOR THE WESTERN BUSINESS FIRM

The Western business firm has been the main vehicle for the transfer process, and individual firms have, of course, an individual right to accept or reject Soviet business in response to their own estimation of the profitability of such sales. There is ample evidence in the files of the U.S. State Department, the German Foreign Ministry, and the British Foreign Office that Western firms have cooperated closely with their respective governments in negotiating for such sales.

Historically, sales to the Soviet Union must have been profitable, although the Russians are reputed to be hard bargainers and there have been numerous examples of bad faith and breaches of contract. Firms have accepted theft of blueprints and specifications,[15] duplication of their equipment without permission or royalties,[16] and similar unethical practices and still deemed it worthwhile to continue trade. This applies particularly to larger firms such as General

[15] Sutton II, pp. 263-67.
[16] *Ibid.*

Electric, Radio Corporation of America, Ford Motor, Union Carbide, and Imperial Chemical Industries, Ltd. There is evidence that larger firms are able to demand and obtain somewhat more equitable treatment from the Soviets, partly by virtue of the fact that respective foreign offices are more willing to back them up and partly because the Soviets are aware of the relatively few sources for their new technologies. But less well-known firms such as Lummus, Universal Oil Products, and Vickers-Armstrongs (Engineers), Ltd., apparently also have found that Soviet business pays.

This profitability must be balanced against possible loss of domestic sales in the face of hostile domestic publicity. American Motors found itself in this trap in 1966, when it had no more than vaguely contemplated sales to the U.S.S.R.[17]—and other firms have suffered boycotts. As long as these sales and the impact of such sales on Soviet capabilities were relatively unknown, however, the possibility of boycotts was not great. It appears that some reevaluation may be in order in the light of the findings of this study; i.e., the factors entering into the tradeoffs in considering such business may change. This applies certainly to sales to Red China, where we now stand at a point equivalent to about 1921-22 with the Soviet Union. It is eminently clear that comparable sales over a period of 50 years could place Red China on an equal industrial footing with the U.S.S.R. The difference between the early seventies and the early twenties is that we now have the example of the U.S.S.R. before us: trade has built a formidable enemy, while hopes for a change in ideology and objectives not only have gone unfulfilled but are perhaps more distant than they were 50 years ago.

IMPLICATIONS FOR SOCIO-ECONOMIC SYSTEMS

The Soviet problem is not that the nation lacks theoretical or research capability[18] or inventive genius. The problem is rather that there is a basic weakness in engineering skills, and the system's mechanisms for generating innovation are almost nonexistent.

Table 29-1 suggests the sparseness of Soviet innovation; engineering weaknesses are implicit in continuing plant purchases abroad—while such purchases continue the Soviets are not building plants using their own laboratory discoveries. Why does the Soviet system have such weaknesses?

There is certainly no choice among competing inventions using market criteria, but if more useful Soviet processes existed they would be adopted whether market-tested or not. Absence of the marketplace is not, then, sufficient

[17]   See *Milwaukee Journal*, January 22, 1967.
[18]   For example of Russian research capability see A. V. Zolotov, *Problema tungusskoi katastrofy 1908 g.* (Minsk, 1969), a fascinating empirical study of various hypotheses relating to the gigantic meteorite that fell in Siberia in 1908.

Table 29-1   INDIGENOUS SOVIET INNOVATION, 1917-65

1917 to 1930	1930 to 1945	1945 to 1965
Primitive tractors	Turbodrill	Electro-drill
	Alumina from nepheline	Aircraft
	Synthetic rubber; SK-B	*Sputnik*
	Once-through boiler	Medical sutures
	Machine guns	Electro-slag welding
		"Scaling up"

Source: Based on table 25-2.

reason to explain the absence of innovation. There may be, as has been suggested elsewhere, no compelling pressures to develop innovation despite the fact that the Party is constantly exhorting technical progress. But the explanation that most adequately covers the problem is one that has been previously mentioned though not heretofore stressed–the "inability hypothesis." The spectrum of engineering skills required to build a complete polyester plant, a large truck plant, a fast large-capacity computer, *and* a modern marine diesel engine just does not exist in the Soviet Union. Sufficient engineering skills do exist for limited objectives—a military structure can be organized to select and marshal the technology of war, or a space program can be decreed and realized through top-priority assignment of resources. But the skills are not present to promote and maintain a complex, self-regenerative industrial structure.

The point to be stressed is that if there *were* adequate engineering ability some innovation would be forthcoming in the form of original new processes, and such innovation would appear in many sectors of the economy. This is generally not the case. In most sectors the West installs the initial plants and subsequent plants are duplicates based on that Western technology. Once the sector has been established, major new innovations within the sector tend to be either imported technologies or duplicates of imported technologies. Therefore pervasive "inability" in engineering seems the most likely basic explanation. For some reason—and this study has not explored the diverse institutional factors within the system that might be responsible—Soviet central planning has not fostered an engineering capability to develop modern technologies from scratch, nor has it generated inputs (educational, motivational, and material) to achieve this objective.

The world is now presented with 50 years' history of industrial development in the most important of socialist experiments, and censorship can no longer hide the problem. Every new Soviet purchase of a major Western technology is *pari passu* evidence for a central lesson of this study: Soviet central planning is the Soviet Achilles' heel.

Bibliography

BOOKS AND JOURNAL ARTICLES

Adler-Karlsson, Gunnar. *Western Economic Warfare, 1947-1967.* Stockholm, Almquist & Wiksell, 1968.

Afanas'ev, L. L., *et al. Garazhi i stantsii tekhnicheskogo obsluzhivaniia avtomobilei.* Moscow, 1969.

Agre, V. L. *Tekhnicheskii progress v chernoi metallurgii SSSR; Prokatnoe i trubnoe proizvodstvo.* Moscow, 1962.

Agroskin, A. A., and Shelkov, A. K. *Rasshirenie ugol'noi bazy koksovaniia.* Moscow, 1962.

Aisenshtadt, L. *Ocherki po istorii stankostroeniia SSSR.* Moscow, 1957.

Akademiia nauk SSSR. *Ekonomicheskie problemy razvitiia i razmeshcheniia khimicheskoi promyshlennosti.* Moscow, 1968.

Aleksandrov, V. G. *Aviatsionnyi tekhnicheskii spravochnik.* Moscow, 1969.

Al'shits, Ia. I., *et al. Apparatura i metody issledovaniia gornykh mashin.* Moscow, 1969.

Andreev, A. V. *Kontsentratsiia napriazhenii v detaliakh gornotransportnykh mashin.* Moscow, 1968.

Andrianov, G. N., and Brodskii, G. D. *Primenenie elektronnykh vychislitel'nykh mashin (EVM) v upravlenii proizvodstvom za rubezhom.* Moscow, 1969.

Androsov, A. A., *et al. Asfal'tobetonnye zavody.* Moscow, 1968.

Androsov, V. F., and Golomb, L. M. *Sinteticheskie krasiteli v tekstil'noi promyshlennosti.* Moscow, 1968.

Andzonov, A. F. *Avtomobil' Moskvich.* Moscow, 1950.

Anisimov, G. "The Motive Forces of Technological Progress in the U.S.S.R. at Its Present Stage of Development." *Problems of Economics,* vol. III, no. 1 (May 1960).

Anokhin, V. T. *Sovetskie avtomobili; Spravochnik mashgiz.* Vol. I. Moscow, 1949.

Antipin, L. N., and Vazhenin, S. F. *Ekonomiia elektroenergii pri intensifikatsii proizvodstva alyuminiia.* Sverdlovsk, 1961.

Artamonov, M. D. *Tiagovye i dorozhnye mashiny na lesozagotovkakh.* Moscow, 1968.

Association of American Railroads. *Railroads of the U.S.S.R.* Report on the Visit of the United States Railroad Exchange Delegation to the Soviet Union during June 1960. Washington, n.d. [c. 1961].

————. *A Report on Diesel Locomotive Design and Maintenance on Soviet Railways.* Chicago, AAR Research Center, September 1966.

Atoian, K. M., *et al. Avtobusy spravochnoe posobie.* Moscow, 1969.

Atomic Energy in the Soviet Union. Trip Report of the U.S. Atomic Energy Delegation, May 1963. Oak Ridge, Tenn., AEC Division of Technical Information Extension, n.d.

Auer, Jaakko. *Suomen sotakorvaustoimitukset neuvostoliitolle.* Helsinki, Werner Söderström Osakeyhtiö, 1956.

Avanesov, Yu. B., *et al. Novye sveklouborochnye kombainy.* Moscow, 1968.

Babichev, A. P. *Vibratsionnaia obrabotka detalei v abrazivnoi spede.* Moscow, 1968.

Babushkina, M. D., *et al. An Industrial Bubbling Column for the Production of Sulfurous Acid Using Calcium Hydroxide.* Jerusalem, Israel Program for Scientific Translations, 1963.

Barch, I. E., *et al. Stroitel'nye krany (spravochnoe posobie).* Kiev, 1968.

Bardin, I. P., ed. *Metallurgy of the U.S.S.R. (1917-1957).* Jerusalem, Israel Program for Scientific Translations, 1961.

Barsukov, A. F., and Elenev, A. V. *Kratkii spravochnik po sel'skokhoziaistvennoi tekhnike.* Moscow, 1968.

Bartosiak, A. *Sistema tsvetnogo televideniia SEKAM.* Moscow, 1968.

Barzifkin, V. N. *Mekhanizatsiia sel'skokhoziaistvennogo proizvodstva.* Moscow, 1946.

Beasant, F. H. *Report on Diesel Workshops and Study Tour—Tashkent, U.S.S.R., 14th-26th April, 1966.* N.p., United Kingdom Railway Advisory Service, November 1966.

Bedran, N. G. *Flotatsionnye mashiny dlia obogashchaeniia uglia.* Moscow, 1968.

Belanovskii, N. G., *et al. Kompleksnaia mekhanizatsiia i avtomatizatsiia kozhevennogo proizvodstva.* Kiev, 1969.

Belen'kii, I. A. *Sektornye varochnye kamery dlia remonta pnevmaticheskikh shin.* Leningrad, 1969.

Berdyuk, V. V., *et al. Stroitel'stvo i montazh nasosnykh i kompressornykh stantsii magistral'nykh truboprovodov.* Moscow, 1968.

Berin, A. L. *Mashinist razlivochnoi mashiny.* Kharkov, 1960.

Bezruchko, V. S., *et al. Spravochnik dorozhnogo mastera.* Moscow, 1968.

Bikchurin, T. N., and Kozlov, F. A. *Sovershenstvovanie rezhimov bureniia dolotami umen'shennogo diametra.* Moscow, 1968.

Blackman, James H. "Transport Development and Locomotive Technology in the Soviet Union." Report no. 3, Bureau of Business and Economic Research, School of Business Administration, University of South Carolina, Columbia, S.C., February 1957.

BOAS International Publishing Co. *Germany, 1945-1954*. Schaan, Liechtenstein [1954?].

Bogdanova, E. N., *et al. Atlas sborochnykh chertezhei oborulovaniia zavolov khimicheskoi promyshlennosti*. Moscow, 1966.

Bol'shaia Sovetskaia Entsiklopediia. 1945 ed. Moscow, 1949.

Book Publishing in the U.S.S.R. Report of the Delegation of U.S. Book Publishers Visiting the U.S.S.R., August 20–September 17, 1962. New York, American Book Publishers Council, 1963.

Borisov, V. I., *et al. Avtomobil' GAZ-53A*. Moscow, 1968.

————. *Avtomobili GAZ-53A i GAZ-66*. Moscow, 1969.

Borisovich, G. F. *Ekonomika promyshlennosti sinteticheskogo kauchuka*. Moscow, 1968.

Borob'ev, K. A. *Konstruktsiia, tekhnicheskoi obsluzhivanie i remont bukhgalterskoi mashiny "Askota" klassa 170*. Moscow, 1969.

Borodin, A. I. *Spravochnik po tekhnologii khlopkotkachestva*. Moscow, 1968.

Braslavskii, M. I. *Sudovye dizel'-generatory maloi moshnosti*. Leningrad, 1968.

Bray, John L. *Ferrous Production Metallurgy*. New York, John Wiley, 1942.

B.I.O.S. [British Intelligence Objectives Subcommittee] Reports:

  The Acetylene Industry and Acetylene Chemistry in Germany during the Period 1939–45. Survey Report no. 30.

  Allen, R. G. *German Filtration Industry*. Final Report no. 485.

  Production of Thorium and Uranium in Germany. Final Report no. 675.

  Report on Visit to Daimler-Benz, at Stuttgart-Untertürkheim. Report no. 35.

  Stirling, J. *The German Agricultural Tractor Industry in the United States and French Zones of Occupation*. Final Report no. 905.

  Urquhart, A. R. *The German Rayon Industry during the Period 1939-1945*. Survey Report no. 33. London, 1952.

British Miners in Russia. Report of the Delegation of the Scottish Area, National Union of Mineworkers. London, British Soviet Friendship Society, 1949.

Bruk, I. *Electronic Computers in the Service of the National Economy*. Santa Monica, Calif., RAND Corp., January 12, 1961.

Budnitskii, I. M. *Ugol'nia promyshlennost'*. Moscow, 1958.

Bukreev, E. M., *et al. Mashiny, mekhanizmy i oborudovanie kommunal'nogo khoziaistva; Spravochnik*. Kiev, 1968.

Bumazhnaia promyshlennost' SSSR 1917-1957 gg. Leningrad, Goslesbumizdat, 1958.

Burchakov, A. S., *et al. Tekhnologiia, mekhanizatsiia i avtomatizatsiia proizvodstvennykh protsessov podzemnykh razrabotok*. Moscow, 1968.

Bushuev, M. N., ed. *Engineering Developments at the Leningrad Metal Plant Imeni Stalin*. Jerusalem, Israel Program for Scientific Translations, 1960.

Campbell, Robert W. *The Economics of Soviet Oil and Gas*. Baltimore, Johns Hopkins Press, 1968.

Chanyshev, R. O. *Malaia mekhanizatsiia v stroitel'stve*. Kiev, 1969.

Chapelle J., and Ketchian, S. *URSS, seconde producteur de pétrole du monde*. Paris, Publications de l'Institut Français du Pétrole, Collection Science et Technique du Pétrole, No. 4. 1963.

Cheftel, Henri, and Thomas, Georges. *Principles and Methods for Establishing Thermal Processes for Canned Foods*. Jerusalem, Israel Program for Scientific Translations, 1965.

Chekmarev, A. P., and Mashkovtsev, R. A. *Iznos prokatnykh valkov*. Kharkov, 1955.

Chemical Processing of Fuels. [Originally published by the Academy of Sciences of the U.S.S.R., 1957.] Jerusalem, Israel Program for Scientific Translations, 1960.

"The Chemistry of the 'Terylene' Process." *Canadian Chemical Processing* (Toronto), November 1955.

Cherkasskii, V. M., *et al. Nasosy, kompressory, ventiliatory*. Moscow, 1968.

Chernyshev, G. D. *Dvigateli YaMZ-236, YaMZ-238*. Moscow, 1968.

Chinese Association for the United Nations. *A Report on Russian Destruction of Our Industries in the North-eastern Provinces*. Taipei, Hsin Sheng Printing Works, April 1952.

Clabaugh, Samuel F. "U.S.-Communist Trade." *Ordnance*, July–August 1967.

———. and Allen, Richard V. *East-West Trade; Its Strategic Implications*. Washington, D.C., Georgetown University, Center for Strategic Studies, April 1964.

———. and Feulner, Edwin J., Jr. *Trading with the Communists*. Washington, D.C., Georgetown University, Center for Strategic Studies, June 1968.

Clark, M. Gardner. *The Economics of Soviet Steel*. Cambridge, Harvard University Press, 1956.

Clay, Lucius D. *Decision in Germany*. New York, Doubleday, 1950.

Clubb, O. Edmund. *Chinese Communist Development Programs in Manchuria*. New York, IPR International Secretariat, 1954.

The Coal-Mining Industry of the U.S.S.R. Report by a Technical Delegation of the National Coal Board. London, July 1963.

C.I.O.S. [Combined Intelligence Objectives Subcommittee] Reports:
    A. G. Sachsische Werke, Espenhain. Report no. XXVIII-23.
    Andress, *et al. Machine Tool Targets*. Leipzig. Report no. XXVIII-10.
    Bavarian Motor Works—A Production Survey. Report no. XXX-80.
    Fay, C. L. *Junkers Aircraft and Engine Facilities, May 1945*. Report no. XXXI-36.
    Handley, E. T., *et al. Synthetic Rubber Plant, Chemische Werke-Hüls*. Report no. XXII-21.

Hollings, H., *et al. A. G. Sachsische Werke, Bohlen (Near Leipzig) Germany, August 17, 1945.* Report no. XXX-13.

I. G. Farbenindustrie, A. G. Works, Leuna. Report no. XXXII-107.

I. G. Farbenindustrie, A. G. Works, Leuna. London, H.M. Stationery Office. Item no. 30, Report.

Investigation of Chemical Factories in the Leipzig Area. Report no. XXXIII-31.

Johnson, Edward, and Wood, Robert T. *The Magnesium Alloy Industry of Eastern Germany.* Report no. XXXIII-21.

Livingston, J. W. *Hüls Chemical Works—I. G. Farben, Hüls.* Report no. XXXI-75.

McBurney, W. G., *et al. German Carbide, Cyanamide and Cyanide Industry.* Report no. XXVII-92.

Notes on Aircraft Gas Turbine Engine Developments at Junkers, Dessau and Associated Factories. Report no. XXXI-66.

Optical Glass Manufacturing at Schott & Gen, Jena, 1946. Report no. XXXII-22.

Optical Grinding and Centering Equipment Used by Karl Zeiss, Jena, 1946. Report no. XXVII-23.

Smith, Leroy, *et al. Synthetic Fibre Developments in Germany*, Parts I - III. Report no. XXXIII-50.

Synthetic Rubber Plant, Buna Werke—Schkopau A. G. Report no. XXII-22.

Synthetic Rubber Plant, Buna Werke—Schkopau A. G. Report no. XXVIII-13.

Weider, R. L. *Survey of Automotive Targets in 12th Army Group Area.* Report no. XXVII-46.

Concise Dictionary, Commercial Expressions, English-Russian. London, British Iron and Steel Federation, April 1961. (New Series, no. 6)

Concise Iron and Steel Dictionary, Continuous Casting, English-Russian. London, British Iron and Steel Federation, July 1959. (New Series, no. 5)

Concrete and Prestressed Concrete Engineering in the U.S.S.R. A Report on the Visit of an American Delegation. Chicago, Portland Cement Association, May 1958.

Cordero, N. G., ed. *Iron and Steel Works of the World.* 3d ed. London, Quin Press, 1962.

Dalin, M. A., *et al. Nitril akrilovoi kisloty.* Baku, 1968.

Dallin, David J. *Soviet Espionage.* New Haven, Yale University Press, 1956.

———, and Nicolaevsky, B. I. *Forced Labor in Soviet Russia.* London, Hollis & Carter, 1947.

Danilin, A. S. *Proizvodstvo kombikormov za rubezhom.* Moscow, 1968.

Davydenko, V. A., *et al. Chelyustnye gusenichnye lesopogruzchiki.* Moscow, 1969.

Dawson, J. K., and Sowden, R. G. *Chemical Aspects of Nuclear Reactors.* London, Butterworths, 1963.

De Gara, John P. *Trade Relations between the Common Market and the Eastern Bloc.* Bruges, De Tempel, 1964.

Degtiarev, F. G., *et al. Kratkii spravochnik mekhanika molochnogo zavoda.* Moscow, 1969.

Dennett, Raymond, and Turner, Robert K., eds. *Documents on American Foreign Relations*, Vol. VIII: *July 1, 1945–December 31, 1936.* Princeton, N.J., Princeton University Press, 1948.

Detali mashin, atlas konstruktsii. Moscow, 1968.

District Heating in the Union of Soviet Socialist Republics. Pittsburgh, National District Heating Association, 1967.

Dobrolyubov, A. L. *Funktsional'nye tsiklogrammy elektricheskikh i gidravlicheskikh skhem avtomatizirovannykh stankov i avtomaticheskikh linii.* Minsk, 1969.

Dochkin, V. G., *et al. Ustroistvo i ekspluatatsiia traktorov T-50Vi, T-54V.* Moscow, 1968.

Durov, V. *Forestry Implements and Machines.* Jerusalem, Israel Program for Scientific Translations, 1963.

Dzhalilov, Kh. M. *The Golodnaya Steppe and Prospects for Its Reclamation; Scientific Information on the Golodnaya Steppe.* Jerusalem, Israel Program for Scientific Translations, 1960.

East-West Trade: A Common Policy for the West. New York, Committee for Economic Development, May 1965.

Ebel, Robert E. *The Petroleum Industry of the Soviet Union.* New York, American Petroleum Institute, June 1961.

Elektrifikatsiia SSSR 1917-1967. Moscow, 1967.

Eliutin, V. P., *et al. Production of Ferroalloy Electrometallurgy.* 2d ed. Jerusalem, Israel Program for Scientific Translations, 1961.

Encyclopaedia of Chemical Technology. 2d ed. Ed. by Raymond E. Kirk and Donald F. Othmer. New York, Interscience Publishers, 1968.

European League for Economic Cooperation. *Economic, Industrial, Scientific and Technical Cooperation between the Countries of Eastern and Western Europe.* Brussels, 1967.

Evans, Medford. *The Secret War for the A-Bomb.* Chicago, Henry Regnery, 1953.

Everhart, John L. *Kholodnoe pressovanie metallov.* Moscow, 1968.

Feigenbaum, E. A. *Soviet Cybernetics and Computer Sciences, 1960.* Reprinted from *IRE Transactions on Electronic Computers*, vol. EC-10, no. 4 (December 1961).

Fishman, I. D., *et al. Burovoi stanok BSV-3.* Moscow, 1968.

――――. *Vrubovaia mashina "URAL-33."* Moscow, 1968.

Ford Truck Illustrations Catalog, 1948-1956. Dearborn, Ford Motor Co., 1964.
Future United States Trade Policy. Roth Report to the President. Washington, June 1969.
Gaidamak, K. M. *Slesar' po montazhu tekhnologicheskogo oborudovaniia khimicheskikh zavodov.* Moscow, 1968.
Galloway, D. F. *Recent Production Developments in the Soviet Union.* Preprint of the 1959 Sir Alfred Herbert Paper. London, Institution of Production Engineers, 1959.
Gemeinfassliche Darstellung des Eisenhüttenwesens. 14th ed. Düsseldorf, Verein Deutscher Eisenhüttenleute, 1937.
Genel', S. V., *et al. Primenenie polimernykh materialov v kachestve pokrytii.* Moscow, 1968.
"German Army Transport." *Automobile Engineer*, October–December 1945.
Germany (Territory under Allied Occupation, 1945— U.S. Zone). Office of Military Government. *Report of the Military Governor.* N.p., March 1949. (Report No. 45)
⸺ . ⸺ . Economics Division. *A Year of Potsdam; The German Economy since the Surrender.* N.p., Lithographed by the Adjutant General, OMGUS, 1946.
Ginnis, R. A. *Beet-Sugar Technology.* New York, Reinhold, 1951.
Ginzburg, A. S., ed. *Grain Drying and Grain Driers.* Jerusalem, Israel Program for Scientific Translations, 1960.
Golodovskii, Ia. E. *Trekhosnyi avtomobil' Zil-157K.* Moscow, 1968.
Golovach, A. F. *Elektricheskie mashiny i elektroprivod, derevoobrabaty-vayushchikh stankov. Moscow, 1968.*
Goodsmit, S. *ALSOS.* New York, Schuman, 1947.
Gornorudnaia promyshlennost' Ukhrainskoi SSSR. Moscow, 1967.
Gornye mashiny dlia dobychi rud. Moscow, 1968.
Gotman, P. E., *et al. Elektro-tekhnicheskie materialy; Spravochnik.* Moscow, 1969.
Gray, R. B. and Pickard, George E. "Planting Machinery." *Encyclopaedia Britannica.* 1958 ed. Vol. 17.
Great Britain. Iron and Steel Institute. *Production of Wide Steel Strip.* London, 1960.
⸺ . ⸺ . *The Russian Iron and Steel Industry.* A Report Prepared by a British Steel Mission to the U.S.S.R. London, April 1956. (Special Report no. 57)
Great Britain. Ministry of Economic Warfare. *Economic Survey of Germany.* London, Foreign Office, 1944.
Great Britain. Ministry of Fuel and Power. *Report on the Petroleum and Synthetic Oil Industry of Germany.* London, H.M. Stationery Office, 1947.
Great Britain. National Coal Board. *The Coal Industry of the U.S.S.R.; A Report by the Technical Mission of the National Coal Board.* Parts 1 and 2. London, 1957–1958.

Great Britain. Parliament. *Parliamentary Debates* (House of Commons), 5th ser., vol. 443 (October 21–November 7 1947).

Grey, C. G., and Bridgman, L., eds. *Jane's All the World's Aircraft.* London, S. Low, Marston, 1932, 1933, 1939.

Groueff, Stephane. *Manhattan Project.* Boston, Little, Brown, 1967.

Groves, Leslie R. *Now It Can Be Told.* New York, Harper and Row, 1962.

Gulenko, N. N., et al. *Putevye mashiny i mekhanizmy; Spravochnik.* Moscow, 1968.

Gumanyuk, M. N., ed. *Automation in the Coal and Ore Mining Industries.* Jerusalem, Israel Program for Scientific Translations, 1965.

Gurevich, I. I., et al. *The KhVS-1,2M; Cotton-Picking Machine Operator's Manual.* Jerusalem, Israel Program for Scientific Translations, 1966.

Gusel'nikov, E. M., and Rott, V. F. *Elektro-gidravlicheskie tolkateli.* Moscow, 1968.

Hague, Douglas C. *The Economics of Man-made Fibres.* London, Gerold Duckworth, 1957.

Hamilton, Peter. *Espionage and Subversion in an Industrial Society.* London, Hutchinson, 1967.

Harbron, John D. *Communist Ships and Shipping.* London, A. Coles, 1962.

Hardie, D. W. F. *Acetylene, Manufacture and Uses.* New York, Oxford University Press, 1965.

Harmssen, G. E. *Am Abend der Demontage; Sechs Jahre Reparationspolitik (mit Dokumentenanhang).* 5 vols. Bremen, F. Trüjen, 1951.

———. *Reparationen, Sozialprodukt, Lebensstandard.* 4 vols. Bremen, F. Trüjen, 1948.

Hasenack, Wilhelm. *Dismantling in the Ruhr Valley.* Cologne, Westdeutscher Verlag, 1949.

Heller, Yu. A. *Instrumental'nye stali.* Moscow, 1955.

Herman, Leon. *Varieties of Economic Secrecy in the Soviet Union.* Santa Monica, Calif., RAND Corp., December 1963. (Report no. P-2840)

Hersh, Seymour M. *Chemical and Biological Warfare.* Indianapolis, Bobbs-Merrill, 1968.

Heymann, Hans, Jr. *The Soviet Role in International Aviation.* Santa Monica, Calif., RAND Corp., December 4, 1957. (Report no. RM-2213)

———. *The U.S.S.R. in the Technological Race.* Santa Monica, Calif., RAND Corp., July 20, 1959. (Report no. P-1754)

Hinde, D. W. *Electric Traction Systems and Equipment.* Oxford, Pergamon, 1968.

Hooftman, H. *Russian Aircraft.* Fallbrook, Calif., Aero Publishers, 1965.

Hoover, J. Edgar. *The U.S. Businessman Faces the Soviet Spy.* Reprinted from *Harvard Business Review*, January-February, September-October 1964.

Hutton, J. B. *The Traitor Trade.* New York, Obolensky, 1963.

Huzel, D. K. *Peenemunde to Canaveral*. Englewood Cliffs, N. J., Prentice-Hall, 1962.

Impact of Oil Exports from the Soviet Bloc; A Report of the National Petroleum Council. Vols. I and II. Washington, October 4, 1962.

L'Industrie cimentière en U.R.S.S.; Compte rendu de mission 9-28 avril 1960. Paris, 1960.

Inter-Allied Reparation Agency. *Report of Secretary-General for the Year 1949*. Brussels, 1950.

Ionas, V. A. *Proizvoditel'nost' trala*. Moscow, 1967.

Iron and Steel Industry in the U.S.S.R. and Czechoslovakia; Report of an Indian Productivity Team. New Delhi, National Productivity Council, March 1963. (Report no. 20)

Iron and Steel Making in the U.S.S.R., with Special Reference to the Urals Region; A Report to the British Iron and Steel Federation by a British Steel Delegation. Rochester, Kent, Staples, 1956.

Irving, David. *The Destruction of Dresden*. London, William Kimber, 1963.

————. *The Mare's Nest*. London, William Kimber, 1964.

————. *The Virus House*. London, William Kimber, 1967.

Islamov, M. Sh. *Pechi, khimicheskoi promyshlennosti*. Leningrad, 1969.

Ivanchenko, S. R. *Schetnye mashiny i ikh ekspluatatsiia*. Moscow, 1968.

Ivanov, A. I. *Rukovodstvo po izgotovleniyu obraztsov iz drevesiny*. Moscow, 1968.

Ivanova, E. P. *Ekonomika promyshlennosti khimicheskikh volokon*. Moscow, 1968.

Jane's Fighting Ships. 1945-47 and 1969-70 eds. London, S. Low, Marston, 1947, 1970.

Japan. Ministry of International Trade and Industry. *Foreign Trade of Japan*. Tokyo, 1954, 1958.

Jasny, Naum. *Soviet Industrialization 1928-1952*. Chicago, University of Chicago Press, 1961.

Jensen, Bartell C. *The Impact of Reparations on the Post-war Finnish Economy*. Homewood, Ill., Richard D. Irwin, 1966.

Jones, Robert Huhn. *The Roads to Russia*. Norman, University of Oklahoma Press, 1969.

Jordan, George Racey. *From Major Jordan's Diaries*. New York, Harcourt, Brace, 1952.

Kalmykov, N. N. *Burovaia tekhnika i tekhnologiia za rubezhom*. Moscow, 1968.

Kamanin, V. I., et al. *Spravochnik shturmana*. Moscow, 1968.

Kardashov, D. A. *Sinteticheskie klei*. Moscow, 1968.

Karpenko, A. N., and Zelenev, A. A. *Agricultural Machines*. Jerusalem, Israel Program for Scientific Translations, 1968.

Kaser, Michael. *Comecon: Integration Problems of the Planned Economies.* 2d ed. London, Oxford University Press, 1967.

Kashuba, B. P., *et al. Traktor T-74, konstruktsiia ekspluatatsiia, ukhod.* Moscow, 1968.

Kazakov, George. *The Soviet Peat Industry.* New York, Praeger, 1956.

————. *Soviet Peat Resources.* New York, Research Program on the U.S.S.R., 1953.

Kazarinov, V. M., and Lamunin, S. N. *Zarubezhnye mashiny dlia mekhanizatsii stroitel'nykh rabot.* Moscow, 1959.

Keller, Werner. *Ost minus West = Null.* Munich, Droemersche Verlagsanstalt, 1960.

Khar'kovskii traktornyi zavod; Katalog detalei traktora DT-2. Moscow, 1968.

Khodorov, E. I. *Pechi tsementnoi promyshlennosti.* Leningrad, 1968.

Khorin, V. N., *et al. Ugol'nyi kombain Donbass-1G.* Moscow, 1969.

Khudiakov, A. V. *Derevoobrabatyvaiushchie stanki i rabota na nikh.* Moscow, 1968.

Kilmarx, R. A. *A History of Soviet Air Power.* New York, Praeger, 1962.

Kitaigorodskii, I. I. *Tekhnologiia stekla.* Moscow, 1967.

Klinkmüller, Erich, and Ruban, Maria E. *Die Wirtschaftliche Zusammenarbeit der Ostblockstaaten.* Berlin, Duncker & Humblot, 1960.

Köhler, Heinz. *Economic Integration in the Soviet Bloc.* New York, Praeger, 1965.

Kogan, L. P., and Kessler, Yu. V. *Odnofonturnye krugloviazal'nye mashiny.* Moscow, 1968.

Korchak, S. N. *Progressivnaia tekhnologiia i avtomatizatsiia kruglogo shlifovaniia.* Moscow, 1968.

Korobov, V V. *Pnevmo-transport shchepy.* Moscow, 1968.

————. *Traktory avtomobili i sel'skokhozyaistvennye dvigateli.* Moscow, 1950.

Kostin, M. I. *Ekskavatory; Spravochnik.* Moscow, 1959.

Kozlovskii, B. K., and Nekrasov, V K. *Spravochnik stroitelia avtomobil'nykh dorog promyshlennykh predpriiatii.* Moscow, 1968.

Kramish, Arnold. *The Soviet Union and the Atom; The "Secret" Phase.* Santa Monica, RAND Corp., April 11, 1957. (Report no. RM-1896)

Kratkii avtomobil'nyi spravochnik. 5th ed. Moscow, 1968.

Krugovoi, V. M., *et al. Avtomobili KrA3.* Moscow, 1968.

Kucher, A. M., *et al. Tokarnye stanki i prisposobleniia.* Vol. II. Leningrad, 1969.

Kusnitsyn, G.I., *et al. Pnevmaticheskie ruchnye mashiny, spravochnik.* Leningrad, 1968.

Kuznetsov, E. V. *Al'bom tekhnologicheskikh skhem proizvodstva polimerov i plastmass na ikh osnove.* Moscow, 1969.

Kuznetsov, K. K. *Rekonstruktsiia, mekhanizatsiia i avtomatizatsiia shakht za rubezhom.* Moscow, 1968.

Lachman, Gisella R. *Manufacturing and Mechanical Engineering in the Soviet Union.* Washington, 1953.

Lagovskii, A. N. *Strategiia i ekonomika.* 2d ed. Moscow, 1961.

Landes, G. A., and Orlov, V. F. *Ekonomicheskaia effektivnost' mashinnoi tekhnologii proizvodstva khlopka.* Tashkent, 1969.

Lantsburg, Ya. B. *Spravochnik molodnogo mashinista ekskavatora.* Moscow, 1968.

Laryukhin, G. A. *Soviet Designs of Hand Seed Drills.* Jerusalem, Israel Program for Scientific Translations, 1965.

Lazharev, A. A., et al. *Traktory, T-100M i S-100 (konstruktsiia ekspluatatsiia ukhod).* Moscow, 1968.

Lee, A. *The Soviet Air and Rocket Forces.* New York, Praeger, 1959.

Le Fleming, H. M., and Price, J. H. *Russian Steam Locomotives.* London, Marshbank, 1960

Leman, G. *Osnovy tekhnologii pererabotki bumagi i kartona.* Moscow, 1968.

Lenin, V. I. *Selected Works.* Ed. by J. Fineberg. Vol. IX. New York, International Publishers, 1937.

Leont'ev, V. F. *Zarubezhnye transistory shirokogo primeneniia.* Moscow, 1969.

Limanov, E. L., et al. *Burenie napravlennykh i mnogozaboinykh skvazhin ustroistvom UNB-KO.* Moscow, 1968.

Little, T. *High Dam at Aswan: The Subjugation of the Nile.* London, Methuen, 1965.

Lloyd's Register of Shipping. London, 1941.

Löwenthal, Fritz. *News from Soviet Germany.* London, Victor Gollancz, 1950.

Lungren, V. G. *Mashiny i apparaty molochnoi promyshlennosti.* Moscow, 1968.

McGinnis, R A. *Beet-Sugar Technology.* New York, Reinhold, 1951.

Machine Building Industry in the U.S.S.R. and Czechoslovakia; Report of an Indian Productivity Team. New Delhi, National Productivity Council, June 1963. (Report no. 27)

Maintenance Manual, Coach Model TGH-3102. Pontiac, Mich., General Motors Corp., GMC Truck and Coach Division, 1958.

Maintenance Manual, Containing Complete Operation, Maintenance, and Repair Information on GM Models TGH-2708 and TGH-3101 Coaches. Pontiac, Mich., General Motors Corp., GMC Truck and Coach Division, 1951.

Makarov, E. I., and Rudnev, A. S. *Mashinist buril'nokranovoi mashiny.* Moscow, 1968.

Malinin, R. M. *Spravochnik po tranzistornym skhemam.* Moscow, 1968.

Mallan, Lloyd. *Russia and the Big Red Lie.* New York, Fawcett Publications, 1959.

Mandzhavidze, N. F., and Mamradze, G. P. *The High Dams of the World; Systematic Tables of Data and Bibliography on Dams over 75m High.* Jerusalem, Israel Program for Scientific Translations, 1966.

Mantell, Charles L. *Industrial Electro-Chemistry.* New York, McGraw-Hill, 1940.

Manual para constructores. 8th ed. Monterrey, Mex., Compañia Fundidora de Fierro y Acero de Monterrey, S.A., 1959.

Marsden, Charles P. *Tabulation of Published Data on Soviet Electron Devices through June 1965.* Washington, U.S. Department of Commerce, National Bureau of Standards, 1965.

Mashinostroenie, katalog liubitel'skaia fotokinoapparatura. Moscow, 1969.

Mazour, A. G. *Finland between East and West.* Princeton, D. Van Nostrand, 1956.

Meimberg, Rudolf, and Rupp, Franz. *Die Reparationsleistungen der Sowjetischen Besatzungszone.* Bonn, Bundesministerium für gesamtdeutsche Fragen, 1950.

Memorandum on Contracts for the Export of Engineering Products to the Soviet Union. London, London Chamber of Commerce, March 1965.

Mendershausen, Horst. *Dependence of East Germany on Western Imports.* Santa Monica, Calif., RAND Corp., July 17, 1959. (Report no. RM-2414)

———. *"Interzonal Trade" in Germany:* Part I, *The Trade and the Contractual relations;* Part II, *Interaction with Early Berlin Conflicts.* Santa Monica, Calif., RAND Corp., July and November 1963. (Memorandum no. RM-3686-PR)

———, and Meyer, Nancy V. *The Concept of Hostile Trade, and a Case Study of Seventeenth Century Japan.* Santa Monica, Calif., RAND Corp., April 1965. (Memorandum no. RM-4433-PR)

Menitskii, I D., and Kaplan, Yu. A. *Universal'nozatochnye stanki.* Moscow, 1968.

Merchant Ships: World Built. Southampton, Adlard Coles. Annual.

Metuzalem, E. V., and Rymanov, E. A. *Televizory "Start," "Start-2," "Start-3" i "Start-4."* Moscow, 1968.

Mikesell, Raymond F., and Behrman, Jack N. *Financing Free World Trade with the Sino-Soviet Bloc.* Princeton, N. J., Princeton University, Department of Economics and Sociology, International Finance Section, 1958.

Miller, S. A. *Acetylene: Its Properties, Manufacture and Uses.* New York, Academic Press, 1965.

Milovidov, G. V. *Montazh tekhnologicheskogo oborudovaniia predpriiatii po proizvodstvu khimicheskikh volokon.* Moscow, Ministerstvo montazhnykh i spetsial'nykh stroitel'nykh rabot SSSR, 1970.

Milyshkin, A. A., and Plekhanov, I. P. *Spravochnik voditelia avtomobilia.* Moscow, 1968.

Minaev-Tsikanovskii, V. A., *et al. Mashiny i oborudovanie promyshlennykh fabrik-prachechnykh konstruktsiia i raschet.* Moscow, 1968.

Misarek, D. *Turbokompressory.* Moscow, 1968.

Mission to Moscow. Report of the Fifth Mission from Leicester and County Chamber of Commerce, September 18th to 22nd, 1967. Leicester, Barker, n.d.

Modelski, G. A. *Atomic Energy in the Communist Bloc.* Melbourne, 1959.

Moncrieff. R. W. *Man-Made Fibres.* New York, John Wiley, 1963.

Monkhouse, A. "Electrical Developments in the U.S.S.R." *I.E.E. Journal,* vol. 76, no. 462 (June 1935).

Moorehead, Alan. *The Traitors.* London, Hamish Hamilton, 1952.

Moorsteen, Richard. *Prices and Production of Machinery in the Soviet Union, 1928-1958.* Cambridge, Harvard University Press, 1962.

Morey, George. *The Properties of Glass.* New York, Reinhold, 1954.

Moroz, I. I., and Sivchikova, M. G. *Khimicheski stoikie keramicheskie materialy i izdeliia v promyshlennosti.* Kiev, 1968.

Motter, T. H. Vail. *The Persian Corridor and Aid to Russia.* Washington, Department of the Army, Office of the Chief of Military History, 1952. (United States Army in World War II, The Middle East Theater)

Nadezhdin, B. N., and Plekhanov, I. P. *Avtomobil' "Moskvich-408" (ekspluatatsiia i tekhnicheskoe obsluzhivanie).* Moscow, 1967.

Narodnoe Khoziaistvo SSSR v 1968 g.; Statisticheskii ezhegodnik. Moscow, 1969.

Nekrasov, A. M., and Rokotyan, S. S., eds. *500 kv Long-Distance Electric Transmission.* Jerusalem, Israel Program for Scientific Translations, 1966.

Nekrasov, K. P., *et al. Khlopkotkachestvo.* Moscow, 1969.

Nekrasov, N. N. *Ekonomika promyshlennosti i tekhnicheskii progress.* Moscow, 1957.

Nemschak, F. *Ten Years of Austrian Economic Development, 1945-1955.* Vienna, Association of Austrian Industrialists, 1955.

Nepomniashchii, I. L. *Koksovye mashiny, ikh konstruktsii i raschety.* Moscow, 1963.

Neporozhnii, P. S. *Electrification and Power Construction in the U.S.S.R.* Jerusalem, Israel Program for Scientific Translations, 1965.

————. *Spravochnik stroitelia teplov ykh elektrostantsii.* Moscow, 1969.

Nesteruk, F. Ya. *Development of Hydropower Engineering in the U.S.S.R.* Jerusalem, Israel Program for Scientific Translations, 1966.

Nettl, J. P. *The Eastern Zone and Soviet Policy in Germany, 1945-50.* London, Oxford University Press, 1951.

Nichols, Robert L. *A 1966 Survey of Russian Merchant Shipping.* Seattle,

University of Washington, Applied Physics Laboratory, October 7, 1966.

Nikitin, S. P. *Avtomobili, rynok kapitalisticheskikh stran.* Moscow, 1969.

Novak, Joseph. *The Future Is Ours, Comrade.* New York, Doubleday, 1960.

Novikov, A. Ia. *Khimicheskie tovary bytovogo naznacheniia (spravochnik).* Moscow,1968.

Novocherkasskii elektrovozostroitel'nyi zavod. *Elektrovoz VL60 k.* Moscow, 1969.

Nutter, G. Warren. *The Growth of Industrial Production in the Soviet Union.* Princeton, N.J., Princeton University Press, 1962.

Opel 1862-1962. Special Issue of the Labor Journal *Opel-Post.* Rüsselheim, Adam Opel A.G., n.d.

Orishich, K. P. *Our Experience in Introducing Complex Mechanization.* Jerusalem, Israel Program for Scientific Translations [1958].

Osadchuk, G. I., and Farafonov, E. S. *Kholodil'noe oborudovanie vagonov i konditsionirovanie vozdukha.* Moscow, 1969.

Pakhomova, V. Ia., *et al. Novye materialy dlia elektroniki.* Moscow, 1967.

Palenyi, E. G. *Oborudovanie samoletov.* Moscow, 1968.

Parkhod'ko, A. P. *et al. Organizatsiia remonta oborudovaniia sveklosakharnykh zavodov.* Moscow, 1969.

Parry, Albert. *Russia's Rockets and Missiles.* London, MacMillan, 1960.

Pauley, Edwin W. *Report on Japanese Assets in Manchuria to the President of the United States, July 1946.* Washington, July 1946.

————. *Report on Japanese Reparations to the President of the United States, November 1945 to April 1946.* Washington, April 1, 1946.

Petrenko, D. S. *Proizvodstvo sul'fata ammoniia.* Moscow, 1966.

Petrov, Vladimir. *Money and Conquest.* Baltimore, Johns Hopkins Press, 1967.

Phillips, C. H. *Glass: The Miracle Maker.* New York, Pitman, 1941.

50 [Piat' desiat] let sovetskaia khimicheskaia nauka i promyshlennost'. Moscow, 1967.

Piiarskii, T. I., and Sheliubskii, B. V. *Spravochnik mekhanika-dorozhnika; Tekhnicheskaia ekspluatatsiia dorozhnykh mashin.* Moscow, 1968.

Planovskii, A. N., *et al. Protsessy i apparaty khimicheskoi tekhnologii.* Moscow, 1968.

Poderni, R. Iu. *Ugol'nia promyshlennost' SShA.* Moscow, 1968.

Pokrovskii, Major General G. I. *Science and Technology in Contemporary War.* New York, Praeger, 1959.

Pomerantsev, S. N., and Dnestrovskii, N. Z. *Kratkii spravochnik go obrabotke tsvetnykh metallov i splavov.* Moscow, 1961.

Pope, Arthur W., Jr. *Summary Report on German Automotive Engines.* N.p., Office of Military Government for Germany, Field Information Agencies Technical [U.S.], January 3, 1946. (Final Report no. 667).

Potiagalov, A. F. *Shlikhtoval'nye mashiny khlopchatobumazhnogo i l'nianogo proizvodstva*. Moscow, 1968.

Pozin, B. L., and Os'kin, V. Ia. *Ekonomicheskaia reforma v stekol'noi promyshlennosti*. Moscow, 1968.

Prityko, V. P., and Lungren, V. G. *Mashiny i apparaty molochnoi promyshlennosti*. Moscow, 1968.

Prokopovicz, Serge N. *Histoire économique de l'U.R.S.S*. Paris, Editions le Portulan, 1952.

Promyslov, V. F. *Razvitie industrial'nogo stroitel'stva v Moskve*. Moscow, 1967.

Protanskii, V. V. *Mashiny i mekhanizmy na lesozagotovkakh*. Moscow, 1965.

Pryor, Frederic L. *The Communist Foreign Trade System*. London, George Allen & Unwin, 1963.

Pulp, Paper and Board Mills: Union of Soviet Socialist Republics. New York, American Paper and Pulp Association, April 1959.

Raitses, L. M. *Teplovoe khoziaistvo proizvodstva viskoznogo volokna*. Moscow, 1969.

Ready Reference Catalog, Parts and Accessories. 1967 ed. Dearborn, Ford Motor Co., 1966.

Registr Soiuza SSR. *Dopolneniia i izmeneniia k registrovoi knige morskikh sudov soiuza SSR, 1964-1965*. No. 1. Moscow, July 1966.

————. *Registrovaia kniga morskikh sudov soiuza SSR 1964-65*. Moscow, 1966.

The Rehabilitation of Austria, 1945-1947. Vienna, U.S. Allied Commission for Austria [1948?].

The Report of the Royal Commission to Investigate the Facts Relating to and the Circumstances Surrounding the Communication, by Public Officials and Other Persons in Positions of Trust, of Secret and Confidential Information to Agents of a Foreign Power; June 27, 1946. Ottawa, 1946.

Report of United States Welding Delegation on Visit to Soviet Union, July 1962. New York, American Welding Society, n.d.

Report of Visit to U.S.S.R. by Delegation from Canadian Electric Utilities, May 14 to June 2, 1960. Toronto, 1960.

A Report on U.S.S.R. Electric Power Developments, 1958-1959. New York, Edison Electric Institute, 1960.

Report on Visit of U.S.A. Plastics Industry Exchange Delegation to U.S.S.R., June 2 to June 28, 1958. New York, Society of the Plastics Industry [1958].

Report—The United States of America Delegation on Industrial Standards and Norms to the Union of Soviet Socialist Republics, April 27 - May 6, 1967. N.p., American Society for Testing and Materials [1967].

Report to the President of the Special Committee on U.S. Trade Relations with East European Countries and the Soviet Union, The White House, April 29, 1965. Washington, 1965.

Rhorin, V. N. *Ugol'nyi kombain "Donbass-1G."* Moscow, 1968.

Rice, H. R. "Iron Mining at Krivoy Rog U.S.S.R." *Canadian Mining Journal* (November 1960).

————. "Vignettes of Russian Mining." *Canadian Mining and Metallurgical Bulletin* (April 1962).

Rizhskii Vagonostroitel'nyi Zavod. *Elektropoezd ER9P: Rukovodstvo po ekspluatatsii.* Moscow, 1969.

Rodin, Nicholas W. *Productivity in Soviet Iron Mining, 1890-1960.* Santa Monica, Calif., RAND Corp., July 7, 1953. (ASTIA Document no. ATI 210792)

Rotrekl, B., *et al. Nanesenie metallicheskikh pokrytii na plastmassy.* Leningrad, 1968.

Rudenko, I. E., and Korzh, M. Ia. *New Developments in Mechanization on the Hog Farms of the Sovkhoz "Kievskii."* Jerusalem, Israel Program for Scientific Translations, 1965.

Rudiia, K. I. *Elektricheskoe oborudovanie teplovozov.* Moscow, 1968.

Rukovodstvo po organizatsii i tekhnologii pervogo tekhnicheskogo obsluzhivaniia avtobusov. Moscow, Ministerstvo avtomobil'nogo transporta i shosseinykh dorog RSFSR, 1969.

Rukovodstvo po trubam neftianogo sortamenta i ikh soedineniiam, primeniaemym za rubezhom (spravochnoe posobie). Moscow, Standarty amerikanskogo neftianogo instituta, 1969.

Ruzanov, N. M. *Vnedrenie novoi tekhniki na konditerskoi fabrike imeni N. K. Krupskoi.* Moscow, 1968.

Ryan, Cornelius. *The Last Battle.* New York, Simon and Schuster, 1966.

Sabinin, A. A. *Avtomobili ZIL-130 i GAZ-53A.* Moscow, 1969.

Salomatin, N. A. *Organizatsiia i mekhanizatsiia upravleniia proizvodstvom na predpriiatiiakh italii.* Moscow, 1969.

Samarskii, G. A., *et al. Petel'naia mashina klassa 01179 firmy "Minerva."* Moscow, 1968.

Sangren, Ward C. *Digital Computers and Nuclear Reactor Calculations.* New York, John Wiley, 1960.

Santalov, A. A., and Segal, Louis. *Soviet Union Year-Book,* 1930. London, George Allen & Unwin.

Schwalberg, Barney K. *Manpower Utilization in the Soviet Automobile Industry.* Washington, U.S. Department of Commerce, Bureau of the Census, June 1959.

————. *Manpower Utilization in the Soviet Automobile Industry.* Supplementary Report. Washington, U.S. Department of Commerce, Bureau of the Census, August 1959.

Shabad, Theodore. *The Soviet Aluminum Industry*. New York, American Metal Market, 1958.

Shcherbatykh, M. A. *Mashiny dlia kompleksnoi mekhanizatsii vovtsevodstve*. Moscow, 1968.

Sheinkman, E. S. *Novye pribory i instrumenty v lesoustroistve*. Moscow, 1968.

Shepherd, R., and Withers, A. G. *Mechanized Cutting and Loading of Coal*. London, Odhams Press, 1960.

Shevakin, Iu. F. *Stany kholodnoi prokatki trub*. Moscow, 1966.

Shiryaev, P. A. "The Economic Advantages of Large Types of Blast Furnaces." *In* Samarin, A. M., ed. *Contemporary Problems of Metallurgy*. New York, Consultants Bureau, 1960, p. 236.

Shishkin, K. A., *et al. Sovetskie teplovozy*. Moscow, 1951.

———. *Teplovoz TE-3*. Moscow, 1969.

Shneerov, L. A. *Nabornye strokootlivnye mashiny*. Moscow, 1968.

Shukhman, F. G. *Setki bumagodelatel'nykh mashin*. Moscow, 1968.

Sidorov, Iu. P., and Rozanov, A. F. *Analiz rabot po avtomatizatsii pitaniia utkom tkatskikh stankov za rubezhom*. Moscow, 1968.

Silin, P. M. *Technology of Beet-Sugar Production and Refining*. Jerusalem, Israel Program for Scientific Translations, 1964.

Sitnikov, G. G. *Tranzistornye televizory SShA i Iaponii*. Moscow, 1968.

Slusser, Robert, ed. *Soviet Economic Policy in Postwar Germany; A Collection of Papers by Former Soviet Officials*. New York, Research Program on the U.S.S.R., 1953.

Smirnov, M. N., and Vydrevich, E. Z. *The Improvement of the Hydrochemical Alkali Method of Processing Nepheline Rocks to Obtain Alumina*. Jerusalem, Israel Program for Scientific Translations [1959].

Sokolov, V. L. "Soviet Use of German Science and Technology, 1945-1946." New York, Research Program on the U.S.S.R., 1955. (Mimeographed Series no. 72)

Sominskii, V. S. *O tekhnicheskom progresse promyshlennosti SSSR*. Moscow, 1957.

Soviet Industrial Research; Report of the Federation of British Industries Research Delegation to the Soviet Union, 7-22 October 1963. London, Federation of British Industries, November 1963.

Soviet Merchant Ships 1945-1968. Havant, Eng., K. Mason, 1969.

Soviet Union: A Survey for Businessmen; Report on the London Chamber of Commerce Trade Mission to the Soviet Union, 1966. London, 1967.

Spivakovskii, A. O., *et al. Transportnye mashiny i kompleksy otkrytykh gornykh razrabotok*. Moscow, 1968.

Spivakovskii, L. I. *Ekonomika trubnoi promyshlennosti SSSR*. Moscow, 1967.

Spravochnik po oborudovaniiu, dlia remonta avtomobilei i traktorov v lesnoi promyshlennosti. Moscow, 1968.

Spravochnik po spetsial'nym rabotam. Moscow, 1968.

Spravochnik po udobreniiam. Minsk, 1969.

Spravochnik po vneshnei torgovle SSSR. Moscow, Vneshtorgizdat, 1958.

Spulber, Nicholas. *The Economics of Communist Eastern Europe.* New York, Technology Press of M.I.T. and John Wiley, 1957.

Stainless Steel. Fagersta, Sweden, Fagersta Steel Works Co., 1954.

Steel in the Soviet Union. Report of the American Steel and Iron Ore Delegation's Visit to the Soviet Union, May and June 1958. New York, American Iron and Steel Institute, 1959.

Stettinius, E. R., Jr. *Roosevelt and the Russians; The Yalta Conference.* New York, Doubleday, 1949.

Stokke, Baard Richard. *Soviet and Eastern European Trade and Aid in Africa.* New York, Praeger, 1967.

Stolper, Wolfgang F. *The Structure of the East German Economy.* Cambridge, Harvard University Press, 1960.

Strachey, J. *The Theory and Practice of Socialism.* New York, Random House, 1936.

Strana Sovetov za 50 let; Sbornik statisticheskikh materialov. Moscow, 1967.

Street, J. H. *The New Revolution in the Cotton Economy.* Chapel Hill, University of North Carolina Press, 1957.

Stroud, John. *The Red Air Force.* London, Pilot, 1943.

Sutton, Antony C. *Western Technology and Soviet Economic Development:* Vol. I, 1917-1930. Stanford, Calif., Hoover Institution, 1968.

————. *Western Technology and Soviet Economic Development:* Vol. II, 1930-1945. Stanford, Calif., Hoover Institution, 1971.

————. "Soviet Export Strategy." *Ordnance* (November-December 1969).

————. "Soviet Merchant Marine." *U.S. Naval Institute, Proceedings* (January 1970).

Svetlichnyi, P. L. *Elektroprivod i elektrosnabzhenie gornykh mashin.* Moscow, 1968.

Sweezy, P. M. *The Theory of Capitalist Development.* London, New York, Oxford University Press, 1942.

Swianiewicz, S. *Forced Labour and Economic Development.* London, Oxford University Press, 1965.

Szklarz, Wladyslaw. *A Technical Survey of Sprinkling Equipment.* Translated from Polish by Centralny instytut informacji, naukowo-technicznej i ekonomicznej. Warsaw, 1964.

Tanatar, A. I., and Meklev, M. B. *Modernizatsiia stroitel'nykh kranov.* Dnepropetrovsk, 1968.

Tarasov, S. V. *Technology of Watch Production.* Jerusalem, Israel Program for Scientific Translations, 1964.

Textile Industry in the U.S.S.R. and Czechoslovakia. Report of Indian Productivity Team. New Delhi, National Productivity Council, November 1962. (Report no. 19)

Toivola, Urho. *The Finland Year Book, 1947.* Helsinki, 1947.

Tokaev, G. A. *Comrade X.* London, Harvill Press, 1956.

————. *Soviet Imperialism.* New York, Philosophical Library, 1956.

————. *Stalin Means War.* London, G. Weidenfeld & Nicolson, 1951.

Torgovo-tekhnologicheskoe oborudovanie; Spravochnik. Moscow, 1969.

Trade Prospects in the U.S.S.R.; A Survey for Businessmen. Report of the Birmingham and London Chambers of Commerce, Trade Mission, May 1963. London and Birmingham, September 1963.

Tynianov, V. N., *et al. Ekspluatatsiia krivoshipnykh pressov dvoinogo deistviia.* Moscow, 1968.

U.S.S.R. Ministerstvo avtomobil'noi promyshlennosti. *Detali gruzovykh dvukhosnykh avtomobilei ZIL-130, ZIL-130G i ZIL-130E, Sedel'nogo tiagacha ZIL-130B1, Avtomobilia-Samosvala ZIL-MMZ-555 i Shassi ZIL-130D2: Katalog-spravochnik.* Moscow, 1968.

————. *Katalog detalei avtomobilei GAZ-69, GAZ-69A, YAZ-450A i YAZ-450D.* Moscow, 1968.

————. *Katalog detalei avtomobilei YAZ-451M i YAZ-451DM.* Moscow, 1968.

————. *Katalog detalei avtomobilei YAZ-452, YAZ-452A, YAZ-452B, i YAZ-452D.* Moscow, 1970.

————. *Katalog detalei avtopogruzchikov 4041M, 4042M, 4043M, 4045M, 4045LM, 4046M, 4049M, 4055M.* Moscow, 1969.

————. *Katalog detalei legkovogo avtomobilia "Volga" GAZ-24.* Moscow, 1969.

————. *Katalog detalei legkovogo avtomobilia "Volga" modelei GAZ-21P, GAZ-21C, GAZ-21H, GAZ-21T, GAZ-22B i GAZ-22D.* Moscow, 1969.

U.S.S.R. Ministerstvo stankostroeniia SSSR. Tsentral'noe biuro tekhnicheskoi informatsii. *Metallorezhushchikh stanki: Katalog.* Moscow, 1949.

United Arab Republic. Maslahat al-Isti'lamat. *The High Dam, Miracle of XXth Century.* Cairo, Information Department, 1964.

United Arab Republic. Wizarat al-Sadd al-Ali. *The High Aswan Dam.* Cairo, 1964.

United Nations. *Development Prospects of Basic Chemical and Allied Industries in Asia and the Far East.* New York, 1963. (E/CN.11/635)

————. *Geological Survey and Mining Development in Europe and in the U.S.S.R.* Report of the Study Group of Geologists and Mining Engineers from Asia and the Far East, August 4 - November 5, 1955. New York, 1958.

————. *Treaty Series.* Vol. 116 (1951); Vol. 130 (1952); Vol. 217 (1955); Vol. 227 (1956); Vol. 240 (1956); Vol. 271 (1957); Vol. 374 (1960).

United Nations. Economic and Social Council. Economic Commission for Asia and the Far East. Transport and Communications Committee. *Report on United Nations Workshop-cum-Study Tour on Problems of Dieselization of USSR Railways.* N.p., May 24, 1967. ([United Nations Document] E/CN.11/TRANS/Sub. 1/L.25)

United Nations. Food and Agriculture Organization. *FAO Technical Conference on Fishery Research Craft. Seattle, Washington 18-24 May.* Comp. by Jan-Olof Traung and Lars-Ola Engvall. N.p., 1968.

———. *Pulp and Paper Development in Asia and the Far East.* Vol. II. Bangkok, 1962. (E/CN.11/547)

United Nations. Secretariat. *The Electric Power Industry in Europe, the United States of America and the U.S.S.R.* Report of the Study Group of Experts from Asia and the Far East on Their Visits to Europe, the U.S.A. and the U.S.S.R. July - September 1956. [New York], October 1957. (ST/TAA/Ser.C/18)

U.S. Atomic Energy Commission. *German Reports on Atomic Energy, A Bibliography of Unclassified Literature.* Comp. by Lore R. David and I. A. Warheit. Oak Ridge, Tenn., Technical Information Service, June 6, 1952. (TID-3030)

———. *Memorandum on the State of Knowledge in Nuclear Science Reached by the Germans in 1945.* By A. M. Weinberg and L. W. Nordheim. Oak Ridge, Tenn., Technical Information Service, November 8, 1945. (German Series, no. G-371)

———. High Energy Physics Advisory Panel. *Report on High Energy Physics, June 1969.* Washington, [1969].

U.S. Central Intelligence Agency. Office of Research and Reports. *The Synthetic Rubber Industry in the U.S.S.R. During the Seven Year Plan, 1959-65.* Washington, 1961.

U.S. Congress. Joint Committee on Atomic Energy. *Soviet Atomic Espionage.* 82d Cong., 1st sess. April 1951.

U.S. Congress Joint Economic Committee. *Comparisons of the United States and Soviet Economies.* 86th Cong., 2d sess. 1960.

——— . ———. *Dimensions of Soviet Economic Power.* Hearings together with Compilation of Studies Pursuant to Sec. 5(a) of Public Law 304 (79th Congress). 87th Cong., 2d sess. December 1962.

——— . ———. *A New Look at Trade Policy Toward the Communist Bloc.* By Samuel Pisar. Subcommittee on Foreign Economic Policy. 87th Cong., 1st sess. 1961.

U.S. Congress. House. Committee on Banking and Currency. *To Amend the Export-Import Bank Act of 1945.* Hearings on H.R. 6649. 90th Cong., 1st sess. April 1967.

——— . ——— . ———. *The Fiat-Soviet Auto Plant and Communist Economic Reforms.* A Report pursuant to H.R. 1043 for the Subcommittee on International Trade. 89th Cong., 2d sess. March 1967.

U.S. Congress. House. Committee on Un-American Activities. *Annual Report for the Year 1965.* 89th Cong., 1st sess. August 1966.

────── . ────── . ────── . *Excerpts from Hearings Regarding Investigation of Communist Activities in Connection with the Atom Bomb. 80th Cong., 2d sess. September 1948.*

────── . ────── . ────── . *Hearings Regarding Communist Infiltration of Radiation Laboratory and Atomic Bomb Project at the University of California, Berkeley.* 81st Cong., 1st sess. April, May, June 1949.

────── . ────── . ────── . *Hearings Regarding Shipment of Atomic Materials to Soviet Union.* 81st Cong., 1st and 2d sess. December 1949-March 1950.

────── . ────── . ────── . *Patterns of Communist Espionage.* Report. 85th Cong., 2d sess. January 1959.

────── . ────── . ────── . *Report on Soviet Espionage Activities in Connection with the Atom Bomb.* 80th Cong., 2d sess. September 1948.

────── . ────── . ────── . *Soviet Espionage Activities in Connection with Jet Propulsion and Aircraft.* Hearings. 81st Cong., 1st sess. June 1949.

U.S. Congress. House. Select Committee on Export Control. *Investigation and Study of the Administration, Operation, and Enforcement of the Export Control Act of 1949, and Related Acts (H.R. 403).* Hearings. 87th Cong., 1st sess., October, December 1961, Part 1; 87th Cong., 2d sess., February 1962, Part 2; 87th Cong. 2d sess., September, October 1962, Part 3.

U.S. Congress. Senate. Committee on Aeronautical and Space Sciences. *NASA Authorization for Fiscal Year 1970.* Hearings. 91st Cong., 1st sess. May 1969, Part II.

────── . ────── . ────── . *Soviet Space Programs, 1962-65; Goals and Purposes, Achievements, Plans and International Implications.* Staff Report. 89th Cong., 2d sess. December 1966.

U.S. Congress. Senate. Committee on Banking and Currency. *East-West Trade.* Hearings Before the Subcommittee on International Finance on S. Joint Res. 169. 90th Cong., 2d sess. June, July 1968, Parts 1-3.

────── . ────── . ────── . *Export Expansion and Regulation.* Hearings Before the Subcommittee on International Finance on S. 813, S. 1940. 91st Cong., 1st sess. April, May 1969.

────── . ────── . ────── . *Government Guarantees of Credit to Communist Countries.* Hearings on S. 2310. 88th Cong., 1st sess. November 1963.

U.S. Congress. Senate. Committee on Commerce. *Extra-High-Voltage Electric Transmission Lines.* Hearings on S. 1472, S. 2139, S. 2140. 89th Cong., 2d sess. July 1966.

────── . ────── . ────── . *The Postwar Expansion of Russia's Fishing Industry.* Report by the Fisheries Research Institute. 88th Cong., 2d sess. January 1964. Seattle, University of Washington.

────── . ────── . ────── . *The United States and World Trade: Challenges and Opportunities.* Final Report by Special Staff on Study of U. S. Foreign Commerce. 87th Cong., 1st sess. March 1961.

U.S. Congress. Senate. Committee on Foreign Relations. *East-West Trade: A Compilation of Views of Businessmen, Bankers, and Academic Experts.* 88th Cong., 2d sess. November 1964.

———— . ———— . ———— . *East-West Trade.* Hearings. 88th Cong., 2d sess., March, April 1964, Part 1; 89th Cong., 1st sess., February 1965, Part 2.

U.S. Congress. Senate. Committees on Interior and Insular Affairs and Public Works. *Relative Water and Power Resource Development in the U.S.S.R. and the U.S.A.* Report and Staff Studies. 86th Cong., 2d sess. May 1960.

U.S. Congress. Senate. Committee on the Judiciary. *Export of Ball Bearing Machines to Russia.* Hearings Before the Subcommittee to Investigate the Administration of the Internal Security Act and Other Internal Security Laws. 87th Cong., 1st sess. Proposed Shipment of Miniature Ball Bearing Machines to Russia. 1961.

———— . ———— . ———— . *Export of Strategic Materials to the U.S.S.R. and Other Soviet Bloc Countries.* Hearing Before the Subcommittee to Investigate the Administration of the Internal Security Act and Other Internal Security Laws. 87th Cong., 1st sess. October 1961, Parts 1,2.

———— . ———— . ———— . *Expose of Soviet Espionage, May 1960.* Prepared By the Federal Bureau of Investigation, U. S. Department of Justice, for Use of the Subcommittee to Investigate the Administration of the Internal Security Act and Other Internal Security Laws. 86th Cong., 2d sess. May 1960.

———— . ———— . ———— . *Nuclear Scientist Defects to United States.* Hearings Before the Subcommittee to Investigate the Administration of the Internal Security Act and Other Internal Security Laws. 89th Cong., 1st sess. December 1964.

———— . ———— . ———— . *Scope of Soviet Activity in the United States.* Hearings Before the Subcommittee to Investigate the Administration of the Internal Security Act and Other Internal Security Laws. 84th Cong., 2d sess. 1956, Part 21.

———— . ———— . ———— . *Soviet Oil in East-West Trade.* Hearing Before the Subcommittee to Investigate the Administration of the Internal Security Act and Other Internal Security Laws. 87th Cong., 2d sess. July 1962.

———— . ———— . ———— . *The Wennerstroem Spy Case; How It Touched the United States and NATO.* Excerpts from the Testimony of Stig Eric Constans Wennerstroem, a Noted Soviet Agent. Subcommittee to Investigate the Administration of the Internal Security Act and Other Internal Security Laws. 88th Cong., 2d sess. 1964.

U.S. Congress. Senate. Special Committee on Atomic Energy. *Hearings* pursuant to S. Res. 179, Creating a Special Commission and Investigating Problems Related to the Development, Use and Control of Atomic Energy. 79th Cong., 1st sess. November, December 1945, Part 1.

U.S. Department of Agriculture. *Soviet Agriculture Today*. Report of the 1963 Agriculture Exchange Delegation. Washington, December 1963. (Foreign Agricultural Economic Report no. 131)

———. Agricultural Research Service. *Farm Mechanization in the Soviet Union*. Report of a Technical Study Group. Washington, November 1959.

———. ———. *Livestock in the Soviet Union*. Report of a Technical Study Group. Washington, September 1961.

———. ———. *Soil Salinity and Irrigation in the Soviet Union*. Report of a Technical Study Group. Washington, September 1962.

U.S. Department of Agriculture. Foreign Agricultural Service. *Cotton in the Soviet Union*. Report of a Technical Study Group. Washington, June 1959.

———. ———. *Grading and Exporting Wheat in the Union of Soviet Socialist Republics*. Washington, February 1961.

———. ———. *Meat Production in the Soviet Union*. Washington, June 1960.

———. ———. *Milk Production in the Soviet Union; Recent Developments*. Washington, May 1959.

U.S. Department of Agriculture. Forest Service. *Forestry and Forest Industry in the U.S.S.R.* Report of a Technical Study Group. Washington, March 1961.

U.S. Department of Agriculture. Soil Conservation Service. *Soil and Water Use in the Soviet Union*. Report of a Technical Study Group. Washington, 1958.

U.S. Department of the Army. *List of All Service Parts for Truck, ¼-ton, 4 x 4, Command Reconnaissance (Ford, Model GPW; Willys, Model MB)*. Washington, October 1949. (Supply Catalog ORD 9 SNL G-503)

U.S. Department of Commerce. *Soviet Excavators* (excerpts). Washington, Office of Technical Services. Washington, February 17, 1960.

———. *The Soviet Logging Industry; Its Resources, Employment, Production, and Productivity*. Washington, Bureau of the Census, Foreign Manpower Research Office, September 1959. (Series P-95, no. 54, International Population Reports)

U.S. Department of Health, Education and Welfare. *Hospital Services in the U.S.S.R.* Report of the U.S. Delegation on Hospital Systems Planning, Public Health Service, June 26 - July 16, 1965. Washington, November 1966.

U.S. Department of the Interior. *A History of the Petroleum Administration for War, 1941-1945*. Washington, 1946.

———. *Recent Electric Power Developments in the U.S.S.R. Report of the United States Delegation Tour to Soviet Russia, August 28–September 9, 1962, under U. S.–U.S.S.R. Exchange Agreement*. Washington, 1963.

U.S. Department of Justice. Federal Bureau of Investigation. *Soviet Illegal Espionage in the United States*. N.p., n.d.

U.S. Department of State. *Background Notes—U.S.S.R.* Washington, Bureau of Public Affairs, Office of Media Services, 1965.

———. *Battle Act Report, 1963.* Mutual Defense Assistance Control Act of 1951. 16th Report to Congress. Washington, December 1963.

———. *Biographic Register.* July 1967.

———. *Foreign Relations of the United States [FRUS].* Vols. IV-VI. Washington, 1944-46.

———. *Promyshlennaia estetika SShA.* Washington, n.d.

———. *Ruchnoi instrument—SShA.* Washington, n.d.

———. *The Sino-Soviet Economic Offensive in the Less Developed Countries.* Washington, 1958.

———. *Summary of East-West Trade in 1958.* Mutual Defense Assistance Control Act of 1951. 13th Report to Congress. Washington, March 1960.

U.S. Department of War. *Coal Mining Industry of Germany.* Prepared By Solid Fuels Branch, Fuels and Lubricants Division, Office of the Quartermaster General. Washington, September 7, 1944. (W.D. Pamphlet no. 31-204)

U.S. Foreign Economic Administration. *U.S. Technical Industrial Disarmament Committee to Study the Post-Surrender Treatment of the German Automotive Industry.* Study by Interagency Committee on the Treatment of the German Automotive Industry from the Standpoint of International Security. Washington, 1945. (T.I.D.C. Project no. 12)

———. *U.S. Technical Industrial Disarmament Committee to Study the Post-Surrender Treatment of the German Electronic Equipment Industry.* Study by Interagency Committee on the Treatment of the German Electronic Equipment Industry from the Standpoint of International Security. Washington, 1945. (T.I.D.C. Project no. 8)

———. *U.S. Technical Industrial Disarmament Committee to Study the Post-Surrender Treatment of the German Iron and Steel and Ferroalloys Industries.* Study by Interagency Subcommittee on the Treatment of the German Iron and Steel Industry from the Standpoint of International Security. Washington, 1945. (T.I.D.C. Project no. 15a)

———. *U.S. Technical Industrial Disarmament Committee on the German Machine Tool Industry.* Study of Interagency Committee on the Treatment of the German Machine Tool Industry from the Standpoint of International Security. Washington, 1945. (T.I.D.C. Project no. 11)

U.S. Oil Men Take a Look at Russia. A Report to the American Petroleum Institute, Based on Observations of the First United States Petroleum Industry Exchange Delegation to Russia, August 2-August 31, 1960. N.p., n.d.

United States Steel Corp. *The Making, Shaping and Treating of Steel.* Pittsburgh, 1957.

U.S. Strategic Bombing Survey. *Aircraft Division Industry Report.* 2d ed., January 1947. Washington, 1947. (Report no. 4)

————. *Ammoniakwerke Merseburg GmbH, Leuna, Germany.* Dates of Survey: 22 April - 6 May 1945. 2d ed., March 1947. Washington, Oil Division, 1947. (Report no. 115)

————. *Auto-Union A.G., Chemnitz and Zwickau, Germany.* Dates of Survey: 10 June–12 June 1945. 2d ed., January 1947. Washington, Munitions Division, 1947. (Report no. 84)

————. *Braunkohle Benzin A.G., Zeitz, Germany; Braunkohle Benzin A.G., Boehlen, Germany; Wintershall A.G., Luetzkendorf, Germany.* Plant Survey: 22 April–6 May 1945. July 1945. Washington, Oil, Chemicals and Rubber Division, 1945. (Report no. 116)

————. *Bussing NAG Flugmotoren werke GmbH, Brunswick, Germany.* Dates of Survey: 8 May-21 1945. 2d ed., January 1947. Washington, Aircraft Division, 1947. (Report no. 15)

————. *Friedrich Krupp Grusonwerke, Magdeburg, Germany.* Dates of Survey: 23 May–4 June 1945. 2d ed., January 1947. Washington, Munitions Division, 1947. (Report no. 91)

————. *The German Abrasive Industry.* Dates of Survey: 5 April–25 June 1945. 2d ed., January 1947. Washington, Equipment Division, 1947. (Report no. 51)

————. *German Electrical Equipment Industry Report.* 2d ed., January 1947. Washington, Equipment Division, 1947. (Report no. 48)

Van Hook, Andrew. *Sugar–Its Production, Technology, and Uses.* New York, Ronald Press, 1949.

Vansheidt, V. A. *Sudovye dvigateli vnutrennego sgoraniia.* Leningrad, 1962.

Vedovato, Giuseppe. *Il Trattato di Pace con l'Italia.* Rome, Edizioni Leonardo, 1947.

Vneshniaia torgovlia SSSR: Statisticheskii sbornik, 1918-1966. Moscow, 1967.

Volkov, O. I. *Ekonomicheskaia effectivnost' mekhanizatsii i avtomatizatsii proizvodstva v mashinostroenii.* Moscow, 1968.

Volzhin, G. N., *et al. Vosstanovlenie iznoshennykh detalei stroitel'nykh mashin.* Moscow, 1968.

Volursus. *The Secret Weapons of the Soviet Union.* Translated by E.W. Schnitzer from *Flugwelt*, November 1953. Santa Monica, Calif., RAND Corp., February 1954. (Report no. T-33)

Vul', Iu. Ia., *et al. Naladka elektroprivodov ekskavatorov.* Moscow, 1969.

Ware, Willis H., ed. *Soviet Computer Technology - 1959.* Reprinted from *IRE Transactions on Electronic Computers.* New York, Vol. EC-9, no. 1 (March 1960).

Ware, Willis H., and Holland, Wade B. *Soviet Cybernetics Technology.* I: *Soviet Cybernetics, 1959-1962.* Santa Monica, Calif., RAND Corp., June 1963. (Report no. RM-3675-PR)

Wendel, K. *Handbuch der Werften.* 1956 and 1960 eds. Hamburg, Schiffahrts-Verlag "Hansa," C. Schroedter, 1956, 1960.

"The Western Origins of Soviet Marine Diesel Engines." *U.S. Naval In-*

the Soviet Natural Gas Industry. N.p., American Gas Association, n.d.
U. S. Atomic Energy Commission. High Energy Physics Advisory Panel. "Report in Response to Questions Pertaining to the Scope of the 200 Bev Accelerator." N.p., January 1968.

———— . ———— . "The Status and Problems of High Energy Physics Today." N.p., January 1968.
U. S. Department of State. Office of Foreign Liquidation. "Report on War Aid Furnished by the United States to the U.S.S.R." Washington, 1945.
"Welding Research and Development in the U.S.S.R." A Report on the Visit of a B.W.R.A. Party to Welding Research Institutes in the Soviet Union. October 1960.

PERIODICALS

ASTM Bulletin, Easton, Pa.
Aero Digest, Washington, D.C.
Aeronautics, London.
The Aeroplane, London.
Air University Quarterly Review, Montgomery, Ala.
American Aviation, Washington, D.C.
American Chemical Society, *Chemical and Engineering News*, Washington, D.C.
American Machinist, New York.
American Slavic and East European Review, Menasha, Wisc.
American Society of Naval Engineers, *Journal*, Washington, D.C.
Automobile Engineer, London.
Automotive Industries, Philadelphia, Pa.
Aviation Week, New York.
Biulletin' tekhnikoekonomicheskoi informatsii, Moscow.
Boeing Magazine, Seattle, Washington.
British Chemical Engineering, London.
British Zone Review, Hamburg, Germany.
Business Week, New York.
Canadian Aviation, Toronto.
Canadian Chemical Processing, Toronto.
Canadian Mining Journal, Ottawa.
CERN Courier, Geneva, Switzerland.
Chemical and Metallurgical Engineering, New York.
Chemical Week, New York.
Die Chemische Fabrik, Berlin, Germany.
Die Chemische Technik, Berlin, Germany.

Chemistry and Industry, London.
Commercial and Financial Chronicle, New York.
Commercial Fisheries Review, Washington, D.C.
Congressional Record, Washington, D.C.
Control Engineering, New York.
Czechoslovak Economic Bulletin, Prague.
Czechoslovak Foreign Trade, Prague.
East-West Commerce, London.
East-West Trade News, London.
Economic Review of the Soviet Union, New York.
The Economist, London.
Electrical Review, London.
Electrical World, Manchester, England.
Electronic Design, New York.
Electronics, New York.
Engineering News-Record, New York.
L'Express, Paris.
Far Eastern Review, Manila, The Philippines.
The Financial Times, London.
Flying, New York.
Fortune, New York.
Gas Journal, London.
Glass and Ceramics, Washington, D.C.
The Glass Industry, New York.
Hosiery Trade Journal, Leicester, England.
I.E.E. Journal, London.
Indian Construction News, Calcutta.
Industrial and Engineering Chemistry, Washington, D.C.
Institute for the Study of the U.S.S.R., *Bulletin*, Munich, Germany.
Institute of Metals, *Journal*, London.
Interavia, Geneva, Switzerland.
Iron Age, Middletown, New York.
Izvestia, Moscow.
Japan Times, Tokyo.
Journal of Metals, New York.
Kommunist, Yerevan.
Kotloturbostroenie, Moscow.
The Los Angeles Times.
Mashinostroenie, Moscow.
Mechanical Handling, London.
Metallurgia, Manchester, England.
Metal Progress, Cleveland, Ohio.

Metalworking News, New York.
Metsalehti, Helsinki, Finland.
Military Review, Fort Leavenworth, Kans.
The Minneapolis Tribune.
Missiles and Rockets, Washington, D.C.
Le Monde.
Morskoi flot, Moscow.
The Motor Ship, London.
Nauka i zhizn', Moscow.
Neue Zürcher Zeitung.
The New York Times.
Nucleonics, New York.
The Oil Weekly, Houston, Tex.
Ordnance, Washington, D.C.
The Oriental Economist, Tokyo.
Petroleum Refiner, Houston, Tex.
Petroleum Week, Chicago, Ill.
Polish Technical Review, New York.
Pravda, Moscow.
Problems of Economics, New York.
Product Engineering, New York.
Promyshlennaia energetika, Moscow.
Railway Age, Chicago, Ill.
Railway Mechanical Engineer, Philadelphia, Pa.
Rock Products, Louisville, Ky.
The San Jose Mercury, San Jose, Calif.
The Shipbuilder and Marine Engine Builder, London.
Shipping World and Shipbuilder, London.
Skinners Silk and Rayon Record, London.
Society of Automotive Engineers, *S.A.E. Journal*, New York.
Society of Glass Technology, *Journal*, London.
Spravochnik khimika, Moscow.
Stal', Moscow.
Stanki i instrument, Moscow.
Steklo i keramika, New York.
Textile Research Journal, New York.
Textile World, New York.
The Times, London.
Trains, Milwaukee, Wisc.
Transportnoe mashinostroenie, Moscow.
Undersea Technology, Washington, D.C.
U.S. Department of Commerce, *Export Control Quarterly*, Washington, D.C.

U.S. Department of State, *Bulletin*, Washington, D.C.
U.S. Naval Institute, *Proceedings*, Annapolis, Md.
Wall Street Journal, New York.
The Washington Post.
Welding Journal, London.
Za industrializatsiiu, Moscow.

Index

Aberdare Cables, Ltd. (U.K.), 331
Aberdeen Proving Grounds, 272
Abraham filter press (for beet sugar processing), 52, 345
Academy of Science, U.S.S.R. (Akademiia Nauk S.S.S.R.), 277, 318-20, 322
Acheson, Dean, 73
Adamian, I., 330
Adler, C.E., 166
Adler Trumpf automobiles, 195
A.E.G. (Allgemeine Elektrizitäts-Gesellschaft, W. Ger.), 90-91, 315, 411-12
Aetna Standard Company, 130
aircraft:
  embargoes on, 53
  helicopters, 368
  high-speed models, 378
  under Lend Lease, 3-5 *passim*, 12-14 *passim*, 254-55, 266, 267-68n.41, 269, 278
  in Tsarist technology, 409, 414n.1
  war planes: Western prototypes, 254-55, 257, 266-67, 269, 279n.82; Soviet models, 254-55, 264, 266-70, 279n.82; rocket models, 269
——— engines:
  BMW, xxix, 119, 258-60, 262, 264, 278
  Junkers, xxix, 119, 258-64, 278, 307
  machine tools for, 305-7 *passim*, 417n.9
  Rolls-Royce, xxix, 255, 257, 263-66, 278
  Soviet models, 262-66, 278
  Western aid to, general, 368, 410
——— industry:
  heavy presses for, 377
  landing systems for, 329, 334, 368
  reparations to, 29, 255-62, 268-70, 414
  Soviet innovations in, 368, 409, 413, 423
  U.K. aid to, 255
  Western aid to, general, 368

Aiton & Company, Ltd. (U.K.), 183
Akademiia Nauk S.S.S.R. *See* Academy of Science, U.S.S.R.
Alco (American Locomotive Company), 64, 215, 219, 249-50, 397
Alexander I, Tsar, 335n.1
Alexandrov, Vladimir, 19
Allied Control Council, 17, 25-26, 27
All-Union Artificial Fiber Research Institute (VNIIV) (U.S.S.R.), 179
Allis-Chalmers Corporation, 213
Almond, Gabriel A., 19
Alpine Monton Company (Austria), 37
Alsthom. *See* Schneider-Alsthom, Société Alsthom
Ambi-Budd Presswerk A.G. (Ger.), 39, 195
American Association of Railroads, 252
American Motors Corporation, 422
American-Russian Industrial Syndicate, Inc., 67
American Welding Society, 131
Amtorg, 72, 212, 266, 321, 412
Anaconda ore cars, 104
Anorgana (New Rokita) briquetting plant (Poland), 141
Ansaldo shipyards (Italy), 227-28
A.P.V. Company (U.K.), 177
Arab Contractors, Ltd. (Egypt), 97
Arcos (U.K.), 412
Ardenne, Manfred von, 236-37
Argonne National Laboratories, 244, 247, 319, 328
armaments. *See* weapons
Artsimovich, Lev, 247
Asahi Chemical Company (Japan), 184
Aschberg, Olaf, 67n.3, 68, 69, 70
Associated Engineering group (U.K.), 119
Astra Romana oil company (Rumania), 38

457

Kahn, Albert, Inc., 413
Kahn, Otto, 72n.72
Kaiser Wilhelm Institute of Biology and
Virus Research (Ger.), 236
Kalmykov, N.N., 59
Kanegafuchi Chemical Company (Japan),
184
Kanegafuchi Paper Company (Manchuria),
187
Kansai Catalyst (Japan), 156
Kaplan electric power technology, 363
Karlstads Mekaniska Werkstad, A/B (Sweden), 176
Katzenbach, Nicholas de B., 400n.56
Kawasaki Aircraft (Japan), 184; motor
boats, 289; steam turbine, 228
Keebush textile plant equipment, 176
Keller copying machines, 310
Keller, Werner, 261
Kellex Corp., 233
Kelley, Robert F., 390
Kellogg acetylene production process, 159n.
30
Kelvin-Hughes echosounders, 291
Kendall & Gent machine tools, 311
Kennedy, John F., 276, 277
Kestner Evaporator & Engineering Company, Ltd. (U.K.), 148, 176
Khaiss, A., 70
Khrushchev, Nikita, xxvi, xxx, 146, 150,
362, 407, 419
King, George (U.K.), 161n.40
Kingfisher echosounding equipment, 291
King vertical lathes, 311
Kirschner, A.G. (Ger.) 178, 306
Kleim & Ungerer (Ger.), 307
Kloeckner-Humboldt-Deutz (Ger.), 223, 373
Koering (U.S.) mechanical dump cars, 59
Kollman (Ger.) machine tool plants, 306
Koppel ore cars, 104
Koppers-Becker coke oven technology, 132,
141-43
Koppers Company, Inc., 142
Korea:
reparations from, 15, 17, 18, 124
war in, 205, 264, 269
Korr, Max, 354
Kosygin, Alexei N., xxvi
Kramator wide strip mill, 128
Kramish, A., 231, 240, 242-43
Krauss-Maffei locomotives, 251n.10

Krebs, Arno, Werkzeugmaschinen fabrik
(Ger.), 306
Krebs et Cie (France), 145
Krotkov, Yuri, 391
Krupp (Ger.), 61, 88-89, 130, 174, 182-83,
251, 273, 291, 392
Krupp financial interests, 69
Krupp-Gruson A.G. (Germany), 172
Krupp-Renn (Ger.) direct-reduction plants,
124, 132
Krutkov, Yuri, 237
Krystal urea crystallization process, 150
Kubek, Anthony, 268n.41
Kuhlmann, R. von, 67
Kuhn, Loeb company, 71, 72n.29
Kurchatov, Igor, 231, 318
Kureha Chemical (Japan), 164
Kurmarkische Zellwoll-A.G. (Ger.), 175
Küttner, Fr., A.G. (Ger.), 175

L&N laboratory recorders, 131
laboratory equipment:
for atomic research, 236, 237
electron microscopes, 85
glass for, 67-68, 174
in reparations, 171, 236
for soils research, 211
in synthetic rubber research, 159
in 1947 U.K. trade agreement, 44
Western prototypes for, 131, 146, 168
See also medical technology
Lagovskii, A.N., 13, 191
Laird, Melvin, 388
Lamont, Thomas W., 68n.6, 72n.29
Lancashire Dynamo Holdings (U.K.), 161n.
40, 162
Lane, Edward, 154n.5
Lang (Hungary) marine diesels, 215, 392
Lange, Dr. (German rocket designer), 269
Lanz, Heinrich, A.G. (W. Ger.), 211, 213
Lattimore, Owen, 34
Latvia. *See* Baltic States
Lazard Brothers & Company, 163
Lazard Freres, 163
leather goods:
boot and shoe manufacture, 83, 353-54, 368
under Lend Lease, 3, 10
synthetics, 354
Lebedev, S.V., 159

www.ingramcontent.com/pod-product-compliance
Lightning Source LLC
Chambersburg PA
CBHW021149160426
42812CB00077B/248